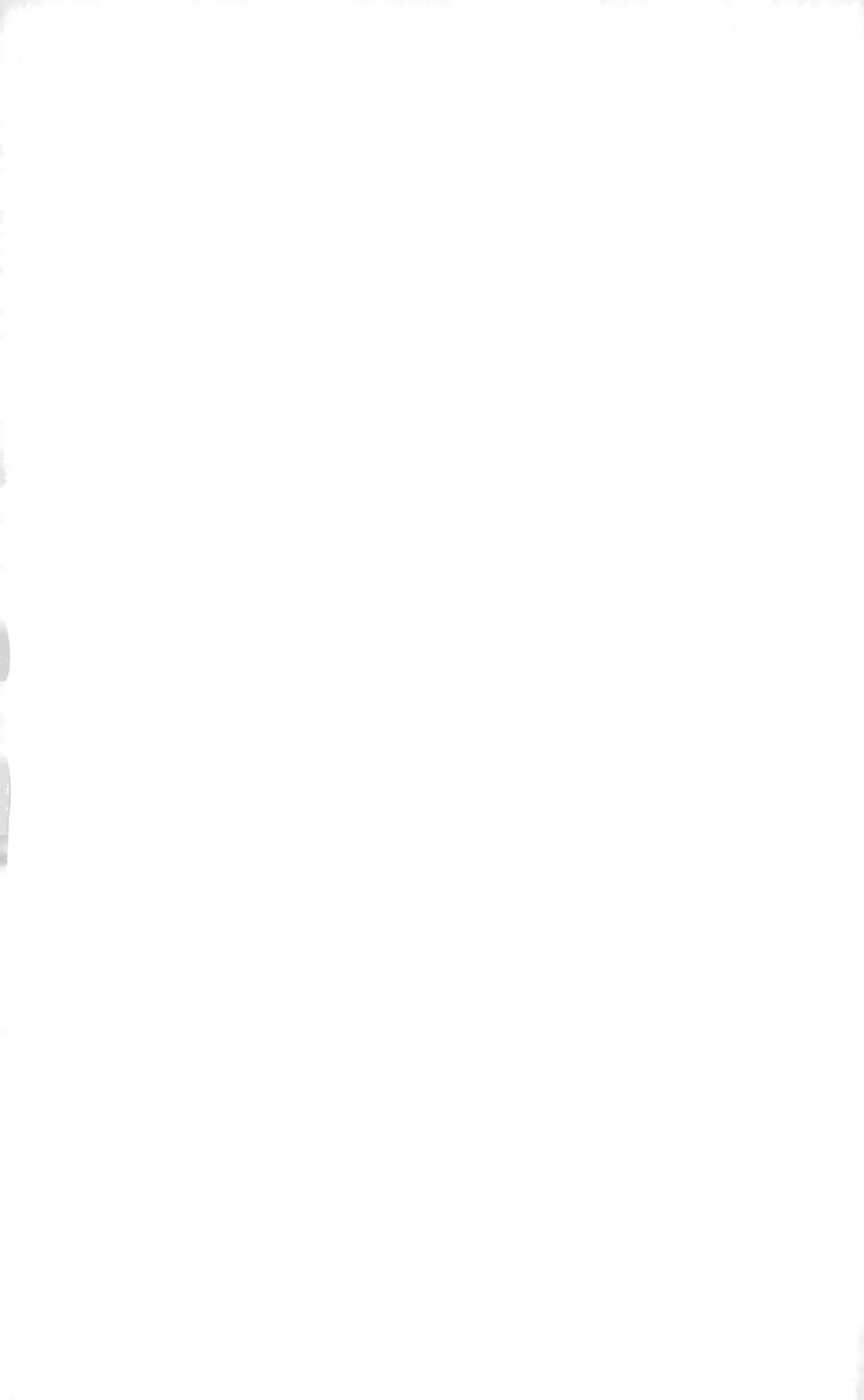

Venice, *Città Excelentissima*

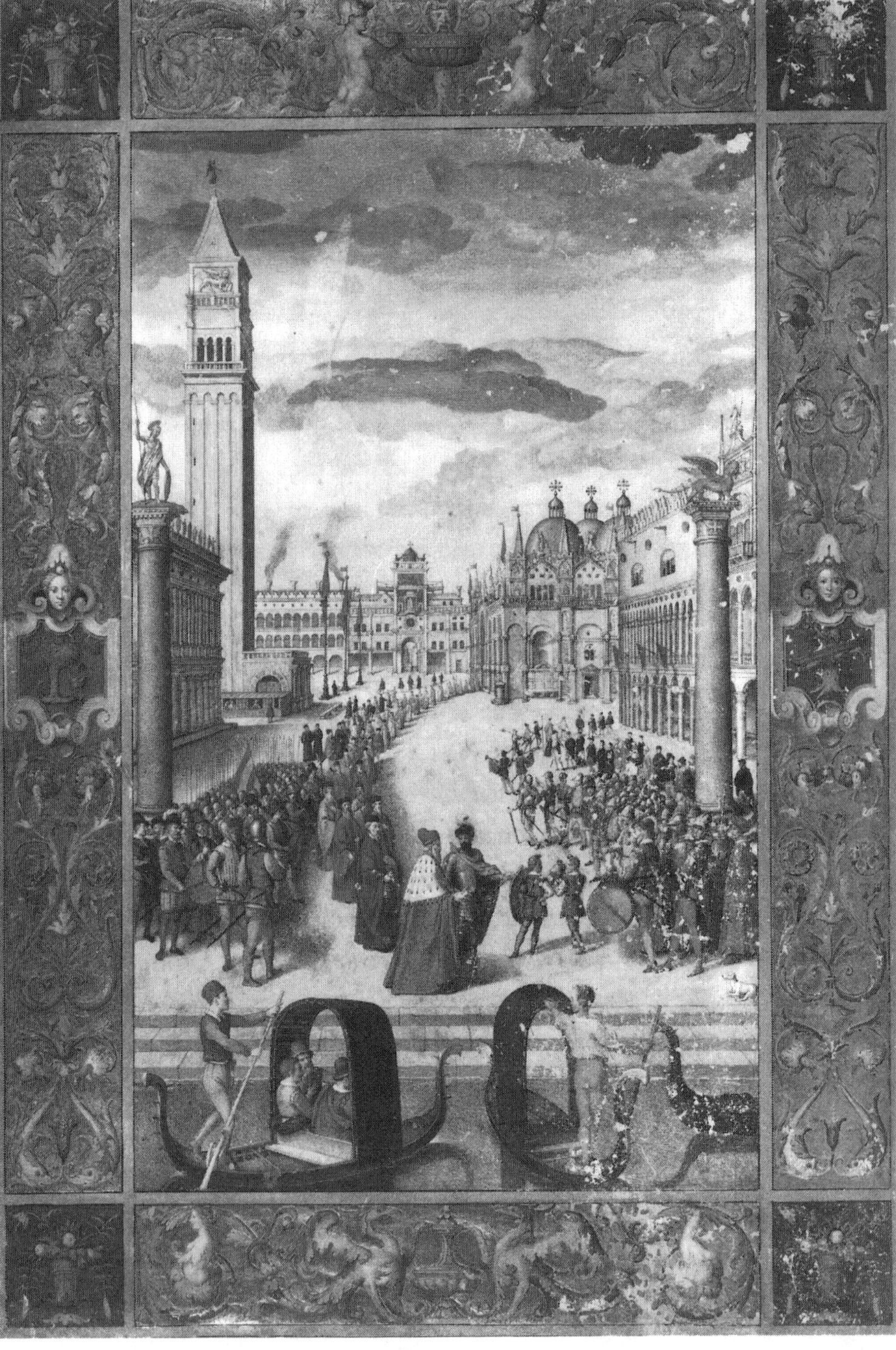

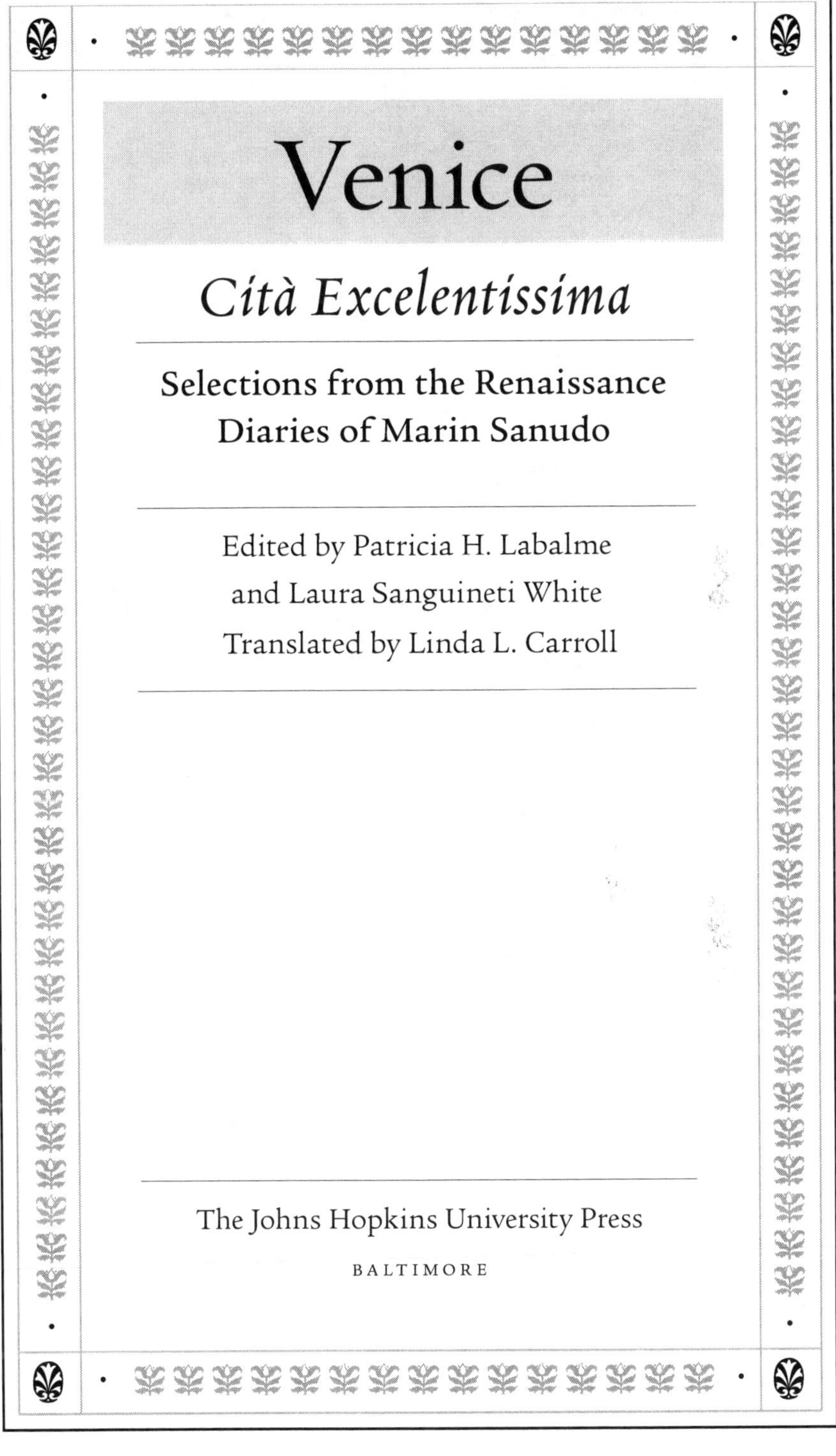

Venice

Città Excelentissima

Selections from the Renaissance Diaries of Marin Sanudo

Edited by Patricia H. Labalme
and Laura Sanguineti White
Translated by Linda L. Carroll

The Johns Hopkins University Press

BALTIMORE

This book was brought to publication
with the generous assistance
of Rutgers University and
Tulane University.

2 4 6 8 9 7 5 3 1

The Johns Hopkins University Press
2715 North Charles Street
Baltimore, Maryland 21218-4363
www.press.jhu.edu

Library of Congress Cataloging-in-Publication Data
Sanudo, Marino, 1466–1536.
[Diaries. English. Selections]
Venice, cità excelentissima : selections from the Renaissance diaries of Marin Sanudo /
edited by Patricia H. Labalme and Laura Sanguineti White ; translated by Linda L. Carroll.
p. cm.
Includes bibliographical references and index.
ISBN-13: 978-0-8018-8765-9 (hardcover : alk. paper)
ISBN-10: 0-8018-8765-8 (hardcover : alk. paper)
1. Venice (Italy)—History—1508–1797—Sources. 2. Italy—History—1492–1559—Sources.
3. Venice (Italy)—Foreign relations—1508–1797—Sources. 4. Venice (Italy)—Social life
and customs—16th century. 5. Arts—Italy—Venice—History—16th century. I. Labalme,
Patricia H. II. Sanguineti White, Laura. III. Title.
DG678.22S26413 2008
945'.3106—dc22   2007024503

A catalog record for this book is available from the British Library.

Frontispiece: Meeting of Doge Andrea Gritti and Francesco Maria della Rovere
in the Piazetta in 1524, from G. B. Leoni, *Vita di Francesco I della
Rovere* (1605). Biblioteca Apostolica Vaticana, Rome.

To the Memory of
Felix Gilbert
(1905–1991)

Tal e tanto è il nome della città de Venetia che, dirò cussì, per tutto il mondo ne è fatto grande estimatione.

Such and so great is the reputation of the city of Venice that, I might say, it is a city held in high esteem by the whole world.

Marin Sanudo, De origine, situ, et
magistratibus urbis venetae

· · ·

Il principe di Bisignano . . . è partito benissimo satisfato di questa cità nostra, e dice le altre terre è ville, e questa li par cità excelentissima.

The Prince of Bisignano . . . left highly satisfied with this our city, saying that all other cities are but villages, but this one seems to him a truly excellent city.

Marin Sanudo, I diarii,
January 23, 1521

· · ·

Niun scrittor mai farà cosa bona delle historie moderne, non vedando la mia diaria, in la qual è compreso ogni cosa seguita.

No writer will ever make much of modern history who has not seen my diaries, within which is contained every event.

Marin Sanudo, letter to the heads
of the Council of Ten, 1531

4. Foreign Affairs: War and Diplomacy 159

Pope Alexander and His Family · Pope Julius · Rome and the War of the League of Cambrai · Pope Leo X · Pope Adrian VI · Pope Clement VII · France's Charles VIII and Louis XII · Francis I · Emperor Maximilian I · Holy Roman Empire and Spain · England · The Ottoman Turks · Foreign Diplomats in Venice · Secretaries

5. Economic Networks and Institutions 227

Sanudo's Experience · Andrea Gritti · Banks and Bankers · Antonio Grimani · The Arsenal · Vetor Fausto · Ships and the Sea · Pirates and Corsairs · Shipwreck · The Pepper Trade · Gifts for the Sultan · The Costs of Cambrai · The Prices of Power · "Everything is for sale" · The Fortunes of Alvise Pisani

6. Society and Social Life 285

A Patrician *Festa* · A Patrician Wedding · Fashion, Taste, and Sumptuary Laws · The Grand Chancellor · *Scuole Grandi* · *Scuole Piccole* · Prostitutes and Servants · Famine and Freeze · Flood · Syphilis · Plague · Germans · Greeks · Jews · Street Entertainments · Rialto Fire · Games of Fortune

7. Religion and Superstition 359

Celebrating a Political Treaty · Processions for Religious Holidays · Earthquake and Propitiation · Plague and Prayers · Chastity in the Convents · Miracles and Monachization · The Church of San Salvador · A Venetian Saint in the Making · Spirits in Chioggia · Witches in Val Camonica · Lutheran Influences · Monstrous Births

8. Humanism and the Arts 427

Humanism in Venice · The Aldine Press · Public Education in Venice · The Concern for History · A Library for San Marco · The University of Padua · Literary Figures · Venetian Artists and Artworks · Arts, Artists, and Monuments in Rome · Venice's Public Monuments · Private Wealth, Private Art, and Public Pride

9. Theater in Venice, Venice as Theater 485

The Patrician Home · *Campi* · Churches · Floats · *Compagnie della Calza* · Patrician Sponsors · Citizen Sponsors · Foreign Groups as Sponsors · Foreign Performers and Organizers · Cherea · Native Actors · Diplomacy in Play · Carnival · The Battle of Pavia · The Diaries

Appendix A. *Money, Wealth, and Wages* 541

Money and Coinage · A Comparative Scale of Annual Wages and Salaries

Appendix B. *Glossary and Terms* 545

Vocabulary Used in the Original · Governmental Terms · Weight and Nomenclature for Candles · Ceremonial Containers · Fabrics and Garments · Boats, Ships, and Nautical Terms · Musical Instruments

Bibliography 553
Index 583

Maps

Preface

I heard much about the Sanudo diaries before I began to work on Venetian history. But when I turned to Venetian history and studied them, I was overwhelmed by their richness. They do not present a connected story, but from day to day give a report about life in Venice. Of course, they are concerned with politics, and they report about the meetings in the Great Council and the Senate and give a picture of the political leaders of the times. But they also depict life in its most varied aspects: religious ceremonies and solemn receptions of foreign ambassadors; marriages and family feuds; floods and fires; the influence of the clergy and news about the religious movements in Northern Europe; then the reports about the Italian wars and discoveries. These fifty-eight volumes show Venetian and Renaissance life in all its aspects.

Felix Gilbert, 1989

The idea for this collection of excerpts from a Venetian diarist originated with Felix Gilbert, a scholar to whom Venetian and Renaissance studies owe so much. Professor Gilbert (1905–91), author of seminal works in these fields as in others, had long cherished the thought that Sanudo's diaries should be shared by a wider audience than historians of early modern Europe, who have continuously mined this immensely fruitful resource for their political, diplomatic, military, cultural, and social histories. To that end he invited Patricia H. Labalme and Laura Sanguineti White to work with him. Letters went out over his signature to colleagues whose work had already drawn on this resource and whose suggestions of excerpts to be included formed the first outline of this work.

Felix Gilbert did not live to see that outline, much less this book that followed from it, but his spirit, learning, and commitment have informed the entire endeavor and guided it to completion. We celebrate his initiative and dedicate this volume to his memory.

This edition is the work of Patricia H. Labalme and Laura Sanguineti White, who made the final selection of the excerpts used and supplied the narrative connections. The large majority of translations were made by Linda L. Carroll. Each translation was reviewed and then edited by Labalme and White. In some instances they supplied the initial translations, which were then reviewed by Carroll. Revisions to all translations involved a multistage, fully cooperative process to which all three contributed, resulting in a final form that was approved by all three. All three contributed to the annotations and footnotes. But the resulting work also owes much to many others.

The original publication of Sanudo's diaries in fifty-eight volume from 1879 to 1903 was a heroic undertaking, a joint achievement involving five senior editors over those twenty-four years. The compilation and translation of the excerpts that form the present single volume, a far more modest project, has taken half as long; even so, it could not have been accomplished without the support of a number of institutions and the encouragement, criticism, and guidance of a great many colleagues. The initial work on the volume was sponsored by the Renaissance Society of America with the aid of a grant from the National Endowment for the Humanities: to both of these early sponsors the editors express their warm appreciation. The facilities of the Institute for Advanced Study afforded the Sanudo project hospitality and ready access to the fifty-eight volumes of the published edition and supporting literature. Over many years, members of the Medieval Seminar at the institute, led by Giles Constable, helped to resolve puzzling textual interpretations, as did a worldwide web of Venetianist scholars consulted electronically.

Among colleagues, the editors wish particularly to acknowledge the support of Patricia Fortini Brown and James S. Grubb, who helped to shape and refine this work from its inception. In the earliest phase of the project, they suggested passages for inclusion, and in the final stages of the preparation of the manuscript, they gave their generous and invaluable assistance. In particular, Patricia Fortini Brown selected all the illustrations. James S. Grubb nurtured the work from the completed manuscript following the death of Patricia H. Labalme through the final stages of production.

Helpful suggestions also came from Linda L. Carroll, Stanley Chojnacki, Robert Finlay, Rona Goffen, Paul Grendler, Margaret King, Michael Knapton, Michael E. Mallett, John Jeffries Martin, Reinhold Mueller, Edward Muir, Dennis Romano, David Rosand, Ellen Rosand, Guido Ruggiero, and the late Felix Gilbert, Donald Queller, and Wendy Steadman Sheard. Their contributions helped the editors to organize the work, and we are very grateful for that early impetus.

In addition to this distinguished list of American scholars who were personally known to Felix Gilbert and whose help he solicited, other scholars offered useful advice and shared the fruits of their own research. Among those, we especially wish to thank Jonathan Glixon, Jeffrey Kurtzman, Michael Putnam, Alan M. Stahl, and Diana Wright. Moreover, many Italian colleagues gave generously of their time and talent. The late Vittore Branca befriended this volume from its start. We are indebted to him for his insights, vast learning, and wide circle of helpful contacts. At various points we sought the advice of Manlio Cortelazzo, Maria Francesca Tiepolo, and the late Gaetano Cozzi, to whom we are indebted for many useful suggestions, corrections, and kind support. Associated research in the Archivio di Stato was facilitated by Michela dal Borgo and Paola Benussi. Generous help was provided by David H. Stam, who read the manuscript, organized the bibliography, and offered timely practical and editorial advice. In addition, we are beholden to scholars of many nationalities whose writings on and references to Sanudo's diaries over the centuries made the task of selection much easier than it would have been without their published works.

Special thanks goes to Angela Caracciolo Aricò, editor of several of Sanudo's most important works. She lent her expertise on Sanudo's language and style to the entire enterprise, reading and reviewing material, and her scrupulous consideration saved us from a variety of uncertainties.

Numerous excerpts from the printed text were checked by the editors against the manuscript word for word. For all the other excerpts used, we are grateful to Sante Marton for his scrupulous work in reviewing the original manuscript and noting any variants from the printed edition. We also thank Loretta Rotunno, not only for her expert technical assistance but also for her full dedication to the project.

Notwithstanding this level of support, errors no doubt remain in translation, identification, and interpretation, for which the editors are entirely responsible. We invite future revisions in what has been from the beginning a participatory undertaking.

The Composition of the Diaries

The origin and composition of Sanudo's diaries are described in the introduction and chapter 1. The original autograph copy exists today in the Biblioteca Nazionale Marciana (BNM), Ital. Cl. VII, 228–86 (9215–73). An examination of these volumes reveals something of Sanudo's system. He appears to have first recorded his observations in notebooks that he kept for each day or a for a few days at a time. The entries in the extant autograph copy of the diaries were a second stage, sometimes combining several days' events into a single entry, although each entry is listed under the earliest of the days covered. An examination of the original full entries shows no change in handwriting or ink color, which would indicate a later addition. Examples of Sanudo's method are pointed out for certain excerpts included in this volume. The diaries are in no way a finished product, however. There are frequent blanks where the author intended to supply names or numbers of people, and many sentences end with "etc." (sometimes omitted in the translations), indicating that Sanudo meant to supply more information.

The History of the Text and the Fulin Edition

The autograph copy of the diaries has its own interesting history. The manuscript notebooks of the diaries were bequeathed by Sanudo to the Venetian government for its use and preservation. They were known and occasionally cited, especially by nineteenth-century historians. In the early nineteenth century, at the time of Austrian occupation of Venice, the notebooks were transported to Vienna, with a handwritten copy replacing them in Venice. Returning to their native city in 1866, the notebooks remained unpublished until a team of Italian scholars edited them in fifty-eight volumes in 1879–1903.

The editors of this volume wish to acknowledge here their debt to the nineteenth-century editors of Sanudo's diaries, in particular Rinaldo Fulin, who launched the enterprise, and Guglielmo Berchet, who completed it. Working with Federico Stefani, Nicolò Barozzi, and Marco Allegri over twenty-four years, these Italian scholars made possible the publication of this rich scholarly resource.

The excerpts translated in the present volume have been checked against the autograph copy. Occasionally we found a date misread by a few days, an incorrect number of troops or ducats, an occasional word omitted or reversed with its neighbor, an abbreviation misinterpreted, more rarely a single manuscript line skipped by transcription error, a possibly (but not certainly) different reading for an especially challenging phrase. Punctuation, which in Sanudo is generally missing or difficult to identify, was sometimes misleadingly added to the published edition; in some cases it has been corrected in the present work by reference to the manuscript or, for vote counts, to documents in the Archivio di Stato of Venice. On the whole, we found few significant variations between the manuscript and the printed edition, and unless the sense was altered, we have not made note of every minor change. Contrary to suggestions by some scholars, we found no deliberate omissions. We have footnoted a number of red-ink rubrics from the early volumes, which Sanudo may have intended to use as headings in a formal history. We concur with the opinion of another Sanudo scholar, David S. Chambers, who has written that while "there has been talk among philologists of the need for a completely new edition . . . , serious need of this seems slight."[1] But we do recommend that the careful researcher into exact chronology, financial figures, or vote counts attentively check the original sources.

The Language of the Diaries

Sanudo chose to write in the vernacular, a choice that may have been imposed on him by a limited classical education. But it was a choice he embraced and justified because of a connection he felt, but never fully articulated, between the vernacular and *la verità*. This connection has been discussed by two Sanudo scholars in particular, Gaetano Cozzi and Angela Caracciolo Aricò. According to Cozzi, Sanudo saw truth and its comprehensibility as intimately interwoven: "The most important aspects of Marino Sanudo's work are the sense he has of news as a document about life, his conception of history as an objective mirror of life, and his conviction of the need for a precise exposition which is comprehensible to everyone."[2] Caracciolo Aricò, in her introduction to Sanudo's *De origine*, sets the author within the broader literary culture of his period, citing at the same time his passion for the force of truth in history

---

1. Chambers 1998a, 7.

2. "L'aspetto più importante dell'opera di Marin Sanudo è nel senso che egli ha della notizia quale documento di vita, nella sua concezione della storia quale specchio obiettivo di vita, e nel suo convincimento della necessità di un'esposizione precisa e comprensibile a tutti." Cozzi 1970b, 348.

which he, as a Venetian patrician, had personally experienced and recorded in his native tongue, his "sermon materno."[3]

Finally, there may have been other, less consciously formulated reasons for his use of the vernacular: if history was a record of not only great matters but also concrete details (foodstuffs, fabrics, commodities, the everyday objects of the lives around him), only a language including vernacular terms, with all their evocative overtones—terms that had no exact equivalence in Latin—could lead to *la verità,* the truth of his narratives, and only the truth could contribute to an understanding of the events of his day. Cozzi also speaks of Sanudo's "scientific" mentality: first the data, then the conclusions.[4] However, it would be incorrect to claim that Sanudo saw himself as a "social historian" before his time. He speculated very little about how future readers would interpret his "history" except to say that they would find it useful and that it would serve the "honor of God and the exaltation of the Venetian state" (34:5).[5]

The Translation of the Diaries

Traduttore, traditore (translator, traitor): translation is always an adventure and never an entirely satisfactory one. Our challenge was to render Sanudo's chancelloresque Italian, his perfunctory and repetitious vocabulary, and his often awkward syntax into a readable text while preserving the lively and living quality of his reports. In some passages that living quality is almost painterly, as if he were describing a theatrical scene replete with costumes, gestures, and words laden with consequence. Nor does Sanudo hesitate to add Latin phrases or classical lines to indicate his own cultural background and his familiarity with classical style. But that was not to be his mode.

As Ludovico Zorzi observed, "The most frequent formula in Sanudo's narrative style is the efficient but hasty run-on sentences that govern the compositions of his periods."[6] This was a text composed with some rapidity and not always legibly. Apart from the problems of Sanudo's syntax, some terms have remained elusive despite every effort to find their appropriate English equivalents. For this reason, many governmental titles have been left in Italian; their approximate English equivalents may be found in appendix B under "Governmental Terms." Certain other Italian terms, such as *comedia* (as in the Venetian dialect), *compagnia della calza,* and *festa,* are left in the original,

---

3. Caracciolo Aricò 1980, esp. x–xiv.
4. Cozzi 1970b, 348.
5. All such citations are to the Fulin edition of the diaries, citing volume and column.
6. L. Zorzi 1971, 24–25. See also Lepschy 1993.

with an explanatory note given at their first use; these terms may be found in appendix B under "Vocabulary Used in the Original."

Names. In order not to overburden the text with proper names, the patronymics of the patricians Sanudo mentions have usually been omitted. Sanudo gives the patronymic out of necessity, since Venetian family names were so frequently repeated in collateral lines; indeed, a 1405 law required that patricians seeking election to office be identified not only by given name and surname but also by patronymic. We have generally retained the Venetian spelling for proper names but standardized Sanudo's sometimes variant spellings of the same name to accord with the form closest to the one in the indexes to his published volumes. Place-names, names of monuments, and names of famous artists and condottieri occasionally have been modernized to facilitate identification. In the footnotes and appendixes, the spelling of names follows that in the indexes of the Fulin edition. Similarly, Sanudo used many variant spellings in naming magistracies and offices. These have been standardized in the editors' commentaries, but Sanudo's versions have been largely retained in the diary excerpts.

Titles. The following titles appear frequently in Sanudo's text: *ser* (occasionally *messer*), usually (but not exclusively) used before patrician names as a title of respect; *dotor* or *doctor,* translated as "university laureate," indicating a university graduate; *k,* for "cavalier," indicating knighthood bestowed by a monarch or emperor or occasionally by the Venetian government; *domino* or *dominus,* a title of respect used for certain laity (nobles, important citizens such as secretaries) or ecclesiastics, here rendered as "domino" or "don."

Ellipses. Sanudo often left blanks for numbers of participants in an event, for financial figures, for a person's age, for a date, or for the rest of a series that he intended to supply later but never did. Sanudo's ellipses are indicated by a dash (——), to distinguish them from editorial omissions, indicated by three or four ellipsis points.

Dates. The date given at the head of each excerpt indicates the date on which Sanudo entered the excerpt into his diaries. However, the event he describes may have taken place some days earlier, and the document he copies or summarizes may date from several days or, in the case of diplomatic dispatches, several weeks earlier. According to the Venetian calendar, the new year began on March 1, a dating system usually referred to in Venetian histories as *more veneto* (Venetian custom), abbreviated as *m.v.* Thus, for example, January 20, 1450 on the Venetian calendar would be January 20, 1451 on the modern calendar; in our text, however, all January and February dates follow the modern calendar.

Hours. In Sanudo's time, the twenty-four-hour clock began near sunset. Thus "two hours" means two hours after sunset. By making adjustments for seasonal differences in the time of sunset, ranging from about 5:00 PM at the winter solstice to about 8:00 PM at the summer solstice, the reader will arrive at the equivalent of the modern hours. For example, Sanudo writes that on June 26, 1514 (18:299–300), a party continued until "nine hours, that is, until full daylight." Since the date was so near the solstice, sunset was calculated as occurring at about 8:00 PM, and "full daylight" therefore at about 5:00 AM. A chart by Michael Talbot based on an eighteenth-century French source offers a calibrated way of converting the old Italian system into approximate modern equivalents. However, it is cumbersome to apply, and the editors have preferred to leave a looser calculation up to the reader, who should calculate the twenty-four-hour day as beginning at sunset, or, as the French commentator put it, "à nuit tombante, et lorsque l'on commence à ne pouvoir lire qu'avec peine."[7]

Bells. For practical purposes, night began with sunset and was further marked by the different bells of Venice. The Marangona—the name literally means "carpenters' bell" and originally referred to the workers in the Arsenal—rang in the morning to signal the beginning of the workday, at noon to signal lunchtime, an hour later for the resumption of work, and in the evening to signal the end of the workday. The Realtina, the bell of San Giovanni Elemosinario a Rialto, usually rang at the third hour of the night and signaled curfew, that is, the extinguishing of all unauthorized fires, and the Mattutina rang one hour before the first Marangona and signaled the end of curfew.[8]

Canonical Hours. The seven canonical hours, each appointed for a religious devotion, were matins, prime, tierce, sext, none, vespers, and compline. Prime indicated 6:00 AM; tierce, three hours later, or 9:00 AM; sext, noon; none, 3:00 PM; vespers, 6:00 PM; compline, before retiring; and matins, with lauds, midnight or 2:00 AM or daybreak. Sanudo uses *tierce* and *none* occasionally to indicate roughly 9:00 AM and 3:00 PM, respectively.

Meeting and Meal Times. Many of Sanudo's entries begin with such expressions as "La mattina fo . . . ," referring to a morning meeting of one of the executive committees, such as the Collegio, or "Da poi disnar fo . . . ," referring to a postprandial meeting of the Senate or sometimes the Great Council. After one of those meetings there might be a meeting of the Ten, and if this continued until particularly late, he described it as ending at "una ora," "due ore," or "tre ore," implying that *disnar* (dinner) was in the early afternoon, roughly at the same time as the traditional Italian *pranzo.*

---

7. Talbot 1985, 52; the chart appears on p. 60.
8. See Cecchetti 1886; Molmenti 1973; Crouzet Pavan 1981; and Scarabello 1980.

Marin Sanudo, His Life, His City, and His Diaries

Marin Sanudo, 1466–1536: His Life

Marin Sanudo, the Venetian diarist, was born in on May 22, 1466, under stars whose configurations he would later carefully document with astrological tables, into an old Venetian patrician family originally descended, he claimed, from a king of Padua. He lived out his three score years and ten in the service of his homeland, which in the half-century before his birth had grown to an empire spanning much of northern Italy, as well as the Adriatic and eastern Mediterranean seas. A French chronicler of the time described Venice as "the most triumphant city," and indeed Venice was a power to be reckoned with throughout Europe and the Near East. It was the center of the commercial world, its trade routes lacing together its various parts, its diplomatic personnel recording its every newsworthy occurrence. This was Sanudo's world, about which he was to leave a fifty-eight-volume manuscript covering the events of almost forty years.[1]

Sanudo grew up in his family palazzo in the parish of San Giacomo dell'Orio on the Fondamenta del Megio, named for the granaries that were so important to the sustenance of the city.[2] His father, Leonardo Sanudo, was a man of some importance in Venetian political life, and his embassy to Rome, where he died when Marin was only eight years old, indicates ability recognized and status acquired. He left an ample family of seven children by two wives, whose fortunes were reduced by the unwise supervision of the oldest

---

1. Sanudo 1879–1903, hereafter often referred to as the Fulin edition. The editors of that edition Tuscanized the spelling of Sanudo's name—*Marino Sanuto*—which in the present work is given in its Venetian form. References to the Fulin edition are to volume and column, as well as, for longer passages, the date of the diary entry. For Sanudo's ancestry, see Sanudo 1980, 13. The often-quoted French commentator was Philippe de Commynes; see Commynes 1970.

2. The city's stores of millet *(megio)* and other grains were situated in a building at the far end of the canal of the same name.

son, Alvise, who after four years of mismanagement gave up the responsibility and left for Syria. Marin's care was taken over by his paternal uncle Francesco Sanudo, who supported his education and must have provided him with sufficient means to live honorably as a gentleman of culture, paying his taxes and collecting an extraordinary library.

Of that education, culture, and library there are some indications: he studied the Latin authors, knew some logic, and attended public lessons in philosophy at the School of Rialto and in rhetoric, history, and poetry at the School of San Marco, although he did not (and perhaps could not afford to) pursue the higher learning available in his day at the University of Padua. He was closely associated with the Aldine press, in 1502 helping to secure for Aldo Manuzio (in Latin, Aldus Manutius) a ten-year patent on the new cursive type, and several early Aldine editions were dedicated to him. His magnificent library of books and manuscripts grew to sixty-five-hundred volumes before the destitution of his last years forced him to sell a number. All these factors argue his full participation in the cultural life of Renaissance Venice.

The focus of his passion, however, soon evolved from the ancient learning associated with Renaissance studies to the contemporary scene. His early writings illustrate this tendency: following his youthful introduction to a course on Ovid's *Metamorphoses*[3] and his "Memorabilia Deorum Dearumque" (1481), a treatise on the gods and goddesses of antiquity written when he was fifteen years old, he produced his *Itinerarium cum syndicis terrae firmae* (1483), a traveler's journal written at age seventeen after a trip through the Veneto with a cousin; his *Commentari della guerra di Ferrara* (1484), an account of a recent war between Venice and Ferrara; and his *De origine, situ et magistratibus urbis venetae ovvero la città di Venetia (1493–1530),* which he began in the early 1490s and continued over the next four decades.[4] The *De origine* was a summary of churches, monasteries, schools, bridges, ferry crossings, prisons, feast days, ceremonies, sights to show foreigners (much as the modern tourist would see), moneys minted, fresh fish, and, most particularly, a careful description of the various magistracies of the city, a section to which Sanudo added revisions in 1515, when his own concern for these magistracies was acute. His *Vite dei dogi (1474–1494)* was a compendium of chronicles and accounts about the lives of the doges, combining historical and political observations, up to the year 1494. Then, with the dramatic descent into Italy of the French king

---

3. The "Praelectio in lib. XIII Ovidi Metamorphoseos."

4. See the bibliography for editions of Sanudo's writings. Sanudo's titles were occasionally in Latin, as if to associate them with the humanistic publications of his day, but the texts of his principal works were in the vernacular. However, Cozzi 1970b, 345, states that according to contemporaries, there was a Latin first draft of Sanudo's *Commentari della guerra di Ferrara.*

Charles VIII and his army in 1494, Sanudo began a history of this campaign, *La spedizione di Carlo VIII in Italia* (1495), which set forth Venice's role in resisting the French invasion and the widening European range of Venetian and Italian affairs.[5] That work concluded with the events of December 1495. On January 1, 1496, his diaries began.

A clear sense of continuity runs through all of Sanudo's writings. All, implicitly or explicitly, were works "to make known for eternity our Venetian state."[6] All were written in the vernacular so that both the learned and the less learned might read them. Most betray Sanudo's passion for detail, for lists, for documents, for the drama of daily events. As each volume of the diaries succeeded its predecessor, Sanudo believed and occasionally promised his readers that he would write a more elegant and formal history when the peace that the French king's invasion had destroyed returned to Italy.

Peace did come to Italy thirty odd years later; the time for Sanudo's revision never came.[7] During 1498, two years after he began the diary, Sanudo was appointed to his first political offices. His hope was that this would be the beginning of a distinguished political career like his father's. But he also knew that the political experience would serve his recordkeeping purpose; it would help to "clarify for myself the truth about what was being contrived in Italy and no less in the world" (2:5). Many times thereafter he considered abandoning his fatiguing journals, but the excitement of subsequent events or discussions to which he was privy seems to have carried him forward. On occasion friends in high places encouraged him; such was the case of the newly elected doge Antonio Grimani (July 6, 1521), who, together with the Signoria, persuaded him to continue in his laborious enterprise (31:7). Companions also sustained him, especially when his political frustrations depressed him: "Marin," one urged him, "do not give up. Follow the path you have undertaken, because 'wife and magistrate are heaven's to designate.' Go on recording the events of Italy and the world" (34:7). And he did, believing in the importance of his work for those who governed his beloved *patria*[8] and for the future. "*Domino concedente* [the Lord willing]," he wrote, "I have decided to continue this task, and so here will be written day by day what news is heard"

---

5. See Caracciolo Aricò 1980, x–xiii, where the manuscripts and published editions of Sanudo's works are listed.

6. Sanudo 1980, 6.

7. For an example of Sanudo's stated intention to reduce his diaries to a history, see diaries, 34:5; there exists no evidence that such an effort ever took place.

8. Sanudo often referred to Venice as his *patria*, a word more resonant with emotion that any of its English equivalents. In the present work it is usually rendered "homeland," with "city-state" as the more traditionally historical term suggested for the extended power of Venice and the other contemporary Italian states.

(34:7). He went on until age and sickness prevented his going further than the fifty-eight volumes he had completed by 1533.

Every writer lives with his work, and a diarist more than others. This continuous recording became, for Marin Sanudo, both "wife and magistrate," a companion, a substitute for political power, a patriotic service for which he eventually became recognized. Seated in his *studio*—his *gymnasium,* as he called it—surrounded by the growing collection of books and manuscripts that were to make his library renowned and by the Latin inscriptions on his walls, he laboriously recorded what news he had gleaned while pacing the *brolo,* a garden area near the Ducal Palace frequented by patricians serving in the government councils, or the spacious hallways and courtyard of the palace, as well as news gathered from merchants and sea captains, bankers and officials, on the Campo San Giacomo, the place of business exchange near Rialto. "For I was continually in the public squares investigating every occurrence, no matter how minimal, how unimportant it was."[9] Sanudo's patrician birth entitled him to participate in all meetings of the Great Council, generally held on Sunday afternoons. And for three decades his abilities were rewarded with a number of elective positions that nourished his hunger for information. All that he gathered there, all that he heard and overheard in the antechambers of the Ducal Palace and in the streets and squares of the city, all the information and documents with which his friends supplied him, he gave to his diaries, an immense undertaking that he always considered a potentially public record.

His intention, however, was that his political career would eventually replace these myriad recordings. It never did. A few of the lower magistracies came his way, as did some terms in the Senate, of which he was immensely proud. Yet continued service in the Senate and election to any of the higher levels of political power eluded him, and he inveighed against the corrupt practices and cabals in which he would not engage to secure office. "But because," he wrote in 1517, "I do not participate in the intrigues that are common today, offering dinner to members of the Quarantia [the Forty, the supreme court of forty judges] and other senators, nor do I attend secret meetings as others do, those who are much younger than I am are elected. Patience! Perhaps some day we will rejoice to remember these things" (24:406).[10] Such righteously advertised integrity did not suit the temper of the times.[11]

---

9. Sanudo to the heads of the Council of Ten, 19 September 1531, in Caracciolo Aricò 1980, xv–xvi.

10. The last words are in Latin: *Pacientia! Forsitan et haec olim meminisse juvabit.* From Virgil's *Aeneid* 1.203.

11. On why Sanudo's political career failed, see Finlay 1980b, 254–58. For a list of government offices mentioned in the excerpts, see appendix B.

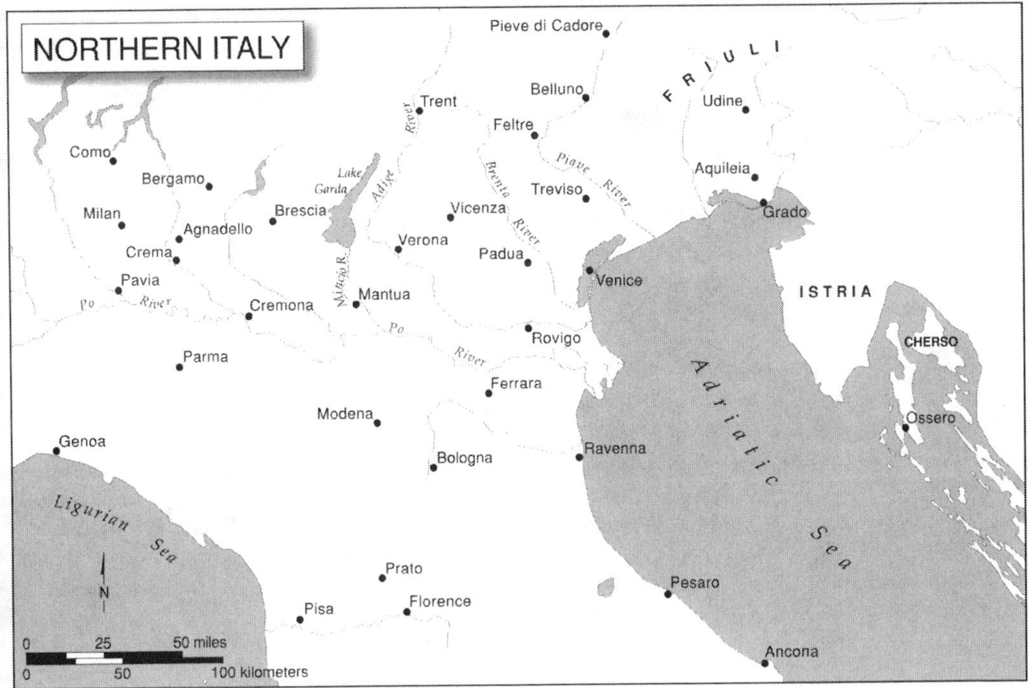

The effort and energy Sanudo might have spent in the political circles of
Venice went instead into his diaries, which soon acquired a reputation of
their own. In 1515 the government, recognizing the value of this growing work
of record, granted his request to see the secret books and letters of the Chancellery. He sought such privilege, he said, in order that he might put his annals into the form of a proper history (20:532).

That attempt to organize his records of twenty-four years, if indeed he
made it, was not sufficient to earn him the post of historian of Venice. A
few months later the post went to Andrea Navagero, who was better known
as a humanist than Sanudo. Sanudo wrote: "And no mention was made of
me because my works are in my maternal tongue" (21:485) and in a style he
later described as "coarse, unadorned, and low" (31:7). Sanudo knew full well
that this was an era when only humanistic Latin was considered worthy of a
state-sponsored history. Yet he also knew that his own works would find an
audience: "They will be read more willingly by everyone than any other, for I
have written fully and truthfully from the arrival in Italy of Charles, king of
France, up to this day [January 30, 1516]" (21:485).

Nevertheless, his gifts were spurned and eventually exploited. Andrea Navagero died in 1529 without a line to show for the annual stipend of 200 ducats

that he had collected for thirteen years. In 1531 a new official historian was chosen. Again it was not Sanudo. The burden and honor fell upon Pietro Bembo, a man of immense literary reputation and small political knowledge who, feeling himself unprepared, requested that Sanudo's diaries be made available to him. Why, cried Sanudo, should I serve him with my sweat?[12] But in the end he did because he had to; it was the price he had to pay for renewed permission from the Council of Ten, the highest government agency, to visit the Chancellery in order to gather materials. Moreover, he desperately needed the annual stipend of 150 ducats, which at last recognized his work as official and which he could enjoy as long as he continued to write his diaries. "Old, ill, poor, and poorer than poor," he had five years left to live, during two of which he continued to write and compete for office, lamenting when he was passed over that this was no way to treat a man who had been recognized by the Council of Ten. In September 1533, without ceremony or sentiment, his diaries came to an end.[13]

That same month he had made his will. He had no legitimate direct heirs; two daughters, born out of wedlock, had been properly married off. His late marriage to Cecilia Priuli had been brief and childless. His books of the "Histories and Events of Italy" (so he referred to the work on Charles VIII's expedition and the diaries) became the property of the Council of Ten; much of his magnificent library was sold to pay his debts. For his mortal remains he ordered a simple tomb with an epitaph informing the stranger or citizen that here lay the bones of Marin Sanudo, "expert recorder of Venetian history by public decree."[14]

Sanudo's last wishes went as unfulfilled as had those of his lifetime. No tomb was built, and his bones have disappeared along with his political dreams and the polished work he never produced. Yet time has confirmed the epitaph. "No writer," he had once claimed, "will ever make much of modern history who has not seen my diaries." No historian of Renaissance Venice and its contemporary world ever has.[15]

---

12. "Non volea dare li suoi sudori ad alcuno." See Bembo to Doge Andrea Gritti, 7 August 1531, ASV, CX, Comuni, filza 14, quoted in Berchet 1903, 95.

13. See diaries, 54:596, for the decree fixing his stipend and his commitment to continuing his diaries; and Sanudo to the heads of the Council of Ten, 19 September 1531, in Caracciolo Aricò 1980, xv–xvi.

14. For Sanudo's will of 1533, see Berchet 1903, 101–7.

15. For Sanudo's statement on future writers of history, see his letter of September 1531 to the heads of the Council of Ten in Berchet 1903, 96; Caracciolo Aricò 1980, xv–xvi; and Bettio 1828, 11–15. The original text is in BNM, Ital. Cl. VII, 375 (8954), fols. 11r–12v.

Venice and the Battle of Agnadello

It was May 14, 1509, six months after a group of European and Italian pow-
ers—France, Spain, the papacy, the Holy Roman Empire, Hungary, Savoy,
Mantua, Ferrara—had signed an agreement in Cambrai to resist Venetian ex-
pansion in northern Italy. Now a French army was in the field, near the river
Adda in the vicinity of Agnadello (about thirty-three kilometers southeast of
Milan), facing a Venetian mercenary force of approximately equal strength.
Sanudo, intent upon following the latest military events, was in the Ducal
Palace to look at a map of Italy with several patricians and secretaries when
the bitter news arrived.

> . . . At twenty-two hours [after sunset] Piero Mazaruol, a secretary, came running
> in with letters in his hand from the battlefield, with many gallows drawn on them.
> Thereupon the doge and the savi read the letters and learned that . . . our forces
> had been routed. . . .
>
> And there began a great weeping and lamentation and, to put it better, a sense
> of panic. . . . Indeed, they were as dead men. They wanted to keep the news a se-
> cret as long as possible but were unable to, since word had already escaped via
> the doge's household that our army had been defeated and that signor Bortolo,
> governor general, had been either captured or killed, etc. And in a very short time,
> within an hour of when the news had arrived, the entire Ducal Palace and the
> courtyard had filled with patricians and others. . . .[16]

The rout at Agnadello, so unanticipated, caused shock and despair. Another diarist contemporary with Sanudo, Girolamo Priuli, wrote: "No one
would ever have imagined that the Venetian mainland state could be lost and
destroyed within fifteen days, as we have now seen."[17] It also dealt a severe
blow to Venice's confidence in its ability to manipulate and control, through
its diplomats and hired troops, the Italian and European powers that had
combined to inflict on it this humiliating defeat.

The crisis of confidence caused by the defeat of Agnadello capped more
than a decade of difficulties.[18] In 1497-98 Vasco da Gama's discovery of a
route to India via the Cape of Good Hope had made possible Portugal's challenge to Venice's monopoly of the spice trade. A year later, in 1499, Venice had

---

16. Excerpted from diary entry dated 15 May 1509 (8:247–48). See chapter 4 under "Rome and
the War of the League of Cambrai," 15 May 1509, for the full text and further excerpts on this
important battle. The gallows drawn on the letters were a sign of bad news. "Signor Bortolo"
was Bartolomeo d'Alviano, commander, or governor general, of the Venetian forces.

17. Priuli 1912–41, 4:15–17, cited in Chambers and Pullan 1992, 160.

18. For an able review of the events of this decade and its aftermath, see Finlay 1994, 45–90.

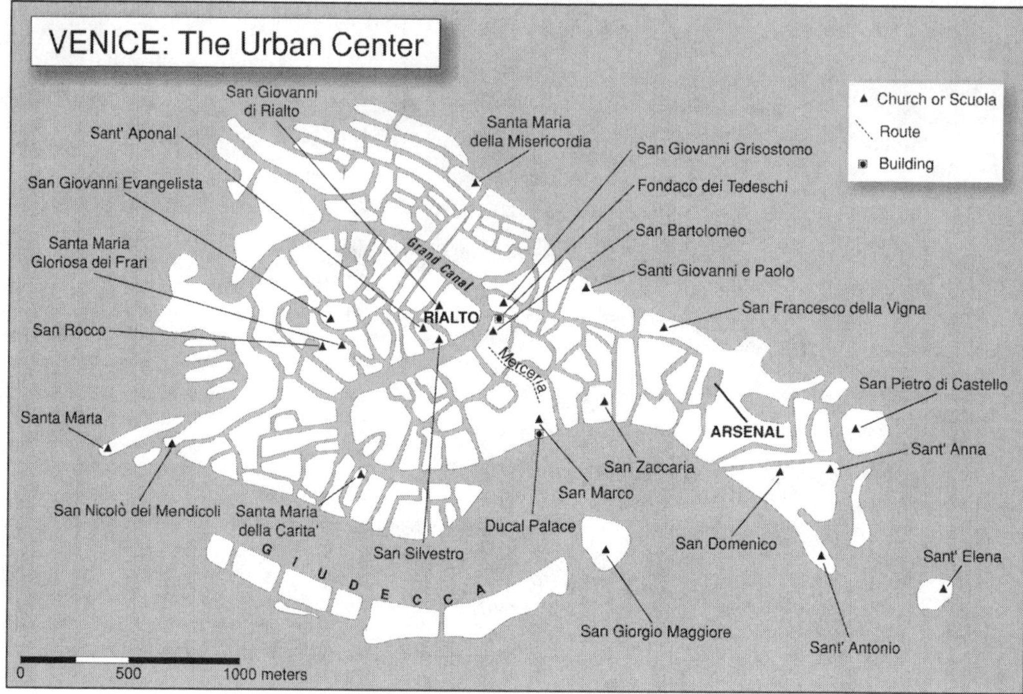

suffered a naval defeat by the Turks at Zonchio, and in 1503, after several years of war, it had made peace with its enemy to the east, to the distress of western powers who had counted on Venice to provide a bulwark against the Turkish tide. Within months of the peace treaty with the Turks, Pope Alexander VI had died, and in the chaos following his death, while his son Cesare Borgia lay ill, Venice had occupied the papal territories of Forlì, Cesena, Rimini, Faenza, and Imola, thereby enlarging its grain supply and commercial opportunities but also invoking the implacable ire of Julius II, the succeeding pope. Early in 1504 it was said in Rome "that the Signoria had made peace with the Turks to become the heir of St. Peter, and at every death of a pope they would take something from the Church."[19] In 1505 the accidental burning of the German warehouse in Venice was considered a bad portent, "together with the news of Coloqut,"[20] at that time a Portuguese trading post in India and a symbol of

---

19. Diaries, 11 February 1504 (5:839). This was the opinion of Giorgio Costa, a Portuguese cardinal from Lisbon, as reported by the Venetian ambassador in Rome, Antonio Giustiniani. *Signoria*, which technically meant the doge, his six councillors, and the three heads of the Quarantia Criminal, was also used as a ceremonial term for the Venetian government.

20. Colocut.

the commercial challenge posed by Portugal (6:126). As a sense of loss began to be felt in the city, Sanudo wrote of strange omens: the sign of the cross on the moon, a communion wafer that gave forth blood and milk. The city's commercial life was at a standstill, with "large warehouses, few goods; lots of banks, little money; many ships, few ventures" (April 5, 1507; 7:42). Peace with the Turks and an aggressive attitude toward its Terraferma neighbors compensated Venice for its losses elsewhere and for its increasing economic insecurity, but by the end of 1508 the diplomatic balance had tipped against it. Pope Julius II led in the formation of the hostile League of Cambrai, and six months later the Venetian troops met the French forces at Agnadello.

Venice's defeat at Agnadello in May 1509 seemed, to its enemies, a just reward for Venetian aggression. In two weeks the Venetian Terraferma as far as Cremona was lost, except for Treviso. Yet over the next eight years, by astute diplomacy and some military success, Venice recovered most of what it had lost, and with it a renewed sangfroid: the doge could boast that by defeating so many enemies leagued against it, Venice would achieve greater fame than ever before, both within Italy and outside (March 16, 1517; 24:79). So it seemed to the Venetians and others as well, and indeed, the decades following the War of the League of Cambrai were in many ways the most celebratory and exuberant in Venetian history. But the shadow of the great defeat at Agnadello was long, and by the time the war ended, for all its rapid recovery of territory, a series of permanent changes marked the city. Whether it was the leap in insurance rates owing to endangered travel routes or the drainage of precious metals from Venice and the disappearance of the gold ducat as a circulating coin; the sale of offices to strengthen the war coffers, the increase in political corruption, and a government dominated by executive councils such as the secret and swift-acting Council of Ten; or the crystallization of the Venetian myth, the congerie of stories that Venetians told about their history and their political and social systems, or the countermyths devised by their enemies about Venetians' insatiable greed for power, Venice emerged from the era of Agnadello profoundly altered. That battle, and the years preceding and following it, came to represent a watershed in Venetian history for whose dimensions Sanudo is our best witness.[21]

---

21. On the importance of the War of the League of Cambrai and the battle of Agnadello for Sanudo, see Chambers 1998a, 24: they "regenerated Sanudo's sense that his diaries were a work of eternal significance, that he was again recording momentous events, important for the whole of Christendom and particularly for Venice, to whose triumphant recovery he was pledged to bear witness." Indeed, it was Sanudo's witness, together with that of his contemporary Girolamo Priuli, that permitted later historians to confirm the importance of that war, that battle, and that apparent recovery. See also Gleason 2000 for a more recent interpretation of the decades following Agnadello and the resolution of Venice's aggressive image into one of conciliation and concord after the Peace of Bologna in 1530.

It was a period dominated by four doges. The first was Agostino Barbarigo, doge from 1486 to 1501, to whom Sanudo dedicated a number of his writings in a vain hope of patronage. The next was Leonardo Loredan, who held the post from 1501 to 1521, an unexpectedly long tenure for a man who was sixty-six when he was elected. Antonio Grimani succeeded him, to Sanudo's great satisfaction, for they were related. Sanudo records in detail the death of Loredan and the election of his relative Grimani. But Grimani's brief dogeship was ended by his death in 1523, and he was succeeded by Andrea Gritti, doge from 1523 to 1538, who outlived Sanudo. Sanudo was critical of Gritti's arrogance, and he carefully recorded the votes against this overproud man (34:157–59) and an opponent's angry statement that he did not wish to make a tyrant into a doge: "Non voio far Doxe tyran" (34:158). At the same time, Sanudo reveled in the civilization that Gritti promoted, and he passionately loved the city the doge personified: still triumphant in its style, shrewd, and confident of its ability to maneuver among the greater powers, more or less successfully, but always with panache.[22]

Selections from the Diaries (1496–1533)

But the story Sanudo tells is not only about Venetian triumphalism. While his diaries were written against the background of the larger events of the period outlined above, they are most compelling for their attention to human details. On June 3, 1530 (53:253), Sanudo recounts the visit of the Turkish ambassador to the doge:

> Then came the ambassador from the Turkish sultan. He disembarked at the quay near the Ducal Palace because it was raining. A handsome, tall, and dignified man, he was dressed in cloth of gold . . . and was accompanied by twelve Turks wearing turbans and fourteen patricians dressed in scarlet. . . .
>
> When he arrived in the Collegio, the doge rose and came forward [to him]. The ambassador, through an interpreter, said that the great lord and the pashas sent a greeting to the doge and the Signoria, and the lord in person had sent him and given him the letter that he presented, and the lord had sent him here to invite the doge to Constantinople to attend the celebrations for the circumcision of the sultan's four sons because of the friendship that the lord feels for the doge and the Signoria. . . .
>
> The doge, with a kindly expression, responded: "Would God that we could come, but we cannot walk, and we are too old." And he spoke laughingly, so that even the ambassador laughed. And then the doge said, "Our ambassador will be there in our name." And the Turk urged that the Venetian ambassador be sent soon; the doge said, "It will be done."

---

22. See Mallett and Hale 1984, 221–27, for an outline of the shifting military alliances between 1509 and 1530.

To be noted: the Turkish ambassador is given ten gold Venetian ducats each day for his expenses.

Again and again in Sanudo's diaries, as in the theatrical performances he so frequently patronized, a scene is set and a drama unfolds. The cast of characters in this most cosmopolitan city was legion: they are always identified, and among them, in addition to highly politicized and articulate patricians, were the world's leading diplomats, traders, and scholars. Their characters are sometimes finely sketched with a phrase, as are their costumes, their conversations, their gestures and expressions, the consequences and costs of their actions. The time of day and the weather are specified. Against the Venetian backdrop of marble-fronted palaces, of sea and sky, senators in their rich robes, women in their finery, Turks in their turbans, and tradesmen and workers in their daily wear carried on the business of their offices and lives, which Sanudo recorded, the simple alongside the ceremonial. It is our good fortune that Sanudo never took the time to reduce his prolixity and narrow his focus. It is his sharp eye, his broad interests, and his indefatigable pen that make the diaries so vivid and privileged a source for this exceptional city in an exceptionally important period.

Beyond Venice, Sanudo is the finest single witness, often the sole witness, to details of the upheavals that were transforming early modern Europe and the Mediterranean basin. During the nearly four decades covered in the diaries, Europe experienced the full force of the Turkish threat, the spread of the Reformation and the beginnings of Catholic reform, the great Italian wars between Habsburg and Valois, the rise of England to world prominence, the development of a mature Renaissance style, and the initial impact of overseas discoveries. The Republic's ambassadors and informants were the most skilled and articulate in Europe, and Sanudo faithfully recorded in the diaries all the news that reached Venice via official reports, treaties, and proclamations; letters from merchants, individual travelers, and spies; street rumors and neighbors' gossip.[23] If his diaries focus on the Venetian center, the extremities are also represented, from Scotland to Constantinople, with personalities ranging from English and Turkish potentates to German and Italian religious reformers, so that this one immense record becomes a remarkably full and variegated record of sixteenth-century life across Europe and the Near East.

Much written history has drawn from this rich source. But while Sanudo's diaries have been the basis for works on topics ranging from the Protestant

---

23. Information that came to Sanudo in documentary form was occasionally interleaved with Sanudo's manuscript text, adding a scrapbook element to his volumes.

Reformation to the Ottoman Empire and from prophecies to theatrical performances, they have not been used so fully as they merit. Even for those with access to the Fulin edition, which is not easily accessible, the sheer bulk of the work makes systematic research daunting. The language is often difficult to penetrate: while Sanudo often repeated the original Italian and Latin of the diplomatic documentation, his own summaries and observations are written in a Venetian chancellory vernacular sometimes laden with technical terms or obscure Venetian expressions. In this volume we seek to introduce the diaries to a larger public through the presentation of translated extracts.

In meeting the challenge of selecting passages from such a large work, we were aided by suggestions from those acknowledged in the preface. To this first list of excerpts, we added many more in response to extensive reading, serendipitous discovery, and the Sanudo-based work of other scholars. General themes began to emerge that we hoped might in combination convey a sense of the period's civilization from a Venetian viewpoint (and from one Venetian's viewpoint in particular). The process of choosing excerpts seemed a metaphor for constructing a mosaic of Venice itself, in which each excerpt represented a tessera of which we asked, Has it a facet that shines; that is, is it of interest in itself? Will it contribute to the mosaic we are composing of Renaissance Venice and its world?

The selection presented here is arranged in topical categories and subsections rather than in strict chronological order. While this arrangement results in some redundancy in references to historical events (i.e., the battle of Agnadello and the defining years of the War of the League of Cambrai), it makes Sanudo's diverse information accessible and gives it organic shape. But that organic shape is protean: to speak in successive chapters of government, justice, foreign affairs, economy, religion, society, culture, and theater is to suggest distinctions where there is overlap and interweave. Is Rialto an economic center or a concourse of diverse societies? Is it a "shrine of the city"[24] or a symbol of both its untidy vitality and its coherent authority? All of these meanings are represented here. In similarly protean fashion, emerging from these excerpts is no single Venice but a multiplicity of insights and images reflecting the tensions and contradictions of the Venetian reality.[25]

Chapter 1 introduces the diarist himself through his own references, revealing his personality, outlining his own story, and, through that story, intro-

---

24. See Calabi and Morachiello 1987, 294.

25. The editors agree with the formulation of Manfredo Tafuri, who described the reality of Venice as one "swollen with visual values, a jealous custodian of its own intimate tensions" (una realtà come quella veneziana, così gonfia di valori visivi e gelosa custode delle proprie intime tensioni). 1985, xx.

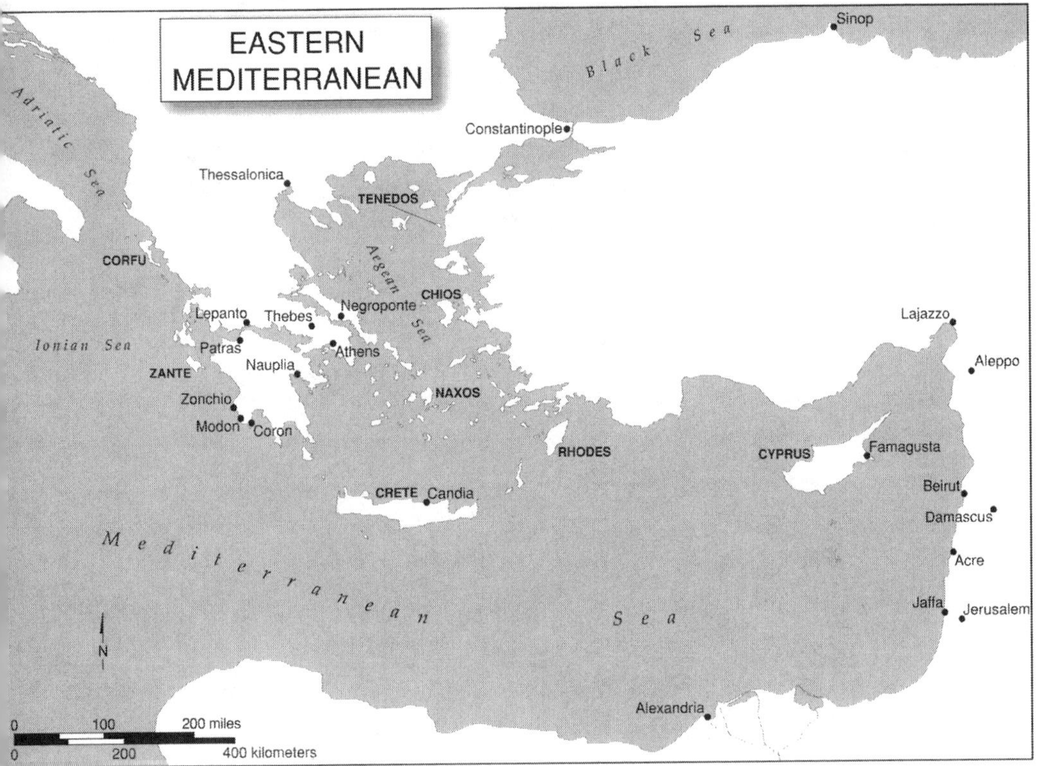

ducing the political framework of the city he delighted to serve as a member of its government. Chapter 9, which concludes the book, is titled "Theater in Venice, Venice as Theater." It was in 1533, the same year in which Sanudo put down his pen, that the Dutch humanist Erasmus, one of the greatest scholars of the era, referred to his sojourn in Venice as an entry into "theatro totius Italiae splendidissimo" (the most splendid theater of all Italy).[26] The chapters in between offer an introduction to the eclectic world of a unique Italian Renaissance city and to some of the European personalities and events of these few decades on the threshold of the modern age.

---

26. Erasmus to John Vergara, 19 November 1533, in Erasmus 1963, 10:321.

Abbreviations

ASV   Archivio di Stato di Venezia

BNM   Biblioteca Nazionale Marciana, Venice

CX   Consiglio dei Dieci (Council of Ten)

MC   Maggior Consiglio (Great Council)

m.v.   *more veneto,* for dating the new year from March 1

n.a.   *numero antico,* for the old numbering of archival folio materials

n.m.   *numero moderno,* for the modern numbering of archival folio materials

Chronology and the Doges

Chronology

1514, January 10–11	Great fire at Rialto
1515	Sanudo granted permission to consult papers of Chancellery
1516, January 30	Andrea Navagero appointed official historian of Venice
March 26–29	Ghetto Nuovo established
1517	Venetian recovery of mainland state (lost in 1509) complete
1527–28	Freeze and food shortage
1530	Pietro Bembo appointed official historian of Venice
	Peace of Bologna, end of Italian Wars
1533, September 30	Final entry in the diaries
1536	Death of Marin Sanudo

The Doges of Venice in Sanudo's Time

Agostino Barbarigo	August 30, 1486–September 20, 1501
Leonardo Loredan	October 2, 1501–June 22, 1521
Antonio Grimani	July 6, 1521–May 7, 1523
Andrea Gritti	May 20, 1523–December 28, 1538

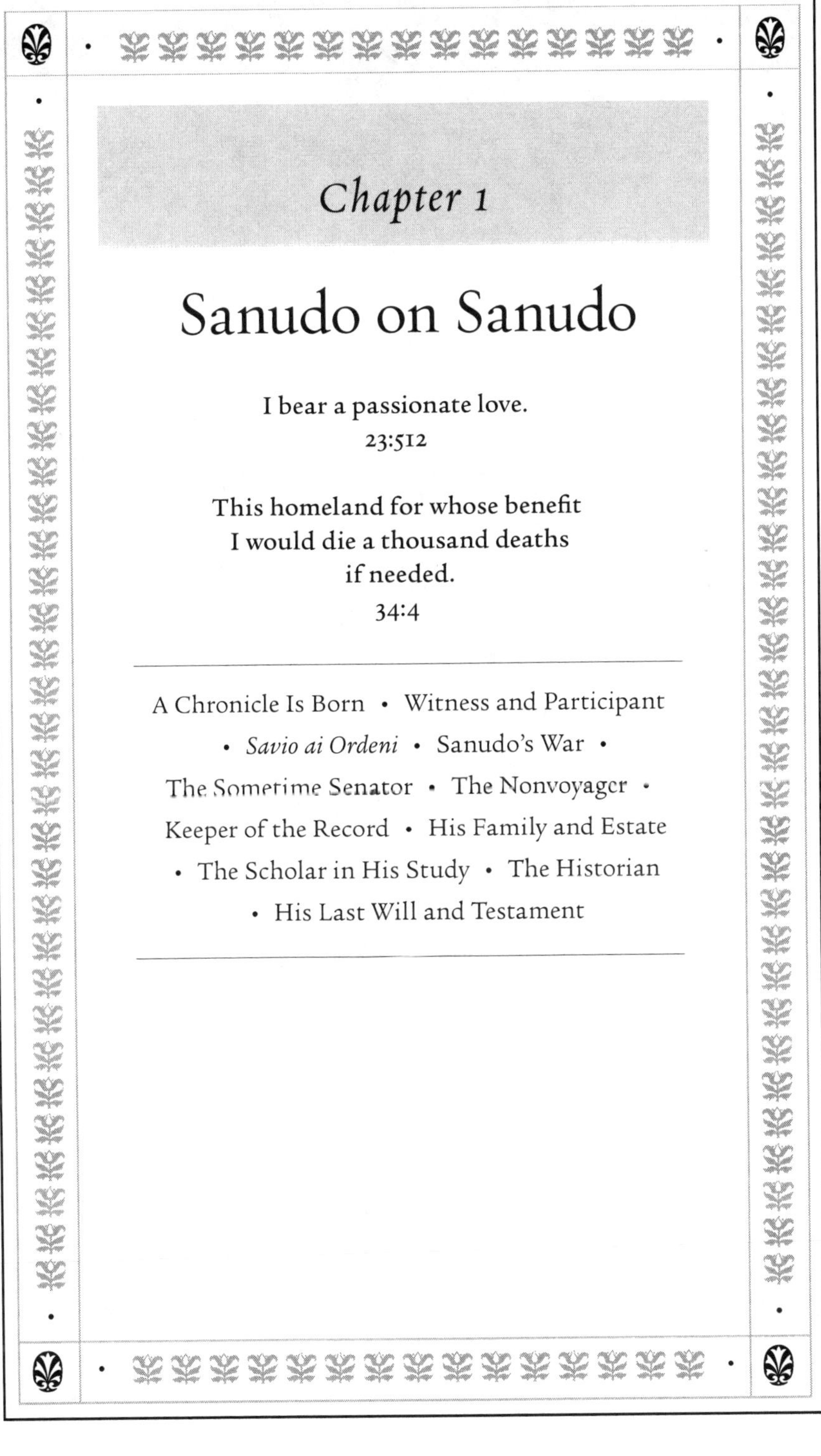

Chapter 1

Sanudo on Sanudo

I bear a passionate love.
23:512

This homeland for whose benefit
I would die a thousand deaths
if needed.
34:4

A Chronicle Is Born

The heavens have ordained that I be the one
to write down each day's memorable events.
1:893

If, as Erasmus stated, Venice was "the most splendid theater of all Italy," the principal European military and political drama upon that stage in the early sixteenth century may be said to have begun with the French invasion of Italy in 1494. In that year the French king, Charles VIII, led his troops toward the Kingdom of Naples, to which he laid hereditary claim. His excuse was that by exercising his right to Naples—contemporaries called it the *impresa di Napoli,* or the Naples campaign—he could set the first stage for a crusade to recapture the Holy Land from the infidels. But this military expedition was actually, and was known to be, an attempt to find glory, spoils, and riches in a peninsula divided into small rival states and easy of access once the Alps had been crossed.

The Italian Wars, initiated by this invasion, loosed upon Italy not only the French armies but also the military companies of the other European powers— the Holy Roman Empire and Spain—Swiss and other mercenary troops, including Italian ones hired by the greater and lesser powers. In the wake of all these armies, Sanudo saw what he called the "overturning of regimes," which he set out to record in his *La spedizione di Carlo VIII in Italia* (History of the Expedition of Charles VIII).[1] But one war seemed to lead into another: the French invasion was not decisive, and the subsequent withdrawal of French troops was not definitive. Great events were still in the offing. So Sanudo undertook a day-by-day chronicle of events in Venice and abroad, not anticipating that this would occupy him for the next thirty-seven years. At the same time, he promised the reader that a more condensed and elegant history would follow. He explains his purpose at the beginning of his diaries:

January 1, 1496 (1:5–6)   Here begins, in the Year of Our Lord 1496 and in the reign of Doge Agostino Barbarigo, Prince of the Venetians, Book One of the Events of Italy by Marin Sanudo.[2]

---

1. The phrase *la mutatione di stadi* appears in the dedicatory preface of bk. 3 in Sanudo 1873.

2. This title was in Latin, a common practice among writers using the vernacular. Cf. Machiavelli's *The Prince* in Machiavelli 1968–82, vol. 1.

Having concluded, not without the greatest daily labors, my account of the French wars that took place in Italy in recent years, and having produced a polished version of it in a large volume, I decided that I should not cease to record what was taking place in Italy even after Charles VIII, king of France, had returned to his kingdom across the mountains. I decided to record these events for two very powerful reasons: one, so that they would not fade into oblivion; and two, because the Kingdom of Naples, also called Apulia, had not yet been completely reacquired by Ferdinand, the second king of the house of Aragon and of Naples. This Kingdom of Naples he wished to retake, even though his forces were very limited, because many of its cities still owed allegiance to the king of France. Furthermore, a primary captain and viceroy, the Lord of Monpensier,[3] had been appointed for the [Neapolitan] realm by Charles; in addition, there were many French and even more Angevins who, with some barons, were on the French side. Thus, help from the Venetians was necessary.

This last sentence is the key to Sanudo's larger purpose in undertaking his diaries: to show what he perceived as the crucial role of Venice in the "great turmoil" transpiring throughout his world. Joining the Holy League against the French invaders, Venice used its naval power to repulse the French from several cities in Apulia, in southern Italy, some of which it retained.[4] It then sent its ships on to attack French positions at Naples and Genoa, and one of its fleets supported Pisa in its effort to free itself from Florence, allied at that moment with the French. It seemed that Venetian support would be needed by anyone wishing to regain or achieve territorial and political status in Italy, a story Sanudo intended to tell. Sanudo's opening statement continues:

For all these reasons, I wished to keep some record. Therefore I have abandoned every other type of composition and here will describe most truthfully all the events that have occurred. God willing, I will continue to describe them briefly, beginning on the first day of January 1495, as the year is reckoned in our Venetian fashion,[5] until peace has come to Italy. I promise my readers that at a later date, when I have more leisure, I will rewrite this book

---

3. Gilbert de Bourbon, Count of Montpensier.

4. The members of the Holy League were Spain (which included Naples), the Holy Roman Empire, the papacy, Milan, and Venice, which joined in February 1495. The ostensible reason for the formation of this Holy League was to defend Christendom against the Turks, but the actual enemy at this time was the invading French army.

5. The Venetian year began on 1 March. See "About the Translation" under "Dates." Except for this passage, all of Sanudo's references to January and February dates have been converted to follow the modern calendar.

in a different style, but for the time being I will set down each day the news that is circulating, beginning with the pontificate of Alexander VI.

In this relatively modest way Sanudo began his immense undertaking. Although he did not reckon how elusive peace would be, he was not deceived in his perception of the importance of the events he witnessed. Some decades later, these same Italian Wars were also to be the subject of more famous works and commentaries by Machiavelli, Guicciardini, Paolo Giovio, and other contemporary Italian historians who saw in this period, especially after 1530, a fundamental shift in the power structures of Europe as all the major Italian city-states except Venice lost their autonomy to the ascending Holy Roman Empire of Charles V.

Sanudo could not anticipate how "overturned" Italian regimes would be, nor did he have the advantage of distance from the events he described. He saw his task as simply keeping an ongoing record, a continuation of the contemporary history he had already written about the invasion of Charles VIII. Indeed, he came to view that earlier effort as the first volume of his diaries, even though it was written as a separate and more formal work, in a style that was as close as he ever came to that of a composed and structured history. Thus, two years after he began the diaries, toward the end of what by then had become a very long first volume, he declared himself to be at the beginning of the third volume of a connected work. At the same time, he made a claim that he was often to repeat: that "the heavens" themselves had ordained his task. It is that sense of destiny that puts him at the center of his diaries and of this chapter.

March 1, 1498 (1:893–94)   Ever since I composed, with no small effort, the history of King Charles of France's expedition into Italy to acquire the Kingdom of Naples, the heavens have ordained that I be the one to write down each day's memorable events until such time as peace comes to Italy. I have often entertained the desire to put an end to these quite fatiguing lamplit studies. But after seeing, in this present age, the various schemes hatched among the powers that govern the world, and after writing another rather lengthy work about the retaking of Naples . . . , and deeming that the affairs of Italy remain in great turmoil, I wish now to begin the third volume, that is, ephemeris[6] or day-by-day account. In it I will record, if the Supreme Creator is willing, the news as I hear it rather than using some polished style. I assure my readers . . . that when I have more time at my disposal I will convert this narrative into

---

6. *Ephemeris* is the term for a table that tracks the movements of the planets day by day through the 360 degrees of the heavens. See Carroll 1992, esp. 126n3. Sanudo compares the events of Venetian life and his discovering and recording of them with the stately progression of the heavens and its study by humans.

more formal prose. Therefore, let whoever wishes to read it do so and not reproach me: he will see here only what happened, plainly presented, beginning with the first day of March 1498.

Witness and Participant

How did Sanudo gather his information? He was, by virtue of his patrician status, a member of the Maggior Consiglio, or Great Council, but this was not so much a deliberative council as an electing body, meeting weekly to exercise its prerogative to staff the many committees that ran the Venetian government. More formative and instructive was his early service as a lawyer in the judicial magistracies of the Ducal Palace, a position he attained on July 8, 1487, at the age of twenty-one.[7] Then, in March 1498, a few weeks after his claim that he was destined to record the passing events, Sanudo was elected a *signore di notte,* a guardian of the Night Watch (1:906). He was one of six, each from a different *sestiere* of the city, who literally watched by night (accompanied by a small guard) over morals and malefactors, prohibiting dangerous nocturnal dances, affairs between Christians and people of other religions, restraining violence and ribaldry, and judging offences of these types. Sanudo held this office for six months (nearly all Venetian offices rotated fairly rapidly, lasting from six months to one year), until on September 27, 1498, he was chosen as one of the savi ai ordeni. This position was the acknowledged first rung of the Venetian political ladder; Sanudo called it "a most ancient and authoritative office" (2:240).[8]

The savi ai ordeni, or Savi da Mar, sometimes translated as "Sages of the Maritime Ordinances," constituted one of the three branches of the Collegio, the leading policymaking organ in Venice, which prepared all business for discussion in the Senate. It is not surprising that a sense of circumstance pervades the passage in his diaries where Sanudo announces his election. "On this day, in the Council of the Senate, there were elected five *savi ai ordeni*." He names the four others and then states: "and I, Marin Sanudo, who was then signor di notte. And for this reason, I shall here cease my description of events and enter into the Collegio and Senate on the first day of this October. And so I make an end to my annals" (1:1114).

But on the very next day Sanudo heard that letters had arrived from France, "which I shall shortly learn about," and he added a concluding line to this large

---

7. Berchet 1903, 84. Sanudo began as one of the minor lawyers—*avocati pizoli*—and within a year was made a staff lawyer attendant upon all the law courts in the Ducal Palace, an *avvocato ordenario per le corte,* or, in Latin, *advocatus per omnes curias* (Sanudo 1980, 144-45). To this experience may be attributed the foundation of his interest in and knowledge of Venetian laws.

8. For explanations of the offices Sanudo held, see appendix B.

first volume, a tentative farewell to his diaries: *"Finis pro nunc:* the end—for the time being." A few days later, he realized he could not give up his diaries because they were part and parcel of his political life. His new commitment would permit him not only to strive for his homeland but also to apprehend "the truth about what was being contrived in Italy and no less in the world" (2:5).

From then on, the volumes grew beneath his pen. "Tutto quel ho visto e inteso ho notado" (Everything I saw and heard I noted down), he wrote (5:1066). He was among the first to arrive in the doge's palace, where the various government bodies convened, and he was often among the last to leave (2:390, 21:98). From official letters, decrees, debates, dispatches, ambassadorial reports, from whatever was spoken or written, he sought *la verità,* the truth of events, "above all, the truth, because that is most powerful in history."[9] He wanted personally to experience the news: he had his own correspondents and sought out eyewitnesses (25:122, 123). Whenever possible, he positioned himself *per mezo,* in the middle, where he could hear it all: "aldì ogni cossa" (20:454).

Indeed, Sanudo was *per mezo.* From the start, he intended to be a participant as well as a witness, for he knew that his political activities nourished his diaries, and they in turn became a personal archive for his political judgments and legalistic statements. "I know the subject matter," he wrote in 1521, "from the history I have written" (31:329).[10] Marin Sanudo was at the center of his work, protagonist as well as scribe, politician and diarist, driven by a fervent patriotism. "Un sviscerato amor porto a questa excelentissima Republica" (I bear a passionate love for this most excellent Republic), he wrote (23:512; cf. 20:284). That passion led Sanudo to trumpet his own actual and potential contributions to his country, political as well as literary. Even when his opportunities for political success wavered, leading him often into depression and self-doubt, his commitment to his diaries endured. But in success or failure, the political aspirant and diarist were one person, their evolutions intertwined.

This chapter contains selections that characterize the diarist, his political successes (which were few but which he always reported, especially the speeches he made), his failures (which were many and bitter), his prejudice against leaving the city and his reputation within it, his financial and emotional family circumstances, the physical setting in which he wrote his works (his *studium*), his hopes

---

9. Sanudo to the heads of the Council of Ten, 19 September 1531, in Caracciolo Aricò 1980, xv.

10. See also diary entry for 3 February 1514 (17:527–28), when, after the fire at Rialto had destroyed tax records of the Provveditori di Comun, Sanudo was able to supply them with a copy he had made "already some years earlier, and they were very grateful"; and entry for 20 June 1516 (22:301), when Sanudo found a law of less than two years earlier that "none of the secretaries was able to recollect . . . and I found it because of the record I keep in my diaries." This was a commentary on both the state of Venetian legal records and the political usefulness of Sanudo's diaries to himself and, he hoped, to future politicians.

for literary recognition (unfulfilled), and his demise ("old, ill, poor, and poorer than poor").[11] At the same time, it is a vivid introduction to the workings of the Venetian government and the patrician class, who were the governors, competing for positions of power and managing the state to its advantage and their own.

Savio ai Ordeni

The first term of Sanudo's service as a savio ai ordeni, from September 1498 to March 1499, was marked by tensions not only within Italy but across the maritime empire that Venice ruled. The Turks, with whom the Venetians had an ongoing ambivalent relationship of mercantile agreements and imperial rivalries, were preparing for war. Sanudo reports his part in a Senate debate over arming thirty galleys against the Turks. In this case, as a member of the Collegio, he supported its proposal, and the measure passed almost unanimously.

January 15, 1499 (2:336)   All the *savi di Collegio* proposed a bill in the Senate recommending that, given the preparations that the Turkish ruler is making, we arm thirty of our light galleys: ten in this city; ten to be divided among Dalmatia, Apulia, and Corfù; and ten on the island of Candia [Crete]. The timing and the means with which this should be undertaken will be at the discretion of the Senate. The bill was opposed by Lunardo Grimani, proveditor of the Arsenal, who said that there was no need for it and that the affairs of the Arsenal were in disarray, and that he had loaned it 1,000 ducats of his own money.[12] By order of all the other savi, I, Marin Sanudo, a savio ai ordeni, went to respond to him, and I was praised by the doge and by everyone for showing the necessity of arming the galleys. . . . The bill passed with 2 abstentions, 4 against, and III in favor.

Sanudo's experience as a savio ai ordeni was not always positive. Later that year, a scene was enacted that would be repeated many times during his life. In the nine months since his senatorial intervention, the war against the Turks had begun, and in August 1499 there was a naval encounter between the Venetian armada, led by Antonio Grimani, and the Turkish fleet at Zonchio, between the Peloponnesus and the Greek mainland. The Venetian armada was badly defeated, to the dismay and anger of the government. On September 14 there was a discussion in the Collegio as to what defensive and punitive action should be taken.

---

11. Sanudo to the heads of the Council of Ten, 19 September 1531, in Caracciolo Aricò 1980, xv.

12. The proveditor was a commissioner. The Arsenal was the large shipyard and armaments depository in the northeastern section of the city. The armaments were in preparation for the war against the Turks (1499–1503).

As a savio ai ordeni, Sanudo supported the proposal that additional defensive forces be sent to Corfu and that four of the disgraced naval leaders be dismissed. At the same time, a group of officials demanded the far more radical action of replacing Antonio Grimani as captain general. Sanudo reported on what ensued.

September 14, 1499 (2:1296)   The first to respond was ser Tomà Donado of the Quarantia,[13] who said that two of his sons had died on the burnt ships but that it was not right to appoint a new captain general. Then Vicenzo Grimani, son of the captain general . . . , spoke well and strongly, requesting the reading of the letters of Simon Guoro, proveditor, to ser Piero Marzello. After these letters had been read, he excused his father by attributing his failure to his not wanting to take the life of any patrician, and he, Vicenzo, begged the senators not to act in haste. All the while, he spoke from the heart as he knelt on the podium. He was answered very wisely by ser Francesco Trun, then by ser Polo Pixani, knight and state attorney, who said that now was not the moment to change [the] captain general. Beneto Zustignan replied, and then Vicenzo Grimani went again to the podium to excuse his father in the face of the criticism against him. After the relatives of the ship masters had left, the bills went to a vote: 4 undecided, 6 against, 59 for ours, and 98 to elect a new captain general, and that passed.[14] And I will not forbear to say this, that I was unjustly spurned because I have always been forceful and on this occasion did not support the vote to make a new captain general since in truth I could not bring myself to do so on this day. Whence, even though I was nominated for *auditor nuovo*,[15] I found myself almost alone and failed to be elected, in spite of all my labors in maritime matters.

In the years that immediately followed, Sanudo was elected a savio ai ordeni three more times, and after a sixteen-month term as treasurer of Verona (1501–2), he served as a savio ai ordeni yet three more times.[16] His political fortunes, how-

---

13. Donado was a member of the Quarantia Criminal, or Criminal Court of the Forty, a body that attended meetings of the Senate. See appendix B.

14. Family members were always asked to leave the council rooms when a relative was being judged. See ASV, Senato, Secreta, reg. 37, fol. 135v *n.m.*, 14 September 1499, where the voting numbers are more clearly presented than in the Fulin edition, where the punctuation is misleading.

15. See appendix B.

16. On the demeaning of this office, see diaries, 26 June 1499 (2:852–53), for the appointment of two administrators for maritime affairs, "executori . . . per le cosse da mar," a new committee sponsored by the Savi di Terraferma and the Savi Grandi that undercut the savi ai ordeni; and 7 October 1511 (13:41) for the waiving of the age limit for serving as a savio ai ordeni upon payment of a contribution to the treasury. Cf. Sanudo 1980, 244.

ever, seem to have leveled out with these relatively minor positions. It may be that his marriage, in 1505, to a wealthy widow may have absorbed him in family concerns, including a physical division of the house he shared with relatives.[17] That marriage lasted only a few years, ended by the death of his wife in 1508. Yet he continued to follow the political scene assiduously, to write his diaries, to bear witness to great events, especially to what was perhaps the central crisis of the years he witnessed, the formation of the League of Cambrai against Venice late in the year 1508, which led to Sanudo's perception that "the world, or better said, Italy and our Venetian dominion," was "in great conflagration" (8:5).

Sanudo's War

That great conflagration began with the disastrous battle of Agnadello and was to continue for the next seven years. The first years of the war were very difficult, even though in the early years after Agnadello the invading forces were initially repelled and much of the Terraferma was restored to Venetian rule. Sanudo tells it all, but with little reference to his own role, because after his seventh term as a savio ai ordeni (1510) he failed in a number of elections—whether for an official position in Cyprus, or as *proveditore alla Camera degli Imprestidi,* or as state attorney.[18] But as the foreign armies swayed the fortunes of war back and forth, Sanudo felt all the more compelled to continue his writing, "praying God that He will allow us to reoccupy our state, and then I will conclude" (21:485). At the same time, he felt equally compelled to intervene on behalf of his country, and so in the summer of 1513, when Venetian Terraferma territories close to home were once again at risk, he made his first speech in the Great Council. He was forty-seven years old.

This was not easy for him. His intervention was in response to a speech by the doge, who wanted patricians to help defend Padua and Treviso, newly under attack by the imperial armies. But, said the doge, all debtors must at the same time pay half of their debts. Those who did not would be forever excluded from the Senate and from all other positions and offices, and they would not be able to occupy offices to which they had been elected during their absence. "And seeing that no one spoke about this matter of great importance, it seemed to me that I should put off every consideration save the good of the homeland, and so I rose from the second bench, where I was sitting, and I made the voting stop and went to contradict" what the doge had said, praying "that God would give me courage because I had never yet spoken in the Great Council" (16:489–90). He began by addressing the doge and the Great Council and describing the need to defend Padua and Treviso:

---

17. See diaries, 15 July 1506 (6:376). See also Chambers 1998a, 15.
18. Berchet 1903, 52–54.

July 10, 1513 (16:490–91)   "Most serene Prince, most illustrious Signoria, most excellent Council, my most excellent fathers and gentlemen . . . :

"These are the bulwarks and suburbs of the city of Venice. For their defense, we must send patricians who will not spare their persons or their purses or anything else in the world. . . . But this proposal, in my opinion, will not have the effect desired by Your Excellencies, because it proposes that those who are debtors, by going, become eligible to be nominated and elected to offices but may not enter into them without paying half of their debt. This is a terrible proposal, because a poor gentleman, for the love of his homeland, will tighten his belt to find some funds and will go to help his homeland by defending these two cities, and Your Excellencies, if this gentleman is nominated to some position, will honor him, but he cannot enter the office because he does not have the means to pay. Although he has spent his own money for arms and has put his own life on the line, he will have achieved nothing, nor will he be able to enjoy the grace of Your Magnificence. Therefore I fervently beseech you, gentlemen, councillors, heads of the Quarantia, amend this proposal so that those who go may, for a while, compete for office and, if chosen, may enter freely into those offices as has been done in the past years. . . ."

We were 1,300 in number, no one spat, and I was praised universally by all. And when I came down from the podium, everyone praised and blessed me, and the doge called me and lauded my opinion, saying, "You have always been dear to us." And the councillors amended the proposal . . . , and it passed.

It was none too soon. The enemy's troops were so close by the fall of 1513 that their devastating fires could be seen from Venice, as Sanudo himself reported, an example of his determination to experience the news firsthand whenever possible.

September 26, 1513 (17:102)   Hearing this rumor of fires at the twenty-second hour,[19] I went to the top of the Bell Tower of San Marco—under reconstruction—to see the truth of it. I saw the terrible destruction wrought by the enemies, who, if they had been Turks, could not have done worse. First I saw the huge fires in the direction of Gambarare,[20] then in the inn and other dwellings of Liza Fusina, and at Moranzan, and everywhere one saw enormous fires that were billowing smoke, so that at the twenty-third hour the sun was as red as blood from the smoke of so many fires. . . . It has been heard around town that the enemy front has crossed the Brenta, burning everything as they

---

19. The twenty-four-hour day began at sunset. In September the twenty-second hour would have been in the late afternoon. See "About the Translation" under "Hours."

20. A village on the Brenta River, southwest of Venice.

go, and that tonight they will burn Mestre and the villages and dwellings and whatever they find, and no measures are being taken! Nevertheless, I did see some infantry sent by the Collegio, that is, the constables, as I shall relate below.

At the end of the following month, on October 27, Sanudo went to the aid of Padua, paying for five men and horses. He stayed beyond the required month, not returning until December 1 (17:258, 261, 268, 278, 320, 352). He would refer to this service later, feeling quite unrewarded for his contribution at that time.

One reason for his failures, he thought, was his refusal to indulge in the politicking then rife in Venice. Such maneuvers, while formally banned, were essential to political success. Sanudo spoke out often against "pregierie" (political importuning), "pratiche" (machinations), "brogli" (intrigues), and "procure" (procurements). At the same time, he recognized that as long as there were impoverished patricians, votes would be for sale, and as a far from wealthy patrician himself, he appreciated the needs of the poorer members of his class. Still, he viewed bribery, along with the ambition that provoked it, as the ruin of the Republic. The Council of Ten tried to deal with the problem of political venality and the class of impoverished nobles whose vulnerability to bribes made it so widespread.

September 13, 1515 (21:70)   After dinner, there was a meeting of the Council of Ten with the zonta[21] and the procurators. Luca Zen the procurator was there. Ser Andrea Corner, of the zonta, was missing because he died yesterday evening. He was a councillor in the last Council of Ten; he was eighty years old, an upstanding and good patrician. It was said that this meeting of the council was for important things concerning the state: either it was held because in the zonta it is rumored that the old ones will lose and the winners will be the ones who give money, or it may have been held to make provisions for a certain number of poor nobles, who are called Swiss.[22] In order to win, a candidate must go to the poor nobles' homes, and if necessary, give them money. Some give forty soldi, some give thirty, some give twenty. The poor nobles are fairly numerous, and it is said[23] that they act in concert. They take off their hats to indicate which candidate they wish to win and touch their beards to

---

21. The Council of Ten had its own additional group, also called zonta, from the Venetian for *giunta,* meaning "addition."

22. The "old ones," or *vecchi,* were not a homogeneous bloc but tended to include the most experienced patricians. It was feared that experience and wisdom would lose out to money and bribes in the elections to be held during September. The Swiss reference is to the mercenary soldiers of Switzerland, who would fight on whichever side paid their salaries.

23. The manuscript has *dicitur,* while the Fulin edition has *dentro.*

indicate which one they want to lose. They have leaders among them: a "captain," "councillors," and a "secretary" called Alvise. Reports about these arrangements have been made to the heads of the Council of Ten[24] so that they can take measures. All the same, it is true that these nobles are poor and have nothing to live on. I do not believe that they are plotting among themselves, but only that whoever is nominated must go and ask their support. The buying of votes is more than ever out in the open; people do not care about the law or anything else. So if they nominate someone, they must be paid. This is the truth: whoever wishes to be nominated now can be so with money.

This was almost the truth. By 1515–16, money made for more political opportunities than ever, not just through bribes but through individual "loans" to the government, which was particularly hard pressed because of the enormous expenses resulting from the War of the League of Cambrai.[25] One still had to be elected, and that did not always follow a proffered loan. But when Sanudo himself managed to put together a loan of five hundred ducats in 1516, he was elected to the Senate, the major policymaking body of the state, and his satisfaction was immense.[26] He lists the names of the twenty-three elected and the votes they received, marking with a cross the three who had higher votes than he did, indicating his rank as fourth in popularity (August 3, 1516; 22:399). On August 16, 1516, having paid his loan, he entered the Senate chamber to cast his votes (22:433).

The Sometime Senator

Two factors besides Sanudo's loan may have smoothed his path to a seat in the Senate. The first was his decision to impose a certain restraint on his own behavior in the debates. Tempted in December 1515 to criticize one rival, he refrained, because, as he piously put it, "disobedience displeases me" (21:361).[27] In February 1516 (21:508) a bill was posted to increase the annual salary of the castellan of Peschiera from twenty-five to fifty ducats. Sanudo considered it a "very bad and deplorable precedent," but he kept his peace: "I confess that I, Marin Sanudo, wished to oppose this — but I chose not to do so out of a certain self-regard"

24. The Council of Ten was run by three heads, or *capi*.

25. For a fuller discussion of these loans, see chapter 5 under "The Prices of Power."

26. Sanudo was elected to the Senate on 6 August 1516 (diaries, 22:409). He had made several unsuccessful offers for lesser sums before this one proved successful—on 20 April 1516 (22:149), for 200 ducats, and 23 April 1516 (22:156), for 400 ducats, to be elected proveditor for taxes, which carried with it entry into the Senate.

27. By contrast, earlier that year he had made several vigorous and successful speeches, one against "expectatives," that is, reserving, usually by payment, a future office for an individual (diaries, 3 April 1515; 20:95), and another against a change in the Senate's voting procedures (10 June 1515; 20:283–87).

(February 10, 1516; 21:508). He knew that his silence might serve him better than any speech in the next electoral contest.

The second factor was his effort, a few months later, to change the law so that the doge's son, Lorenzo Loredan, might become a procurator of San Marco. This was contrary to all measures that sought to protect the government from dynastic threats, measures that, moreover, it had been stipulated could not be changed during any doge's lifetime. Sanudo looked through his records and came up with a precedent. The way was further smoothed by a Loredan's loaning the state fourteen thousand ducats, an enormous sum. Sanudo explained the legal circumscription with delicacy: "The first cause was God, then me, who persuaded the Great Council to consider a bill pertinent to the sitting doge." And he recorded with satisfaction that he had attended the lavish celebration dinner (June 1, 1516; 22:257–59, 261–62). Making it possible for Loredan to become a procurator most certainly helped Sanudo's electoral chances a few months later.

On his first day in the Senate, Sanudo wrote that his Senate position would make his recordkeeping easier: "With greater facility I will note the truth of the events that occur daily" (August 18, 1516; 22:440). It undoubtedly did. He also thought it would lead to higher office. It did not. Even during his tenure in the Senate his bids to enter the upper echelons of the Collegio as a *savio di Consiglio* or a *savio di Terraferma* were unsuccessful. He would not himself solicit votes, and remarks in his diaries betray both his chagrin, because he judged himself as worthy as others who were chosen, and his anger, because he had no help from his family. This was a major impediment, for success in the Venetian political system depended on commandeering blocs of votes, sometimes from whole clans at a time. A large, rich, and supportive family could make an appreciable difference in nominations and balloting. Sanudo's family was neither large nor rich, and there was considerable friction within it.[28]

March 30, 1517 (24:128)   After dinner there was a meeting of the Senate to choose the savi di Collegio, for which there was a lot of campaigning. Even for the Savi dil Consejo and the Savi a Terraferma, people campaigned for votes every morning on the stairs to the Quarantia,[29] except for me, Marin Sanudo, who alone had no help, not even from brothers or from other relatives; rather, I was opposed by them. And may this be remembered for all eternity and

---

28. In 1527, a year when Sanudo was not reelected to the Senate or its Zonta, there were twenty members of the Sanudo family in the Great Council. Twelve other families had fifty or more representatives (45:569–72).

29. Because the members of the Quarantia sat and voted in the Senate, their support could be critical for nominations.

especially by ser Marin Sanudo, savio a Terraferma, my cousin, who, to keep me from blocking his entrance into office, does whatever he can to obstruct me.[30] Nevertheless, God be praised, I was very well treated, and I am pleased with the votes that I had.

Yet that modest success carried its own liability: Sanudo was sure that his "competitors and enemies" had conspired against him and thwarted his efforts on behalf of his beloved country.

June 25, 1517 (24:406)   After dinner, the Senate was convened to choose the savi di Collegio. . . . I, Marin Sanudo, was nominated and did poorly in the balloting; and this is the reward for my labors, both in composing this history and in the speeches that I made opposing the entire Collegio, when my point of view triumphed for the good, the advantage, and the glory of this Republic. But because I do not participate in the intrigues that are common today, offering dinners to members of the Quarantia and other senators, nor do I attend secret meetings as others do, those who are much younger than I am are elected. Patience! *Forsitan et haec olim meminisse juvabit* [perhaps some day we will rejoice to remember these things]."[31] The friends of those who have been nominated, and the nominees themselves, and both my rivals and my enemies all feared that I would succeed; they did not want me, saying that "the other time he received 104 votes and now he has been making fine speeches and could have even more ballots," so all of them are intently against me. May God forgive them and give them what they deserve.[32]

In spite of his frustration, Sanudo continued his political efforts. In the fall of 1517 he reported in his diaries a speech he had made in the Great Council. With the fiery tone of a reforming prophet, he had attacked the excessive ambition and selfishness that he felt was ruining the Republic, exhorting his fellow patricians to set aside personal ambition and approve a new magistracy that would enforce adherence to the laws.

September 13, 1517 (24:656–57)   After dinner a meeting of the Great Council was held. . . . Zuan Batista Adriani read the bill that was passed in the Senate yesterday to create two censors. He wanted to read it from the tribunal of the

---

30. On certain higher government bodies it was not permitted for two members of the same family to serve at the same time.

31. The line, a well-known tag, is from Virgil's *Aeneid* 1.203.

32. The 104 votes were for a proposal supported by Sanudo that won with such a margin that he considered it a tribute.

Signoria, but I made him come to the bench so that everyone could hear him. Once it had been read, ser Bernardo Donado, head of the Quarantia, opposed it, using the same reasons that he used yesterday. I, Marin Sanudo, at the urging of my conscience and because I am distressed at the kind of electioneering that is occurring, went to answer him. With the great attention of the entire council, so intense that no one even spat, I gave a good speech, defending the good, just, and holy bill to eliminate electioneering:

> The laws exist, but who applies them?[33] There is no longer anyone who executes them and cites the old law; it used to be that the Senate considered the good of the Republic, but it is no longer what it used to be, being now composed of those who do whatever they want. Thus the savi di Collegio, like the ambassadors and proveditori, and even the judges that went around the Brescian and Bergamasque territories, alluded to the well-founded republics that were governed by laws, such as Athens, Sparta, and Rome, none of which survived more than 600 years. But our Republic has survived for more than 1,100 years because it was founded by Christians in the name of Christ and fortified by excellent laws, though they are poorly enforced at the moment.[34] And it will last a long time if we do not choose to ruin it. To preserve it, we must vanquish this ambition, worst of all evils [*omnium malorum pessima*], for if it continues, it will be the ruin and corruption of this state. In these years our state has endured great travail and suffering because of the conspiracy of the entire world, so to speak, against Your Excellencies. Nevertheless, through the grace of Our Lord and our good administration, our empire was recovered, and it will long endure and increase.[35] But after this good fortune, Venice contracted a plague, an illness that devastated this most excellent Republic, and that plague is ambition, which affects the Senate most of all. So that political deals are made on the stairs of the Senate, in the chamber of the Quarantia, in the Basilica of San Marco, and at Rialto, a lobbying for office that even involves friars, nuns, and others; everything is political plotting.[36]

Nevertheless, Sanudo was undeterred in his efforts. At the end of September 1517 he itemized ten speeches he had made in the Senate during the year of his service and added that no one had spoken from the podium more often than he had.

---

33. Cf. Dante, *Divine Comedy, Purgatorio,* canto 7: "Le leggi son, ma chi pon mano ad esse." This allusion provides an insight into Sanudo's culture. The text that follows appears to be Sanudo's speech, or a summary of it, although there are no quotation marks in the manuscript.

34. The traditional date for the founding of Venice was 25 March 421.

35. By the winter of 1517 the War of the League of Cambrai had been concluded, with Venice having regained almost its entire Terraferma empire.

36. The speech continued at length, citing historical precedents from the fifteenth century and the weakening of earlier controls brought on by the War of the League of Cambrai. He ended by exhorting his listeners to put aside their selfish ambitions and approve the new magistrates (diaries, 24:657–58).

But, he concluded, it had all been in vain. Such virtue as his went unrewarded.

September 29, 1517 (24:705)   I never thought I would speak in the Senate, but recently, in the Great Council, when I spoke in favor of the bill to establish two censors, to the rapt attention of the whole Great Council, my advocacy passed the bill by 400 votes. And this I did having achieved my fiftieth year and having taken enormous pains to write continuously the history of this city, as I still do. My reward for these great labors was to be nominated censor, yet I failed to achieve the necessary votes in the Great Council. The following day, nominated twice for the Senate, I was defeated, failing to gain even half the votes in the Great Council. And likewise I failed three times to be elected savio a Terraferma. . . . So I shall turn my thoughts to a quiet existence, etc. But I wanted to leave this record so that all might realize what happens in republican states.[37]

This was surely a moment of despair for Sanudo. He had thought he could conclude his diaries when the War of Cambrai was over. But his political involvement was such that he felt he could not, for the two activities were by then so closely interwoven. Even when illness kept him from the public spaces where the news was to be had, informants supplied him with the proposals before the Senate or the news from Rome (25:277, 302). At the same time, his success and energetic interventions as a senator seemed to have been for nothing, and he thought his public life was over. However, this time his disavowal of public life was premature. When the next year's elections came around in September, he made another speech, one in which his diaries and his passion for the law served him well, a speech that shows not only the complex dynamics of Venetian politics but also the role of oratory, argument, and, in Sanudo's case, knowledge of the law.

Made in the Great Council on Sunday, September 26, 1518, the speech concerned the election of two new members to the Council of Ten. As always, the candidates were voted on successively. When all the votes had been tallied, one nominee, Batista Erizo, had handily won his election to the Council of Ten by garnering the highest number of supporting votes, 810, according to Sanudo's register. The next most favored was Francesco Foscari, who won 665 votes (with 635 opposed), followed by Francesco Donado,[38] with 649 votes for him and 601

---

37. This negative comment about republics, his own and those of the past, recurs occasionally in Sanudo's diaries, proud as he was of the Venetian Republic. See 22:172, 54:622, 56:875.

38. The family name was changed by the nineteenth-century diaries' editors to Donato, a Tuscanized form of the Venetian Donado/Donà. We have used the original here as more authentic.

opposed. The usual procedure would have been to declare Erizo and Foscari the winners, but, as Sanudo recounts, some political manipulation took place.

September 26, 1518 (26:64–66)   Although Foscari had won, some of the councillors wished to resubmit Donado for a separate vote, contrary to legal procedures and obligations, because by reballoting only him the Great Council would make him win. It was an effort promoted by ser Antonio da Mula, councillor, Donado's dearest friend, and ser Luca Trun, councillor, Foscari's worst enemy. Trun had, on other occasions, cited ser Francesco Foscari in the Senate as having practiced contraband with steel, but he had not been arrested. So then they had a revote for Donado, who, in this second round, won with 668 votes and was declared victorious.

The three state attorneys, seeing that injustice had been done to Foscari, rose while the next round of voting for the Senate was proceeding and went to the Signoria, saying that Donado should not have had a second vote. And the councillors, acting as one and seeing that what had been done was ill done and contrary to the law, told the state attorneys that they should proceed. The state attorneys advised the six councillors to propose to the Great Council a declarative vote: should the second vote stand or not? Predictably, three of the councillors (including Donado's advocates da Mula and Luca Trun) were for the validation of the second vote; the three other councillors were not. The ballot clerks prepared to collect the votes on each side of the question. And then, at this point in his account, Sanudo himself intervenes, reminding his listeners (and readers) whose son he was and in whose tradition of patriotic service he intervened.

I, Marin Sanudo, son of the late ser Leonardo, was on the second bench wearing a mantle of mourning for the death of Lorenzo di Prioli, savio dil Consejo, my relative. I was melancholic, grieving that I was fated not to win a seat in the Senate and that ser Alvise Salamon . . . and ser Zuan Batista Memo, who had promised to support me, did not nominate me today, and both of them were elected to the Senate. Then I heard of this proposal, which was contrary to justice, to the well-being and tranquillity of our Republic: it gave authority to the councillors to elect whom they chose in disregard for the will of the Great Council and to the disgrace and ruin of poor Francesco Foscari, who was — old and who would fail to be elected. This was contrary to justice, contrary to the will of those who had cast the first round of votes.

So Sanudo was moved to speak, even though Francesco Donado was a close friend with whom he had served as savio ai ordeni. He knew that the decision should not be put to the Great Council in that way, for if it had to decide which vote was legitimate, Foscari would lose, since he was very unpopular.

Moved by my conscience, inspired by the Divine Majesty, I rose from my seat to protest. Three times I told myself to stay put, but it was God's will [*ita volente Deo*] that I go up. Once I had mounted the podium to protest, all the Great Council rose to hear me, because the Great Council too was displeased at this procedure.

The nominees had already left the room, that is, the supporters of Foscari and Donado and their relatives inside the Great Council and ser Francesco Donado, the knight, himself. Eternal God inspired the words and introduction as I spoke them. I showed how it distressed me to have to speak about this matter and against my friend domino Francesco Donado, because of his age and because we had been colleagues as savi ai ordeni. Then I discussed the laws and the proposals put forward by the councillors, who should not have proposed them, and even less should they have reballoted Donado.

Sanudo told his audience of certain voting technicalities that had been violated. He argued that the councillors had acted illegally and that the state attorneys should suspend the second balloting and the councillors should withdraw it. Then Foscari would remain elected.

Having spoken a few more words, I took my leave and came down from the podium, and the entire Great Council was pleased with my reminder of the laws, and everyone praised me, saying that this was not a man to be excluded from the Senate, as I had been this year, and they wanted to make me a member of the zonta.[39] And the state attorneys, who should be commended for this, seeing that my reminder was excellent and legal, did not become obstinate, as perhaps others might have, and promptly formulated a proposal.

Their proposal was that the reballoting of Francesco Donado be rescinded so that the first balloting would be reinstated.

And ser Luca Trun, the councillor, went to the podium to justify the councillors' revote. He made a bad speech—so God willed it [*ita volente Deo*]. Furthermore, the points he raised spoke against his argument. And ser Nicolò Michiel, university laureate, the state attorney, responded to him, praising me to

---

39. The zonta of the Senate was elected by the Great Council from nominees proposed in the Senate. See Finlay 1980b, 39.

the skies for the reminder I had given and saying that the state attorneys also wished to do it [i.e., rescind the second vote] but that the councillors were of a mind to put their proposal forward. But since, in the end, my reminder had been valid, Nicolò Michiel too agreed with the opinion that the second ballot was against the law. The Great Council silently listened to what he said. The motion of the state attorneys [to quash the second balloting of Donado] was put to the vote: it received 914 votes in favor, 322 against, 11 undecided, and it passed. The election of ser Francesco Foscari to the Council of Ten was announced, and the entire Great Council praised me, predicting that they would want to make me a member of the ordinary zonta.

And some days later they did. Sanudo was rewarded with election to the Senate's zonta, that additional group coopted and conjoined to the Senate. His joy was unbounded at his restoration to what he considered the heart of the political body:

September 30, 1518 (26:72)   The election for the zonta was held. . . . Only fifty-two were elected, among whom I, Marin Sanudo, formerly of the Senate, was included by a wide margin, thanks to this most excellent Great Council, and with so much glory and honor that no one, in a number of years, has entered the zonta more favored than I was and, one might say, "without entitlement," because my title of senator was through a loan.[40] But now I have been chosen because of the speech that I gave Sunday, which pleased the Great Council, whom I shall serve for all eternity. I consider myself repaid for my every labor, since they have received me into the most excellent Senate with such great honor. Present in the Great Council were 985 members.[41]

Sanudo served for the next year with his usual vigor. His positive mood is reflected in the preface to volume 27 of his diaries, in which he sees the diaries as essential political instruction for those who served Venice then and in the future:

March 1, 1519 (27:5)   In the past years I have described as they occurred all the events of Italy and beyond, with no little fatigue, producing a work of great length and an enduring record of past events, an excellent instruction for patricians, senators, and others who take pleasure in history and aspire to the

---

40. The coveted title *senator* (or *di Pregadi*) was not awarded if the entry to the Senate had been facilitated by a loan, as had Sanudo's entry in 1516.

41. A few days later, on 3 October, Francesco Donado's supporters were able to get him elected to the Council of Ten to finish out the term of a member elected to the Collegio as a *savio grande*. Diaries, 26:102.

government of the state. Therefore, without further introduction, I shall continue this undertaking. I shall here write daily whatever seems to me worthy of note for the eternal memory of my country, beginning with the first day of the month and year according to the Venetian custom, that is, the month of March, and I shall daily go on writing as I have done in the other volumes.

The energy and confidence of these remarks, recorded after a holiday in Aquileia,[42] sprang from his participation in the debates of the Senate. "Whenever I see that my words can recall a useful matter for this state, I will speak out, without reservation," he had said during a speech in January (January 18, 1519; 26:376). In that instance, he summarized his speech fully (26:374–76), even though he had not succeeded in persuading the Senate to reject a proposal concerning diplomatic relations with the Turkish sultan. Much more satisfying were his triumphs: "I cried from my seat that this motion could not be put . . . and the motion failed" (April 4, 1519; 27:133–34). Such vehemence, however, whether in vain or successful, may have been politically reckless. In September 1519 he rotated off and was not reelected. Once again he sounded his bitter refrain: "And this happened as my reward for the efforts I made this past year in the Senate, as well as those I am making in writing down these events" (September 25, 1519; 27:672).

But his reputation for probity endured. A few months later, in January 1520, the doge referred to him in the Senate as "our ser Marin Sanudo, upholder of the laws, who when he sees something proposed contrary to the laws does not let it pass. He deserves great praise and should be in all the councils because he who wants the laws upheld maintains the republics." Sanudo recorded the words he had not been in the Senate to hear.

The Nonvoyager

It may also be that Sanudo's political viability suffered from his unwillingness to leave the city. In his earlier years, his family, unlike those of many young patricians, had not sought employment for him as one of the "bowmen of the quarterdeck" *(ballestrieri della popa),* in which job he might travel on a galley and gain experience of the sea and the overseas dominion.[43] At the beginning of his career, he had spent sixteen months (May 1501–September 1502) as treasurer *(camerlengo)* in Verona.[44] Not only had this not led to positions of higher prestige but it had made it necessary for him to rely on the diary of Pietro Dolfin for the news of that whole period, a dependency he regretted and never openly acknowledged.[45]

---

42. Cf. Chambers 1998a, 29.
43. On "bowmen of the quarterdeck," see Lane 1973b, 344–45.
44. Diaries, 4:8, 329.
45. Sambin 1944–45. When Sanudo returned to Venice, he begged the indulgence of those who

Apart from a patriotic stint defending Padua in 1509, a voluntary military service, Sanudo would not accept positions elsewhere. Even a week's family trip to a fair in Treviso induced him to arrange for a substitute recorder—"having left someone to investigate the things that were happening" (October 28, 1521; 32:68). In 1520 he vigorously objected to his nomination as inspector in the Levant; had he been elected—he was not—he might have advanced his career through a three-year tour of the Venetian colonies, inspecting complaints of maladministration in the *stato da Mar,* the sea dominion. It was an important and well-paid office, but Sanudo wanted a political career in Venice, not one that removed him from the center of his world and the news hub that nourished his assiduous recording, to which he variously referred to as a history, annals, or diaries. For him, it was indeed all three.

February 9, 1520 (28:247)   By chance, speaking with ser Zuan Antonio Memo, the head of the Quarantia, I learned that yesterday I was nominated inspector, which pained me in two ways: in the bad luck that I have had this year and in the ill will of someone who was the enemy of my every good fortune. Thus, I have never let myself be nominated for this office in the past, and to everyone who asked me, I refused, because my age and my condition and my status do not deserve this. Moreover, I want to stay here and supervise those who supervise [*voglio star qui e synichar chi va synichi*],[46] not wait for three years to be nominated to any other office. Even if you gave me one hundred ducats a month and expenses, I would never wish to leave here. I have never sailed. I have held the rank of *zonta ordinaria.* It is against my principles to do harm to anyone just to win; my concern is to obey the laws and serve my country. Sometimes while giving a speech either in the Great Council or in the Senate when I am there, I express my opinion without reservation. Moreover, [if I went away,] the history that I am writing, which I started —— years ago, and my annals and diaries would be stalled.[47] Thus it should be plain to everyone that I did not want to be nominated, and I have said this openly to everyone [*palam locutus sum omnibus*]. But I suffer from that unjust person, that enemy who caused me to be nominated, whose only reason was malevolence,

---

would read his diaries: "Forgive me for having written from word of mouth" (4:320). And he assured his readers that from that time on, "I will describe every event, day by day," so that the reader would find a summary of what was happening (4:329).

46. Sanudo's words are a clue both to his ambition and to his failure to achieve it. He wished to stay home and compel his fellow patricians to obey the laws, many of which he could cite to them from having recorded them in his diaries.

47. The references here were apparently to his history of Charles VIII's invasion of Italy, *La spedizione di Carlo VIII in Italia,* which he always considered the first volume of his diaries; or *Le vite dei dogi,* which was annalistic in form; and to the diaries themselves.

because, since I did not want the office, no one should have done me this wrong. Patience! God will give him what he deserves, and if I can find him out, sooner or later, I will never forget him.

Keeper of the Record

Once more Sanudo's patience was rewarded. In September 1520 he was reelected to the zonta of the Senate in for a third term. But again, after a year he was not reelected. Recriminations and bitterness reappear in the diaries. Indisposed by illness for much of 1522, he expressed his frustrations in an introduction to the volume he began on March 1, 1523, with a long musing upon his sense of mission, his patriotism, his rectitude, his mortification at his mistreatment, and finally, his commitment to continuing his records. He reiterates his conviction that these records themselves will serve his country and its leaders even if his political misfortunes keep him from active office. If his own voice could not be heard in the chambers of the Ducal Palace, his records, condensed into a proper history, would "inform and instruct" all those who would be governors. It was that responsibility to his future readers that he was determined to fulfill, anticipating the solemnity of his task by weaving Latin phrases and a vernacular colloquialism into his text.

March 1, 1523 (34:5–7)   I have written and composed so many volumes of my history, beginning with King Charles's incursion into Italy and continuing to this first day of March 1523, works of great utility to those who, wishing to attain public office and also to learn of the events of modern times, will read them. And although the books do make a fat diary, if they were reduced to a history, they would fit into only four volumes, a work that, if God grants me a long enough life, I wish to complete and publish so that everyone may be informed and instructed. And this in spite of my having been sick and in bed, with my life at no small risk, almost this entire past year of 1522, whether by the disposition of the heavens or because of my own sins. And I have spent great sums to be cared for by numerous doctors and surgeons. Yet God be praised for all things. But since I am still competent to perform some good deeds in this life, to the honor of the Almighty and the exaltation of the Venetian state, I cannot fail to do so, having been born into this homeland, for whose benefit I would die a thousand deaths if needed, despite having been abused, beaten, and mistreated in our councils in the past year and dropped from the zonta, to which I had been elected two years before. For when I was in the Senate, I always helped my homeland with my speeches, and the other senators paid attention to me and honored my opinions and promptings even when they went against the recommendations of the Collegio.

To Sanudo, it must have seemed that his passionate patriotism and moral integrity on behalf of his city counted for naught. Committed to recording the truth in his diaries, committed to speaking the truth (as he saw it) in the political debates, using his God-given "gift of persuasion," his "vast memory," his "knowledge of events" gained from having so assiduously recorded them, all in the service of his *patria,* he sought some explanation for his defeats.

It was envy that harmed me; things would have gone differently if I had kept quiet and applauded this one and that one, as people do these days, and let the bill pass even though it would harm my beloved country, and if I had acted against the laws that preserve the governments of cities. Although I was not a state attorney, to whose office the protection of these laws is committed,[48] when I saw others remain silent my conscience goaded me to speak, since God has granted me the gift of persuasion, a vast memory, and a knowledge of events that has come from having described them for many years and seen all the books of our Chancellery.[49] Thus it seemed an offense against myself not to speak about the matters under consideration. I know that those who proposed the bills were displeased to be contradicted, and others were vexed because they would derive certain benefits from this legislation. But I was heedless of anything but the public good; nothing mattered to me save supporting the Republic in whatever way I was able. The outcome was that those whom I had thwarted did not want any opposition, and they were joined by their children and relatives, both their contemporaries and their elders, who had been blinded by envy. They neither wanted nor knew how to speak, and perhaps even less how to act, although they are the first to be elected to the Senate.[50] Then others who for their own reasons wish ill to those who do good managed to have me dropped from the Senate, despite the fact that in the old days [*antiquitas*] he who spoke for the public good was rewarded above all others. Now the opposite pertains. But enough of this [*Sed de his hactenus*]!

The hostility Sanudo perceived had incapacitated him, he wrote, both psychologically and physically. But even while ill, he had kept up his diaries and let his friends confirm that he was destined to bear witness to the truth and to the great events of the world, the struggle of Christianity against the "frightful" power of the Turks.

---

48. This office, *avogador di comun,* was among those that Sanudo most coveted and never attained.

49. See below for Sanudo's receiving access to the government archives in 1515.

50. Sanudo's speech illustrates what some historians have called his "legalistic and righteous posturing" and his combination of "pugnaciousness with unrelenting pedantry." See Chambers 1998a, 8; and Finlay 1980b, 256–58.

I confess that this rejection has inflicted more than a little pain on me and has been the cause of my illness. Again this past year I was nominated to the zonta, but it was no surprise [*nil mirum*] that I lost because, since I had not left my house for many months prior to the elections, many believed that I was dead or so ill that I could no longer serve. However, God in his goodness wished to spare me, and as I said, I finished last year's diary; sick as I was, I did not refrain from including the daily news that was brought to me by friends, thus adding another volume to my work. Sometimes I think about giving up this task that I have begun, but then, in my mind's eye, I see those compatriots who love me and who say, "Marin, do not give up. Follow the path you have undertaken, because 'wife and magistrate are heaven's to designate' [*moglie e magistrato dal ciel è destinato*]. Go on recording the events of Italy and the world because you are witnessing great preparations against Christianity, if Christians do not unite together. The Turk has captured Rhodes, although his father and grandfather were never able to do so, and he has taken Belgrade in Hungary. He is a frightful sovereign." For this reason, the Lord willing [*Domino concedente*], I have decided to continue this work. So I will describe here day by day whatever news I hear, under the pontificate of Adrian VI, who has taken the right path for the good of Christianity if he is followed by the other rulers.[51]

Even when he was deprived of a voice in the Senate, Sanudo continued to speak in the Great Council, to which, as a patrician, he had assured access. There he defended the laws, maintaining his reputation as the epitome of integrity, and ridiculed those who would tamper with constitutional custom. In June 1525 he protested a proposal to raise the age of those chosen for the Quarantia Criminal, upholding the ancestral wisdom of allowing younger patricians to be elected to the body so that they might learn to govern the Republic and add their warmer blood to the cooler blood of their elders to make a *bon composito,* a good mix.

June 5, 1525 (39:24–25)   After dinner there was a meeting of the Great Council, which the doge did not attend. . . . The members of the council proposed a bill to change the organization of the three councils of the Quarantie.[52] Sponsored in the Senate by ser Bernardin Justinian, head of the Quarantia, the bill had passed that body on the thirtieth of last month.

---

51. Adrian VI had come to the papal throne on 9 January 1522. But during his brief papacy—he died on 14 September 1523—he proved no more able than his predecessors or his successors to organize a crusade against the Turks.

52. The three judicial councils of the Quarantia, with forty members each, were the Quarantia Criminal, the Quarantia Civile Vecchia, and the Quarantia Civile Nuova. See appendix B under "Governmental Terms."

The first to speak was ser Zacaria Trivixan, savio ai ordeni, who had opposed the bill in the Senate. He was in a great rush to speak because he had gone to the council at tierce. I wanted to be first, but he insisted on going, and in his hurry he came close to knocking down Alexandro Busenello, who had read the proposal, as he descended from the podium. His opening remarks were very nice, but he said nothing against the bill. Of me he said, "Ser Marin Sanudo, a man of great integrity, wished to speak first, but since I had spoken in the Senate I wished to speak first here as well." And he came down from the podium.

Then ser Bernardin Justinian, the former head of the Quarantia and the sponsor of the bill, spoke at length.[53] His address was in the stilted style that old men use; he said that the bill would do nothing but change the order of election to the councils of the Quarantie, that it is good for candidates to be first elected to the Quarantia Criminal, which judges the lives of men and the state. He talked for a long time, saying that it was God who inspired him to propose the bill.

After he finished, I, Marin Sanudo, went to the podium. The council followed my words closely as I said that it pained me greatly that in matters of such importance people had spoken in a ridiculous fashion and that I would demonstrate that this bill was against the law, against that which our ancestors wanted, fruitless, and a source of confusion. . . . I also spoke about how necessary it was for young people to be in the Senate to learn how to govern the Republic, citing a decision of the Quarantia Criminal dated April 23, 1441, which they made so that . . . young men and the three ages should always be there. And I referred to a painting in the chamber of the Senate showing great, medium, and small trees, which are like cold, warm, and hot blood: when combined, they make a good composite. . . .[54] And I said that if something is not broken, it need not be fixed. . . . The council understood immediately that I was telling the truth. I then concluded that this change should not be made, recapitulating what I had said. Holding everyone's attention, I gave an admirable speech.

When Sanudo had finished, Bernardin Justinian, the bill's sponsor, went to the podium to defend it. But the Great Council would not hear him, kicking their feet against the benches. The bill failed to pass, with 864 voted against it, 457

---

53. Bernardino Giustiniani, identified above as one of the heads of the Quarantia when he sponsored the bill in May, had by June rotated out of his two-month term in that office. Diaries, 38:139.

54. It is worth noting here the adumbration of the idea of a "composite" Venetian constitution, more fully developed in this same period by Gaspare Contarini. See Gleason 1993, 110–22, esp. 116–17.

for, and 2 undecided. Sanudo claimed the responsibility and the honor: "It was defeated to the great shame of Justinian, called 'Mortaella,' and the more honor to me who had caused the proposal to fail."

For Sanudo, success was sweet but infrequent: after five years, he earned a re-entry into the Senate zonta, but only for a year.[55] Sensitive for his reputation, he once more became cautious in his speeches. In February 1526, in a debate about where certain shops should be built on the Rialto bridge, Sanudo, although he held strong opinions on the subject, which he confided to his diaries, chose not to speak: "For there are newcomers in the Senate who will say, 'Marin talks about base matters'" (February 22, 1526; 40:855). Again and again, frustrated by his political failures, he threatened to discontinue his diaries (January 10, 1529; 49:352). And he reminded himself and his future readers that his father had died and was buried in Rome, and he vowed that his own bones should not rest in his patria, which had "rewarded" him, as he says, with heavy irony for his immense labors:

September 29, 1529 (51:611)   Six senators were elected. I, Marin Sanudo, was nominated by my half-brother Antonio; it has been ten years since I was first elected to the zonta ordinaria, and again two other times. Today I was rejected as a reward for my labor in composing these many volumes that number — not counting my other books and without any recompense.[56] Wherefore, seeing that I am not accepted by my homeland, I will write no more, dedicating myself to living out the small amount of time that is left to me: even that will pass bitterly. I am sixty-three years old, son of one who died for his homeland as ambassador to Rome, where his bones are buried, and I would like to say, as has been said, "Ungrateful homeland, you will not have my bones" [*ingrata patria non habebis ossa mea*]. So tomorrow I will close this last book.[57]

55. After election to the Senate in 1516, Sanudo had been out for a year (September 1517–September 1518); then in for a year as a member of the zonta (diaries, 26:65, 78); out again in September 1519 for a year; in again in September 1520 for a year (29:218); out for four years; in from October 1525 to September 1526 (40:17, 21; 42:319, 513); out for six years; and in for three more years as a member of the zonta (January 1531 [55:368]; September 1532 [56:1033]; September 1533 [58:750]). Besta 1899, 72, suggests that Sanudo's absence from the Senate from 1525 to 1531 may be explained by the fact that the loan to become a senator was limited to 500 ducats, and many able men were available for that sum.

56. Sanudo has himself lost track of the number of diary volumes already completed. By this time there were more than fifty volumes, plus many works that Sanudo had begun earlier, to some of which he continued to add during the decades when he was writing his diaries.

57. The use of Latin expressions such as the one quoted here, incorrectly borrowed from Valerius Maximus, *Facta et dicta memorabilia* 5.3.2b, is not unusual for Sanudo, who liked to show off his classical education in this way. The exact words, spoken in the text by Scipio Africanus, were *ingrata patria ne ossa quidem mea habes*. See diaries, 10 June 1526 (41:540), for this same expression of disdain. We have kept some of the Latin phrases, especially in this first chapter, to better render Sanudo's style.

The above entry was written on September 29, the Feast of St. Michael, when most of the offices rotated. On September 30, without further complaining, Sanudo recorded that day's electoral events; and the next day, contrary to his earlier statement, he commenced writing volume 52. Thus he continued to play his chosen roles: keeper of the record, conscience of the Republic, guardian of tradition, gadfly to his contemporaries.

Sanudo could not have been an easy political colleague. Often, when he reported a successful speech, he would report the embarrassment of his opponent. For example, on one occasion when his proposal won, he wrote: "I was greatly praised, and the head of the Quarantia [who opposed him] remained red-faced and scowling" (July 31, 1510; 10:885). Outspoken in his opinions, quick to protest what he perceived as unjustified changes, he could be vociferous in his objections to any action he felt was illegal, unwarranted, or untraditional, whether it was to cite a law, argue the warrant, or protest an alteration in the physical fabric of the city.

September 9, 1530 (53:541)   I note that in these last few days the procurators of the Basilica of San Marco wanted to place those two stone lions that are currently in the baptistery upon the two columns that stood at the gates of Acre. They had the scaffolding put up. It is all very shameful[58] to move those ancient pieces, and I made such an outcry against this that the doge heard me; he absolutely refused to move them, and today the scaffolding was dismantled.[59]

To the end of his recordkeeping, Sanudo continued to follow his conscience. In his last volume, of 1533, there are still references to his *conscientia:* "And I, Marin Sanudo, moved by my conscience [*motu conscientiae*], went to the podium . . . and made a most beautiful speech praised by everyone" (June 26, 1533; 58:374); "And I, Marin Sanudo, obligated by my conscience, went to the podium . . . and contradicted [the proposal of the Savi] . . . with quite wise and appropriate words. . . . I made an excellent and fine speech that was praised by all" (July 31, 1533; 58:498).

What seems to have been often overlooked by those writing on Sanudo's career is that at the very end of his record, on September 30, 1533, he was once more elected to the zonta of the Senate. What caused him to end his diaries after this date was certainly not despair; perhaps it was a combination of preoccupation, fatigue, and illness. His last electoral triumph is worth recording:

---

58. The manuscript has *E'tutto cosa. . .*, while the Fulin edition has *e tutto. Cosa. . . .*

59. The "Pillars of Acre," or *pilastri acritani,* now to be seen on the south side of the Basilica, were actually from the church of St. Polyeuctus in Constantinople. See P. F. Brown 1996, 17.

September 30, 1533 (58:750)   St. Jerome's Day. The Senate zonta was voted on with great order, nor was there any error, and the ballots were cast in secret. One thousand sixty-one ballots were given out. Only fifty-seven members of the zonta were voted in; it is still short by three.[60] I, Marin Sanudo, formerly of the zonta, son of the late Leonardo, was among those chosen. I had 602 votes for me, 462 against.

His Family and Estate

In contrast to his full descriptions of his political interventions, Sanudo used few words to describe family members and familial events, apart from his many references to the revered figure of his father, Leonardo Sanudo. Again and again in moments of disappointment he refers to his father and regrets that his example does not weigh more in the balance of his own political fortunes. In his will of 1533 he refers to the help he received from family members to pay debts but also to pieces of real estate and funds shared, administered, and sometimes contested with family members. Generally in the diaries his references to his family, when he is not grumbling about their lack of political support, are brief, and occasionally he betrays impatience that such obligations distracted him from his political observations. His references to his own wedding are slipped into the same paragraphs with the political record, as if reminders to himself but irrelevant to his chronicle.

February 15 and March 29, 1505 (6:132, 144)   On the fifteenth there was a meeting of the Council of Ten. And in the morning, in the eighteenth hour, I was betrothed to the daughter of the honorable ser Constantin Prioli, who is the widow of ser Hironimo Barbarigo and has a dowry of 5,500 ducats, as is stated in the contract [*ut in contractu*]. . . . And on the twenty-ninth, after dinner, I announced my betrothal in the presence of the families and pledged my hand publicly to my wife, Cecilia Prioli. And then the Senate met and elected the five savi ai ordeni.[61]

The marriage was brief. Three years and nine months later Sanudo's wife died, and another personal note was slipped into his record of those bleak days:

November 27, 1508 (7:672–73)   At none my dearest wife Cecilia died after an illness that lasted forty-nine days. May God grant her peace and rest.

---

60. The Senate zonta numbered sixty.

61. Cecilia Priuli was related to Antonio Grimani, a powerful figure who at that time was in exile but who would later be doge (1521–23). Her dowry was of good size. The terminology of the Venetian marriage procedure mentioned in these excerpts—*Jo mi maridai* and *Jo fici el mio parentado e ditti la man publice*—is discussed in Labalme and White 1999, 44.

After dinner there was a meeting of the Senate for the Paduans. Very few attended, but it was held anyway. Ser —— [Alberto] Trapolin spoke for the Paduan community until two hours after sunset. No one answered him; it has been deferred to another meeting.

So it went until the thirtieth of November, when the diaries stretch out once again to include the meeting of the Great Council and long summaries of letters from Milan. As for the wedding arrangements, two years later, of Cecilia's daughter (his stepdaughter), he made clear how reluctantly he had interrupted his political duties to fulfill this domestic obligation:

April 8, 1510 (10:114)   After dinner there was a meeting of the Senate. But I had to be present unwillingly [*me nolente*] at the conclusion of the marriage contract for my stepdaughter, with no public invited [*nos omnibus inscientibus*]. She is the daughter of the late ser Hironimo Barbarigo and married ser Vicenzo Malipiero. The marriage took place at Ca' Emo and caused me to miss the Senate meeting because later they did not open for me.[62]

But for all Sanudo's preference for the political scene (which family obligations occasionally interrupted) and for all his scanting of his personal life, every now and then his personal emotions force his hand, as in his grief for the death of a beloved sister and his melancholy at the monastic investiture of four young girls, including a great niece:

January 27, 1517 (23:534)   At tierce my dearest and sweetest only full sister, Sanua, died.[63] She was the wife of ser Zuan Malipiero, of the parish of Santa Maria Formosa. The poor little martyr suffered from a relentless disease that had confined her to her bed since St. Martin's Day.[64] She died a very Christian death. I was present and can say without doubt that her soul passed to celestial glory. Her age at death was —— years; this coming February 8 she would have been married for twenty-eight years, and one may truly say that she lived with her husband without quarrel [*sine ulla querela*]. I pray God to grant her eternal peace. She died in the highest esteem and was mourned by all who knew her. She was honorably buried the following day after dinner in the

---

62. Once the deliberations had begun, the doors to the Senate were closed and latecomers could not enter. This explains Sanudo's ill humor. It is worth noting that the names mentioned in connection with Sanudo's personal life—Priuli, Barbarigo, Malipiero—all refer to important patrician families. He was well connected.

63. The Fulin edition incorrectly gives Sanudo's sister's name as Sancia.

64. 11 November.

church of San Francesco di la Vigna, as she had requested, in a tomb near the bones of my dearest and most excellent mother, madonna Letizia. I took little note of any other news, my sorrow was so great. But since there is no remedy, the wise thing is to accept God's will, and so enough said [*et de hoc satis*].

May 22, 1526 (41:375)   I attended the ceremonies for Corpus Domini, where I heard many Masses. Four women took the veil; among them was a daughter of my nephew ser Francesco Sanudo, named Marieta, who is thirteen years old . . . , and it disturbed me greatly to see them led into a convent, where they will never be seen again.

Other family events brought him more satisfaction, such as the advantageous matches he made for his dependents. Of these he was proud enough to make notice in his diaries. In 1530 he records "for all time" the engagement of one of his two illegitimate daughters, for both of whom he was able to arrange honorable alliances.

May 9, 1530 (53:201)   On this day, as I record for all time, I betrothed my illegitimate daughter Candiana to Zuan Morello. May God grant them good fortune.

Candiana's marriage took place the following June 13 (53:268). The other daughter, Bianca, was engaged to Angelo di Grattaroli on July 29, 1533, and married on August 10 (58:495, 541). From the dates, it would seem that these illegitimate children were born after Sanudo was widowed in 1508 at fifty-two years of age.

The dowries that went with these daughters in marriage, the wherewithal to accumulate a magnificent library (see below), and the ability to pay his taxes are not discussed by Sanudo, but the financial anxieties were surely there. Only a few hints exist of the straitened circumstances of his life, and they are revealing. One was his concern in the great Rialto fire of 1514 that La Campana, an inn in which he had a share, might have burned (January 1514; 17:458). Fortunately, it was unharmed, and he tells us that "from this I, Marin Sanudo, . . . derive my living; it pays a rental income of 205 ducats in addition to income from the shops below." But toward the end of his life Sanudo had to forfeit to his brother Leonardo his income from the inn in repayment for his brother's having sold his own share of the inn to cover one of Marin's debts.[65] This was most likely the debt that led to his horrendous overnight imprisonment.

---

65. See below under "His Last Will and Testament."

December 19,[66] 1516 (23:343)   In the morning the dreadful occurrence took place. Thinking that I would make my way to San Marco as usual, I was [accosted] by that traitor Zuan Soranzo, with whom I have been in litigation for the past six years. He is very sure that I owe him more than one hundred ducats and the forty-seven ducats remaining from two court judgments on what it appeared he was owed from old bills. And to do me outrage, he had me arrested at San Cassian, and I had to appear in court at San Marco before Zaneto Dandolo. But all these charges were suspended by ser Marchio Nadal, *auditor vecchio*. So I was released the following day. This vendetta I will leave to no one else.

From these few references and his self-description in his 1531 letter to the heads of the Council of Ten as "old, ill, poor, and poorer than poor" and from the codicil to his will (see below) we learn how difficult the last years of his life were.

The Scholar in His Study

Sanudo's solace and his sustenance from personal and political loss remained his work, his library, and his reputation as a man of letters. We learn more about his library from others than we do from him.[67] The kind of information he gives is very casual, such as the fact that in the summer of 1509, as enemy armies swept through the Terraferma, Padua became crowded with refugees, among them local peasants who were selling goods looted from the empty houses in the countryside. Some of those homes had belonged to Jews, most of whom had fled to Venice for safety. Sanudo, who was in Padua to help defend the city, was able to acquire a Hebrew Bible at a very good price, and he records the transaction with satisfaction:

July 17, 1509 (8:525)   There were ten thousand outsiders in Padua, although many today left with their spoils to go home, especially peasants from Gambarare and other places in the Paduan countryside, some carrying one kind of acquired spoils and others other kinds. And by chance I met one of these who had a most beautiful Hebrew Bible made with fine paper, worth twenty ducats, and to my good fortune he sold it to me for a *marcello*.[68] I took the book as a memento with the intention of putting it in my study.

Over the years, Sanudo continued to purchase books, and the reputation of his collection attracted important visitors. On July 20, 1513 (16:517), he remarks that

---

66. The Fulin edition misdates this entry as 18 December.

67. See, e.g., see Aldo Manuzio's praise for Sanudo in chapter 8 and the praise of others in Berchet 1903, 55–67.

68. A coin whose value was half that of the *lira*. See appendix A.

two envoys from Pope Leo X, Pietro Bibbiena and don Pindaro (Sindesio Gentile), who had made the standard visits to see the jewels of San Marco and the Arsenal, "came the other day to my house to see my *studio*." A number of manuscripts from Sanudo's library record poems of praise for his collection.[69] Sanudo decorated his library's walls with Latin verses celebrating it as a sanctuary of the muses and the seat of historical and poetical learning:

> "This place is dedicated to the nine sisters;
>   May he who is without art, untrained, and a prattler, withdraw afar."
> "This place contains historians, this place also contains poets;
>   Those whom earth itself scarcely contains, this one place contains."[70]

This library was his *locus,* his place; it contained his cultural world, which was dedicated to his city and formed part of his patriotic contribution. In a note of 1516, and in the context of another electoral disappointment, he adds the library to the list of services he had rendered his patria. The notice comes as he recounts how so many of the most powerful and generous patricians were not elected to a procuratorship in spite of their generous offers of funds to the state. "I will put it this way: the city is ungrateful. . . . That is how things are in these days. . . . So that we have to accept the ways of our city however they go" (April 28, 1516; 22:172). Then he speaks of his own disappointments, in spite of his service as a historian and his purchase of books, as if this too had served his homeland, along with his paternal heritage and his speeches in the Great Council, all to no avail:

April 28, 1516 (22:172)   It is no wonder [*Et nil mirum*] that I, Marin Sanudo, failed to be elected state attorney, I who have already put such great effort into writing for the past twenty-four years, who have served in the Collegio seven times and in other magistracies and offices, who have made a library of 2,800 books, for which I have spent 2,000 ducats and more, born of the family I come from and son of one who is buried in Rome, having died as ambassador from this Republic, I who have spoken three times in the Great Council! So do Republics treat those who do such deeds!

His disappointment in 1516, however, did not moderate his bibliophilia. A few years later he mentions that he had acquired and still had a work of Martin Luther, who in 1517 had publicly entered the controversies surrounding the reform

---

69. BNM, Lat. Cl. XII, 210 (4689), 211 (4179).
70. Berchet 1903, 59.

of the church with his ninety-five theses. By June 1520 Luther's writings had been ordered destroyed, and his works were banned in Venice.

August 25, 1520 (29:135)   August 25, Sunday. Don Octavian Britonio, the vicar of the most reverend patriarch, appeared before the Collegio today and presented a printed brief from the pope that had come from Rome. It condemns the writings[71] and works of the German brother Martin Luther, of the Augustinian Friars; no one, under pain of excommunication [*sub poena excomunicationis*], is to read or to keep any of the aforementioned books in his home. The vicar obtained permission to send the police captains to the home of the German bookseller Zordan, who lives at San Maurizio, to confiscate these aforesaid works, which were printed in Germany and sent to this city to be sold. Thus the Collegio sent Thomà di Freschi, secretary of the Council of Ten, with the vicar to take care of this, and they seized the works that he had. Nevertheless, I have had, and still have, one in my study.

By 1530 Sanudo's library collection included sixty-five hundred books and manuscripts and was famous enough to be sought out by men of high station, such as the Prince of Salerno.

April 27, 1530 (53:173)   The Prince of Salerno arrived accompanied by six Venetian gentlemen sent by the Collegio to bring him to the Signoria; they were dressed in scarlet. He is twenty-one years old, his name is Ferrante, of the house of Sanseverino, and he appeared in the Collegio. The doge embraced him warmly and went to meet him at the tribunal and offered him [the keys of] the city. Then he went to see the Basilica of San Marco ——. I note that the aforementioned prince sent one of his men to me, Marin Sanudo, saying that the prince desired to see three people: ser Pietro Bembo, with whom he stayed in Padua, I, Marin Sanudo, because of my fame as a historian, and Zuan Soro the cipher master. He cared about nothing else because he is a scholarly man and a lover of letters, and he wished to see my study. I made my excuses because I did not want him to come.[72]

---

71. The manuscript has *sententia;* the Fulin edition has *scritura.*

72. Prince Ferrante di Sanseverino, evidently wanted to visit the sites that important visitors to Venice were usually shown: the basilica and treasury of San Marco, the Arsenal, the armory of the Council of Ten, the Rialto, the glass factories of Murano, the many shrines of sacred relics, and so on. Sanudo does not bother to list them here, but he knew that his *studio,* with its codices and chronicles, *mappa mundi,* drawings, and paintings, was also famous. The cipher master Zuan Soro, whose skills were important for Venetian diplomatic codes, was also well known in Venice (see chapter 4), as was Pietro Bembo, with whom Sanudo would have painful dealings a few months later (see below). On Pietro Bembo, see chapter 8.

The Historian

Sanudo's diffidence about showing his library to an important visitor in 1530 may have been due to his chagrin at the lack of official recognition for his efforts to record the history of his homeland day by day over the previous thirty-four years. Not that he had been entirely ignored. His early and ongoing commitment to recording the events of Italy and the world and his repeated promise to his readers (1:6, 8:5, 34:4) that these diaries would be reduced to a proper history when time permitted finally received some recognition from the government in 1515, when Sanudo requested and received permission to consult the secret archives of the government.

August 17, 1515 (20:532)   I, Marin Sanudo, once again appeared this morning in the Collegio before the heads of the Ten, ser Nicolò Prioli, ser Alvise Grimani, and ser Francesco Foscari the knight. As I have already been working for twenty-two years to write the history of these times, an important and copious work that began with King Charles's incursion into Italy and continues to this time, and as I have seven times been savio ai ordeni by the grace of this state and have written whatever has come to pass and now wish to reorganize my work, I requested again that I be permitted to see the secret books and letters so that I may write the truth, as has been granted on other occasions to others. The heads of the Ten consulted together and praised me greatly. And so today the Council of Ten, after conferring with the doge and the most illustrious Signoria, decided that I should be shown everything I asked for and ordered the grand chancellor to make a record and decree of this.[73]

But even though Sanudo had access to the sources, his literary ambitions would be as frustrated as his political hopes. A year after the permission granted above, Andrea Navagero, not Sanudo, was appointed official historian, at an annual salary of two hundred ducats. Sanudo recognized that he had been passed over because he had written "in lengua materna," in his own tongue (January 30, 1516; 21:485).[74] But it was all the more galling because Navagero produced nothing,

73. The permission, granted on 20 August 1515, was patterned on that given to Andrea Mocenigo on 28 June 1515. Sanudo's permit was reconfirmed on 27 September 1516. See ASV, Notatorio dai Capi X, fol. 68v.

74. Sanudo chose to write in the vernacular so that, as he wrote in his dedication to the doge (1873, 17), his work would be accessible to learned and unlearned alike, "because it is better to labor for everyone than for the rare and few." His reasoning, never made fully explicit, seems to have been that the completeness of the information he offered would serve the truth and that truth set forth in the common tongue would educate the patricians of Venice for service to their homeland.

while he, Sanudo, had for so many years written his "history of the events occurring in Italy," pursuing "with enormous labor . . . the investigation of verifiable events," believing himself worthy "of some reward, if not a stipend such as others have received who write nothing, at least some honor from my homeland, which I have so greatly exalted and raised to eternal memory" (March 1, 1522; 33:5). In 1529 Navagero died, having still written nothing and all the while having collected his stipend, as Sanudo noted bitterly (50:372).

Sanudo was not chosen to replace him. Instead, a Venetian patrician and literary figure whose fame had spread throughout Italy, Pietro Bembo, was appointed. Sanudo was fully aware of Bembo's distinction. He copied into his diaries a letter from Bembo's nephew Zuan Mathio [Bembo], who was seeking reprint privileges for certain of Bembo's many important writings (March 22, 1530; 53:65), and a fulsome letter from an admirer naming Bembo "the true light and father of our language" (53:387). But Bembo, for all his literary prominence, was not, in Sanudo's lexicon, the *humanista* that his father, Bernardo Bembo, had been, for the son had withdrawn from the Venetian political scene, in which the father had played such a large role.[75] So Sanudo, as if distancing himself from Bembo's appointment as official historian of Venice, dryly records on two occasions the terms of Bembo's employment: subsidized housing for Bembo's use, supervision of a collection of books that would form the nucleus of Venice's public library, and access to the government archives:

September 26, 1530 (53:568)   A bill was passed that the honorable ser Pietro Bembo, who lives in Padua, be the one to write the history of Venice in Latin, succeeding Navagero, who died after drawing 3,000 ducats' salary and not writing a word. The aforementioned Pietro Bembo will be paid for his housing, that is, the rent where he lives, up to sixty ducats a year, nor will other provisions be made for him.

December 21, 1530 (54:186)   A noteworthy item: in these days, by decision of the Council of Ten, the management of the books of the late Cardinal Bessarion, which are held in the Ducal Palace in strongboxes above the room of the thirty savi, was assigned by the procurators to the reverend ser Pietro Bembo.[76] He has been charged with writing the history of Venice in Latin, something that ser Andrea Navagero did not do. Even though he was paid 3,000 ducats for that purpose, at 200 ducats a year, he wrote nothing [*et nihil scripsit*]. What this monsignor will do, I do not know. He was given a mandate

---

75. For a broad survey of the civic nature of Venetian culture, see Branca 1998; and chapter 8.

76. The collection of books that later became part of the Biblioteca Nazionale Marciana was the gift of Cardinal Bessarion to the Venetian Senate in 1468 (see chapter 8).

by the heads of the Ten to have access to the [government] books and letters and writings from —— to the present.

Pietro Bembo's access to the government archives profited him little; he had no patience or time to sift through piles of documents. Learning of Sanudo's preselected record, he requested access to that. Sanudo demurred. In a long letter to the heads of the Council of Ten in September 1531 Sanudo gave his reasons: he had labored mightily all those years in the hope that his work would achieve fame; he had hoped thereby to do honor to his beloved country; he had wished—and who does not? he asked—that he might earn a goodly sum from a work that all would want to read, especially since it was written in the common tongue. Such a work would be indispensable to future historians, and it was an achievement in whose creation he had grown "old, ill, poor, and poorer than poor, having no income." He complained that "for more than thirty years I have earned nothing from offices, I have neglected my own affairs, and I have dedicated myself completely to writing."[77] So the government made a financial arrangement with him: Bembo would see the diaries, and Sanudo would receive 150 ducats a year to continue his work.[78]

September 19, 1531 (54:596)   A bill was passed to give me, Marin Sanudo, for my labors in writing fifty-three volumes of this history and diary, a stipend of 150 ducats a year. I will be paid by the office of the governors of revenues, which paid ser Andrea Navagero to write his history. For this I am also to allow ser Pietro Bembo to make use of my books to write his Latin history, and I am to continue to write as long as I live. All this was contained in the bill, which received a unanimous vote.[79]

---

77. This is a typical case of Sanudian exaggeration, since he had held some public offices. The exaggeration is in service of the larger truth that he had been elected to only a few, that they had not been lucrative, and that he had not taken financial advantage of them.

78. For Pietro Bembo's letters requesting access to Sanudo's diaries—to the doge on 7 August 1531 and to the Council of Ten on 2 September 1531—see Berchet 1903, 94–95; and ASV, CX, Comuni, filza 14, inserted in a minute of 19 September 1531. It appears that in Berchet's time a number of the archival copies of official documents and relevant correspondence were gathered together in this minute with a pink paper enclosing the documents. But as of June 2001 several documents were not there, including Bembo's letter of 7 August 1531 to the doge and the Council of Ten's decree of 19 September 1531 giving Sanudo a stipend of 150 ducats—the title *pars provisionis ducatos 150* is there, but not the document. Nor is the decree of 26 September 1531 from the heads of the Council of Ten allowing Sanudo access to the government archives, except for material especially designated as secret. See Berchet 1903, 99. For Sanudo's letter to the Council of Ten, see BNM, Ital. Cl. VII, 375 (8954), fols. 11r–12v; Berchet 1903, 95–97; Caracciolo Aricò 1980, xv–xvi; and Bettio 1828, 11–15. For Sanudo's letter to Pietro Bembo and Bembo's response, see Berchet 1903, 98–99; BNM, Ital. Cl. VII, 375 (8954), fol. 10r; and Bettio 1828, 16–17.

79. See diaries, November 1531 (55:103), December 1531 (55:211), March 1532 (55:655), for Sanudo

His Last Will and Testament

The government decree of September 19, 1531, determined that Sanudo was to be compensated for his "history and diary" as long as he lived. But he had sufficient health, energy, and conviction to continue the diaries for only two more years. The diaries would end, without formal conclusion, on September 30, 1533. A few weeks earlier Sanudo had made his last will and testament.

The will may still be seen today in the Archivio di Stato of Venice.[80] On the back is the notary's statement in Latin, citing the date (September 4, 1533); the place (Rialto); and the testator, Marin Sanudo, son of the late Leonardo Sanudo, of the parish of San Jacomo de Lorio [Giacomo dell'Orio]. The notary also verified that the document, closed and sealed, represented the testator's wishes and that there was nothing further Sanudo wished to add. The notary's statement was attested by two witnesses.

The first sentence—the text is in the same Venetian chancellory language as the diaries—remarks on the importance of ordering one's affairs before sickness interferes. The second praises the laws of succession, which protected the testator's last wishes against noncompliance. And then Sanudo's personality, his anxiety for the future security of his life's work, breaks through the otherwise objective prose: "And this happens to those who have no legitimate children; such a one am I, by my unfair destiny, thus my great labors and my works must pass into the hands of strangers! So for these reasons, I, Marin Sanudo, son of the late ser Leonardo, of the parish of San Jacomo de Lorio, by the grace of God sound of mind and body, make my testament by my own hand. This is the fifth testament I have made; I have destroyed all the others, and this I will give into the hand of the notary in the presence of witnesses."

The document then follows a typical pattern. The testator commends his soul to God and asks to be buried in the habit of the Scuola di San Giovanni Evangelista, of which, he writes, he had been a member for many years. His body, after twenty-four hours in his home, is to be carried into the church of San Zaccaria, where there should be no funeral canopy, "only one double candle at

---

as a "historico publico" (public historian). His usefulness as such was especially evident in December 1531, during a discussion of the time of day when a trial in the Great Council should take place. Sanudo cited the trials of Antonio Grimani in 1499 and Anzolo Trevisan in 1510: both had been condemned in the morning. Pietro Bembo's *Historiae venetae libri XII*, published in Latin in 1551 and in Italian in 1552, dealt with the years 1487-1513. The work was a disappointment to the Venetian government, which edited it considerably before releasing it to the public. The work did not acknowledge Sanudo as one of its primary sources, and after its moment of literary fame had passed, it has been largely unread. Cf. Berchet 1903, 100n1; and chapter 8, n. 5.

80. ASV, Sezione Notarile, Testamenti in atti di Gerolamo da Canal, busta 191, n. 546. A copy of the will is in BNM, Ital. Cl. XI, 324 (7135). Berchet transcribed the will and the later codicil (1903, 101–7); see also Caracciolo Aricò 1980, xiv–xv.

the head." There, in one of the vaults belonging to the Sanudo family, he is to be buried in a simple casket of pitch-treated larch and placed in a tomb on which is to be carved the Cross, his family arms, and the letters *M.S.* And, adds the distrustful testator, should the nuns of San Zaccaria resist assigning his body to its rightful place, let them be reminded of the many benefactions given to their order by his ancestors.

For the funeral cortege he requests the chapter of his parish, twenty parish priests chosen by his *scuola,* and sixteen Jesuati, to each of whom should be given twenty soldi, and to the school should be given twenty double candles: "Nor do I wish other priests or beneficed ecclesiastics, because it is all a waste; still, one must conform for one's worldly reputation."

Then he lists as executors two procurators *de ultra* whom he trusts: one was a Corner, son of the famous Zorzi Corner, who often appears in the diaries; the other was Sanudo's nephew Marco Antonio, "whom I have always regarded as a son." He expresses his confidence that, working with Antonio di Marsiglio, they will faithfully execute his wishes in spite of current criticism that the procurators do not fulfill their testamentary duties. And then follows the paragraph encapsulating his life's ambition, namely, that he should be remembered as a historian of Venice. Below his simple, old-fashioned tomb he wished there to be a stone inscribed with the following epitaph, containing the self-description and the title he coveted:

> Whether you are a stranger or dweller in the city,
> Do not spurn the tomb you see:
> Here lie the bones of Marin Sanudo, son of Leonardo the distinguished
> Senator.
> He was an investigator of ancient deeds
> And expert recorder of Venetian history by public decree.
> This I wished you to know. Now fare thee well.

Numerous bequests and financial adjustments follow, including arrangements for prayers for his soul, for the "deserving poor." There are bequests for servants and relatives, with an occasional personal comment thrown in, almost defiantly: "I have lived honorably as a gentleman in his home; I have paid my taxes and married off two daughters. May God be praised for all this."

But the most personal aspect of the will lay in his disposition of his library and his personal papers:

Item: I wish and command that all of my books on the history and happenings of Italy, written in my hand, which begin with the arrival of King Charles of France in Italy, which books are all bound and have covers and are in an armoire and number fifty-six, shall belong to my most illustrious Signoria, to which they are to be presented by my executors; the books will be kept where it suits and pleases them, under the supervision of the heads of the Council of Ten, for it was this supreme council that established my stipend of 150 ducats a year—which I swear to God was nothing compared with the enormous labor I have had!

I wish and command that all my other printed books, which are in the large study on the ground floor, and those manuscripts that are in my armoires in my bedroom be sold by my executors at public auction. . . . They are more than 6,500 in number and have cost me a lot of money, and they are rare and beautiful objects, many of which one no longer finds. I have an inventory of these with the price that each cost me, and those marked with a cross I sold in my time of need. And I beg these procurators and stewards not to throw away these books, especially the manuscript books, because they are beautiful things and cost me much money, all of which may be seen in the inventory, and those that are boxed were printed in Germany and were quite costly. I made these great expenditures for books because I wanted to make a library for some monastery or leave some to the library of San Marco, which library I doubt will ever be built. However, I have changed my mind and wish them to be sold. These books are worth much more than they cost me because I bought them advantageously in time of scarcity and had them at a good price, which is why Father Zuan Batista Egnazio and ser Antonio di Marsilio, when they see the index, will find much to value and will not throw them away, as is the custom.

Item: the other works written in my hand, and especially [*et potissimum*] the three books of the chronicle of Venice that I composed,[81] the three books on the magistracies,[82] and the other books that are in a chest and an armoire in my bedroom, all written in my hand—these I do not wish sold. Instead, an inventory of them should be made, because I did not do one in my lifetime, and they should all be put in a strongbox and carried to the Procuratia to be given to whom and at what time I shall specify below. For I wish all of these to go to someone in my family, and unless I order otherwise, I wish them to belong to Marin Sanudo, son of my brother Leonardo, who is not yet one year old, and they shall remain locked up and bound until he is twenty years old, and then all of these shall be consigned to him by the *signori procuratori*.

A clause follows these dispositions bequeathing to the church of San Sebastian "a most worthy relic of a bone of San Sebastian, which used to belong to the dogaressa of Ca' Moro, née Sanudo, and our house has always been preserved from

---

81. Sanudo, 1989–2001.
82. Sanudo 1980.

the plague. Not having given it in my lifetime, I wish it to be given now, because in my illness I vowed it should be so given." And then, to protect his nonliterary goods, he voiced his concern that because of his political and literary preoccupations he might not have sufficiently safeguarded his other properties.

Item: I wish that from all my papers, which are in a strongbox in one room, be made an inventory of the important ones and [that it be] well kept in the Procuratia, because by this means my holdings can be seen and defended against whoever wishes to torment me, and also what is owed to me can be recovered, because I have always attended to matters of the state and to reading and writing, as one can see from the many books written in my hand.

Nearly a page and a half of the densely written three-page document follows, listing his properties and sums owing to him, so that his executors would know what was rightfully his beyond his furniture and books, "because I am certain that after my death, many who in my lifetime would not dare to open their mouths will make demands."

Finally, a penultimate paragraph leaves his residual wealth to his three nephews, sons of his brother Leonardo, with a warning that should they or their father contest any part of the will, that bequest will be forfeited. And then, after leaving five ducats to the notary for the public registration and processing of his will, he signed the document he had himself devised and written, "I, Marin Sanudo, with my own hand."

Three years after this will was written, and only two months before his death, Sanudo added a codicil.[83] His government stipend had ceased when he stopped keeping his diaries, and his poverty weighed on him. He was now infirm in body, although "sound in soul, mind, and memory." In contrast to the feisty testator of the will, the codicil's author breathes despair and resignation. Reiterated were two bequests that his will had placed "before all else," bequests to faithful servants who had tended him without pay during his impoverished years.[84] He revealed that his library had had to be dismantled to pay his debts. He was not sure where his body would be buried. He had earlier stipulated that it should be placed near the tombs of his family in San Zaccaria; now he stated that it should be placed there or in San Francesco della Vigna, "where God will inspire me." No longer confident even that a proper tomb would be built, he replaced the line in his original epitaph that read "Do not spurn the tomb you see" with "Do not spurn the tomb which you do not see." For all the splendid funerals that Sanudo

---

83. ASV, Sezione Notarile, Testamenti notaio Diotisalvi Benzon, busta 97, n. 470; Berchet 1903, 108–9.

84. Berchet 1903, 103.

had witnessed and described, he appeared unsure that even his modest requests would be fulfilled.

His doubt was justified.[85] The tomb has never been found, and either the tombstone was never erected or it was soon destroyed. But what he could not anticipate was how justified his faith in his diaries proved to be. Replete with primary sources not found elsewhere, the diaries remained to support (at least in certain respects) his claim that no one would make much of modern history without them, and in that way they continued his patriotic service to a homeland with writings that have made Venice central to the history of much of the larger world about it. More enduring than any monument could ever be, these writings are the true legacy of Marin Sanudo, "investigator of ancient deeds and expert recorder of Venetian history by public decree."

85. Ibid., 109, states that his named executors refused the responsibility.

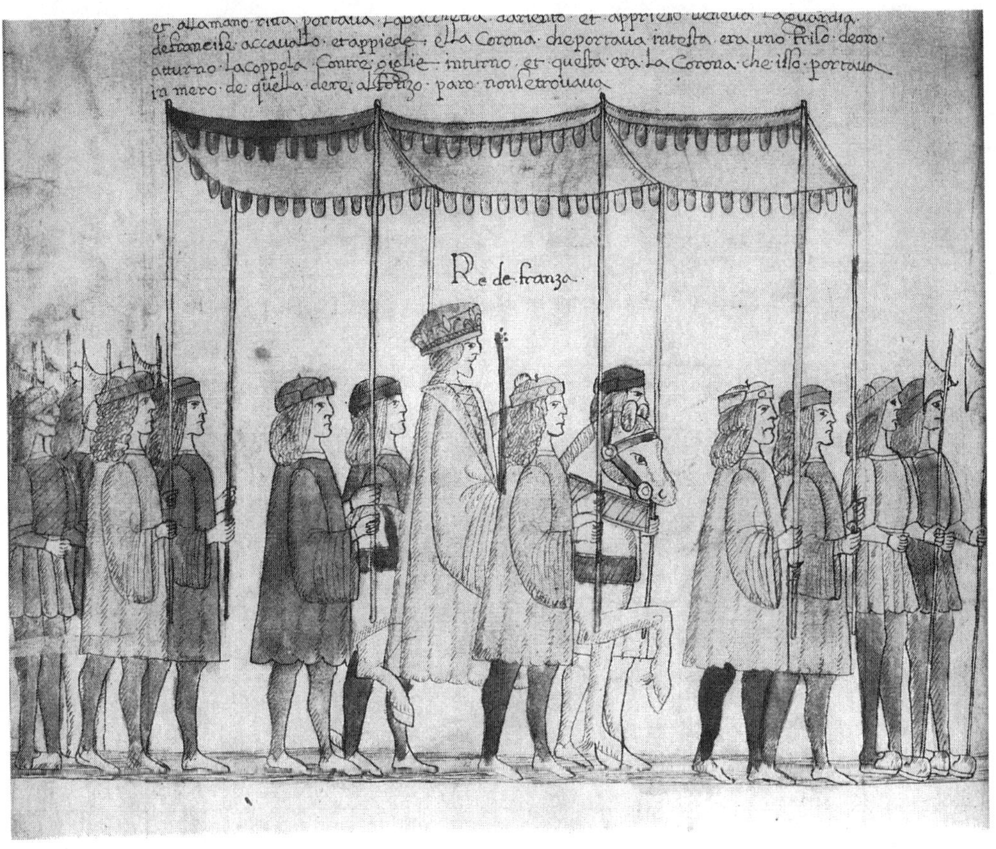

Charles VIII, king of France, entering Naples in 1494 or 1495. Ferraiolo, *Cronaca della Napoli aragonese*. The Pierpont Morgan Library, New York.

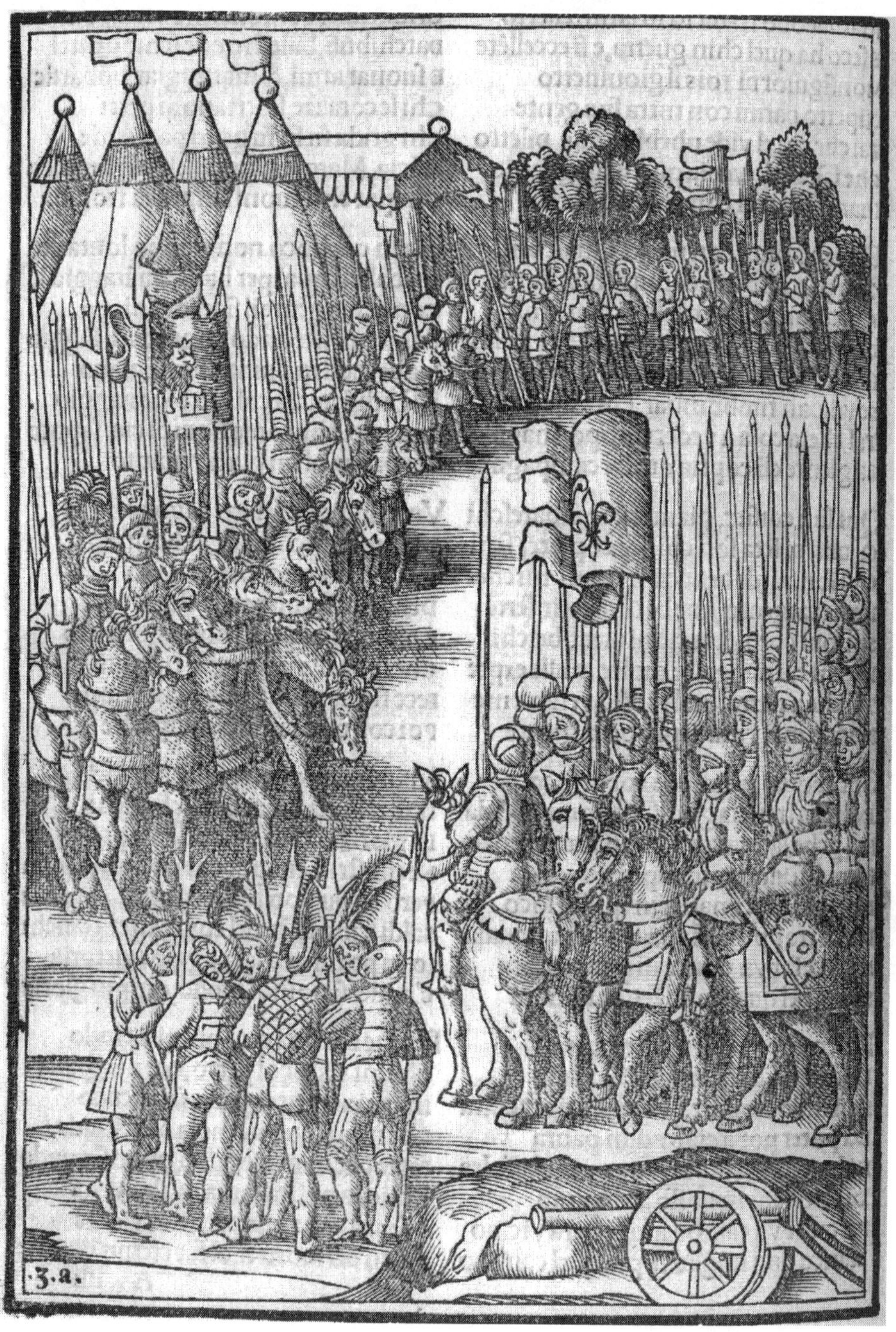

Preparations for the battle of Agnadello. Reproduced by permission from Niccolo degli Agostini, *Le successi bellici seguiti in Italia del fatto darme di Gieredada del MCCCCCIX fin al presente MCCCCCXXI* (Venice: Nicolo Zompino & Vincenzo de Venetia, 1521). © British Library Board. All rights reserved. G.11109.

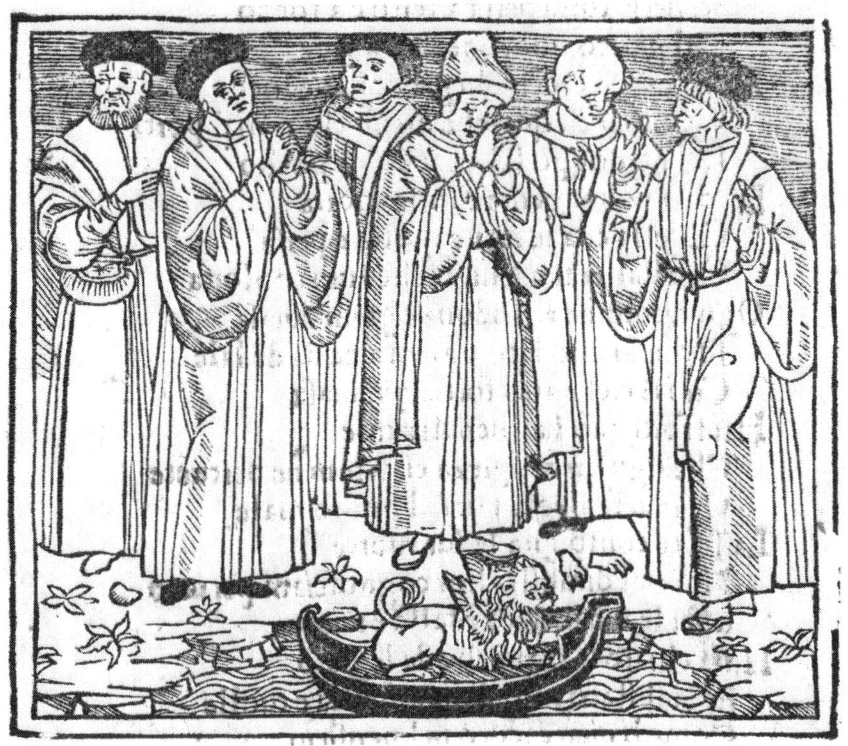

Venetian grief over defeat at the battle of Agnadello. Frontispiece, *Lamento de veneciani* (Ferrara, 1509). The British Library.

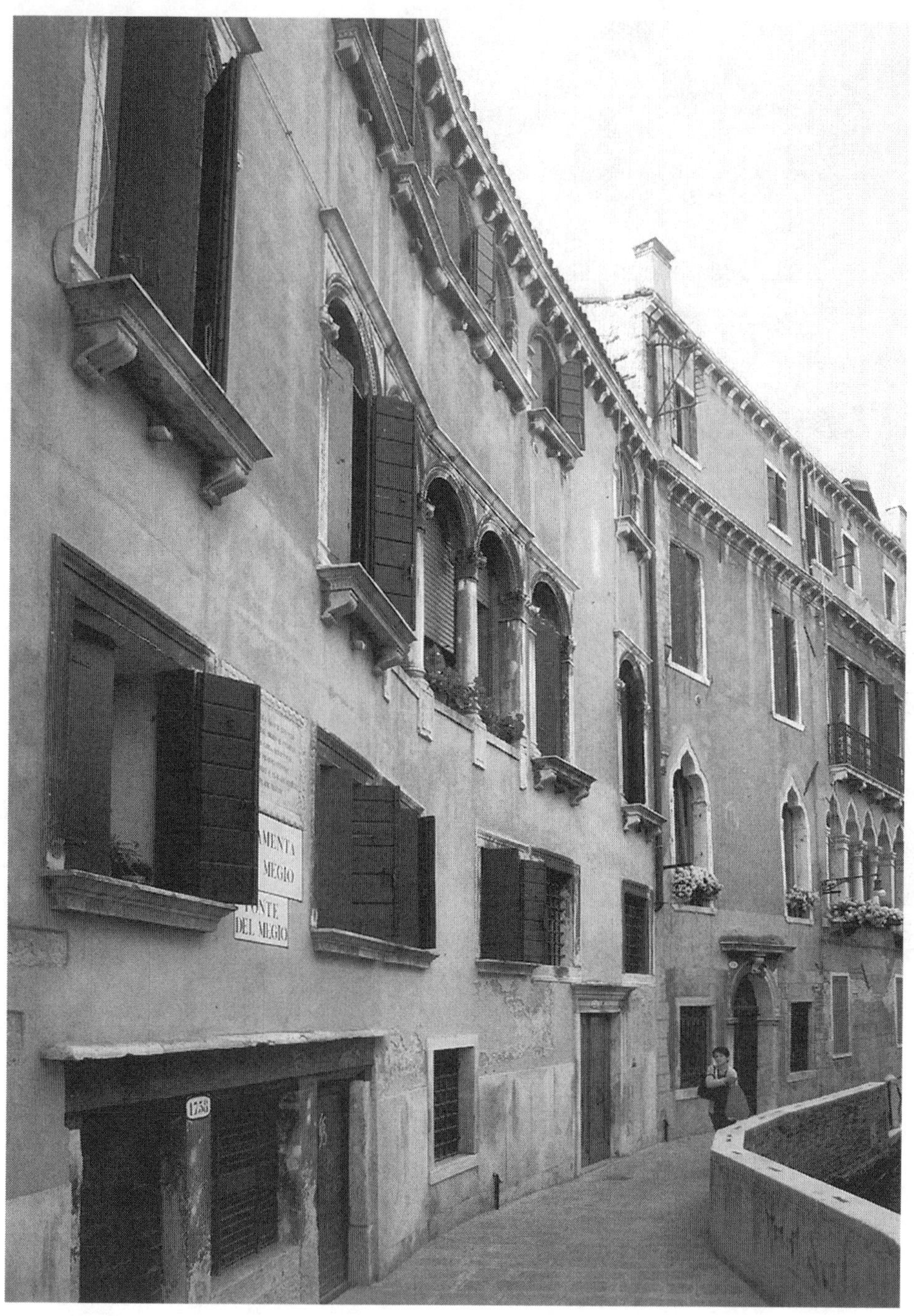

Ca' Sanudo on the Fondamenta del Megio near San Giacomo dell'Orio. Photo courtesy of P. F. Brown.

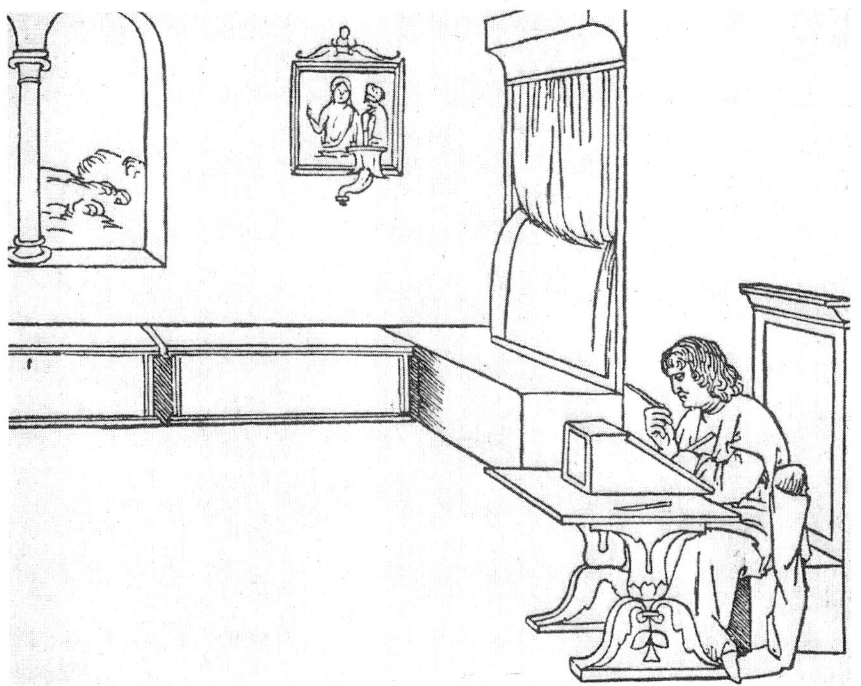

Polifilo in his study, from *Hypnerotomachia Poliphili* (Venice: Aldine, 1499).

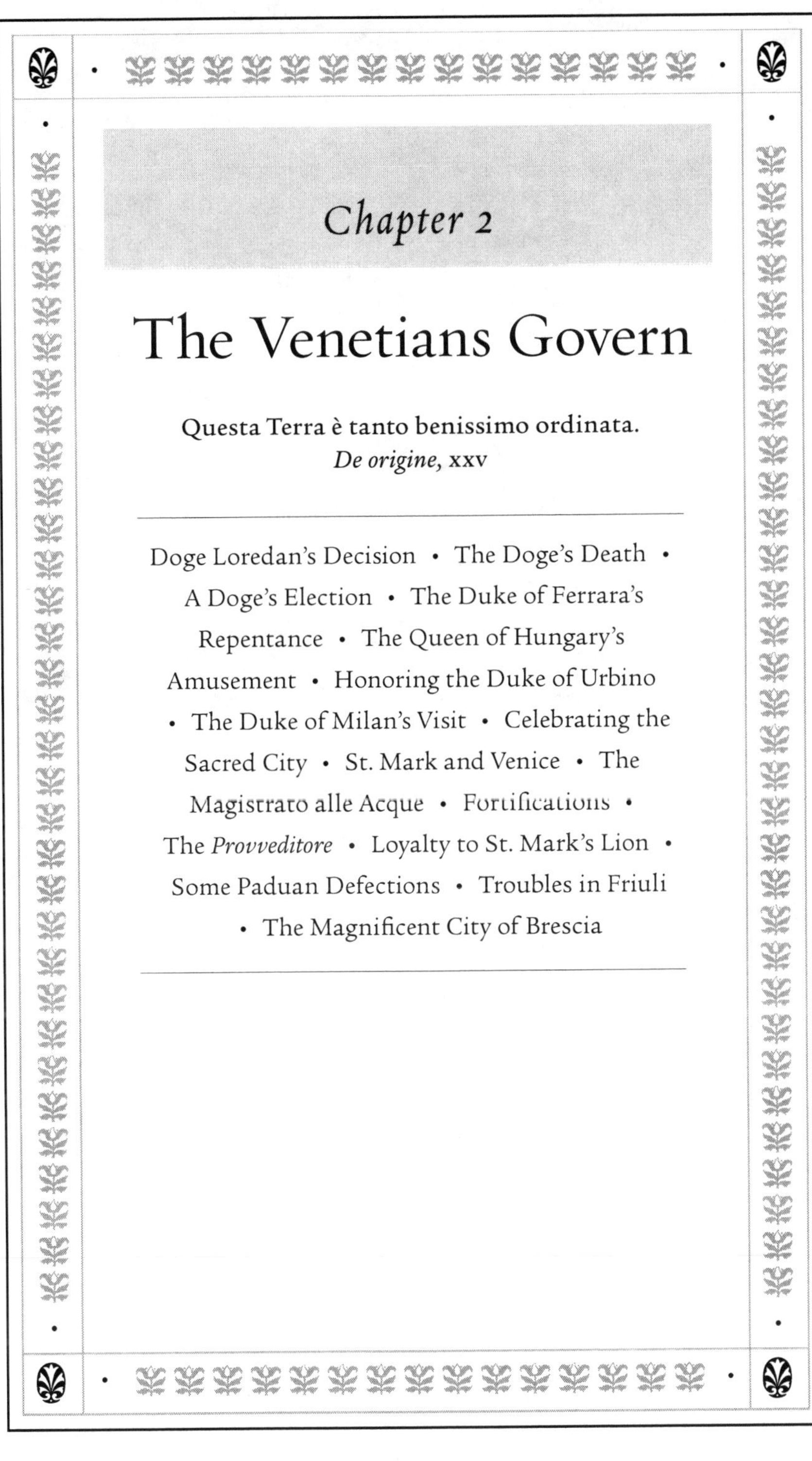

The Venetians Govern

Questa Terra è tanto benissimo ordinata.
De origine, xxv

Sanudo's annalistic and political endeavors, these twin commitments, were presented in chapter 1 as a consistent and interwoven story, although consistency was not inherent in the diaries. The information that flowed from Sanudo's industrious pen was a collection of assorted items that he found "noteworthy," among which his references to himself form a very minor part. His often-confessed intention was someday to cull, from the vast collection of information he had accumulated, the materials with which he would construct a formal "history." That day never dawned for him, and his interest in the entire variety of news that he faithfully recorded in his diaries endured as long as he wrote.

The chapters that follow here, thematically structured as they are under the general rubrics of government (both within the city and over the dominion), crime and justice, foreign affairs, economic networks and institutions, society and social life, religion, cultural concerns, and theater, retain a measure of that variegated quality. As already seen in the excerpts on Sanudo's own life, the most consistent focus of his attention was the government, in both its domestic and its imperial aspects. The final purpose of the information he accumulated was to celebrate his city and its government. As he wrote in his early account of the origin and magistracies of Venice, "The renown of the homeland of Venice is such and so great that the whole world holds it in high esteem."[1] That esteem, he surmised, was due to the order and effectiveness of its polity. Thus he intended to join his writings to a growing body of literature on the city's history and political composition produced to satisfy contemporary curiosity—both native and foreign—about the beginnings, unusual location, and workings of the Venetian homeland.

Sanudo's early work on the origins, site, and magistracies of Venice was one to which he continued to add during much of his lifetime. Its composition parallels the period during which he was writing his diaries and shows that his preoccupation with the Venetian structure and practice of government took several forms: the summaries and explanations that formed his *De origine* and the daily descriptions of elections, debates, decrees, and administrative concerns that contributed to the raw material of his diaries.

Moreover, his interest in the actions and operations of the government was shared by most Venetian patricians. From the age of twenty-five, and sometimes earlier, male patricians were allowed to sit in the Maggior Consiglio, the Great Council, which in 1513 numbered more than twenty-five hundred members

---

1. From the dedication to Doge Agostino Barbarigo in Sanudo 1980, 6.

and was the elective body for about eight hundred positions, most of which rotated every year or every six months. Those who proved most powerful and popular might be elected to the Senate, to one of its two higher branches (the Savi Grandi and the Savi di Terraferma), to the Quarantia (the supreme court of forty judges), as councillors to the doge, or as state attorneys. Particularly prestigious and important were the Council of Ten and the procurators, from among the latter of which the doge was usually selected. If Sanudo's own story describes the government from the perspective of a largely unsuccessful political aspirant who did not progress beyond the lower governmental levels, the following extracts on the dogeship frame a view of the top, filtered through this one observer's keen eye.

Doge Loredan's Decision

At the apex of the governmental pyramid was the dogeship itself. Although its powers over the past centuries had become increasingly circumscribed, the office commanded enormous prestige and men worked hard to attain it. The doge was still the leading member of Venetian society, the high priest of the state, the celebrant of Venetian communal life.[2] Along with the procurators, he had a life tenure and therefore a chance to influence public policy in the long term.[3] He represented the state in its glory, and in times of danger he was expected to show courage and resolution. Sanudo was appalled that at the news of the defeat at Agnadello in 1509 Doge Leonardo Loredan would not allow a motion that he go to the front himself to hearten the troops; that he appeared "more dead than alive"; and that he did not wear the traditional golden robe to the Ascension Day ceremonies to show that "he was not dismayed" (May 15–16, 1509; 8:251–52, 257, 266). A few months later, the diarist was equally ready to report a fiery speech made by the same doge in which he recriminated against the Venetians for their unpaid debts, their sins and arrogance, and their pusillanimity in an effort to rally their support for the war in which Venice was by then fully engaged.

July 8, 1509 (8:496–97)   After dinner there was a meeting of the Great Council. There were not many of us, about 1,200, because many did not attend, even though there are more patricians in the city than ever before, perhaps 2,000 or more who could have come to the council. . . . The doge was persuaded that he should speak, so after the ballot boys were sent outside he stood and spoke. He finished by charging those who were debtors [to the government] to pay the monies owing for the war, for there were many wealthy men who refused to pay; and he said that our money will be of no use to us if we lose

---

2. See Cozzi 1993, 5, citing Tenenti.
3. For an overview of ducal elections and ducal power, see Finlay 1978a.

the war because our enemies, all conspiring against us, will torture us and take our money and silver and gold, as happened at Constantinople when the Turks conquered it: someone brought the signor Turco [the sultan] a lot of money, and the Turk had him cut in two, saying, "What good will this money do you now?" And then the doge said that it was because of our arrogance that all these powers were allied against us, because we thought we were as high as the sky. Everyone is spending money, everyone is lining his clothes. In his day, he said, people wore garments that were simple from the waist up, and now everyone wears ducal sleeves, which in former times only the doge and doctors could wear.[4]

Then he returned to our vices and how we should fear God and do justice so that God will help us and we shall regain our empire. And [patricians should] serve as rectors and treasurers and castellans, as they used to, and pay taxes as was done at the time of the Genoese war, when, if there was a tax, people ran to pay it. The city was in far more danger in the time of that Genoese war of Chioggia.[5]

Doge Loredan then contrasted the Veneto towns' willingness to supply infantry with the stinginess of the Venetians:

And he said that today letters had come from the camp in Treviso and that it was absolutely necessary to maintain our army, that 400 Brescian infantry had arrived and wanted their pay and a good number of those came from Valtrompia. He said that they had had reports that from Padua to Bergamo the people supported San Marco and that if they had a little backing [from the Venetians], they would cut to pieces all the French and Germans because they were poorly treated by the French. He said that when he had asked for a loan, the Collegio and the Senate together could only find 13,000 ducats, and then finally another 32,000, which was shameful considering the wealth of the city. Those who have wealth ought to put it in the service of the city for the financial needs of the army in the field and acquiring arms. He said that some laws that were passed yesterday in the Senate will be read to the public, and he said that everyone should go to fight for our freedom. And when he said this, the Great Council cried, "Let's go, let's go!" And the doge was distressed because the implication was that His Serenity had not gone himself

---

4. For ducal sleeves, which were ample and open at the wrist, as a sign of status and wealth, see Newton 1988, 12, 22–24, 87–88, 98, 104, and fig. 20.

5. The War of Chioggia with the Genoese took place in 1379–81. Felix Gilbert points out that in the rare speeches this doge made in the Great Council, he stressed the moral responsibility of the Venetians for their difficulties (1973, 277). See diaries, 10 July 1513 (16:489–90), 2 October 1513 (17:119–20); for a similar speech in the Senate, see 8 July 1513 (16:479).

after the army was routed [at Agnadello]. And the doge said that there was no need to act impetuously; the right time will come . . . that we had twice as many soldiers as the French . . . , that if we support our army, we shall in the end be victorious.

Loredan was right, although it took eight long years for his prophecy to be fulfilled. And old as he was—seventy-three—he lived to see the war concluded and the Venetian dominion almost entirely recovered. His longevity was in spite of the frailty of his health, upon which Sanudo commented frequently, for frailty affected Loredan's commanding role.[6] Symbolic and ceremonial as that role was, it was still a central and powerful role. Even in ordinary times the doge's behavior and mien were constantly scrutinized. His physical presence or absence, his appearance and carriage, his costume and conversation, were scrupulously observed and commented on. Consequently, no event in the internal politics of the Venetian state was more dramatic than a doge's death and the election of his successor. This was especially true in the case of Doge Loredan, whose dogeship had been unusually long (1501–21).

The Doge's Death

In the following excerpt, Sanudo describes Doge Loredan's final illness and the medical reports that circulated throughout the city.

June 19, 1521 (30:370)   In the morning it became known that the doge's health had worsened so much that there is no longer any hope that he will live, and the doctors have said that there is no way to cure him. The doctors treating him are Agustin da Pexaro, Bartolomeo da Montagnana, and his usual physician, Lunardo Butiron. Thus, early this morning he took Holy Communion. *Item:* the doctors removed from his toe a gangrenous spot that yesterday was bleeding but by today had stopped. Yet he felt no pain, and nothing issued from the wound, so the doctors concluded that he could not last many more hours and that his vital spirits are ebbing. He had his eighty-fourth birthday last November and is in a very weak state. Tonight . . . the moon is full, and that bodes ill.

The sick doge clung to life, but the end was assured. So the ducal family had to find other lodgings.

---

6. See, e.g., Sanudo's comments on Loredan's health in the spring of 1519: 26, 27, 29, 30, 31 March, 3, 10 April (27:107, 108, 111, 116, 118, 127, 158).

June 19, 1521 (30:380)   The news is that the Ducal Palace has begun to be vacated, and the doge's children have rented the house of the *primicerio* at San Filippo Jacomo and are sending their things there.[7] Today they openly had the firewood loaded on barges and transported to the new house, and this went on all night.[8] The only things that remain are the benches and what is in the [private] rooms, especially in the doge's room, to protect him from contamination. His Serenity remains the same: he is slipping away. The doctors have concluded that he may linger two or three days. There is a full moon tonight. It is believed that he will not live until morning.[9]

An entry in the diaries made a few days later indicates that the doge had died and the government was attempting to control the news until the family had vacated the palace. This was important for separating the state from its connection to the dead doge and his kin.

June 22, 1521 (30:387)   This morning at eight hours past sunset[10] I heard for certain that our Most Serene Prince had died but that it is being kept secret. I was[11] in the Ducal Palace, and his son ser Lorenzo Loredan, the procurator, was in the hall with many patricians, and they were saying the doge was doing better, and yet he was dead.

They sent word of the death to the Signoria, who decided to ring the death knell at sixteen hours in order that the doge's son ser Alvise, who is ill, could move at none from the Ducal Palace to the house of the primicerio that they have rented at San Filippo Jacomo.

Another entry that same day carries the story forward to the public announcement of the doge's death.

June 22, 1521 (30:387–88)   The savi were dismissed, and the Signoria, with the heads of the Quarantia and the councillors, remained alone to decide what

---

7. The primicerio of the Basilica of San Marco, appointed by the doge, was its chief ecclesiastic, acting as chaplain to the doge and his government and dean of San Marco itself.

8. See below, the excerpt dated 26 January 1531 under "The Magistrato alle Acque," on the value of wood as a household commodity.

9. The manuscript has *si tien non viverà;* the Fulin edition has *si tien viverà.*

10. In June, when the sun sets quite late, this hour was about 4:00 am, indicating that Sanudo was abroad in the city very early in the morning. The canonical hours referred to in these excerpts are tierce and none, the third and ninth hour after prime, the first hour (6:00 am), therefore about 9:00 am and 3:00 pm, respectively. See "About the Translation" under "Hours" and "Canonical Hours."

11. The manuscript appears to have *fui* corrected to *sui;* the Fulin edition has *fui,* accepted in our text.

should be done, although at first they had wanted to call the Senate and then toward evening have the death knell rung.[12] Then they decided to ring the bells at sixteen hours and to have the Signoria spend the night in the Ducal Palace, which was the subject of heated words among them. Finally, at fourteen hours they decided to ring the bell of San Marco nine times. And so the patriarch ordered that all the churches ring their bells when those of San Marco rang, and so it was.[13] And the doge's gold signet ring, the one that has *Voluntas Senatus* written on it,[14] was broken; the stamp for the leaden [ducal seals] was also broken. A new signet ring for marking wax was made, with [the lion image of] St. Mark and the Erizzo arms of ser Batista, the eldest councillor.[15] Letters announcing the death were ordered sent to all of the towns of our dominion, as is the custom; a copy will be included below. And they sent for the admiral[16] and other sailors from the Arsenal to guard the Ducal Palace, as is customary, and the gates of the palace were locked. However, the councillors and the heads of the Quarantia stayed in the palace and took their meal there, as the laws prescribe; they cannot leave. They decided to dine and not to quit the palace until the election of the new doge, which will take several days.

Meanwhile, preparations for the interval between the doge's death and the election of the next doge were under way.

June 22, 1521 (30:388–89)   So the councillors and the heads of the Ten remained in seclusion with their secretaries to consult about the laws that will need to be proposed about the election of the new doge, and they decided not to take the body of the doge to the Sala di Piovegi[17] tonight, as is customary, but early tomorrow morning. The Signoria will accompany the body, as is required by law; so it will stay in the palace tonight, something that has never

---

12. The Signoria normally included the doge, his six councillors, and the three heads of the Quarantia Criminal, but in this case it obviously met without the doge.

13. The patriarch of Venice was the chief ecclesiastical authority in the city. His church was San Pietro in Castello, on an island in the northeastern section of the city, at some distance from the center of government.

14. The inscription implies that as doge, Loredan simply fulfilled the will of the Senate. The destruction of the ducal ring signified that the dead doge's association with the ducal office was severed. See Muir 1978, 147.

15. The eldest councillor served as the vice-doge and would therefore serve as the chief government officer until a new doge was chosen. This ensured the transfer of ducal authority to an elected official of the patrician hierarchy. See ibid., 148.

16. The admiral from the Arsenal was an administrative functionary and not the leader of the Venetian fleet.

17. The meeting room for the *giudici del piovego* (see appendix B under "Governmental Terms"). This venue was also used, as it still is, for ceremonial occasions.

been done before. In the evening, the body was placed on a bier in the hall, and the Ducal Palace was opened. Everyone went to view it, but they could not see the body; the arrangements were handled badly. And twenty-two patricians were elected to stand, morning and evening, in the Sala di Piovegi around the doge and to accompany him to his interment, which will take place after dinner in the church of San Zane Polo [Santi Giovanni e Paolo], where he will be buried. As a sign that even if the doge is dead, the Signoria has not died, they will go dressed in scarlet with scarlet stoles; the law requires them to wear scarlet hoods, but since these are no longer the fashion, they are to wear red stoles. These twenty-two patricians were all chosen from the Senate by ser Lodovico Barbarigo alone; he belongs to the zonta but is young. He sent them word of their selection, commanding that they pay a fine of fifteen ducats[18] if they refuse the assignment. So they will come tomorrow morning.

Those who want to succeed the doge are caucusing with their supporters. They include ser Antonio Grimani, ser Zorzi Corner, ser Leonardo Mocenigo, ser Alvise Prioli, ser Andrea Gritti, and ser Domenego Trivixan; very little of this is being done by ser Antonio Trun, although everyone says he will win. Ser Alvise da Molin also wants to have some votes.[19]

The next day was given over to the funeral ceremonies:

June 23, 1521 (30:393)   Sunday. In the morning after tierce, the deputies dressed in scarlet with scarlet hoods arrived at the Ducal Palace, where the body of the doge dressed in his ducal robes lay on the bier, which was covered with cloth of gold lined in ermine, and he was dressed as a penitent. Upon him lay the mantle of gold with its collar and the ducal *corno*[20] upon a cushion of gold cloth. His sword was laid at his left side; spurs were placed on his feet backward, and a cross upon his breast.[21] Next came the cathedral chapter of San Marco with a cross preceding them; the canons came to take the doge's body to the Sala di Piovegi, where it will remain for three days so that everyone may view it. And in this way the canons came down from the palace carrying small lit candles in their hands; next came twenty squires dressed in mourning capes, each with a four-*libra* wax torch in hand;[22] then half of

---

18. The manuscript has *XV ducati;* the Fulin edition has *10 ducati.*

19. Antonio Grimani would be elected doge a few days later and would rule for two years (1521–23); Andrea Gritti succeeded Grimani, holding the office for fifteen years (1523–38).

20. The distinctive horn-shaped ducal cap, which was usually made of sumptuous materials and occasionally bejeweled.

21. While the bier itself was splendidly covered and the symbols of ducal office were displayed, the doge's body was dressed as a *batudo,* as a member of a penitential confraternity.

22. Candles were often described by their weight. See appendix B under "Weight and Nomenclature for Candles."

the patricians dressed in scarlet; at last the doge's bier appeared, carried by the sailors, and then the other half of the patricians dressed in scarlet. Following them came all of the notaries of the Chancellery and the councillors and heads of the Quarantia, who entered the aforementioned hall, where the bier was placed upon a high platform surrounded by four lit double candles weighing sixteen libre apiece in four very large brass candleholders. First the doge's shield was brought in; for the moment it was placed on a column at the foot of the bier, then the members of the Signoria sat on a high, unadorned bench, and a psalm was read. Then the canons with the primicerio, who used to be the rector of Sant'Aponal, went into the Basilica of San Marco, where a solemn funeral mass was sung. This will be continued for three days.

Prior to its embalming, the defunct body was disemboweled. Sanudo reports all the medical details:

June 23, 1521 (30:394)   An important item should be made known: the day before yesterday in the evening, the doge was cut open so that his intestines could be removed and he could be embalmed. Although he is extremely thin, his intestines were found to be full of fat because he ate only refined foods. *Item:* they found a black stone in his liver. Similarly, a white stone was found in ser Augustin Barbarigo, the previous doge. *Item:* they found a stone in his bladder, even though this doge never had kidney stones or pain from stones.

Plans for the funeral went forward, hastened by the warm weather.

June 24, 1521 (30:395)   The funeral ceremony has been ordered for tomorrow, after none; a message has been sent to all senators to come at none. The body of the doge has begun to stink, and the face has become distorted, to the point that it is fearsome to behold, even though just yesterday he looked as if he were sleeping. And so, at five hours after sundown, his sons had him put in a coffin sealed with pitch upon his own catafalque. On top of the coffin were placed the gold cloth, the robe, cushion, sword, spurs paired with the scarlet stockings, and the corno on the cushion.

The next day was the feast day of St. Mark, but no celebration took place: it was the day of the doge's funeral (30:396). Sanudo summarizes the letters that came in from abroad. The obsequies for the dead doge continued, with Sanudo participating as a member of the Senate's zonta. The body lay in state in the Sala di Piovegi and then was carried by the Arsenal sailors to the church of San Zane Polo, where it was interred. The funeral oration was given by ser Andrea Navagero, "who has a public stipend to write the history of Venice, etc. The oration was long" (30:398–400). And then the following day the government turned to the matter of choosing the next doge.

A Doge's Election

The election of a new doge was no simple matter: it involved a complicated sequence of committees designed (since 1268) to moderate factions and rivalries. Thirty members of the Great Council, none of whom could be related, were chosen by lot and then reduced by lot to nine. These nine then elected forty, each of whom had to receive at least seven votes. Twelve of the forty were then chosen by lot to elect twenty-five more, who had to receive at least nine votes each. The twenty-five were reduced by lot to nine, who elected forty-five, each having at least seven votes. Eleven of the forty-five were chosen by lot to elect another forty-one, each receiving at least nine votes. These forty-one, which could include no one who had been on the committees of the Nine, the Eleven, or the Twelve, thus sifted in stages from the entire Venetian aristocracy, had to elect a doge by a majority of at least twenty-five votes.

The last two committees, the Eleven and the Forty-one, were the critical ones. Among Sanudo's loose papers is an autograph list dated March 1530 that gives the names "of those who would be the Forty-one,"[23] a list that must have been entirely speculative on Sanudo's part, for the current doge at that time, Andrea Gritti, would live for another eight years. But it shows the enormous interest even during a doge's tenure about his successor and who might be responsible for that future choice. No sooner had the old doge died than a meeting was held about the process to elect his successor.[24]

June 24, 1521 (30:395)   After dinner the councillors gathered alone with the heads of the Quarantia, except for ser Bortolamio da Canal, who because he did not feel well this morning, had gone home. That left eight, who closed themselves in together without any secretaries in a room on the ground floor of the palace, where there had been plans to put a chapel but which had been furnished with hangings and benches for the Collegio. Here they stayed from vespers until twenty-three hours after sunset, alone, consulting about how to elect the doge because ser Luca Trun wants to make changes in the election process. It is said that they want to double the [number of] elections; others

---

23. Zorzanello 1950–79 describes this sheet of manuscript in the BNM, Ital. Cl. VIII, 375 (8954), fol. 23, as "1530 marzo li 41 sarebbe," with the names of forty-one possible electors of a new doge.

24. On the election process, see Maranini 1931; Finlay 1978a, 100–104; H. F. Brown 1973; and Sanudo 1980, 85–90.

want to eliminate the consuls;[25] others say that they want to make a law that no ducal candidate can have sons or brothers who are priests and that they want to do this because of ser Antonio Grimani and ser Zorzi Corner, who have two sons who are cardinals, and because of ser Alvise Pisani, father of another cardinal, when his time will come.[26] Still, it is not yet clear how this will be done. Secretary Zuan Jacomo Caroldo is in the palace along with Zuan Batista di Lodovici, of the extraordinaries,[27] and there they will stay.

At the same time, the Great Council made arrangements for the government's fundamental work to continue, establishing that for urgent and important matters of public concern the Senate and the Council of Ten could be convened while the doge's office was vacant and his successor's election was in progress.

June 27, 1521 (30:421–22)   From the statute (June 28, 1521) of the Great Council proposed by the correctors of the ducal *promissione*.[28]

The election of our Most Serene Prince is necessary and, as everyone knows, of great importance; yet when that office is left vacant, as it is at present, our state must not completely suspend those other important activities that may need to be dealt with, so that no necessary and short delay such as this one might be called a hindrance. Therefore, to remove any doubt or difficulty that could obstruct such activities, it is moved that in the present and in all future vacancies of our dogeship, until the forty-one electors of the Most Serene Prince have entered closed session, for matters of importance and immediate concern to the state the Senate and the Council of Ten may be convoked together. However, they are not empowered to handle, and must not handle, anything except matters that are of public concern and are pertinent to our state, as is just: for 1590, against 49, abstaining 4.

---

25. The "consuls" were three elected officials who resolved the problems concerning commerce. See Cappelletti 1992, 105.

26. Domenico Grimani was made a cardinal in 1493, Marco Corner in 1500, Francesco Pisani in 1517. The Venetian government guarded itself against pressures from Rome exerted by clerical relatives (called *papalisti*) of incumbent magistrates. "When his time will come" may refer to Alvise Pisani and imply that he too would someday compete for the dogeship, which he might well have done but for his early death in 1528.

27. The "ordinary" secretaries were higher-ranking and better paid than the "extraordinaries"; they normally held office for life and were often entrusted with state secrets and diplomatic missions. The extraordinaries were entry-level notaries, but they constituted a reserve pool from which the ordinaries were usually chosen.

28. This is an example of how Sanudo added material from a later day or days to his diaries under an earlier date, in this case the day before. The correctors of the ducal *promissione*, or promissory oath, on the basis of an analysis of the previous doge's actions, drew up the oath that the new doge had to swear to observe.

After a week of considerable delays and maneuvering, Doge Antonio Grimani (1521–23) was elected. Sanudo describes the pageantry of his installation, the popular celebrations, Grimani's background, his earlier fortunes and misfortunes, and the wealth and reputation that contributed to his election. Sanudo also proudly mentions his personal connection to the new doge and does not fail to describe the gratifying recognition the new doge extended to him as he attended the Great Council with other officials.

July 6, 1521 (30:480–83)   And thus they [the new doge and a number of officials] went to sit in the Great Council, and then came the state attorneys and the heads of the Council of Ten, dressed in silk, and His Serenity's son, ser Vicenzo Grimani, dressed in gray cloth because he has taken a vow and refused to wear a colored garment. The doge's grandsons ser Marco and ser Vetor Grimani, the sons of his late son, ser Hieronimo, were there on the tribunal dressed in silk, and there were pages holding fans and bringing a cool breeze to His Serenity, and all of the kinsfolk of the Grimani house and others were there, dressed in silk and in scarlet cloth. And the whole city came to take his hand, and he welcomed them all. And I, Marin Sanudo, attended because I was related and well liked by His Serenity, and he greeted me warmly, kissing my cheek four times, and I kissed his hand, weeping with joy.

The whole city ran into Piazza San Marco. It was decided that at twenty-two hours the doge would be carried into the church and around the Piazza. Bells were rung at San Marco and in all the churches, and this evening there will be fireworks and bells, and it will go on like that for three days. The Signoria immediately sent word to the Mint to strike coins with the name Antonio Grimani Doge, coins worth 16, 8, and 4 *soldi*. Thus 300 ducats were struck. . . .[29]

The ducal cortege then proceeded to the Basilica of San Marco with the doge's forty-one electors and his relatives, entering the Basilica by the "little door" and mounting up to the *pergolo,* a large elevated enclosure reserved for the doge to the right of the altar screen. He was introduced to the congregation by the oldest prior,[30] who praised his "virtues and worthy condition," from which, he said, the state could "hope for its well-being and preservation." To which the new doge replied that "since it pleased the Divine Majesty to put him in this position, he promised abundance, justice, and the preservation of peace; and if war

---

29. See appendix A under "Money and Coinage."

30. In the final phase of the ducal election three priors, or presidents, were chosen from among the forty-one electors to manage the process, and the oldest of these introduced the new doge to the people. See H. F. Brown 1973, 1:304.

should come, he would wage it valiantly and go in person, and everyone began to cry 'Viva,' etc." (30:481).

Then His Serenity descended from the pulpit and, with the forty-one electors following him, went to the high altar of San Marco. He kissed the chief canon, the former rector of San Silvestro, who then invested him. And there, on the missal, he swore to preserve the state and the honor of the Basilica of San Marco in good faith and without fraud. This canon, in the name of the chief priest, invested him and gave him the red banner of St. Mark with his arms upon it. This will belong to the doge personally, and the government will pay for it; the doge gave the canons fifteen ducats. Then the doge gave the banner to the admiral of the Arsenal to hold. And having come to the choir stairs, he climbed up on a red wooden platform with St. Mark painted on it,[31] which was carried by the Arsenal sailors on red poles ——. This platform is square.

The doge was seated, and behind him went two of his grandsons, ser Marco and ser Vetor, and in front of him was a silver basin that belongs to the admiral as part of his regalia, and the sailors who brought it were paid —— ducats. In this fashion the doge left the church and was led around the Piazza, throwing coins, that is, gold ducats and half-ducats and coins worth 16, 8, and 4 soldi that were minted today with his name on them. . . .

The ceremonies continued for a while, as does Sanudo's account of them (30:482–83). And then the diarist supplies for his eventual readers a summary of the new doge's life:

This doge is eighty-seven years old. He was born in 1434, on January 17 at the eighth hour. He is a man of great prosperity who has always been fortunate in his dealings, a rich man who has amassed great wealth through luck. He has been esteemed in this Republic. . . . He has served as savio di Terraferma, attorney to the Council of Ten, and a savio di Consiglio. Twice he was captain general of the fleet. Twice he was ambassador to Maximilian when he came to Milan in 1496. And he was ambassador to the current king of France in Milan when Francis came and went to Bologna to speak with the pope, where Grimani accompanied him.[32]

Grimani, by the will of the Venetians, was captain general of the fleet during the war with the Turks in 1499, when Lepanto was lost; [as punishment] they voted to bring him to prison in leg irons, and thus he came. And he was

---

31. Most probably the lion of St. Mark, often used as the evangelist's symbol.

32. For these secret talks of 1515 in Bologna between Francis I and Pope Leo X, for which no written records exist, see chapter 4.

led into the Great Council by the state attorneys. . . . They undertook their deliberations and chose the harshest sentence, that is, to confine him for life to Cherso and Ossero with a price on his head [should he violate his exile].[33] He went there but could not stand it, so he went to Rome, where he had a son who was a cardinal, who is still alive and is one of the most important cardinals of the papal court. . . . So the [future] doge lived in exile in Rome . . . and bought a vineyard and built himself a house there.[34]

At last, in this war [the War of the League of Cambrai, 1509–17], the members of the Collegio, seeing that our Republic had need of such a senator, presented a bill in the Great Council to allow him to return to the city even though he was still formally exiled. It was passed by the whole council, and he came back, and he was again elected procurator of San Marco for the church, he who had been procurator *de citra* before.[35] Thus he entered the Collegio, and he has always helped his country, and that is why he has been accorded this high honor. He rebuilt the bell tower of San Marco and the new buildings around the Piazza, projects to which he dedicated all of his energies as procurator.

On the next day, which was Sunday, the ordinary life of the city was resumed. There was Mass in the morning, and after the noonday meal the Great Council met and Grimani made his first speech as doge.

July 7, 1521 (31.7–9)   Now then, on Sunday, July 7, 1521, His Serenity the new doge entered the Basilica of San Marco with the ambassadors. . . . After Mass was heard and the doge accompanied to the Ducal Palace, he took his leave of the ambassadors and the other patricians and the more than 150 friends and relatives who had been with him. And it was a beautiful thing to see so many garments of silk, velvet, damask, and satins and scarlets. . . .[36]

After dinner there was a meeting of the Great Council, which the doge attended; even his son, ser Vicenzo, who has not attended in months and years, was present. And after the announcements had been made, the doge stood

---

33. Only exceptional cases such as this were tried in the Great Council. See diaries, 1 October 1499 (3:5), for the *odium* in which Antonio Grimani and his family were held because of this defeat at Lepanto, also called the battle of Zonchio. For Grimani's condemnation, imprisonment, and eventual exoneration, see chapter 3. Grimani's exile was to Cherso and Ossero, two towns on the island of Cherso between Istria and the Dalmatian coast.

34. See chapter 4 under "Pope Julius" for a description of this house.

35. See diaries, 17 June 1509 (8:411), for Grimani's pardon. Cardinal Domenico Grimani's role in detaching the pope from the League of Cambrai was a factor in changing public opinion about his father.

36. "Scarlets" were a kind of fine woolen cloth, not necessarily red in color. Dotson 1994, 76; cf. Molà 2000, 129.

up. But before that, when he came up to sit in his chair, he knelt before the chair, gazing at that depiction of the majesty of God while he held the corno in his hand. After praying, he sat down with alacrity. All were greatly moved by this act. After he stood up, he said that since, by the grace of Our Lord God, he had achieved this ducal dignity, of whose every benefit he was aware, he wished to call to mind three things. First, that all should act in a just fashion, for this leads to great good, and he offered his aid that this might be achieved. Second, that he promised to keep the city prosperous, sparing no expense in that endeavor. Third, that he would preserve the peace, and when it could not be preserved, that he would wage war valiantly against those who opposed us, joining the fight in person both on sea and on land. Then he sat down.

Two years after Grimani's triumph, he was dead. But the kaleidoscopic character of his naval and political career long remained in the Venetians' memory. His successor was Andrea Gritti, who would govern from 1523 to 1538, outliving Sanudo.

By the time he came to the dogeship, Andrea Gritti had gone from strength to strength. A successful grain merchant in the trade with Constantinople, he had established a reputation as a bold and able representative of the Venetian commercial community there. Returning to Venice after a stint in a Turkish prison, he had immediately been elected to public office. When the War of the League of Cambrai began, he entered military service and established a heroic reputation. His progress toward the dogeship was promoted by some patricians, deplored by others.

Sanudo reported fully on Gritti's ducal election. Two decades earlier, he had expressed his appreciation for Gritti's handsome appearance, generous nature, and eloquent speech (April 1, 1501; 4:254), and for his military service he had pronounced him "a most worthy man [who] merits every praise" (March 15, 1517; 24:63–64). At the same time, Sanudo shared many of his colleagues' distrust of Gritti's arrogance (March 26, 1523; 34:41), and he demonstrated his own ambivalence toward this controversial figure by his inclusion of negative details surrounding his choice as doge:

May 20, 1523 (34:156–57)   After dinner, at the nineteenth hour, which was vespers, it was learned that the Forty-one had held its third vote and elected domino Andrea Gritti, procurator, [as doge]. He is sixty-eight years old and had 25 votes. . . . The doors of the Forty-one were opened, the bells of San Marco were rung, and the Signoria went inside to congratulate His Serenity, who was dressed in crimson satin with modified ducal sleeves and a new cap of crimson silk, which he had made this night in the French style. And so they rose from the Senate chamber and came into the Golden Room, near the tribunal, where they took their seats. The room had been decorated with tapestries under the late doge for the supper [that he gave on] the feast of the Sensa,[37] and the decorations had not been removed. Crimson silk and two hangings with the Gritti arms had been added. When His Serenity had been seated, a great rush of people came up to see him, and patricians came to take his hand. I made my way there with the greatest effort, and he greeted me very pleasantly.

There follows mention of the joy of the French ambassador, who gave a great party with fireworks "because it is known that this Gritti is a partisan of the French" (May 19, 1523; 34:157). Then Sanudo lists the names of fourteen of Gritti's opponents in the Forty-one—an indication that few secrets were kept about these highly contested elections—among whom were Alvise di Priuli and Antonio Tron, about whom he had additional anecdotes to tell:

May 20, 1523 (34:158)   I note that ser Alvise di Prioli said in one of the committees[38] that it was inappropriate to make doge someone who had three bastards in Turkey, and ser Andrea Gritti sought out this Alvise, who was sitting with ser Zorzi Corner, procurator, saying that he wished to speak with him. Prioli answered, "Then you can speak in front of messer Zorzi." To which Gritti replied that he regretted, since they were close relatives, that Prioli had used such words about him and he hoped that he would accept him as doge. Prioli said, "Messer Andrea, it is true that I said this, and I have never wanted, nor will I ever want, you [to be doge] because I do not want to make a tyrant doge." Then there was a big argument between them.

And it should be known that children made a doge doll with a beard. It was small, like Antonio Trun, and they took it around the Piazza crying "Trun, Trun."

Indeed, earlier, when Tron himself had announced in the Basilica that Gritti had been elected, "no one cried 'Gritti'; rather they said, 'You, you!'" (34:158). But Tron, who had adamantly refused to campaign, had said that if elected, he would reject the office (May 9, 1523; 34:133). When Tron died a few months later, Sanudo wrote of his high reputation as a patrician and added that "everyone wished he had been doge" (January 10, 1524; 35:324).

Gritti's election ceremonies continued the next day. Both religious and secu-

---

37. The annual marriage of Venice to the sea, held on the feast of the Ascension.

38. *Su le banche,* "on the benches," given as the location of the conversation, could refer to any of the meetings of these patricians in council or in one of the election committees.

lar, they included the Mass, the oath to obey the ducal *promissione,* the reception of the banner of St. Mark, the scattering of coins to the crowds in the Piazza, and the "crowning" with the jeweled corno on the great outside stairs in the courtyard of the Ducal Palace. About all this Sanudo commented:

May 21, 1523 (34:159)   It should be known that very few shouted "Gritti." He was elected to the discontent of the people and of nearly everyone. Nevertheless, he is there, and I pray God it will be for the good of our Republic. But according to the astrologers, this morning there are many bad planetary aspects, and it is not a favorable day.

Even Gritti's attempt to curry favor by distributing cheap grain failed to win him a following.

It should be known that this doge, having imported from Turkey much grain for his business and having in the warehouse a certain quantity of his flour, ordered that it be made available at twelve soldi less than the market price, and he wants to offer 2,000 *stera* of his flour at such a price. Nevertheless ——, everyone deplored his election.

Nor could Sanudo resist commenting on the size of Gritti's ducal corno. For the high ceremonies of May 22 he wore a corno "that was small and suited him very poorly." Two days later, Sanudo commented that at least the corno "was larger than the other and suited him better" (May 22, 24, 1523; 34:185, 188).

Predictably, once he was doge, Andrea Gritti wished to assert in every way Venetian power and his association with it. He had a medal struck at the beginning of his reign that featured his portrait on both sides, an innovation that was not well received:

December 9, 1523 (35:269) I record the following noteworthy item. In the last few days the doge, being obligated to give the patricians a silver coin to commemorate the present festivities, had a medal struck by Vetor Gambello, who works in the Mint. On one side [are] the head of the doge and the words "Andrea Gritti, doge of the Venetians";[39] on the other is a standing figure of St. Mark, before whom the doge, holding the standard of Venice, is kneeling.[40] Many people believed that such a thing could not be done in silver, recalling

---

39. "Andreas Gritti Dux Venetiarum."

40. Sanudo is mistaken in his description of the original design. The reverse did not have the kneeling doge and St. Mark, but the saint seated at a lectern writing. The editors thank Alan Stahl for this information.

what happened when Doge Nicolò Tron had a coin struck with his head on it. The coin was called a 'tron' and was worth twenty soldi. As a result . . . , a law was passed by the Council of Ten that such coins could no longer be struck by the Mint, nor could the head of a doge be put on any coin.[41] For this reason, the past heads of the Ten suspended the coining of [Gritti's] medal in the Mint. In a resolution solicited both by the proveditor of the Mint, ser Andrea Mudazo, and by members of the Raxon Vechie[42] charged with giving this present, the councillors decided that a medal with a head should not be made. Instead, the medal should bear on one side an image of St. Mark with the doge kneeling in front of him. Around the edge should be inscribed the legend "Andreas Gritti [Doge] of the Republic of Venice," and in the middle of the other side, the legend "Andreas Gritti, Doge: Gift of His First Year."[43] That gift coin began to be distributed about fifteen days ago, and it is an ugly coin. It is being dispensed by the office of the Raxon Vechie with ill grace.

The Duke of Ferrara's Repentance

The doge's role as ceremonial head of the government consisted largely in the reception of important visitors. Along with the rituals of governmental process and judicial procedures, state receptions served the mystique of Venetian power, expressing the Venetian ethos and reaffirming Venetian self-esteem. To Sanudo, such rituals were worth describing in all their details—the reception of foreign dignitaries, the greetings, the costumes, the types of boats that met and accompanied them, the locations of these encounters, diplomatic precedence, and festive dinners. All these reflected and served a dual governmental policy: to impress visitors with the wealth and power of Venice and to provide the Venetians with entertainment and reassurance as to the political stature, reputation, and stability of their homeland. As bearers of such messages, they formed a significant part of Sanudo's record. All during the period of the diaries, which spanned the rules of four doges, Sanudo described the major ceremonial receptions of distinguished guests. Four of these receptions are described below, each with its own character, depending on the occasion and the honored guest, all contributing to the carefully crafted public image of Venice.

Among the earliest receptions described in Sanudo's accounts was the visit in 1497 of Ercole I, the Duke of Ferrara, to Doge Agostino Barbarigo. This was a vis-

---

41. Nicolò Tron was doge from 1471 to 1473. The innovation of his placing his portrait on coins aroused objection on republican principles, and by a law of 2 August 1473 the Great Council forbade the practice to his successors. See Tucci 1996, 769, 788.

42. See appendix B under "Governmental Terms."

43. *Andreas Gritti S.M. Veneti; Andreae Gritti munus anno primo.* See Papadopoli Aldobrandini, 1893–1919, 2:146–71; and Montenegro 1907, 107–9.

it of reconciliation, for Ercole had fought a bitter war against Venice in 1482–84, and in 1494–95 he had given the invading French king, Charles VIII, free passage through his territories. Now the duke sought an alliance with Venice, putting aside his French connections (and fashions) and demonstrating his loyalty to the doge, who received him in a manner reminiscent of the parable of the prodigal son.

November 19, 1497 (1:820–21)   On November 19 Duke Ercole da la ca' di Este, the Marquis of Ferrara, arrived in this city with his second son, don Ferrante, who had been at the court and on the payroll of the king of France. The duke was accompanied by about two hundred people, most of whom were no longer wearing French styles, as they used to, but Spanish and Ferrarese styles. Don Ferrante, who is a very handsome young man, was also dressed in the Spanish style.[44] Several patricians were sent to Chioza [Chioggia] to receive the duke honorably. He did not bring a large barge with him, but came on smaller, flat-bottomed boats.[45] He was honorably welcomed by Beneto Trevixan, knight and governor of Chioza. He was also accompanied by Bernardo Bembo, knight and doctor, who is our *visdomino* in Ferrara.[46] When they reached Malamocho, they found the patricians who had been sent there to greet them, as is customary. The Senate had decreed that [the city officials] would go forth to meet him in the Bucintoro,[47] so today, which is Sunday, the doge and the ambassador of Spain (although he was in mourning for his king's only son),[48] as well as the ambassadors of Naples, Milan, Monferrato, Rimini, and Pisa, went forth. Also attending were the members of the Signoria, many richly dressed patricians, and knights wearing cloth of gold. Because of the lateness of the hour and the tide, the Bucintoro went as far as Sant' Antonio,[49] where it met the boats from Chioza bearing the aforemen-

---

44. Don Ferrante had been in France since 1493, receiving an annual pay of 13,000 ducats and the title of royal chamberlain from Charles VIII. He had accompanied Charles into Italy in 1494, but now, since August 1497, as part of the duke's reconciliation with Venice, he had been ordered by his father to leave the French court and accompany him to Venice, where he was to be invested with the title of *condottiere della Repubblica di San Marco* (military captain in the service of the Venetian Republic).

45. The types of boats mentioned here—the *ganzara, burchiele,* and *paraschelmi*— were among the many different types of water craft used in the Venetian lagoons. See appendix B under "Boats, Ships, and Nautical Terms."

46. Bernardo Bembo (1433–1519) was a distinguished patrician, senator, and ambassador and father of Pietro Bembo (see chapter 8). After the War of Ferrara ended in 1484, Venice exercised a kind of protectorate over Ferrara, with Venetia authority represented there by a resident Venetian consul known as a *visdomino*.

47. On the Bucintoro, the doge's ceremonial galley, see Sansovino 1968, 449–50.

48. Juan of Aragon, who had died on 4 October 1497.

49. Sant' Antonio is on the Pellestrina litoral between Chioggia and Venice.

tioned duke. When they had disembarked on the Piazzetta, the doge greeted the duke warmly. The duke was wearing a floor-length, tight-sleeved robe of black damask lined with marten. Over it he wore a cape of black cloth because he is in mourning for his daughter, the Duchess of Milan;[50] on his head was a cap of black velvet. After boarding the Bucintoro, they proceeded along the Grand Canal until they reached his house, which had been prepared for him.[51] Several heavy fishing boats accompanied them, as is customary, and boats filled the Grand Canal. When they had disembarked, the doge accompanied the duke as far as his chamber, where he left him to his repose.

On the morning of the following day, the 20th, the duke was joined by the knights and patricians who had been sent to bring him to the public audience on flatboats. When he reached the Piazza San Marco, our doge, along with the members of the Signoria, in order to give the duke every sign of affection, came out to meet him on the landing of the stairs to the tribunal. The doge grasped the duke's hand and led him to sit near him, with the duke's son on his left. The duke then spoke some very sweet words, saying that he wished to be a most devoted son to this state, offering himself, etc. And the doge skillfully responded to him publicly in a voice that could be heard by all. After the duke took his leave, he returned to his dwelling.

On the 21st, after dinner, the doge, together with the members of the Signoria and many patricians, went on flatboats to the marquis's house to visit the Duke of Ferrara. Then just the duke and the *visdomino* went to the Ducal Palace to speak in private with the doge. Thus did the duke begin to repent, protesting his desire to be a good and loyal son of this Signoria.[52]

The Queen of Hungary's Amusement

One of the most elaborate (and expensive) state visits by a foreign dignitary to Venice was that paid by Anne de Foix in the summer of 1502. This seventeen-year-old Frenchwoman, "small, beautiful, and soft-spoken" (July 31, 1502; 4:288), was

---

50. Beatrice d'Este, wife of Ludovico Sforza, who had died at age twenty-two in January 1497.

51. This house, the Casa del Marchese, was a palazzo given to Nicolò d'Este, Marquis of Ferrara, in 1381, confiscated from the Estensi in 1482, as it would be again in 1509. In 1497 it could still be referred to as belonging to the duke. Later it was given to Julius II and used by several papal legates thereafter until it was again restored to the Estensi in 1527. See Tassini 1970, 278. It was often used by the government to accommodate high-ranking guests. In 1621 it became the Fondaco dei Turchi (Turkish Warehouse).

52. See chapter 3 for reference to the beginning of the Duke of Ferrara's reconciliation with Venice, some months earlier, in January 1497. It is worth noting here that Sanudo included information from two days later under the date of the diary entry. These diaries were evidently a second stage in Sanudo's accumulation of daily notes. On Sanudo's method and style, see "About the Translation" under "The Composition of the Diaries."

highly connected. Cousin to the wife of the French king, Louis XII,[53] she was now en route as bride to Ladislas VI, king of Bohemia, Hungary, and Poland. Since she could intervene with the kings of France and Hungary in favor of an alliance against the Turks, her reception in Venice by the government of Doge Leonardo Loredan (1501–21) was sumptuous, and the entertainments provided were extensive. The queen—for so she was already entitled—arrived on July 31 and was met in style and lodged at the Casa del Marchese. A joust in her honor was to be held a few days later. Sanudo's pride in Venice's display of magnificent hospitality is evident:

August 4, 1502 (4:295–96)   At sixteen hours after sunset the platforms were put up in the Piazza; the barriers and the sand had been set out the day before. All this took place because the Hungarians wanted to hold a joust to show off their large horses and fine trappings. Fifty-four women had arrived, bedecked with jewels, etc.; they mounted the platforms, where the heads of the Ten had already seated themselves to prevent anyone else from going up there. While they waited there for the queen to arrive with the doge and the Signoria, word reached the Collegio that the horses that were to be used for the joust were in Treviso and would arrive the next day. So a message was sent to the women to come down from the platforms and go to the Ducal Palace for the festivities because the joust was not yet ready, and they did so. The festivities were presented by the compagnia of the Elect[54] and began at about eighteen hours. The doge came forward to greet the queen and lead her onto the platform. In the midst of this came a great wind and rain storm that lasted an hour and a half. The festivities were held in the palace; the queen danced with Lord Galeazzo Visconti, of Milan. Then the refreshments were served; they were very nice and cost 300 ducats or more. A hundred and ten persons attended, as will be described in detail later; next came the *momaria* [mummery].[55] After it ended, at twenty-three hours, the queen went home.

This was a costly visit, complicated by Anne's retinue of seven hundred Hungarian horsemen and her inability to leave the city for Hungary until her dowry arrived from France. In addition to reporting the expenses, Sanudo weighs the cost against the political advantage such entertainment might bring:

---

53. Sanudo may have been particularly interested in this "very worthy woman endowed with every quality," for he had entertained her earlier in Verona, "where I was treasurer and bore the considerable burden of honoring her." Diaries, 31 July 1502 (4:287). Given that Sanudo's term as treasurer in Verona (May 1501–20 September 1502) extended through the period of Anne de Foix's visit to Venice, he describes her visit in remarkable detail.

54. On these *compagnie,* see chapter 6.

55. For mummeries, see chapter 9; and appendix B under "Vocabulary Used in the Original."

The expenses involved in honoring this most serene queen, which amounted to more than 400 ducats per day, began to be regretted. Nor is there any discussion of when she might leave, because the Hungarians have been charged not to take her from here until they have received the 40,000 ducats in dowry promised to her by the king of France. Many of the French who accompanied the queen, seeing that the matter would take a long time, are leaving and returning to Milan. Some of the Hungarians are returning by way of Treviso. Thus the queen remains here with a retinue of sixty to seventy mouths. A light galley and another long-oared ship[56] were prepared for her, to take her to Segna[57] in comfort. An election was held in the Senate to choose one of the lords of the Arsenal, who currently are ser Alvise Marzelo, ser Tomà Duodo, and ser Piero Lando, to serve as the captain of the galley that accompanies the queen. The winner was ser Piero Lando, the youngest, handsomest, and wisest. It seems that now, however, people are saying that the queen does not want to go by sea, but by way of Treviso and then through the lands belonging to the king of the Romans.[58]

Sanudo reports not only the splendor of the festivities but also the gracious exchange of appreciative comments between the future queen and the doge:

One thing is that in the past days she has been here with about 600 mouths to feed, counting the French, the Hungarians, and the Milanese. A great deal of money has been spent and a lot of resources consumed. Word is out that two Frenchmen and two Hungarians are making a record of all the honors paid to the queen in our mainland cities and here in Venice so that it may be shown to the king of France and the king of Hungary. And the queen, who is very perceptive, told the doge that she had not known what it meant to be a queen until her arrival in Venice and that she will therefore commend this state to His Majesty the king and that she wishes always to be a daughter of this most illustrious Signoria. To which the doge replied with kind and fitting words that this was nothing in comparison with the feeling in Venice's heart for her.

For the next two days, the queen toured Venice. She went to Murano to watch glass being made. She visited the relics of the body of St. Barbara at the Crosech-

---

56. A *fusta*. See appendix B under "Boats, Ships, and Nautical Terms."

57. A seaport on the Croatian-Dalmatian coast.

58. Maximilian I was called "emperor" by his contemporaries and still is called known by this title. However, because he was never crowned by the pope, technically he held only the title "king of the Romans" until his death in 1519. See Hale 1981, 205.

ieri.[59] She went to Santa Maria Mazor to see where the monastery was going to be built. She attended a concert in Cannaregio, where music of all kinds was played (4:298). And on Sunday she was invited, along with other members of the foreign community, to the regular meeting of the Great Council. However, behind the facade of pleasurable activities, Anne de Foix's situation was quite entangled in diplomatic negotiations over her dowry, and the costs continued to escalate. But the legendary Venetian hospitality prevailed, and Sanudo summarizes the situation with the popular wisdom of a proverb:

August 7, 1502 (4:298)   The queen did not come to the Great Council meeting, but the French and Hungarian ambassadors did. Arrangements for the election of the new members of the Ten were begun. Then in the evening the queen went to vespers at the Celestia and then to the Vergini to hear the nuns sing.[60] Thus she is not yet ready to leave, because the French do not want to give the 40,000 francs to the Hungarian ambassadors, who are here until the king has received the bride into his home and consummated the marriage. And the Hungarians have been told that she may not come to Hungary until she has the money. So Her Most Serene Highness is in a bad mood. Letters have been sent to Milan, to the king of France, and to Hungary; in the meantime she will remain here. Every day she goes to visit churches and monasteries, and she continues to stay at our expense. In eight days 4,500 ducats have been spent. Our officials have had to close their eyes so as not to lose the benefits of her visit; it has been said in this regard that "if you can drink a sea, you can drink a river."[61]

Honoring the Duke of Urbino

Many of the ceremonial occasions celebrated by the Venetian government were planned to coincide with religious holidays, among which were those honoring the patron saint, St. Mark. Three separate feasts were associated with this holy figure, so identified by the Venetians as their saint: the translation *(translatio)* of

---

59. Many relics were brought to the church of the Crosechieri (Crociferi) for safekeeping in the fifteen century. The church, located near the lagoon, burned in the Rialto fire of 1513, and the relics were destroyed. See Lunardon 1985, 42 and n56.

60. The references are to the Chiesa di Santa Maria Celeste, also known as the Celestia, which no longer exists, with its adjacent convent (Lorenzetti 1926, 377), and to Santa Maria delle Vergini, which Sanudo 1980, 62, lists among the notable things to show important visitors and where one could hear "the nuns singing."

61. "Chi beve el mar, puol bever el fiume." The suggestion is that the Venetian government, which had already invested so much in the queen's visit, hoping by that investment to find favor with the kings of France and Hungary and to enlist their aid against the Turks, could well invest a little more. It was another fortnight before the queen finally left Venice, on 22 August.

his body from Alexandria, celebrated on January 31; his apparition *(apparitio* or *inventio),* which represented the saint's self-revelation of his body in the church after it had been lost, celebrated on June 25; and his martyrdom *(passio),* celebrated on April 25. In the excerpt below, the arrival in Venice in 1524 of its military leader, Francesco Maria della Rovere, Duke of Urbino, is arranged to take place on the feast of the Apparition, when he was ceremonially honored by Doge Andrea Gritti.[62]

June 25, 1524 (36:429-31)   Today, Saturday the 25th, was the feast of the Apparition of San Marco. His Serenity the doge, dressed in a toga and cape and corno of crimson satin, entered the church to hear Mass with the ambassadors of the pope, the emperor, the Archduke of Austria, Milan, Ferrara, and Mantua, and with four procurators. . . . Also present were the rest of those assigned to accompany His Serenity these past months.

Note: because of a decree announced at Rialto on the 23rd of this month that today is the feast of St. Mark and that people must observe it and not work, this day is being observed and the shops are closed.[63]

Then, since this day was planned as the arrival day of Francesco Maria de la Rovere, Duke of Urbino and our governor, who was elected the captain general[64] and is thirty-four years old, after dinner the doge appeared dressed in silk cloth of gold and wearing a corno of cloth of gold. With him were all the ambassadors who had attended this morning, except for the French ambassador, who no longer comes with the Signoria, although he is in town.[65] Ser Marco Dandolo, doctor, knight, and councillor, was dressed in gold; none of the other knights was present. Attending were —— procurators. They came by land as far as San Salvador, where they heard vespers, and His Serenity saw the church with the renovations that have been completed and those that still are under way.[66] In the midst of this, the Duke of Urbino [and his company] arrived on flatboats from San Zorzi [i.e., San Zorzi di Alega (San Giorgio in Alga)], and he disembarked at the Fondaco di Todeschi, where the German

---

62. On French relations with Venice, see Mallett and Hale 1984, 288-90. Francesco Maria della Rovere (1490-1538) was a protégé of his relative Pope Julius II and had been adopted by his uncle Guidobaldo da Montefeltro, Duke of Urbino, whom he succeeded in 1508. He was deprived of the duchy by Leo X, who gave it to a Medici relative in 1516, but it was restored to him in 1521. He was appointed captain general of the Venetian forces on 22 June 1524.

63. In this commercial city, a governmental decree determined, according to the importance of the occasion, whether the civic offices and the shops would be closed.

64. He was made governor general of the Venetian army in September 1523, then promoted to captain general in June 1524.

65. Eleven months earlier, on 29 July 1523, Venice had abandoned its longstanding alliance with France for a treaty with Emperor Charles V.

66. For renovations to the church of San Salvador, see chapter 7.

merchants had prepared tapestries at the doors and benches for seating on the ground floor. When he heard this, the doge left the church and came to meet the duke outside the door of the Fondaco. Once they had greeted each other, they walked together across the Rialto bridge and boarded the Bucintoro. The duke was dressed in black velvet with a short tunic and a scarlet cap. With him was the ambassador of the Duke of Milan. . . , whose name is ser [Scipione] di la Tella, a Milanese. Included in his group were ser Janes and Camillo Orsini, our condottieri, and other leaders of his and important men. . . .

And with a grand triumphal procession of a great number of boats, the Bucintoro passed along the Grand Canal from the other side of the Rialto bridge, where it had been, preceded by heavy fishing boats; leading them all was the armed light galley whose commander was ser Polo Justinian, which departs the day after tomorrow. The duke was accompanied to the lodgings that have been prepared in the house of St. Mark on San Zorzi Mazor [Giorgio Maggiore], the doge remaining with him until he reached his chambers, as is customary.[67] On the Bucintoro were about 150 gentlemen dressed in silk and scarlet, including those who are going to San Zorzi di Alega [San Giorgio in Alga] and to Liza Fusina. Thus the city was in great jubilation, and the ceremonies were approved by all. . . .

A noteworthy item: this evening the office of the Raxon Vechie ordered that a supper be prepared for him, that he be given fifty ducats a day for expenses, and that they would buy twenty boats for his use. He had a new boat built in this city that had twelve oars, was furnished, and had a most beautiful cabin covering of brocaded silk.

During the Duke of Urbino's stay some military consultations took place, but in Sanudo's account the ceremonial events loom larger. He describes the boats, decorated with flags and tapestries, that carried the duke and his retinue and the compagnia members and their ladies down the Grand Canal and entertainment of a gondola regatta, all concluded by an elegant torchlit supper:

July 3, 1524 (36:457–58)   The Duke of Urbino, our captain general, came informally and reiterated that the fortification of Verona and Padua needs to be completed. . . .

The council meeting was not held after dinner because of the feste taking place on the Grand Canal, with a marvelous one [under the sponsorship] of

---

67. These were state accommodations in the Benedictine monastery for honored guests, located in a separate building called the *casa nova* at the time of the visit. See P. F. Brown 1990, 138–39.

the compagnia of young men called "The Valorous," who named ser Almorò Dolfin lord of the festivities.[68] First they prepared two heavy fishing boats, and these were covered with light sailcloth awnings and flags, below which they were decorated with tapestries, and benches were set out for the women to sit on. About —— women were seated, dressed very well and adorned with gold chains and with jewels, that is, pearls. The members of the compagnia were all wearing short jackets. They sent for the captain general [Francesco Maria della Rovere] and his military officials and the current ambassador of Milan, who is with him, and ser Piero of Ca' Pesaro, the procurator, who always accompanies him, together with ser Domenego Zorzi of Santa Marina. The duke, together with the women and the compagnia members and his own group, boarded the barges and proceeded along the Grand Canal, the compagnia members dancing with the women aboard. As they were about to pass under the Rialto bridge, they separated one boat from the other, and once they had passed [under the bridge], they joined them together again and proceeded down the Grand Canal. It was twenty-two and a half hours after sunset when the barges, which were heading toward Ca' Foscari, passed the gondola regatta that was being held, with four men per boat; they rowed from Castelli to Ca' Foscari, at San Simion, and the prizes were ——.[69]

Afterwards, the barges went all the way along to the tip, where a plank floor had been laid on the flatboats with tables on top, such that —— persons could sit at table. When they arrived . . . supper was prepared by the light of wax torches and lamps, and everyone had supper there, including the Duke of Urbino and the other foreigners. Supper was finished at —— hours, and they danced a little, then everyone went home.

The festivities went on for several more days and included a women's regatta, a momaria, a meal for five hundred people, many thick (and therefore costly) candles, and a grand display of silver:

The real festa will be held tomorrow at Ca' Foscari, at San Simion, where they have built a large stand along the bank in front of the house. They are making a bridge across the Grand Canal, and there will be another bridge at Corpus Domini, where they are preparing a wonderful momaria with giants and platforms, etc., under the direction of Maestro Tonin. . . . There will also be a meal served on silver for the five hundred guests, with 250 wax torches of ten libre apiece; those who will be carrying them will be wearing breastplates

---

68. On the compagnie della calza, see chapter 6; and appendix B under "Vocabulary Used in the Original."

69. See chapter 9, excerpt dated 15 February 1520, for a party of the Immortali at this house.

loaned to them by the Arsenal. Ferigo the barber steward is preparing this meal, for which he can spend forty ducats, which includes his responsibility for the silver.[70]

Today there was an infinite number of boats on the Grand Canal, and the use of each boat from none on cost six lire or more; thus for the entire day the houses along the Grand Canal were celebrating. Tomorrow the women's regatta will take place. . . . Thus, the compagnia members will spend more than one thousand ducats on these festivities.

The list of compagnia members follows. The festivities offered by the compagnia continued over the next two days at Ca' Foscari with more women's races, a triumphal carriage and a figure of Faith presented to the Duke of Urbino, a sugar eagle to the imperial ambassador, and a snake, the symbol of the Visconti and Sforza dynasties, to the Milanese ambassador, as well as gifts to other dignitaries present, with dinners and dancing and a momaria on the abduction of Helen by Paris (July 4, 1524; 36:458–59). In this way the whole city participated in celebrating the arrival of the Duke of Urbino and his appointment as Venice's military commander. It was an assertion of Venice's imperial and triumphal style.

The Duke of Milan's Visit

One of the most elaborate secular ceremonies was the one honoring a visit by the Duke of Milan in 1530, the first time a Milanese duke had visited Venice. Among the chief concerns of Venetian ceremony was the proper ranking of the various attending dignitaries; precedence was often an issue among ambassadors. The positioning of Doge Andrea Gritti vis-à-vis his visitors was another matter, and a certain flexibility was sometimes necessary.

October 10, 1530 (54:35–36)   From Chioza there were letters from the governor and ser Gabriel Venier, the ambassador, which were written yesterday evening. . . . They related how the duke, upon his arrival in Chioza, was greeted by the governor, ser Andrea da Mula, and various gentlemen. They came forth to meet him in small boats; once they had met on the other side of Chioza, they boarded his barge, where ser Gasparo Bembo, university laureate, recited a very beautiful Latin oration. His Excellency thanked him very much. . . . Then they continued on to Chioza, disembarked . . . , and took up their lodgings in the palace. . . .

---

70. "Et ha ducati 40 e tuò li arzenti soprà di sè." It appears that this Figaro-like barber majordomo was responsible for renting the silver, a common practice in this period. For Maestro Tonin, see chapter 9; and for the weight of the candles, see appendix B under "Weight and Nomenclature for Candles."

Many of the members of the compagnia the Royals came to the Collegio and requested the use of the hall of the Great Council so that they could give a little festa and a comedy for the duke; in addition, they wanted to hold a banquet. His Serenity and the Collegio said that they were willing to let them use the hall but that they did not wish there to be any banquet, since such a thing had never been done. Thus [the compagnia members] began to decorate it with tapestries for the festa that will be held on the 18th, Tuesday. But first, on the 17th, they will put on a festa and a mock sea battle, or *neuthomachia,* with the Bucintoro on the Grand Canal; that evening they want to hold a banquet for him.

I note that the Signoria wished to invite the ambassadors to go to meet the Duke of Milan, [and the ambassadors of] the emperor, France, and the king of England sent word yesterday to His Serenity that they would come but that they did not want to be placed below the Duke of Milan. Thus it was decided to invite neither them nor the papal legate. *Item:* it was decided by the Collegio that the chair should be removed from the Bucintoro and replaced by [a bench covered in] crimson satin, as is done when cardinals visit, so that the duke will be equal to our doge.

The reception of so important a person had several exceptional elements, such as the doffing of the doge's ducal corno and the disembarking of the duke in Piazza San Marco itself rather than in an outlying point of the city. A carefully planned program followed, with the two principal players, the duke and the doge, accompanying each other in mutual honor.[71]

October 11, 1530 (54:37–38)   After dinner, this being the day designated for the arrival in this city of the most illustrious Duke of Milan, Francesco Sforza, the five heavy fishing boats were prepared; in spite of their costing ten ducats apiece rather than the usual five, they were very small and not very nice. Dressed in gold with a corno and a collared mantle of crimson satin, His Serenity boarded the Bucintoro without any ambassadors; the chair having been removed, he sat on a crimson satin bench. Present were the following procurators: ser Domenego Trivixan, knight, ser Alvise Pasqualigo, ser Lorenzo Pasqualigo, ser Hironimo Zen, ser Andrea Lion, ser Marco da Molin, ser Francesco Prioli, ser Antonio Prioli, ser Vicenzo Grimani, and ser Zuan da Leze. Only ser Marco Dandolo, university laureate, councillor, and knight, wore a gold stole; there were many other patricians, though there were few silk robes, and none of the knights wore gold ones. They went to San Chimento [Clemente] to await the duke. . . .

---

71. See Casini 1996, 288–89; and Mitchell 1979, 147.

His Serenity, who was waiting for the duke in the church, went forth to meet him. The duke took off his cap, and our doge did the same, although by law the ducal bonnet may be doffed only for a king or a cardinal or an imperial elector; however, a duke of Milan has never before come to this city. Once the necessary greetings had been made, they boarded the Bucintoro together. The duke has difficulty walking ——, and his ambassador, who lives here, went along with him, giving him a hand to help him. His Excellency was followed by his brother and preceded by the ambassador of France; present also was the ambassador of the Duke of Ferrara, who went to meet them. Together they boarded the Bucintoro, followed by those other gentlemen and nobles in parity with the senators, all dressed in black. They disembarked at the columns of the Piazzetta, between which they passed after the gangway had been put in place. The Piazza San Marco was half full of people, and it took some effort to cross it. The duke usually travels on a small mule, which was actually there in the Piazza, but today he wanted to go on foot. I should not neglect to mention that don[72] Andrea di Franceschi was dressed in crimson velvet, and the other secretaries of the Collegio, that is, the secretaries of the Council of Ten and others, were wearing scarlet.

For so distinguished a visitor, lodgings were prepared in the Piazza San Marco itself, in the home of one of the procurators, which had been richly decorated with rugs and tapestries. Upon its walls hung the coats of arms of the doge and the duke together. Sanudo observed the choreography of greetings and leave-takings, as well as the physical and psychological qualities of the guest:

The duke was taken to the Procuratia and the house where the patriarch of Aquileia, domino Marco Grimani, is staying. It was very nicely prepared with very beautiful tapestries, etc.; on the balconies were large, very fine rugs from Cairo [*tapedi grandi caiarini finissimi*].[73] Also placed there on the facade on canvas were two Sforza coats of arms with the Grimani coat of arms beneath. In addition, ser Andrea Lion, procurator, had himself prepared his house very well, although it is always kept in good order; other houses were prepared for other gentlemen, as were all the inns. The doge accompanied the duke

---

72. This use of the title *don* for one of the secretaries of the Signoria is an instance of this title of high courtesy being attached to a Venetian citizen. Below it is used for the patriarch of Aquileia.

73. The Procuratorie, the official homes of very highly ranked Venetian procurators, were choice lodgings for this important guest. See P. F. Brown 1990, 139. For the rugs, see Erdmann 1966, 539–41. Sanudo 1980, III, 248, explains that the office of the Raxon Vecchie kept "tapestries and other necessary furnishings of adornment to prepare the houses" for such distinguished guests.

upstairs; after he had stayed there a while, he took his leave. The duke accompanied him as far as the door of the room and sent his brother and some other gentlemen to accompany him to the Ducal Palace. It was sunset then, and nothing else took place. This evening a supper was held for the duke. . . . Tomorrow he will rest, and the next day he will go to the Signoria. This duke is — years old and very melancholic; he has difficulty using his hands and walks poorly.

Twelve days later, the festivities continued with an elaborate naval battle staged for the Duke of Milan in front of the Ducal Palace, facing San Zorzi Mazor. An exceptionally large crowd of spectators watched the two heads of state meet at the top of the palace stairs and proceed to their appointed seats to witness this theatrical event.[74]

October 23, 1530 (54:79–81)   It was the day designated for the festa and the naval battle, [which took place] after dinner. First, the platform in front of the facade of the Ducal Palace that looks toward San Zorzi Mazor was very nicely decorated, and above the little columns an enclosure was built for the doge and the duke, and both were covered with crimson silk.

A beautiful wooden castle was brought on rafts to the middle of the canal and anchored there so it would not move. Soon about a hundred women gathered on the platform; however, their costumes did not exceed the sumptuary law. Then the doge arrived, well accompanied by all the young procurators and other senators both in the Senate and formerly in the Senate—except that I, Marin Sanudo, did not wish to attend.[75] But there was a huge number, because whoever wished to go, went. The doge was dressed in cloth of gold with a matching corno.

Then the compagnia members went to fetch the Duke of Milan, who came with his companions, and when he arrived at the top of the palace stairs, the doge was there, and they went together to the appointed place. And I do not wish to omit from the written record that the whole Piazza was packed with people as far as the Terra Nuova and the entire quay of San Zacaria.[76]

In the naval battle, twenty-four armed brigantines attacked a castle that was defended by a captain and his armed infantry. After the canonical stages of a re-

---

74. See chapter 9 for another naval battle.

75. Perhaps because one month earlier Sanudo's pride had once again been injured by the appointment of Pietro Bembo as historian of Venice. Nevertheless, he was evidently persuaded to join the observers (see below).

76. The Terra Nova, an area of reclaimed land just west of the Piazzeta, was replaced by the Mint, which now houses the Sansovino Library. See Tassini 1970, 478.

quest to surrender and the defiance of the defenders, the assault took place. Clay pots were launched, and there were mock executions until the castle was taken.

Item: two ships were brought into the canal, one belonging to ser Mafio Bernardo dal Banco — and the other of 400 *botte*[77] belonging to ser Marco Bragadin and ser Nicolò Michiel. This ship is going to Barbary, and I boarded it, and together with this ser Marco Bragadin, I went to watch. These ships and many other watercraft were full of women and men, and so were other large vessels, so that it seemed an armada was gathered in front of San Zorzi Mazor. There were so many people between there and San Marco and all about that the crowd was estimated at 100,000,[78] not to speak of an infinite number of little boats full of people. The Duke of Ferrara in disguise stayed up above, together with his retinue, on the balcony of the Great Council.

Everyone having gathered, two members of the compagnia had charge of this naval battle: ser Etor Contarini and ser Michiel Salamon, who, wearing their [compagnia] jackets, were on little barges. They proceeded to organize the festa. There were twelve armed brigantines, that is, longboats, on each side, which made twenty-four, each containing artillery and ladders to breach the castle, and each armada had a captain—for one, Zuan Papa, and for the other, Francesco da Pozo, both sailors. And in the castle was a captain of infantry called Gatin da Bologna with infantry armed with wooden swords and artillery and enough powder and clay pots to fire.[79]

Now, both armadas having arrived and surrounded the castle, and those within saluting them by firing their muskets and doing other things, two brigantines were sent to request the castle [to surrender], and they responded by showing their weapons. Then one of the armadas approached on one side, and the other on the other, and they began to make general war on the castle, while those inside defended themselves by launching clay pots. And when the ones with the ladders attempted to scale the castle, two were captured and "hanged." After that, the battlements were destroyed, and those inside pushed down the attackers, who fell into the water. In the end, a few valiant ones climbed up the ramparts, and those within retreated with their ensigns to the citadel, which was also then attacked and captured.

Elaborate as this event appears, it did not satisfy Sanudo's expectations. He was more impressed with the feast that followed and the display of sweets molded

---

77. A measure of a ship's loading capacity. See appendix B under "Boats, Ships, and Nautical Terms."
78. Sanudo tended to exaggerate his numbers.
79. Metal was too expensive to waste in mock battles.

into political symbols, the sugared meringues in animal shapes, and the large number of servers:

And this did not last very long—there should have been at least one more battle. The castle was taken, but it was in bad shape. After this was finished—and in my opinion it wasn't successful, this thing that in Greek is called a *neumachia*[80] and had never happened before—they began to serve the meal, which was carried out through the main door of the palace. Each member of the compagnia had, as presents for each guest, an infinite number of molded sweets. The first was ser Leonardo of Ca' Pesaro, and his was the molded sweet for the duke decorated with a large St. Mark's lion and the [Visconti] snake with a Guelf in its mouth. Then came the doge's sweet, a large St. Mark's lion bearing the Gritti coat of arms and the ducal corno. Then there were seven St. Mark's lions ——. Afterwards, there followed the other members of the compagnia, with various kinds of sugared meringues and certain nymphs with the arms of all the members of the compagnia and other animals made of sugar and various confections: cookies, pine-nut cakes, filled pastries, pistachios, confections, ring-shaped cakes, wafers, flat-bread,[81] etc.; so that there were twenty-three members of the compagnia, with servants in various liveries and especially hats. Among them was a compagnia of German bakers, well dressed, and everything in silver: goblets, salvers, candy dishes, large cups, wine jugs, pots, vessels,[82] and other [containers]. Altogether those who served the meal numbered 250, which made it a magnificent and sumptuous event, although it was difficult to make space [for the servers]. But the members of the compagnia vigorously wielded clubs, and two people died from the crush. Nevertheless, the entire meal took place on the platform, and then, after the little columns had been removed, [the participants], using a stair from the platform, went above to the Signoria, where he [the duke] was presented to everyone, the senators as well as the ladies.

Sanudo also notes the absence of all ambassadors save that of Milan, for reasons of diplomatic precedence. Then the doge and duke returned to their lodgings, while some of the women danced on into the night.

And it should be noted that not one of the ambassadors was at this festa except the Milanese. The reason for this I wrote above: the royal ambassadors did not wish to be seated beneath the duke. Not even the papal legate wished

---

80. Sea battle. Sanudo spells it *neumachia* instead of *naumachia.*
81. "Terzie, pignochae, calisoni, pistachee, confetti, bozoladi, storti, fugazine" (54:80).
82. "Cope, bazili, confetiere, tazoni, bocali, ramini, vasi."

to come. The ambassador of Ferrara did not come; neither the ambassador of Mantua nor the ambassador of Urbino would give way. Before and after the meal, there was dancing on the platform, the women dancing with the members of the compagnia. After the meal, a difference arose between the two captains of the armadas over who should get the castle, and it was decided that they should fight each other. And one armada fought the other with wooden swords, which was nice to watch for a while.

At sunset the doge left with the duke. A few members of the compagnia accompanied the duke to his lodging, with their trombones and shawms[83] going on ahead, while the duke greeted everyone. . . . More than a hundred wax torches were brought onto the platform, where some of the women continued to dance and some took their leave.

But after such extravagant entertainment, Sanudo found some of his fellow Venetian hosts betraying their greed rather than extending their courtesies to the visitors:

I do not wish to omit that a most elegant collation was served, but badly apportioned, because the Milanese gentlemen seated on the ladies' viewing platform had nothing, while many senators stuffed their sleeves with confections, to the great chagrin of those who observed them, and among the others was ser Vetor Moresini da San Polo, who stowed away plenty of confections.

Celebrating the Sacred City

Whether in the regular cycle of feast days or in the occasional visits by foreign dignitaries, the ceremonial life of the city was a combination of religious and civic celebration. Of all such events, no ceremony was more central to the ritual life of the city than that of the Sensa. Sanudo's description here focuses less on the meaning of Venice's asserting its dominion over the Adriatic (and beyond), which he takes for granted, than on the persons attending, their costumes, the ritual symbols of sword and ceremonial barge. For it was in these details that the mystical power of Venice was reified, and it was the strong desire of the doge at this time, Andrea Gritti, that the import of every such ritual be enhanced through the magnificence of its enactment.

May 9–10, 1526 (41:307)   After dinner today, which is the eve of the Ascension, the Most Serene Doge [participated in the customary ceremonies], dressed in

---

83. See appendix B under "Musical Instruments," s.v. "trombe e pifari."

a very beautiful mantle of sumptuous gold cloth and a gold flowered corno, and beneath that, a toga of crimson heavy silk. . . . [Those attending] came to hear vespers in San Marco, as is customary. The doge and the ambassadors were in the pergolo, and they were so numerous that the sword-bearer and his companion were not able to sit there; the primicerio sat in the choir.

May 10 was the feast of the Ascension. The Most Serene Doge, dressed in gold and with a mantle of white-gold damask and a corno of the same damask of white gold, went with the aforementioned ambassadors in the new Bucintoro to marry the sea and to hear Mass at San Nicolò on the Lido. Carrying the sword was ser Alexandro Contarini, who will be captain of the galleys in Beirut, dressed in crimson velvet. His companion was ser Zuan Donado, dressed in crimson damask. Other assigned companions and dinner guests [attended], among whom I saw ser Nicolò Michiel; he is a member of the Raxon Nuove, and, it should be noted, was wearing a — black toga with a crimped collar in the French style, which caused a great deal of talk, and sleeves in the modified ducal fashion.[84]

I wrote "new Bucintoro" because this is the first time that this Bucintoro has been used. It was made this year in the Arsenal; it is larger than the other one by — and wider by — and is a most beautiful piece of work. They have barely finished gilding it; indeed, they were still working on it yesterday. It is very beautiful with lots of gold, which cost six hundred ducats or more.

St. Mark and Venice

The following excerpt, from the last volume of Sanudo's diaries, is yet one more description of the feast of the Apparition of St. Mark but emphasizes the relics of the saint: his body, his ring, and his book. These possessions certified Venice's claim to an apostolic patron and the special dispensation that its ceremonies solemnized. For in the end, it was St. Mark who symbolized, ruled, and protected the city. To do him honor on this occasion, the city closed its offices (but not its shops).

June 25, 1533 (58:372–73)   Today, the 25th, was the feast of the apparition of the body of St. Mark. The governing bodies do not meet today, but the shops are open. His Serenity wore crimson damask; after the Low Mass he repaired with the councillors and the heads of the Ten to the parlor, where they met with the papal legate. . . .

Then he went to the Basilica for the [Solemn] Mass and the procession to-

---

84. See above, n. 4.

gether with the legate and the ambassadors of the emperor, France, and England, since the ambassadors of Milan and Ferrara are not in the city, as well as the primicerio and at least two procurators, ser Carlo Morexini and ser Antonio Capello. Besides the censor, there were only twenty-two of us. In the procession, each of the scuole carried only twelve high double candles, and they went behind the high altar, which is believed to contain the body of St. Mark, which emerged from a column in the chapel of San Lunardo with its arm extended. The Scuola di San Marco carried the saint's ring, which used to be kept in the Dolfin palace.[85] The book of the Gospel of St. Mark, with golden covers, written by his hand, was brought from the church of San Marco and was carried by twelve members of the scuola of the Strazaruoli [secondhand clothing dealers]; it was carried under the umbrella and accompanied by wax torches, six preceding it and six following it.[86] Friars and priests also participated in the procession; as it was leaving the door of the Ducal Palace, a great rain came down, so that the procession entered [the Basilica by] the door of the baptismal chapel so as not to get drenched. And thus it concluded.

The Magistrato alle Acque

To elect its officials, manifest its ethos through ceremony and ritual, and keep the civic peace through its laws and judicial system (see chapter 3) required much of the government's attention; so did the organization and protection of the livelihood of the city, a matter in which Sanudo also took pride. "This city," he wrote, "is administered as well as any city in the whole world ever was or will be; everything is organized, and that is what maintains it and increases it."[87] That tutelage engendered a vast series of governmental bodies to deal with matters such as customs, health, the grain supply, and the ever-important struggle to keep the city's lagoons, canals, and other waterways from filling up with silt. The

85. This ring was considered to be the one received from the hand that St. Mark extended from the pillar at the time of his apparition by a pious member of the Dolfin family, and it was retained by that family until it was given to the Scuola Grande di San Marco.

86. The "Gospel of St. Mark" was brought to Venice in 1420 from the newly acquired territory of Friuli. In actuality, the manuscript was a sixth-century codex, and only a partial one at that, a portion of it having been given by the patriarch of Aquileia to his half-brother Charles of Bohemia in 1355. See Tramontin et al. 1965, 69–70. Its position "under the umbrella" was a signal honor since usually the doge himself proceeded under his ceremonial umbrella, which reportedly had been given to him by Pope Alexander III in 1177. Here the conflation of St. Mark's gospel with the saint himself includes the doge as the saint's ceremonial representative in the city. See also Law 1988, 143.

87. "Sì che questa Terra è tanto benissimo ordinata quanto terra che fusse, né sia mai al mondo; hanno in tutto ordine, et questo è quello la si mantiene, et augmenta." Sanudo 1980, 30.

Magistrato alle Acque will serve here as one example of Venetian administrative concerns as reflected in Sanudo's diaries.

Sanudo himself described this magistracy in his *De origine:* "There are three *savi sora le acque.* They occupy the office for two years. They meet at the Rialto, and they are chosen by the Senate. They have no salary, but sit in the Senate without having a vote . . . ; their concern is to see that the waters keep their flow, that the waterways do not become choked with silt, and that no one interferes with the common waters."[88]

The following two excerpts from the winter of 1517 deal with the machinery and the money needed to dredge the canals and maintain the free flow of waters through them:

February 19, 1517 (23:590)   Ser Carlo Contarini, ser Moisè Venier, and ser Luca Trun, the provedadori sora le acque, appeared before the Collegio. They spoke of the city's need, caused by a continuous silting of watery areas, to dredge out the Grand Canal, and [to do so] they had to build the apparatus that is in the Terra Nuova, and it is very fine, but more money is needed.

March 7, 1517 (24:45)   A very long bill was proposed [in the Senate] by ser Zuan Alvise Soranzo, ser Zacaria Prioli, and ser Antonio Grimani, provedadori di comun [city commissioners], and ser Carlo Contarini, ser Moisè Venier, and ser Luca Trun, provedadori sora le acque. It concerns the making of some provision about the silting of canals, which is visible every day, and large shoals are forming in the canals of the city, so that it has become almost impossible to navigate them. For that reason, they propose that all monies dedicated to the dredging of canals be spent solely for that purpose and that one of the provedadori di comun set up a single account for such monies for the entire term of his office, and he alone shall handle all funds in that account. The other fund shall be managed for half of the term of office by each of the other two provedadori. *Item:* all those who are obligated to bring money to this office must take it under penalty of law to the officials; as it

---

88. Ibid., 116: "Attendino a far che l'acque habbino il suo corso, et che le fiumare non atterrino; anchora, che niun non toglia le acque del Commun." See also pp. 82, 103, 252. Protecting the flux of waters through Venice for their salubrious cleansing power and the lagoon's channels for the commercial transportation on which the city's economy depended was always a central focus of the government. The first savi sora le acque were appointed in 1415; in 1501 three savi were elected from the Senate by the Council of Ten; and in 1505 a committee of fifteen was created to aid the savi in their deliberations and the implementation of their decisions. In the diaries as in other documents, *savi* and *provedadori* are both used as titles for these magistrates. See Ferro 1845–47, 1:35, s.v. "Acque." See also B. Giustiniani 1722, bk. 1, col. 8, for the importance of maintaining the viability of the lagoons; and Labalme 1969, 265. The Magistrato alle Acque still exists and has a large purview as a general ministry of public waterworks.

says in the law, these officials, once their term of office has expired, cannot be nominated again without a written statement from the provedadori. *Item:* that the dry docks on land be obligated to dredge the area in front of them at their own expense.[89] *Item:* because the Jews who have gone to live in the Ghetto are throwing their trash in the canals, be it stipulated that a trash pit be built at their expense, along with other clauses stated in the law, and that their canal be dredged at their expense. There were 177 yes votes and 8 no votes.

But machines and money could not be effective against the continuous encroachment of private construction upon the public waterways. In 1521 yet another attempt was made to remedy this situation.

January 19, 1521 (29:561–62)   [A law of] January 18, 1520 [*m.v.*] passed in the Senate. Regulations were previously passed that stipulated, with regard to the canals and the Grand Canal and our lagoons along the edge of this city, that no wharves[90] could be constructed, nor pilings sunk, nor any building be built on pilings. All this is to prevent the flow of water from being blocked and the lagoon from filling up with silt. However, for some time many have acted against the provisions of the regulations, building wharves and other buildings on pilings, sinking pilings, and building boat shelters, contrary to what they should and could have done and causing great damage to the flow of the water and consequently to our lagoon. Our savi sora le acque, in attempting to carry out their duties, have found that many of our patricians and others resist and prevent the removal and destruction of what was illegally built, threatening and insulting the functionaries of the savi sora le acque and even throwing rocks at them, so that if a remedy for this situation is not found soon, it will deteriorate.

Therefore, it is proposed that by the authority of this council, all those, of whatever social status, both ecclesiastics and lay people, who are found to have wharves,[91] boat shelters, or other buildings constructed on our lagoons, on the Grand Canal, or on the canals and byways of this city in violation of what they are allowed to have, within eight days of the publication of this law must have torn down or destroyed all those constructions. Similarly, they are to have taken away and removed all the pilings standing more than half a

---

89. Since these dry docks did not stand at the edge of the canal but had a slipway in front of them running down to the canal onto which the boats were hauled, their owners may have tried to claim exemption from a contribution by saying that they did not occupy the actual banks of the canals.

90. The manuscript has *pontili;* the Fulin edition has *ponti.*

91. Again, the manuscript has *pontili,* but the Fulin edition has *ponti.*

foot from the beams,[92] that is, the embankment of the canal. Exempted from this are the pilings located near the ferries to assist passengers in alighting from the boats; these are to be regulated and modified only in such ways as all three of the savi judge to be best. Once the eight days have passed, the savi must have these things removed, and the pilings and the lumber will belong to the ministers of the office who remove them in order that the office expend the least amount of money in having them removed.

Doge Andrea Gritti was particularly interested in maintaining the viability of the lagoons. Toward their protection, as well as toward the needs of certain industries, he promoted the reforestation of those Terraferma woodlands that had been denuded by their proprietors.[93]

January 26, 1531 (54:262–63)   In the Council of Ten with the zonta. Each member of this council has the wisdom to understand how important firewood is to our city because, beyond the fact that wood is frequently used to purify the air and make it healthier for the inhabitants of this city, it is a most urgently needed commodity, especially soft wood, because the operation of the Mint and many other professions, including dyeing, glassmaking, and others, can use no other kind. For this reason, if that swift, appropriate, and necessary provision is not made, everyone will not merely worry but be certain that there will be not so much a shortage of such wood as a complete lack. The kinds of wood that used to be sold on the banks of rivers at six lire *per passo*[94] are now worth fourteen lire and more, and even worse, they often cannot be found. The reason for this is that many *campi*[95] have been deforested and converted to farming, even though deforestation is forbidden by our laws, as everyone knows. In addition to this problem, deforestation causes another one: it is the very evident cause of the silting of our lagoon, there being no way [to slow down] the rains and floods or keep them from flowing into the lagoon, as the trees used to.

Seeking, therefore, a swift and effective solution to these three problems, while preserving all the current laws and regulations on the matter of wood . . . , a bill is proposed that by the authority of this council it be ratified that all those who for the past forty years have cut down forests of whatever type, no matter whom they belong to, whether they be ecclesiastics holding whatev-

---

92. The manuscript has *luntan de i travii over fondamente;* the Fulin edition has *luntan de le fondamente.*

93. See Barbarigo 1972, 40.

94. See Boerio 1856, 479: "è un'altra Misura Veneta d'un braccio e mezzo quadrato, con cui si misurano le legne"; a *passo* would be somewhat smaller than the American cord.

95. See appendix B under "Vocabulary Used in the Original."

er title they might claim or laymen, with no exceptions, situated and located in the Patria of Friuli or in the territories of Treviso, Mestre, or Padua, or in the area from Rovigo to the Po, or in the Dogado,[96] or in the territory of Cologna,[97] be required to reforest eight campi for each hundred that have been deforested during that period. Moreover, the forests that currently exist may not in any way be cut down, under all the penalties of our most severe current laws pertaining to this matter. However, excluded from the present bill are all deliberations made by this council at other times concerning communal lands; the present deliberations are not intended in any way to countermand them.

So interested was Doge Andrea Gritti that on at least one expedition he paid his own way to survey the commission's work:

March 1, 1531 (54:318–19)   Our Most Serene Prince, having officially announced that he would accompany the savi sora le acque to observe some of the lagoon, went out this morning by boat despite the cold and a strong wind. With him were ser Andrea Trivisan, knight and savio dil Consejo, ser Agustin da Mula, the former councillor, ser Francesco Donado, knight and councillor, all three of whom are savi sora le acque, as well as ser Hetor Loredan, ser Gabriel Vendramin, and ser Marco Contarini, the executive officers of the commission, Vicenzo Sabadin, notary, and others of this magistracy. The commissioners traveled at government expense, while the doge paid his own way. They went to Marghera and entered the Dese River.[98] The doge dined on his boat, the others on land, then they continued on toward — and saw everything, and at twenty-two hours they returned home.[99]

Fortifications

Beyond its preservation of the peace, prosperity, and integrity of the city and its canals, the government of Sanudo's day attended to a great empire. In the early sixteenth century it stretched from Crete, Cyprus, and the Morea (Peloponnesus) in the east to Brescia, Cremona, and Bergamo in the west. In addition, the Adriatic litoral was for the most part in Venetian hands, as were certain pockets

96. The piece of land that ran from the island of Grado to Capo d'Argine, or Cavarzere, which is near the mouth of the Adige, south of Chioggia. See Mutinelli 1851, 127.

97. On the banks of the Po River.

98. A river flowing from the north into the Venetian lagoon.

99. The editors acknowledge with gratitude G. Zorzi 1959–60, which facilitated the selection of the excerpts above.

in Lombardy, Romagna, and Apulia. This disparate collection of territories was administered by Venetian civil, military, and ecclesiastical personnel and ruled by a system that was both centralizing and relatively tolerant of local custom and style. It was a dominion acquired over time, and each territory, with its own character and problems, challenged the Venetian administrative systems.[100]

Among the principal burdens imposed on the Venetian government were the protection of this empire from its enemies and the balancing of its competing needs. Which part most urgently required fortification was often the subject of review and debate in the political councils. The following excerpt summarizes a report made by one of Venice's military leaders concerning Corfu, Crete, and Nauplion and shows how the frontiers of the Venetian dominion might have to compete for scarce funds.[101]

November 13, 1518 (26:200)   This morning Janus di Campo Fregoso, a condottiere in our army, came before the Collegio. He returned yesterday from an inspection tour of Corfù, Candia [Crete], and Napoli di Romania [Nauplion] whose purpose was to determine how best to fortify those cities against all eventualities. He sailed as far as Istria on the galley commanded by ser Bernardin Taiapiera. Reporting on what he had seen, he concluded that those cities can be fortified at little expense and that if their inhabitants want to hold them, particularly against the Turks, they will be able to do so, especially if a strong armada is available. He went on to report on all the important things that he had seen. The doge, with a pleased expression, thanked him for the trouble he had taken, saying that he should talk to the savi and remind them of what was needed.

But when the proposal was made to fund these fortifications with monies taken from funds established to fortify Padua, Verona, and Brescia, it was much debated. It was only passed after the argument was made that the fortifications of Padua, Verona, and Brescia "did not matter so much, for there was nothing to fear from the emperor, with whom there is a truce. And anyway, no other funds were available to aid [in the fortification of Corfu, Candia, and Napoli di Romania] but these" (26:228).

100. The shape of the Terraferma was, in the words of one Venetian military commander in 1579, "long and narrow . . . nothing but frontier"; that of the *stato da Mar*, as the sea possessions were called, was "a series of clusters of islands and ports ending in two widely spaced and weighty pendants, Crete and Cyprus." Mallett and Hale 1984, 412, 429.

101. See Mallett and Hale 1984, 431–32, 468; for a debate on Cypriot fortifications, see diaries, 24:237, 263.

The *Provveditore*

For the purpose of governing these extended territories, the patrician class itself was not wanting in military and naval skill.[102] The Venetian system of commissaries or proveditors connected the governing class to the practical details of military matters, including such decisions on fortifications as were made above. A high degree of professionalism was achieved by these civilian proveditors. They liaised with commanders of infantry and men-at-arms. They recruited spies, detected traitors, saw to the billeting and feeding of troops, and above all were the information network of the Venetian government. In the spring of 1509, at the time of Agnadello, Venice had thirty-seven proveditors in the field.[103] Sixteen of them became prisoners after that battle. Such dangers were real. During that summer, as the imperial troops invaded Friuli, Zuan Paulo Gradenigo, who was serving there as proveditor general, undertook to relieve the siege of Cividale, in Friuli, because he saw that the stradiot (light) cavalry[104] would absolutely refuse to ride there if he were not present. Sanudo summarizes Gradenigo's account written after they left the city of Udine:

August 3, 1509 (9:18–19)   And so I immediately mounted a horse and made all the stradiots come with me and the crossbowmen . . . so that we left the city with more than 500 horsemen. . . . [Encountering the enemy], the stradiots fled in a manner too disorderly for me to remedy. Therefore, I and a few valiant men who remained with me made a sally and engaged [the enemy] two or three times, so that in a short time all our men escaped to Udine. And if we had not made this sally, in truth many would have perished. And even now we are not able to verify whether more than twenty-two of our men died and whether about ten were captured. But among our forces who were really fighting, [only] a few died and a few were wounded, including me. I received three wounds in fighting: one lance wound to my neck, which drew a great quantity of blood, and two rapier wounds. . . . Nevertheless, I hope I will not be badly off. Still the fact is that we accomplished what we set out to achieve: the entire enemy decamped from the city and abandoned the siege it was engaged in, so that [the city of Cividale] had time to tend to its repairs and necessary defenses. When the enemy returned, it saw the city better prepared than it had been before, and, perhaps thinking we might attack again, they took off and went to the devil. For all of which we thank the Lord and Our Lady. . . . And I

---

102. The section "The *Provveditore*" is indebted to Hale 1979. See also Mallett and Hale 1984, 227, where "the unremitting nature of Venice's military commitment" is examined for the period 1509–30.

103. Hale 1979, 12.

104. See appendix B under "Vocabulary Used in the Original," s.v. "stradioto."

do not wish to complain about the grave peril I was in, because I was able to secure that city, whose loss might have led to the loss of the entire Patria.

In addition to the dangers, the proveditors had to deal with the continuous shortage of funds. "Money is needed" was their incessant plea.[105] There were also the difficulties and discomforts of military life, frequently described in the proveditorial dispatches. On November 16, 1509, Sanudo summarized five letters from ser Piero Marzello, proveditor general, sent to ser Bernardo Donado from Noale, in the Trevisano, and Vicenza (9:314–19). Two letters written on November 11 vividly describe the delay of a reconnoiterer because he had only a "bad and exhausted horse," the lack of money to pay the crossbowmen and stradiots, German plans to sack the territory, the population in full flight. Then came a letter written on November 13, which Sanudo records a few days later:

November 16, 1509 (9:316–17)   Letter of the same [Piero Marzello], written on the 13th, from Camisano.[106] He writes that yesterday morning, at the twelfth hour, he had left Noale with his men, in such a downpour as destroyed the world, and that by evening he had arrived at Camisano. There he was poorly lodged and without food until the night, and he had to sleep on a bench, as he would also have to do this night. They had hoped to enter Vicenza but had remained outside the city. And since this morning, November 13, when they left Camisano, where they had been billeted, itself eighteen long miles from Noale, they had ridden all day, soaked, in their armor, without food or drink, without dismounting until dark, deprived of every comfort. Having arrived this morning, they went on until they were under the city walls with the light calvary and infantry. Finally, not seeing any sign of an agreement, which they had hoped to see, they decided to draw the artillery up to the Borgo San Piero gate, which faces Padua. And after many rounds of canon and *falconeti* [guns] had been fired, and the first gate of the guardhouse destroyed, and a breach made in the wall, some infantry jumped inside. They were rebuffed, and many were killed. And when night finally came, Lactantio da Bergamo stayed there with part of the infantry and light cavalry, and the captain of the infantry was sent to the Pusterla district with the rest of the infantry and light cavalry. All day their proveditors—some on one side and some on the other—were exhorting [the men to fight], under a rainstorm so heavy that it dispersed the infantry and men-at-arms. It was a pitiable sight.

---

105. Letters continued to abound from Zuan Paulo Gradenigo describing his military adventures and often asking for money—"Vol danari." See, e.g., diary entries for January and February 1510 (9:466, 507).

106. Near Vicenza.

The life of a proveditor was a generally arduous existence. A year after the above letter, a message intercepted from a papal envoy described the endurance of these proveditors as superhuman:

September 22, 1510 (11:397)   He praised these Venetian gentlemen, who day and night [surrounded by] artillery, rally the men-at-arms, the infantry, stradiots, Turks, and victualers, etc. He says that he would not have believed [their energies]. The proveditors never sleep; they have one meal a day, at dusk, and have diabolical constitutions, which are never worn out.

Because of the difficulties and dangers of the military life, many a patrician refused to serve or gave excuses.[107] The government responded with heavy penalties for such refusals. But such service, when it turned out well, could have its own rewards. Andrea Gritti is a case in point. In 1513, after more than seven years of service in the field and a period of captivity in France, he was elected proveditor general in command of the defense of Padua. On this occasion, his protests were unavailing.

July 8, 1513 (16:476)   A bill was read and posted by Piero Trun, savio a Terraferma, to elect immediately a proveditor general for Padua, who would have ten horsemen, including his secretary, a manservant, and two squires, at a salary of 120 ducats per month for expenses, of which he need make no accounting. The fine for refusal was 500 gold ducats in addition to all other penalties [e.g., disqualification for other offices]. He could be chosen from any ongoing position or office. He should immediately report for service and leave forthwith, as the bill stated.

Andrea Gritti, savio dil Consejo, went up to the podium and protested, saying that this bill was directed at him and that he had borne enough burdens and could not serve. Moreover, there was no need: there were two rectors [in Padua], and to install two proveditors would lead to confusion, etc., and he spoke vigorously against the bill. Piero Trun answered him and praised him, saying that in formulating this bill he, Trun, had considered only the good of the country and that if Gritti were elected, which it was certain he would be, he would go to serve his country. Trun said he had proposed the bill, not because those rectors and proveditors were not enough, but because they were not experienced in military affairs. Trun then declared that first [before voting] there should be read out loud[108] a letter from the governor [of the army] to the Signoria that says that ser Andrea Gritti is needed in Padua.

---

107. Hale 1979, 23.
108. The manuscript has *fe'lezer;* the Fulin edition has *de'lezer.*

Others also spoke in favor of the election, which was held later that same day, with a predictable result: Gritti was chosen with 165 votes; his competitors had 45 votes and 36 votes, respectively (16:477).

Four years later, Gritti, having not only secured Padua but reoccupied Brescia and Verona, made a triumphal return to Venice, where he was honorably received in the Collegio, acclaimed by the populace, and praised by Sanudo.

March 15, 1517 (24:63–64)   This morning, after the doge had joined the Collegio, Andrea Gritti, procurator, arrived. Having recovered Brescia and Verona as proveditor general, he returned from the front dressed in purple [*paonazo*] cloth[109] and accompanied by a large escort. . . . He reported very little of substance, referring to his report to the Senate, and he rendered his accounts, etc. And when he was finished, the doge praised him lavishly and took, one by one, the hands of the chief captains [in attendance], whom this proveditor Gritti praised, saying they had acted well in this war. . . . Then the doge had himself carried to his residence, and Gritti went along to accompany him . . . , and the Piazza was full of people who had come to see him. He is a most worthy man and merits every praise.

Six years later, Andrea Gritti was elected doge. His military achievements—and Gritti could claim a long record of them—were not forgotten, though Sanudo's admiration would later to change into disapproval of Gritti's arrogance.

Loyalty to St. Mark's Lion

Just as important for the defense of the dominion as physical fortification or the quality of its civil and military personnel was the loyalty to Venice of the different communities it ruled. This loyalty depended partly on their previous history, partly on location, partly on the social level of those involved. But since Venetian administration was at best a guarantee of peace, justice, and order and at worst less oppressive than the alternatives, the populace of the Venetian dominions tended to favor the Venetian overlords. This was made abundantly evident in a number of incidents concerning the Venetian symbol of St. Mark's lion during the War of the League of Cambrai.

The following report from Bergamo, the westernmost town of the Venetian dominion, occupied by the French shortly after the Venetian defeat at Agnadello, describes the sentiments of the townspeople:

---

109. According to Newton 1988, 19–21, *paonazo*, which was an ambiguous color, indicated a mixture of happiness and sorrow.

June 28, 1509 (8:448)   A certain Gotardo of — arrived today; he was the constable in charge of one of the city gates of Caravaggio,[110] appointed by ser Antonio Sanudo, the former civil governor [*podestà*] there. He left Bergamo recently and says that the Bergamasques, that is, the popular class and part of the citizen class, from the leaders on down, are unhappy. . . . He also said that there were certain French troops in the [Caravaggio] fortifications and that all of the large artillery pieces had been confiscated and taken to Milan. The large gilded statue of the lion of St. Mark that had been in the Piazza, the one with the kneeling doge, had also been taken down and sent to Milan. And as it was being taken down, one voice [from among] the people could be heard saying, "He's going to Milan because he will soon be the ruler of Milan." And the French did not like these words but were not able to discover who had said them.[111]

Moreover, when an accident befell the sculpture in its journey to Milan, the Bergamasques present interpreted it as a bad omen for the French and an opportunity to cheer for Venice.

July 3, 1509 (8:478)   A certain Thomaso arrived today; he is the son of the late Francesco di Conti, who used to cast artillery at the Arsenal and who was sent to Bergamo to cast certain artillery pieces. He is young and was captured near Bergamo by the French and made a prisoner of Lord Antonio Maria Palavixim [Pallavicino], but he escaped by dressing up as a muleteer, and fled here [to Venice]. . . . He reports that there are only a few French in Bergamo, a hundred in the castle and an equal number in the chapel. But they don't want to stay there and are saying, "The king is going back to France and is leaving us here to be cut to pieces by the Venetians." They are going around selling iron and lead shot and whatever they can, and then fleeing. The French have taken the St. Mark's lion and set it up in the piazza in Milan; while they were crossing the River Adda during the journey, the cart that [the statue] was on tipped over and fell out but landed on its feet. This is an ill omen for the French, as was noted at the time. And the populace of Bergamo is crying out, "Marco! Marco!"

Over the next eight years nearly all of the various communities that composed the Venetian Terraferma, including Bergamo, were restored to Venetian rule. The

---

110. In Lombardy. A constable was the head of a unit. See Mallett and Hale 1984, 377, 381.

111. The sculpture, showing Doge Francesco Foscari kneeling before St. Mark's lion, had been on the facade of the Palazzo della Ragione in Bergamo. In the following excerpts, Sanudo references to St. Mark's lion are to sculptures, either bas-reliefs or statues, of the lion identified with the saint. See Rizzo 1996.

last city to be reacquired was Verona, which on January 17, 1517, was returned to Venice by French military leaders to whom the emperor had ceded it, crowning the diplomatic and military success of the Venetians. The lion of St. Mark once again ruled in that city.

January 20, 1517 (23:500)   Letters from Verona, from our proveditors general Gritti and Gradenigo dated the 18th at four hours after sunset, were read in the Collegio this morning. They relate that on that morning a Solemn High Mass was celebrated in the cathedral, where the most illustrious Lutrech, the governor,[112] the proveditors and other French captains, and many members of the citizen and popular classes had gathered, filling the church. At the conclusion of the Mass came the announcement of an eighteen-month truce with the emperor. Next, a writ by the most illustrious Lutrech that concerned making the annual payment in fifteen days was read. . . . Then [Gian Giacomo] Caroldo[113] read a letter patent from the Signoria pardoning all the Veronese. Everyone was very happy to hear it, calling out "Marco! Marco!" Even the citizens in the packed church were calling out in loud voices, and when they tried to leave, they found the streets so crowded that no one could move. The French marveled at the great love and devotion that the populace manifested toward our Signoria. A number of stone images of the lion of St. Mark that had been buried [for safekeeping] were carried in procession in the church and through the town on platforms covered with carpets. Legends were placed around them saying, "The truth has risen up from the earth, and justice has looked down from the heavens."[114] For the entire day the only activity in the city has been the making of jubilant noise: people have been crying out "Marco! Marco!", the bells have been ringing, weapons have been discharged, and in the evening lanterns and fires have been lit. Many members of the citizen class who were not equally loyal have remained in their homes, fearing that they will be cut to pieces by the people.

Some Paduan Defections

Less easily accommodated than the people [*popolo*] of the Terraferma was the nobility, disaffected by Venetian taxes and chafing under alien rule. In Padua, for example, nearly all the members of the upper classes embraced the invading armies of Emperor Maximilian in the spring of 1509. Shortly after Venice recon-

---

112. Viscount of Lautrec, Odet de Foix (c. 1483–1528), appointed governor of Italy in the name of France.

113. A ducal secretary who had become an adjutant to Andrea Gritti and then had been sent to Milan to accompany Lautrec.

114. "Veritas de terra orta est et justicia de coelo prospexit."

quered the city on July 17, they found themselves under strict surveillance; some were even sent to live in Venice, and some were sent to be executed. When the emperor besieged the city late in the summer, they were the subject of renewed scrutiny.

September 25, 1509 (9:184)   An order was given by the heads of the Council of Ten to the Paduans and Trevisans who are confined here, who twice a day are required to present themselves at the Office of the Seal to register with Alvixe de Marin, assigned to this task. Specifically, they are no longer to come to the Ducal Palace or to Piazza San Marco or to Rialto unless they are passing through, under pain [of penalties], etc. Instead they are to come to the Chapel of Saint Thodaro, behind the Basilica of San Marco, to register twice a day. The reason for this is that they have again been eavesdropping and writing to their comrades in the enemy camp.[115] This order was given with the support of the Collegio.

A few days later, on September 29, Maximilian mounted a heavy bombardment of the city, but the Paduan walls held fast, and the imperial troops were subjected to a massive defensive barrage by the Venetians. Maximilian canceled the siege and withdrew his troops. As a result, the stringent control of the Paduans in Venice was somewhat relaxed:

October 15, 1509 (9:256)   A bill was passed that the Paduans, who had been required to report twice a day and could not come to the Piazza San Marco, may now go wherever they please and are required to present themselves only once a day to register. And they [the Council of Ten] wish within a week to process the ones held in prison, so the Collegio is meeting continuously to complete the examination of the remaining cases.[116]

Nearly eight years later, in early 1517, when the War of the League of Cambrai was in its final months and Verona had been returned to Venice, thus completing almost entirely the reconquest of the Terraferma, a group of Paduans petitioned the Collegio to restore their privileges to them:

January 25, 1517 (23:527)   Eight ambassadors from Padua appeared before the Collegio; because there is no council [in Padua] and because they are support-

---

115. That is, using their trips to the Ducal Palace or the Piazza San Marco as an opportunity to eavesdrop on conversations at the seat of the government.

116. See chapter 3, excerpt dated 1 December 1509 (9:358–59), reporting that four of the leading citizens of Padua had betrayed the city to the emperor and were hanged.

ers of Venice, they were chosen by the Venetian governors and their fellow citizens.[117] The speaker was ser Gasparo Orsato, a university laureate, who had been confined in the "cages"[118] and then freed. A good man, he gave a long address in the vernacular, rejoicing at the retaking of Verona, and went on at length. A written copy of his speech will perhaps be attached below. And in closing he asked for three things: the first, that the university resume its activities as before the war; the second, that they be allowed their city council; the third, that they have the vicariates that they had before the war. The doge said that we were pleased to see them, that we were certain of their fidelity because they were extremely loyal, and that the university would be reopened.[119] Regarding the other two requests, he would meet with the savi and give them an answer.

Troubles in Friuli

Particularly critical was the Patria of Friuli, a large subalpine territory that originally had been part of the Holy Roman Empire, had been conquered from its immediate ruler, the patriarch of Aquileia, in 1420, and in the sixteenth century was dominated largely by its quarrelsome nobility.[120] Its size, its origin as an ecclesiastical principality, and its unlegitimated conquest led to the retention of its nomenclature as a patria, that is, a separate and defined community within the Venetian dominion, and to the military-sounding title of its Venetian governor, the *luogotenente* (lieutenant)[121] Considered by the Venetians to be of critical importance as a buffer against invasions of Turks, Austrians, and Hungarians, Friuli was difficult to rule, for it lacked any central authority and was subject to disorders because of poverty and endemic factional violence. In 1511, during the War of the League of Cambrai, at the very moment when Friuli was threatened by an invasion of German troops, the tension between two Friulan clans, the della Torre and the Savorgnan, erupted in a vendetta of pillage and bloodshed, which the Venetian authorities attempted, with varying degrees of success, to control.

The first report of the riots and deaths came from the luogotenente, who described how the sparks of long-term antagonisms had been ignited by rumors of invasion and led to the Carnival massacre of 1511.

---

117. The governing bodies of Padua were still suspended.

118. The punitive *gabbioni*, in which traitors were held and sometimes died.

119. The university would not reopen for about a year, and we know from Sanudo that the subject was revisited. See, e.g., diary entries of 10 September 1517 (24:670–72), 4 November 1517 (25:66), and 1 December 1517 (25:120), the last confirming reports that the university would reopen.

120. For background to and a full narrative of the events of this section, see Muir 1993.

121. A title given to governors in those territories on the frontiers where attack might be expected.

March 1, 1511 (12:5–6)   The heads of the Council of Ten, ser Piero Capello, ser Bernardo Barbarigo, and ser Andrea Loredan, entered the Collegio for the reading of letters of the greatest importance addressed to them by ser Alvixe Gradenigo, luogotenente of the Patria of Friuli, sent on February 27, which was the Thursday of the Chase.[122] They tell of an event that has taken place there in Udine: there has been a hostile outburst in that area, namely, by the faction of don Antonio Savorgnan against don Alvise di la Torre and other castellans belonging to his faction. As a consequence, don Alvise has been killed, along with don Sydro di la Torre and other castellans, including don Ypolito da Coloredo, etc.; in all, eight of the leaders and as many as — other men of theirs have been killed. The houses of di la Torre partisans have been sacked, and twenty-two of them have been burned, including don Alvise's. During these events don Antonio was in the castle with the proveditor and did not wish to go down [to the street], saying that he was not armed. It is said that the cause was the longtime enmity between the Savorgnan, the most distinguished family of the Patria,[123] and the di la Torre, whose side has been taken by the majority of the castellans. The partisanship had earlier resulted in the deaths of some members of the household of the di la Torre, and the Signoria brought the heads of the two factions to the Collegio on another occasion to arrange a peace between them. The preceding day, which was Wednesday, the luogotenente again established peace between the heads of the two factions. It appears that on Thursday news arrived that two hundred German cavalry from Gorizia and five hundred infantry troops were coming to raid Udine, so the city armed itself and went to guard the gates with artillery from the armory. Now, some armed men were in the house of the aforesaid don di la Torre, and it happened that they used certain words of [the di la Torre] household against Udinese partisans of the Savorgnan, and a fight broke out. All of Udine being against the di la Torre, the killings described above took place. And it is said that some of don Antonio Savorgnan's enemies went to a village belonging to him near Udine . . . , and they pillaged it and burned the houses. This is how this disturbing event of great importance took place.[124]

The luogotenente writes that all of Udine was armed and involved in the uprising, that public artillery was used to knock down the door of the house, that the luogotenente had sent to Gradisca for one hundred infantry to guard

---

122. The day during Carnival on which the bull chase was held.

123. As usual, Sanudo follows the government in supporting the Savorgnan clan to the point of admitting some of them into its patrician ranks.

124. As with so many reports of armed conflict, the exact sequence of events is not fully clear. The luogotenente's attempt at a truce and the debacle that followed are described in two other accounts, which Sanudo reports in diaries, 12:17–19 and 12:26–30. See also Muir 1993, 152ff.

the city, and other details. I will give all the details below, where I may write at greater length; the letters contain copious material on the subject. Thus, all [extraneous persons] having been ejected from the Collegio, a meeting was held to decide what was to be done. It was agreed that a meeting of the Council of Ten, with the zonta, would be held today so that steps could be taken.

So grave was the situation, and so important was the control of this territory deemed to be, that later that same day the Council of Ten determined to send a special envoy to help deal with the violence. The appointment was not without controversy, for the patrician chosen was a former governor of Friuli known to favor the Savorgnan, a bias that some found alarming but that for Sanudo justified the appointment.

March 1, 1511 (12:8)   The Senate having been adjourned at twenty-two hours after sunset, the Council of Ten, with the zonta, convened to deal with the matter of Udine, remaining in session until five hours after sunset. After a heated debate, a letter was written to the luogotenente, and it was decided to send a head of the Ten to Udine with orders as stated in the bill. Ballots were cast, and Andrea Loredan, a former luogotenente of the Patria of Friuli, was elected; his election was not well received in the city. He will leave immediately. Some would have preferred to send someone else, saying that he is a friend of the Savorgnan, but it seems to me that his friendship with Savorgnan is probably the chief reason why he was chosen.[125]

Two days later, letters reached Venice describing new outrages and disorders, which the Venetian luogotenente apparently was helpless to control.

March 3, 1511 (12:15)   This morning it was heard that letters have arrived from Udine saying that the disturbances have continued and that two castles belonging to the di la Torre faction have been burned: Villa Alta, which is four miles from Udine, and Porpet [Porpetto], which is thirteen miles away.[126] The widow of don Alvise di la Torre was captured and tortured to try to learn the whereabouts of her children. Thus this matter is still in tumult, and many castellans have fled to Pordenone to save themselves because the entire Patria is up in arms. And I [Sanudo] saw, in the Basilica of San Marco, don Jacomo da Castello, the university laureate, one of the highest-ranking men of the

---

125. The controversy surrounding this particularly sensitive appointment suggests the complex issues involved in appointing Venetian officials to the territories of the Venetian dominion.

126. Porpetto is about 20 kilometers south of Udine, toward the sea.

Patria, who has often come to Venice as the ambassador from Udine, wearing a ceremonial robe.[127] Along with others who have fled from the Friuli, he was in the Basilica, standing behind ser Piero Capello, one of the heads of the Ten. The heads met at length with the Collegio about these matters, and in the evening ser Andrea Loredan, one of the heads of the Ten, left for Udine. He took with him ser Alvixe Zamberti, the notary to the State Attorneys' Office, and his orders were to take measures to handle the situation together with the luogotenente. In addition, the Collegio voted to send Malfato, the constable, with two hundred infantry, whom he will recruit here. Thus the drummer went around the town [announcing the recruitment effort].

Other correspondence was received from the Venetian treasurer in Udine, addressed to his father and listing the murdered members of the della Torre clan, the homes sacked, and the ineffectual attempts to control the disturbances. Sanudo summarizes this letter:

March 3, 1511 (12:19)   Yesterday evening the luogotenente dispatched a messenger on horseback to Gradisca with orders to send one hundred infantry. They should arrive at any moment, and he hopes that once they have arrived, there will be no further disturbances. This morning they sent away a number of peasants, the majority of them, but many of them are still there. They wanted to sack the Jews; however, steps were taken immediately, and they were not allowed to do any harm. The luogotenente never failed to take every step and to command and to protest on behalf of the most illustrious Signoria and of the excellent Council of Ten that they were not to do those things. He has always been there in the midst of firearms and crossbows, insisting that they retreat and threatening them with the gallows if they would not. Yet not a single honorable man, or man of any kind, listened to him or obeyed him.

A few days later there was news from the special Venetian envoy Andrea Loredan, who, together with the luogotenente and Antonio Savorgnan, was making every effort to control the disorder.

March 7, 1511 (12:31)   Letters from ser Andrea Loredan, a head of the Council of Ten, addressed to the heads arrived from Udine. He wrote of his journey [to Friuli] and how along the way he found peasants at the castle of Fratta who

---

127. The manuscript has *vesta da contor;* the Fulin edition has *vesta da cantor.* This term does not appear in any of the Venetian lexicons, but uses of it cited in Bistort 1969, 355, and Molmenti 1973, 2:478–79, suggest a ceremonial gown. See also Labalme and White 1999, 61n54.

wanted to sack it, but he stopped them. When he arrived in Codroipo,[128] he sent an adjutant to order them to put down their arms, and he was obeyed. Yet the entire Patria is in arms. On March 5 he entered Udine and was met by the luogotenente and don Antonio Savorgnan and all the others, etc. He will try to hold the trial and to complete the return to peace, which he has been commissioned to do.

For several weeks more, clan leaders from Friuli lobbied in Venice, especially Antonio Savorgnan and his adherents, who blamed the uprisings and murders of the di la Torre on "the fury of the people" (12:104, 109). Meanwhile, Venetian troops in Friuli went unpaid; earthquake, famine, and plague racked the Patria; and the Germans crossed the Piave River into Friuli. Here, as in Padua, many of the nobles welcomed the imperial forces, and by September Antonio Savorgnan had been enticed into negotiations with imperial messengers. On September 20 he entered Udine with imperial prefects, betraying his long alliance with Venice. The Council of Ten confiscated his property and offered a reward for his assassination. On May 27 of the following spring he was murdered by an opportunistic Friulan lord and avenging partisans of the della Torre clan.

June 4, 1512 (14:282–83)   From Udine, from ser Andrea Trivixan the knight, who is luogotenente and proveditor general of the Patria of Friuli. He has heard from a reliable source of the death of the traitor Antonio Savorgnan, which occurred as follows. At Villach on May 27, a Thursday, at nine hours [*hore nove*],[129] Antonio Savorgnan came out of the church where he had heard Mass, accompanied by some of his entourage. He was assaulted by one Zuan Odorigo, from Spilimbergo, whom Savorgnan had caused to be banished from the cities and territories belonging to Venice. Zuan Odorigo pursued him in order to kill him and obtain the bounty promised to his killer by the Council of Ten, which amounts to 3,000 ducats.[130] He dealt him such a forceful blow to the head that his brains fell out, and he cut off his hand, and then Savorgnan died. Other wounds were delivered, and one of his entourage was killed, and a second injured by those who were with Odorigo, who were also from the Patria and included five who had been banished, as I recounted above. Once they had killed him [Savorgnan], they immediately took horses and set off upon the road to Hungary. After they had crossed the —— River,

---

128. A town in Friuli south of Udine.

129. If the hours are counted with regard to the season being very near the solstice, the time might have been around 5:00 am, when an early Mass could have been celebrated.

130. According to Ventura 1964, 211n84, the reward was 5,000 ducats.

they destroyed the bridge. They were followed by some who tried to catch them, but they found the bridge destroyed, so the murderers easily escaped. And this was the end of this proveditor [Savorgnan], who died without legitimate heirs, leaving only don Nicolò, a bastard who is a canon of Udine, and even he is in Germany.[131] I note: his cousin don Hironimo Savorgnan, who belongs to the zonta, did not wear any sign of mourning, because this Antonio has brought shame upon his house.

From that time forward, Venice placed less trust in any single leader, although Hironimo Savorgnan, the murdered Antonio's cousin, who had been coopted into the Venetian government, was granted his request to occupy the superior position in the Friulan parliament, which his family had always enjoyed. It was only over a long period that Venice could wean itself from a system of favoritism in this particular province, and factional rivalries continued to cause trouble in Friuli.

December 14, 1519 (28:121)   After dinner the Council of Ten met with the zonta. . . . They considered the matter of Lord Hironimo Savorgnan, who, now that the parliament of the Patria has been convened, wishes to take his place above all seven of the deputies, a seat that has always been occupied by his ancestors, who were leading and valued citizens of our state.[132] Francesco Donado the knight, who is luogotenente in the Patria, said that it did not seem right to allow Savorgnan to take that place without a further order from our Signoria, and he wrote to the Council of Ten about the great grumbling heard among the castellans. Now these heads of the Ten . . . proposed a bill that he be given the seat. There were speeches against it, and it did not pass.

December 15, 1519 (28:121)   This morning there were no letters worth talking about. After dinner there was a meeting of the Council of Ten with the zonta to conclude this Savorgnan matter. . . . At the end of the meeting, after much debate, it was decided that in light of the merits and fidelity of our most beloved patrician Hironimo Savorgnan and of his ancestors toward our state, he be allowed to sit above the seven deputies of Udine in the parliaments that they will hold among the castellans and in other places, and this with the approval of our Signoria.[133]

---

131. Nicolò was himself assassinated six years later by some revengeful castellans. See Muir 1993, 244; and Ventura 1964, 211n84.

132. Girolamo, Antonio's cousin, had ingratiated himself with the Venetians by serving in the Venetian army and distinguishing himself in the successful battle of Cadore (1508) against imperial forces. In a controversial decision, he was elected an honorary member of the Senate's zonta, an honor that, to his hosts' dismay, he decided to take seriously. See Muir 1993, 239.

133. Sanudo's papers contain, in his own hand, the following few verses composed by Girola-

The Magnificent City of Brescia

The challenges posed by Friuli may have been more severe and therefore more dramatic than those posed by the other territories and cities of the dominium, but each required particular accommodation. More typical than the accounts of divided loyalties in Padua and violence in Friuli were the routine reports from governors such as the following one of 1520 from the returning governor (podestà) of Brescia, a commune that, since its acquisition in 1426, had proved the most profitable of all the Terraferma territories to Venice.[134]

October 31, 1520 (29:334–35)   This morning ser Piero Trun, who has just returned from being governor of Brescia, came before the Collegio, dressed in purple wool, and gave his report, which I stayed to hear.[135] He said that he would not expend words on the excellence of the magnificent city of Brescia, as all were acquainted with its qualities, but wished to limit his remarks to its fortifications. He said that something needs to be done immediately about Canton Monbello because it is in the greatest danger. He said that construction work on the Pille Gate continues with all due diligence; the work has been under way for two years, and another two years will be required to complete it. The expense has been divided three ways: one-third to be borne by the Signoria, one-third by the city, and one-third by the surrounding territory. The same arrangement holds for the rest of the fortifications, and the Tor Longa gate should also be fortified.[136]

He praised Antonio di Castello, who holds the castle with twenty-five infantry; he is a man of great military deeds and is very devoted to our Signoria.[137] In the Castello Antonazo da Peroza [is serving as constable] in the place of Zuan Jacomo Rochon, who was sent to Cyprus.

The city numbers 50,000[138] souls, and the surrounding territory, 200,000, that is, Valchamonicha, 50,000 souls; Val di Trompia, 50,000 souls; Val di Sabia, 40,000 souls; and Riviera di Salò, 50,000 souls.

---

mo Savorgnan in praise of Sanudo and Sanudo's studio: "Di Minerva d'Apollo et de le Muse / Tutte le discipline et tutte l'arte / Qui dentro el mio Sanuto tien richiuse" (BNM, Lat. Cl. XII, 211 [4179], fol. 8v). [Herein my Sanudo holds enclosed / All branches of learning and the arts / Of Minerva, Apollo and the Muses.] Their friendship explains Sanudo's favorable view of this member of the Savorgnan clan.

134. See Muir 1993, 62–63.

135. Sanudo was a member of the Senate's zonta at this time.

136. The Fulin edition omits the word *fortificar* before "la porta di Tor Longa." Canton Monbello, a buffer area, is now known as "spalto San Marco," or the glacis of Venice; the Pille Gate is now Porta Trento, and the Tor Longa is now Porta Venezia.

137. The punctuation here follows the manuscript; the Fulin edition has the period after *Castello.*

138. The manuscript has 50,000; the Fulin edition has 30,000.

The treasury receives 70,000 ducats per year [from the city and its territory], but the expenditures are great. The tax imposed is 29,000, and the budget allowances of the governors cannot supply [the rest]; in addition, 200 ducats were raised there for the Monte Nuovo.[139]

The city has six *podestarie*[140] in its territory—Axola, the Orzi, Lonà, Chiari, Valchamonicha, and Salò—and about fourteen vicariates, which have large villages under their jurisdiction, as well as castles. Brescia is an extremely wealthy city; everyone wears silk, women as well as men. The city is full of shops, and it does not look as if it had ever been sacked. They live off the products of their land and look forward to grain shortages;[141] they do not live from commerce as their ancestors did, but they amuse themselves by keeping up with fashion.

He spoke of the grain market that is held in Desenzano.[142] Most of it goes to German lands. The Brescians would like a noble proveditor [to regulate] it, who would receive a salary; they have been to see the Signoria about it, but to no avail. It would be appropriate there.[143] The income to Brescia from grain is good because of the abundance of water and the canals that carry it where they want it to go; and all is "gold" that comes from the Ojo [Oglio] River,[144] which fattens the land.

He said that he sought to administer justice impartially and to punish the bad because when he arrived there he found it to be a lawless city.[145] One assassin had even escaped to Mantuan territory. Trun wrote to the marquis, who had him captured in church and sent to Trun, and he saw that justice was done. He also told of the case of the bishop of Recanati, who was killed in Bergamasque territory; he found the criminals and recovered some silver items and a mule. As he reported, he turned all of this over to the bishop's brothers, and he has the receipt for it.[146] It was just five cavalrymen and four infantrymen who committed the crime. He also recounted the events of the fair of Crema, when the crowd panicked and he had one hundred light cavalry stand in formation and one hundred light men-at-arms, and he sent some

---

139. See appendix B under "Governmental Terms."

140. Communities having a Venetian podestà, or civil governor.

141. Grain shortages enabled them to sell at higher prices.

142. On the south tip of Lake Garda, between Verona and Brescia.

143. The manuscript has *lì* (there); the Fulin edition omits it.

144. The manuscript has *et è tutto oro vien dal fiume Ojo;* the Fulin edition has *et tuto oro vien dal fiume Ojo.* The river provided irrigation and cheap transportation for the lucrative grain trade and thus was a liquid form of gold.

145. On the difficulty of administering justice in Brescia and elsewhere during this period because Venice had allowed local nobles to take justice into their hands during the war, see Zamperetti 1991a, 234–35.

146. That is, he did not keep any of it for himself.

of them here and some of them there, so that the people who went to the fair had their safety assured. . . .

He said that he had held this office, for three months with ser Jacomo Michiel as military governor, for whom he expressed his respect. The rest [of his tenure] was with ser Nicolò Zorzi, whom he praised. The treasury is well run: he praised above all the reverend domino Piero Pagnan, the treasury clerk, but he complained about the fifty ducats per year paid to that Paulo Agustini, the other clerk. He praised his court,[147] which accorded justice to all and tried to keep the city prosperous. If they had not made provisions, the price of grain would have risen, harming poor men. The doge praised him, as is customary, and said that he deserved a commendation.

Thus Piero Tron concluded his *relazione,* a somewhat typical report on an important city in the Venetian dominion. Of all the aspects of Venice's administration that he mentioned, none was more significant than its administration of justice. Venice depended upon the reputation of that justice, both at home and abroad, as will be seen in the next chapter.

147. The manuscript has *laudò la sua corte;* the Fulin edition has *laudò la corte.*

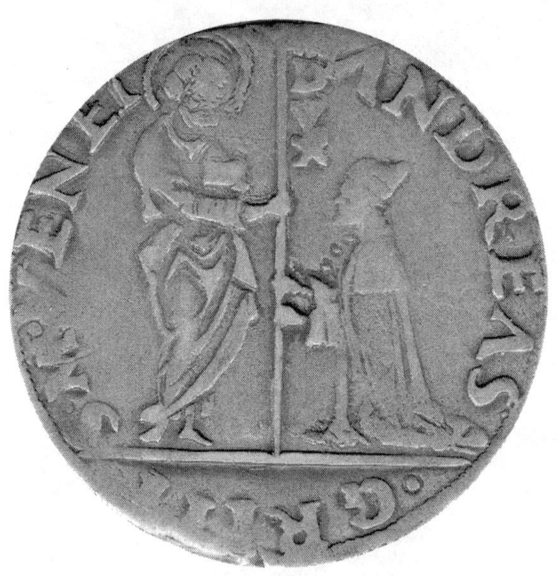

Doge Andrea Gritti (1523–38) kneels before St. Mark, Venice, *mocenigo*.
Photo courtesy of Guy Clark, www.ancient-art.com.

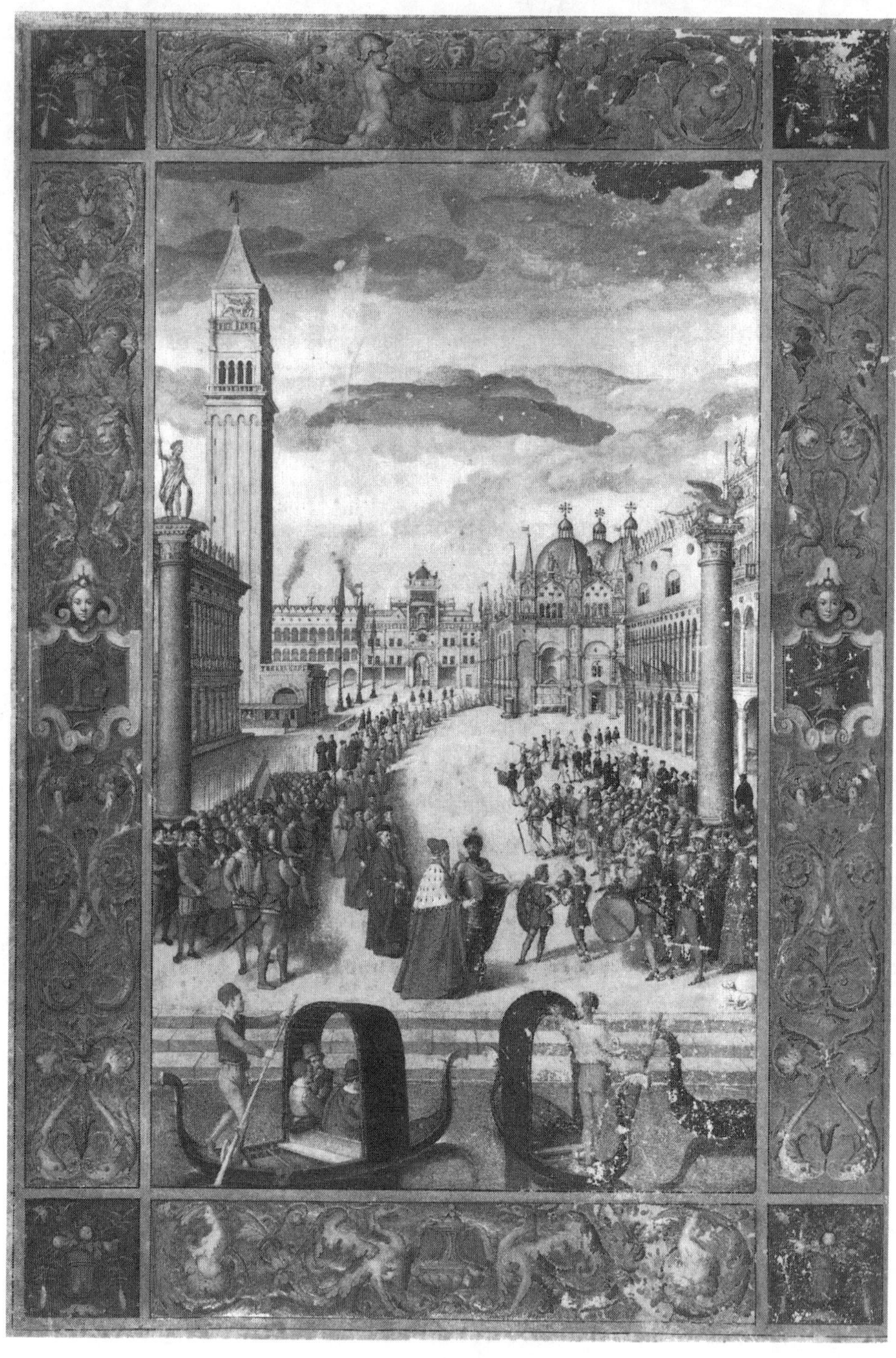

Meeting of Doge Andrea Gritti and Francesco Maria della Rovere in the Piazetta in 1524, from G. B. Leoni, *Vita di Francesco I della Rovere* (1605). Biblioteca Apostolica Vaticana, Rome.

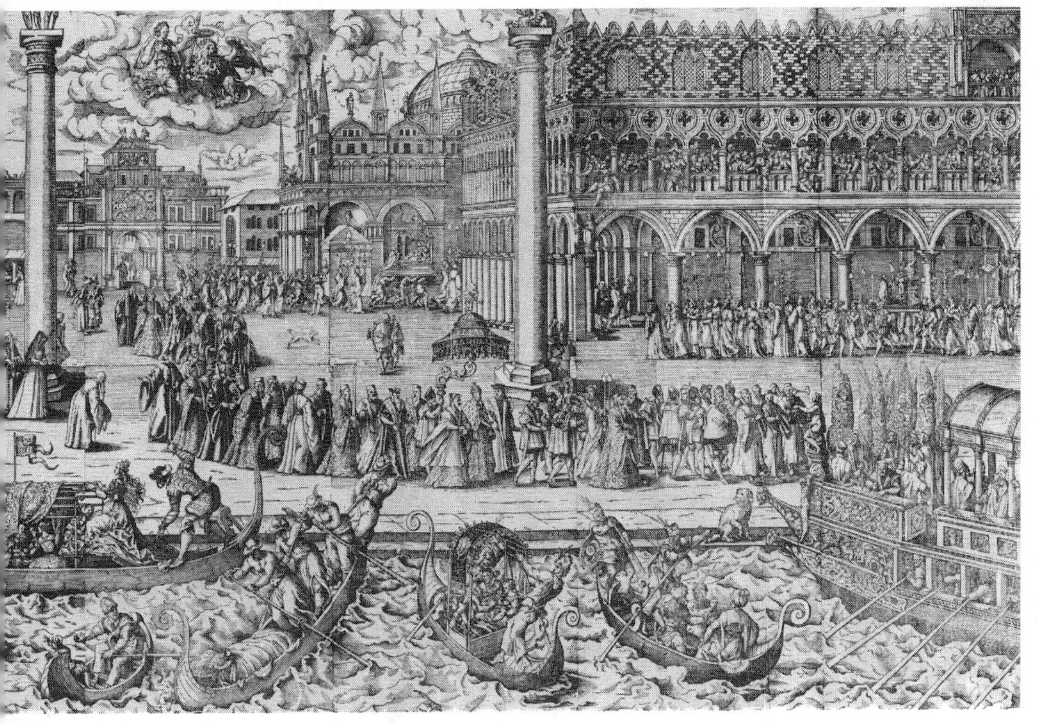

Jost Amman, *Feast of the Sensa,* woodcut, 16th century. Metropolitan Museum of Art (49.95.5).

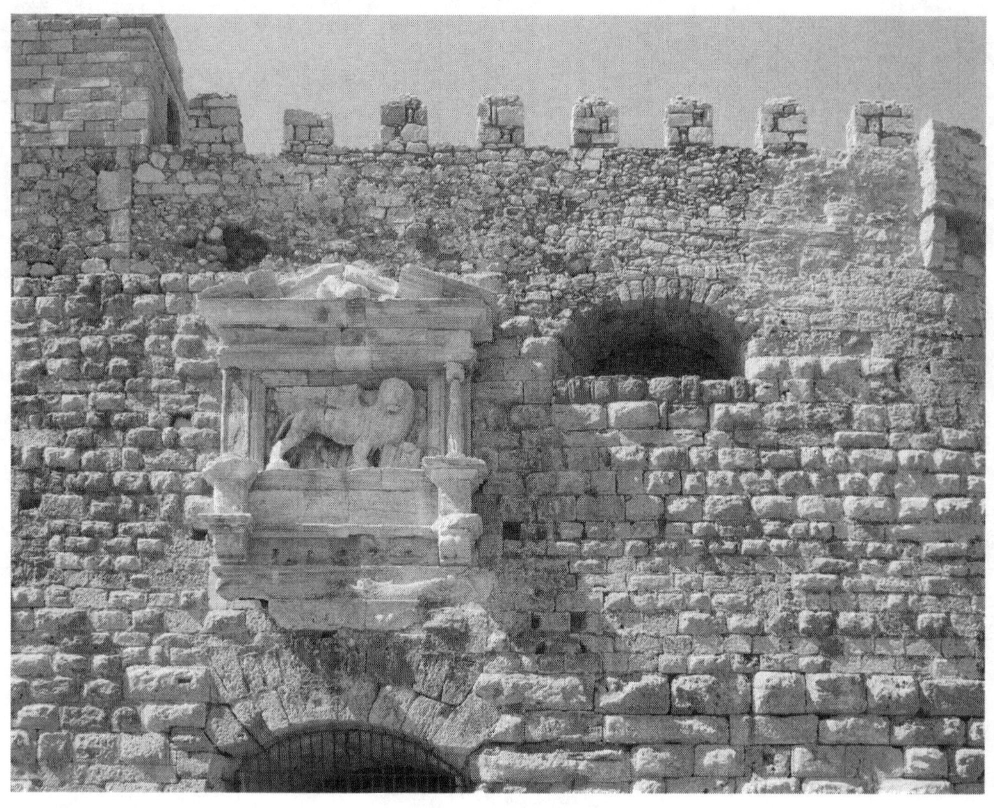

Lion of St. Mark on the Koulès fortress in the harbor of Candia (Heraklion), Crete, 16th century. Photo courtesy of P. F. Brown.

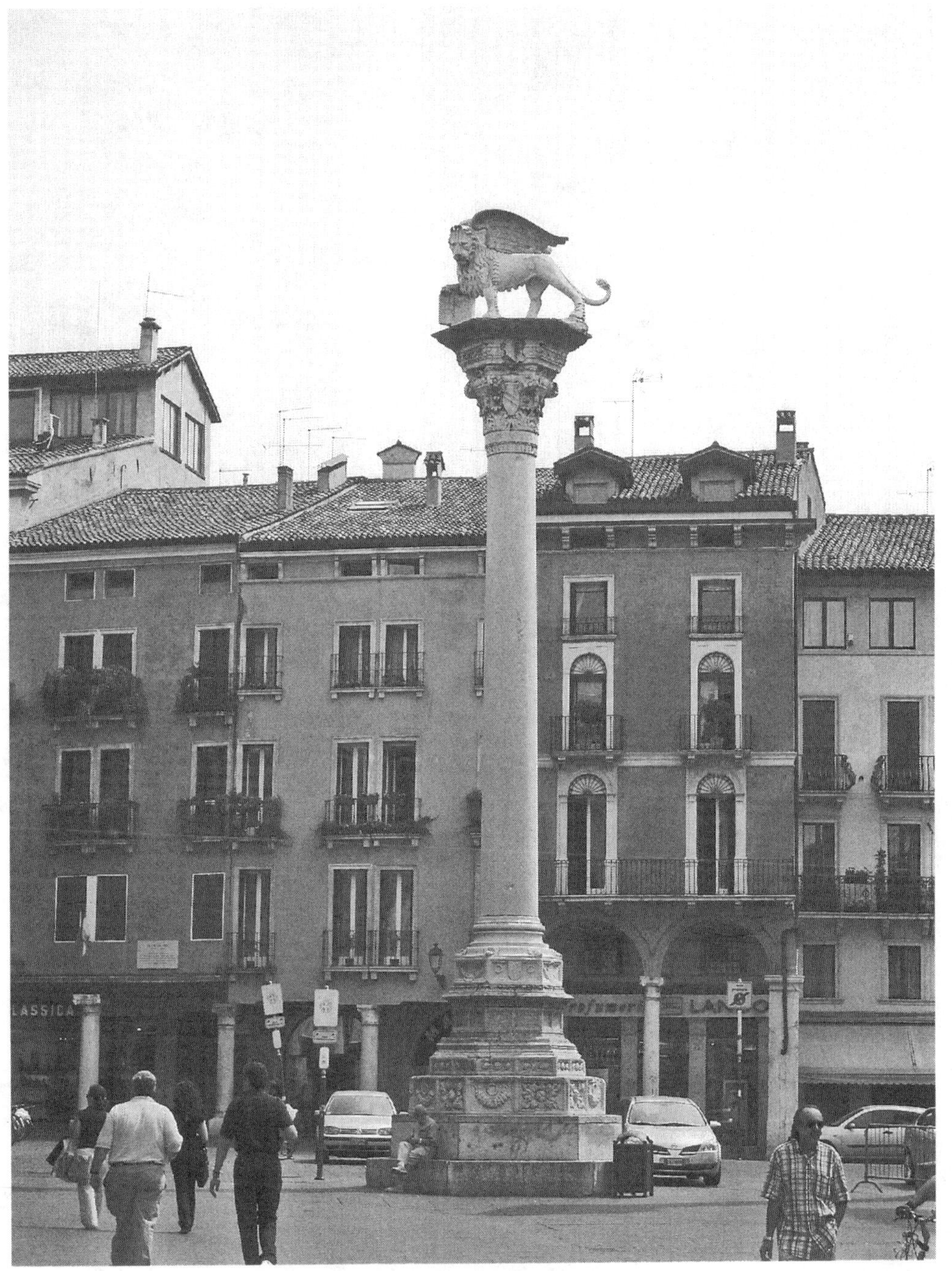

Lion of St. Mark in Piazza dei Signori, Vicenza, 1464. Photo courtesy of P. F. Brown.

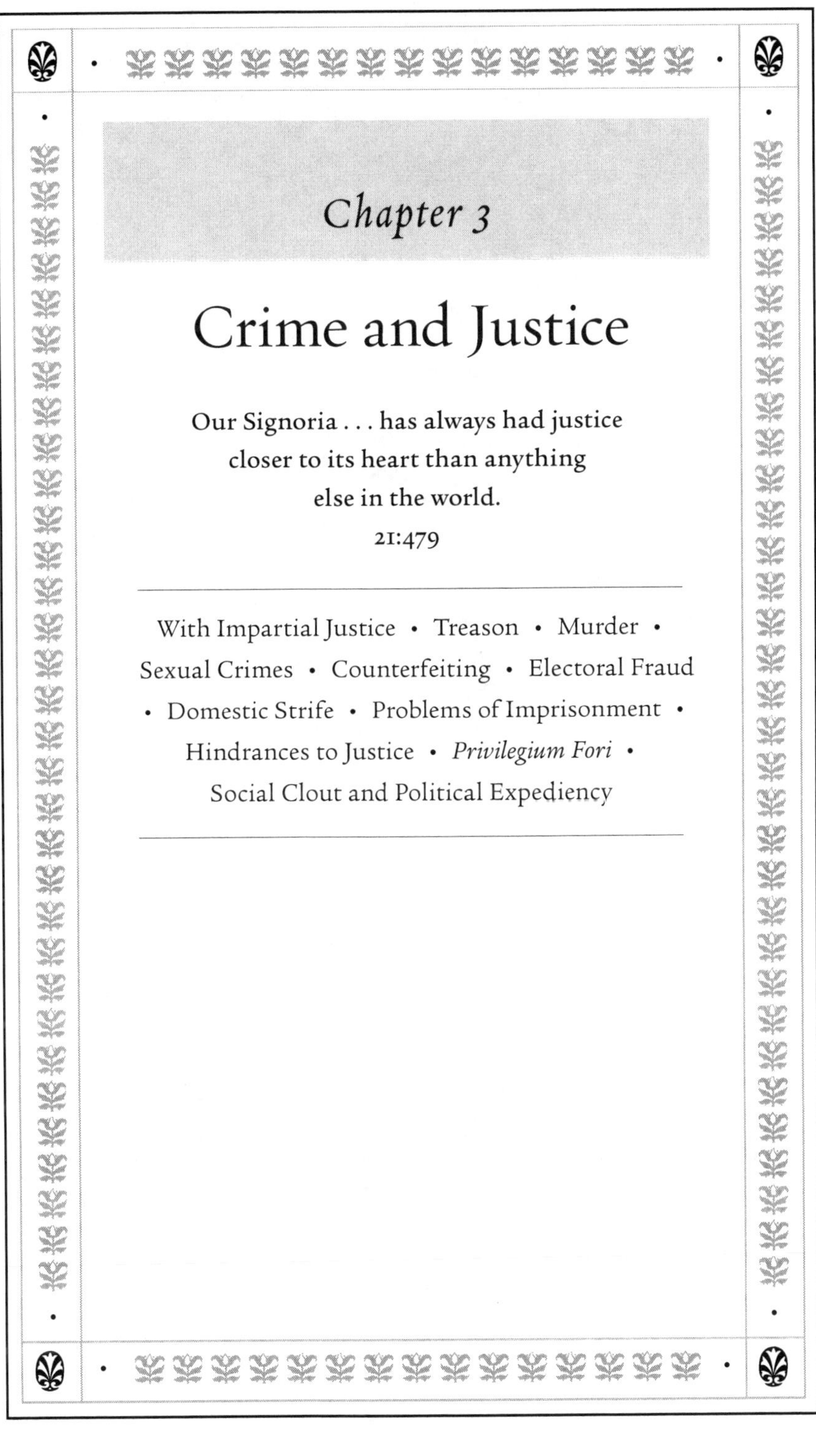

Chapter 3

Crime and Justice

Our Signoria . . . has always had justice
closer to its heart than anything
else in the world.

21:479

With Impartial Justice • Treason • Murder •
Sexual Crimes • Counterfeiting • Electoral Fraud
• Domestic Strife • Problems of Imprisonment •
Hindrances to Justice • *Privilegium Fori* •
Social Clout and Political Expediency

As important as magistracies, ceremonies, and a connective administrative framework were to the Venetian government's reputation and self-esteem, even more critical were its laws and judicial organs. When the doge entered the Basilica of San Marco, the first charge upon him, as inscribed in the chapel of San Clemente, was "to love justice."[1] Law and justice were considered the foundations of the Republic, guaranteeing its order and longevity, maintaining the unity and structure of its society. The legal activity of so many of the political committees and councils ensured patricians a broad exposure to the legal system, as Sanudo had had in his early training. Sanudo retained a particular interest in the Venetian legal record and practices, and his frequently articulated belief was that "he who believes in observing the laws maintains republics" (January 25, 1520; 28:206). Debates about the laws, the texts of new legislation, and accounts of crimes and their punishments (often in considerable detail) form an important element in his quotidian record.

Yet here too, in what Sanudo writes about the workings of justice, an element of the exceptional persists. Some of his reports are brief records of the punishments executed upon criminals as justice went its normal way. But the longer passages deal with unusual crimes or more legally complex cases or illustrate points he wished to make, such as the validity of Venice's reputation for having an impartial system of law.

With Impartial Justice

In his early work on the origin, magistracies, and sights of the city, Sanudo described the figure of Justice that decorated the prow of the doge's ceremonial galley, the Bucintoro, with these words: "The prow has a seated and gilded figure of Justice with sword and scales in her hands, a sign that the Venetians serve everyone with impartial justice."[2] That impartiality was not absolute: laws were sometimes bent or ignored to accommodate influential persons. But the ideal remained sufficiently strong to enlist Sanudo's pride, palpable in the following excerpt from his first volume, where he points out that Venetian principals of equity applied to foreigners as well as to patricians and citizens.

---

1. Gallo 1967, 6.
2. Sanudo 1980, 37.

FLORENTINE VS. VENETIAN

January 31, 1497 (1:496)   During this month of January a very noteworthy event occurred in this city. That is, it seems that one Lorenzo Tornaboni, a Florentine, was owed a certain sum of money by a Venetian patrician named Andrea Bragadin, of San Sovero, so he sent his agents to Venice to claim the said money. The matter having been referred for judgment to the Office of the Merchants' Consuls [Consoli dei Mercanti],[3] this Bragadin defended himself. The case was open to debate, given the pacts that they had agreed upon. The arguments were presented, and a decision was handed down in favor of the Florentine. The Venetian patrician appealed, the decision was suspended, and the case went to the Quarantia, one body having been made from two branches.[4] Finally, on the tenth of the present month, after long debate, the case was again decided in favor of the Florentine. The important point is the greatness of Venetian justice; even though there are some frictions with the Florentines, a Florentine still swiftly won the case against our patricians, something that would not have happened elsewhere.[5]

THE CASE OF GASPARE VALIER

Another example of how sternly impartial Venetian judges could be was the trial and execution of a young and handsome patrician, Gasparo Valier. The story unfolds in Treviso, on the mainland, and in Venice and begins with the condemnation to death of Rocho, the head state courier in Treviso, who guarded contraband but also dealt in it. This condemnation by the Cinque Savi alla Pace permitted the killing of Rocho by any person, who then might collect a bounty or be exonerated of some crime of his own.[6] But then Rocho's condemnation was canceled by the Council of Ten, who took Rocho under their protection, probably in exchange for his reporting on illicit activities by other smugglers in Treviso. However, either in ignorance of Rocho's pardon or in defiance of it, a young patrician called Gasparo Valier, himself also a smuggler and perhaps a competitor, murdered Rocho in hope of collecting a bounty.

---

3. See appendix B under "Governmental Terms."

4. That is, two branches of the Quarantia—the Quarantia Civile and the Quarantia Criminal. See ibid.

5. The Venetians at that time were supporting the Pisan rebellion against Florence; hence the reference to "frictions."

6. See Cozzi 1973, 293–95, on the custom of involving the general public in the execution of justice via incentives such as bounties or forgiveness of the vigilante's own criminal penalties. Cozzi's essay deals with the competition and distinctions between two of the chief judicial organs, the State Attorneys (Avogadori di Comun) and the Council of Ten.

April 26, 1511 (12:137) In the morning letters arrived from ser Andrea Donado, podestà and military governor [*capitanio*] of Treviso, dated yesterday. He
wrote to say that Gasparo Valier was there in Treviso. He is the one who murdered Rocho, the head of the horsemen, who had been assigned to guarding
the wine and contraband and who was under the protection of the Council
of Ten. The doge and other members of the Collegio deplored his action and
decided to take measures concerning it. . . .

After the Senate had adjourned, the Council of Ten convened and decided
to arrest ser Gaspare Valier, who had murdered Rocho in Trevixo and who
every year has maintained a continuous heavy traffic in contraband. Thus,
this night he was taken into custody by the Council of Ten's constable and a
number of officials, in his house at the Zatre [Zattere], near San Trovaxo. He
defended himself stoutly, especially with some large dogs, who helped him a
great deal. But he was captured and placed in a cell.[7]

A month later, the trial began in the Council of Ten. The council used its own
secret and swift judicial procedures, known as the *rito*. To quote Sanudo's own
description in his *De origine,* "Those who fall within the Council of Ten's jurisdiction may not defend themselves with lawyers. When they are examined, the
Ducal Palace is barred." A judicial committee called a *collegio* is formed with four
members: a ducal councillor, a head of the Council of Ten, a state attorney, and
an inquisitor (one of two such officers chosen monthly by the Council of Ten
from its own membership). Any one of these, should he so choose, may defend
the suspect. Upon the recommendation of this collegio, the Council of Ten acts.
"And what is decided by the Council of Ten is firm and valid and may not be
countermanded except by the Council of Ten."[8]

In this way the council moved the trial rapidly along, as was often the case
when a patrician was involved. At the same time, there was strong resistance
from Valier's family and allies, who claimed that the council had acted illegally
in canceling Rocho's condemnation. If that were true, Gasparo Valier could not
be condemned for killing Rocho. Their efforts were to no avail.

May 21, 1511 (12:186)   The Council of Ten met without the zonta . . . and expedited the trial of ser Gasparo Valier, who killed Rocho, head of the horsemen,
in Treviso. They decided that he should be beheaded on the 24th between

---

7. *In camera,* i.e., in the Ducal Palace. See Scarabello 1979, 56–59, for cells in the Ducal Palace.
8. Sanudo 1980, 99, 242. On the *rito,* see Cozzi 1973, 308–9; Fulin 1870; and Labalme 1984, 224.
For a detailed account of the Council of Ten's use of the *rito* in an eighteenth-century case, see
Cozzi 1988.

the two columns,[9] he and a peasant who was with him. This verdict was kept secret for two days, then communicated to Valier by the head of the Council of Ten and the state attorney. Once it became known, the entire city reacted strongly against it. It was said that the decision to have him beheaded had been made by a single vote and that the doge had fulminated against him.[10]

Even the patriarch tried to intervene, using an argument frequently employed in seeking exoneration, that is, that the accused was a cleric and therefore under the jurisdiction of the church:

May 22, 1511 (12:186–87)   In the morning, our patriarch appeared before the Collegio to see if he could help ser Gasparo Valier, to keep him from being beheaded. He said that Valier was at his first tonsure. The heads of the Ten were present, and the patriarch was sent away with the admonition that the decisions of the Council of Ten must be implemented. And given that many talked at length and offhand about this matter, saying that it is bad to kill a gentleman who killed someone in Treviso, the heads of the Ten warned them not to speak of this matter.

The state attorneys became involved, leading to a confrontation between two powerful judicial authorities: the state attorneys and the Council of Ten. But the Council of Ten rejected their interference, as it had the pleas of the patriarch, patrician relatives, and the people, and fired the state attorneys from their positions.

May 24, 1511 (12:188–90)   In the morning. This is the day chosen for carrying out the order of the Council of Ten to behead ser Gasparo Valier. His relatives, ser Marin Zorzi, university laureate, ser Marin Morexini, ser Alexandro Gradenigo, his mother's brother, and other family members and friends, in all a large group of patricians, went to the state attorneys. . . . They complained that Rocho had been banished by the Cinque di la Paxe [alla Pace] and that the cancellation of his sentence had not followed the procedures established by law. They entreated the state attorneys to set aside the cancellation, after which the most excellent Council of Ten could discuss the matter and suspend the execution. The state attorneys, consulting the laws, noted that in effect the verdict against Rocho had been canceled against duty and the law. Having been given permission by the heads of the Council of Ten to be heard,

---

9. The columns of San Teodoro and San Marco in the Piazzetta, the location for most executions.

10. Note the telescoping of several days' events into this single diary entry.

they decided this morning to go to the Quarantia Criminal. After one of the state attorneys had presented the case, all three proposed [that the Quarantia] rescind the cancellation of the verdict against Rocho, who is already dead, because it was done against the prescriptions of the law. Their proposal received unanimous support. A very large number of patricians filled the Senate, waiting to hear what would follow. Next, the heads of the Ten, ser Andrea Loredan, ser Andrea Magno, and ser Hironimo Tiepolo, seeing that their Council of Ten had been overruled, went to the Collegio. Then the entire Council of Ten was summoned; they all came immediately and gathered together. The state attorneys wanted to enter, but they were sent to their offices below.[11] But first, and swiftly, all those patricians were cleared out of the Senate chamber by Gasparo di la Vedova [dalla Vedova][12] and the constable of the Council of Ten. Next, the Council of Ten, all seventeen members, convened until well past none. When they had adjourned, ser ——, one of the heads of the Ten, went to the door of the state attorneys' office because all three of the state attorneys were listening to cases. He called them by name and used the familiar *ti* form with them, as is the custom of the Council of Ten, saying, "The Council of Ten has deemed that you are no longer worthy to hold this office; please leave the premises." So all three left and went home. It was decided that they would be banned from holding the office of state attorney permanently and from being elected to the secret council[13] for two years. And people said that they were very close to being put in jail. It should be noted that ser Nicolò Dolfin is the doge's nephew and was a member of the Eleven when [Loredan] was made doge[14] and was devoted to the doge. But they were given this sentence anyway, and [Piero] Contarini was three days away from finishing his term of office.

Once the state attorneys had been removed, the sentence against Gasparo Valier was carried out by authority of the Council of Ten. Sanudo, always the conservative defender of Venetian authority, concurred with their action, although most of the city sided with the state attorneys.

---

11. The Collegio's meeting room was on the fourth floor of the Ducal Palace, while the offices of the State Attorneys were on the second floor. Lorenzetti 1926, 243, 253.

12. The manuscript has *et prima, destro modo, per Gasparo di la Vedova;* the Fulin edition has *et prima, destro modo, sier Gasparo di la Vedova.* Gaspare dalla Vedova had a long civil-service career with the higher councils of the government. See Neff 1985, 573–74.

13. That is, the Council of Ten.

14. Nicolò Dolfin is called the *nipote,* meaning "nephew" or "grandson"; in this case it more likely means "nephew." As a member of the Eleven, he was involved in the penultimate stage of the election of the doge, having been selected by lot to choose the final electoral group of forty-one. See chapter 2; and Finlay 1980b, 141–44.

After dinner there was a meeting of the Council of Ten with the zonta, and a new group of state attorneys was inaugurated: ser Zuan Arseni Foscarini, who was already elected, and ser Marco Loredan, who had been elected a year ago. At the first meeting of the Great Council one more attorney will be chosen to replace ser Zuam Trivixan, who has only been in office for a short time. Then at vespers, between the two columns, Gasparo Valier was beheaded. He was a young man . . . with a beard and quite handsome. The square was full of people, and he passed through it kissing groups of people. When he had climbed the scaffolding, he dawdled quite a bit. Then he spoke forth freely: "I know that my death displeases all of you, and I beseech you to pray to God for me." And the executioner doffed his cap, asked for his forgiveness, and urged him to prepare himself. In the end he did so, and his head was cut off. He was dressed in a light toga lined with vair and wore a soft cap on his head.[15] The body and the head were taken down immediately and placed[16] in a coffin and taken by boat to be buried. Valier was rich, with an income of 300 ducats; he had many friends, and his traffic in contraband netted him many ducats per year, and he had made a will. He left the Venetian government — ducats as reparation; and to his relatives and to a certain ser Piero Trun, his companion, a large portion of his possessions. That he died in such a manner troubled the entire city, especially because Rocho was disliked. And they say that this will be the making of the careers of the three state attorneys who wanted to help him. However, the state attorneys deserved their sentences, because once a decision has been made in the most excellent Council of Ten, it must be carried out, because the council is the rudder of this city. And also beheaded was a peasant who had been with him and had assisted in the murder of Rocho.[17]

Treason

The Council of Ten's intervention in the case above was based, not on the crime of murder, which was usually judged by the Quarantia, but on the situations of the victim and the perpetrator. But among the major crimes, certain categories were specifically reserved for the Council of Ten, and the number of these tended to increase over time. Treason, conspiracies, counterfeiting, sodomy, and questions relating to the *scuole grandi* and the Chancellery were within the purview of the council. Sacrilege in monasteries was added in 1513, and blasphemy

---

15. For vair, which was much used in this period, see appendix B under "Fabrics and Garments." For the soft cap, or *scufia,* see Newton 1988, 43–44, 67.

16. The manuscript has *e posto;* the Fulin edition has *posto.*

17. For another account of this case, see Cozzi 1973, 318–19.

in 1514. Indeed, the Council of Ten was, in Sanudo's words, a "very fearsome" magistracy."[18]

A SECRETARY'S BETRAYAL

The following case of treason illustrates the Council of Ten's judicial swiftness and secrecy, which led to the enlarging of its sphere of control.[19] It involves the ducal secretary Antonio di Landi, his kept woman, a former member of the Chancellery now in the service of a foreign power, and a commoner. Sanudo, witness to the denouement, provides the dramatic narrative: the encounter of two conspirators in the darkness, a spy hidden behind the bed, the language code used for their communication (in this case Latin), and the hint of foul play in the prisons.

March 26, 1498 (1:917–19)   On this day [Monday] there was a meeting of the Council of Ten with the zonta, even though there had been one on Saturday; and in the evening, at about three and a half hours after sunset, an event occurred of which I shall now write.[20] On the morning of Tuesday, March 27, while I was going as usual to San Marco, everyone was saying, "This night justice was done." And indeed, when I reached the Piazza, there was our [Chancellery] secretary, Antonio di Landi, aged about seventy, hanging between the two columns. He had access to secret matters, translating letters written in cipher and attending the Senate. All the city marveled because no one had known anything about it, and he had been hanged in the full-sleeved robe of his office, and at night. It should be known that this was for having revealed secrets to one Zuan Battista Trivixan, who was formerly in the Chancellery but had been dismissed and was virtually a secretary to the Marquis of Mantua. It was discovered in the following way. This Antonio di Landi, although he was an old man and had an annual salary of 180 ducats from our Signoria,[21] kept a woman called Laura Troylo, who lived at Santa Trinità, and this Zuan Battista also frequented the place, and in the evening they chatted together in Latin.[22] This Laura told another friend of hers, named Hironimo Amai, a member of our popular class, who hid behind the bed and heard these two discussing matters of state and the secrets of the Senate. And the

---

18. "È magistrato . . . molto tremebondo." Sanudo 1980, 100.

19. The justification for this enlargement of power was the council's concern for political security and the preservation of secrets. See Mallett and Hale 1984, 249–50. For a review of the council's increasing authority at the expense of the State Attorneys, see Cozzi 1973.

20. The first part of this translation is based largely on Chambers and Pullan 1992, 92–93.

21. A relatively high salary for a Chancellery secretary. See the salary scale in appendix A.

22. The manuscript has *latine;* the Fulin edition has *latino.*

said Laura did not have the courage to go herself and make an accusation against him, but sent the said Hironimo.

The two men were quickly arrested and sentenced. Sanudo fills in the details—Antonio's economic condition, his refusal to eat or to repent, and, at the end, the macabre treatment of his body:

The heads of the Council of Ten were Troylo Malipiero, Antonio Trun, and Alvise da Molin, and when the council had been called, it was decided to arrest these men and also the said Laura. And so on Sunday morning this Antonio (who was lying ill at the said Laura's house) was arrested, as was Zuan Battista, who on Monday was on his way from Mantua in a boat and was seized by the captain, [Girolamo] Zenoa, and taken to prison. And when the judicial committee had been balloted, the choice fell upon Lorenzo Venier, councillor; Troylo Malipiero, a head of the Council of Ten; Nicolò Michiel, university laureate, knight, and state attorney; and Marco Antonio Morexini, knight and inquisitor.[23] On Monday morning they closed off almost the whole Ducal Palace, and after examining the men, they quickly sentenced them after dinner, that is, that this Antonio be hanged during the night just as he was found. Zuan Battista, not having had access to any secret council, and because there is no law carrying the death penalty unless one does have such access, was sentenced to life imprisonment within the walls of Retimo [in Crete] with a price on his head, if he should escape, of 3,000 ducats if taken alive and 2,000 ducats if dead. If captured, he is to be hanged, as is stated in the judgment. And the said Antonio was left all day on the gallows, and in the evening he was taken down and sent away to be buried. And it is worth noting that the said Antonio had spent forty years in the Chancellery, but he was very poor.[24] He had a wife who lived in Padua, and from the time he was arrested until he was hanged he refused either to eat, to make his confession, or to take Communion. And when he was to be hanged, since there was no rope to be had nor to be bought because the shops were closed, [the officials] sent to the Arsenal for some pieces of rope, and thus they hanged him. And while they were hanging him—it was reported—he fell and broke an arm, and then he was pulled up again, and the captains did not allow anyone to stay

---

23. These four officials—councillor, head of the Ten, state attorney, and inquisitor—made up the usual judicial committee for serious crimes. For a useful study of judicial procedures, see Fulin 1871. See also Cozzi 1973, 303–9 and passim; and Labalme 1984, 222–31, for the different judicial procedures of the Council of Ten and the State Attorneys.

24. This was in spite of his high salary, perhaps a clue to why he may have been selling secrets to the city-state of Mantua.

in the Piazza, and no cry was heard. Many were of the opinion that he died in prison but was then hanged, because hanging was the proper way to do it. One thing is certain: this is the way things happened. Zuan Battista was taken from where he was being kept and sent to the prison of Toreselle.[25] Provisions were made by the Council of Ten for this Hironimo Amai who made the accusation; he was given a lifetime [lease] on two flour and grain shops in Piazza San Marco, one of which is already available, and the next one that will become available, which yield and will yield him — ducats once he has them both, and he will also have three ducats a month for life and until he assumes this office. A further item: Laura Troylo was given twenty-five ducats, and that is all.

I note that I saw the rope tied to [Antonio's] neck with two knots without a loop and the back of his gown soiled with dirt, as if it were a body that had been killed upon the ground. Others believe that he was strangled in prison.[26]

Sanudo concludes his account with a reference to the broader diplomatic repercussions of this event and a philosophical reflection on the mercurial nature of Italian politics in his era:

I do not wish to omit from my account that with this act of treason, which happened as it did, the Marquis of Mantua has not only lost his hope of reconciliation with our Signoria but also brought great disgrace upon himself, as well as the hatred of the entire city. And just as some people felt compassion when he was cashiered [as a military leader in 1498], in the present situation everyone condemns him. The Duke of Ferrara, together with his sons, is [currently] in our good graces, although in the beginning he was out of our favor. This is the way the world works: one person rises as the other falls.[27]

---

25. See Scarabello 1979, 57-58, for a description of this little tower, which remained from the earlier fortifications of the Ducal Palace and was used as a secure prison for political detainees.

26. The judicial record of the Council of Ten is suggestive, if not explicit, about this point. The case came to the Council of Ten's attention on Saturday, 24 March 1498, and the council moved swiftly to examine Antonio di Landi and Zuan Battista Trevisan, using torture if necessary. The record states that Antonio di Landi "expired early in the morning" (mane expiravit) on Monday, 26 March, having confessed to his treachery. Because justice for this great crime could not be done to the living man, it was determined that it should be "done to his cadaver as a fearsome example to all" (contra eius cadaver fiat talis demonstratio que sit exemplaris omnibus et timorosa). Zuan Battista Trevisan was condemned to life imprisonment. ASV, CX, Miste, reg. 27, fols. 195-96 *n.m.* (fols. 153-54 *n.a.*).

27. See below for the Marquis of Mantua's later volatile relationship with the Venetian state.

FOUR PADUAN TRAITORS

Another case of Venetian dealings with treason took place during the first months of the War of the League of Cambrai, when the city of Padua was briefly under imperial rule (June–July 1509) and then reoccupied by Venetian forces, on July 17. Padua was under siege by Maximilian's troops from late August until the end of September. These experiences made the treason of certain Paduan nobles and citizens eager to exchange Venetian for imperial overlordship particularly galling to the Venetian government, and a large crowd gathered to witness their punishment.

December 1, 1509 (9:358–59)   This morning, Saturday, at tierce, according to the decision made in the Council of Ten with the zonta, four of the leading citizens of Padua were hanged. The Piazza was completely filled, to the point where I may say that I have never seen so many people. [The four] were led out of the prison accompanied, as is customary [*de more*], by the Scuola di San Fantin and by four Observant friars of San Francesco [di la Vigna], including Fra Lodovicho of Chioza.[28] [The prisoners] all had beards and were dressed in long robes with tight sleeves and the scuola's habit of coarse black cloth; around their necks were a red cross and a noose. Leading the group was Alberto Trapolin, the brother of the late ser Piero, who was a most excellent, learned man; Alberto belonged to the Council of Sixteen, which governed Padua, and is a man of great intelligence.[29] His grandfather too was hanged in Padua in 1437, during the time of the uprising of Marsilio of Carrara.[30] Second came Lodovico Conte, recently knighted by the current emperor [Maximilian I]. The third, Bertuzi Bagarotto, university laureate, who held a public lectureship in canon law [*publice in jure canonico*] in Padua and received 300 ducats per year from the Signoria, was rich and famous.[31] The fourth was Jacomo da Lion, university laureate, knight;[32] he delivered the oration to the

28. The Scuola di San Fantin had as its special job the accompaniment of the condemned to the gallows. Lorenzetti 1926, 508.

29. The Council of Sixteen governed Padua during the six-week period in which it was an imperial city. See Bonardi 1902, 341.

30. In 1435 Marsilio of Carrara, backed by emperor-elect Sigismund of Hungary, attempted, but failed, to regain control of Padua, which had been lost to Venice over thirty years earlier. See Grubb 1988, 41–42.

31. See Sanudo's diary entry of 17 May 1514 (18:199), which mentions the marriage of Bertuzi Bagarotto's daughter to Nicolò Aurelio, for whom Titian painted *Sacred and Profane Love* (c. 1515). Nicolò Aurelio was secretary to the Council of Ten from c. 1509 to 1523, and his marriage to the daughter of a traitor, even with the permission of the doge and the Council of Ten, caused quite a stir. On Titian's painting, see Goffen 1997, 33–44.

32. The manuscript has *cavalier;* the Fulin edition omits it.

emperor when the Paduans gave their city to him, saying many bad things about the Venetians.

Once they had been led forth, these four were comforted by the friars, as they also had been during the night, when, it is said, their wives and families came to the prison to say their good-byes. It appeared that the four were reconciled [with their deaths]. The first to be hanged was Trapolin, who, when he had reached the top stair, said many psalms and prayers. He did not appear to fear death; indeed, he said to the executioner, "Would you like me to jump?" The second, Conte, was distraught and said little. The third was Bagaroto, who said that he went to his death innocent and had not been a rebel and recommended his son to the Signoria because he had not been a rebel. He was wearing a gown of vair. The fourth was Lion, who recited prayers and was distraught, although he had said to Lodovico Conte when it was his turn to climb the gallows, "Go as a valiant knight." When the other three had been hanged, Lion raised his eyes to look at them and became very upset. There were many Paduans in the Piazza,[33] and many women watched from boats. Once hanged, they remained there until one hour after sunset, when they were taken down and placed in coffins. The Chapter of San Marco[34] then came with fourteen wax torches and accompanied the four coffins by boat to San Francesco di la Vigna, where they had been ordered buried. This is the burial spot of Zuan Francesco da Ponte, the Paduan, who also was recently hanged. Be it noted that the goods of these four were confiscated and taken by decision of the Council of Ten. It remains for the rest of the Paduans to be dealt with. I will record what happens to them. The Trevisans were at the balcony of the Forty, where they are being held, and the Marquis of Mantua stuck his head out [of his prison] to look at them.[35]

---

33. See chapter 2 for excerpts dealing with the many rebels who had been arrested in Padua when the city was retaken in July 1509. These had been sent to Venice, where they lived at large but reported to a Venetian official once a day. They were not meant to frequent the Piazza San Marco but on this occasion were undoubtedly compelled to witness the traitors' punishment. See Bonardi 1902, 389. The fame of these executions was to prove awkward a few months later, when the Veronese, under imperial control, were invited to submit to Venetian troops. "And then be hanged, like those Paduans?" they replied. See Mallett and Hale 1984, 340, citing ASV, CX, Miste, reg. 33, fol. 16.

34. The corporate body of clergy serving in San Marco.

35. This Marquis of Mantua was Gian Francesco Gonzaga, mentioned above in connection with the spy discovered in 1498, who had fallen out of favor for his association with this act of treason. A decade later, sought after by Venice as a military commander, he refused, and he became party to the anti-Venetian League of Cambrai in 1509. He was captured by the Venetians in August of that same year. Then he agreed to lead the Venetian forces, changed his mind, and again switched sides before he ever took the field. See Mallett and Hale 1984, 221–22, 285–86.

Murder

A DIABOLICAL PLAN

In addition to treason, murder was among the major crimes reported in the diaries, sometimes in vivid detail. In the following account, the court involved was the Quarantia Criminal, and the criminal was a prostitute who had murdered a Venetian blacksmith in a particularly horrible and premeditated way and who was condemned to death, on four counts, in an exemplary public execution.

January 26, 1506 (6:288–89)   This morning, in the Quarantia Criminal, the state attorneys . . . presented the case that occurred on the eighteenth of this month at Santa Sofia. It happened like this. There was a woman . . . , a prostitute from Miran,[36] of Paduan origin, who first had lived there as a married woman and then was widowed. She was —— years of age and of diminutive stature. It seems that she became acquainted with a blacksmith who lived in the neighborhood of Santa Sophia, in the campo across from the church. It happened that one night she stayed over to sleep with him; he had no one working for him in the shop and was an excellent blacksmith. In his shop he had a few ducats and items belonging to other people that he was holding in hock. Once the blacksmith had gone to bed, a diabolical plan came to this woman, which she executed without thinking twice, as she confessed. Pretending that she suffered from some pain, she remained by the fire. She filled a pot with linseed oil, which she heated to the boiling point. The blacksmith having fallen asleep, she approached him with a knife and plunged it into his breast. Immediately, as he tried to jump up, she took the hot oil and threw it in his face, causing him to pass out. Then she picked up a candlestick and hit him on the back of the head with it and beat him senseless. She next grabbed two bags of coins and his purse and certain belts and other items, but, as it is rumored, she was not able to open the box where he kept his money. Then she set a fire under his bed and left. That night his entire home caught fire and burned, as did the one above it, which belonged to the Longin family, of the popular class. When this woman tried to leave [the city], she was arrested on suspicion of thievery. I do not know how the crime was uncovered, but once she was examined by the judicial committee, she confessed the truth, as recorded in the trial. Today she was led before the Forty, and the matter was expedited.

Don Andrea da Bolzan, university laureate, and Marin Querini, both attorneys, spoke on her behalf, requesting that she be given a lesser sentence

36. Mirano, a village on the nearby mainland.

so that she would not lose her soul. The state attorney charged her with four crimes: theft, homicide, arson, and assault [*furto, homocida, incendiaria et assassinamento*]. Three proposals were made: the proposal of ser Hironimo Pixani, head of the Forty, which I include, was that her head simply be cut off, and it had five votes. The winning proposal was as follows: next Wednesday, on the 28th of this month, she is to be taken along the Grand Canal on a platform, as is the custom, as far as Santa Croce. She will disembark at Corpus Domini, whence, on another platform, she will be taken by land to Santa Sophia. There, on the spot [where the crime occurred], she will have a hand cut off. Then, again by land, she will be taken to San Marco, where, between the two columns, she will be struck senseless and have her head cut off. The head will be hung up at San Zorzi, and the body is to be burned. And so it was done.[37]

THE WOMAN TURNED DEVILISH

Exemplary punishments were not infrequent. In 1521 the murder of a grocer by his wife of twenty-two years was judged to be a particularly heinous crime. That the husband had physically abused his wife is mentioned as a contributing factor, but it was not accepted as an extenuating circumstance. The criminal's cunning deception, her astute planning, her rupture of domestic trust, and her attempt to involve her daughter in the crime all implied an intolerable rejection of her role as wife and of the hierarchical structure of the family. For all these reasons, a brutal punishment was mandated in order that the end of this "Fury" provide "an example to everyone."

August 2, 1521 (31:163–65)   After dinner there was a meeting of the Council of Ten with the zonta, and the charge made in the Forty on the first of this month was reviewed. The speaker was ser Alvise Mocenigo, knight and state attorney. He brought before the Council a woman named Bernardina . . . , who has been married for twenty-two years to Luca from Monte Negro, called

---

37. Cf. Muir 1981, 247, where the ritual aspects of the punishment are described: the severance of the offending hand and the procession from prison to the crime scene and then to San Marco for her execution both cleansed the city of this crime and reasserted the judicial power of the state over its every part. The case is recorded in ASV, Avogaria di Comun, Raspe, reg. 3660/20, fols. 131–33 *n.m.*, 26 January 1505 *n.a.* The woman is identified as "Marieta sive Faustina," and the blacksmith as "Ambrosius fabbri." The crime is described as "horrendous" (*immanissima*), and its prescribed punishment emphasizes its public aspect: the platform on which she was carried and the platform on which she was executed were both to be "very high" (*eminenti*), and a herald was to accompany her on her journey through town, "proclaiming her crime." Prior to her beheading, she was struck—*descopata*, a term that has been interpreted both as a hard blow to the nape rendering the victim unconscious or a severe beating (see Battaglia 1961–2000), expressed here as "struck senseless."

"the Jew." He lived in the neighborhood of San Antonin and was a grocer. His fortune amounted to 1,000 ducats and more, and he lived in the houses of the Coco family, and by his wife he had an unmarried daughter by the name of Diana. This woman [Bernardina] turned devilish because her husband beat her. In 1514 — he, after being detained by the state attorneys, gave a surety of 200 ducats that he would be a good companion to her and was released from prison.[38] On May 1 of this year, after dinner, when her husband had fallen asleep on the footboard of the bed in the daughter's room, this Fury,[39] an accursed woman, for some unknown reason gave him three blows on the head with a carpenter's tool. One of these[40] blows hit a gold ring on his finger that was worth twelve ducats. Then [the accused] dealt him two more blows, so that, without being able to confess his sins, he died.

In the meanwhile, the daughter had gone up to the roof, and when she came down, the mother told her that she had killed the father. Since the daughter kept crying, the mother threatened her and dragged the body[41] into a storage room, where it spent three days unburied. Then the woman called for a cousin of hers named Thomaso, who was an officer serving with Novello,[42] and she told him that she had killed her husband and asked him to help her bury him. He responded, "You will be quartered." In the end he bought a shovel, dug the grave, and the two of them buried [the corpse] there in a storage space under the stairs. The wife gave everyone to understand that her husband had left the city, and no one knew where he had gone. In the end she thought up a plan to have a fraudulent letter written, apparently by someone in the town of Santa Maria di Loreto in the house of Curtio the blacksmith.[43] It informed him[44] that her husband Luca had gone there in fulfillment of a vow[45] and that he was going to Rome and would soon return, and it reminded her of some business of his, all of which appears in the letter. The wife showed this letter to an uncle of her husband's, and he took it and made inquiries about its nature and sent [for information] as far as Ancona and found that

---

38. See Romano 1987, 39–40, for a fourteenth-century case of non-noble wife-beating that came before a notary. In that case, the husband agreed not to abuse his wife physically or verbally but retained the right to correct and castigate her "moderately and decently" for disobedience.

39. Sanudo uses *Erine*, the classical word for Fury.

40. The manuscript has *desse*, i.e., *d'esse*; the Fulin edition has *disse*.

41. The manuscript has *lo*, indicating the body; the Fulin edition has *la*, suggesting the daughter.

42. Giacomo di Novello, head of an infantry troop employed by the Venetians.

43. The manuscript has *fabro*; the Fulin edition, *Favio*.

44. The manuscript has *lo*; the Fulin edition, *la*.

45. The house of the Virgin Mary was believed to have been miraculously transported from the Holy Land to the town of Loreto, in the Marches, in 1291. The cult of the house grew noticeably in popularity in the late fifteenth and early sixteenth centuries.

the letter was false. From that point [the uncle] began to suspect that the wife had killed him.

Even as suspicions developed and the authorities became involved, the "devilishly" clever behavior of the culprit continued to argue her innocence.

Captain Novello reported her to the state attorneys. Once the trial had been set in motion, the said Bernardina was sent for, and when her statement had been taken, she justified herself so well that the attorneys, especially Alvise Mocenigo, knight, let her go. She had taken into her home a certain Vicenzo Zarla and his wife, and I believe that he turned her in, because after the daughter had been called, he told everything in his deposition. The said Bernardina was arrested, and she confessed the truth in every detail as I have recorded above, without being tortured. The notaries of the state attorneys were sent to oversee an excavation, and they found the dead body[46] in the said storage space. The matter was discovered because after she had been to see the state attorneys the first time, she wanted to move the body from where it was, and she took Zarla into her confidence. He told her that it would smell too much and went to turn her in to the state attorneys.

When this case was brought[47] publicly before the tribunal of the Quarantia Criminal, many people came to hear[48] it. The said attorney Mocenigo spoke, saying she was guilty, along with that Tomaso [who helped her], who was present in the courtroom. All of the written material was read. She was defended by ser Zuan Donado, the attorney for the prisoners, who spoke of the terrible life that that husband of hers[49] had made her lead. All three attorneys posted a bill to proceed, which was supported by all thirty-eight [members] of the council.[50] Two punishments were proposed. . . . According to [one proposal], the said woman today, Saturday, August 3, will be placed on a high platform on a barge and taken along the Grand Canal as far as Santa Croce, with her offense being called out by an officer. Then she will be taken off the barge and led by a land route, with her offense still being called out, as far as Santo Antonin, where she lived. There her right hand will be cut off, and with it hanging from her neck she will be led between the columns of Piazza San Marco, where she will be struck senseless and torn in four parts, which parts will be hung from the gallows, as is customary. On the other side, ser

---

46. The manuscript has *corpo morto;* the Fulin edition has *corpo posto.*
47. The manuscript has *menato;* the Fulin edition, *venuto.*
48. The manuscript has *udirlo;* the Fulin edition, *vederlo.*
49. The manuscript has *esso so' marito;* the Fulin edition omits *esso.*
50. That is, the Quarantia Criminal.

Luca Trun, councillor, and ser Jacomo Barozi, vice-head [of the Ten], agreed with this proposal, except that they wanted her head to be cut off; they did not want her to be beaten senseless. The proposals were presented for a vote: . . . Trun's received 9, and that of Erizo and the others received 28 and won.

Note that no other case has been found of a woman who, whatever her crime, was quartered. This is the first one. This was a very important case: it is quite true that other women have killed their husbands, but none with so much ferocity.

Thus today she was executed in the manner prescribed by the Forty: she was struck senseless and took a long time to die. Even when she had been stabbed in the heart and in the throat, she continued to move. She was dressed in white, wearing a gown and with a clean soft cap on her head. Then she was torn in four parts, which were sent to be hung on four gallows as an example to everyone. And this is the first woman to be quartered in this city.[51]

Sexual Crimes

SERIAL RAPE

Sexual crimes were treated with varying degrees of severity, depending on the circumstances and the social level of those involved. In the following cases of serial rape, because of the number of victims, capital punishment was administered.

August 1, 1513 (16:579)   This morning in the Quarantia Criminal the proposal of ser Zuan Capelo, state attorney, and his colleagues was accepted. That is, tomorrow a certain Gasparo d'Arquà will be quartered. This man, using the pretext that he had a trembling disease in his head, made certain very ugly movements, twisting his head backward, and thus he went begging for alms. More than a year ago he found a traffic for himself: he brought many wet nurses and women from the country here and [took] others from this city out [to the country]. Once they were on the road, he took them into a certain wood and assaulted them and took the possessions and the money that they had on them, threatening to kill them. Then he would leave, and the poor women who had been shamed and who had lost their belongings were left there. He did this to more than eighty of them, including eleven maidens, whom he raped; the number from this city [whom he attacked] was sixteen,

---

51. On this case, see Viggiano 1994, 833–34. Crouzet-Pavan 1992, 2:815, points out that women were only rarely the protagonists of criminal conflicts: they cause them and are involved, but only exceptionally are they enactors ("Elles les occasionnent, les suives, mais ne sont qu'exceptionnellement actrices"). This may explain why Sanudo took such interest in the two preceding cases.

as is noted in the trial records. He was recognized in the street at San Fantin by one of these women, who said to him, "You assassin, here you are." She grabbed him and turned him over to the officials. It was decided that he be held in the custody of the Forty, and he made a full confession. His sentence was to be taken along the Grand Canal on a barge, as is customary, tomorrow at none. Then he will be disembarked at Santa Croce and dragged from a horse's tail [*a coda di cavallo*] to Piazza San Marco, where his head will be cut off and he will be quartered, with the quarters hung on the gallows, etc.[52]

SYMBOLIC RAPE

Some cases, such as those described below, involved symbolic rape. In both instances cited, the flouting of public mores was viewed as a serious crime because patrician women were involved and because the actions against them undermined the formal procedures of betrothal and marriage to which patrician families subscribed.

May 13, 1500 (3:314–15)   I will not omit something that I heard, that the son of Andrea Morexini, the former state attorney, was brought before the Senate for having kissed a woman and taken a jewel from her. And he said publicly [of his son]: "Hang him! Off with his head!" And so he was condemned.

There is no further mention in Sanudo's diaries of this charge or its punishment, which he certainly would have recorded had it taken place. Thirty years later, similar miscreants were punished, although not in the capital manner advocated above.

May 29, 1530 (53:234)   Bortolamio Comin, the secretary of the Council of Ten, made public two guilty verdicts handed down yesterday in the most excellent Council of Ten against ser Zuan Soranzo and ser Marco di Garzoni. On the tenth day[53] of the present month, the feast of St. Job, they loitered around the

---

52. Two days later the sentence was executed. The rapist, before his mortal punishment, pleaded "with the state attorney that before he died he be given some privileges and [said that] he wanted to do 'that thing' once more" (diaries, 16:582). See ASV, Avogaria di Comun, Raspe, reg. 3662, fols. 85r-v, where the criminal, identified as Gaspar de Faedo, "vicevicarius arquadi" (vicevicar of Arquà), was declared a "crudelissimus et immanissimus assassinus" (most cruel and horrendous assassin) who lured these women with promises of "faciendum bonum salarium" (making good money). Cf. Romano 1996, 120. Sanudo's statement about being dragged by a horse is ambivalent. *A coda di cavallo* could mean "from a horse's tail," although a horse would have to cross many bridges to get from Santa Croce to San Marco, or it could mean, more metaphorically, "roughly." Battaglia 1961–2000 translates the phrase into Italian as *sconsideratamente*.

53. The manuscript has *a dì X*; the Fulin edition has *a dì 11*.

door of his church and took handkerchiefs out of the hands and belts of the women, setting a bad example. Since something needs to be done about this, these two will be banished for four years from Venice and the surrounding area, with a reward [to the informer] of 1,500 ducats' worth of their goods to be levied if they violate the terms of the banishment. If they are caught, the reward is to be paid, and they are to be sent back into banishment, which will begin all over again, since the four years are to be continuous. Their goods are to be bound over for payment of the reward, and if these are not sufficient, the reward is to be paid with money belonging to the Signoria. They cannot be pardoned except by vote of five-sixths of this council, in its stated number of seventeen.[54] This verdict is to be announced at the next meeting of the Great Council.

ABDUCTION IN BRESCIA

A more politically complicated case, threatening the sexual integrity of a young woman, occurred in Brescia in the decades between the first and second incidents of symbolic rape described above. It concerned the abduction of a wealthy ten-year-old heiress. The abductors were a powerful provincial family, important to the Venetian government as military leaders, and the heiress's stepfather was equally well connected in Venice. It was a situation requiring cautious procedure, secret decisions, and restorative diplomacy.[55] The case opened in the Council of Ten in April 1518:

April 28, 1518 (25:368)   A wealthy young girl, a member of the Cavrioli family, was living in the country. Her mother is married to one of the Averoldi who has two sons, one of whom has [married] the girl's sister. The second son wants this girl, who is ten years old, with her mother's permission. But the Contin[56] Martinengo, who is a condottiere in our army and the son of Count Vetor, who was made a member of our nobility, went to the house where she was . . . , with a number of other armed men, as is recounted in the letter [*ut in litteris*]. He abducted the girl while distracting the mother with chitchat and took her to Brescia. He placed her in a certain monastery of Santa Iulia,[57]

---

54. The group in charge was the Consiglio semplice, the Council of Ten meeting with the doge and his six councillors, but without its additional zonta of fifteen. It was this more restricted group that had first taken cognizance of the case on 17 May 1530 (diaries, 53:214), and it was hoped that the narrower body, "congregato col prefato numero di 17," would be less exposed to pressure from relatives eager to have the exiled culprits pardoned than an enlarged council would be.

55. For a more detailed presentation of this case, see Labalme and White 1999, 66–68.

56. His name was actually Camillo (see next excerpt). Sanudo calls him Contin, "Little Count," because he was heir to the title of Count of Martinengo.

57. The manuscript has *monastier di Santa Iulia;* the Fulin edition has only *monastier. . . .*

where some of his relatives are nuns, with the idea of giving her in marriage to a brother of his. . . . The mother then came to Brescia to the Venetian governor to lodge a complaint about this insult, and the governor immediately had the girl brought to him. He kept her in the governor's palace — days, then had her taken to another monastery to keep her very safe under his protection. He then wrote a report to the Venetian government about what had occurred.

Thus there was a great debate today in the Council of Ten with the zonta because a bill to send a state attorney to Brescia had been posted.[58]

A few weeks later the state attorney who had been sent to hear the case in Brescia returned to Venice and made his report, whereupon the Council of Ten acted with utmost secrecy because of to the high social position of those involved.

May 21, 1518 (25:420)   In the Council of Ten, ser Lorenzo Orio, who is a university laureate and a state attorney, reported on what he did in Brescia and had the trial record read; it was signed there by ser Filippo Zamberti, his notary. The council then decided to arrest Contin Martinengo, called Camillo, who is in this city, and some others; I will give details below. This decision was kept extremely secret. It should also be said that Julio Averoldo, whose stepdaughter was kidnapped from his house, is a relative of the papal legate, and this legate is pressing the Venetian government quite hard about this matter and opposing the Martinengo because of the force used.[59] So a bill was posted to arrest Martinengo, who is in this city. After it passed, the greatest secrecy was ordered.

The following day, the offending Contin Martinengo and a number of his followers who were in Venice to argue their side of the story (25:363) were seized and confined in several prisons.

---

58. Under the date 29 April 1518 this case begins to appear in the Council of Ten's records. See ASV, CX, Criminali, reg. 2, fol. 217v *n.m.*, with an order to keep the young count and one of his relatives, Teofilo, from leaving Venice without permission. At the same time, a message was sent to the authorities in Verona to restrain two others of the Martinengo clan. The case continues on fols. 218, 219, 220v *n.m.* under the date 21 May 1518. The abduction, under the guise of a social visit, is similarly described in the judicial record: "Et sub specie affinitatis et visitationis violenter rapuerunt et asportarunt honestissimam puellam Franciscam, filiam quondam D. Hieronmymi Capreoli ac dicte D. Marinae" (And under the guise of a social visit, they violently seized and carried away the respectable girl Franceschina, daughter of the late Girolamo Caprioli and the said Marina).

59. The Fulin edition eliminates the following passage, probably considering it repetitive: "In questo conseio di X con la Zonta sier Lorenzo Orio, el dotor, Avogador di comun, tornato di Brexa, fece la sua relatione et fe lezer il processo formato a Brexa contra il Contin di Martinengo, condutier nostro di cavalli fiol dil conte Vetor, zentilhomo nostro, per il forzo fato di quella puta in caxa di domino Julio Averoldo, et cussì fu posto di retenirlo, il qual è in questa terra."

May 22, 1518 (25:420)   This morning Contin da Martinengo was summoned to appear before the heads of the Council of Ten ser Alvise Malipiero and ser Alvise Gradenigo; the third, ser Hironimo Contarini, was absent. And so he came with many of his servants, armed with swords. They were made to remain below in the Senate chamber, and only Contin entered [the council's chamber], where by order of the heads he was arrested. In addition, summonses were issued for Gabriel da Martinengo, called "the knight," who is not one of the family,[60] don Theofilo da Martinengo, the son of the late ser ——, and Gasparo da Martinengo, the son of the late don Lodovico, a Venetian nobleman, who were all here, as well as for a certain Franzi, his [Contin's] squadron leader.[61] The rest of his men left the Ducal Palace and are to leave the city immediately. The ones who had been arrested were placed in various prisons: Contin in the prison of the Signori di Notte, others in the office of the tax collectors, others in the house of the prison warden.

A judicial committee was formed (25:420) that one month later reported back to the Council of Ten. The reading of the hundred-page dossier and the extensive debate took place over two days (25:493), and on June 23 sentences were pronounced against Contin Martinengo and his henchmen, most of whom were relatives. Contin Martinengo's *condotta* (military contract) was abrogated, and he and one relative were exiled from "Verona and the Veronese and all the Venetian territory beyond Verona" for five years. Three of the others were exiled for three years. For the one who was a servant and had physically enacted the crime, a ten-year period of exile was imposed, and should this last miscreant be apprehended in violation of the exile, he should suffer, before the door of the house from which he seized the child, the amputation of his offending hand (25:495–96).[62] Two further actions followed to repair the public reputation and image of the two injured parties. The first concerned the child, and it was legislated that her virginity, lineage, and heritage should be considered intact:

June 25, 1518 (25:495)   The girl is to be returned permanently to the place from which she was kidnapped and is to retain the status, being, and legal position that she enjoyed before her abduction.[63] This decision is to be published on the stairs of Rialto and in the city of Brescia so that all might know it.

---

60. The manuscript has *qual non di Martinengi;* the Fulin edition omits the phrase.

61. See ASV, CX, Criminali, reg. 2, fol. 218 *n.m,* where he is called Contin Martinengo's "armiger," or armor-bearer.

62. Ibid., fols. 219r–220v *n.m.* In the judicial record, the guilty servant is named Giorgio Grande. See ibid., fol. 248v *n.m.*

63. The judicial language is *in eo statu esse et juribus in quibus erat antequam raperetur.* See ibid., fol. 219 *n.m.*

To mollify the child's stepfather and guardian, whose relationship to the papal legate earned him particular consideration, a knighthood was granted:

July 4, 1518 (25:522)   This morning Julio Averoldo appeared in the Collegio. He is a citizen of Brescia and relative of the papal legate, and he was in the city because of the episode that occurred in Brescia involving Contin Martinengo, who abducted one of his stepdaughters. And after the case was tried, he wished to be knighted, and so the doge knighted him[64] with a gold chain placed around his neck and spurs put on by ser Polo Capello and ser Andrea Trevixan, knights, and then, accompanied by trombones and many companions, he went through the city to the house formerly belonging to the Duke of Ferrara, where together with the legate, his relative, he is lodged. He held a ball all that day for some patricians, and some days later he departed thence and returned to Brescia much satisfied.[65]

SODOMY

In the case above, the sexual crime was averted, and the social injury was redressed by exiling the perpetrators, proclaiming the sexual integrity of an heiress, and bestowing a knighthood on a provincial patrician. A type of sexual crime that could not be easily redressed and was treated with particular severity was sodomy. To some extent, acts of sodomy were considered more of a threat than rape, for those men who allowed themselves to be sodomized were considered by their society not only to have demeaned themselves but also to have violated the god-given sexual order of nature. During the War of the League of Cambrai, when such behavior was considered to contribute heavily to the sins of the city, the death penalty might be incurred, as in the following case of sodomitic rape.

March 22, 1510 (10:56)   I note that today someone called "Buzi"[66] was burned for having raped a son of the late officer Andrea, etc. [The penalty] was the result of the deliberation held yesterday in the Council of Ten.

---

64. The manuscript has *e cussì il principe lo fece cavalier;* the Fulin edition omits the phrase.

65. Within months of the sentencing of the culprits, their Martinengo relatives and their allies in the government and the military forces began to urge a reconsideration of the trial. See diaries, 26:40, 479; and ASV, CX, Criminali, reg. 2, fols. 237v, 239v *n.m.* Their first attempts failed, but they persisted, the "governador nostro" describing Contin or Camillo as a good servant, a courageous man, whose military company was suffering from not being paid. Diaries, 19 February 1519 (26:479). In December 1519 every one of the miscreants was pardoned. See fols. 247v–248v *n.m.* Contin, restored to his military command, was later accused of plotting with the emperor, imprisoned for fifteen months, and once again pardoned. See diaries, 33:563, 34:362 and 371, 35:184; and ASV, CX, Criminali, reg. 3, fol. 183r *n.m.*, 10 November 1523.

66. This name is suggestive. *Buggerare,* whose Venetian equivalent is *buzarar,* means "to de-

Sodomitic acts between consenting adults were harder to certify. Those involved were divided into the agents, or initiator *(agenti),* and those who permitted the act upon themselves, the passive parties *(pacienti).*[67] In 1516 the "agents" were to be induced by promises of absolution and monetary awards to identify their passive partners, which led to some ribald mockery by foreigners in Venice.

July 29, 1516 (22:386–87)   This morning a bill was announced at Rialto that passed yesterday in the Council of Ten. . . . The bill is the following: there are in this city men in their thirties, forties, fifties, and sixties who have themselves sodomized. For that reason, let it be approved that if the active parties accuse the passive parties [of acts committed] over the last five years, they will be absolved and will have 300 ducats from the criminal's goods or from the funds of the Council of Ten, and this within eight days' time, if these accusations are verified; [if the eight days are] exceeded, they will incur the penalty, etc., as is stated in the bill. This bill was of great importance and gave great attention to the city. When it was announced, I was at Rialto and heard it, and many foreigners laughed about it, saying that the old men have themselves worked over [*dicendo li vechii si fano lavorar*]. Thus this news will travel all over the world. Nevertheless, the most excellent Council of Ten decided it, so one must obey it and praise it.

Responses to this law did not always lead to conclusive guilt, however, and the following case, according to Sanudo, may even have involved a political vendetta.

August 12, 1516 (22:425)   This morning . . . ser Anzolo Tiepolo, of the Quarantia Criminal, was detained. The captain of the Council of Ten having thrown a cape over his head,[68] he was led into the chamber, and the appointed [judicial] committee came immediately to interrogate him. The Council of Ten without the zonta had decided yesterday to arrest him and accuse him of passive homosexual acts. It was said that ser Zuan Barbo made the accusation that he had worked Tiepolo over, and it was for this reason that the poor man was arrested. The judicial committee is composed of ser Andrea Baxadona, councillor, ser Domenego Capello, head of the Ten, ser Hironimo Contarini,

---

ceive" or "to have sodomitic intercourse with." See Boerio 1856, s.v. "buzarar," for the former meaning; and Durante and Turato 1975, s.v. "busarare/buzarare" for both.

67. See Labalme 1984, 225, for the legal distinctions between these two terms. The agent was usually considered the more reprehensible criminal.

68. One assumes that this was so that Angelo Tiepolo, himself a patrician member of the Quarantia Criminal, could not see his judges.

inquisitor, and ser Lorenzo Venier, university laureate and state attorney. After dinner they will question him again.

Sanudo was clearly on the side of "the poor man." The following excerpt explains why and suggests that in this case as in others, the charge of sodomy may well have been brought for political reasons.

August 13, 1516 (22:430)   The zonta of the Council of Ten having been excused, the simple council continued its meeting, but only for a short while. It should be known that the judicial committee appointed for ser Anzolo Tiepolo met this morning and again after dinner but found nothing, because it was all a piece of chicanery.[69]

The case continued through the next ten days. Anzolo Tiepolo confessed nothing, not even under torture; nor did his maidservant, who was also tortured.[70] But in the end, in spite of talk of pardon, he was banished for five years, as were commoners implicated in similar acts two years later:

January 9, 1518 (25:190–91)   *Item:* one Francesco, a wine porter, convicted of practicing sodomy with a woman, who is absent, was banished to the sodomites' boundaries [*ad confinia sodomitarum*].[71] If he returns, his head will be cut off, and his body will be burned. *Item:* a certain woman[72] convicted of being a procuress for sodomitic acts was condemned to being placed on a platform between the two columns and crowned[73] on Thursday, and then banished, etc.

---

69. Sanudo's word is *jotonia*. See Boerio 1856, s.v. "gioton," equivalent to the Italian *coglione* or the English slang *balls*. Sanudo also appears to use the term in the sense of "scam."

70. See diaries, 14, 19, 22 August 1516 (22:431, 446, 454); and ASV, CX, Criminali, reg. 2, fols. 179v, 181v, 182 *n.m.*

71. The Venetian laws defined these confines as beyond the Piave and Mincio rivers on the side of the land and the Quarnero (Kvarner) Gulf (which lies between Istria and Venetian Dalmatia) on the side of the sea. The Mincio, near Peschiera del Garda, is at the westward terminus of the Venetian land state, while the Kvarner Gulf, near Fiume, is at its eastward terminus. In 1492 the question arose whether Ravenna was inside or outside those boundaries, because the Mincio River changed its name there. Ravenna was declared beyond the Mincio and therefore habitable by exiled sodomites. ASV, CX, Miste, reg. 25, fol. 152v, 25 August 1492. For other cases, see Labalme 1984, 233n66.

72. The manuscript has *certa;* the Fulin edition omits it.

73. The judicial record refers to this "crown" as a "devil's mitre," sexual deviation being associated with diabolical influence. See ASV, CX, Criminali, reg. 2, fols. 211r–v *n.m.*, 4 January 1518. Cf. a case of incest in which the female culprit was crowned with a "mitre painted with devils" and, after due public exposure between the two pillars, perpetually banned from Venetian territories (diaries, 57:104–5).

Counterfeiting

In addition to crimes of treason, certain cases of murder, and sodomy such as described above, the Council of Ten dealt with acts of counterfeiting, which would weaken Venice's reputation for commercial probity.

January 9, 1518 (25:190)   Several prisoners' cases were expedited. One, named Cocha, was condemned to having his eye gouged out for having brought counterfeit coins to this city. He was also banished from the city and its territories with a price on his head; if he returns, his hand will be cut off, and he will be banished again.[74]

June 1, 1520 (28:571)   Hironimo di Pasin, who was absent but who was legitimately subpoenaed for counterfeiting, has been condemned to perpetual banishment from Venice and the surrounding area and from all the cities and territories of the Venetian dominion, both on the mainland and overseas, from here to the Menzo [Mincio] River and from here to the Gulf of Quarnero [Kvarner Gulf]. If at any time he is caught, he is to be taken between the two columns and have one eye gouged out and be banished again. And if he is caught a second time, he will have a hand cut off, and the person who catches him will have a reward of 1,000 *lire di pizoli*, with Hironimo's goods used to pay for the reward.[75]

Electoral Fraud

Other types of crime might be less seriously punished but were viewed no less seriously. Among these was electoral fraud. In a system of government in which elections were continuous and rivalries for positions intense, electoral fraud was as frequent as it was ardently condemned. In the following excerpt the one patrician clearly involved was tortured to discover the truth and then exiled, as were the *ballotini*, or ballot-box clerks.

August 21, 1496 (1:275–76)   I note that on August 18, by order of the Council of Ten, several members of the ducal staff whose job it was to carry the ballot boxes in the Great Council were arrested.[76] These men, Salvador Nocente and

---

74. The judicial record may be found in ASV, CX, Criminali, reg. 2, fol. 211v *n.m.*, 4 January 1518.

75. See ibid., reg. 3, fol. 78 *n.m.*, 31 March 1520, and fol. 82 *n.m.*, 1 June 1520. On *lire di pizoli*, see appendix A under "Money and Coinage."

76. The margin of the manuscript contains the following notation in red ink in Sanudo's hand: *scelus in comitjis perpetratum*, that is, "crime perpetrated in the committees." This would indicate that the diaries were to serve as a legal reference source. On the ballot-box clerks, see appendix B under "Governmental Terms," s.v. "ballotini."

Francesco Triuli, were discovered in a way that would take too long to relate; [they had found a means by] which they could help those whom they wished to get elected to offices in the Great Council. They were discovered by Zuan Battista Foscarini as follows: He had been elected to the Senate, and one of the ballot-box clerks said to him, "I helped you." And he knew nothing about it.

The organizer of this fraud was identified as the patrician Zuan Jacomo Bon. Arrested on his ship at Porto Pisano (he was a captain involved in the Venetian attempt to support Pisa against Florence), he was sent to Venice for judicial examination.

September 13, 1496 (1:303)   Finally, the proveditor of the fleet, having called the said captain to his galley, arrested him and sent him in chains over land to this city with [a guard of] eight crossbowmen who were in Pisa with the company of Sonzin Benzon. He was immediately called before a judicial committee and was subjected to several jerks of the rope. He was blamed for being the cause and the inventor of the scam [*jotonia*] that I described above, involving the ballot-box clerks and changing no votes to yes votes. Under examination he continued to deny it, although the truth was almost gotten out of him. Hieronimo Friso, one of the clerks, said to his face, "You made me do it." Yet he continued to deny it.

A few days later, the sentences were handed down and made public since the major elective body had been involved. Although Zuan Jacomo Bon had confessed nothing, Sanudo considered the evidence against him sufficient to warrant his punishment of strict confinement on the island of Cyprus.

September 18, 1496 (1:323–24)   On September 18 the sentences of Zuan Jacomo Bon and the three ballot-box clerks that were passed in the Council of Ten with the zonta on the 14th of this month were announced in the Great Council. First, the said Zuan Jacomo is sentenced to perpetual confinement in the city of Famagosta [Cyprus] with the provision that every day he must present himself to the Venetian prefecture. If he violates his confinement, he is to be captured and brought to the Strong Prisons,[77] where he will be kept for a year and then banished again, and this as many times as is required [*et*

---

77. The Preson Forti, which were better guarded and locked than the other cells. They are not to be confused with the Strong Prison, which was under the jurisdiction of the Ten. Scarabello 1979, 56. The prisons were described by a contemporary as "vermin-ridden" and closed by four doors. Ibid., 31, 56.

hoc tociens quociens]. It should be known that he was given seventeen jerks of the rope. He never confessed anything, but the evidence was very clear. If he violates his confinement, whoever catches him will have 3,000 lire from his possessions, which will be set aside for that purpose; and if they do not suffice, the reward will be paid from our Signoria's money. The sentence against him was made public because it was brought about by what happened regarding the Great Council.

The other participants in the scam, including the ballot-box clerk who manipulated the fraudulent system, also received sentences of banishment.

September 29, 1496 (1:338)   On the 29th of the present month, the sentence that had been decided upon by the Council of Ten with the zonta against Hieronimo Friso, who carried the ballot boxes, was read in the Great Council. He has been confined in perpetuity to Baffo, which is on the island of Cyprus, and is obligated to present himself to its military governor every day. And if he breaks his banishment and is caught and brought back in chains, the person who captures him is to have two thousand lire from the heads of the Council of Ten. When he has been brought to this city, he must stay locked in the Blind Prison[78] and live on bread and water for the rest of his days. This punishment is for his being essentially the inventor and initiator of the ballot-box crimes.[79]

Domestic Strife

Among the Sanudo's diary entries that read like tabloid news are those reporting unusual incidents of domestic strife. These incidents might be tragic or grotesque or comic, but they became the talk of the city and found their way into his record as "noteworthy." And sometimes he added his own sociological reflections, indicating lesson that might be drawn from the events.

April 17, 1515 (20:126)   Today at none a most heartrending event took place in this city, which should be recorded. That is, ser Hironimo di Mezo . . . wounded his father in the stomach with a sword. As a result of the wound,

---

78. The Orba, the Blind Prison, named for its lack of windows, was one of the prisons on the ground floor of the Ducal Palace. See Mutinelli 1851, 311; and Scarabello 1979, 12, 26–28, 31.

79. The judicial records for this trial are in ASV, CX, Miste, reg. 27, fols. 85v, 86, 87, 89v–90r, 93v *n.m.* According to this official record, Hieronymus Friso claimed that he was a *clericus,* in clerical orders, and thus had to be examined by the patriarch. But that did not protect him against the secular punishment of exile, also imposed on the other two *ballottini,* Salvador Nocente and Francesco Triuli, who were sent to Rettimo in Crete.

the father died. . . . All the same, he forgave his son. Moreover, when he gave his statement to the signore di notte, he said that he himself, not his son, had inflicted the wound. He did this to spare his son from banishment. However, the truth is that the son wounded him, and because of the wound the poor father died. Thus the entire city is full of this case, the like of which has not been seen here for many years, except for the case of Lodovico Fioravante, who was killed by his son Lodovico while he was listening to the sermon in the church of the Friars Minor [the Frari] on Holy Friday evening.[80] The son [Lodovico] later was given a safe conduct because of things that he had done in France benefiting the Venetian state and is [now] in this city.[81]

Sanudo continues under the same date with another unusual event, concluding that such deplorable events are caused by pardons too easily obtained by money.

Another noteworthy event took place on Sunday. There was a woman named Paula Cavrasecha, very beautiful and a courtesan. A paramour [*inamorato*] of hers, named ser Bernardo Grimani ——, seeing that she no longer wanted him but others, entered her house and took hold of her nose with his teeth and bit it off, so that she was given stitches. Such strange happenings are taking place in this city in these times. The reason is that every sorry miscreant hopes to rectify his crime with money and ransom himself from banishment.

Prostitutes were often involved in problems of domestic strife. In 1532 a patrician was discovered to have married two women, the first a prostitute, the second a patrician whose dowry he had begun to claim, perhaps leading to the exposure of his bigamy:

April 24, 1532 (56:95–96)   Today, after dinner, the Quarantia Criminal met. It is an unusual thing to have any council meet when the doge is out of the Ducal Palace. Ser Filippo Trun, the state attorney, introduced the case of ser Paulo da Canal, who is accused of having taken two wives. First he married a prostitute named ——"Balla le oche."[82] Then he married a sister of ser Bertuzi Valier —— months ago and had collected about 400 ducats of the dowry. The said ser Paulo was subpoenaed in Castello by his first wife, who obtained a judgment against the second [wife, affirming] that she [the first wife] was the

---

80. This same Fioravante—the son—would be a leader in a 1497 jailbreak, described below.

81. Here, service to the state was used to justify a pardon for the otherwise unforgivable crime of parricide. The priority of the public good outweighed private guilt.

82. A sobriquet meaning "Geese Dance."

true one. Therefore, the state attorney recommended that he be arrested and received a unanimous vote. [Ser Paulo] absented himself.[83]

Problems of Imprisonment

Exile was a convenient punishment because it solved the double-faceted problem of detention: where to put the prisoners and how to ensure their confinement. The following excerpt describes a nearly successful jailbreak by prisoners in Venice who could not complete their escape only because they lacked a boat, an incident that Sanudo also found "noteworthy."

August 5, 1497 (1:704–5)   It happened during the night in this city that a number of prisoners who were serving life sentences at prisons in Piazza San Marco — decided to escape together. They chose a captain; he was Lodovico Fioravante, who had his father killed[84] at the church of the Friars Minor on Holy Friday evening. The leaders were Marco Corner, "of the beard," serving a life sentence for sodomy, and Beneto Petriani, for thievery, and quite a few others. In the evening of the fourth, when the guards went to make their rounds of the prison, the prisoners had the chance to take them and disarm them. Thus they went from prison to prison,[85] breaking out. Gathering strength, they got as far as the very new prison and were very close to breaking out completely. Many bows and arms were kept there. And it happened that on that night two Saracens wanted to be the first to escape through a privy, and one escaped, and the other one drowned. The one who got away started to call for a boat in the night. One of the boats of the Council of Ten was passing, and when it stopped to pick him up, the [boatmen] began to wonder, since he was dark-skinned, if he was escaping, and they frightened him. From him they heard about the escape plot hatched by the prisoners.

The officials were called, and a strong guard was posted for the night. On the morning of the fifth, the heads of the Council of Ten were called: this month they are Cosma Pasqualigo, Nicolò da ca' da Pexaro, and Domenego

---

83. The court records of this case add a number of interesting details, among them that both wives were named Cecilia and that Paolo da Canal's crime was considered one of "deperdite audacie et iniquitatis . . . in contemptum legum et sacri matrimonii" (depraved audacity and iniquity . . . in contempt of the laws and holy matrimony). See ASV, Avogadori di Comun, Raspe, reg. 3667, fol. 20v *n.a.*, 28 May 1532. The sentence levied upon the bigamist was perpetual exile to Cyprus or lifetime service on Venetian ships.

84. In this excerpt Sanudo writes "che fe' amazar il padre," while in the excerpt above dated 17 April 1515 he writes "che fo amazato . . . da suo fiol."

85. Sanudo consistently uses *prexon*, which literally means "prison." But these are not distinct institutions, but sections within a complex.

Beneto.[86] Together with a number of officials, they went to the prison, and the prisoners were very stubborn. In the end, burning straw was used to force smoke through all the windows of the prison, so that the smoke suffocated them. The heads of the Council of Ten issued a decree that if on the third try they did not respond and show obedience, they would all be hanged by the neck. Thus Marco Corner was the first to surrender, and then the others. They were put back in their prisons with more care, and the guards were ordered to pay more attention. I decided to include this incident because it is noteworthy.[87]

Hindrances to Justice

DISORDER AND DELAY

Sanudo's concern that the laws be applied and not circumvented, misused, or misinterpreted had some foundation. The Venetian judicial system involved so many governmental bodies that there were bound to be delays, competing jurisdictions, difficulties of interpreting legal procedures, and attempts to purchase judicial relief. Sanudo reports several cases that illustrate these problems. In the following excerpt, the government sought to impose on the lower courts the same criteria as were followed in the higher courts (both criminal and civil) of the Forty with regard to when cases should be pleaded, how they should be remanded, which of the judges should not absent themselves, and other "excellent" measures.[88]

January 27, 1516 (21:479–80) [Statute proposed and passed by the Great Council upon the recommendation of the] heads of the Forty . . . :

Our Signoria is continually vigilant in regulating the councils, committees, and offices of our city. This is especially true in the administration of justice, where it is a question of the rights of the litigants, [and where our Signoria] exerts every care and study to find the means and the form to conclude litigation and save all parties the obstacles and causes that can draw out the process. In this way neither its citizens nor foreigners will lose their time and fortune in endlessly prolonged suits, which would also bring a very grave loss of their rights. These regulations and laws, in the prosecuting of cases before the councils of the Forty, are excellently and fully observed and executed without the slightest modification of, or threat to, justice, as everyone knows.

---

86. The heads of the Council of Ten rotated every month.

87. See Sanudo's entry for 19 August 1514 (18:445–48) for another jailbreak.

88. See Cozzi 1973, 316; 1980, 122ff.; and Gullino 1996a, 370–71, for other examples of attempted reform under Doge Andrea Gritti. See also diaries, 21:477.

But the cases that are argued before the Colegio de le Biave[89] suffer from much disorder and [are subject to much] damage because of the indifference of those whose obligation it is to come to the collegio to judge them. This must truly give grave offense to the Divine Majesty, and it is a situation that is entirely opposite to the intention of our Signoria, which has always had justice closer to its heart than anything else in the world.

On many occasions, and with a variety of means and ordinances, provisions have been made concerning this collegio, and little or no result has been seen from the bills dealing with it, because they have not been executed. It is therefore our moral duty, and most necessary, to make provisions concerning such disorder, which causes much harm both to our citizens and to foreigners.

Therefore, a bill is proposed, not superseding any of the laws and ordinances taken in the past relative to this body, that in the future those presiding over the collegio may not allow any case to be pleaded if they do not immediately proceed to its conclusion, continuing the second and third sessions according to the laws of the city. They must observe in all cases the procedure and order of trying the cases and giving counsel that are observed in our Quarantie Civil.

UNCLEAR JURISDICTIONS

In another case, competing jurisdictions provided a highly complicated situation in which Sanudo showed off his own legal learning, based on the records of legal decisions he had kept over many years. As he had said on an earlier occasion, "None of the secretaries knew how to retrieve the law, and I found it and therefore record it in my diaries" (June 20, 1516; 22:301). But what the following case also shows is the knowledge of legal procedures on the part of the criminals' relatives who intervened through the state attorneys and the Council of Ten.

September 14, 1520 (29:181–82)   I note that today, in Piazza San Marco, justice was to be administered to four people. First, an eye was to be gouged out of someone, and that was done. Then two young thieves were to be hanged for having robbed a woman of about 120 ducats, and it is a good profit.[90] . . . And something worth noting happened. Once all three had been led out, the first one had his eye gouged out, and the two thieves were waiting in the square at the foot of the gallows to be hanged. While they were waiting, some of

---

89. For the Collegio alle Biave, see appendix B under "Governmental Terms."

90. After "120 ducats," the manuscript has *et ei bº fruto,* which could mean "and it is a good profit." The Fulin edition omits this sentence.

their relatives went to the state attorneys. . . . They told them that in justice these thieves should not die because the Zudexi [Giudici] di Proprio[91] had been of three opinions concerning their fate, that is, ser Alvise Zusto thought their eyes should be gouged out and a hand cut off; ser Michiel Basadona thought one eye should be gouged out and one hand cut off; ser Andrea Dandolo thought they should be hanged by the neck until[92] they died. According to the law, when the judges are of three different opinions, they are to go to the doge, and whichever sentence he agrees with is the one that applies. They did that, and the doge agreed with Dandolo's sentence, and for this [reason] they are to be hanged. But their relatives say that that law applies in civil matters, not criminal ones, and that the doge has no freedom in criminal cases. For this reason, they have sent Valerio, an assistant of the Ten, to suspend the hangings for one hour. One of the criminals had already mounted the stairs of the gallows when word of the suspension arrived. They were then returned to prison. Next the state attorneys extended the suspension for two days because they wanted to take the matter to the Forty, eliminating the doge's decision and having the three Zudexi di Proprio come with their three opinions to the Forty, who will read the documents in the case and make their own decision. . . .

The entire city thought it unprecedented that this had been done so late [in the process], because these thieves had been sentenced days ago. And so that those who come after us may understand the cause for the suspension, I will write the law below. It is in the Correction to the Civil Statute and says that the doge has this freedom in civil sentences but not in any death sentence. The letter of the law is this: . . . "And if it is the case that the judges of an odd-numbered group that already exists or that shall exist have a diversity of opinions in their sentences, so that a majority does not agree upon one opinion but their opinions number three or more, they must come to the doge and tell him what their consciences say, and whatever sentence the doge agrees to will be the sentence in the case."[93]

INCORRECT PROCEDURE

A few years after this case, in 1523, Andrea Gritti became doge, and he attempted to establish more consistency and efficiency in the legal practices of the city, largely without success. Nor were his own actions in one legal case beyond criticism:

---

91. On the Giudici di Proprio, see appendix B under "Governmental Terms."

92. The manuscript has *sì che;* the Fulin edition has *sinchè.*

93. Sanudo then copies the 1346 law (29:184–85) and four days later reports that the Quarantia decided that each of the three thieves should lose an eye and have a hand amputated (18 September 1520; 29:193–94).

August 19, 1532 (56:775)   In the morning, ser Vetor Grimani, the procurator, came before the Collegio complaining of a judgment rendered on the 16th in the morning and published by the doge. It was against Vicenzo Bembo, the illegitimate son of the late ser Francesco Bembo, who was the chancellor of the Lower Chancellery, and it was posted by the doge without either summoning Bembo or giving him a hearing. Moreover, the doge had chosen in Bembo's place Antonio di Marsilio, the custodian of the Procuratia de ultra, who is certainly a worthy man. Here Grimani spoke in stentorian tones, saying that His Serenity the doge had raced through the matter at top speed without hearing and taking into consideration the justifications [of the accused] regarding the charges against him, even though Vicenzo Bembo had been approved at one time by the most excellent Collegio. Grimani further said that Our Lord God, when he wished to condemn Adam, set this example: he went about the earthly paradise saying, "Adam, Adam, where are you?" [*Adam, Adam ubi es?*] And this is practiced by every administrator of justice, who never condemns anyone without first summoning him to defend himself. Grimani also said other things. The doge replied that the chancellors of the Lower Chancellery and their entire staffs and the canons of San Marco are under his jurisdiction and that he hires them and fires them as he pleases. And if he did wrong, the city has its procedures and [Grimani should follow them by] going to the state attorneys.

PRESSURES AND PROCEDURES FOR PARDON

The above delays, competitive bodies, and confusions were not the only hindrances in the legal structure. Justice was also thwarted by the procedure of *gratie,* pardons that could be had for money; for good service to the state, such as the killing of an outlaw; for military service;[94] for financial loans; or owing to the pressure of powerful relatives. Such *gratie* at times belied the vaunted impartiality of Venetian justice. Yet it has been argued that such pardons may also be viewed as introducing a needed flexibility into the judicial system.[95] That such flexibility was exploited is not surprising, although the persistence and degree of pressure was in some cases remarkable, as in the case of Zuan Emo below.

The case first appears in Sanudo's records in October 1516 (23:33, 51–52, 87–90, 93–94). Zuan Emo, former state treasurer, was accused of stealing as much as 28,000 ducats from the city's treasury. Charged with being "seditious," a "tyrant," and the "worst administrator, committing private and public theft"

94. See above, "Abduction in Brescia," for an example of a *gratia* granted on the grounds of previous good service to the state.
95. Romano 1983.

(23:88–89), he was banished to Crete. Thereupon his father, Zorzi Emo, began an intensive campaign over the next six years, offering monetary compensation, volunteering to resign his procuratorship, and making tearful speeches and urgent pleas (he wore a beard in mourning for his absent son) in the attempt to get his son's sentence lifted or commuted (24:585, 633). Each entry in the diaries outlines the offers made, such as this one, one year after the original crime surfaced and the ban was declared:

November 27–28, 1517 (25:112, 113–14)   After dinner there was a meeting of the Council of Ten with the zonta. The relatives of ser Zuan Emo tried to negotiate a deal, believing that the heads of the Ten wished to consider his pardon, as . . . one of the heads promised to do in the last Council of Ten meeting. However, there was no time and nothing was done ——.

[The next day] the bill, or rather pardon, of ser Zuan Emo, son of ser Zorzi, knight and procurator, was read [in the meeting of the Council of Ten with the zonta]. He is in exile, and his father is petitioning in his name to loan our Signoria 6,000 ducats in cash for two years . . . or else to give the Signoria 2,000 ducats outright so that he may have his banishment lifted and be allowed to return home. There are other clauses involving the payment of whatever money he took from the Signoria, and his father will give surety of this in the amount of 8,000 ducats.

These efforts extended into the following summer, but to no avail. Indeed, Sanudo thought the intense lobbying was counterproductive (March 18, 1517; 24:82). By August 26, 1518, it was declared that any further proposals would be considered against the law, and their proponent would be fined 1,000 ducats (25:613–14). For a year, Zuan Emo's cause is not mentioned. His name was read forth each March as one of the publicly cited thieves, but in his case, unlike in the thirteen others mentioned on March 13, 1519 (27:46–48), Sanudo does not explain the crime, because it was notorious, "per esser cosa nota." That the years 1518–20 were unusually free of pressing military expenses made the continuing monetary offers of Zuan Emo's father more resistible.[96] The discussions continued, but the opposition of the state attorneys remained firm.

By 1521 Zuan Emo had returned to Venice and was hiding in the church of San Zane Polo (Santi Giovanni e Paolo), where he received visitors, including Sanudo (July 7, 1521; 31:28–29). Two months later a decree was issued charging priors who were hiding outlaws to declare the criminals' presence within three days or themselves suffer pain of perpetual banishment (September 24, 1521; 31:459–60).

---

96. Mallett and Hale 1984, 318.

Amnesty was proposed, and the vote went against it (January 10, 1522; 32:343–34). But by early September 1523 the opposition had weakened. On September 3 and 5 the vote failed, but on September 7 it passed, perhaps because one of the opposing state attorneys had just accepted the *podestaria* of Padua and was absent (September 3, 5, 7, 1523; 34:393, 395, 397). On September 26, 1523, Zuan Emo was seen in the Basilica of San Marco (34:456); by November he had moved back into his house, which had been rented out (November 17, 1523; 35:202); and by December 27 he had resumed his place in the Great Council (35:302). The seven-year effort to reinstate Zuan Emo was finally successful.

The following two cases had more expeditious outcomes for the criminals involved. On the same day that Zuan Emo returned to the Great Council, December 27, 1523, a fracas took place in the scuola of San Giovanni Evangelista that led to a young noble's death (December 27, 1523; 35:203). A year later, on December 4, 1524, Piero Trivixan, the man held responsible for that young noble's death and punished by exile, was voted into the Great Council as one of the Barbarelli. This was a custom by which a number of patricians who had reached the age of eighteen but were still some years short of the legal age of admission to the Great Council were chosen by lot on December 4 (St. Barbara's Day) for early admission to that body. That this could happen to a young man still in exile for murder indicates how certain his pardon was believed to be.

January 18, 1525 (37:448)   [The Council of Ten with the zonta] took under consideration the pardon of ser Piero Trivixan, banished by the Forty for homicide. He has made a donation of 300 ducats [to the state]. It was approved. . . . The said ser Piero has had his banishment lifted; this [past] year, while he was still in exile, he was elected by golden ballot on St. Barbara's Day for admission to the Great Council.

A year later there was another case of lifted exile for a murderer. This time the quid pro quo involved the capture and killing of a wanted criminal peasant.

December 24, 1526 (43:502)   This morning the Quarantia Criminal lifted the banishment of ser Francesco Zen, who killed ser Lorenzo di Prioli.[97] This was for his having captured a peasant who had been banished in his absence from [Venice's] cities and territories, with a price on his head, by ser Jacomo Corner, then governor of the Patria of Friuli. [The peasant] was living in the

---

97. A few months earlier, in April, these two young patricians had fought over women and wounded each other, and Priuli had died two days later of a severe abdominal wound (diaries, 41:189).

Trivixan countryside, and this ser Francesco called him out of his house in a very friendly way one night, then tied him up and cut his head off. He took it to ser Alvixe Bragadin, civil and military governor of Treviso; once it was certified as authentic, ser Zuan Alvise Navaier, the state attorney, went to the Quarantia and petitioned for Zen's absolution, as in the bill [of banishment]. There were 35 yes votes and 2 no votes; thus the banishment was lifted.

Privilegium Fori

Particularly awkward for the functioning of justice were those cases involving priests and tonsured clerics, who were normally tried in church courts. This special procedure was viewed with alarm by the doge and the Collegio, for it encouraged young patricians to take minor orders in order to circumvent secular legal procedures. Sanudo himself condemned this practice as undermining the integrity of the law:

September 26, 1520 (29:206)   I note that the gallows are still standing. They were supposed to be used to hang a thief who killed seven people, but the [execution] has been stayed. He is a priest, and he never said this in any of his testimony,[98] so the execution has been suspended.

But when they heard this, the doge and the Collegio summoned the papal legate and the vicar of the patriarch, complaining of these things and saying that everyone is becoming a priest [to avoid punishment for their crimes]. They said that they wanted to see if it was the truth and [if so,] whether the matter should proceed. In addition, those two thieves were supposed to be hanged, but then the Forty decided that they should have an eye gouged out and a hand cut off; the execution was stayed because they are men of the cloth. Thus justice is not done.

For this reason, more than fifty young patricians on various occasions have gone to the papal legate asking to be given minor orders, and he has complied. It is a bad thing, and harmful to tolerate it.[99]

Social Clout and Political Expediency

Hindrances, delays, deviations, and pardons: if equity remained the ideal in the Venetian system of justice, social position remained its main variable. In No-

---

98. The manuscript reads *in alcun suo constituto;* the Fulin edition has *in alcun constituto.*

99. For other contemporary cases of disputed jurisdiction between civil and ecclesiastical courts, see diaries, 20:40; 29:45, 256, 282; 34:436–37; 41:196.

vember 1499 Antonio Grimani, whose barometric career would be legendary, suffered the fierce opprobrium of the city for the great naval defeat at Zonchio, for which he was held responsible. On that occasion he was brought to Venice in chains to be tried by the Great Council. And the entire city said he deserved "a thousand gallows" upon him because of the disaster they blamed on him.[100] But by the spring he was still alive in prison, awaiting sentencing, and not without the consolation of his friends.

June 8, 1500 (3:380)   It should be noted that the trial of Antonio Grimani is being conducted in the Great Council by the state attorneys; nonetheless, the other evening a beautiful serenade was sung for him at the prison by all the virtuosi.

That trial ended in Grimani's exile. Nine years later, a month after Venice's defeat at Agnadello, Grimani was forgiven. His position, his family, his wealth, and his influence through the position at the papal court of his cardinal son, Domenico, as well as the rivalries between the different judicial bodies of the government, worked to his advantage. Here again, as in other cases, public service was the justification for a reversal of his sentence.

June 17, 1509 (8:411–12)   After dinner there was a meeting of the Great Council. And before the proposal to hold elections had been announced as usual, ser Vicenzo Grimani . . . and other relatives gathered together in one group and appeared before the Signoria to ask them to put to the vote the bill that was formulated yesterday concerning his father. And so, because of the merits of ser Antonio Grimani in these times and those of the most reverend cardinal, his son, and those of his family, and because the state attorneys have invalidated the [earlier] trial in which this ser Antonio was condemned, for it was done outside their mandate, it was proposed that this ser Antonio, by the authority of this Great Council, be permitted to enter this city and live here as one of our patricians . . . and that his condemnation to exile be rescinded. And his relatives having been excluded from the chamber, the vote was put: 4 undecided, 200 against, 1,261 for, and the proposal carried.[101] . . . A courier was dispatched to Rome, and today ser Vicenzo left for Ancona to meet his

---

100. Diaries, 3:47. See chapter 1 for Antonio Grimani's replacement as captain general; this chapter, above, for his condemnation to prison and exoneration ten years later; and chapter 2 for his election as doge in 1521 and Sanudo's personal connection to him.

101. That the large total of 1,465 attended this meeting of the Great Council for this matter was owing to the Grimani relatives having lobbied for the votes in advance. See Cozzi 1973, 299.

aforesaid father, with the greatest joy. . . . So that the stars have taken a turn that favors this family, which suffered the nine-year exile of its most prominent citizen, Antonio Grimani. He is a great enemy of our doge, who was his rival. Had Grimani not been exiled, the present doge would never have been elected.

Twelve years later, on July 6, 1521, two weeks after the death of his former rival, Doge Lunardo Loredan, Antonio Grimani was elected doge.[102]

102. See chapter 2 under "A Doge's Election" for Grimani's election. For a discussion of the factors involved in Grimani's naval defeat, see Lane 1973b, 359–60. The vicissitudes of fortune experienced by Grimani would become a popular topos in Venetian culture. See Giannetto 1985, 223–24.

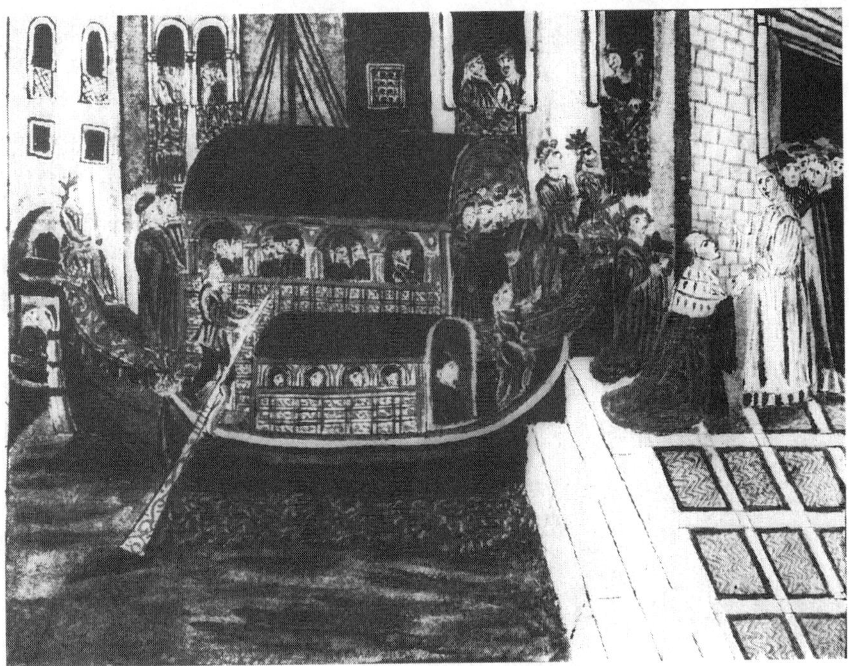

The Bucintoro before 1526, with statues of Venezia-Justice on both the prow and the stern and a *peota* at the side. Museo Correr, Venice.

Overleaf: The site for executions on the Piazzetta, detail from Jacopo de' Barbari, *View of Venice,* woodcut, 1500. Photo by Osvaldo Bohm, 912.

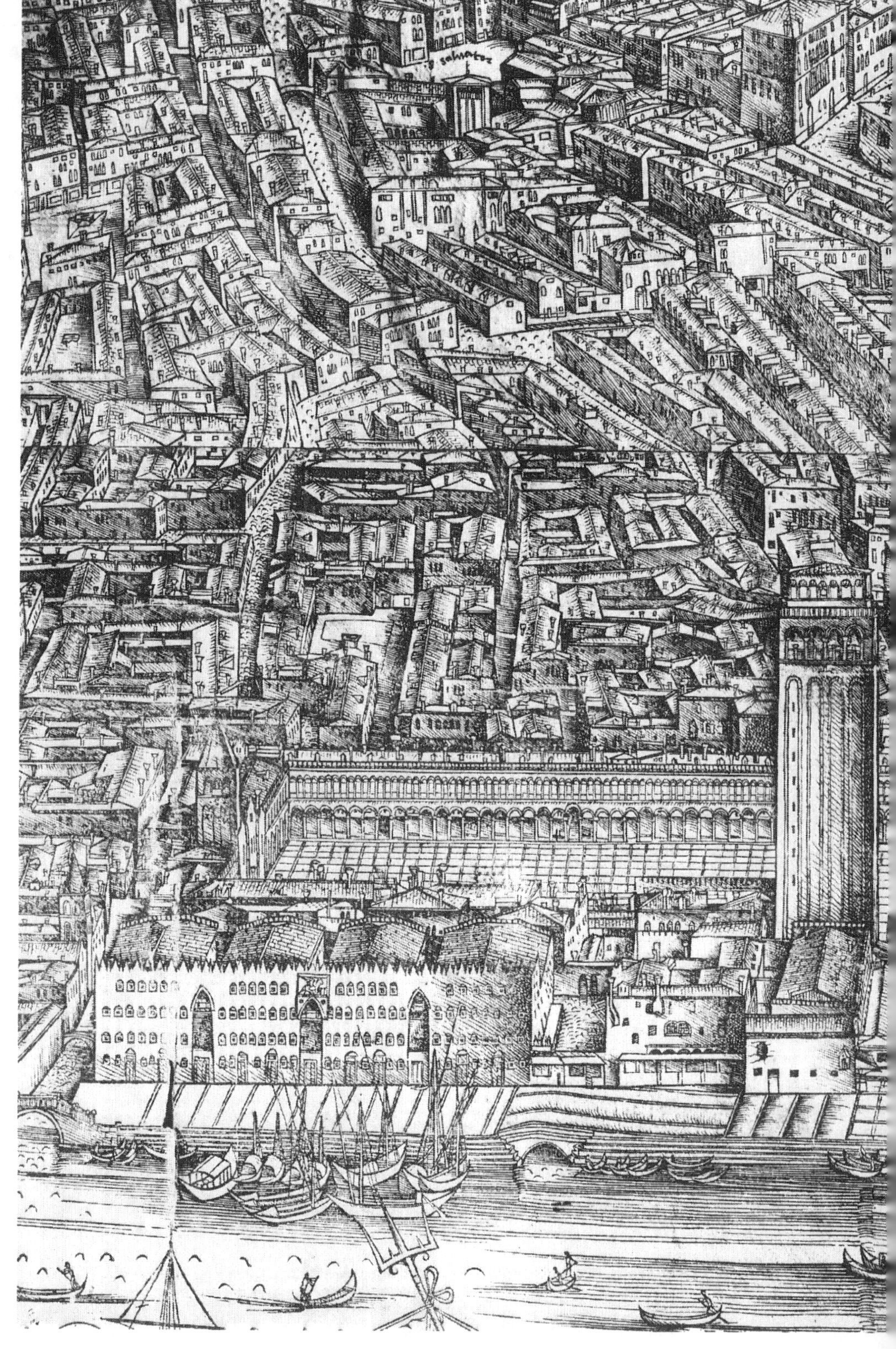
saluatar

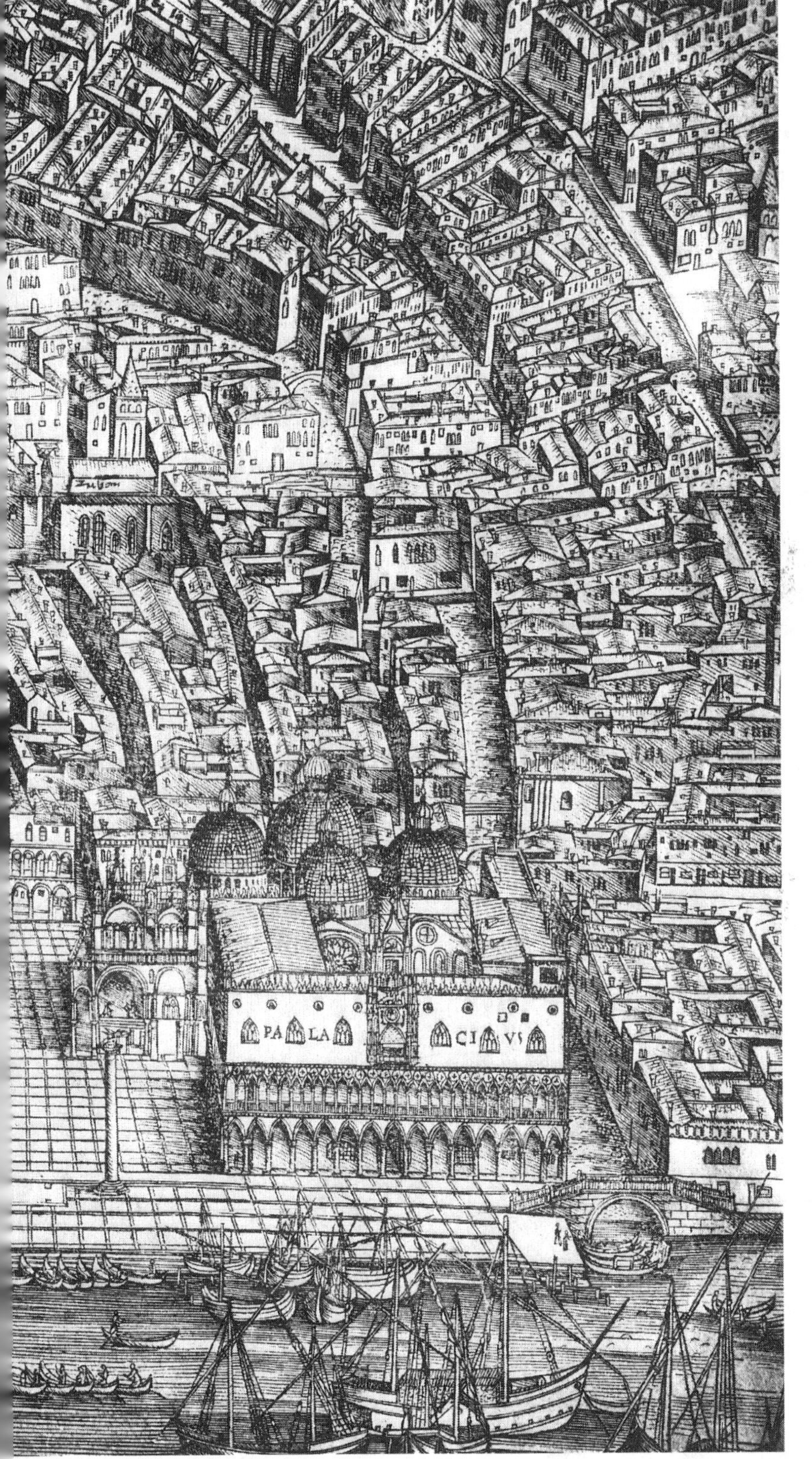
PA LA CI VS

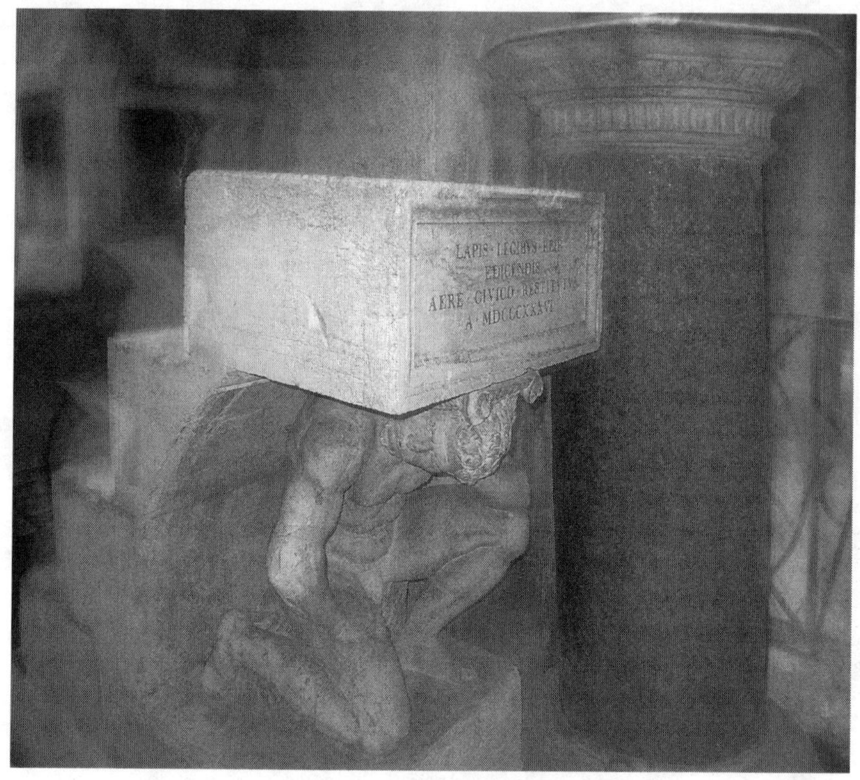

Colonna de Bando and Gobbo di Rialto supporting a staircase on the Campo di Rialto where announcements, proclamations, and sentences were read. Photo courtesy of P. F. Brown.

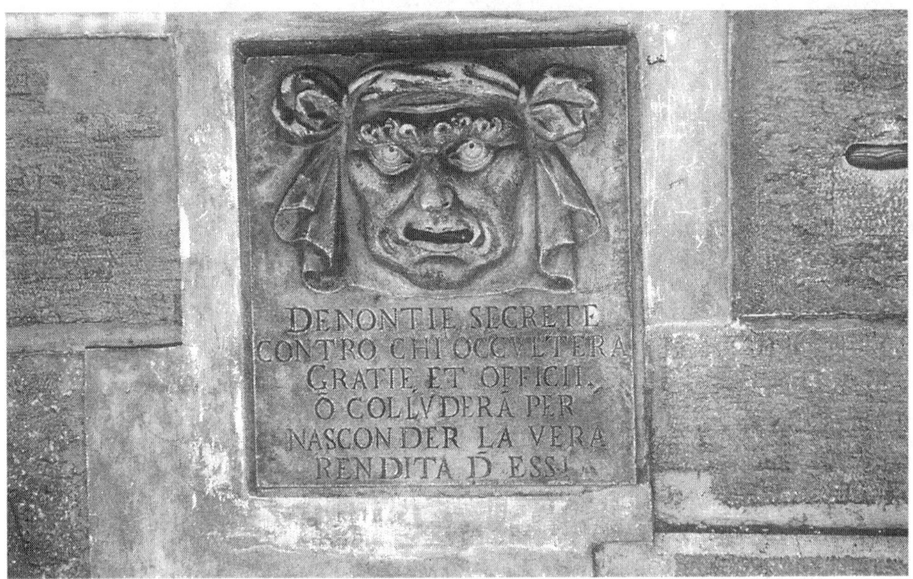

Buca di segrete denuncie: mail slot in the wall of the Palazzo Ducale where secret denunciations were deposited for the Council of Ten. Photo courtesy of P. F. Brown.

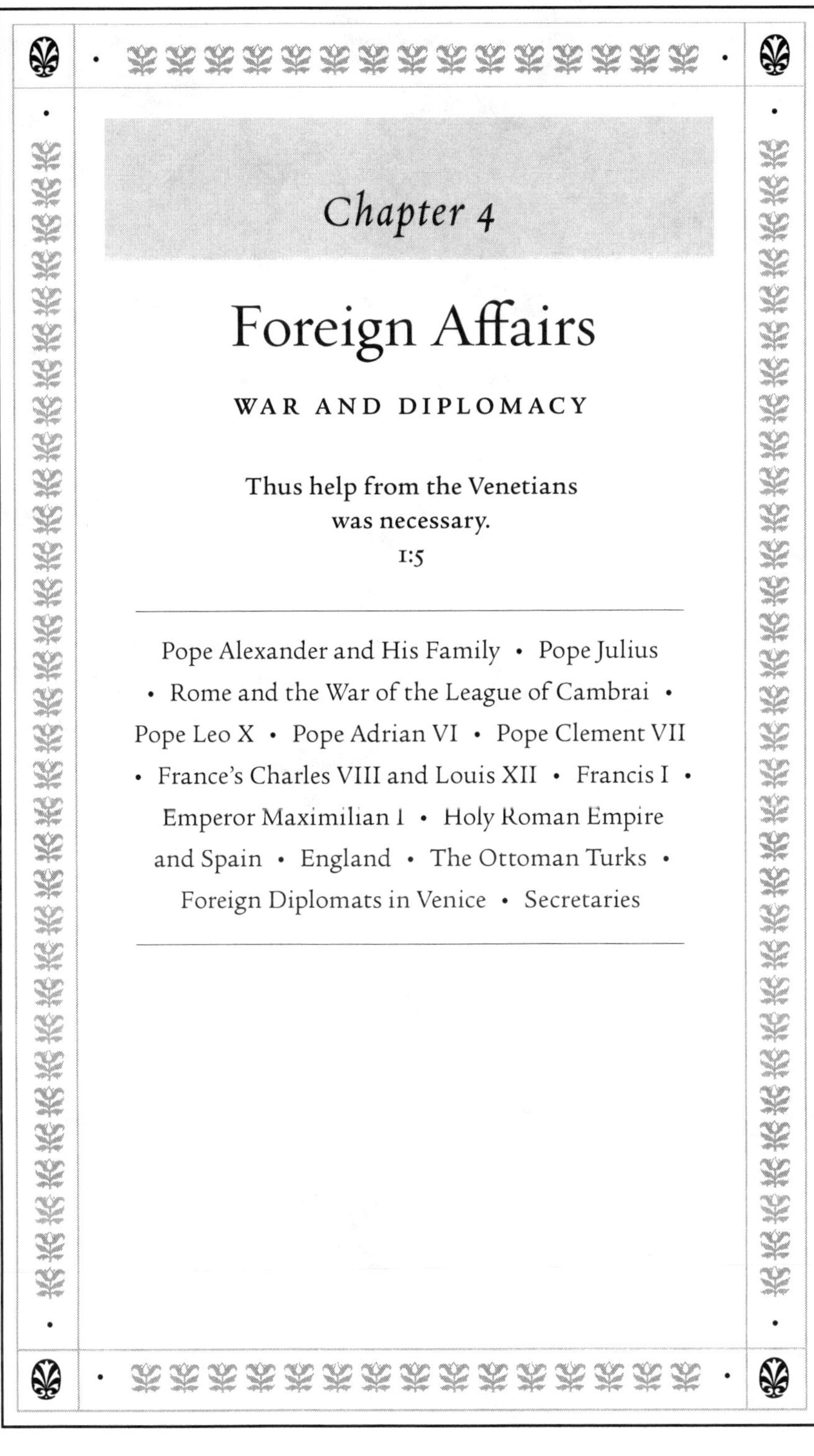

Chapter 4

Foreign Affairs

WAR AND DIPLOMACY

Thus help from the Venetians
was necessary.
1:5

Pope Alexander and His Family • Pope Julius
• Rome and the War of the League of Cambrai •
Pope Leo X • Pope Adrian VI • Pope Clement VII
• France's Charles VIII and Louis XII • Francis I •
Emperor Maximilian I • Holy Roman Empire
and Spain • England • The Ottoman Turks •
Foreign Diplomats in Venice • Secretaries

From their start in the midst of the Italian Wars, Sanudo's diaries were intended as the raw material for a history of foreign affairs, with "foreign" including all the non-Venetian Italian states, as well as France, the Holy Roman Empire, Spain, Portugal, England, and the Islamic lands of Egypt and the Near East. The Latin title Sanudo gave this account was, *De successu rerum Italiae* (The unfolding events of Italy). He included the many ultramontane powers engaged in the Italian Wars and the threats from powers such as the Turks that impinged, sometimes force-fully, on the Italian scene. His record was based very largely on reports from Venetian diplomatic representatives and merchants in foreign countries, all over Italy, Europe, and the Islamic world. These Venetian diplomatic representatives and merchants were everywhere at work, observing, consulting, maneuvering on behalf of the Venetian Republic, and enhancing its power as a player on the international scene. Most of their reports went to the Venetian government, but many went to relatives or friends or business associates, and copies of these often fell into Sanudo's hands, providing him a record from which he intended to compose a history.

As quoted in chapter 1, in the document dated January 1, 1496, he said at the beginning of the diaries: "I promise my readers that at a later date, when I have more leisure, I will rewrite this book in a different style, but for the time being I will set down each day the news is circulating, beginning with the pontificate of Alexander VI" (1:6). For this reason and because of the central diplomatic role of the papacy, the "foreign affairs" treated in this section begin with the Papal States, whose successive rulers offer some introduction to the politics of the Italian peninsula and its invaders during the period of Sanudo's diaries. Milan, Florence, and Naples, highly individualized city-states, were also of great dip-lomatic importance, each following an independent policy carefully tracked by Venetian observers, especially Milan, which shared a common, much-disputed boundary with Venice. But they will not receive special treatment here, nor will the smaller Italian powers such as Ferrara and Mantua, in which there was keen interest and whose ambassadors often appear in the diaries, occasionally as individual representatives of their respective states but more often as part of the diplomatic corps in Venice.

Following the Papal States, the principal European powers, France and the Holy Roman Empire, will then be treated, as Venice, as well as the other Italian city-states, oscillated between them until the predominance of imperial strength became formalized in the Peace of Bologna in 1530. England, important to Ven-ice as a trading partner and as a pendant in the Franco-imperial scales, also re-ceived Sanudo's attention, but in a less concentrated and continuous way. Spain, which until 1519 and the accession of Charles V was an independent power, long involved in the Kingdom of Naples through the kings of Aragon, will serve here as a window on the New World as it was being discovered and described. And lastly, we devote a section to the Ottoman Turks, whose increasing domination of the eastern Mediterranean and whose incursions into the Balkans, Hungary, and Friuli made them very much a European presence, a threat to Christianity, a preoccupation of the papacy, and a particular challenge to Venice's overseas commercial empire. Some excerpts follow on the activities of the representatives of these nations in Venice, and a look at the secretaries and cryptographers of the Venetian government concludes this chapter.

These soundings, selected from the great number of materials dealing with foreign affairs that found their way into the diaries, do not form, either in Sanudo's record or here, a coordinated history. Some excerpts do indeed report on the dramatic events that shaped this period. Some focus entirely on magnificent receptions and the accouterments of power, which were important in assessing foreign nations and national self-esteem. Some contain more gossip than anything else, for Sanudo thought that gossip had its own value. Some provide character sketches, the character of political leaders being considered a key part of political analysis.

Using Sanudo's diaries together with other sources of the period, some modern historians have traced the transformation of Venetians' confidence in their independent political position into a circumspect acknowledgment of the secondary role Venice came to play in the struggles of the larger nation-states and empires.[1] Sanudo, so close to these events, does not himself draw that conclusion. To him, as to his fellow Venetians and most of their European contemporaries, the importance of Venice, with the largest standing army in Europe and its large fleets patrolling the Mediterranean, remained paramount, no different in the early 1530s than in the late 1490s, when Venice's aid or enmity figured in the Italian Wars. So Sanudo continued to collect what came his way, seeing all of it as raw material for the history he hoped to write. His instinct to include everything, along with the rawness of the material itself, is what makes the diaries so appealing.

Pope Alexander and His Family

In Sanudo's day, not only were Rome and the Papal States at the geographical center of the Italian peninsula but the papal court was the fulcrum of Italian diplomacy.[2] For this reason, there had been a resident Venetian embassy in Rome

---

1. See Finlay 1999; and Gleason 2000.

2. For an introduction to the complex role of the papacy and the interests of the other major Italian city-states in Charles VIII's invasion, see Mallett 1995.

since 1431, and Sanudo often identified letters from Rome as "Ab Urbe," or from The City, as if Rome, with its imperial heritage, represented the quintessential model of civilization. In his fifty-eight volumes Sanudo deals often with events at the papal court during the pontificates of Alexander VI (1492–1503), the Borgia pope, father to Cesare and Lucrezia Borgia; Pius III (1503); Julius II (1503–13), the warrior pope; Leo X (1513–21), the son of Lorenzo de' Medici; Adrian VI (1522–23), the Dutch pope; and Clement VII (1523–34), the second Medici pope.

So politically powerful was the Roman Catholic Church's influence considered by Venetian rulers that within Venice every effort was made to insulate the government from its reach and to control its personnel. The patriarchal church was on an easternmost island at some distance from the governmental center of San Marco; patricians whose family members held high positions in the Roman Catholic Church were considered *papalisti,* that is, subject to papal influence, and therefore were excluded from voting on matters relating to the church; and Venetian bishops, unlike their counterparts in other European countries, were ineligible for political office.

Externally, the most experienced and skilled Venetian diplomats were sent to Rome, and their reports swell the pages of the diaries because the pope's every move or inclination was of interest. Thus, after the brief introduction justifying his work, the first volume of Sanudo's diaries opens with the ambitious plans of Alexander VI to reroute the Tiber River through the Castel Sant'Angelo for reasons of safety and convenience. This was four years into his papacy and two years since the French invasion had initiated the Italian Wars. No background is provided: the initial passages of this excerpt remind the reader that Sanudo had completed his own book on "the French war in Italy," and he seems to have felt either that this recent history was too familiar to need iteration or that it could be supplied later, when he rewrote his text. But the excerpt illustrates the insecure position of a pope threatened not only by enemies within Rome but also by the now uncertain fortunes of the Italian peninsula and the financial stringencies imposed on the papacy by the current wars.

January 1, 1496 (1:6–7)   In Rome, the pope continued to fortify and rebuild the Castel Sant'Angelo. His intention was, through changing the surrounding walls, towers, and moats, to have the Tiber River flow through [the fortress]. But this plan had no chance of success; it has become widely known that over the course of construction this pope would have to spend about 80,000 florins on it. He often rode around to view this work.

His ill humor was increased by the fact that the French were no longer coming to Rome to seek bulls for benefices, [whereas] he had previously derived a large income from that region and the Gallic nation, and so the church was suffering a great loss. Nevertheless, Pope Alexander remained loyal to the League.[3]

The cast of foreign representatives at the papal court is then introduced by the names by which they were known, not always the proper names they bore. And included was some news about cardinal legates and their financial situations:

[At that time], the Venetian ambassador to His Holiness was Hironimo Zorzi, knight; the Milanese ambassador was don Stefano Taverna, who very much wanted to be made a cardinal—although he had not taken holy orders—with the help of Vice-Chancellor Ascanio [Sforza], who has been able to obtain anything from this pope. From Spain there was dom Garcilasso de la Vega, and from Naples, don Girolamo Sperandio, university laureate. The ambassador from the king of the Romans at that time was dom Cristoforo Sorovestener.[4]

And it should be noted that this year Cardinal Curzense[5] was the legate to Fuligno [Foligno], and Cardinal de Luna,[6] of Pavia, was the legate to Terni, whereas in earlier times bishops used to be the legates, and now there are these two cardinals because they are poor [and need the income]. And it happened that on the feast of San Silvestro [December 31], after Mass in Rome, the pope suffered a collapse and was carried into the palace, where for twenty-three hours he remained in a feverish paroxysm. But soon after he was given medications, he recovered. Moreover, the plague was nipping [*pizegava*] in Rome, and those who stayed in the city did so with some trepidation.

The diaries then continue with a survey of events in Genoa, Lyons, Mantua, Pisa, Florence, and Naples, as the various threads of Italian political life lead the diarist on. What had begun as a grand survey lapses into daily reports, copies of letters, the raw material from which the diarist intended to form his history. Again and again he returns to what was happening in Rome, reported back to Venice through ambassadorial or private correspondence to which Sanudo had access.[7] Some accounts that Sanudo records concern matters of state; some fall

---

3. The league formed after Charles VIII's invasion that had successfully expelled the French king from Italy after the battle of Novara in 1495.

4. For Ascanio Sforza, who was suspected of murder, see below, n. 13; the king of the Romans was the emperor-elect, Maximilian; Sorovestener is listed in the index to the Fulin edition also as Scrofsteu and Scroften.

5. That is, Cardinal Raimondo Pérault of Gürch.

6. Bernardino Lunati.

7. Much of the existing history of the Italian and European powers is based on·what Sanudo reports from these letters and on his copies and summaries of official documents for which no other copies are extant.

into the category of colorful gossip gleaned from more private letters, copies of which he had seen, especially concerning this Borgia pope's personal life. An example of the latter is the following, written six months after Sanudo began his record, which describes a tragic event in the turbulent family history of the Borgia family: the murder of Juan Borgia, Duke of Gandia, a beloved son among the progeny of Alexander VI. It was included in a letter of June 17, 1497, written to a gentleman in Ravenna by a cleric in Rome.[8]

June 24, 1497 (1:658–59)   On the evening of Wednesday the fourteenth, his lordship the Duke of Gandia, who had recently been given Benevento, Terracina, Pontecorvo, etc. [in fief], was amusing himself by riding around Rome on a mule, accompanied by a groom, as was his custom. He sent his groom to fetch his arms; in the interim an acquaintance of the duke's appeared and was allowed by him to ride behind the saddle. When the groom returned, his master was nowhere to be found. The mule was found in Rome, going toward home,[9] with only one stirrup strap, the other having been cut. On Thursday the situation remained unchanged, with very few people knowing about it. But that evening and the following night a concerted search was made. By Friday morning it was relatively certain that the duke was not to be found. A Slavic boatman who during the night was watching his boats on the bank leading to Santa Maria del Popolo, where there [are] a St. Jerome[10] and a fountain on the bank of the river, said that Wednesday evening at perhaps four hours after sunset two soldiers arrived at that out-of-the-way spot. They looked around for a while, and after quite some time someone [rode up] on a beautiful white charger carrying a gilded dagger. Then, from the bridge in the place I have described, *unum in Tiberim funus dejicitur,* a corpse was thrown into the Tiber.[11] A voice then was heard to say, "Has he gone under, that is, has he drowned?" And someone answered, "Yes, sir." Finally, on Friday several boatmen set about dragging the river with many grappling hooks and other similar instruments. At midday, as we were returning from the scripture reading [of the divine office], the body was found, to the amazement of all. The entire city was shocked. Indeed, it seemed almost as if public mourning had been declared. Everyone returned home filled with fear, and the shops were hastily closed.

---

8. One of a number of letters copied into or summarized in the diaries that describe the incident, including a report from Nicolò Michiel, the Venetian ambassador (1:651–52), and official notices from the pope to the Duke of Milan and the Venetian Signoria (1:657–63). Each added or varied certain details.

9. The manuscript appears to have *a casa,* "toward home"; the Fulin edition has *a caso,* "wandering about."

10. A St. Jerome statue or shrine.

11. The sentence in Latin is repeated in Italian.

The body was taken in a small boat up the Tiber to the fortress [of Sant'Angelo]. There it was washed, readied, and clothed in brocade. Meanwhile, I was on the bridge, always eager for news, and I heard a howling and crying of many people such as I had never heard before. I believe that the pope's voice was among them, for one person cried loudly. It is believed that His Holiness will suffer terrible grief, because that son was truly his right eye, in whom he placed his hope of progeny and glory [*in quo spes prolis erat et gloriae*]. Last evening, which was Friday, after a [procession] of many torches[12] and infinite wailings and weepings, [his body], covered with brocade, almost more handsome than when he was alive, was carried with all the traditional ceremony from the fortress to Santa Maria del Popolo, and there was enormous sorrow and compassion for the poor lord. It is said that he has nine or ten wounds; but the main thing is that his throat was cut, an unheard-of and stunning event. Even stranger is that there is no one who can conceive the motive or the author of such a deed, although someone says that the pope immediately said, "I know well who killed him."[13]

The pope's mourning extended over the ensuing months, and his confessed disinterest in matters of the church is fully reported in the diaries (June 20, 1497; 1:653–55). Yet he continued to intrigue for the aggrandizement of his family "and did everything to create states for his sons," the most notable among whom was Cesare Borgia. To this end, he negotiated with Federico of Aragon, king of Naples, against the interests (and possessions) that Venice had in Apulia, "so that he is not a good pastor, but he is greedy for acquiring new power"[14] (February 17, 1498; 1:879). Venetian attention was focused during the earlier part of Alexander VI's reign on supporting the Pisan rebellion against Florence and during the latter part on Venice's war with the Turks, which ended in 1502. Venetians' confidence ran high.

Pope Julius

It was during the reign of the next pope, Julius II, that the aggressive territorial expansion of the Venetian city-state over the previous century and some of its recent and current actions came home to roost. The power of the Borgia clan, so effective during the reign of Alexander VI, collapsed upon his death in 1503, when Cesare Borgia's illness prevented him from retaining the territorial domain

---

12. The manuscript has *funali;* the Fulin edition has *fanali.*

13. Among the prime suspects were Cardinal Orsini, of the powerful Roman family; Cardinal Ascanio Maria Sforza, of the reigning Milanese family; and, according to F. Guicciardini 1971, 3:13, Cesare Borgia, the victim's brother. See Sanudo 1987, 47n5; and Mallett 1969, 153–57, on Juan Borgia's death and the uncertain identity of his assassin.

14. "Sichè, non è bon pastor; ma è cupido di novità."

he had established in Romagna. The Venetians seized certain of these territories, an act that would eventually cost them the support of Julius II. But in the earlier part of Julius's reign, diplomatic relations were cordial, as shown by the following report of the reception of a Venetian embassy by that pope in 1505.

May 16, 1505 (6:165–66)   On the fifth of May a public audience was given to the Venetian ambassadors, who went to the [papal] palace with their entourage, properly attired and adorned, so that everyone considered this a beautiful sight to behold. After they had been brought into the consistory, they kissed, as was customary, with great [reverence], the feet, the hand, and the cheek of His Holiness, the pope. When they had returned to their places, a most elegant Latin oration was given by don Hironimo Donado, university laureate, on whom this office fell by reason of his age. So weighty, so full of meaning, so eloquent, so well enunciated [was this oration] that nothing better could have been hoped for. When it was finished, His Holiness the pope replied, with as much solemnity as was appropriate. And then when they were gathered in a circle around His Holiness's feet, the attendants came one by one to kiss his foot. Because of their number and quality, it appeared to all to be a great tribute. This done, His Holiness was accompanied into the Parrot Chamber, where he disrobed. The eldest of the group, Bernardo Bembo, university laureate and knight, was designated to carry his train. And after receiving [the pope's] benediction, the company took their leave. And they accompanied the most reverend Cardinal Grimani to his house, where they remained for dinner with his lordship, who invited and entertained them there. And this banquet was very abundant and sumptuous.

A few pages later Sanudo includes a long description of this elaborate dinner. As a resident cardinal at the court of the pope, their host, Domenico Grimani, cardinal from 1493 until his death in 1523, was expected to provide succor and style to the Venetian presence in Rome. The wealth of his household and the quality of his hospitality formed as much a part of the political record as had the pope's reception. For this reason, Sanudo copies a letter written by one of Grimani's stewards, who scrupulously describes the virtuosic entertainment and impressive feast, complete with successive dishes decorated with pennants of St. Mark.

May 31, 1505 (6:171–75)   Summary of a letter from Rome describing the undertakings of our ambassadors, their public audience [with the pope], and the banquet of the most reverend Cardinal Grimani . . . on May 16, 1505.

On Monday, May 5, a public consistory was held for the audience that His Holiness gave to the ambassadors of the most illustrious Signoria, receiving them in the most kindly and gracious manner. . . . [Our ambassadors] pledged their obedience [to the pope], as is customary. Then they took their departure, going with the most reverend Cardinal Grimani to his residence. The group was accompanied by the cardinal's entire retinue, festively dressed and not wearing mourning as they had been for the death of his mother, but elegantly attired in velvet and in purple and scarlet gowns.

The narrator then accompanies the visitors as they process through a series of visual experiences, moving up the stairs and then through a series of antechambers, chambers, and courtyards before returning to the first room, where their host met them for the feast:

The group arrived at [the cardinal's] palace, and upon entering, the first thing they saw was the door at the top of the staircase, richly adorned with garlands in the classical style, with the papal arms, and with the cardinal's arms. There were also many [symbols of the lion of] St. Mark in gold and high-quality colors.[15] [To the accompaniment of] a large wind band and tambourines, a large crowd cried out, "Marco, Marco" and "Grimani, Grimani." The whole world seemed to ring with joy. The group then entered the courtyard, which is large and spacious. It was bedecked with beautiful figured tapestries, classical garlands, coats of arms, and [lions of] St. Mark: a lovely sight to behold.

At the entrance to the first room, [they saw] a door that was similarly well decorated. The room was hung with beautiful tapestries in foliage patterns, arranged as if they were large paintings. Between one tapestry and the next were white columns with capitals and bases carved in the classical style. And above these columns, under the beams, were placed the papal arms and the cardinal's arms and a large lion of St. Mark, all beautifully wrought in gold and fine colors. And beneath, all around the room, were tables that had been beautifully set.

At the entrance to the second room they found a door adorned in similar fashion. There was also a large and spacious door hanging [*antiporta*] with a beautiful field of gold, and the room was hung with lovely figured tapestries. At the head of the room was a grand and ornate credenza holding numerous large gold and silver vessels. They were in various styles, and all bore noble classical decorations including [geometrical] shapes and foliage, some of which were in relief and some engraved. Because of the great quantities involved, many estimated the vessels' worth at 15,000 to 20,000 ducats. Near the first credenza was another credenza holding cups, large and small bowls, and saucers made of gold and silver, as well as other small silver implements

---

15. San Marco was often depicted by his leonine symbol.

for use at meals at all the courses. These were in addition to the objects on the large credenza. The writer of this letter was in charge of all tableware made of precious metals, both gold and silver.

As the group exited that room to enter the most reverend cardinal's chamber, they beheld at the door a curtain of rich purple velvet [whose pile was cut] in two heights. Embroidered upon it in gold in antique fashion was the cardinal's coat of arms. His lordship brought all the ambassadors into his chamber, which was hung with purple cloth as a sign of mourning. The room next to his chamber is his library, which he showed them. It is furnished with great quantities of exquisite books and numerous marble statues and many other classical objects, all of which were discovered in the ground of his vineyard during the course of excavations made for the building of the palace that he is erecting within it.[16]

The tour of the splendidly decorated public rooms having been completed, the company was invited to the dinner tables, where they were seated according to rank on richly covered chairs. A parade of gourmet dishes ensued, each served with appropriate wine and accompanied by carefully selected music and entertainment, as if all the senses were to be beguiled in a procession of sensual delights.

Once all of these things had been seen, the most reverend cardinal, together with the ambassadors, emerged into the first room. To the sound of a wind ensemble and tambourines, rose and lavender waters were brought in basins and vessels of gold and silver. They were offered to all seventy-four persons who were at table, including the ambassadors and other gentlemen who were with them, so that they could wash their hands. Each was seated according to his rank, with His Reverence at the head of the first table, seated on a chair of purple velvet. The ambassadors and some other gentlemen were seated on chairs covered with cloth of gold, or crimson [silk], or green or purple velvet, or other colors. All of the chairs had heavy fringes and gold pommels nobly worked with sculpted foliage and friezes; all of the pommels were in the form of classical vases or other different and noble styles.

Once the guests had washed their hands and everyone was seated at table, the first course was ordered by ser Zuan Bolognese, the cardinal's personal steward, who organized and presented the meal. Damascened, that is

---

16. The family vineyard and excavations for a new Grimani palace were on the Quirinale. The classical marble statues referred to here formed the original core of what came to be, during the sixteenth century, the famous Grimani collection of antiquities. At his death in 1523, Grimani bequeathed to the Republic all his antique bronzes and marbles, on the condition that they be displayed in a room in his honor. See Perry 1978, 215, 217.

candied, fruit appeared on plates of gold and silver; included were candied squash, citrons, lemons, and muscat pears, ceremoniously presented with flowers and roses. Served with it was muscatel malmsey wine; a musical accompaniment was played by a wind band.

Next came eighteen silver and gold sweet platters filled with seventy-four gilded pine-nut cakes and the cookies eaten with them, to an accompaniment of tambourines and harps.[17] Then each ambassador was served a dish of whipped cream with sugar and rose water; all the others had to share a dish with another person. Accompanying this was soft music, which lasted until the beginning of the next course, consisting of elderflower [*fior sanbucho*] fritters with sugar and rose water and decorated with flowers and roses. They too were carried in on eighteen gold and silver platters.

Following that were eighteen dishes of *suppe de duca,* with gilded sweetbreads and kids' heads, each with its gold pennant bearing a St. Mark [lion] and the cardinal's arms, accompanied by the music of *trombe squarzate* [ceremonial trumpets].[18] Next seventy-four deep dishes of pullet prepared in the Catalan style, with one dish per person. They were brought to the table with similar pennants, to the sound of harps, cymbals, and stringed instruments.

Then came eighteen platters of small roasted meats, including ten quail, six pigeons, and six pullets per platter, with bitter oranges and cherries in the dish, flavored with hollandaise sauce [*salsa bastarda*]. They were served with sweet San Severin wine and accompanied by more excellent music, which lasted until the bringing of the small casseroles in sauce, carried in after the roast meats in silver and gold bowls, with one bowl per person. Eighteen platters of medium-sized roast meats came next, with two pheasants and one peacock per platter. Each one had its neck and tail dressed with its own feathers, and the breasts were fully gilded. The birds were served with a soup of broom flowers and flavored with royal sauce.[19] Accompanying them were some buffoons who made contorted movements with their bodies, mouths, eyes, and noses. They cavorted around and did a lot of other funny things that made people laugh. Each of the[20] dishes in this course had its own little pennant.

---

17. Given the ostentatiousness of the banquet, the reference to gilded pine-nut cakes *(pignochate dorate)* here and the references to other gilded foods below are taken to mean that the foods were actually gilded with gold leaf, not just glazed in a culinary manner. For the gilding of foods, see chapter 6, n. 56.

18. See appendix B under "Musical Instruments."

19. For such dishes as *fior sanbucho* or *bianco manzar* and such sauces as *sapore camellino,* see Faccioli 1987, 74 *(bramagere),* 75 *(brodeto camelino),* 84 *(sambugado zoè lacte con fior de sambuco);* for *salza reale,* see the earlier edition, Faccioli 1966, 64. Manlio Cortelazzo kindly served as a consultant on this passage, as on several others.

20. The manuscript has *tutti li preditti piati;* the Fulin edition has *tutti preditti piati.*

Next were eighteen plates of a poultry stew [*miraustro*],[21] with eight pigeons per plate, served with sweet oranges and dry white wine and accompanied by two Spanish buffoons. They carried silver cymbals in their hands, improvised songs in competition with each other, and said many delightful things. This continued until the large roast meat course, brought in on eighteen platters. This included ten pounds of veal rump, a kid, a mutton shoulder, two capons, and four pullets per platter, served with a spicy sauce, a soup of new peas, and sweet Grignano wine. The buffoons continued their act until the pies were brought, similarly displaying pennants, which happened after the *miraustro*.

Then followed eighteen platters of boiled meats, each one with ten pounds of breast of veal, ten pounds of mutton, half a kid, four capons, and four pul-lets. They were accompanied by a pudding of strips of blancmange, lemons, a green sauce, and a dry San Severino wine and by harp and viola music. All of the dishes had similar pennants, including the eighteen platters of gilded preserved meats, with a half-side of bacon, two tongues, and a ham, brought in after the boiled meats.

Then came eighteen platters of timbales, three per platter, with lemons beaten with sugar and salt. They were accompanied by some buffoons who pantomimed a ball game without a ball. They tossed the ball and batted it back, made points, and chased it, catching and missing it. They also talk-ed and argued with each other with all the gallantry in the world—"that's a penalty," "that's not true," "it's mine," "not so," "let's get a referee," etc.—as usually happens when people are really playing. All the dishes had similar pennants.

Served next were eighteen plates of covered capons, with four capons per plate, two covered in white sauce with pomegranate seeds and two with purple sauce, with white Foligno confections and accompanied by eighteen plates of large Bologna sausages, all gilded, with four sausages per plate. Along with them came an Albanian buffoon, whose name is Barleta, dressed all in gold and carrying some kind of a drum with silver fittings. He had a companion, who played a *violeta*.[22] Together they sang sweet songs that were refined, deli-cate, and worthy. All the dishes bore the pennants described above.

Then came eighteen plates of wild boar, roe deer, and hare, each with its pepper sauce and each with its pennant, like the others. Harps and *violete* ac-companied this course.

---

21. According to Battaglia 1961–2000, 10:525, *miraustro* was a poultry dish classified as a *mines-tra,* in which the meat is first roasted, then boiled in broth, and then flavored with spices and either lemon or orange juice. Manlio Cortelazzo suggests here the Spanish *mirrauste,* which included almonds and pine nuts.

22. A stringed instrument of the viol family.

This was followed by sixty-four cups of gilded gelatin and dry Corso wine, with more musical pieces no less sweet and worthy than the others. It continued until eighteen plates of brightly colored cakes with fresh beans and both cooked and raw artichokes were brought, together with pepper and Sardinian cheese on plates of gold and silver. Both of these were brought after the gelatins, and each had a pennant and was garnished with fresh fennel and candied fennel on saucers of gold and silver.

Next came whipped ricotta with sugar, rose water, and borage flowers. Two little boys dressed as shepherds appeared with them, carrying rustic cheeses, which they presented while reciting verses in praise of the most illustrious Signoria, the most reverend cardinal, and the ambassadors.

This was followed by eighteen marzipans on eighteen gold and silver plates, and as many plates laden with candied peaches, each plate bearing a gilded pennant with the arms described, to the accompaniment of a refined morris dance [*moresca*] performed in a gallant style.

Next towels were brought, and rose water was dispensed for the washing of hands, accompanied by shawms, trumpets, and tambourines. Small confections were distributed, including [sugared] Palermo coriander seeds, gilded sugared cinnamon, melon seeds, Foligno anise [seeds], almonds, pine nuts, and cookies. A musical accompaniment was provided by Iebia and two companions, who played two large viols [*viole grande da archeto*], to the great pleasure and appreciation of all.
Written by Raynero di Fideli to Alexandro Calzedonio.

Rome and the War of the League of Cambrai

The substantive political news from Rome was, of course, contained in the official diplomatic dispatches sent home by Venetian ambassadors. Only three years after the splendid reception of the Venetian ambassadors by Cardinal Grimani, the relationship with Julius II had worsened as the central crisis of the Venetian Republic in Sanudo's lifetime, the War of the League of Cambrai, drew near. The hostility toward Venice engendered by its acquisitions and continuing ambitions in northern Italy during the fifteenth and early sixteenth centuries had increased with its aggressive actions since the eruption of the Italian Wars. Venice had taken advantage of the confusion of the French campaign against Naples to strengthen its holdings in Apulia. It had sided with Pisa in its rebellion against Florence, abetting its struggle with military and naval support. It had seized certain papal territories in Romagna during the chaos after the death of Alexander VI and the illness and subsequent death of his son, Cesar Borgia. Venetian diplomacy failed to avert the formation of the hostile League of Cambrai, which began to take shape in December 1508 and eventually was made up of Pope Julius II, Louis XII of France, Emperor Maximilian I, Ferdinand of Spain, and Hungary, plus Ferrara, Savoy, and Mantua. In the following spring, on April 27, 1509, the pope pronounced a ban of greater excommunication against the Venetian empire unless the Venetians restored all the Romagnol cities to the Holy See within twenty-four days.[23]

As the excerpts below show, Julius threatened the Venetian ambassadors and printed six hundred copies of the excommunication. He absolved Orsini and other Venetian military commanders of their contractual commitments and refused to let them return the money they had received from Venice to maintain their troops.

May 8, 1509 (8:182)   [Summary of letters] from Rome of May 3 and 4. Although our ambassadors wanted to go to the pope to protest this excommunication, he refused to speak with them. Thus they are in great danger; indeed, they fear they will be taken into custody. Six hundred copies of the writ of excommunication have been printed up and distributed; the pope wants to send them to Venice and to the entire world.[24]

Excommunication was a formidable papal weapon. The following excerpt shows that the pope sought to detach from Venice its current military leaders, members of the Orsini family.

May 8, 1509 (8:183)   *Item:* a report has also come from Rome that the Orsini are serving as guarantors to the pope and thus are neither against the church nor in the employ of the Venetians. When they wished to repay the money [to the Venetians], [the pope] told them that in no way should they do so. Moreover, he gave them absolution for holding such money, since it came from excommunicates, and he absolved them from the promise they had made. They said to him, "Holy Father, we do not want to blacken our reputation." And the pope replied, "Do not in any way repay that money," etc.[25]

---

23. For well-documented accounts of the formation of the League of Cambrai and its consequences, set against the larger events of 1507-17, see Setton 1976-84, 3:51-171; and Finlay 2000.

24. The Latin text of the excommunication was copied by Sanudo (8:187-205). The excommunication would last ten months.

25. The Orsini were a distinguished Roman family. Nicolò Orsini, Count of Pitigliano and Nola, was captain general of the Venetian forces at this time, and several relatives of his were also on the Venetian military payroll, including Mario and Corrado Orsini, whom Sanudo refers to in a review of military personnel as "conduti e non veneno," under contract but not present (10 May 1509; 8:218).

Meanwhile, the French forces under Louis XII (1498–1515), who had claimed and occupied Milan, were moving toward the Venetian forces on the Lombard plain, and on May 14, 1509, they met at Agnadello, where the Venetian forces were routed.

May 15, 1509 (8:247–49)   The savi were in the midst of their meeting, consulting about a certain issue concerning the Council of Ten. I was there to look at [the map of] Italy with some other patricians.[26] At twenty-two hours [after sunset] Piero Mazaruol, a secretary, came running in with letters in his hand from the battlefield, with many gallows drawn on them.[27] Thereupon the doge and the savi read the letters and learned that our forces had been routed.

And there began a great weeping and lamentation and, to put it better, a sense of panic. Indeed, they were as dead men. They wanted to keep the news a secret as long as possible but were unable to, since word had already escaped via the doge's household that our army had been defeated and that signor Bortolo [Bartolomeo d'Alviano], governor general [of the army], had been either captured or killed, etc. And in a very short time, within an hour of when the news had arrived, the entire Ducal Palace and the courtyard had filled with patricians and others. The Collegio decided to convene the Senate immediately; indeed, the senators were already beginning to arrive. The call went out for the procurators, and at Rialto for the senators; the doge descended half-dead. [The Senate] having convened with those who could come, the letter from Brescia, with its most bitter news of our defeat, was read. . . .

Sanudo went on to describe, over the next eight days, the city's "foul mood" *(malla voglia)*, the anger and recriminations, the lack of decisive leadership, with a doge "half-dead" and the Collegio almost paralyzed with indecision (May 17, 18, 1509; 8:265–66, 280–81). With the enemy so close, there was fear for the provisioning of the city and fear of internal commotion. So serious was the situation that the great feast of the Sensa had to be canceled.

May 23, 1509 (8:301–2)   There is no news from the Collegio; everyone is as if dead, and ill-humored. [Our forces at] both Brescia and Bergamo have been routed, and there is fear for Venice. Discussions were held in the Collegio with

---

26. This map of Italy, which was in the Collegio's antechamber, measured about 5.7 meters wide and 2.8 meters high. It was considered "so perfect in its dimensions [*misure*] that a number of contemporary rulers asked for copies." See Sansovino 1968, 323; and Gallo 1954. For the attempt in 1506 by the Marquis of Mantua, Francesco Gonzaga, to have a copy made, see Chambers and Pullan 1992, 406. Mallett and Hale 1984, 253, date this map to 1505.

27. Gallows were a sign of bad news.

the heads of the Council of Ten about security measures, that is, in addition to the officials [i.e., the signore di notte], to appoint one maritime guard per neighborhood, who, together with twenty-five men who are also sailors and good Venetians, will vigilantly patrol his *sestiere* at night, etc. And the heads of the Ten will give each of the leaders five ducats per month and the men two and a half. It should be noted that there were many soldiers in this city who were armed, such that there was fear of an uprising. And because it is the feast of the Ascension, with booths set up in Piazza San Marco, it was decided that each of the booth[keeper]s should be commanded to take all his goods away this morning and that by tomorrow morning all the booths should be taken down. This was done, but there was a lot of grumbling about the dismantling of the festival, which usually lasts until Saturday. In addition, all captains and officials [of the *sestieri*] were ordered to present themselves at the Ducal Palace in the morning by half past tierce. The maritime guards were also ordered to come, although they were not told the reason. Everyone was talking about the canceling of the festival and the calling up of these men. They want to hang someone tomorrow morning; a lot of people were saying that the Count of Pitigliano[28] would be brought to Venice and have his head cut off. Some said one thing, some said another. The next morning a large crowd gathered in San Marco, but nothing happened.[29]

But while Venice despaired, Rome rejoiced. The ambassadors were ordered home, the pope at first refusing to release them and looking to profit from Venice's defeat by expanding his territorial powers:

---

28. Niccolò Orsini, the captain general.

29. In the search for the causes contributing to this disastrous defeat and someone to blame, Sanudo records numerous letters and judgments, such as the pusillanimity of allied princes and captains who deserted to the enemy or the forceful counterattack of the French army led by its king, but most blamed the impetuosity of d'Alviano, which was considered both ill-advised and compromised by the caution of his commanding officer, Captain General Niccolò Orsini, Count of Pitigliano, and the two provveditori, or military advisers, from the Venetian government. Cited were d'Alviano's insubordinate statements and actions, such as his bold statement to his patrician advisers: "Most honored provveditori, if you wish to order me not to cross [the river Adda] with so fine an army, put it in writing and I shall obey you; otherwise I intend to cross." Which is exactly what he did. See report from the Venetian provveditori, in diaries, 6 May 1509 (8:173). A letter of 15 May 1509 written by Francesco Corner, in Rezzato (southeast of Brescia), to his brother states: "The opinion is that the rout was caused by Signor Bortolo [d'Alviano], who chose to heed no one unless it was done his way, and if anyone uttered a word, he accused him of being a good-for-nothing. The captain [general, Niccolò Orsini] went along and did not say a word. We would have been well served had he [d'Alviano] been killed three months ago" (8:257). Cf. Finlay 2000, 994–95; and diaries, 8:247–50, 256–58, 268–70, 286–89, 397. Yet four years later d'Alviano returned to Venice from his French imprisonment and was received as a hero in the Senate, where he presented his own version of the battle of Agnadello. Diaries, 12 May 1513 (16:236–40).

May 25, 1509 (8:310–11)   [Summary of letters] from our ambassadors in Rome dated May 19. They recount that, having received our letters with orders to request leave, they attempted to speak with the pope, but he continually refused to speak with them. They then sent him a message requesting permission to return to their homeland and an escort, and the pope ordered the letters [of permission] and the escort. In the meantime, [news of] the appeal [to a general council] of the excommunication reached the pope, who became so enraged that he suspended his permission. Our cardinals have been to speak with him, telling him that the ambassadors[30] knew nothing about it, as indeed was the case. The pope sent [an agent] to their homes to take their oath, and they swore that they had not been involved.

Item: one thousand or more ducats of the money obtained here from the Orsini have been returned through letters of credit.

Item: on the date — the pope received the news of the defeat of our army. He was very happy about it and celebrated in the Castel Sant'Angelo, and he ordered the cardinals to do the same. He then related this news in the consistory with great joy, etc.

Item: he absolutely refuses to grant any more audiences to our ambassadors, who are excommunicated.

Item: he is sending soldiers into Romagna, intending to profit [from their presence], and sending money to his troops in the hope of acquiring towns.

Item: he has written to the king of Hungary inviting him to come and fight against us.

May 25, 1509 (8:312)   It was proposed that a letter be sent to our cardinals in Rome, Grimani and Corner,[31] to inform them that we have been defeated, have lost our territory as far as the Mincio, and will not be able to withstand the French, and that the pope should have mercy on us, sons of the Holy Church, for we will be destroyed [if he does not], and that we want to return his lands to him. They should narrate all of this to the pope with great submissiveness and request his pardon, etc. And the bill passed.

It was not until nine months later, on February 24, 1510, that a reconciliation between Pope Julius II and the Venetian state was finalized. The War of the League of Cambrai continued, but now, with the papal troops participating on their side, the Venetians had some relief as they sought to regain and defend their Terraferma dominion. Nevertheless, once again, in the fall of 1513, the imperial forces came impressively close to Venice. Sanudo himself witnessed from the

---

30. The manuscript has *li oratori;* the Fulin edition has *i nostri oratori.*

31. This is according to the manuscript, Corner being Marco Corner, cardinal of Santa Maria in Portico. The Fulin edition gives the names as Grimani and Condulmer.

Campanile the destructive fires burning on the mainland.[32] Not until 1516–17 were the threats of invasion removed and a truce finally arrived at. By that time Pope Leo X had replaced Julius II.

Pope Leo X

Pope Leo X (1513–21), formerly Giulio de' Medici, had long been an important person on the Florentine political scene. In a report of a secret visit the then Cardinal de' Medici (and his brother Piero) paid to the Collegio in 1499, Sanudo describes him as "a big man, but with an ugly face, not much presence and unrefined."[33] The report was inaccurate in one respect: Leo X proved to be a very cultured pope. But his election to St. Peter's chair on March 11, 1513, was unexpected by the Venetians, and the news astounded the city.

March 12, 1513 (16:28)   This evening, at the first hour of night, one of our couriers arrived from Ravenna . . . with letters from our ambassador ser Francesco Foscari, knight, three lines long, sent on Friday the 11th at the 14th hour.[34] [He reports] that in that hour the most reverend [cardinal] Medici was elected pope. This letter was read in the doge's chamber with ser Zaccaria Dolfin, savio dil Consejo, present by chance—he had gone there with his daughter to take the doge's hand on the day of her wedding. And having heard the news, the doge immediately sent word to Pietro Bibiena, Florentine, a Medici partisan, and other members of the Collegio. The city was full of the news, and it surprised everyone, because the Medici [cardinal] was not in line for the pontificate, being only thirty-six. He has an income of 10,000 ducats, no more, of which 4,000 ducats derive from Monte Cassino, which he has bequeathed to the Benedictines after his death. He did not accomplish it by simony, because he has no money, nor benefices to give away, but miraculously by God's will [*ita volente Deo miraculose*] he was elected, although of the twenty-five cardinals in the conclave, twenty-two were older than he. Nevertheless, they elected him. He is very worthy, learned, and leads an exemplary life.

Leo would need the current good reading of his character and abilities. The problems he faced were formidable and familiar: the hostilities between the larger European powers and the mercurial shifting of alliances between these powers and the Italian city-states. Together, these made a concerted effort against the Turks very difficult. The new pope had sworn, in an agreement with

32. Finlay 2000, 999. See also chapter 1, above; and diaries, 4, 6, 8 March 1514 (17:102, 113, 118).

33. "Homo grande, ma bruta efigie, et pocha vista, homo grossolan." Diaries, 11 August 1499 (2:1060).

34. This was a very fast journey, Rome to Venice in thirty-five hours, even for such important news.

all the cardinals, to "defend the faithful . . . against the perfidious Turks" (March 31, 1513; 16:101), and it remained a fixed, if unfulfilled, aim. But barely two weeks after Leo's election, at the signing of the Treaty of Blois, on March 23, 1513—in the midst of the Cambrai wars—a French-Venetian alliance was formed to recover Milan for the French and the Veneto for the Venetians, and this agreement was eventually followed by a holy league of the Germans, the English, and the pope to thwart these efforts. Meanwhile, Turkish invasions continued to threaten the eastern frontiers of Christianity, and a few months later Archbishop Giovanni Laski, the Polish ambassador who had led a delegation to do obedience to the new pope, begged for his aid.

June 18, 1513 (16:385)   [Summary of] a letter from ser Vetor Lippomano [in Rome], with this news.

Yesterday . . . the ambassadors from Poland had their audience [with the pope]. That bishop made a worthy oration, offering obedience to the pope and imploring his aid against the Turks. The pope and others were in tears.

It would take more than tears to deal with the Turks, who threatened not only Hungary, Poland, and Christian lands to the east. Turkish corsairs were appearing in Italian waters during this period and in one episode in 1516 were found cruising off Civitavecchia, while nearby the pope's hunting party ran for their lives. "The news came to Rome," the Venetian ambassador wrote, "that the pope had nearly been captured, something many desired, then the truth became known."[35]

Meanwhile, the Venetians had their own interests to protect. On October 17, 1513, the Venetians renewed their truce with the Turks, which assured their commercial safety in major Turkish ports and their suzerainty over ports and lands already under Venetian control as well as those it might acquire in the future from other Christian states. It was a long document, dealing with such common concerns as slavery, piracy, debtors, naval encounters, local taxes, and annual tributes and including the promise, on both sides, not to interfere in the wars of the other power as long as attacks were not directed against themselves. Negotiated by the Venetian ambassador Antonio Giustiniani in Adrianople, the treaty was fully accepted by the Venetian government on December 3, 1513.[36]

The Turks were relentless in their progress. In November 1514, news of the Turkish victory over the Sophì (the Persian ruler) reached Rome, and the Venetian envoy wrote in cipher to the Signoria describing the pope's reaction:

---

35. See diaries, 1 May 1516 (22:184), 17 June 1514 (18:278–79), and 11 July 1514 (18:346–47).

36. See the full account in Setton 1969, 380–81 and n54, based on ASV, Documenti turchi, busta 1, document dated 17 October 1513 at Adrianople (Shāban 919); and ASV, Senato, Secreta, reg. 46, fol. 28v.

November 5, 1514 (19:210) The pope . . . had letters from Ragusa with the copy of the letter from the sultan [signor Turcho] to Constantinople about his victory over the Sophì. . . . He sent for all the ambassadors and had them read this letter, saying how he had not slept that night because of the bad news for Christianity. He said that we must prepare to defend the faith, and not wait, and that he wanted to unify the Christian princes. Therefore, all of the ambassadors are to write to their rulers about this and send a copy of this news and the letters received, and for his part he will use every means to defend the church and will write briefs to all the rulers and send legates, etc.

Item: our ambassador was not able to attend at that time, but he went later and was given a copy of the letter.

The ambassador's absence from the audience may have been intentional, although he had the excuse of suffering from gout. But it may also have been part of the Venetian double game, renewing their treaty with the Turks on October 17, 1513, listening to the papal exhortations, and cautioning their ambassador in Rome to steer clear of commitments while at the same time professing their Christian loyalty. It was their standard position, and one that persisted.

November 6, 1517 (25:71) After dinner the Council of Ten met with the zonta. A letter to our ambassador in Rome was composed directing him to avoid attending papal conferences on Turkish affairs. Instead he is to tell him that this state has always fought on behalf of Christianity against the Turks, nor will it ever fail to do so once it sees that the other rulers wish to react with deeds and not just words, because whenever they begin the enterprise, we will be the first to go.

Pope Leo's hope for a crusade was never realized. The powers of Europe, including the city-states of Italy, gave precedence to their own individual concerns. In a sense Leo did likewise. The report of a Venetian ambassador in March 1517 characterizes Leo's nature and his preoccupations on behalf of his Medici relatives:

March 18, 1517 (24:90) . . . The pope has completed his 42nd year as of last December 11th. He has some internal sicknesses with congestion and catarrh. And it is not proper to talk of another matter, that is, a fistula. He is a fine man, very generous and good-natured, who would rather not exert himself if he does not have to. But he makes an effort for his own family. His nephew Lorenzino is astute and likely to accomplish things, not as much as Valentino [Caesar Borgia], but falling little short of him. That splendid Giuliano, [his brother] who died, was a worthy man, and two days before he died . . . he beseeched the pope not to harm the Duke of Urbino [Francesco Maria della

Rovere] or take his state away from him, because the duke had been so helpful to the house [of Medici] and taken them in when they were exiled from Florence. His Holiness told him, "Giuliano, concentrate on getting well," and refused to make him promises, saying that it was inappropriate to speak of such matters. He did this because, on the other hand, Lorenzino was pressing him to take Urbino. And in this connection, [the Venetian ambassador] said that when the pope was elected, he said, "Giuliano, now that God has given us the papacy, let us enjoy it."[37] Thus, this pope wants neither war nor undertakings, but his relatives involve him.

The letter continues with more details about the family and contains Lorenzo de' Medici's well-known characterization of his three sons—"I have three sons: a good man, a wise man, an insane one. The good man is Giuliano, the wise man is the pope, the insane is Piero of the big head, etc."—along with the ambassador's explanation.

Lorenzino was Piero's son and may have shared his folly. Historians have more usually called him Lorenzo de' Medici after his more famous grandfather. His uncle Leo X secured him Urbino in August 1516, but it was retaken by the ousted duke, Francesco Maria della Rovere, in January 1517. Eight months of warfare followed before Urbino was recovered for the young Lorenzo, costing Leo X a fortune of 700,000 ducats (September 15, 1517; 24:669).

History does not judge Leo to have been especially wise, especially about papal finances. Pope Julius II had left him a full treasury, about 250,000 ducats in cash, 150,000 ducats in jewels, and 80,000 ducats in silverware (March 4, 1513; 16:11). Even subtracting 30,000 ducats spent on the funeral events and other outlays for the cardinals, this was "the richest patrimony that had ever been left by a pope in the world, after St. Peter."[38] It was quite otherwise when Leo X died:

January 13, 1522 (32:356)   Summary of a letter from Rome sent January 8 to ser Justinian Contarini. . . .

An epitaph was written on the sepulcher of Pope Leo and quickly removed, and I was told that the gist was that the passerby should not marvel at the large size of the sepulcher, that is, of the tomb, because it is small compared with the grandeur of Leo. For never had a pope so closely resembled the Trinity as Leo, and this because he had disbursed the funds of three papacies, namely, those of [his predecessor] Julius, who at his death left a balance of 600,000 ducats; his own; and those of his successor, who [will] rise [to heav-

---

37. The manuscript has *godiansi;* the Fulin edition has *godianci.*

38. "Più rico patrimonio che mai fusse lassato da pontifice al mondo poi San Piero." Diaries, 12 March 1513 (16:30).

en] before he will have paid Pope Leo's debt. I do not believe I can get hold of this epitaph, which is beautiful and is no lie.[39]

Venice had been very glad to receive news of Leo's death the previous December, and Sanudo recorded the harsh judgments made about the deceased as the "miracle" of Leo's election gave way to the "miracle" of his death.

December 5, 1521 (32:207)   Early this morning the crowd went to San Marco to hear the miraculous and excellent news for our Republic, and gentlemen rejoiced with one another as if some great victory had been won, because in effect [Leo] was our[40] great enemy, being a Florentine. He sought to diminish this state in order to exalt Florence and his own Medici family, and he did not believe that the Turks were set on the destruction of the Kingdom of Hungary or that Christianity could suffer other kinds of damage, and he fostered continuous war among Christians, as [he did] in Lombardy against the French, and between the imperial majesty and the French king in Flanders, Burgundy, and France. So the whole city was very happy, even the shopkeepers and the artisans, saying that [with Leo's death] "a Turkish captain general had died, and one who was ruining[41] Christianity." And everyone rejoiced; nor could any better news have come. And people were saying that this is done by God and is a miracle in our eyes, because we heard about the sickness and the death at the same time, therefore may the Lord God be blessed for it all.

Pope Adrian VI

Leo X was succeeded by a Dutch pope, Adrian VI. He had been the tutor of Charles V, and the Venetians were not overly enthusiastic about his election.[42] But as with other popes, careful attention was given by Venetian diplomats to his character, and his parsimony was realistically if not sympathetically portrayed in a report resulting from the Venetian embassy sent to proffer obedience.

May 25, 1523 (34:222–23)   [Taken from the] summary of the journey of our ambassadors who are in Rome to make obeisance to Pope Adrian VI.
    This pope gets up well before daybreak, says his office, and then returns

---

39. Leo X died on 1 December 1521. His successor, Hadrian VI, was elected on 9 January 1522, the day after this letter was written. For references to other anti-Leo *pasquinades,* as these satiric writings were called (because affixed to the statue of Pasquino in Rome), see diaries, 26 November, 29 December 1521 (32:289, 302).

40. The manuscript has *nostro;* the Fulin edition omits it.

41. The manuscript has *ruinava;* the Fulin edition has *minava.*

42. Setton 1969, 424n213.

to bed until dawn, when he [rises and] celebrates Mass. Having taken off his vestments, he spends several hours in prayer and after a while has his chaplain say Mass while he attends it. Only after that does he let others see him, giving a small number of audiences. In this he is quite parsimonious, partly because his lack of experience makes him irresolute, so that his first response in any matter, whether it be large or small, is "Videbimus" [We shall see]. He refuses to seek advice from any of the cardinals, not trusting even the most reverend [cardinal] Campeggio, who has helped him considerably, so that he expedites few matters and everyone is unhappy. . . . The pope wishes to spend a large part of each day in study; he is not content just to read but also wishes to write and compose. This distracts him from his papal duties, so that between masses, prayers, dinner, naps, study, the divine office, and supper, much of the day is occupied, so that he can give only a few audiences. On top of that, there are the ordinary consistories three mornings a week, Monday, Wednesday, and Friday, in addition to which there are often special assemblies of the cardinals.

The pope spends only one ducat a day on his food. In the evening he himself takes it out of his own pocket and gives it to his personal steward, saying, "Buy tomorrow's food with this." His victuals consist of some veal, beef, chicken, sometimes coarse and very plain[43] fish soups of the kind one eats on feast-day vigils. He brought with him a woman from his own country who cooks for him and makes his bed and washes his clothes. Behind his chamber he keeps a study full of books, where he studies and holds the majority of his most secret audiences. He gave a couple of them there to our ambassadors, inviting them to sit down and cover their heads [to put them at ease]. In the penultimate audience, having been asked by one of the ambassadors if they could see Veronica's veil[44] along with the other relics of St. Peter's, the pope with some reluctance gave them permission.

Pope Clement VII

After Pope Adrian's brief reign, he was succeeded to the papal throne by a second Medici, Clement VII. In the shifting politics of the Italian peninsula, the French king Francis I was defeated and captured at the battle of Pavia, in February 1525 and then, to offset Charles V's imperial power, the new "Holy League," also known as the League of Cognac, was formed on May 22, 1526. Signatories

---

43. The manuscript has *parcissime;* the Fulin edition, *farcissime.*

44. The headcloth with which, according to tradition, Jesus, on the way to Calvary, wiped his face, leaving his imprint upon it. It had been a venerated relic of St. Peter's since the fourteenth century.

to this league included France, England, the papacy, Venice, Florence, and the deposed Duke of Milan, Francesco Maria Sforza. But this loosely constructed alliance did not attempt to stop the southward march of imperial troops in the winter of 1526–27. Francesco Maria della Rovere, the Venetian commander, tracked their progress but avoided battle, and it has been suggested that this was the policy of Andrea Gritti, based on his own military experience.[45] The unruly imperial army moved down the peninsula, cutting swaths of destruction. Its Spanish soldiers and German halberdiers [landsknechts], accompanied by Italian mercenary companies and some riffraff, were scarcely under the control of their leaders; they demanded pay and booty and were bent on reaching Rome.

On May 6, 1527, they swarmed over its walls and sacked the city. It was the most shattering news from Rome in all the period of Sanudo's diaries, not just for the Venetians, but for the Christian world. Sanudo records forty-two dispatches from thirteen correspondents about this event. Two are given here, from eyewitnesses (although not all their information is correct). One was a priest, and the other was a servant of the Venetian ambassador to Rome; both escaped from the city a few days after the ordeal.

May 21, 1527 (45:167–68)   Report made to the doge in his chamber on May 20 by a friar of San Salvador, who left Rome on May 12, 1527, and a servant of the ambassador of our most illustrious Signoria, both ransomed.

On the 6th [of May] at eight hours after sunset, the landsknechts and the Spaniards had begun to do battle in Rome near Ponte Mollo[16] and two other city gates. At first they were beaten back, with some loss of life, by the Banda Nera, [the company of] ser Giovanni de' Medici. But then had come a fog so thick that one could not see two steps ahead, and the landsknechts climbed over the walls without being recognized. In this first assault of the landsknechts, the Duke of Bourbon was killed by an arquebus, and more than 3,000 others died; almost all of our men fighting with the Banda Nera died, but none of the commanders.[47]

The enemy soldiers who entered Rome sacked the city from one end to the other, cutting to pieces friars, priests, nuns, and anyone else who stood fast

45. See Finlay 2000. Only Giovanni delle Bande Nere, a Medici cousin of the pope's and a condottiere of considerable reputation, attempted to interrupt the progress of imperial troops south. In a battle near Mantua he was mortally wounded, but his company continued to fight on the side of the papacy.

46. The manuscript has *Mollo;* the Fulin edition has *Molle.*

47. Charles, Duke of Bourbon, Count of Montpensier, and constable of France, was one of the imperial leaders, having quarreled with the king of France, who confiscated his large domains. He had helped to defeat the French at the battle of Pavia (February 1525) and was created Duke of Milan in 1526 to replace the deposed Francesco Maria Sforza. His death removed the last possible element of control over the imperial troops. On the sack of Rome, see Hook 1972.

in their homes. All those in the hospital of Santo Spirito were killed except a few who fled; the same happened to the foundlings of the Pietà, and many were thrown out the windows onto the street. All of the convents were thrown open and sacked, and the nuns were raped and some killed. In general, priests and friars were killed, though some were wounded and some taken prisoner. They burned a number of palaces; both the Spaniards and the landsknechts carried the take of all their plundering through the [Vatican] Borgo, each to his own lodging, since it seems that they have established headquarters in the Borgo and are making it their stronghold. All of these troops have chosen from among themselves eight captains to govern them, of whom three are landsknechts, three are Spanish, and two are Italian. Next to enter the city was Cardinal [Pompeo] Colonna, accompanied by 12,000 peasants and villagers seeking revenge for the burning of their homes. They too began plundering, going so far as to strip the iron fittings, no matter how small, off of houses and walls.

Our sources say that every single one of those left alive and taken prisoner, even small children, must pay a ransom, some a larger one and some a smaller one. But the landsknechts take no prisoner who does not pay a ransom; thus all get the edge of the blade. The Spaniards take prisoners, as do the Italians, and they allow them to live. They have sacked the palace of Cardinal Colonna, for those people are not afraid of him. They did the same to the palaces of the ambassador of Portugal, the Marchioness of Mantua [Isabella d'Este Gonzaga], the Orsini, and other patricians.

Four cardinals were killed: Ponceta, Cesi, Santiquattro, and Aracoeli.[48] [Of the other cardinals,] Colonna has taken [della] Valle, [Alessandro] Cesarini, and Siena [Giovanni Piccolomini] prisoner. Como [Scaramuzza Trivulzio, cardinal di San Ciriaco], who foresaw the ruin of Rome, fled to Civitavecchia with all his belongings and his household before the sack started. [Tommaso Vio], cardinal di la Minerva, and his nephews fled on foot shoeless, and he was found in the street. Cardinal [Francesco] Pisani is in Castel Sant'Angelo; otherwise, all of the Venetian prelates had fled to the home of the Marchioness of Mantua and were taken prisoner. The same is true of the Venetian ambassador [Domenico] Venier with his secretaries and household, ser Marco Grimani the procurator, and don Hironimo Lipomano. Each one of these is prisoner of a Mantuan count named Nogara and must pay a ransom.[49] They

---

48. Ferdinando Poncetti, cardinal of San Pancrazio; Paolo Cesi, cardinal of Sant'Eustacchio; Lorenzo Pucci, cardinal of the Santi Quattro Coronati; and Cristoforo Numai, cardinal of Araceli. The last was roughly treated by imperial soldiers and died in 1528, probably from his injuries. See L. Guicciardini 1993, 108–9, 149.

49. This account is at odds with other reports, according to which Isabella d'Este Gonzaga was one of the few nobles to survive the sack with all of her retinue and goods; she was living

say that more than 12,000 have died and that up to the day that this account was made the bodies lay unburied in the street. They have turned St. Peter's and the papal palace and chapel [in the Vatican] into stalls for their horses, and a silver image of Christ that was in the center of the church was cut into four parts and divided among them. The pontiff, the rest of the cardinals, and other gentlemen are in Castel Sant'Angelo; they have already given a ransom consisting of 500,000[50] ducats, the four installments of back wages owed the soldiers, the promise that the pope and the cardinals will go to Spain, and the surrendering of all goods in the castle. It is said that the soldiers had already begun to dig trenches and to attack the castle, which, however, is strong, well stocked, and well provisioned with men and munitions.[51]

The gates of Rome stand open, unguarded, and everyone is free to come and go as they please, since the troops have gathered in the Borgo, on the other side of the Tiber, and fortified themselves and keep there all the treasure and the plunder they have gathered. The roads are all impassible, and at every turn there are people waiting to plunder and to take prisoner anyone they can who is fleeing with plunder from the city of Rome.

Reports a month later were no better: rape, robbery, and the desecration of relics and images were rampant as the center of the Christian universe lay devastated and abandoned.

July 1, 1527 (45:435–36)   Copy of a letter from Rome, sent June 15, 1527, written by a [certain] Vincenzo da Treviso [secretary of the archbishop of Spalato].

… As far as matters in Rome go, everyone has been taken prisoner, the Colonna and their adherents no less than anyone else; indeed, especially them, and they are treated worse than the others. The other convents of Rome [have become] bordellos, and such is the fate of all Roman women; the head of St. John has been found in a ditch[52] in the gardens of the Sancta Santorum. The heads of St. Peter and St. Paul have been similarly stripped and ruined; the costume of Our Lady with all the relics has been thrown on the ground; all the silver has been stolen, as has everything else in Rome. All of the account books and registers of the banks have been cut up. Picotino, whose ransom was 250 scudi, has escaped the hands of the Spaniards. He had himself shaved bald so that the Spanish and the landsknechts would not recognize him.

---

in a Colonna palace and managed to escape, taking a number of refugees with her, including Domenico Venier and Marco Grimani. See Setton 1976–84, 3:280–82; for a detailed and moving account of the sack, see ibid., 3:269–90.

50. The manuscript has *500 milia;* the Fulin edition has *300 milia.*

51. The precautions taken by Alexander VI in 1496 (see above) later proved useful.

52. The manuscript has *fosso;* the Fulin edition has *pozzo.*

They have divided the pearls into bowls, and they are all[53] made of gold. The lowliest groom has three or four thousand ducats. Mass is no longer said, nor are church bells rung in Rome. There is no image of Christ in the churches that has fewer than one or two hundred knife wounds, and St. Peter's sarcophagus and the case containing Veronica's veil have been smashed. I would not be capable of recounting to you the cruelties that have been committed and are being committed in Rome.

This disaster in Rome and the inability, perhaps unwillingness, of the Italian states, especially Venice, to interfere in the imperial attack led a few years later to Clement's alliance with Charles V; the Peace of Bologna, which settled this phase of the Italian Wars; the coronation of Charles by Clement on February 24, 1530; and the subsequent hegemony of the Empire over much of the Italian peninsula. France, so important to Venetian diplomacy in the early decades of the sixteenth century, was phased out of its long contest for control of Italy.

France's Charles VIII and Louis XII

But in the late fifteenth and early sixteenth centuries Venice gave no European power more consideration than it gave France. The Venetian alliance with the French king, "the most Christian king" *(il re cristianissimo),* was usually the hinge of its policy. Whether Venice found itself opposed to that power, as in the earliest passages of the diaries on the French campaign, fearing the preponderant role France might play in the politics of Italy, or allied, as in the League of Cognac, it was clear that the role of the French monarch and his armies loomed large, drawing alternately Venice's admiration and its apprehension.

Charles VIII did not long survive the expedition to Italy that had been the subject of Sanudo's most historical book and had prompted its continuity in the shape of the diaries. Charles died in 1498, to be succeeded by his cousin Louis XII, whose Orléans inheritance included a claim to Milan. The Italian Wars now continued with a focus on northern Italy, and Sanudo's summary of a *relazione,* or report, by the former Venetian representative at the French court conveys the complex analysis that this situation required: study of the king's character, description of the king's priorities, identification of his chief officers and possible marital alliances, and estimates of his military strength.

October 12, 1498 (2:30–31)   Zuan Piero Stella, our secretary, having arrived from France, presented his report to the Collegio.[54] First: His Majesty the

---

53. The manuscript has *tutti;* the Fulin edition has *tutte.*

54. Stella was one of the most successful Venetian civil servants, a nonpatrician who would rise to the highest citizen rank, that of grand chancellor. See chapter 6.

king [Louis XII] sent his greeting and recommended himself to the most serene prince and Signoria of Venice. He is forty years of age, distrustful, and most avaricious. The taking of Milan is very important to him, and he bears great ill will toward Lord Lodovico [Sforza], the present Duke of Milan. He has told him [i.e., Stella]: "You will say to the Signoria that while it is my ally, it need fear no power on earth." The king's favorite, the Monsignor of Ligny, who is twenty-eight years old and Savoyard, is in negotiations to marry him [Louis XII] to the daughter of King Federico [of Naples]. She is in France, and a grand master of Brittany is also negotiating with her. Our secretary reported that this Monsignor of Ligny is the son of the late Count of St. Paul, whose head was ordered cut off by King Louis [XI], the father of the late king Charles. Ligny has only three thousand ducats per year in income.

In France many have died of hunger because of the levies ordered by Charles, principally from Paris south. When our ambassadors arrived in France, two opinions circulated in the court: one was that the Signoria would not tolerate the king's taking Milan, [because it did not want] to have someone of this kind and power[55] so near. The other was that the Signoria would not mind, because the king had no children and never had been able to have children with any woman; he would conquer the state of Milan, and then the Signoria would have it after his death, as happened in the case of the Monsignor of Andrages with Pisa, etc. Our secretary believes that the king has formed a union with the queen [of Brittany], who is the widow of King Charles, called Lady Anne, at San German,[56] near Paris, where he found the king and her and another man alone in a chamber.[57]

His Majesty claimed to have 3,000 men-at-arms, that is, 500 in Burgundy in that undertaking, 500 moving toward Spain, and 500 with ser Zuan Jacomo di Trivulzi in Asti; our secretary, however, does not think it is 300.[58] He [the king] has become friends with the Marquis of Monferrat and ser Constantin and has sent[59] them money. The Duke of Savoy, Philiberto, currently is on the side of the Duke of Milan. The Monsignor of Ligny, together with the Duke of Lorraine and the Monsignor of Rouen, now a cardinal, commend themselves to the Signoria.

---

55. The manuscript has *di questa sorte e potentia;* the Fulin edition has *questa forte potentia.*

56. The manuscript has *German;* the Fulin edition has *Zerman.*

57. Two months after this report, in December 1498, King Louis XII obtained a divorce from Jeanne (daughter of Louis XI), and early in 1499 he married Anne of Brittany (widow of Charles VIII) in order the keep this important duchy for the crown. In spite of the speculation, this match produced two daughters, Claude (who married the future Francis I) and Renée, who married Ercole II d'Este.

58. The manuscript has 300; the Fulin edition has 3,000.

59. The manuscript has *e li amanda danari* (probably *ha mandato*); the Fulin edition has *e li manda danari.*

The Monsignor of Clarius [William of Poitiers, Monsignor of Clariens], a native of Provence and former intimate friend of the king who went chasing after women with him when they were young, is completely on the Aragonese side. He is the one who arranged for Federico's ambassadors to come to France, and he thinks[60] that he will handle those matters, since the king is more concerned with the Milanese undertaking, saying that that duchy pertains to him, while the kingdom [of Naples] does not. The king has found no money remaining in King Charles's treasury and has spent 60,000 francs for his funeral. He does not wish to impose new levies, and his soldiers were paid in four quarterly installments, that is, four times per year. All of the king's revenues come from Languedoc and Normandy. There is no money in France, and they are poor, and little money circulates between Paris and Italy. The queen, wife of the late king Charles, was traveling toward Brittany, which is hers as part of her dowry.[61] The daughter of Madame de Angoulême is in negotiations to marry the Marquis of Monferrat.

The reign of Louis XII saw a number of invasions into Italy as the French king pressed his claims to Milan. He joined in the War of the League of Cambrai against Venice, occupying Milan and Brescia and leading his own troops to victory at Agnadello, but then he saw his territorial conquests slip back into Venetian hands. Brescia was taken back by the French in 1512, but soon it was lost again with the death of Gaston de Foix, Louis' military commander. A new attempt at recovery met with a new defeat at the hands of the Swiss (at Novara on June 6, 1513), and the Venetians, who were allied with the French at this point, suffered once again as their Terraferma possessions were plundered by Spanish and German troops. Louis died during the night of December 31, 1514, leaving the kingdom to the Valois line and the young, dashing Francis I (1515–47), whose tastes were as Italianate as his ambitions. Dreaming of military glory, he renewed the alliance with Venice on June 27, 1515 (July 31, 1515; 20:436), and set forth for Italy. The Venetians went out to meet him with a suitable retinue.

Francis I

August 30, 1515 (20:495)   A bill was posted by the aforementioned savi to the effect that given His Most Christian Majesty's journey to this side of the mountains, four ambassadors should now be elected from among the leaders of this city to honor His Excellency, from every governorship and current of-

---

60. The manuscript has *et crede;* the Fulin edition, *et credo.*
61. The manuscript has *ch' è soa di la sua dotte;* the Fulin edition has *che è di là soa dote.*

fice ... and that they should each take thirty horses, as well as a secretary, an assistant, a manservant, and four attendants, at the expense of our Signoria. Each one is to be given thirty ducats for baggage, strongboxes, etc., as specified in the bill, which passed.

A few weeks later (September 13, 1515), French and Venetian forces won a victory at Marignano [Melegnano]. In October Francis entered Milan (21:233–34, 236ff.), and in December a meeting with Pope Leo was arranged in Bologna, but "between the pope and the king no written agreements were exchanged" (21:396). All the while, Sultan Selim was extending the Ottoman Empire eastward, defeating the Persians near Tabriz in the late summer of 1514 and trumpeting his victories. Leo continued to hope for a crusade, and Francis was willing to strike a pose of Christian obedience and cooperation, as may be seen in a discussion that took place in Paris three years after the Bologna meeting, as reported in a letter from that city:

December 27, 1518 (26:302–3)   The recently arrived letters sent from Paris on the 9th were read. [They tell of] how Bibbiena, the most reverend legate, cardinal of Santa Maria in Portico, having requested that the king grant him an audience to obtain his response on a matter of importance to Christianity, His Majesty agreed to accept his agency in this matter and gave him an audience. With His Majesty were the Monsignor of Lanson, the grand constable, and the Monsignor of Vendome, all of royal blood; also present were the Duke of Ferrara, Monsignor the grand maistro, and the grand chancellor and other lords. The king wanted the legate to speak in the vernacular so that he could answer him himself, and since he did not know Latin, he would be required to use others to speak for him. He wanted everyone to witness what [the legate] will offer to do, so that, should he not do it, he might be held as untrustworthy. And so the legate made a most elegant speech in the common tongue, conveying the danger to the Christian religion from the Turks, exhorting His Majesty to take up arms as the firstborn of the Holy Church and the most Christian king, for he had all the qualities necessary for this undertaking—experience in the military art, generosity of spirit, a strong body, youth, prosperity, and great power. Therefore he should aid the Holy Church and Italy, menaced by the Grand Turk, who was now puffed up as a result of his victories. And now that His Majesty had made peace and matrimonial arrangements with the most serene kings of Spain and England, he could turn at present to this Christian task that was so needed. . . .

His Majesty himself then wished to answer in the common tongue. First, he praised the pope, who, like a good shepherd and catholic head of Christianity, had this wish: to be with the Christian princes and to inspire them to defend Christians against the Turk. And so His Majesty offered, for the defense of the Holy Church and Christianity, 40,000 foot soldiers, half of whom, that is 20,000, would be Swiss, landsknechts, and English, and another 20,000 would be from his country, plus 3,000 men-at-arms, that is, 2,000 French[62] and 1,000 Italians, with a good force of artillery; moreover, if it became necessary, he would come in person. And he wished to make this offer whether or not a union of Christian princes was actually formed, and he volunteered all the resources of his kingdom in the event that it did form. The monsignor legate was very satisfied and wrote to the pope.

It was a brave gesture, but an empty one. Nothing came of Francis's promises. It has been suggested that the decline of Latin in diplomatic circles was symbolic: the universal language and the universal church were going down together.[63] The French and Spanish kings' ambitions for the imperial crown in 1519 set the stage for a decade of competing territorial claims, with Venice attempting to find a role negotiating between Francis and Charles. The election of Andrea Gritti as doge in 1523 did not clarify things. Considered to be all French, Gritti found it politic to first make an alliance with the emperor and then make a secret alliance with Francis, which resulted in a defeat of French forces in 1525 at the battle of Pavia, in which the French king was captured and taken to Spain as the emperor's prisoner. The decade played out in the drama of the League of Cognac against the Empire, the sack of Rome in 1527, and Francis I's betrayal of his alliance with Venice by signing an accord with Charles V in August 1529 (51:322). All this was tracked and reported in the diaries, and Venice played its cards as carefully as it knew how. But in the final reconciliation between the emperor and the pope in 1530 at Bologna, Venice was effectively ignored.

But war and peace were not the only stuff of interest to contemporary Venetians. French culture continued to fascinate and attract their attention. Of particular interest to the Venetians were French fashions in food, furnishings, costume, and entertainments. Their attention to these details, as in the report of the feast and entertainments in Rome above, should be viewed in conjunction with descriptions of Venetian ceremonies and hospitality (as in chapter 2), for such comparisons formed part of the political competition and self-assessment of that period, as Francis I's remarks in the following excerpt illustrates. The classical references are significant in that they reflect contemporaries' interest in classical authors and heroes.

---

62. The manuscript has *300, zoè 200 francesi;* the Fulin edition has *3000, zoè 2000 francesi.*
63. Setton 1969, 367.

March 11, 1533 (57:598–600)   Summary of a letter of ser Marin Justinian, ambassador to France, from Paris the last day of February 1532, written to his brother-in-law ser Tomà Lippomano. It recounts some feste held there.[64]

As I wrote on the 21st of this month . . . , there have been so many elegant and formal banquets during this Carnival season that never have I seen the like, both for the abundance of the many dishes and the great orderly process maintained in those suppers and for the settings, which were such as will scarcely be believed. And there were so many elaborate costumes and masks that one marvels to hear of them. I have told you of the banquet [given] by the most illustrious high commander to which I was invited. Three other formal banquets were given following that: that is, on Carnival Sunday by the most serene dauphin, the following Monday by the most serene queen, and Tuesday by the most Christian king. I was invited to all of them, as were the ambassadors of the pope, the emperor, England, and Ferrara. The ambassador from Portugal was not invited because of the dispute over precedence that he is having with the ambassador from England.

The tables were set in two very large rooms decorated with very rich hangings, the first with a hanging of green velvet whose elaborate embroidery retold the stories and deeds contained in Virgil's *Bucolics*. Under each of the scenes the very letters and verses of Virgil were embroidered; this is a very elaborate object of such great excellence and richness that never have I seen any embroidery, even a small one, richer or equal. There were many hangings that went entirely around a great room, the second of the two, which was larger [than the first], perhaps the size of our library.[65] At the head of this room stood a dais much larger than that of our doge, which was decorated with a hanging made half of cloth of gold and half of violet velvet, and on the velvet was a very rich raised embroidery of some genealogical trees.[66] Around the rest of the room hung tapestries newly made at the order of this king, whose scenes in rich threads of gold, silver, and silk displayed the deeds of Scipio Africanus. As I was admiring their beauty—because ambassadors usually are seated there only when there is a banquet—the most Christian king stopped to speak with me, declaiming to me the high quality of the illustrations. He said that before they were woven, they were painted by Raphael of Urbino, from which paintings the tapestries were then derived. His Majesty, comparing these tapestries with the ones that the same Raphael of Urbino

---

64. This is a good illustration of Sanudo's ability to get hold of letters that, although private, evidently circulated among the patricians.

65. Perhaps a reference to the upper room in the Basilica of San Marco where Bessarion's books had been housed since 1531. See chapter 8.

66. See Battaglia 1961–2000, s.v. "tronco."

made for the pope,[67] affirmed that his own were much richer. All the musicians were gathered near the platform; there were many of them, and they were dressed [by the host] in cloth of gold.

The buffet, or credenza, as we call it, was very large and laden with dishes and numerous other large pieces of gold-plated silver, which produced an air of regal majesty. None of those was used, but there numerous other pieces that were used and that had not been set out in arrangements to be admired. What made me marvel the most was that the infinite number of masked guests participating in each of these four banquets wore costumes so long that they swept the ground. Some of them were made of gold brocade, some of silver brocade, some of crimson velvet, or velvets of the following colors: old rose, violet, green, yellow, ash, and every other color. There were so many of these that one took no notice of the maskers dressed in damask and satin.

During the daytime on Carnival Sunday and Monday, before the guests went to the banquets, they engaged in valorous jousts. On the first day, which was Sunday, the king and all of the other princes and great gentlemen participated. The most serene dauphin also jousted, with smaller lances; his contender, however, did not wish to break any lance and avoided touching him. His Serenity the dauphin, though, broke a number of lances in the manner described. The most illustrious Duke of Orléans, the son of the present king, participated in the same way. At the banquet of the queen, the most serene queen [Margaret] of Navarre, the sister of the most Christian king, came to converse with three of the ambassadors: the imperial ambassador, the English ambassador, and myself. Since the other two ambassadors were standing on each side of the queen, it was necessary for me to stand at something of a distance, so she had a chair brought and placed across from her. She began to discuss a number of subjects with us, including the fact that those embroideries had been both commissioned and in part made by the hands of her late mother the queen and herself. She said that not a day had passed that she had not worked continuously for some six or seven hours at her mother's command; her mother did this to make her avoid idleness, the root of all evil. She then told us how she came to marry the most serene king of Navarre,[68] praising greatly his chaste and devout life, and spoke of many other things that would take too long to narrate. The leave-taking of this majesty from this city has been put off until next week. The reason is said to be the postponement of the joust that was to be held the Tuesday of Carnival, which was

---

67. The manuscript has *forno fatti dal papa, fato per ditto Raphael;* the Fulin edition has *forno fatti per il papa da ditto Raphael.*

68. Henry of Navarre, whose daughter, Jeanne d'Albret, was the mother of Henry IV of France (1589–1610).

not held then and will now be held next Sunday. That will be the first Sunday of Lent. . . .[69]

It did not seem that the Turkish threat to Christianity was much on these courtiers' minds. If the Spanish occupation displaced the French as the sixteenth century wore on, French fashions continued to impress and influence the Venetians. And it is perhaps worth noting that at the end of the eighteenth century it was a French ruler, Napoleon, who accomplished what no other ruler had in the thirteen centuries of the Venetian Republic's much-vaunted existence: its demise.

Emperor Maximilian I

If France was one of the dominant European powers in Italy, the Holy Roman Empire was the other.[70] The motives and military movements of the German ruler, Maximilian I (1493–1519), and his grandson Charles V (1519–56), who brought Spain into the empire, were of critical concern to Venice. The counterweights these rulers provided to French preponderance and their dealings with the popes, who had the authority to crown them, who cajoled them into promises of a crusade against the Turks, and who resisted any assertion of imperial control in northern Italy, were carefully observed and measured by the Venetian diplomats accredited to the imperial court. The following excerpts from the reports of one such diplomat, Alvise Mocenigo, the Venetian ambassador to Maximilian I in 1503, illustrate the difficulty a Venetian ambassador might have in discovering the German ruler's mind and activities, especially with regard to his political alliances with the papacy and France, which would threaten the balance of power in Italy to Venice's disadvantage.

Alvise Mocenigo was commissioned as ambassador to Maximilian on November 15, 1502, and had joined the colleague he was replacing in Augsburg by December 9. The situation that he found and on which his predecessor reported the following February, when he had returned to Venice, was one of flux (4:694–97). It was not an easy legation for either of these patricians, as the following letters written by Mocenigo in the spring of 1504 reveal.

March 18, 1504 (5:1008)   [Letters] from Germany, from our ambassador, written in Innsbruck on March 5. [Our ambassador recounts] that don Mateo Lang, the royal secretary, told him of a three-year truce that had been finalized between France and Spain, which includes the king of the Romans and

---

69. During Lent, Sunday was the only day of the week on which fasting and abstinence could be broken.

70. On the Valois-Habsburg rivalry in Italy and the Venetian responses to it, see Finlay 2000.

the Archduke [of Austria].[71] [Lang also said that] Certayner [Gaspare, Lord of Persene], returning from France, would be here within six days.[72] Our ambassador said he would remain until the king returns from his journey to consult with the advisers of the late Duke Zorzi about Bavarian matters. *Item:* the Milanese are here and despair about the truce [that threatens Milan's independence from both European powers]. *Item:* the envoys of Duke Alberto [the king's brother-in-law, Albert IV] and the Count Palatinate are still there at the court. *Item:* the king will go to Bavaria, and it is thought that the Kingdom of Naples, by the treaty being negotiated, will belong to the archduke.

In his effort to assess the king's disposition, the Venetian ambassador weighed every gesture (such as a gift of fish) and used every means to gather news, including placing one of his company as a spy among the king's couriers:

March 18, 1504 (5:1008–9)   From [our ambassador in Germany], dated March 8. [Our ambassador recounts] that the king sent him a gift of two trout and twelve carp, while to the Spanish ambassadors he has sent nothing but a message that His Majesty wishes them to consume the gift with him and therefore they should pay him a visit. *Item:* [our ambassador] will be on the lookout for any letters or *nunzios* coming from Rome; he has a good system for hearing about them. He has sent one of his men to stay with Zanetto [Jean de Taxis], the head of the king's couriers, with the excuse that he was not able to find decent lodgings for him elsewhere. *Item:* it is believed [in Germany] that the king of France is consumptive and that he will [soon] die. *Item:* the king will come to Italy in any case; if he does not come soon to Innsbruck, our ambassador will go to visit His Majesty.

Each week, sometimes daily, the Venetian ambassador reported on his progress (or lack thereof) in gathering information and in attempting to win the king's confidence, but his task was made more difficult by the lack of directives from Venice. For nearly two months, he complained, he had had no word from home.

---

71. Maximilian is referred to in this and following passages as the king of the Romans until he took the title "Roman emperor elect" in 1508. Mattias Lang, bishop of Gurk at this time, was a powerful force at the imperial court. Some years later, after the defeat at Agnadello, Venice tried to purchase his help in detaching the empire from the hostile alliance. Setton 1976–84, 3:74.

72. Editors of the Fulin edition suggest that this may refer to an imperial secretary who was chancellor of the Tyrol and ambassador to France. But since Sanudo also spells the name *Siristayner, Chersayner, Serentainer,* or *Certainer,* it is impossible to make a definitive identification.

March 27, 1504 (5:1044-45) Letters from Germany, from our ambassador, written in Augsburg on March 16, partially in code. [Our ambassador relates] that in the peace accord being negotiated between His Majesty and the [French] king there are certain clauses that require the French king to oppose our Signoria, and if Milan or the Kingdom of Naples were to end up in the hands of the archduke, it would be very bad [for us], etc. Therefore, he reminds us that it would be better to communicate with that king with more than words, doing things that would be pleasing to His Majesty, etc., as is stated in the letter, in code.

From the same, of the 17th. He has been to see the king; having heard that letters had come from Rome, he tried to glean something about them. The king would not tell him anything, but they spoke together of various matters, and of the peace accord between France and Spain. Yet he seems to have been firmly set against our Signoria. *Item:* concerning Bavaria, our ambassador believes there will be a war, because the king wishes to have the matter settled and to take a piece of it for himself.

From the same, of the 18th. He spoke with someone from the entourage of ser Constantin Arniti, the king's ambassador in Rome, who had received letters from Rome, and he describes their tenor, etc. Nevertheless, the ambassador complains that he is not advised by our Signoria about these urgent matters, that he has not had letters from our Signoria since January 26, and that he does not take as a good sign the fact that the king has not told him that he has had letters from Rome, therefore, etc.

The next day, however, the ambassador had some news of the negotiations between the pope and the German ruler.

March 25, 1504 (5:1060) Letters from Germany, from our ambassador, written in Augsburg on March 19. Our ambassador has heard from a good source that the pope [Julius II] will give the king the money for the crusade. However, he wishes three things from the king in return: first, that His Majesty go soon to Rome to be crowned; second, that he swear to defend and guarantee the rights of the church; third, that he spend that money against the infidels and for the church. The king has replied that he does not wish to agree to these stipulations, first, because he cannot come to Rome so soon, and especially not now, because of the disturbances in Germany; second, that in Italy and anywhere else he might be, he will defend the rights of the church as a good emperor; as for the money for the crusade, he does not wish to obligate himself.

The Venetian ambassador Mocenigo's difficulties with Maximilian and Maximilian's relationship with the papacy were compounded by the following problems: Maximilian wanted to be crowned in Rome, but Venice would not give passage to him through its territories unless assured that he came "in peace." Meanwhile, Julius II wanted Venice to return to the Papal States the towns of Faenza (seized by Venice in November 1503) and Rimini (purchased by Venice from its Malatesta rulers in December 1503), which Venice had taken from Cesare Borgia and was holding, it claimed, for the "glory, benefit, and convenience of the Apostolic See." This was the phrase used in the most recent letter received by Mocenigo and referred to above,[73] and it was a claim vigorously disputed by the pope, whose hostility toward Venice would grow during succeeding years, until it issued in the League of Cambrai (December 10, 1508).

March 30, 1504 (5:1063–64)   Letters from Germany, from ser Alvixe Mocenigo the ambassador, written in Augsburg on March 20 at one hour after sunset. He makes[74] an issue in the beginning of the letter of his doubts about the sincerity of the warm treatment he has received from the king, who he fears may undergo a change of heart or of mind. Our ambassador is suspicious [of the king] because he did not inform him of the news[75] he received from Rome, as he had promised to do. The king answered him four days ago, yet it was only today that his answer was sent. Don Matheo Lang, the king's secretary, told him that the king himself wants to tell him whatever news he has from Rome; thus he [fore]sees important consultations with those gentlemen.

Item: as far as Bavarian matters go, the king appears to want a part of it,[76] saying that it belongs to him [as an inheritance] from Federico I, who was Bavarian; thus a great war will take place in Germany. The king having received [a promise of] the money for the crusade from the pope, he then received the entire sum. Of that, ser Rigo Bulfo took the 3,000 ducats in florins owed to him; the king has already spent the rest. He closes by stating that there will be a great war in Germany for Bavaria and that within the next three days the king will deliver his opinion on this. He entreats us to elect his successor so that he may return home.

Frustrated as Mocenigo may have been, his diplomatic service had some compensation. On May 9 a letter arrived from Germany reporting that Alvise Mocenigo had been knighted (6:21). From then on, Sanudo would refer to him al-

---

73. ASV, Senato, Secreta, reg. 39, fols. 164v–165r *n.m.*, 26 January 1504.
74. The Fulin edition has *gran principio;* in the manuscript the word *gra*ⁿ is erased with a line.
75. The manuscript has *quanto;* the Fulin edition has *quello.*
76. The manuscript has *il re par ne voi;* the Fulin edition has *il re par voy.*

ways as "cavalier." By June 17 he had been replaced and was back in Venice, and four days later he made his report (6:34, 36).

The lessons of those years taught Venice to be more circumspect, seeking a more neutral balance in its dealings with Charles V, whose political strength it came to assess more accurately. From its earlier proclamations of its own pre-eminent presence as a powerful, militant state, a serious player on the European scene, one whose help "was necessary," it would come to mint a new image of Venice as a city of peace and concord that could teach its contemporaries the art of successful government.[77]

Holy Roman Empire and Spain

Among the most interesting passages in Sanudo's diaries are about the discoveries being made by explorers and their new-found worlds, reports of which came to Venice via Spain. In 1497 such a report concerned a "Saracen king" from the Canary Islands, sent as an exotic gift to the Signoria:

May 17, 1497 (1:628–29)   Francesco Capello, knight, who was ambassador to Spain, returned with the Barbary galleys, whose captain is Piero Contarini, called Rosso, bringing with him a Saracen king, or to put it better, a king of light brown skin from the Canaries, the islands recently discovered by the king of Spain.[78] The Saracen king was given to the ambassador by the king of Spain to present to the Signoria, as I wrote above when, in his letters, he informed us of this gift made by the Spanish king. He also brought several types of parrots of many different colors. The next morning he went to the Collegio, and then to the Senate on the 20th, to report on his legation of about two years. . . .

Item: he related how, on his return journey, he disembarked at Tunis and was greeted by this king of Tunis as a Venetian envoy. He presented to the Signoria this black king, who was very well behaved but could not speak; nevertheless, he had been baptized. The savi di Collegio discussed what to do with him. Some proposed to send him as a gift to the Marquis of Mantua, and on the — day of June it was decided by the Senate that he would go to live in Padua in the palace of the *capitano*. He would be given a house and would have an allowance of five ducats per month from Paduan revenue for his expenses, and two ducats for his servants. He would also be provided from time to time with clothes according to his needs. This was done[79] in recognition of the

---

77. See Gleason 2000; and Finlay 2000.

78. The term *Saracen,* which was used somewhat indiscriminately for Arabs and Moslems, is applied loosely here.

79. The manuscript has *facto;* the Fulin edition has *scrito.*

gift sent by the Catholic king and queen of Spain. That Saracen king said he thought he was in paradise. It is said that he previously had two thousand mouths to feed, and in his country they eat human flesh, that of executed people. Along with six other kings, he was brought to Castile by the caravels and the Spanish soldiers who went to take command of those islands. It is said that before they were captured, these leaders put up a valiant defense, etc.

The king walked in front of the doge on the feast of Corpus Christi and entered Padua with Fantin da Pesaro, who was going there, as *capitano*, on June 18, 1497.[80]

A few decades later we find a description of Yucatan, which Spanish explorers had just discovered:

March 26, 1520 (28:375–76)   Section of a letter of ser Francesco Corner the knight, our ambassador to Spain, written in Valladolid on March 6, 1520.

Yesterday after dinner His Majesty sent for me and showed me the present sent to him by the ruler of the land called Yucatan, recently discovered by his caravels. It is a pagan god holding a scepter in his hand, sculpted in a great round disc of gold measuring six ells in circumference and of the thickness of a ducat; the god is surrounded by a number of other figures, and the disc weighs about as much as 4,000 ducats.[81] There is another object of the same type and size made out of silver. In addition, there were some sacks of gold in granules, like pepper, as is found in those countries. Moreover, there were many vestments and headdresses, which are customary in those countries, made of canvas and wool and birds' feathers. There were also many heads of wolves, tigers, and other animals that had been decorated with gold and plumage of parrots and other birds unknown to us, and other unusual objects with minute stone intarsias, which truly show that the people in that part of the world are very artistic. There were three men and two women the color of Abyssinians, whose faces were very deformed; the flesh above the chin of each one was as perforated as a marcello, and where the flesh had been they put a piece of multicolored stone mounted in gold. They say that in fact[82] in their country there is a great deal of gold and silver.

In the fall of 1522 Gaspare Contarini, the Venetian ambassador in Spain, wrote to the Signoria about various matters. He included a long letter with news of the

---

80. See Caracciolo Aricò 1996.
81. See appendix A for the weight of a gold ducat.
82. The manuscript could read *L'è vera*, "it is true"; the Fulin edition has *revera* in italics.

Indies, which Sanudo copied a few days later into his diaries. It is particularly interesting for its references to golden objects, pagan worship, and cannibalistic practices:

November 10, 1522 (33:501–3)   Most Serene Doge, etc. The emperor having received news of the Indies in the past few days from individuals who have returned from that region, including items worthy of being brought to Your Serenity's attention, I will not fail to communicate them to you. May Your Excellency know, then, that the visitor is don Hernando Cortes, the governor of His Majesty on the island of Cuba; it is he who in past years discovered Yucatan and sent to His Majesty several presents offered by the people of Yucatan as a token of their obeisance. They included a sun made of gold and a moon made of silver and some other gifts, of which Your Excellency was informed by our most worthy procurator, the then ambassador Corner, in his letters. After landing, Cortes continued his journey and discovered that Yucatan, which he had believed to be an island, was joined to the mainland,[83] which continued on to the west. He penetrated the interior and discovered various cities and castles inhabited by peoples of a higher level of civilization than have heretofore been encountered. He then arrived in a city named Tlascala,[84] which is governed communally and which is a very large city. They are at war with a prince whom I will name below, who claims to have jurisdiction over that city, while the people wish to be free. Cortes and his men having arrived there, as I said, they soon persuaded the people, for the reasons I have given, to pledge obedience to and recognize [as their sovereign] the present Holy Roman Emperor, since the Spanish told them that His Highness was ruler of our world. The Spanish then penetrated more than sixty leagues into the interior, where they found a lake with a circumference of sixty leagues; its water[85] is salty and rises and falls, as do most seas. In the middle of that lake they discovered a very large city called Temistitan,[86] which they said had more than 40,000 hearths. Its ruler is that great prince I mentioned above who claimed to have jurisdiction over Scalteza; he is the lord of more than one hundred leagues of land all around this area. He is held in awe by all of his subjects and is scrupulously obeyed. The inhabitants are very civilized except in the matter of religion, because they worship pagan gods and make human sacrifice to them. Moreover, they are set in the following custom: when they go to war against their enemies, they eat all of those who die in battle.

---

83. The manuscript has *per me;* the Fulin edition has *ferma.*
84. In Yucatan, spelled *Scalteza* by Sanudo.
85. The manuscript has *la qual;* the Fulin edition has *lo qual.*
86. In Mexico, also spelled *Tenustitan.* The manuscript spells it *Tenuscitam* and later *Tenusitan;* the Fulin edition has *Temiscitan.*

Their homes are comfortable and nicely decorated with cloths made of cotton that they use for their garments. They have a great quantity of gold, which they do not use as coins; rather, they revere it and use it to make a variety of ornaments. All of their commerce is conducted by bartering one item for another. However, for small items that they need to buy and that are not easily obtained by bartering, they employ as currency a small fruit similar to an almond that is rare. This city and its prince surrendered to the Spanish when they arrived. However, when the majority of the Spanish had left, they rose up in rebellion and killed those who remained, eating them as is their custom. When the Spanish captain don Hernando Cortes learned of this, he dispatched many Spanish with artillery and many citizens of Tlascala, who were enemies of Temistitan. They recaptured it, and the prince resumed his obedience to the emperor.

The inhabitants of the island described above eat bread made of Indian grain and meat and drink a potion similar to beer. They do not have an alphabet, but write the most important things with pictures of animals or other things, in the manner used by the ancient Egyptians. These characters, however, are not adequate for all matters. This is all that they related about those islands.

It was later said by the Spanish that they received letters [from their explorers] who remained there about how they traveled so far that they came to the sea, although they did not specify whether the sea they found was on the west or on the south. Then on the sixth of this month there arrived in Sybillia [Seville] one of the five ships that the Spanish king had sent three years ago to discover the spice routes with several Portuguese who had fled from the most serene king of Portugal. . . . They returned by the Portuguese route, the eastern route, thus they went entirely around the world, as will be explained more clearly and completely to Your Serenity in the letters. They brought 600 hundredweights [*cantere*] of cloves and samples of every other kind of spice. September 24, 1522 in Valladolid.

England

Another European power of interest to Venice was England. Southampton was a major port of call for Venetian galleys, which brought back to Venice cloth to be dyed, along with tinware and pewter. The Venetian community in London numbered more than forty as early as the fifteenth century.[87] Still, England was considered by some in the government so peripheral that Sanudo records a debate as to whether it was worth the expense to keep an embassy there.

---

87. See Lane 1944, 123.

May 3, 1533 (58:115–16)   A bill was posted by the savi di Consiglio (excepting ser Alvise Mocenigo the knight), the savi di Terraferma, and the savi ai ordeni to elect an ambassador to the Most Serene King of England in place of ser Carlo Capello, who has repeatedly asked to be relieved. The ambassador is to have 140 gold ducats in gold per month for expenses, and he will take with him eleven horses, including the secretary and two servants, and will leave when and with whatever mission this council will decide.

Ser Alvise Mocenigo, the knight and savio di Consiglio,[88] proposed a contrary bill to postpone the election, citing the disturbances presently occurring in England, in which the Holy Roman Emperor and the king of the Romans have intervened.[89]

The first to speak was ser Alvise Mocenigo, who said what little good has been served by sending an ambassador[90] to England, that we have never had anything but words from him, and that our ancestors did not send an ambassador there.

Ser Andrea Trivixan began to speak, and then ser Andrea Badoer was sent to assist him; he spoke at length of disturbances, divorces, etc., saying that it was a good idea to postpone this election for the time being.

Ser Bernardo Capello, member of the Forty and brother of the ser Carlo who is the ambassador to England, answered him saying that it is necessary to have an ambassador in England, whose king is the third most important in the world,[91] and that not to send one would be to insult him. He then spoke of his brother's need to return home to care for his six children and his elderly father-in-law, who is on his deathbed. The bill was voted upon: 153 for the proposal of the savi, 53 for Mocenigo's, 2 no, 3 abstentions.

This debate took place during Carlo Cappello's long embassy (1531–35) to King Henry VIII. Cappello's reports have supplied historians with detailed descriptions of the tortuous process of Henry's divorce from Queen Catherine of Aragon and his marriage to Anne Boleyn (see below, 58:201). Beyond that, Cappello provides an example of the personal trials a Venetian ambassador might suffer. He arrived in England in August 1531 only to learn that his wife, the mother of his six children, had died. After seventeen months in London, he began to request the election of his successor, as mentioned in the excerpt above. Not until a year later was his successor chosen, but he refused to serve. Another year elapsed

---

88. This is the same Alvise (di Tommaso) Mocenigo who was ambassador to Germany in 1503 (see above).

89. The king of the Romans was the brother of Emperor Charles V, Ferdinand of Austria. The disturbances had to do with Henry VIII's divorce from Catherine of Aragon.

90. The manuscript has *orator;* the Fulin edition has *oratori.*

91. That is, after the emperor and the king of France.

before a new replacement was chosen and dispatched, and that only in response to Cappello's brother's plea to the government that Carlo was needed at home by his children and his dying father-in-law.

In the following two reports, Cappello describes the situation in England in May 1533, in the midst of Henry VIII's divorce (sought since 1527) from Catherine of Aragon and his marriage to Anne Boleyn, characterizing the canny and irascible monarch, his curiosity about continental politics, his admiration and suspicion of Venice, and the importance of Venice's commercial ties to England.

May 24, 1533 (58:200–201)   Letters from England, from our ambassador Capello, [written] from London on April 16, received on May 21 in the evening. He writes this one by way of Antwerp: a gentleman came from the king before noon to tell me to go to the court of Granuzi [Greenwich] to dine. Thus I went, and I was there at the beginning of the meal, and I dined with the grand chancellor the Duke of Norfolch,[92] the Marquis of Ancor,[93] and the father and brother of Queen Anne, who were most pleased to see me and told me that the king wished to speak with me. After I finished dining in their company, I entered the king's room, where he was with many gentlemen and Queen Anne with many ladies and damsels. His Majesty immediately took me by the hand, and I congratulated him in the name of our Signoria with general words, wishing him every happiness. His Majesty showed that he was pleased to hear them. Then he asked me if I had any news, and I said[94] no. His Majesty told me that the current imperial ambassador had confirmed that the Signoria has entered into a league with the pope and the emperor, and I said that it was not true. He said that it had been confirmed, that it was very true, that the Signoria was pretending that it had not entered the league, and that a proclamation of the league had been printed that included the Signoria. At that point our ambassador denied such a claim, saying that the Signoria had been solicited to join the league but had refused and that the proclamation had been printed in Bologna [in the papal territories] and not in Venice, and had been done as they [the league members] wished. His Majesty appeared to be satisfied by this, saying that the pope and the emperor were making this known to give greater authority to their league. Then he said, "You have passed a law that upon pain of capital punishment all are prohibited from divulging matters of the Council of Ten and the Senate." He is of the opinion that the Signoria governs most prudently and that this decision was very wise, saying, "I can affirm that most of your matters have reached many ears." He showed that his words were meant kindly, indicating

92. The Duke of Norfolk, Howard Thomas II.
93. The Marquis of Exeter, Edward Courtenay.
94. The manuscript has *li dissi;* the Fulin edition has *io dissi.*

this with words and with gestures. He then told me that he had heard that the Signoria had recruited 30,000 foot soldiers in the region between Padua and Treviso and nearby places. I answered, "These are standing troops, who are passed in review at this time." And His Majesty said, "I believe it." Then he asked when I thought the galleys would be here. I said that I believed that it would be at the end of the coming November. His Majesty told me that when I had news of Italy or of the Turks, I should tell him. Then he took me to Queen Anne, and I greeted her.

May 24, 1533 (58:201)   From the aforementioned ambassador, written April 27, received May 21. By royal order, all the guilds of this city [London] were warned not to dare speak of this new marriage or of Queen Anne unless they spoke favorably, and [they were told] to prepare the entertainments and expenditure that are customarily made by the city for the coronation of a queen, which will be celebrated this Pentecost.

They have also ordered the four mendicant orders not to allow anyone to preach without license from the archbishop, and the reason was that although the preachers had been ordered to admonish the people to pray to God for the king and Queen Anne, one preacher at Westminster not only spoke against this marriage but publicly urged the people to pray for the king and Queen Catherine and the princess [Mary]. They have also prohibited, on pain of death, the mention by anyone of Queen Catherine.[95]

The Ottoman Turks

Of paramount concern to the Venetians were their relations with the Ottoman Turks, whose conquest of Constantinople in 1453 had fully awakened the West to the potential danger of this Moslem power. During the entire span of Sanudo's diaries, only one actual war took place between Venice and the Turks, from 1499 to 1503. But that conflict began with a humiliating naval defeat for Venice in 1499,[96] and in the following decades Venice pursued an ambivalent and careful policy toward this power, which shared two thousand miles of common borderland with the Venetian empire, whose naval and military strengths were formidable, whose hostility was always possible, and whose alliance—never formalized politically but sealed in commercial terms—was discussed, pursued, and found useful in the diplomatic power games with Austria, Hungary, France, and the Empire. Especially during the tense days and months after Agnadello, the controversial question of seeking Turkish support, and at what diplomatic level it should be done, was ardently discussed.

---

95. See R. L. Brown, 1871, 398.
96. See above, chapter 3, on Antonio Grimani and the Venetian defeat of 1499.

August 28, 1509 (9:100)   A most secret matter of the Turks was raised. Some wanted to send an ambassador, others an official secretary, others a private secretary. Yet others wished to negotiate through the *bailo*,[97] who is elected by *scrutinio*[98] in the Great Council, etc. Each expressed his view. There was disagreement. Ser Alvise da Molin spoke for his opinion: I think he wants the bailo. Ser Antonio Grimani spoke for his: he wants to send a secretary. Ser Luca Zen the procurator contradicted them: he does not want Turkish help. Ser Zuan Corner, savio a Terraferma, wanted to speak, but because it was late the matter was postponed[99] to another session of the Senate after the morrow. . . . and the Consejo sworn to secrecy.[100] Nevertheless, in the city one heard that they are about to call in the Turks, and everyone was for it. And would to God it had happened![101]

In spite of all the talk of a crusade against the infidel during the period of Sanudo's diaries, Venice managed, after hostilities ended in 1500 and a peace was finally signed in 1503, to retain a relationship with this same infidel, keeping contact through its commercial representative in Constantinople, sending embassies of congratulation to the new sultans, and receiving the occasional Turkish envoys. These envoys always came for a special purpose: to formulate, confirm, and renew the peace treaty of 1503 (Sanudo recorded four visits); to protest incidents of hostility along the common Dalmatian frontier and the shared trade

---

97. See appendix B under "Governmental Terms."

98. A procedure in the Senate whereby a candidate was nominated from the floor to be voted on alongside those nominated in the Great Council by a group of committees, usually four, themselves chosen by lot.

99. The manuscript has *ma l'hora tarda rimesso;* the Fulin edition has *ma per l'hora tarda fo rimesso.*

100. The manuscript has *il Consejo;* the Fulin edition has *in Consejo.*

101. Sanudo had already expressed his own view on the day after the defeat of Agnadello in 1509. He wrote in his diaries that had he been a member of the Senate, he would have advocated sending two ambassadors to the sultan, which "they have never wanted to do." Diaries, 15 May 1509 (8:251). Cf. the entries of 6 December 1513—"Erano letere cative di Roma; e tutti cridava si dimandi aiuto al Turco" (17:365) [Bad letters came from Rome; and everyone was crying out that the Turks should be asked to help]—and 30 December 1513—"De lì in Roma se dice, per tutti, che turchi vien in Italia in aiuto di la Signoria e passerano in Puia" (17:423) [There in Rome everyone is saying that the Turks are coming to Italy to help the Venetian government and that they will land in Puglia]. The debate about the diplomatic level of contact was still going on in 1519, when Sanudo himself participated, arguing for a higher level than won out (18 January 1519; 26:373–77). In addition to Setton 1969, see the detailed analysis of Veneto-Turkish relations from 1523 to 1534 provided by Finlay 1984, 78–118. Finlay follows the career of Doge Gritti's illegitimate son, Alvise Gritti, whose residency in Constantinople and close friendship with Suleiman's grand vizier, Ibrahim Pascià, both afforded Venice both a special connection with the Ottoman court and an awkward exposure to the ambitions of a partially renegade Venetian. It also increased the suspicion among Italian and European powers that the Venetians had connived with the Turks in order to divert Charles V from Italy (9 July 1529; 51:45). See also Gleason 2000, 172.

routes of the Mediterranean (seven visits); to insist on duties owed, that is, for Cyprus, after 1517 and on certain customs payments in Dalmatian ports (four visits); to announce the enthronement of a new sultan (two visits); to invite the doge to celebrate the circumcision of the sons of Suleiman (one visit); and more frequently than any of the above, to announce a military victory (nine visits). The Signoria always ostensibly rejoiced in these announcements, which often took their own peculiar form.[102]

August 24, 1516 (22:460)   Sunday, the feast of St. Bartholomew. Approximately eight patricians dressed in scarlet went to fetch the ambassador of the sultan. He made his entrance into the Collegio dressed in a gold tunic, flanked by ser Sebastian Foscarini and ser Zuan Baxadona, university laureates. Behind him, one of his attendants brought a dried head stuffed with straw on top of a pole,[103] which is said to be that of a captain of the Egyptian ruler, the Sophì subjugated by the sultan, that is by his army, which the ambassador brings to the Signoria as a token of [their] victory. When the ambassador arrived in the Collegio, the doge came toward him a little way and greeted him warmly. The ambassador then took a seat and with the help of an interpreter explained in Greek that his sultan was sending greetings to His Serenity the doge and to this Signoria. The sultan wished also to advise them of his victory[104] against the army of the Sophì, composed of 15,000 horse, compared with the Turkish army's 10,000. Yet the Turks defeated them and cut off the heads of eighteen important captains, which they brought to their lord, and 10,000 noses, and this [head] which they had brought to the Signoria was of a captain called ——.

There was further talk between the doge and the Turkish ambassador of their mutual interest in pursuing and punishing pirates, whether Venetians preying on Turkish ships or vice versa, and of victories won by the Venetians against their enemies (in the War of the League of Cambrai) and by the Turks against theirs. The doge greeted the ambassador warmly "with sweet words," and the ambassador took his leave, "and left the aforesaid head to the guardian of the door of the Colegio."[105]

There were many such victories for the Turkish sultan to boast about. During the summer, fall, and winter of 1516–17 Selim wrested Syria and Egypt from its

---

102. See Zele 1989, 258–59.

103. The following line was omitted from the Fulin edition: *uno di soi havia in zima di una maza.*

104. The manuscript has *vitoria auta;* the Fulin edition omits *auta.*

105. For other heads presented to doges as proof of military victories, see also diaries, 24 August 1516 (22:462), 10 July 1519 (27:465–66).

Mamluk rulers, "with great slaughter of mamluks and golems" (24:162), rounding up fifty-four "admirals," Mamluk officials, who were beheaded in public although they had been given safe-conducts. "And this was so that the people would lose hope." Fifteen hundred lesser officials were sent to Alexandria, where they were similarly dealt with. "At present, the Turkish sultan has begun to destroy the Arabs with great cruelty, even little children" (July 30, 1517; 24:440).

Meanwhile, the captain of the Turkish armada wrote a letter to the Grand Master of the Knights of Rhodes:

July 30, 1517 (24:440–41)   ". . . Now the sword of the Moslems has been delivered into the hands of the lord sultan Selim, lord of the world . . . but you, you mangy herd dog . . . if you act against this commandment [to recognize the lordship of the sultan] . . . if you think that fear will keep us from coming to your herd of pigs and taking it, this devilish thought will bring great harm upon your head. . . ."

But with the Venetians, the Turkish sultan continued to talk about the "love and good peace and friendship that will always exist between us":

May 16, 1518 (25:416)   Sultan Selim sach, son of Sultan Bajesit Cham the Emperor of Emperors,[106] Emperor by the grace of God, Greatest Emperor of Asia, Europe, Persia, Syria, unconquered Lord of Arabia and Egypt, etc.

Hitherto there was always an oath of good friendship and peace between the Most Serene Doge of Venice and us, and at present the aforesaid Most Serene Doge of Venice, ser Leonardo Loredan, has sent ser Bortolo Contarini and ser Alvise Mocenigo the knight, his worthy gentlemen, to my high and glorious court to show the love and royal friendship and ancient peace that existed between us, and to affirm it and work together to improve it. And I swear by that God who created heaven and earth . . . that love and good peace and friendship will always exist between us. . . .

Selim died in 1520, to be succeeded by his son, Suleiman the Magnificent (1520–66). Marco Minio, a seasoned Venetian diplomat, was elected to lead an embassy of congratulation to the new sultan on November 7, 1520. But he did not receive his commission until May 14, 1521, leaving Venice one week later, and he did not arrive in Constantinople until September 27, to the sultan's vexation. Within a few months, however, Minio had confirmed with Suleiman the previous Turco-Venetian treaties, resolved a number of commercial disputes, and taken his leave (his last dispatch from Constantinople was dated January 9, 1522) to

---

106. The manuscript has *Imperator Imperatorum;* the Fulin edition has *Imperatoris, Imperator.*

proceed to Candia in Crete, where he had been appointed duke. Sanudo reports on these dispatches:

February 27, 1522 (32:498–99)   There were —— letters from Constantinople from our ambassador Marco Minio, that is, from —— to December 29.[107] He writes of those urgent events and negotiations with the pasha lords to conclude the agreement, which was finally reached and signed by the sultan, not without much hard labor. The provisions included the old ones that had been in force with his father and two new ones, namely, that should a battle at sea occur with Turkish pirates, any deaths will be their own responsibility, but those taken prisoner will be sent to the sultan for the dispensing of justice. *Item:* if ships or other vessels of the Turks or of the Venetians encounter military ships or vessels, and the former are commercial vessels, they must lower their sails.[108] If they do not, it is permissible for them to be captured. There were also other clauses, as stated in the letters. *Item:* concerning the damage to the light galleys [*fuste*], we arrived at the agreement that the Mosta ship, which was captured and taken from Alexandria, was his, and damages will be dispensed with because the peace agreement had not been concluded when it was taken. The [captured] ship, however, had not yet arrived in Constantinople, even though it had left Alexandria, and it was feared lost at sea. Our ambassador writes that he has received a robe from the Great Lord, from whom he has taken his leave, and that he will embark upon the galley in two days' time to go to Candia and assume his governorship there. He writes that there are no preparations for an armed fleet.[109]

After concluding his mission to the Porte (Constantinople), Minio fulfilled the duty of every Venetian ambassador and composed a *relazione,* a long report on his embassy that included, as prescribed, his assessment of the political and economic strength of the country visited and the character of its ruler. This was sent on to Venice and was read in the Senate by his secretary. Sanudo's summary of this report captures both the ambassador's respect for the extent of Turkish

---

107. Note that it took sixty days for this last letter to reach Venice. It is also worth remarking here on Sanudo's gift for summary.

108. The great galleys of Venice carried large crews to man the oars needed for entering and leaving port. These crews could also be used to defend the ships, along with marines and bowmen who might be aboard. The lowering of sails could provide a signal that this ship was on a commercial rather than a military mission. See Lane 1944, 49.

109. However, in June 1522 the Turkish expedition against Rhodes was launched, and on 20 December the Knights of St. John surrendered. Suleiman's preoccupation with Rhodes gained Venice some respite from immediate danger, and an envoy was elected on 4 March 1523, to congratulate Suleiman on his success. At this point the Fulin edition has many ellipsis points, as if a part is missing. The manuscript has a blank half-page, followed by a new summary.

power and his awareness of the arbitrary nature of the Turkish government, so alien to the legalistic procedures of the Venetian state:

April 8, 1522 (33:314–16)   Summary of the report of ser Marco Minio, our former ambassador to the sultan, sent from Candia to our Signoria.

The sultan has huge resources of manpower, authority, an income of three million gold,[110] and tax revenues of one million two hundred thousand in personal taxes [from Christians].[111] These are collected every day, with additional collections four days per week. The money is put in the treasury: sacks holding 220 weight were full of money. The aspers that are collected are weighed in the same place that the governors hold audiences. The principal tax is the one on sheep, so much per thousand. The mines yield 800,000 ducats per year; salt production gives 400,000; all other commerce yields 400,000. His Majesty spends a great deal on the 10,000 janissaries, who are paid quarterly and who cost him 75,000 ducats annually; at the present time, however, he has a smaller number than that. He has about 10,000 cavalry troops, paid quarterly, who cost him 95,000.

He maintains three households. There is his own. There is also the one for 200 children, where they receive instruction in reading and writing and armsbearing until they are eighteen or twenty years old and then are clothed, given a horse and provisions, and sent on their way. Finally, there is one for the women. He has made many provisions in Pera[112] for instructing the older children. There used to be many Greek Christians living in the Morea [Peloponnesus]; at the present time he has taken away their subsidy.

It is not known whether he has money in the treasury, but it is clear that he is assiduously obeyed. While I was there, he had a Salitar pasha hanged; he was one of the leaders of the Salitars, a group of cavalry, and had many slaves at his command. The sultan sent an agent to his house, who told him, "You, the sultan has decided that you will be hanged." Without further ado, he was led out and hanged while his company wept. No more was said.

He has one hundred large galleys and ninety-two light galleys between Constantinople and Gallipoli, but they are in poor condition. The arsenal he built recently has 114 bays [*volti*], within which there is continuous construction. It is not closed off; rather, since it is made partly of masonry and the rest of wood, one can peer through. He has begun to build an arsenal in Gallipoli;

---

110. The unit of currency is not given, but it was probably the asper. In 1509 fifty-two aspers were roughly equivalent to the Venetian ducat. See Spufford 1986, 290.

111. These personal taxes were imposed on all Christians living in Moslem lands. Battaglia 1961–2000.

112. The Venetian district of Constantinople.

eight bays of it have already been built. . . . This sultan is a perfect Turk and very observant of his own law; he is the enemy of the Christians and the Jews and mistreats the Jews in his territories, which did not happen in the days of Selim, his father.

This is a person who informs himself, who does not like to be told what to do but who instead forms opinions that he clings to stubbornly. I do not believe that he will be a peaceful person, but will soon show that he is most warlike. Now that he has taken Belgrade,[113] he thinks that he holds the keys to Christendom in his hands. They say that Mustaphà Pasha, who is beyler-bey [governor] in Greece and a friend of ours, wants to make war in Hungary. And in our discussions, this Mustaphà told me that our Signoria should not show favor to that king. At the present time, he wants to arm one hundred[114] galleys and send them forth from the strait [Dardanelles].

The sultan is twenty-three years old and hot-tempered; he has dark hair, pale skin, and deep-set eyes. He wears a turban well down over his eyes, which gives him a secretive air. I believe him to be of medium height, but I have only seen him seated, never standing. In the space of a few days three of his children have died, two boys and one girl; two died before he returned from Belgrade, and one since then. He has only one child over one year of age left alive, and two were born a few days before I left. If the sultan were to die, the state would be[115] in the greatest confusion.

The life of the Turkish lord is judged to be very self-indulgent. He makes frequent visits to the women's quarters, creates a lot of disturbances, and often goes sailing. On Fridays he goes to the mosque to greet people, accompanied by his pashas. At the moment he has four pashas. Perì, who is of Turkish birth, answers everyone; he is astute and well versed in government matters. However, he is not very regal in his manner. It is assumed that without him the Porte would be poorly governed; sometimes he has feigned illness. He came very close to being dismissed because of Belgrade and is sixty years old. The second pasha is Mustaffa, who is Slavic by birth; he is a very discreet and courteous man. Good-looking and well built, he is forty years old. He is also the sultan's brother-in-law, being married to the woman who used to belong to Mustazi Pasha; he shows fondness for us and has always helped this Signoria in our dealings with the sultan. The third pasha is Fercal,[116] from Sibenico [Šibenik], who is about thirty-five or less. A warlike man, he went to

---

113. Belgrade surrendered to Suleiman's forces on 8 August 1521 (Setton 1976–84, 3:199), a significant loss to Hungary and the defense of Christendom.

114. This is the number in the Fulin edition; the manuscript has an unclear mark.

115. The manuscript has *restaria;* the Fulin edition has *restava.*

116. The manuscript has *Fercal;* the Fulin edition has *Fereal.*

Syria to expel Gazeli; he is proud and daring. Cassin Pasha, an elderly Turk, is the fourth. He is believed to be a well-intentioned man [*molto dabene*] who does not allow himself to be bribed; he is not very aggressive and says little; people say that he will be dismissed because the beylerbey wants to take his place. These pashas[117] have an income of 25,000 [aspers?] each per year. The beylerbey of Greece is thirty years old and was born in the Morea; he is plump, cheery, and warm hearted. He brought about the downfall of the sanjak [military and civil governor] of Bosnia, who ousted the one from Sibenico, and he soon will be pasha. It is said that as far as the peace accord goes, the pashas were concerned with only two stipulations: that if our ships encounter the sultan's armada when they are at sea, they are to lower their sails, and that if any ship belonging to a subject of his causes damage [to a Venetian ship] and [the offending ship] is captured, it will be sent to the sultan, who will punish them [the captain and crew]; if they happen to be pirates, justice is to be meted out on the spot. He said that the sultan sent with him as a gift two tunics of cloth of gold and 5,000 aspers.[118]

The relationship with the Ottoman Empire was no more resolved when Sanudo's diaries ended than when they began, except that the peace, or extended truce, continued until 1537, the year after Sanudo's death. In these four decades Turkish power continued to play a significant role in the foreign affairs of Venice, as it did in those of the Holy Roman Empire and the papacy. The grave losses that Sanudo witnessed in his lifetime—the loss of the Venetian port of Modon in August 1500, of the commercially important states of Syria and Egypt in 1516–17, and of the strategically significant island of Rhodes in 1522; the defeat of the Hungarians at Mohacs in 1526; and the nearly successful siege of Vienna in 1529—show that these Turkish aggressions continued.

Cyprus was lost in the same year as the victory of Christian forces over the Turkish fleet, in 1571; later, in 1669, most of Crete would fall to the Turks. There would be no satisfactory conclusion to the rivalry and interdependency of these two empires, and every Venetian accommodation with the "infidel" drew charges of betrayal and collusion from Christian powers. A letter written in 1526 by a Venetian merchant in Buda says that the Venetians were much blamed by the Hungarians, "who say that the Venetians secretly give favors and money to the Turks and that all the engineers [with the Turkish forces] are Venetian. For which reason I encounter continual problems with them" (August 18, 1526; 42:417–18). In 1529 a savio di Terraferma stated in the Senate that there was no one who

---

117. The manuscript has *bassì;* the Fulin edition has *bassà.*
118. For another dispatch, see diaries, 27 February 1522 (32:498).

did not believe that the Signoria had brought the Turks into Germany to divert them from Italy, especially because Doge Gritti's son Alvise was with them (July 9, 1529; 51:45). But it was such accommodation, judicious neutrality, and diplomatic dexterity that gave the Venetian empire its long lease on life, without which the history of Europe in this period would have been very different.

Foreign Diplomats in Venice

No picture of Venice's relations with the Italian, European, and Turkish foreign powers would be complete without reference to the presence in Venice of ambassadors from these countries, the concern of the Venetian government for their proper reception and well-being, and the occasional problems posed by a diplomat's sense of entitlement and privilege or a too-close relationship formed between a Venetian host and his foreign guest.

Foreign diplomats were regularly invited to attend the ceremonial events of the Venetian Republic and were often to be found at the elaborate dinners held in the homes of wealthy patricians. A particularly interesting entertainment was presented in the spring of 1513, while Venice was in the midst of the War of the League of Cambrai. The occasion was a *festa* celebrating an engagement between two patrician families. Among the people in the audience were three ambassadors.

May 2, 1513 (16:206–7)   After dinner not much happened, just a meeting of the savi. The reason was that the wedding of ser Ferigo Foscari to the daughter of ser Zuan Venier, head of the Ten, was held at Ca' Foscari. She is the granddaughter of our most serene prince.[119] Upon her arrival, there was a superb banquet, with special honor given to the ambassadors of the pope, Spain, and Hungary and other high-ranking senior patricians. Three of the doge's sons attended. . . . Also present were the prior of San Zanne dil Tempio and Martini, a Knight of Rhodes; they dined in a room apart on a silver service. Permission [to use silver] was given because of the ambassadors whom I mentioned. About ninety-six women were seated at table in the central hall, and between these and others in the adjoining rooms, there were 420 people seated at the main tables. Everything was carried out in splendid order, and it was a fine meal."[120]

---

119. The bride is described as *neza*, which can mean "niece" (the meaning chosen by some historians in this case) or "granddaughter." For the identification of this young woman as the daughter of Doge Loredan's daughter who married Zuan Venier, and therefore the doge's granddaughter, see Finlay 1980b, 82; and diaries, 4:143.

120. The permission to use silver refers to sumptuary laws that, among other strictures, sought to control the expense of wedding celebrations. See below for specific examples.

After the feast came the entertainment, an elaborate series of scenes, separated by dances, in which the women usually participated, and sometimes by musical interludes.[121] More usual were the ceremonial greetings offered to visiting diplomats, such as that provided to the legate (i.e., the papal ambassador) in 1498. Here, as when Venetian ambassadors arrived in Rome, there was a formal ritual involving other ambassadors and high government officials. Receptions in Venice, however, often were vulnerable to inclement weather:

September 11, 1499 (2:1276)   Although today is Wednesday, it was chosen as the day on which the cardinal legate [Juan] Borgia, the great-nephew[122] of the pope [Alexander VI], who has been authorized to come as legate *a latere*,[123] is to be met with the Bucintoro and five fishing boats. In spite of a heavy rain, after dinner the doge and the ambassadors . . . and other prelates and many patricians went aboard the Bucintoro to San Biasio Catoldo[124] to wait for the cardinal, who was coming from Chioggia by sea. . . . It was raining very hard when he disembarked there, and the doge welcomed him. They were all soaking wet when they climbed on the Bucintoro, which proceeded along the Grand Canal as far as the house of the Marquis of Ferrara, which had been prepared for the cardinal. The doge accompanied him to his chamber. I will not neglect to say that all the fishing boats were decorated in the usual manner by the savi ai ordeni.[125] The banners were soaked and ruined; there was extensive damage on my [boat] as well.

Some ceremonial receptions for foreign ambassadors were elaborate enough to provide urban entertainment. Those involving ambassadors from the sultan were among the most scrupulously reported in the diaries, partly because of their exotic aspect but also because the ambassadors always came for a particular, often sensitive purpose and were never resident. Zanne Sius (or Giovanni Symix) had arrived in Venice on June 21 to announce the enthronement of Selim I (1512–20).[126]

---

121. For a description of the complete event, see chapter 9.

122. The Fulin edition has *nepote,* but the legate was actually the grandson of Alexander VI's sister. The index to the Fulin edition incorrectly identifies him as Cesare Borgia. This is not the same Juan Borgia whose murder in Rome is recounted above under "Pope Alexander and His Family."

123. A personal representative of the pope, usually a cardinal, sent from Rome to act in the pope's name in matters of diplomacy, meetings, or celebrations.

124. A small island adjacent to the Giudecca.

125. The manuscript has a period here; the Fulin edition does not.

126. See Zele 1989, 275.

June 23, 1512 (14:410–11)   In the morning, since it had been decided in the Collegio that forty gentlemen of the Senate dressed in scarlet were to be sent to fetch the ambassador of the sultan and bring him to the Signoria, the gentlemen passed through St. Mark's Square [on their way to the ambassador's lodgings]. From San Moisè they accompanied him on land to the Ducal Palace. First came four small Turkish pages preceding him, then the ambassador himself wearing a tunic made of cloth of gold and lined with sable; he was flanked by ser Nicolò Michiel,[127] university laureate, and ser Anzolo Sanudo. The interpreter[128] was ser Piero Zustignan, the son of ser Francesco the councillor, and there were others . . . ; they wore turbans[129] on their heads and silk tunics, while the other patricians around them were dressed in scarlet. At the end [of the group] came four janissaries; in all there were twenty Turks. The courtyard of the Ducal Palace and the square were filled with people coming to see the ambassador arrive. The audience chamber had been decorated, and the doge, who was dressed in velvet, and the members of the Collegio, who wore scarlet, processed as far as the staircase to meet him, greeting him warmly and honorably. When they had entered the palace, and the ambassador had been seated next to the doge, he presented his letter of credentials, written in Greek. This will be translated and a copy of it transcribed below. Then, with the help of a Venetian gentleman who had been a merchant and a prisoner in Constantinople, the ser Piero Zustignan mentioned above, [the ambassador] asked the doge how he was and greeted him on behalf of his lord.

But it was not always easy to satisfy an ambassador's expectations:

December 24, 1514 (19:331)   The news this morning was that the Turkish ambassador had been to the Collegio.[130] He complained that we have not given him a gold brocade tunic lined in sable like the one given to the other ambassador to Venice, Alibei.[131] He refused [a gift of] cash.[132] As of now I do not

---

127. The manuscript has *Nic° Michiel;* the Fulin edition has *Marcho Michiel.*

128. The Fulin edition has a period after *interpetre,* whereas the manuscript seems to have it before.

129. The manuscript has *sexe;* the Fulin edition has *fexe.* According to Battaglia 1961–2000, 18:792, s.v. "sexe," this is a strip of cloth wound as a turban.

130. Zele 1989, 276, identifies this ambassador as "Mechanet is Pachmogam . . . ambasciatore dal nome incomprensibile." He had come to Venice to report on Selim I's victory over the shah [Sophi] of Persia. He stayed in Venice from 3 December 1514 to 9 January 1515.

131. The manuscript has *Alibei;* the Fulin edition has *Aly Bei.*

132. Ali Bey had been in Venice a few months earlier, from 29 January to 25 February 1514. He had received five hundred ducats, whereas this ambassador was offered only four hundred. Zele 1989, 269n92.

know how it will be resolved. He came down from the Signoria and went to see the Basilica of San Marco and the jewels. Ser Andrea Gritti, the procurator, was there with him and showed him the jewels; they had met when Gritti was in Turkey. When the ambassador saw the bejeweled ducal corno, he said, "This corno was made especially for your head. You will be doge."[133]

Some Turkish ambassadors became well known in Venice, among them the Ali Bey mentioned above, who apparently was known for his provocative comments, as in the following excerpt:

November 7, 1517 (25:72–73)   This morning Alibei, the interpreter and ambassador of the sultan, arrived.[134] Several elderly patricians were sent on barges to meet him, [along with] the heads of the Forty and the savi ai ordeni, to increase the size of the group, for of the many who were ordered to meet him twelve were absent. He was wearing a dolman of crimson velvet and a tunic of cloth of gold with a sable lining; part of his entourage was dressed in silk, and part in scarlet. He has with him only seven men, however. Once he had entered the Collegio, he took his leave. The doge spoke gracious words to him of the good peace that our Signoria wants to maintain with his lord, saying that he respects his lordship more than all the others in the world and that he hopes that his lord has the same attitude toward our Signoria. He also hopes that, should something happen, [Ali Bey] would intercede to put things right with his lordship, and he also said other things. He said that we are writing to our *baylo* to say that in the matter of the debt of Nicolò Zustinian the Signoria has no obligations, because he [Nicolò] does not have an [official] contract, as has our baylo, but has his own business undertaking, etc.[135] This Ali responded in part through the interpreter and in part on his own, for he knows Latin,[136] saying that he will undertake every favorable office with his lord and that he wants to maintain the good peace. He touched on the idea that it would be wise to renew [the treaty] now, then took his leave. He was accompanied by the same gentlemen, and when the weather is right he will

---

133. This came to pass nine years later.

134. Ali Bey was a dragoman, or professional interpreter. Turkish interpreters were occasionally used for diplomatic missions, which in this period of the Ottoman Empire were handled ad hoc by a variety of civil servants, there being no regular diplomatic missions. This was his second mission to Venice, 26 October to 11 November 1517, and its purpose was to solicit the tribute Venice had owed the sultan for the island of Cyprus since the Ottoman victory over the Mamluk Empire earlier that year. Zele 1989, 278.

135. Nicolò Zustinian had been bailo in 1514, three years earlier, when he was acquainted with Ali Bey. See Zele 1989, 276, 278; and diaries, 18:203–4.

136. This could be either Latin or a Latin-based language. Ali Bey knew both Latin and Italian.

leave. His expenses have been taken care of, great friendship is being shown to him, and great honors have been paid him. He is a shrewd man and an evil one, and wherever he goes he spies for his lord.[137]

Apropos of this, I wish to record that last Saturday, the last day of October, he wanted to climb the Bell Tower to see the city of St. Mark from it, saying that it had been so well restored. The savi ai ordeni were sent to accompany him, and a collation of malmsey wine and confections [*confeti*], etc., was prepared for him, and off he went. Once he was up there, he asked how one could approach the city by sea. He was told that it could be done with large ships by way of the two castles but that the port, or the channel, did not stay in the same place, that seasoned pilots were brought along to plumb it continuously, and that at times it represented a danger to ships and galleys and other large vessels. And he said, "If my lord came with 300 galleys to this port and armed the boats with good artillery, he would come inside." The savi ai ordeni said, "And then what? The inhabitants of the city would be there to oppose you." Then he said, "But couldn't you come by way of Chioza?" He was told that that would only work with small boats because of the shoals. Then he asked how far away dry land was, and he was told five miles to Liza Fusina and Mergera [Marghera]. Next he asked, "Don't your enemies come?" And he was told that they did. Then he asked, "Why don't they advance with their artillery loaded on rafts[?]" and he said, "When my lord goes on an expedition, he has so many people with him that if each one carried just one bundle of sticks, he could make a bridge that would reach this city." The answer given to him was, "Those who would be defending the city would not let them get close, and ten would be enough against one hundred." Then he asked where Friuli was, on what side. It was shown to him. He remarked that one could ride horseback to a distance of only five miles from the city. And the savi ai ordeni said, "My lord ambassador, we are telling you that in this recent cruel war [of the League of Cambrai], in which all the kings of the world joined to defeat Venice, not a single man of this city died. Everything was accomplished with money and the deaths of foreign soldiers, and this city is still as packed as an egg with people, nor is it possible to conquer it," and other such words. Then they came down from the Bell Tower.[138]

137. Ali Bey was known to Sanudo from his first visit, in 1514. See Zele 1989, 276 and references to vol. 17 of the Fulin edition. That earlier visit had also concerned the renewal of the 1503 treaty.

138. There is no better example of Venetian triumphalism than this, turning the disastrous experience of Agnadello and the grueling recovery of Venice's Terraferma empire into a paean of self-praise. Cf. Leonardo Loredan's speech in diaries, 16 March 1517 (24:79). See also Finlay 2000, 1005–6, converting the defeat of Agnadello into a heroic triumph over Venice's combined enemies. Ali Bey's questions justify Sanudo's declaring him a spy. More than a decade later,

Because of the complex, ambivalent relationship with the Turks, some associations between their representatives and Venetian patricians was permitted, but only if the occasion was an official courtesy and did not involve giving sensitive information. The following excerpts indicate that it was permitted for a Turkish ambassador to be the house guest of the governor of Mestre but that it was not permitted for him to receive privileged intelligence ten days later.

June 5, 1522 (33:278–79)   I note that the Turkish ambassador named — has been to this city on a previous occasion. At that time, ser Zuan Francesco Mocenigo, who now holds the dual post of civil and military governor of Mestre, was a savio ai ordeni. The two of them became great friends, and now the ambassador is asking for him and has written to Mestre to say that he wishes to see him. The governor invited him to supper there, and he said that he would come to supper and dinner. Thus, on the morning of the 5th[139] he went there to dinner, and he stayed for supper and spent the night. The governor paid him great honor.

June 16, 1522 (33:309)   It should be known that there was a great deal of complaining and talk in the Council of Ten about ser Valerio Marzello, the former savio di Terraferma and the owner of the Corner house at San Samuel, where the Turkish ambassador was staying. [Marzello], having made friends with the ambassador, had given him a map of Dalmatia and Istria. This matter has caused great displeasure on the part of the entire Collegio, and he came very close to being put on trial for it.

But just as often, Sanudo includes encounters that were quite friendly and indicated a cordiality beyond the formal requirements of diplomatic converse:

June 3, 1530 (53:253)   Then came the ambassador from the Turkish sultan.[140] He disembarked at the quay near the Ducal Palace because it was raining. A handsome, tall, and dignified man, he was dressed in cloth of gold . . . and was accompanied by twelve Turks wearing turbans[141] and fourteen patricians dressed in scarlet. . . .

When he arrived in the Collegio, the doge rose and came forward [to him]. The ambassador, through an interpreter, said that the great lord and the pashas sent a greeting to the doge and the Signoria, and the lord in person had sent him and given him the letter that he presented, and the lord had sent

Sanudo disapproved of taking Turks up into the Bell Tower unless the tide was high enough to hide the channels (27 September 1525, 39:479).

139. The manuscript appears to have *a dì 5;* the Fulin edition has *a dì 3.*

140. Identified by Zele 1989, 283, as "Chusem," who stayed in Venice from 2 to 21 June 1530.

141. The manuscript has *sessa;* the Fulin edition has *fessa.*

him here to invite the doge to Constantinople to attend the celebration for the circumcision of the sultan's four sons because of the friendship that the lord feels for the doge and the Signoria. . . .

The doge, with a kindly expression, responded: "Would God that we could come, but we cannot walk, and we are too old." And he spoke laughingly, so that even the ambassador laughed. And then the doge said: "Our ambassador will be there in our name." And the Turk urged that the Venetian ambassador be sent soon; the doge said, "It will be done."

To be noted: the Turkish ambassador is given ten gold Venetian ducats for his daily expenses.[142]

Occasionally, envoys other than the Turks presented difficulties. The Spanish attendants to the papal legate proved acquisitive guests in the house of the Marquis of Ferrara, the premier guest quarters of the Signoria:

September 25, 1499 (2:1351)   It should be noted that the [papal] legate left this morning for Padua. [The governors] there have been sent written instructions to honor him. Two carpets and some sheets . . . belonging to our Signoria were stolen by his Spanish attendants from the house of the marquis, where he was staying.

And some decades later the French ambassador complained about how he was treated by his hosts:

April 25, 1521 (30:169–70)   After vespers the savi gathered to hold an audience. It should also be known that yesterday, after vespers, the Signoria went to the doge's chamber to hear the Ferrarese ambassador, as I have written. The French ambassador arrived, saying that he wished to speak to the doge alone in secret. This seemed strange to the doge, who said to the councillors, "We wish to hear him in your presence." But it was clear to the Collegio that the ambassador wanted to have a meeting alone with the doge, and the Collegio and the heads of the Ten directed the doge to hear him. Thus the councillors and the Collegio went upstairs. The French ambassador came with two sacks of stuff, that is, sheets and bed covers that were torn, saying, "Look at the manner in which your Raxon Vechie treats me." He had the [bedding] emptied out in the doge's chamber, saying that if the Signoria would not give him good [bedding], he would buy it himself. He spoke in high dudgeon. The

---

142. The ambassador was also given five hundred ducats as a parting gift and clothes for his attendants. See Zele 1989, 283, on this embassy. He appears frequently in vol. 53 of the diaries. See index to the Fulin edition, s.v. "Choseim."

doge expressed his concern, saying that they would take care of it, and the orator departed, leaving the stuff where it had fallen in the doge's chamber. Then the Collegio came back downstairs; after hearing the story, they concluded that the French ambassador was shallow and ill-tempered. A message was sent to Alexandro Frizier, the majordomo of the Raxon Vechie, who is in charge of such matters, telling him to give the ambassador what he wants. Frizier said that he had given the French ambassador as much as [he had given] three other ambassadors.

Secretaries

Crucial to the support of the Venetian diplomatic network were the diplomatic secretaries who accompanied ambassadors to their foreign posts, sometimes themselves representing Venice between the departure of one ambassador and the arrival of his successor. These secretaries were chosen from the citizen class and represent the degree of responsibility such men could achieve in the diplomatic activities of the Venetian government.

May 11, 1526 (41:322)   A bill was proposed by the councillors, the heads of the Forty, and the savi di Consiglio and di Terraferma concerning the expenditures of Andrea Rosso, our secretary to the most Christian king [of France]. [He purchased] a gown of black velvet, called a *saio,* and a robe of lightweight black damask for the sum of forty-eight ducats, as appears in his letters. Since it is not proper for him to be out of pocket for these items, it was proposed in the bill that the forty-eight ducats be paid by our Signoria. It passed.[143]

Of equal and occasionally superior importance were those civil servants and citizens who prepared documents and dispatches sent out by the Venetian government or helped to decipher those received. The following excerpts concern Zuan Soro, a famous Venetian cryptologist who was called "the father of Venetian cipher" by one of his juniors in the ducal chancellery.[144] The excerpt below tells of Zuan Soro deciphering an intercepted letter about the condition of hostile imperial troops toward the end of the War of the League of Cambrai.

April 8, 1516 (22:114)   From Lodi, from signor Marco Antonio Colonna, the captain general of the imperial army, April 2, in code. It was deciphered by our [secretary] Zuan Soro with great difficulty. He [Colonna] writes that he

---

143. See above under "Charles VIII and Louis XII" for the secretary Zuan Piero Stella's report from France to the Signoria in 1498.

144. According to R. L. Brown, 1869–71, vol. 2, app. 2, p. lxx.

is there, and he asks the emperor, to whom he is writing, to please either send him the money to pay the landsknechts or come in person. The 20,000 ducats that they are expecting from the king of England will not be paid by that king's agents to anyone except the Swiss soldiers, and the English king will not send any more, and he [Colonna] needs 4,000 more to give to certain other Swiss soldiers. *Item:* if the money is not sent within eight days, the Swiss soldiers will leave. [He also writes] that for reasons of provisioning, it is better for them to leave Lodi and to move camp.

A decade later, another intercepted letter was brought to Zuan Soro for deciphering, this time by the papal legate:

June 18, 1526 (41:616)   The papal legate, the bishop of Pola, arrived bearing a letter in code that had been intercepted. It was from the imperial ambassador in Rome, the Duke of Sessa, who was writing to Naples. He [the papal legate] says that it must be decoded here by Zuan Soro, the secretary, who is unique in all the world for his ability to decipher codes. The Collegio therefore ordered that it be decoded.

Such an ability as Zuan Soro's was not only useful to the Venetian diplomatic network but also enhanced Venice's reputation. Thus a Venetian secretary, Andrea Rosso, could write from France that in that country Zuan Soro was "held to be divine" because he had deciphered certain letters sent for that express purpose from Poitiers to Venice" (August 26, 1526; 42:473). No wonder the Venetians were confident in their foreign relations: from their most senior patrician diplomats to their employed clerks, an unusual degree of professionalism was evident and secured their reputation, if not always their security.

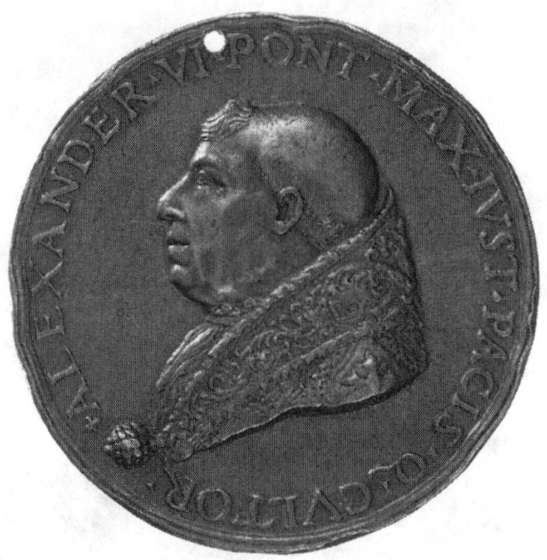

Medal of Pope Alexander VI (Rodrigo Borgia), 1492. Edward
E. MacCrone Fund, Image © Board of Trustees, National
Gallery of Art, Washington.

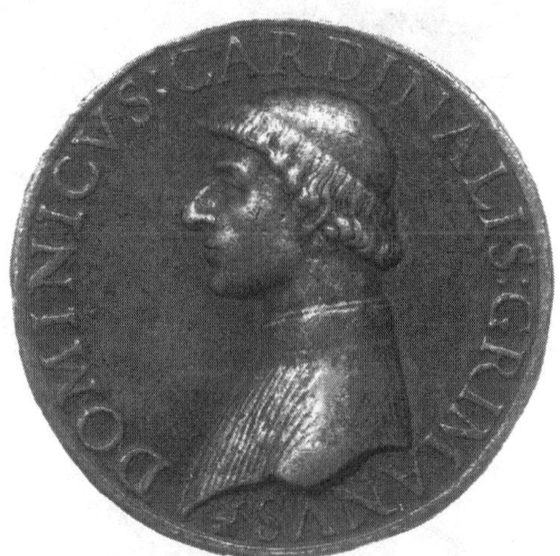

Vettore Gambello, Medal of Cardinal Domenico Grimani,
1493. Samuel H. Kress Collection, Image © Board of Trustees, National Gallery of Art, Washington.

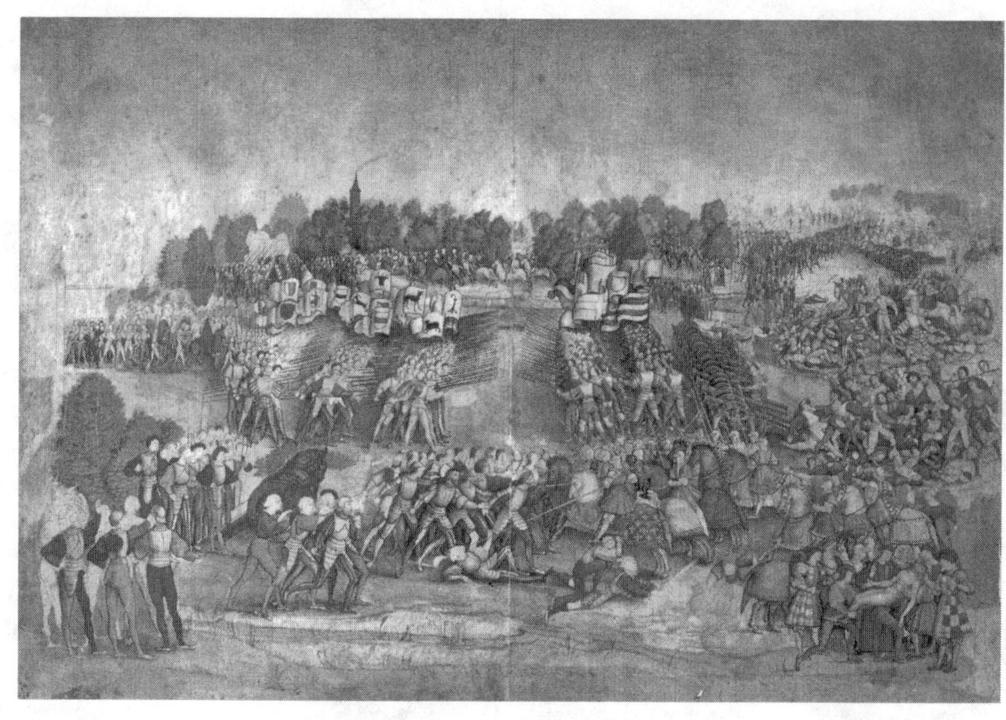

Maitre a' la Ratiere, Battle of Marignano in 1515. Musée Condé, Chantilly, France. Réunion des Musées Nationaux / Art Resource, NY.

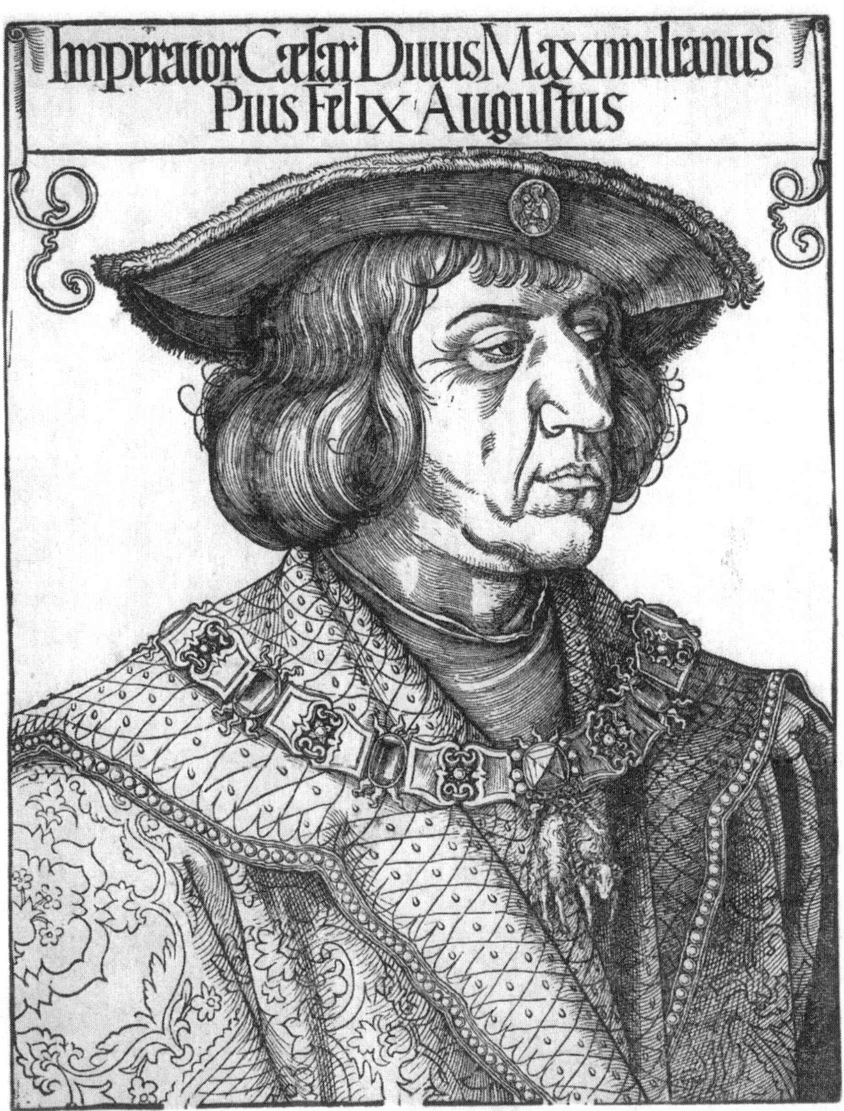

Albrecht Dürer, *Emperor Maximilian I*, woodcut, c. 1518. Rosenwald Collection, Image © Board of Trustees, National Gallery of Art, Washington.

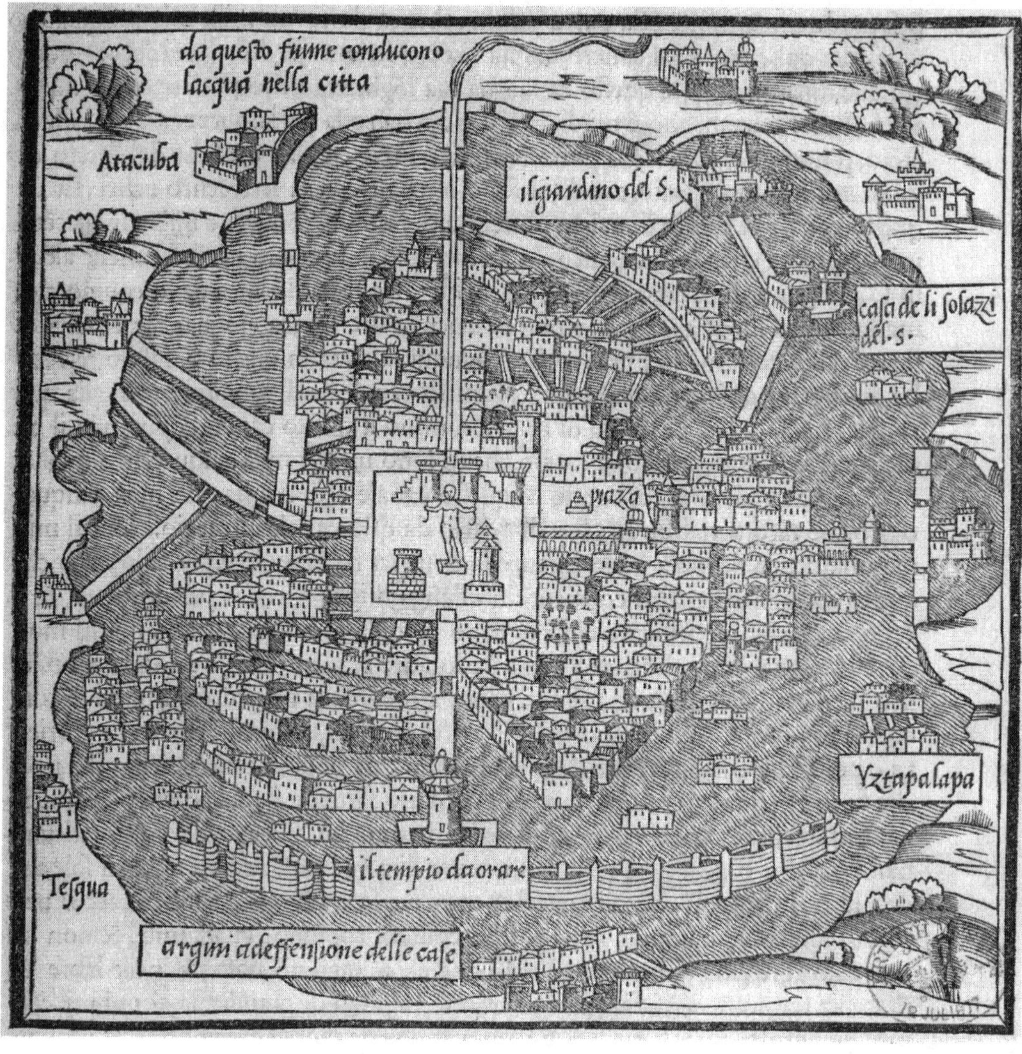

The great city of Temistitan (Tenochtitlan), from Benedetto Bordone, *Tutte l'isole del mondo* (Venice, 1528), x. © British Library Board. All rights reserved. Maps. C.7.b.10.

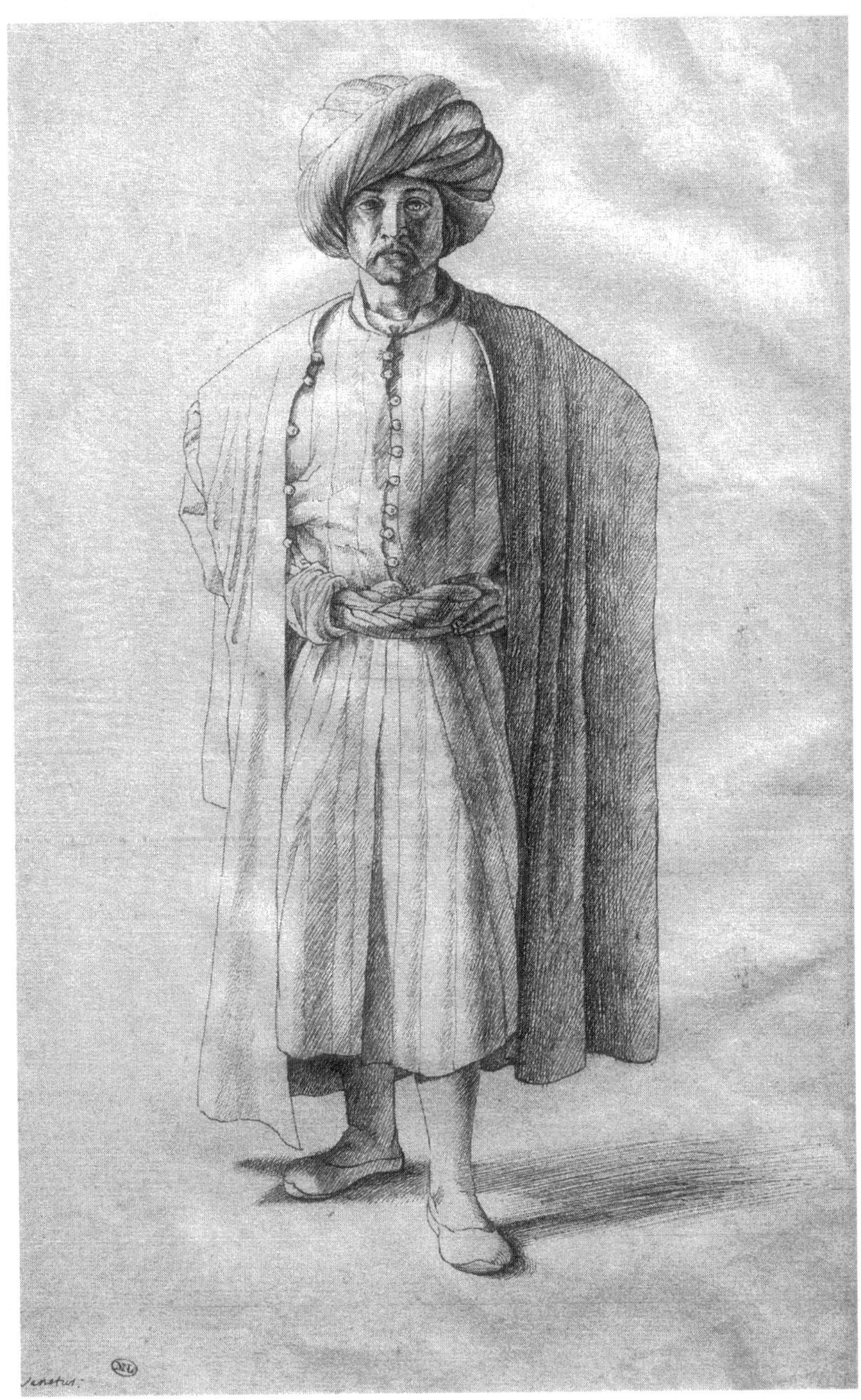

From the workshop of Gentile Bellini, drawing of an Ottoman Turk, late 15th century. Louvre, Paris. Réunion des Musées Nationaux / Art Resource, NY.

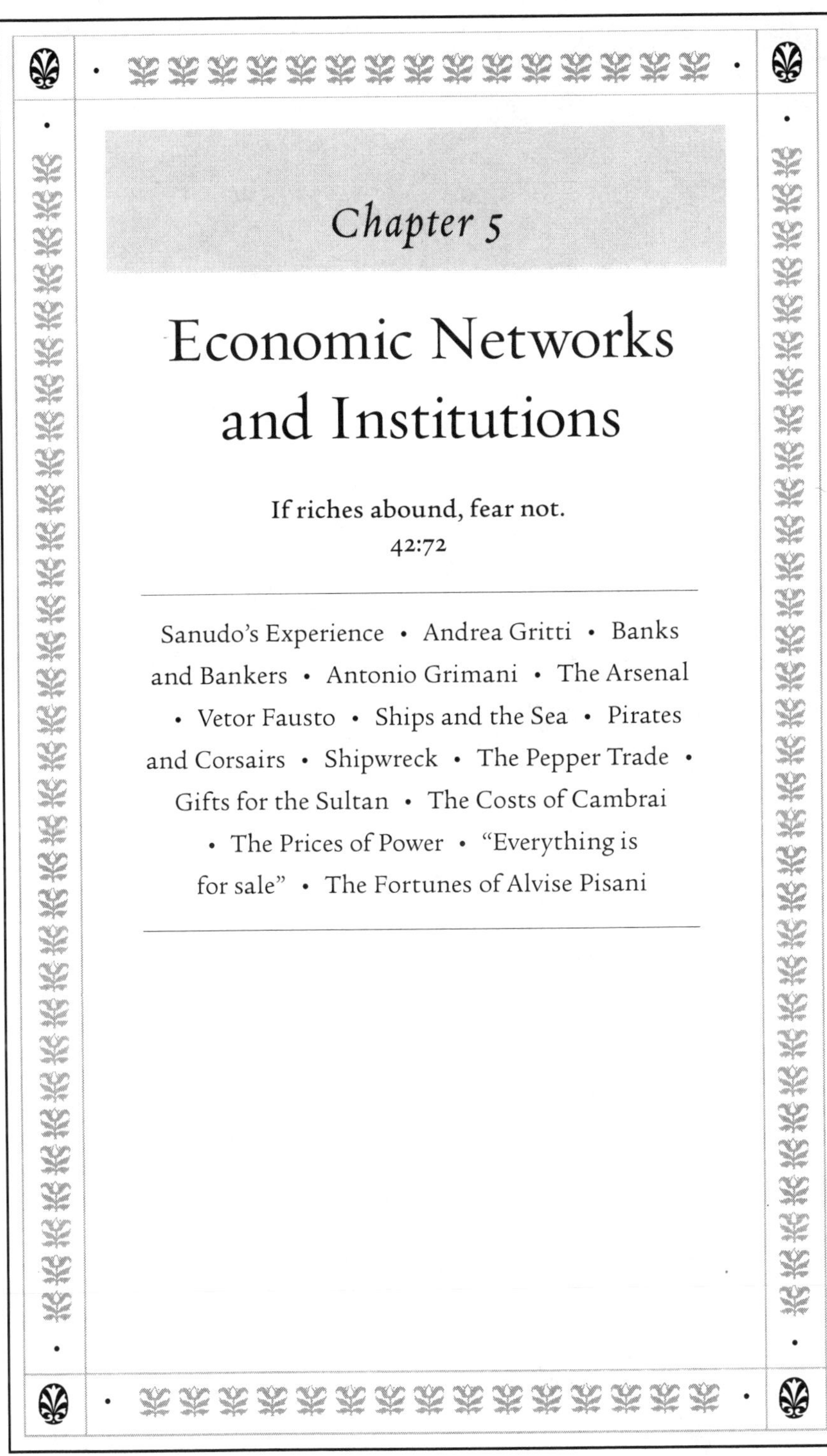

Chapter 5

Economic Networks and Institutions

If riches abound, fear not.
42:72

In the first volume of his diaries, Sanudo describes the arrival in Venice of four Portuguese ships carrying sugar from the island of Madeira. He adds some background on the sugar industry there and remarks on how the quality of that Portuguese commodity had debased the prices of sugar from Cyprus, Alexandria, Syria, Dalmatia, Sicily, Valencia, and other places. He then adds, apologetically, that he wanted to include this information "although it was not relevant to the war."[1]

Having undertaken his diaries to describe the French invasion and subsequent wars that began in 1494, Sanudo only casually began to include such economic information. But over the course of his thirty-seven-year record, much more came to be encompassed: the focus of government officials (Sanudo among them) and the general populace on nautical concerns, Venetian merchants abroad and within the city, banking and government finance, urban industries such as the shipbuilding in the Arsenal and the luxury trade, pirates, shipwrecks, and the venal competition for government office. These were subjects the diarist could hardly ignore, for they were part of the very fabric of Venetian life. They provided the city with its livelihood, affected its political practices, supported its lifestyles, and funded its every enterprise. To be sure, Sanudo described them as a journalist, not an economist, often including them because of their newsworthy aspects. But in supplying a record of these activities, he offered insights into the economic substructures of the city.[2]

Sanudo's Experience

From his earliest experience in the government, Sanudo was exposed to financial and commercial matters. He had begun his career as one of the "little lawyers" (*avocati pizoli*) of the Ducal Palace. He was attached to the Giudici di Petizion, a court whose purview included commercial suits between Venetians up to the sum of fifty ducats. His first important governmental position, as a savio ai

---

1. "Licet non sia a proposito di guerra." Diaries, 17 August 1496 (1:271). Chambers 1998a, 2, points out Sanudo's sense that in any classical work of history, war was the greatest theme. But Sanudo's practical perception that this kind of economic information would be critical to any future understanding of events is indicated by the continuation of that sentence: "Still, I wanted as a matter of course to describe this here, for a permanent record."

2. Much of this chapter is based on the work of two great scholars, Frederic C. Lane and Felix Gilbert, to whose vast learning all students of Venetian history are indebted. It was Lane and his colleague Reinhold Mueller who described Sanudo as more a modern journalist than a modern economist (1985, 100n19), "more interested in the spectacular than the ordinary." Lane 1966d, 147.

ordeni, a position he held seven times between 1498 and 1510, entitled him to a seat in the Collegio and introduced him to the complexities of Venetian maritime concerns and the problem of finding and funding the crews of the Venetian merchant galleys, which provided the city with its economic sustenance. He had hardly entered upon his duties as a savio when, on October 11, 1498, the three state attorneys had to decide how to pay crews who had returned from the voyage to Barbary and were shouting for their wages on the stairs of the Ducal Palace. "And I, Marin Sanudo, savio ai ordeni, being chief for that week, was given this matter to settle" (2:27).[3]

A month later he was sent to the Lido to inspect a group of cavalry seeking employment by the Signoria. He reported back that the government should not hire them "because the horses and the men were so woebegone" (November 23, 1498; 2:146-47). The following winter and spring he was busy with the selection of patrician bowmen and deck hands for the ships (February 22, March 2, July 1, 1499; 2:466-67, 491, 869).[4] In addition, he found himself negotiating with crews hired for commercial voyages who, anticipating that their ships would be coopted into the war fleet, wished to be paid, not at their usual commercial rate, but at the higher rate that the crews on warships were currently earning in the war against the Turks (1499-1502). Sanudo records his explanation of this problem to the Collegio:

June 23, 1499 (2:844-45)   *Item:* I explained that crews could not be found to serve on the great galleys at eight lire a month. Instead, they want to serve in the armada at twelve lire a month, [the same wage] being paid to man the narrow war galleys. Therefore, by order of the Collegio, we made an announcement yesterday in the Piazza that they will be paid four months' salary [at eight lire a month] and that whoever does not go now will not be able to go on any galley for five years. Nevertheless, this did not work, and the galleys for Flanders, which used to be easily provisioned, could not be manned. Then there was considerable discussion, and the Collegio ordered that today we should make every effort to punish these ruffians, because if one was successful, everyone would claim the same. By dint of my efforts, I fixed the price at eight lire per month. Thus, it was my job to see to the manning of the Flanders galley whose shipmaster was ser Fantin Querini . . . , the Beirut galley whose shipmaster was ser Jacomo Corner, and the Alexandria galley whose

3. Cf. 2:323, 25:205; and Lane 1987b, essay 10, p. 25. For the composition of the Collegio and the roles of the state attorneys *(avogadori di comun)* and the savi ai ordeni, see appendix B under "Governmental Terms."

4. The patrician bowmen, sometimes called "bowmen of the quarterdeck," were young patricians whom this employment gave experience at sea and a chance to trade in foreign parts. On Sanudo's role, see Lane 1987b, essay 13, 158nn47-49.

shipmaster was ser Trojan Bolani; and for this reason we, the savi ai ordeni, went to the recruiting benches with the shipmasters.[5]

But finding and funding crews was not easy. The following year it was established that back pay *(refusura)* would be given, one-third at the hiring and two-thirds on board (April 22, 1500; 3:251). The next day, April 23, crew members demanded the back pay all at once (3:253). And the day after that, they got what they wanted. "There was a discussion about the *galioti* who would not sign on for the galley voyages because they wanted their entire back pay, and it was determined they should have it" (April 24, 1500; 3:254).[6]

Such naval and commercial training led to what Sanudo hoped might be for him the first of increasingly significant appointments, that of treasurer *(camerlengo)* in the subject commune of Verona, a post he held from April 1501 to October 1502 (4:8, 329). The treasurer was the fiscal officer who served under the *podestà,* or civil governor, and the *capitanio,* the military governor. He rarely alludes to his Veronese experience in his diaries, but he was in charge of supervising the collection and transfer of funds to Venice (see 4:235 for payments made in February 1501, just before his term) for expenditures for defense, for the entertainment of dignitaries such as the queen of Hungary (4:287–88), or, together with the podestà and the capitanio, for reviewing the damage caused by the flooding of the Adige River (4:265).[7]

---

5. These shipmasters, or *patroni,* of the great merchant galleys "gained their positions by making the highest bid for the galley when the government put up to auction the charter for their operation on specified commercial routes." If they represented a group of investors, they were the ones whom the others had selected to go with the ship to look out for their interests. Lane 1973b, 53. "With Turkish intentions doubtful all through the spring of 1499 the great galleys had been auctioned for the usual voyages and the crews contracted for at the usual commercial rate of eight *lire* per month." Lane 1987b, essay 8, p. 158, and essay 10, p. 21. However, Sanudo's success in holding the crew to that rate was short-lived. Some ships arrived at the battle fleet undermanned (diaries, 2:918, 1063), and the next year the crew's wages were raised to twelve lire per month (3:266).

6. Lane defines *refusura* as the balance due upon dismissing a crew. 1987b, essay 10, p. 25. The problems of manning the ships persisted, not merely because of the pressure to raise wages but also because of the difficulty of finding men and turning them into an effective crew (diaries, 3:1546). Sanudo reports on the sicknesses that seemed to afflict crews from Lombardy (9 February, 12, 21 March 1501; 3:1419, 1544, 1581), on the endemic lack of a sailing complement (21 March 1501; 3:1581–82), and on the unruliness of the dissatisfied sailors and the efforts made to control their behavior in Venice (27 April 1501; 4:27). As Lane wrote, "Not lack of ships but lack of men limited Venetian sea power." 1973b, 364.

7. On Sanudo's experience in Verona, see Chambers 1998b, essay 8, pp. 37–66. Chambers points out (p. 41) that for information about Venice during this period, Sanudo relied, "often word for word," on the contemporary diary of Pietro Dolfin, as well as the reports of his friends. There are some interesting indications of this reliance (never openly acknowledged), such as an entry of 28 January 1502 (4:214) about the arrival in Venice of two ambassadors from the king of the Romans, to which piece of information Sanudo adds: "I believe this happened in February, but I

This experience with financial matters was surely useful, although Sanudo's position in Verona did not result in a step up the career ladder in Venice. After his sixteen months in Verona, he returned to Venice only to be reappointed to the savi ai ordeni. But financial concerns were part of the business of government and as such always remained of great interest to Sanudo.

Andrea Gritti

Others were able to use their fiscal and commercial experience more effectively. Nowhere is this better illustrated than in the career of Andrea Gritti and his activities during these same years of the war with the Turks. Like all traveling merchants in Sanudo's period, Andrea Gritti was expected to provide useful political and military information to the Signoria. In the late 1490s, because of the imminent war with the Turks, such information about Constantinople was especially needed.

A grain merchant resident in Constantinople at the time, Andrea Gritti began to act as a leader for other Venetian merchants who were also there to trade with the Levant. Some years earlier, the official bailo, usually the representative of the resident community to the sultan, had become *persona non grata* to the sultan because of his spying activities.[8] So when the sultan instituted an embargo against the resident Italian merchants shipping grain from the area, and this at a time of great scarcity in Italy that had forced up the price of bread beyond what most could afford, it was Andrea Gritti who stepped into the diplomatic breach and resolved the problem.

February 8, 1497 (1:508)   It was learned from letters sent from Modon[9] by Francesco Bembo, proveditor there, that the export of grain belonging to the Turkish lord had begun again and that Andrea Gritti, our patrician, who was at that time a merchant in Constantinople, after receiving permission from the Sultan to export, had rented ships to load with grain totaling 20,000 *staio*.[10] This was good news, and the cost of flour in the Venetian warehouse suddenly fell by eight soldi per *staio* and grains fell by twenty soldi per *staio*.

Clearly, this diplomatic achievement was not only critical to the well-being of Venice but also profitable to Andrea Gritti himself. Yet in the next few years, as

---

inadvertently wrote it down here." See also an entry of 20 September 1502 (4:320), where he comments on his return from this post and begs forgiveness for any errors because he had written what he had heard, *per relazione*. That he considered the news in Venice, even secondhand news, more important to report than his own experience *in* Verona indicates his priorities.

8. For this entire section on Andrea Gritti, see J. C. Davis 1974, esp. 100, for the loss of the Venetian bailo in Constantinople.

9. A Venetian port in the Peloponnesus, known today as Methone.

10. Lane (1992, 245) defines a *staio* as eighty-three dry liters or two to three imperial bushels.

the situation with the Turks worsened, he undertook the personally hazardous role of conveying to his government the size and movement of the Turkish forces; so as to escape the notice of the Turkish authorities, he used a disguised commercial language. Sanudo called such a code "sub enigma" (December 15, 1498, 2:208) and appeared confident of its translation even though the meaning at times seems far from obvious:

January 2, 1499 (2:292)   A letter of November 9 written by Andrea Gritti and consigned to the bailo in Pera was received . . . saying in a parabolic fashion [*scrita in parabula*] that a pirate had captured a ship of 200 *botte,* which means that the Turkish lord is putting together an armada of 200 sail.[11]

January 29,[12] 1499 (2:372)   A letter received from Andrea Gritti . . . in Constantinople. "Things here are calming down rather than otherwise. I do not see a sure profit from cornering the market"—as if to say that the armada is forming slowly and its departure is uncertain.

March 28, 1499 (2:559)   Letter received from Constantinople . . . from ser Andrea Gritti, under the guise of a debtor in prison, who said he wished to leave in the month of June, meaning that the Turkish armada would go forth by the end of June.

Gritti's secret reports were particularly valued because they proved more reliable than the rumors circulating at the time:

July 1, 1499 (2:869–70)   After dinner there was a meeting of the Great Council. And a brigantine arrived, so that the entire city was full [of news] that the Turkish armada had set sail because so it was said by the master of the brigantine. Then the doge came up to a meeting with the savi di Collegio, and the letters were read. The truth was seen, and the master was sent for and greatly rebuked by the doge for having spread this falsehood. The master answered that his men on Corfù had told him it was so. . . .

A communication from Andrea Gritti, consigned in Pera, was read. It is dated May 27 and is written in a cipher using a kind of business-transaction language. It states that the [Turkish] armada is assembled and will sail to Corfù within fifteen days and that the land army is organized and will go to Greece; he writes briefly using his code.

---

11. Gritti's "parabolic fashion" was not a unique device. In 1482–83 a Florentine businessman wrote partly ciphered and unsigned letters from Milan to a business associate in Pisa, who sent them directly to Lorenzo de' Medici's Chancellery in Florence. Decoded from cipher and perhaps even from their business reference, they proved to be analyses of current Milanese policy. See Mallett 1994, 242.

12. The manuscript gives the date as 29 January; the Fulin edition dates it 27 January.

This mercantile code must have been standard enough to be easily understood by Sanudo, who served as a savio ai ordeni for much of this time. Perhaps for the same reason, as early as January 1499 Gritti had begun to write of the "great danger" of sending messages over land (2:542). In late July 1499 some of his letters were intercepted, and by August 1499 he was imprisoned [for espionage] along with many other Venetians, including other merchants and workers in the Venetian community of Constantinople (2:1073, 1128; 3:15, 1494, 1554–55).

The detention was to last two and a half years, for much of the period of the war between the Turks and Venice, 1499–1503. In the beginning, Gritti was not well treated, and his goods, along with those of other merchants, were auctioned off by his captors. But the discovery that he had served as a kind of ambassador gave him some protection. News came a year later, in August 1500, that he and the other Venetian merchants "were well and had hope" (3:596, 1555).

By December 1501, through the intervention of a pasha (4:72), a ransom of 10,000 ducats was levied for the entire group of sixteen, with Gritti's share, by far the largest, specified at 2,400 ducats (4:181, 243). Early the next spring, the group was released, and on a Sunday in March Gritti made what appears to have been a triumphal return to Venice:

March 13, 1502 (4:244)   On Sunday ser Andrea Gritti arrived in this city. He had been imprisoned in Constantinople and ransomed, as reported above. His cousin Alexandro Gritti was with him, and some others. . . . The whole city was pleased at his arrival. The next morning Andrea appeared in the Collegio and, together with the heads of the Ten, reported many things to them; the session lasted until none. It is said that he is here to negotiate peace, and it is rumored in the city that he will be made a savio a Terraferma or a councillor in order to have him in the Senate. And his son and his followers are maneuvering to have him made councillor for [the *sestiere* of] Santa Croce.

Their efforts were successful, and on April 3, 1502, Andrea Gritti, merchant, began his important political career with his election as one of the doge's six councillors:

April 3, 1502 (4:254)   The new councillors from the far side of the Grand Canal were elected. Ser Andrea Gritti, recently returned from Constantinople, won by the *scrutinio*. It is the first elected office he has held in this Republic; nor was he on any earlier ballots, except that the other day in the Senate he was nominated to be a savio di Terraferma but lost, being short of votes. This ser Andrea Gritti will be a worthy citizen, because he has every good quality. First, he is handsome, generous, well spoken, etc.; one could even say that "his worth is the more pleasing because it appears in a handsome body."[13] He was elected in recognition of his merits, in that to warn his homeland, he wrote letters from Constantinople, giving information to our Signoria of the events and the actual preparation of a fleet the Turks were undertaking. His letters were found, so he was [imprisoned by the Turks and] in danger of having his head cut off.[14]

Sanudo would be less enthusiastic about Gritti's dogeship, but in this early phase of Gritti's career he shared the general appreciation of this patriotic merchant turned successful diplomat and politician.[15]

Banks and Bankers

At the same time that Andrea Gritti was composing "under his enigma" informative but risky letters to the Venetian government, several family banks in Venice were undergoing their own high-risk business. Their histories make clear the intricate familial and economic relationships between the patrician politicians who ran the government, the patrician traders whose economic activities made possible the armies and argosies upon which the reputation and viability of the city-state depended, and the bankers, who were either patricians or wealthy members of the citizen class and whose funds provided emergency loans to bridge the gap between what was collected in taxes and what was needed by the government to pay its mercenary forces.[16] Among these family banks, that of the Garzoni was the oldest.[17]

By 1499 the Garzoni bank had been established for nearly seventy years. But

---

13. "Gratior et pulchro veniens in corpore virtus." Virgil *Aeneid* 5.344.

14. Translation based on J. C. Davis 1974, 106. It should be noted that Gritti's return and election, described above, may not have been directly witnessed by Sanudo, since his term as treasurer of Verona did not officially end until October 1502.

15. While Gritti's political rise over the next two decades was quite spectacular, it was not unique. J. C. Davis points out that of the thirty-six doges elected between 1300 and 1550, fourteen were known to have been merchants, nine probably were not, and thirteen may or may not have been, although the likelihood is that they were and that it was so unremarkable a pursuit that it went unmentioned, whereas governmental honors were always mentioned. 1974, 98.

16. See Gilbert 1990, 29, 34–35. On banking as a form of commerce, see Lane 1966c, 76; and Tucci 1996, 787, 790–91, 798.

17. The following section is greatly indebted to Lane 1987a and 1966c, 69–86. An earlier account based on Sanudo's diaries, although lacking specific references, is Brunetti 1950. See also Tucci 1996, 787–99; and Mueller 1997, 241–51. Lane points out (1987a, 1–2) that the physical bank was a booth set up near the market in Rialto, and that the banker sat in this booth entering financial transactions into a journal. The coin itself was stored with the state treasurers or in the Mint for safety, and merchants transferring funds could do so simply by asking the banker to transfer funds in writing from one account to another. The depositors' risks were real; the banker's risks were enormous, as the diaries bear out.

on January 29 of that year Sanudo remarked on some strange activities of the doge and other members of the Signoria, excluding the savi ai ordeni and the heads of the Forty. He later discovered that these activities were an effort to deal confidentially with the financial difficulties of this bank, whose solvency the government hoped to maintain.

January 29, 1499 (2:377–78)   This morning the doge did not convene the Collegio, but called to his chambers the heads of the Council of Ten, the councillors, and the savi,[18] and no one else was allowed to enter. Seven times we savi ai ordeni entered along with the heads of the Quarantia, and then we were sent out. They were [called] into session, as we later learned, at the behest of the Garzoni bank, which was on the verge of bankruptcy and requesting the support of our Signoria. [The Garzoni] said they needed several thousand ducats from our Signoria and were pleading for help, and they had been to the doge the evening before to tell him this. And in all secrecy it was decided that the honor of this city lay in keeping this bank on its feet, so it was determined to provide it with some funds without fanfare. But there were no funds available from our Signoria because of the heavy expenditures and the wars on two fronts,[19] so it was agreed to borrow funds from the office of the procurators and other banks . . . , and all were willing to lend. In addition to sending for the members of the Garzoni bank so that they would not be suspected [of being the borrowers], they sent for the banker Hironimo Lipomano and the banker Mafio Agustini, and I believe they even sent for the banker ser Alvise Pixani. They too provided some funds, which I saw being carried into the doge's palace in sacks; and these Garzoni were given ——, and ser Piero da Pexaro, the official cashier, was sent to Rialto [to reassure creditors]. But nothing availed, as I will describe below, because everyone was furiously withdrawing money.

The Garzoni were not popular at this time. Rumors circulated that for four years they had been buying silver at a price above the Mint's ratio to increase their specie reserves, and they had lost 30,000 ducats in that speculation. It was said that they had allowed their relatives heavy overdrafts and that a Florentine had been permitted to withdraw 45,000 ducats,[20] although Venice was at war with Flor-

---

18. When *savi* appears, as it does here, without further description, it refers to the six savi grandi, or savi di Consiglio, that is, the senior group as distinct from the five savi ai ordeni and the five savi di Terraferma.

19. That is, the government was maintaining an army in northern Italy, where even after the withdrawal of the French army under Charles VIII the situation remained volatile, as well as preparing to fight a naval war against the Turks.

20. See Mueller 1997, 241; and Lane 1987a, 2.

ence in this period. Yet the Garzoni were given safe-conduct by the Venetian government for a year for their persons and their goods, lest they be seized by angry creditors, an action that did little to reassure those same Venetian creditors.[21]

February 1, 1499 (2:391)   This morning at Rialto a considerable crowd gathered at this bank to withdraw money, but even by a late hour none of the Garzoni had come to the bank. Therefore, everyone became suspicious, and there was much grumbling throughout the city. And I do not wish to neglect recording that 500 ducats that my mother had received from a legacy had been deposited in this bank. Since I knew what was happening, I ordered ser Lunardo, my brother, to withdraw it, and so he did, so that on the eve of the holiday he withdrew from the bank these 500 ducats and had that number of Hungarian gold ducats.[22]

The Garzoni stated that they intended to pay back all their creditors, for they had the funds but not the cash. Sanudo surmised that money was tight everywhere because of the wars Venice had been fighting, the continual levying of taxes to fund these wars, and withdrawals from banks to purchase Monte Nuovo bonds, which were shares in the public debt.

February 1, 1499 (2:391-92)   [The Garzoni say] that they have 45,000 ducats owing to them, of which 10,000 are owed by bad debtors; they have 15,000 in jewels and silver and 45,000 in real estate.[23] And the members of the Garzoni family said they wanted to pay everyone but needed time, given that everyone wanted to withdraw his money and they did not have the cash. . . . But I must state what I heard, that the money of the Venetians has disappeared largely because during four wars taxes have been raised in the city, that is, for the War of Ferrara [1482-84], 37 *decime;*[24] for the war with Austria [1487], 5 *decime;* for the invasion of Italy by Charles VIII, king of France [1494-99], 18 *decime;* and in this war against the Florentines [1496-99], 10 *decime* up to this point.[25] And huge sums of money have been spent in the purchase of Monte Nuovo bonds and the building of homes and the expenditures on luxurious dress, so that the city is in financial straits.

---

21. Lane 1987a, 2; 1966c, 76-77.

22. On the circulation of foreign coins in Venice, see Tucci 1996, 769, 786, 799-800; for an illustration of such coins, see Pezzolo 1996, 721.

23. The manuscript has *in stabele ducati 45 milia;* the Fulin edition has *in stabeli ducati 43 milia.*

24. The *decima* was a direct tax inaugurated in Venice in 1463. See Mueller 1997, 454.

25. By August 1499 Venice had a military force of 14,000 on the Italian front and 20,000-25,000 embarked on its fleet. See Pezzolo 1996, 727; and the diary entry for 31 August 1499 (2:1176-79).

Another meeting was held in the ducal chambers. The creditors pressed for some guarantees and wanted more control over the process of repayment through a committee of creditors, which the Garzoni protested against as humiliating for so ancient and accommodating a bank. The government continued its mediation between the two groups:

February 4, 1499 (2:401)   The doge spoke of the good intention of these Garzoni to pay everyone and said that, God willing, after Easter they would make a beginning, and they had many debts to call in. He exhorted the creditors to quiet down, saying that the Garzoni intended to pledge their entire fortune to their creditors. They would place the money they collected from their debtors in the care of our government treasurers; [the Garzoni] would keep one key and would give the other to the heads of the creditors' group, etc. The creditors were still complaining about not having their money, and they wanted to name the heads for their group to oversee the bank's books. And so, somewhat subdued, these Garzoni went to the bank, but they wrote nothing and did nothing and were scowled at by everyone, and this caused great pain to ser Andrea, who was the senior member of the family and a very good man.[26] And in one vote, two were elected by the Collegio who, in the name of the Signoria, would keep the key to the Garzoni funds, and they, in place of the heads of the creditors' committee, would view the Garzoni account books.

The loss of confidence in the Garzoni spread to other banks in the city. Hard pressed were the Lippomano, the Pisani, and the Agustini.[27] By May the Lippomano bank had lost a quarter-million ducats' worth of deposits and had to be given a moratorium similar to that given the Garzoni, to the great distress of the Lippomano creditors.[28] The Pisani saw the handwriting on the wall and through the efforts of relatives were in a position to dispense 100,000 ducats. The creditors, who previously had been adamant in their demands to withdraw their funds, now tried to reinvest.

May 17, 1499 (2:726–27)   The heads of the Council of Ten—ser Benedetto of the Pexaro family, ser Piero Loredan, and ser Nicolò di Prioli—arrived [in the Collegio] and with great vehemence sent everyone outside, and this was because of what had happened at the Pisani bank. This morning ser Alvixe

---

26. Lane says that Sanudo, having gotten his family's money out of the bank, was prepared to be charitable toward this senior Garzoni. 1987a, 4.

27. The Lippomano and Pisani were patrician-family bankers; the Garzoni and Agostini were *popolani*-family bankers. There was also a patrician Garzoni family.

28. Lane 1987a, 4; diaries, 2:723, 726–27, 731.

Pisani wanted to write in the bank journal as usual, but there were so many who wished to withdraw funds, saying "Make this entry,"[29] that the pen was snatched from his hand. Whereupon, seeing such vehemence, he raised his pen and said, "Signori, one by one, each of you will have what belongs to you," and he sent word to his uncle ser Piero Loredan, mentioned above, and to ser Beneto Zustignan, his father-in-law, who ran to the heads of the Ten. Then our Signoria, after consulting with the Collegio, undertook this remedy: these heads of the Ten were sent forthwith to Rialto, together with ser Marco Antonio Morexini, knight and councillor, ser Filippo Trun, procurator and savio dil Consejo, ser Alvise Venier, savio di Terraferma, and Zacharia di Freschi, secretary. When they arrived at the bank, they made the whole crowd give way, and the herald announced that this bank was giving surety funds amounting to 100,000 ducats, naming the guarantors. Thereupon, just as everyone had earlier wished to withdraw his deposit, now everyone shouted at the same time, "Take my pledge for me." . . .

Nevertheless, after dinner, money was frantically being put [into the bank], and the reason for this was the failure of two banks, and the city was complaining that safe-conducts had been issued by the Council of Ten.[30] And this morning I saw ser Beneto Zustignan come into the Collegio followed by many merchants and patricians, who were shouting that the safe-conduct for the Lipomano should be withdrawn, etc. And they were told to come back tomorrow. *Item:* it should be noted that ser Mafio Soranzo, who was the silver supplier for the Lipomano, is bankrupt by 20,000 ducats; also, the [moneychangers] Perduzi and Alvixe Nicheta, who ran small banks across from the consuls [of the merchants], are bankrupt.[31]

The economic tremors continued to spread. Four military leaders were asking for their troops' wages. The government responded that this was not the moment, that it would be taken care of in the future. In short, what the petitioners received were what Sanudo called "good words," *bone parole* (2:731), but not wages to pay their troops or themselves. Then there were the masters of the Beirut and Alexandria galleys, "dismayed that because of the failure of the Lipomano

---

29. "Fè questa partida."

30. The failed banks were the Garzoni and the Lippomano, whose members obtained safe-conducts in order to leave the city.

31. Lane 1987a, 5. On the Garzoni (and others') dealings in silver, see Mueller 1997, 239. On moneychangers, who could be quite unscrupulous, see Sanudo's report on 7 July 1525 of a patrician, ser Francesco Michiel, who cheated the poor by claiming to change "clipped coins" into good but whose claimed full-weight coins were also *stronzadi,* from the verb *stronzar,* which Boerio defines as "with a scissors or file or other instrument cutting off the edge of coins." Michiel was arrested by the captain of the heads of the Council of Ten (diaries, 39:180). For the *consoli dei mercanti,* see appendix B under "Governmental Terms."

bank, they were unable to move ahead and to post the bonds [as required] because the shareholders' money was tied up in that bank" (2:732). At least for these, some solution was found. Sanudo, who had found and suggested the solution, recorded it proudly: "And during the discussion in the Collegio, I registered an opinion that was praised by everyone, which was to propose in the Senate that the 200 ducats loaned to the Arsenal be recalled, as well as the 200 ducats that used to be given to the captain to buy biscuits. And so [the shipmasters] were called in by the doge, who said, 'This will be expedited for you by the savi ai ordeni'" (May 18, 1499; 2:732). Meanwhile, the German merchants were frustrated by the financial paralysis and came with their lawyer and commercial representative to plead their own situation:

May 20, 1499 (2:736)   Then there appeared [in the Collegio] German merchants from the Fontego dei Tedeschi, with messer Zuan Batista, their lawyer, and Zuan de Cheler, who manages the affairs of the Focher.[32] They pressed their demands because of the failure of the Garzoni bank and, recently, that of the Lipomano; they had deposited about 30,000 ducats in the Garzoni bank and 10,000 ducats in the Lipomano. And they complained that they were told by the Garzoni to wait until Easter, and then at Easter to wait until the feast of the Ascension, and now the Garzoni say they want fifteen days to think about deciding the time when they would be able to satisfy their clients. Therefore, the German merchants wished that the safe-conduct, at least for the Garzoni's goods, would be cancelled so that either the Garzoni could give some of those goods that they have in their galleys to their creditors or even that these German merchants could themselves prolong the time [until which they had to repay their own debts].[33]

The merchants received the same temporizing reassurances that the Garzoni wished to pay back everyone and that there would be further consultations. The government's temporizing was forced by a severe shortage of bullion in Venice. Historians have pointed out that the interruption of gold shipments from Barbary and the diversion of German silver to Lisbon, prompted in part by the news of Vasco da Gama's circumnavigation of Africa (1497–98), led to a serious drop in Venetian imports of gold and silver, which added to the crisis caused by the government's heavy borrowing to pay for its military needs.[34] To increase the circulation of bullion, the government ordered the Mint to work on holidays, for which it had to seek ecclesiastical sanction: "The patriarch was asked to permit

32. Johannes Keller was the factor of the Fuggers in Venice. Mueller 1997, 245.
33. Cf. Lane 1987a, 5, and, for Lane's version of the following excerpts, 6–7.
34. See Lane 1966c, 81; and 1987a, 10.

[the Mint workers] to work on feast days. He answered that he could not do so but that he would absolve those who did" (August 23, 1499; 2:1121).[35]

All this time the Garzoni were rallying their allies and their funds. Before their moratorium expired in February the following year, they opened a new bank with the blessings of the government and the church but without the usual musical fanfare, a wise forbearance since their new venture failed six weeks later.

February 3, 1500 (3:96–97)   On the feast of San Biagio. In the morning a number of delegates were sent by our Collegio to accompany ser Andrea di Garzoni, along with his sons and nephews, to attend a High Mass at San Zuan di Rialto. Meanwhile, a great many gold ducats, many bags of coins, and a stack of *mocenigo* coins[36] fresh from the Mint [were put] on top of their counter. [The total] was estimated at 60,000 to 70,000 ducats, and the bank journal was prepared. All around were the captains of Rialto with officials, to keep back the crowds. After the mass, the delegates arrived, each flanked by a Garzoni; that is, the Garzoni were dressed in black, and they did not want a wind ensemble.

When all the officials and the Garzoni had assembled, a herald announced the reestablishment of the bank in the traditional terms:

In the name of the Most Holy Trinity, Father, Son, and Holy Ghost, it is made known by the magnificent and illustrious signori, governors of the fisc of our most excellent Signoria of Venice, that the magnificent and generous ser Andrea di Garzoni, with his sons and nephews . . . has given to this office his oath and guaranty of 50,000 gold ducats for the reestablishment[37] of his bank. Which guaranty has been voted acceptable as sound, secure, and sufficient for three years, according to the law of November 27, 1455, established by the excellent Senate in regard to pledges and guaranties. In addition, our most illustrious Signoria has given surety of 20,000 ducats for the specified period of three years, as stated above, so the bank could be opened. It was so authorized by the Senate, which on this past January 30 deliberated upon and passed the bill, mindful of the merits and other excellent and praiseworthy conditions of the Garzoni family and their bank. The Garzoni above cited, with God's help, promise everyone to fulfill their duty, as has always been the practice of this family. The total guaranty of this bank amounts to 70,000 ducats. And long live San Marco! "Et viva San Marco!"

---

35. Mueller 1997, 245, points out that the German merchants could not sell the silver they had imported because nobody had sufficient liquidity to buy their bullion.

36. See appendix B under "Vocabulary Used in the Original."

37. The manuscript has *per el rellevar;* the Fulin edition has *per el revelar.*

And then this ser Andrea di Garzoni went to the bank and opened the journal and began to write.

Sanudo lists some of the depositors who came in turn to be inscribed—an agent of Antonio Grimani's and men from Lucca and Florence—and he rejoices that this will be a good bank, pleasing to God and a great honor for the city. But six weeks later he had a different story to tell:

March 16, 1500 (3:148)   This morning the Garzoni bank failed again. There was great resentment in the city that the bank had been reopened and then, after funds had been deposited, failed. And the doge said in the Collegio that the Marranos[38] had withdrawn 30,000 ducats from the bank and that the Garzoni are going to a monastery, and it is said that they have the money [with them there]. After dinner there was a proclamation in Rialto that all the creditors should gather forthwith at San Giovanni di Rialto because they intend to choose the heads of the creditors' group for this Garzoni bank.

Official inquiries were made at the Garzoni home about their whereabouts, but relatives of Andrea di Garzoni said they did not know where they were. Nor would they respond to a demand that they turn over the account books and records: "they did not know; so it will be difficult." Threatened with imprisonment, the next day the Garzoni made the books and records of both the old and new banks available to the authorities, and the creditors' committee met. "There was much noise but nothing was accomplished" (3:148).

The succeeding months witnessed the continued crises of the Garzoni, Lippomano, and Pisani banks. The Lippomano were imprisoned but escaped (3:716, 1066; 4:827–28, 108). Embittered creditors railed against the bankers, citing the hardships their failures had imposed: monasteries and hospitals were unable to function, citizens were forced to sell their homes because they could not pay their taxes, young women became prostitutes for lack of dowries, the suddenly impoverished died of melancholy (4:244–45, 518). In the end, the Lippomano settled with their creditors in March 1504, giving sixty-five ducats on a hundred.[39] The Pisani remained a powerful family (see below). "Time," remarked Sanudo, whose own small fortune was not at risk, "will take care of everything" (4:108).

38. Spanish Jews who had converted to Christianity but remained suspect of secret Judaism, especially in times of financial stringency.

39. Lane 1987a, 9–10. At the time of the Lippomano bank's default, the depositors numbered 1,248, of whom 700 were patricians. Diaries, 3 January 1504 (5:654–55). Because of the number and prominence of their creditors, these banks, with their fortunes and misfortunes, were of concern to the entire city. See Tucci 1996, 790.

Antonio Grimani

Meanwhile, one Venetian was able to profit politically from the bank failures. During the spring of 1499, as the Turkish fleet prepared for war and Venetian banks faltered and failed, the Venetian government tried to ready its forces and find funds to pay for them. On April 12 the savi and four of the councillors (Ferigo Corner and Antonio Grimani not among them) proposed to the Senate that the Great Council elect a captain general of the sea to lead the Venetian naval forces against the Turks. "And ser Antonio Grimani went to the podium and excused himself, saying he did not wish to be made captain at this time. He offered [instead] to meet the need and to arm ten galleys with his own funds" (2:613). Two days later, in spite of his disclaimer, Antonio Grimani was easily elected captain general (2:619–20). And a week after that election he appeared prominently in public, resplendent in his new naval garb, and standing next to a counter stacked high with coins, he made good his offer to hire the crews and arm the ships.

April 21, 1499 (2:637–38)   Sunday, in the Collegio. The doge, with the ambassadors and the usual ceremonies, that is, [accompanied by] patricians, went to San Ziminian at the head of the Piazza. This solemnity should take place on the morning of Pentecost Sunday, but it occurred today.[40] And also today, as soon as the doge had been accompanied to the Ducal Palace and after the ambassadors departed, ser Antonio Grimani, procurator, captain general, dressed in crimson velvet, with a velvet cap, came down the stairs in the midst of procurators, councillors, knights, and others, so that whoever had accompanied the doge went on to accompany the captain general to the opening of the recruitment bench. On the counter, for the manning of the ships, were five piles of gold ducats of different sorts, including Venetian, and one pile of mocenigo coins, and many small sacks of marcelli,[41] each containing ten ducats' worth, so that the total was said to be 40,000. Grimani's sons were seated there; the captain general stayed a while, then left, and everyone went home.

---

40. "La qual solennità dovea andar la matina de la domenega di Apostoli." Pentecost was on 19 May, the seventh Sunday after Easter, which was on 31 March that year. Diaries, 2:733, 563. In this case, the ceremony may have been advanced into April to assert the stability of the government and the reliability of its political and military representatives, that is, the doge and the captain General, so to assuage anxiety about the bank, a not unusual use of religious ceremony to serve a political purpose. San Gemignano was the church at the western end of the Piazza. It was later destroyed by Napoleon to permit a grander entrance to the Piazza.

41. See appendix B under "Vocabulary Used in the Original."

Grimani's fate would take a sharp downturn a few months later when he led the naval forces to a shocking defeat, but at this moment his popularity stood high, and it would return later to carry him toward the highest office.[42]

The Arsenal

Most of the galleys manned and provisioned with government funds and private contributions such as Grimani's were refurbished in the government's shipyard, the Arsenal. This immense shipyard, storehouse, and armory had been famous in the fourteenth century, when Dante compared that crowded part of hell where sinners boiled in pitch to the workplace of the Arsenal's caulkers and other employees.[43] In his *De origine* Sanudo describes this enormous installation as "truly one of the finest things in the world. . . . Here every skill in building galleys and other craft is practiced. . . . Here there are innumerable caulkers and ship's carpenters; there are ironsmiths at work here making every kind of ironwork; included here is every skill necessary for this purpose. . . . And lastly, it is the most beautiful and marvelous thing to see our Arsenal so well provisioned."[44] For this reason it has been called by a modern historian "a genuine industrial concentration";[45] everything needed for the final product—a hemp factory, timber yards, gun foundries, sail makers—was contained there. And for the same reason, the Arsenal was a wonder to contemporaries, a site visited ceremonially by the doge and honored guests of the city.[46]

By any count, the Arsenal was a remarkable complex. Oversight was provided by a patrician board of three *patroni al Arsenal,* or lords of the Arsenal, who served overlapping terms of thirty-two months.[47] Its workers—as many as two thousand—formed a little city within the city. Sanudo, whose interest was sharpened by his own considerable exposure as a savio ai ordeni, includes many passages about the Arsenal in his diaries. Its most important personnel and their wages are listed in 1503 (5:107): "These are the salaried employees of the

42. For Grimani's fall and rise, see chapter 2, "A Doge's Election."

43. Dante, *Divine Comedy, Inferno,* canto 21, lines 7–15. The Arsenal had been founded in 1104. R. C. Davis 1991, 104.

44. Sanudo 1980, 36–37.

45. Lane 1968, 60. R. C. Davis 1991 states that it was "among the earliest and largest examples of state capitalist industries in modern Europe" (47). As to its size, Sanudo gave it as "a circumference of twenty *stadii,*" which, according to Lane 1992, 146, was equivalent to sixty acres.

46. See, e.g., diaries, 49:357. The Arsenal was part of the usual itinerary for distinguished guests, along with the jewels of San Marco, the glassmakers on Murano, etc. On one occasion it was shown to the Turkish envoy Ahmed, and "it pleased him greatly, for the excellent order of everything there" (29:411). But on a later occasion the Arsenal was not included in a tour because it was "lacking in materiel" *(disfornito)* (33:443). Sanudo dined there on the feast of St. Martin, 11 November 1521 (32:122), as the guest of Lorenzo Falier, whose brother was a lord of the Arsenal.

47. See Sanudo 1980, 107, 246–47; and R. C. Davis 1991, 48.

house of the Arsenal, in this year 1503, on September 20." The list includes the foremen for the outfitting, arming, and manning of the ships; the foundry workers, the doorkeepers who monitored those entering and leaving the shipyards *(portaneri)*, the guardians *(vardiani)*; the arms steward *(masser)*; the supply master *(provisionato)*; and some of the main employees on the ships, such as the scribe, who maintained records of the cargoes *(scrivan)*, and the mate *(nochiero)*.[48] There were also the guardians for the *casa* itself, as the Arsenal was called, including the bell ringer *(sonar la campanella)* and timekeeper *(conzar le hore)*, the customs bookkeeper *(scrivan a doana)* and letter clerk *(tenir conto di le lettere)*, and external supervisors such as those charged with supplies of wood *(legnami)* and hemp for ropes *(canevi)*, which came principally from Treviso, Montagnana, and Istria.[49]

A major concern of the government was to keep the supplies of wood and hemp from the Terraferma flowing into the Arsenal. Protection of the forests led to a number of laws concerning land use.[50] The need for high-quality hemp for the Tana, the rope factory adjacent to the Arsenal, presented its own problems. The best hemp came from Bologna, and it was a coup for Venice in 1476 to lure away from that city one of the expert hemp growers, Michele di Budrio. In 1503 the Senate appointed Andrea di Budrio, a descendant of Michele's, with a good salary (which would pass on to his son) and the use of a castle as a reward for improving the hemp of Montagnana:

January 19, 1503 (4:631)   It was proposed by all [the committees] to give three ducats per month for his needs to a certain Andrea di Budrio, who brought the hemp of Montagnana to a quality equal to that from Bologna. *Item:* after his death the same three ducats a month will go to his son. *Item:* and [he may live in] the castle of Montagnana, though it will serve as lodging for the lords of the Arsenal when they go there. The bill had 23 against, 80 for, and it passed.[51]

While each craft group within the Arsenal complex had its particular identity, the workers as a whole were known as the *arsenalotti* and had special privileges and responsibilities. During the interregnum between doges, they formed an honor guard at the Ducal Palace, served as torchbearers at ducal funerals, and

---

48. Lane 1992, 17, 157. Lane 1966b, suggests that *masser* also means "rope-layer" (276n35) and "shipper" (279n54).

49. For another extensive list, see diaries, 5:928–30; and for a later period (c. 1560), see Lane 1992, 161–63. See also Rossi 1996 for Arsenal personnel and their wages.

50. See chapter 2 under "The Magistrato alle Acque"; and Appuhn 2000.

51. Lane 1966b, 282. Lane remarks that for his desertion of Bologna, Michele di Budrio was perpetually banished from the Papal States, and his property there confiscated, for which he was amply compensated by the Venetian government.

carried the newly elected doge on their shoulders around the Piazza. They alone could work as laborers in the Mint. In times of tension they guarded Piazza San Marco, and for every meeting of the Great Council their chiefs provided armed guards under their admiral (who was the chief non-noble supervisor) for the portals of the council chamber.[52]

So important were the activities of the Arsenal that when it suffered a devastating fire and explosion in 1509, the entire city was afflicted. It occurred in the uneasy months before the battle of Agnadello, when military preparations were under way and the news from the Terraferma was ominous.[53]

March 14, 1509 (8:17–19)   There was a meeting of the Senate after dinner. And I saw letters from Cremona written on the 12th, full of news from Milan, which I will summarize below. And while the Senate was meeting, at about twenty-one hours after sunset something important happened: two huge blasts of cannon and powder exploded into the air, so that the houses and the Ducal Palace and the stars in the sky shook. And this happened because a fire had started—or been started—in the Arsenal, in the powder supply, and it burst into flame in this manner. At this, everyone ran to the Arsenal to see; I was among them, and I saw appalling things, terribly upsetting, as I will relate. And the entire Senate came down [from their chamber], fearing some disaster. Then they went back up, except for ser Polo Capello, knight, who is in charge of the armaments for the Council of Ten; the *executori,* ser Hironimo Capello and ser Marco Antonio Loredan; *arsenalotti;* and ser Daniel Dandolo, lord of the Arsenal, who today had been moving his things to stay there because he had just taken up this office. They went [to the Arsenal] with others to make provisions. . . .

Now first, on my way there, I met the captains [of the guard], in boats and on the land, with four whom they had taken into custody and whose heads were covered. The captains said that these men had fired the powder and were from Trieste.[54] Others said that they were Frenchmen caught in the Arsenal, and others said they were taken in the church of San Martin, and they charged them [with this crime]. Then further along I encountered the many bodies pulled from the ruins, some burned, some mangled, some without a head, without an arm, some half-crazy,[55] unable to speak, with faces like Saracens, blackened by the fire, who were being carried out on planks. Among

52. Lane 1992, 186–87; R. C. Davis 1991, 162ff.

53. This is one of three major fires described in this volume of excerpts, a reminder of how much of the city was made of wood and how devastating fire could be. For the Rialto fire in 1514, see chapter 6; and for the burning of the Corner house in 1532, chapter 8.

54. They might therefore have been loyal to the emperor-elect, Maximilian.

55. The manuscript appears to have *mezi pazzi;* the Fulin edition has *mezi parti.*

these I saw ser Francesco Rosso, foreman, a very worthy man, and everyone grieved for his death because of the fine galleys he had built and his good design.[56] And I saw [the bodies of] Vicenzo Zenaro, the son of the steward, in full gathered sleeves, and another, who—it was said—was a gentleman, with full sleeves and a robe lined with marten, placed in the church of San Martin. It was said that he was ser Alvise Loredan, newly made a galley commander, but it was not true: he was Carlo Bontempo, the scribe of the Cinque, who had accompanied Zenaro there. So that in the end it is thought that more than sixty have died, and many were badly wounded, among whom many boys and porters and other worthy men who worked in the Arsenal. And the stones of the wall fell like rain in the Arsenal and did great damage to the poor wretches who found themselves in such a storm.

The explosions caused the roofs of the artillery storehouses belonging to the Council of Ten and other offices to cave in and did dreadful damage in the Arsenal. As for the powder, only about twelve thousandweights burned because, by God's will, two days earlier 4,000 barrels of this powder had been loaded on barges, and had it not yet departed from the Arsenal for Cremona and elsewhere, and had those barrels remained there, and had the fire also gotten into the large powder storehouse, the entire Arsenal would have burned down. Many of the old houses in the district of Castello were ruined, and the monastery of San Daniel suffered great damage to its roofs and glass windows; but especially distressing was the death of so many valuable men. There was a high wind. Many measures were taken to see that the fire did not reach the galleys. All the porters one could find at Rialto or San Marco were sent there to help with the damage.

The men who had been retained by the captains of the guard were examined for a long time; however, no decision was reached to put them under torture, and they were released. But the public was enraged. The archbishop of Crete, hearing of the tragedy, visited the Arsenal with his entourage, but his garments in the French style drew suspicion, the officials mistreated him, and he had to flee to a nearby church. All the next night the lords of the arsenal stayed up with those sent to work in the Arsenal. Wine and bread were supplied to the porters, and all the while bodies continued to be found. And then the true cause of the disaster was discovered:

Now it should be made known that the true cause of the fire was revealed the following day. It was learned from one of the half-dead porters that in order

---

56. Note the use here of the honorific *ser* before the name of a nonpatrician. See R. C. Davis 1991, 54, for the translation of *sesto* (normally "the curve of an arch") as "ship design."

to seal a casket in which there was powder, a nail was struck with a hammer, and a spark flew off, and this ignited the powder and caused the damage.[57] And if it had not been for a certain large round ship that was being worked on nearby and protected many who hid there, there would have been a great loss of the master craftsmen of this Arsenal; this large ship became warped by the fury [of the fire]. The storehouses and the hemp storage rooms at the Tana were destroyed, as were the walls of the Arsenal on that side. The master craftsmen set to work in the morning and rebuilt the wall. And it should be noted that one other time, in 1476, on December 9, a fire ignited the powder in this Arsenal because a horseshoe had struck a spark. From that time forward, the horses working there went unshod.

The damage was not as great as was believed, except for the death of the men, and especially master Francesco Rosso, lamented by the whole city. The next day he was carried to be buried at San Zuane Pollo, and all the masters of the Arsenal came to do him honor.[58]

Francesco Rosso was only one of several shipwrights in Venice who achieved fame in these decades, for the economy and reputation of Venice depended upon its ships. The names of several others stand out in the diaries: Leonardo Brexan, famous for his armed round ships; Vetor Fausto, for his quinquereme (see below); and Francesco de Theodoro da Corfù, called Zoto, who was so sought after that in 1529 the captain general insisted that he sail with the armada, while one of the lords of the Arsenal insisted that he remain on duty at the Arsenal:

June 25, 1529 (50:552)   Hironimo da ca' da Pexaro, who is soon to depart as captain general of the sea, has requested that the Signoria allow him to take with him on his galley in the armada Francesco Zoto, [master] carpenter in the Arsenal. It was therefore proposed by the savi ai ordeni, except for Hironimo Trun, that the aforesaid captain be allowed to take Zoto along and that he receive, while in the armada, the [same] pay of forty-two soldi that he earns per day in the house of the Arsenal, without further wages, and that his shipyards [in the city] be maintained for him, just as was done with Lunardo Brexan.[59]

And ser Piero Orio, lord of the Arsenal, went to the podium and objected, saying that this man is one of the top carpenters of the Arsenal, because Lu-

---

57. Note the passive construction, which tells how it happened but does not attempt to identify who did it.

58. See Lane 1992, 61–62, for a paraphrased translation of this passage.

59. Shipwrights who worked at the Arsenal often had their own private shipyards, or *squeri*.

nardo Brexan is now an old man. And for this reason he should not be moved from the house [of the Arsenal]. . . .

And he was answered by Hironimo da ca' da Pexaro, who will go as captain general and is [currently] savio di Consiglio, saying that we have an armada of fifty galleys, and in such an important situation do we want to refuse him a man he has personally requested, a man necessary for the armada in many respects? And the vote passed: 5 undecided, 88 against, 109 for.

Vetor Fausto

Perhaps the most colorful and curious of the ship designers was Vetor Fausto. He did not come from a family or milieu of shipwrights, as did those others mentioned above. On the contrary, he was a humanist of the "original citizen" class who, through his studies with Hironimo Maserio and Marco Musuro and his wide travels, became skilled in classical languages, especially Greek, and in mathematics.[60] Convinced of the relevance of classical literature to current concerns, he proposed to design and build a quinquereme such as had been used in antiquity, that is, a galley propelled by five rowers to a bench, a concept that was beyond the contemporary practice of three or four rowers to the bench. He even produced a "most beautiful model" of such a vessel in 1525 (diaries, August 15; 39:322). He found some support among the skilled shipwrights (September 17, 1525; 39:440), and eventually he was given a dock at the Arsenal and the materials and personnel necessary to build his experimental ship. This was done in great secrecy and in an atmosphere of considerable skepticism; "most think it will not succeed," wrote Sanudo in April 1529 (50:227). Its fledgling trial created such excitement that it was planned for a Sunday afternoon, and the meeting of the Great Council that normally took place at that time was moved to the Thursday before that (50:344). Sanudo described the events of the race:

May 23, 1529 (50:363–64)   After vespers His Serenity invited all the ambassadors. . . . Accompanied by many nobles, [they] went in boats to the castle called Castel Nuovo, where seats had been adorned with tapestries and shaded from the sun for them.[61] And there were an infinite number of boats outside the two castles[62] and along the canal . . . and boats from as far away as Padua with people inside, and an infinite number from Chioza, and today some have paid eight or ten lire for a gondola just to see such a thing. I saw many

---

60. See chapter 8 for Girolamo Maserio da Forlì and Marco Musuro. In 1518 Fausto was appointed to the Chair of Greek in the School of San Marco.

61. Castel Nuovo, also known as the Castello di Sant'Andrea, made up part of the defenses on the Lido islands.

62. The second was the Castel Vecchio of San Nicolò.

ladies [*donne*] in boats, and procurators, and even the most reverend Cardinal Pixani with the archbishop of Nicosia, Poldacataro,[63] in a small boat with don Lippomano, the primicerio [of the cathedral] of Padua. Now, at the hour agreed upon, when the signal was given, the said galleys came rowing, racing one another, and in front came the [trireme] *Cornara*,[64] but when they had almost arrived at the castles, the quinquereme was ahead and the *Cornara* hugged the land so closely that it passed in front of His Serenity, and so came ahead rowing as far as San Marco, with so many boats in the canal, along with sails of large ships that had returned from the high seas, that it seemed like an armada. It was most beautiful to see.

This quinquereme has its own rowing slant, whose angle, however, is not much forward of the other light galleys', so that Vetor Fausto, who was in charge of the design, will be immortal.[65] And afterwards, when the Signoria had returned to San Marco, the said quinquereme went rowing up the Grand Canal as far as Cà Foscari, where it turned around, but with very great difficulty because it was twenty-eight paces long, more than three paces longer than the light galleys. Many boats were in the Grand Canal, and I was there among them, and the celebration lasted till evening.[66]

Ships and the Sea

The excitement and festivity of this race conveys something of Venetians' fascination, commitment, and even romance with ships and with the sea. The sea was their essential element, and they were committed to maintaining control of the Adriatic—which they referred to simply as their "gulf"—and of the established commercial lanes of the Mediterranean.[67] As Sanudo put it in 1532, "In matters of the sea, this city uses every possible diligence to maintain its ancient reputation" (September 24, 1532; 56:992). Sanudo's descriptions convey both the romance and the dedication. The flawless launching of a new ship was "a good

---

63. The manuscript spells his name *Poldacataro;* the Fulin edition, *Podacataro.*

64. Ships often were named for the patrician families that financed or owned them, but in the feminized form of the surname—Cornara, Pasqualiga, Foscara, etc.

65. Cf. Concina 1984, 108–34.

66. The translation of this entry is based generally on Lane's translation in Lane 1992, 66–67. Lane also quotes the original text of the central passage, which describes the race itself ("Now at the hour fixed . . ."), because the words are "difficult to translate, although I have done my best with them" (66). Vettor Fausto continued to design boats in the Arsenal and in private shipyards until his death in late 1546 or early 1547. See diaries, 24 September 1532 (56:992–93). His influence continued into the next century. Lane 1992, 67–71. For his biography, see Piovan 1995; and for a more negative opinion of his abilities, see Gullino 1996b, 100.

67. Tenenti 1991, 8, states that Venetians in history as well as Venetian historians have demonstrated "una pronunciata nostalgia per la supremazia marittima."

augury" (4:51); the swift passage of a galley from Messina to Southampton in "only 42 days . . . was a most beautiful event," attributed to the skill of its designer, Francesco Rosso (2:187); the arrival of a long-awaited cargo-laden ship from a commercial voyage fraught with great danger was a divinely sanctioned event: "it escaped great danger, and at last, by God's will, made safe harbor" (1:379–80); and the departure of a great ship under sail, leading an armada forth, was a thing of beauty, "a castle upon the waters":

April 18, 1497 (1:607)   On this Tuesday morning, April 18, Andrea Loredan, captain of the great round ship of the armada, who had boarded the ship in the name of Christ on April 9, set sail for Istria. This ship is very well provisioned, with 450 men on board and more than 400 pieces of artillery and large cannons for bombarding any large city—they fire stones weighing 150 pounds each. It is furnished with munitions and victuals, large quantities of biscuit. . . . Many went to see it because it is one of the [most] beautiful sights that in these years and in many past years has appeared on the sea, and the ambassadors of the League [against Charles VIII] went to see it. . . .

And on the following day, the other state ship, whose shipmaster is Daniel Pasqualigo, armed with 300 men, also set sail. This great round ship of the captain had a capacity of 2,000 botte; its sails could be seen at a great distance, and it looked like a castle upon the waters.

It was an appropriate image, for these great round ships served a defensive as well as a commercial function. The purpose of the two described above was to protect the eastern and western Venetian trading routes. The description continues:

And on the aforesaid date [April 18], the Senate commissioned this ship to sail to the mouth of the Adriatic Gulf together with the other round ship, the *Pasqualiga,* to protect the ships of Syria, which had already been anchored for several days near the harbor awaiting those two round ships as escorts. Once this captain has arrived at the mouth of the gulf, he is to sail in the direction of Sicily to protect the grain ships, and he is to remain near Cao Bon[68] for all the coming July, pursuing and preying upon corsairs and enemies of our Signoria. Then he is to leave and go to the east. And the *Pasqualiga* ship alone is to go to escort the ships from Syria, because at present there are no reports of pirates roaming about in the Levant. And in this way the [trade routes of] east and west have been provided for.[69]

---

68. Capo Bon, at the extreme northeastern tip of Tunisia.

69. A few days was a short time to wait for an escort. In an entry in 1519 Sanudo writes of a

Pirates and Corsairs

The protection afforded by the great round ships to convoys of galleys was necessary because the danger from pirates was almost constant, so taken for granted that Sanudo has to explain why he mentions it at all in the following passage:

August 22, 1497 (1:722–23)   On the 21st of this month it was made known by the shipmaster of a merchant ship belonging to Andrea Loredan, our patrician, that this merchant ship, laden with copper and other merchandise, as it was going toward Sicily and was off the coast of Calabria, encountered three long ships and two large galleys of French corsairs.[70] The merchant ship was taken captive, and the master and some others with him fled on land. Then, upon the arrival of our two Barbary galleys [from northern Tunisia], captained by Bernardo Zigogna, this merchant ship was recaptured with its merchandise, and the [corsairs'] long ships and large galleys took flight. I wanted to record this news, not because it was of much moment, but to point out that notwithstanding the truce, the French are mounting raids and doing damage.

The difference between pirates, operating independently, and the corsairs, whose activities were increasingly affiliated with some political structure, was shadowy. The search for plunder dominated, even as the pirates and corsairs on both sides of the religious divide called themselves castigators of "the infidel." It was an uninterrupted, immense struggle in which the battles and betrayals,

---

ship called the *Matio Verga,* which left Venice for Constantinople in February 1519. It was "very rich," and probably for that reason the Senate mandated that two ships escort it beyond Corfu (22 February 1519; 26:486). Letters from Corfu confirmed that the ship had to delay there for two months while it waited an escort. Eventually appropriate escorts were arranged, and later letters indicate that by June the plan was that this wealthy ship would go on to the island of Zante and then join the Venetian armada in Napoli di Romania (Nauplion), on the east coast of Morea (Peloponnesus). However, a letter dated in July finds the ship only in Coron (Corone), on the southern Greek coast of Morea. Through this correspondence the ship was tracked as it made its way from safe port to safe port. The original orders of the Senate were that escorts of one sort or another should accompany the ship until Cape Malea, the most southeastern point of Morea, whence it was thought the ship could make safe journey to its destination. The ship eventually reached Constantinople sometime later in the year. On 7 January 1520 Sanudo notes that the bailo of Constantinople arrived in Venice, having left Constantinople on this ship, and then, at the island of Lesina, off the Dalmatian coast, switched to a faster brigantine *(gripo),* the sooner to reach Venice. Thus the ship's journey lasted almost a year. For the *Matio Verga*'s journey, see 27:219, 243, 389, 576, 632–33; 28:162.

70. The Fulin edition dates this excerpt 21 August; in the manuscript the date is 22 August. The merchant ship is identified as a *maran,* a mercantile ship used in the Mediterranean in the fifteenth and sixteenth centuries. The three long ships were *fuste,* which were smaller than a galley. See Lane 1992, 261; and appendix B under "Boats, Ships, and Nautical Terms."

regardless of truces and treaties, were often bloody and cruel, with no quarter given.[71]

December 3, 1501 (4:178)   On the morning of December 3, the scribe from the ship of ser Bortolo da Mosto arrived [in Venice]. . . .

Among other things, this scribe told how Erichi, the Turkish corsair, with three long ships, was raiding the island of Melos at night, and two of the long ships were wrecked, but thanks to the skill of his pilot, his own landed on a beach. And Erichi asked, "Where are we?" The pilot answered: "We are on *terra ferma*." Erichi said, "Very well, what shall we do?" The pilot said: "We will draw the ship up on the land so we are safe, and then we will go to the castle." And while they were drawing this ship onto the beach, the pilot went to the castle and said: "Open up, because I have brought you a great prisoner! Erichi is here on this island with his ship beached." And first thing that morning, Erichi was captured by the inhabitants with all his men. And he said right away: "Don't kill me. I will deliver Camalì[72] into your hands." Nevertheless, he was put to death, as I will tell you below.

In an entry one month later the circumstances of this corsair's fate are made known:

January 3, 1502 (4:205-6)   A letter from the captain general[73] written on Corfù and sent from Melos on December 12. . . . Erichi, the Turkish corsair, happened to land on Melos on his way back from Barbary. His ship went aground in a storm on this island. Aboard were 132 Turks, and he was taken alive with 34 Turks. The rest were drowned or killed by the islanders, but we kept this one in our grasp. On December 9 we roasted Erichi alive on a [spit made from] the handle of a large oar. He lived in this torment for three hours. Thus he finished his days. We also impaled the pilot and mate and a galleyman from Corfù who betrayed his faith. And we shot full of arrows and drowned another. . . .

This pirate Erichi in times of peace with the Turks did great damage to our [ships] and even to the carracks of the Turks.[74] A complaint was lodged with the sultan, who, by offering a reward, tried to have him captured and brought

---

71. Alberto Tenenti, on whose work this section is based, uses the terms *pirate* and *corsair* almost interchangeably. See Tenenti 1960, esp. 235-36, 259; and 1991. Much of Tenenti's material is drawn from Sanudo's diaries.

72. Camalì (Kemal) was, along with Erichi and Curtogoli, who is mentioned below, one of the most famous corsairs. The spelling of these names varied.

73. Benedetto da Pesaro was the captain general of the Venetian fleet at that time.

74. See Lane 1992, 41, for an illustration of a carrack from a 1490s painting by the Venetian painter Vittore Carpaccio.

to the Porte. . . . It happened that ser Ambruoso Contarini in 1491 was seeking to load grain on his small cargo ship at Salonika, and he agreed to go in convoy with this Erichi [for protection]. After he had loaded his ship, the sailors told Erichi that this Ambruoso wanted to capture or kill him.[75] Wherefore, on this suspicion, after a long battle, Erichi captured this Ambruoso, who was wounded in four places, and he roasted him and killed all the sailors.[76] And for that reason, our captain general also put Erichi to death and roasted him alive.

Much of the correspondence of this period reported encounters with corsairs, such as the following letter written in Kotor by a galley commander to his brother, with its casual reference to the curios he had acquired in his victory over the pirate "Il Moro" and how he intended to advertise his triumph.

February 25, 1520 (28:282–83)   Summary of a letter from ser Zuan Antonio Taiapiera, galleymaster, written to his brother, ser Piero, from Cattaro [Kotor] on the first day of February 1519 [*m.v.*], received on the 20th day of this month. . . .

It was the feast of St. Paul, which was the 25th of January. At daybreak I discovered the long ship of Moro da la Valona, a mile out of the port of Durazo. I went toward it, but it took flight below Durazo, etc. As it fled, I released two shots from my artillery but did not hit it. Once I saw it had reached the walls of Durazo, I turned my poop toward it to pursue my journey toward Corfù. But the pirates, eager to revenge themselves for the ship destroyed at Cape Cesta,[77] having boarded as many valiant men as seemed to them sufficient for their galley, began to follow me. When I perceived them following, I readied my ship and drew them 5 miles into the open sea, and there we attacked each other in a battle that lasted 7 to 8 hours, and I cut them all down, among them Il Moro with 4 other shipmasters of the long ships. And from what I understood from some on board who were slaves, there were about 220 Turks on the bark. . . . On my galley 7 men died and 93 were wounded, but except for 3, nobody in critically.[78] One I killed [in pity]; he was my chief bombardier. Others were also badly wounded; they will be blind and lame, but we hope they will heal. I had only a lance wound in my thigh; it was superficial despite the force of the blow. Still, I had this satisfaction, that in the final struggle they leaped on my prow, and with my own hand I killed two of them, and

---

75. The manuscript has *o amazarlo;* the Fulin edition has *e amazarlo.*

76. Lane's interpretation is that the deal involving the pirate's protection led to a quarrel, as Sanudo's account indicates. See 1987b, essay 8, p. 165.

77. On the Dalmatian coast, near Šibenik.

78. The manuscript has *ma 3 solum, nesu^n di pericolo;* the Fulin edition omits *nesu^n.*

that was when they wounded me with the lance point. . . . I have captured the castanets, the drums, the banners, and the head of Il Moro, described above, which I rightfully will display on the prow of my ship.

The letter ends with the galley commander's request that his brother order a new banner to be made in time for him to parade in commemoration of his victory:

Item: have made for me a military banner with fields of yellow and blue divided by a third field dotted with turbans, and make it big, and as soon as possible send it to me in Corfù so I will have it on the first of May to carry in the parade review, because my other one was burned; and if it seems appropriate to you to add something to it, do what you think best, and have some hooks made on which to hang our trophy armor.[79]

In the year after this incident (and it was not isolated), a Venetian diplomat, Marco Minio, negotiated the renewal of the complex treaty with the sultan, which included a peaceable way to handle such encounters.[80] But it made little difference in practice. Some years later a well-known Anatolian corsair, Curtogoli, fired two blank shots ("without stones") at a Venetian ship, which responded by a live shot that killed fourteen of his men. "And in anger he went for that ship and took it, and [his men] having taken whatever they could, burned it and killed all its crew. And it seems that then he went to Modon to sell the cloth, etc. But hearing that there were seventeen Venetian galleys in those waters, Curto goli weighed anchor and left in fear" (August 21, 1527; 45:649–50). Only superior numbers provided protection from pirates.

Shipwreck

To the difficulty presented by piracy were added the primitive challenges of wind and weather. The length of voyages was a variable of the commercial life. A voyage from Corfu to Venice might take eleven days (January 23, 1519; 26:388) or twenty-nine (May 13, 1521; 30:218). From Cyprus, among the furthest of Venetian outposts, it might take a ship thirty-five days (28:653) or ninety-four (33:412) to arrive in Venice. Venetian traders, their families, their clients, and governmental authorities lived in an uncertain world. And many a voyage ended in disaster. Sometimes a survivor described a shipwreck from start to finish, as in the fol-

---

79. The first of May was a traditional moment for bringing military companies out of winter quarters and inspecting them, paying advances, etc., and therefore a perfect occasion to show off military trophies. For trophies carried in parades on hooks, a classical custom continued in the Renaissance, see *Triumphs of Caesar*, by Andrea Mantegna (1431–1506), at Hampton Court. The editors thank Michael Mallet for the information in this note.

80. See chapter 4 under "The Ottoman Turks," 32:498–99.

lowing letter from Cyprus, "a very pitiful tale" with its loss of life, hardships, near cannibalism, and moralizing conclusion.

March 3, 1517 (24:24–25)   Summary of a letter . . . from Famagosta on Cyprus, written on December 30, 1516, by Nicolò Michiel, university laureate, to his cousin. . . .

Today, messer Nicolò Bragadin arrived here. On his way to his post as consul in Alexandria, he escaped the shipwreck of the Alexandria galley with about fifty other people. This is his story: On the 22nd of this month the galley, en route to Alexandria, about 250 miles out to sea, was so damaged by a storm that it shipped more water than it could cope with. And at dawn the next day, Monday the 23rd, the ship broke into three parts, one from the forward mast to the galley, and the poop broke in two parts. The high seas and the pressure from the weight or the crashing of the copper bars had this effect.

The abovementioned messer Nicolò Bragadin and about eighty-three others boarded the [landing] boat, into which many others were throwing themselves, but ten to twelve unsheathed swords blocked the others from boarding. In the end, about fifty of the eighty-three survived; the others died of hunger, thirst, and cold. Some may have gone to relieve the hunger of the others;[81] they had already decided to butcher the little scribe, who was young, fat, and rosy-complexioned, in order to drink his blood. He escaped with many others as they reached land here in Famagosta; so said the abovementioned messer Nicolò and others.

This messer Nicolò landed naked with only a small coverlet wrapped around him. They were in the boat from Monday through the following Sunday. It was dawn on Monday when they reached this island. . . . So great was their desire to land that they did not really try to land on a beach, and the place [they landed] was so treacherous that some drowned in getting off [the boat], and those who did get off arrived on all fours because that was the best they could do. Among the survivors is a young Soranzo [*Soranzeto*], who is so ill that he holds his life by his teeth, and ser Vicenzo Magno, the shipmaster. However, he is very sick and will probably die—so it has been said this evening. A Barozi is missing. Also surviving is a Badoer, son of ser Zuan Andrea. He is said to have vowed to become a friar, as did that Soranzo, and certain other survivors will present the boat as a holy offering to the True Cross. Some will go barefoot on one pilgrimage, and others on another; all have made various vows. They claim to have seen several saints; and an astonishing thing is that

---

81. The manuscript has *Et forsi qualche uno è andato per campare la fame a li altri, zà;* the Fulin edition has *Et forsi qualche uno è andato per campar la fame, e li altri zà.*

at times they saw giant swells as big as the Basilica of San Marco, and they made the sign of the Cross, praying in the name of God and Our Lady that the swells would part and not harm them. Thus it appeared that the waves parted, as a very great sign of God's mercy.[82] In addition, saints appeared in the sky with lit candles, a remarkable event. They were at sea seven days and seven nights, always in a storm, with a sail made out of two sacks tied with strings and two rudders for the boats made out of two other oars and a spar for the mast[83] made from a strip of flat wood. They drank urine and ate the shirts off their backs and even stranger things so as to have some food.

This is a very pitiful tale: sea voyaging entails many excessive dangers, and all for greed.[84] I can't tell you what passage home I shall find. This morning again I had masses said to the Holy Ghost and Our Lady, so great has my fear grown of traveling with the old galleys, having seen the wreck of this Alexandria ship.

In other cases, and these may have been the most heartbreaking, the news of a shipwreck came slowly over a period of months, first as a rumor, then as pieces of evidence, then through the report of an eyewitness:

August 21, 1497 (1:721–22)   Letters came from Bruges, written on the first and fifth of this month, from Andrea Trivixan, en route to England as our ambassador. . . . [And his news included the following]: *Item:* nothing has been heard of the ship called *Tiepola,* whose shipmaster is Polo Foscari, nor had it arrived in England by the last day of July, and there has been no word of it since the storm that occurred in the channels in June. But they believed that from there it had taken refuge in the Bay of Biscay.

December 5, 1497 (1:846)   In these past days, through the return of ser Piero Contarini di Zucon from the west, we have the truth about the ship *Foscara,* that is, the ship of which Polo Foscari was shipmaster: it broke apart, and the main mast and the scribe's strongbox have been found.

January 3, 1498 (1:849)   On this day there arrived in the city, by land from the west, Jacomo Foscari, by whom the news of the shipwreck of the Tiepola was verified. . . . His brother Polo Foscari was its shipmaster, as I wrote above, and there were 310 men aboard, and two patrician officers of the quarterdeck [*gentilhomeni da pope*],[85] that is ——. Memo, son of ser Lodovico and —— Donado, [son of] ser Thomado. . . . And Foscari reported that for many reasons it

---

82. The manuscript has *ch' è la clementia;* the Fulin edition has *de la clementia.*

83. The manuscript has *fata l'antena;* the Fulin edition has *fata l'altena.*

84. The manuscript has *et tutto la ingordissia;* the Fulin edition has *et tutto per la ingordizia.*

85. Defined by Battaglia 1961–2000 as second in command.

was quite certain that this ship was lost: first, that nothing has been learned[86] concerning the whereabouts of this ship since the month of June, that is, since its departure for England, but a main mast was found that was said to belong to this ship. Moreover, ships arriving in England from every direction, that is, from Biscay, from Galicia, from Brittany, from Portugal, from Scotland, and elsewhere, had nothing to report, and they said they had not seen this ship since it left Lisbon to continue on its course. Whence it was concluded that it had not broken apart but sank straight down because it carried much more cargo than it ought to have, so that at the shoals of the Seine it went to the bottom.[87] And if this ship had completed its trip safely, it would have earned a good profit; but that was not God's will, and everyone drowned. And many patricians had invested in the ship. . . .

When the Foscari brothers of the shipmaster heard what truly happened, they put on mourning, and our Signoria most graciously was moved to compassion for the two young patricians who had drowned. A vote was taken in the Great Council to grant the father and brothers of each of these [young men] a place as bowman of the quarterdeck for four years, one place for each family on the merchant galleys, as a compensation for their loss.[88]

The Pepper Trade

Among the most valuable cargoes that Venetian ships carried were spices. In an age without refrigeration, spices were necessary to preserve meat and make it palatable to consume. Northerners in Germany, Flanders, and England developed a taste for food highly seasoned with Eastern spices that the Venetian "galleys of Flanders" brought to western markets centered in Bruges; on their return voyages, these same galleys carried back to the entrepôts of the East silver, copper, and woolen cloth. The spices themselves arrived at these entrepôts via several routes. Before the Portuguese circumnavigated the Cape of Good Hope (1497–98), the two main routes were through the Red Sea to Jiddah and thence by camel caravan to Damascus and ports such as Acre; or through the Red

86. The manuscript has *nulla si haveva saputo;* the Fulin edition omits *saputo.*

87. The information given in these excerpts puts the ship out of Lisbon on its way to England in June 1497. Storms in the English Channel could have driven the ship "from there," *de lì* (diaries, 1:722), to the Bay of Biscay to find calmer waters. Southampton is almost directly across the channel from Le Havre and the mouth of the Seine, the apparent reference of Sanudo's *Saym.*

88. Although three families were involved in this tragedy, the Foscari, the Memmo, and the Donado, only the latter two were compensated. Perhaps some responsibility for the loss lay with the Foscari family, whose relative had overloaded the ship. Furthermore, the Foscari who was the *patron,* or shipmaster, was not paid, while the deck officers were. Foscari (and his family investors) would have taken any profits, and they would have taken the risk. Since he was not salaried by the state, there was no reason to compensate him.

Sea either to Suez and Cairo and thence to the port of Alexandria or to Quseir and from there, by descending the Nile, to Cairo and Alexandria. An incident in Alexandria early in the sixteenth century illustrates some of the perils of this profitable trade.

Cargoes included a great variety of spices, among them cloves and cinnamon, nutmeg and mace, and various kinds of ginger. Chief among the spices was pepper, and the pepper market in Alexandria was a keystone of the Venetian economy. But that market was controlled by the soldan of Egypt, who, in 1505, disgruntled that the new Portuguese trade with the Indies had interrupted the predictability and diminished the supplies of pepper reaching him via the old routes, raised prices exorbitantly and then tried to force Venetian traders in Alexandria to accept his new terms. Instead of a fixed price of 80 ducats per *sporta,* or bale, of pepper and a fixed number of 210 *sporte* acquired by the Venetians in exchange for a fixed number of copper bars, the soldan insisted on a price equivalent to 192 ducats per *sporta,* which the Venetians considered "an insupportable price." Then he added to their distress by literally dumping an additional 250 *sporte* into their loading areas and demanding that these also be bought and loaded onto the Venetian galleys. He even menaced the Venetian merchants with incarceration and sent his servants to ransack the Venetians' strongboxes in a search for coins (6:199–200).[89]

These difficulties had been brewing throughout the winter of 1504–5. The galleys had been in Alexandria since December, having sailed from Venice in October 1504 (6:70). In February 1505 a letter arrived in Venice that had been sent from Crete in mid-January, reporting on the "complications with the pepper of the soldan" (February 27, 1505; 6:136). Letters from Alexandria about the ongoing intrigues arrived in March (March 8, 1505; 6:140). That same month it was learned that ser Zuan Francesco Venier, a Venetian merchant in Alexandria who was Sanudo's brother-in-law, had died of the plague. The danger presented by contagion was serious, the political situation was worsening, and the time for the galleys to depart, set by Venetian law, was long past.

The captain of the Venetian galleys was ser Polo Calbo, and the story that follows is about his run for freedom.[90]

89. For types of spices, see Lane 1968, esp. 50n2. For the spice trade in general, see Lane 1973b, 71–72 (with a map of trade routes) and 285–94. The *sporta* was equivalent to about 475 English pounds. Lane 1992, 250.

90. The full description of this adventure came several months after the event in a document dated 8 August 1505 but added to the diaries under the date 31 July 1505 (6:199–207). It took the form of a directive to the new consul leaving Venice for Alexandria, so that he would be aware of the dangers of his position. It contains the reaffirmation of the terms necessary for Venetians to continue their trade with Alexandria and a list of personnel in Alexandria to be trusted or avoided. It was to be two more years before a new agreement about the pepper trade was reached with the soldan. In the end, he restored the terms under which the Alexandria pep-

July 31, 1505 (6:202–3)   Our captain, aware that the galleys' long stay in port had continued four months past the mandated departure date, was seeking to obtain a departure permit from the Mamluk admiral in charge. The admiral therefore had to write the soldan to learn what he wished done about this permit, because from several signals that the captain had given—pulling out to the lighthouse,[91] coming about often and staying in the rushes—the admiral had concluded that he might well leave, even without a permit, and therefore he [the admiral] wanted the soldan to tell him what to do.[92]

And the soldan wrote him in reply that if he suspected that this would happen, he should send a message to the captain demanding the sails and rudders of the galleys. And if the captain did not allow them to be kept in the city, this official, together with [the official] in the fortress, should bombard the galleys and send them to the bottom.

Having received this order, the lord of Alexandria came to the lighthouse with all his Mamluks and a large crowd of others carrying square banners, and there he set up and pointed the artillery toward the galleys, and he fired a mortar across a galley bow to strike terror in them. Right away, he sent his admiral of the harbor and others of his officials to demand from the captain the sails and rudders of all the galleys. The captain refused to do this. [Then the admiral] commanded him at least to withdraw further inside the harbor than where he stood [at anchor] in the mouth of the harbor, near the lighthouse. Our captain, well informed about the hostile intentions, fearful of the danger, also refused to budge from the place he was in, excusing himself [by saying] that he was more secure there from the sea and at better anchorage.

The [Mamluk] lord, seeing that he had not obtained either request, asked of the captain that he promise upon his faith not to leave within [the next] eight days so that in the meantime he could write to Cairo to negotiate a valid

---

per trade had long operated, which were favorable to Venice. The soldan's chief envoy in these negotiations was a Mamluk whose long stay in Venice made him a somewhat familiar figure around town. He even attended a patrician betrothal banquet with ten of his entourage in October 1506 (6:437). For the diplomatic context of the Alexandria incident, see Setton 1976–84, 3:18–22; for the Mamluk's later negotiations in Venice, see Wansbrough 1963; for the treaty itself, taken from a Venetian archival document more accurate than Sanudo's record of 31 May 1507 (7:220–24), see ibid., 521–30.

91. The manuscript has *Farion;* the Fulin edition, *Assarion.*

92. The departure permit was called the *licentia,* a technical term meaning "clearance to sail," implying that all business had been properly concluded. Wansbrough 1963, 526n1. It should be noted that the title given in the Venetian report to the Alexandria official in charge, *admiral,* is the same title as that used for a principal officer in the Venetian Arsenal. Cf. Lane 1992, 151n21, for the several uses of this title. See also Rossi 1996, 597–98, 622n31, stating that the term refers to various professionals of high technical and organizational responsibility in maritime matters.

[departure] permit for him. And so the captain promised him and kept the promise, not just for eight days but for more than eighteen days.

At this point, the captain, having waited more than the requisite number of days and seeing that his patience had not been rewarded with a permit to leave,[93] took matters into his own hands:

July 31, 1505 (6:203–4)   Finally this captain saw that permission [to leave] had not been given to him [and would not be forthcoming] and that the [Venetian] council and merchants were chained and imprisoned in Cairo. He also saw that despite the money the Venetians had managed to collect, they had not been able to content the soldan, who kept threatening to expel them from the country and who wanted [to deal with] other nations so that ours could not do business there. [Moreover, the captain] saw that there was a considerable plague in Alexandria, that many of the Venetians in the city had died, and that the contagion had even begun to appear on their ships, since they had been there for so many months. He thus decided to leave and not await further permission.

In addition, the captain had learned that the soldan had not negotiated in good faith but was determined to bombard the Venetian ships. Toward this end he had engaged the ships of other trading nations to attack the Venetian convoy so that he could acquire the Venetian ships, men, and wealth, which he then intended to turn against the Portuguese, who had stolen his trade (April 25, 1505; 6:156–57):

Once he had made that decision [to leave], the captain was informed by his good connections and spies that the signor soldan wanted above all to take the ships in the port and would do so by aiming the mortars of the lighthouse at them. He had also sought the help of some foreign ships that were in the port of Bechieri,[94] whose arrival at the mouth of the harbor to attack and capture these galleys had been plotted by the signor soldan. [The soldan]

---

93. According to the terms of the later, 1507 treaty (see diaries, 7:220–24, for the terms), based on earlier practice, once the *muda,* or period during which the business was to be transacted in a foreign port, had passed and the departure permit had been requested, the galley was expected to wait six to eight days for the merchants to make their payments and consign their goods. "And should the eight days pass without their having got leave, the captain shall be free to depart with these galleys without any hindrance." 7:220–21; Wansbrough 1963, 526. The term *muda* was also applied to a group of merchant ships traveling together. See Lane 1966d, 136.

94. The port of Abukir, not far from that of Alexandria.

thought that he would thus get his hands on the wealth and the persons of our merchants, as well as the galleys and sailors of our Signoria.

This news spurred the Venetian captain to act promptly even though a favorable wind was lacking and even though the artillery of the port had been trained on their ships and a warning mortar had already been fired:

Therefore the captain, very prudently, started sailing his ship in a light wind out of the harbor before the abovementioned [foreign] ships could come, and he gave this order to the rest of the convoy. Since the wind was not sufficient, he was forced to stand still for some time, so that from the fort they [the Mamluks] could fire all their mortars and artillery set up many days previously for this purpose. Night and day they had been on guard, [ready] to discharge their artillery at the first sign of movement by the captain. And so on March 15 the departure took place, [and the Mamluks] bombarded the ships and damaged them, especially the Trivisana galley, whose mast was almost broken. In response, the captain and our galleys, although they had large culverins [*pasavolanti*] and short-barreled bombards [*cortaldi*][95] and other heavy artillery, fired nothing so that our men would not be blamed for this incident. But with the help of God they escaped from the harbor and were free. And because the captain saw that the mast [of the Trivisana] was in danger, he went to Bechieri to have it fixed. There he found two French ships, whose masters informed this captain that they had been provoked by the soldan and by his consul Filipo da Paretollo, who was in Cairo, to attack the Venetian galleys as written above, and they showed him letters containing these plans. At this point the captain saw the ill will of the soldan toward our nation, and he left Bechieri for Cyprus and then went to Candia [Crete] to tell what had happened so that those wishing to sail to these parts should exercise caution, and then he arrived safely in this city [Venice].

Captain Calbo's arrival in Venice on April 29 was triumphant. The Venetians had followed the news from Alexandria with considerable concern, and when the story of the escape reached Venice a week before the captain himself arrived, "many praised this captain, while others deplored the misfortune that might derive [from his action]" (April 22, 1505; 6:154), for the escape of these Vene-

---

95. The *passavolante* was a large culverin, that is, a long-barreled piece firing metal shot of 25–35 pounds. It was fairly modern and was usually sited in the bows of galleys. The *cortaldo* was a short-barreled bombard firing stone shot. It was somewhat old-fashioned by Sanudo's day. It could be fired from the waist of the galley or the deck of a ship, as its trajectory was "up and over," like that of a mortar, and it therefore had little recoil. Personal communication from Michael Mallett.

tians did not improve the lot of those still incarcerated in Cairo. But there was "great rejoicing" in the city when the galleys arrived, and the captain was kissed three times by the doge, who greeted him with these words: "Warm welcome to this magnificent captain" (April 29, 1505; 6:158). A month later, when the captain made his final report to the Senate, he was "praised to the highest heaven" (May 29, 1505; 6:170).

Venetians served as middlemen for the exchange of pepper and other spices, but there were also native industries apart from shipbuilding. The Mint, which employed as many as two hundred workers, produced coins from imported bullion, and there were manufactories of such basic products as salt and soap. Then there were luxurious glass pieces produced by the glass factories on the island of Murano, so famous that visits to these shops were as obligatory in the sixteenth century as they are today. There were the fine fabrics that Sanudo often describes the Venetian dignitaries and patrician women wearing.[96] And of special interest to Sanudo were the jewels and jeweled objects that were produced in the city for sale in the East, some of which he describes in considerable detail.

Gifts for the Sultan

The Venetians of Sanudo's time often had particular purchasers in mind for some of their more exotic products. Suleiman the Magnificent (1520–66) was known, at least in the earlier part of his reign, as the sultan who "loves jewels." In 1527 Sanudo saw and described a magnificent chess set on exhibit in the Senate; its patrician owners hoped the government would purchase it as a gift for the sultan, and they planned to use the proceeds of the sale to fund the dowries of two daughters:

January 7, 1527 (43:599)   I note that this morning I saw a beautiful object in the Senate chamber. It was a round high chess board, large and very beautiful. It was wrought of gold and silver and set with chalcedony,[97] jasper, and other jewels. The chess pieces are made of the purest crystal. It belonged to ser Jacomo Loredan, of the Santa Maria Formoxa branch of the family, who gave it in dower to two of his daughters, who married ser Christofal and ser Marco Donado of the San Polo branch of the family. It was brought to the Ducal Palace because ser Piero Lando, their uncle, wanted to show it to His Serenity and the Collegio to see if they wished to buy it to send as a gift to the signor Turco with ser Marco Minio, who is going to Constantinople as our ambassador. . . .[98] They are asking 5,000 ducats for it.

96. For a description of the silk industry, see Molà 2000.
97. A type of quartz that includes agate, carnelian, and other colored gems.
98. See chapter 4 for Marco Minio's earlier mission to Constantinople in 1522.

Constantinople was considered a good market for such luxuries. A few years after the above notice, Sanudo reported on an unusual piece of jewelry that the son of a Venetian representative in Constantinople hoped to sell in that city.

October 2, 1531 (55:14)   This morning in the Jewelers' Street I saw ser Francesco Zen, whose father Piero is bailo in Constantinople;[99] he was holding a gold ring. Mounted on it was a very beautiful and well-crafted[100] watch that shows the time and chimes. He wants to send it to Constantinople to be sold.

The following spring, a magnificent helmet, a fine saddle, and a saddlecloth were created for that same emporium, and specifically for the sultan, Suleiman the Magnificent. Sanudo dwells on these "jewels of great worth," the financial projections, and the route of transport, planned for maximum safety:

March 14, 1532 (55:634–35)   This morning I, Marin Sanudo, saw on Rialto a most memorable object that deserves to be recorded. It was a gorgeous gold helmet covered with jewels, made by the Caorlini.[101] It has four crowns set with very expensive jewels and a finely wrought gold aigrette on which are set four rubies, four large beautiful diamonds worth 10,000 ducats, large pearls weighing twelve carats apiece, a long and beautiful emerald weighing — carats, and a large and very lovely turquoise. All these are jewels of great worth. The aigrette holds the plumage of an animal that lives in the air and lives on air[102] and has very fine feathers of many colors. It comes from India and is called a chameleon, and it is worth a fortune. It is said that this helmet was made to be sold to the signor Turco for 100,000 ducats or more. It was commissioned by a partnership; [the partners] are the sons of ser Piero Zen, our ambassador to the Turks, ser Jacomo Corner, ser Piero Morexini, the Caorlini mentioned above, and some others who joined in the venture. They are having it taken to Constantinople by ser Marco Antonio Sanudo, who is a member of the Senate. They are giving him 2,000 ducats for eight months and are paying all his travel costs; if he stays longer[103] in Constantinople they are giving him — ducats per month. If he can sell it for more than 100,000 ducats, ser Marco Antonio will receive a commission of 2 percent. This helmet is part of

---

99. Piero Zen was actually the vice-bailo in Constantinople at that time. On the Zen family's relations with the Ottoman court, see Concina 1994.

100. The manuscript appears to have *lavorà;* the Fulin edition has *lavora.*

101. Here Sanudo refers to a particular family of goldsmiths. Caorle, a city on the coast just north of the Venetian lagoon, was known for the work of its goldsmiths.

102. The manuscript has *sta in aiere et vive di aiere;* the Fulin edition has *sta in aiere et vive in aiere.*

103. The manuscript has *stando più lì;* the Fulin edition has *stando poi lì.*

a set with a jewel-studded saddle and saddlecloth commissioned by another group, which are also worth 100,000 ducats. They are to depart within two weeks, going by sea as far as Ragusi and from there to Constantinople by land with a large escort. This sultan loves jewels; this is the first time that anyone in the Ottoman family has ever liked or appreciated them.[104]

The economic networks implicit in the descriptions above, the patrician dowries gained by the sale of a luxurious object to the sultan using diplomatic channels, the government's compensation to families devastated by loss of members and wealth in a shipwreck, and its guarantees for failing banks all illustrate the intimate connection between patrician investments and the regime controlled by and dedicated to the interests of the patrician class. It was not unusual for members of the same extended families to make the investments and to supply the necessary governmental support. The existing boundaries between private and public tended to be porous, especially where money and political power were involved.

Nowhere was this connection more apparent than during that major conflict of Sanudo's period, the War of the League of Cambrai (1509–17). It was a war whose lessons may well have been written on the placards displayed in a later procession: "All things obey money"; "If riches abound, fear not"; "Whoever has wealth may sail with fair wind and govern fortune as he wills" (July 8, 1526; 42: 68, 72). These were the inscriptions carried by floats in the 1526 celebration of the League of Cognac against Charles V. They were the fruit of experience, much of it gained over the previous two decades.[105]

The Costs of Cambrai

That experience began to crystallize in December 1508 as news of the formation of the hostile League of Cambrai reached Venice (7:689, 693, 703). The Senate recognized the need to prepare for a war that would be waged, as were all Ve-

104. A few weeks later, on 2 April 1532 (56:10), Sanudo listed the jewels used in the helmet, along with their values, for a total of 144,400 ducats, that is, 44,400 ducats more than the projected price of the sale to the sultan. But when the helmet was sold for 115,000 ducats, the Venetian partners claimed a 100 percent profit. According to Pazzi 1995, 31, the helmet was made to suggest the papal tiara, with its three crowns, to which a fourth was added to indicate the greater power of the sultan. Cf. Kurz 1969. For a summary of more recent scholarship on this unusual item, see Necipoğlu 1989, which indicates that the composite crown was based on the papal tiara, the emperor's mitre crown, and Habsburg parade helmets, all combined to illustrate Ottoman supremacy (413). Among those involved in the consortium were Vincenzo Livrieri and Alvise Caorlini, both among Aretino's correspondents. See Aretino 1060, bk. 2, no. 55, and bk. 1, no. 74. Piero Zen, mentioned here as orator to the sultan, was actually the vice-bailo. The Marco Antonio Sanudo mentioned in this excerpt was not a close relation of the diarist.

105. The following section is closely based on an unpublished article by Felix Gilbert, Gilbert 1983, cited here by permission of Mary Gilbert. For the 1526 inscriptions, see Cozzi 1982, 133.

netian wars, by mercenary troops and mercenary leaders under the purview of civilian patrician proveditors. Bartolomeo d'Alviano was among those condottieri favored by Venice, and the pressing question of the day was where his wages and those of his troops would be found. But there was also the matter of how the army itself should be constituted. The Collegio met to formulate a proposal for the Senate, and Sanudo, as he often did, provides the terms and course of the debate and identifies its participants, following the proposal from the small council of the Collegio to the larger council of the Senate and back again:

December 12, 1508 (7:688)   A bill [to fund the salary of the governor general of the army] was posted by the savi di Collegio, with the exception of Andrea Gritti, a savio di Consiglio, Alvise Prioli, and Alvise Mocenigo, the knight, both savi di Terraferma.[106] This was in response to the many requests that our governor general Bortolo (Bartolomeo) d'Alviano has made about where the funds would come from to pay the 30,000 ducats per year of his salary. It was thus proposed that 20,000 ducats from the fisc of Verona and 10,000 ducats from the fisc of Vicenza be assigned to him. Speaking against the bill was Andrea Gritti, who said that it is better first to limit the number of troops and that the fiscs of Verona and Vicenza are already so greatly encumbered that they can produce nothing more, and that we have expenditures of 249,000 ducats per year, and the *limitation*[107] on all the mainland income is only — ducats, and for that reason it is better to curb the number of troops. Zorzi Emo, a savio di Consiglio, responded to him.

The next to speak was Francesco Trun, a councillor, who proposed that the decision be postponed and that the council [of the Senate] be convoked for Friday or Saturday to deal with this matter and that the members of the Collegio come with their proposals about how to reorganize the army. After him came Zuan Paulo Gradenigo, the former governor of Brexa [Brescia], who shared Trun's opinion, saying that it is better to reorganize the troops first, and the limitation, etc. Alvise da Molin, savio di Consiglio, spoke in support of the bill, then Zorzi Corner, the knight, whose words were listened to intently. He said that we must not give signor Bortolo a hollow cane, because there is no money, the limitation is already high, and there is no hurry. He had had a letter about this from signor Bortolo saying that as long as he is given sound and good funding, he wishes nothing else, and it is a good practice to pay those who serve us well.

---

106. In reporting these debates in the various consultative bodies, Sanudo does not always make clear which "council" he is referring to. In the text that follows this sentence, the debate on the bill posted by the Collegio takes place in the Senate. The Senate then unanimously remands the bill to the council of the Collegio for revision.

107. The *limitation* was an assessment upon dominion towns to pay for their defense.

All were in agreement with Trun's proposal to postpone a decision and to [let the matter] come to the Senate later. And [the postponement] received a unanimous vote from the Senate.

It is clear from the above that the major part of the costs of the anticipated war was to be paid by the subject cities of the Terraferma. But even if they could pay the established amounts of tribute—and some doubt was expressed that they could—that would not be sufficient. The question remained, *"Quid fiendum?"* (What should be done?) (7:689). Four days after the postponement of the earlier bill, the Collegio proposed a revised schedule of levies on the subject towns that they deemed would cover the payment of the military leaders and their troops.[108]

December 16, 1508 (7:690) And the bill was passed, that is, the limitation on the mainland fiscs was raised; I will give a detailed account below. The limitation was increased by —— ducats. Included are 12,000 ducats from Cremona that used to be assigned to the Council of Ten and 5,000 ducats from Crema that had been set aside for fortification of the city's walls but are not needed at the moment. *Item:* a bill to pay all of signor Bortolo's 30,000 ducats from the income of Vicenza was passed. Vicenza has a limitation of 27,000 ducats, so the total is short by 3,000 ducats, not much. *Item:* [a bill was passed to pay] the Count of Pitiano [Pitigliano], the captain general, from the fiscs of Padua and Brescia, as was the case previously.

The old limitation and the increases:

Padua, which used to be 42,250 ducats: increase—2,000 ducats
Vicenza, which used to be 26,750 ducats: increase—2,000 ducats
Verona, which used to be 34,450 ducats: increase—4,000 ducats
Brescia, which used to be 52,000 ducats: increase—5,000 ducats
Bergamo, which used to be 19,000 ducats: increase—1,000 ducats
Crema, which used to be 5,000 ducats [for fortification of the city walls],
    then its purposes were achieved—5,000 ducats
Cremona, which used to be 12,000 ducats given to the Council of Ten,
    now to be brought back—12,000 ducats

The sum to be collected (including monies from other Terraferma cities not mentioned above, such as Udine, Treviso, and Rovigo) was calculated, according to

---

108. These decisions were made more difficult by the fact that Venice had no budget at all until the second half of the sixteenth century, and no war was budgeted for, nor was an accounting made at its conclusion. Mallett and Hale 1984, 461.

Andrea Gritti, at 249,000 ducats (see the preceding excerpt).[109] With this were to be paid the yearly salaries of twelve condottieri, including those of the captain general (the commander in chief), Niccolò Orsini, Count of Pitiano, fixed on December 23, 1508, at 36,000 ducats, and Bortolo d'Alviano, governor general (the deputy commander), fixed at 26,400 ducats. The condottieri were to be paid in eight installments over the rest of the year, and from these sums they would pay themselves and their troops.[110]

But these arrangements were hardly possible after the defeat at Agnadello on May 14, 1509. Nearly all the subject cities on the Terraferma were captured, and it would be years before the tribute they were intended to provide would be made once more available. The Venetian government had to look to other sources through direct and indirect taxes. But these, whether property taxes, which increased from three levies in 1508 to twenty-four in 1509, or duties on imports and exports such as wine and oil, or revenue from the salt monopoly, or exactions from the Jews, were still insufficient. So the government turned to loans.

The Prices of Power

Loans to the government were not new. Two mechanisms to handle such loans already existed long before the outbreak of the War of the League of Cambrai in 1509: the Monte Vecchio, established in the late fourteenth century to consolidate the state's funded debt, which dated back to 1262;[111] and the Monte Nuovo, established in the 1480s. Then, after the war commenced, a third, the Monte Novissimo, was established. Shares (which the Venetians called "capital") paid out interest averaging 5 percent and were considered a good investment. But those voluntary deposits were still not enough to meet the government's military needs, which by early 1510 were twofold: to field an army against France and the Empire on the Terraferma and to strengthen the fleet to secure the Venetian sea routes if the Terraferma was occupied by enemy armies. So in the early years of the War of the League of Cambrai there a new system of loans made in exchange for political privileges and positions:

109. Gilbert puts the total needed at 240,000 ducats and points out that this was the sum calculated to conduct a campaign for one year, beginning in the spring and lasting through the summer. Of this sum, 100,000 ducats were for the commanders of Venetian towns, islands, and fortresses along the Adriatic and Greek littoral and were therefore not an emergency expense. Gilbert 1980, 26. See ASV, Senato, Terra, reg. 16, fols. 78v–80v, 23 December 1508, for a list of the taxes to be imposed on the Terraferma communities, amounting to 290,195 ducats.

110. For the sum needed for one year's campaign, see diaries, 7:688, 690; for the commanders' salaries, 7:705–6; and for the increase in property taxes, 20:9–11.

111. This funded debt made Venice the first European state to fund its debt so that interest was regularly paid to all bondholders equally. Lane 1973b, 150.

March 6, 1510 (10:23)   After dinner the Council of Ten met with the zonta on finances. An offer made by Leonardo Emo was read: he will serve the Signoria as the commander of a galley for six months and will loan the Signoria 1,500 ducats. Of this sum, 1,000 ducats will be used to buy shares for him in the Monte Novissimo, and 500 will be put toward taxes that will be levied on him. In recompense, when he returns, he will be permitted to go to the Senate for one year. While he will not have the vote, he will have the title "of the Senate" . . . as in the offer. After the offer was read, the heads of the Council of Ten proposed that it be accepted and that up to ten other patricians be allowed the same terms. Candidates will be voted on by the Council of Ten with the zonta, and those receiving the support of more than half [of the members] will be considered elected.[112]

On the morning of March 7 the entire city was talking about this bill about commanders. Some praised it, and some condemned it, but most of all people believe that a sufficient number [willing to accept the conditions] will not be found and that the bill will have to be revised.

The most significant innovation here was the admission to the Senate, even for a limited period and without a vote. It gave Emo the privilege of adding *di Pregadi,* that is, "Senator," after his name, a privilege that continued even after his senatorial term was over. This implied that the offices open only to members and former members of the Senate, including membership in the zonta or any additional council that aided the Council of Ten in its work, would be available to him and to others who followed his example. As a result of this provision, by April 16, forty days after Emo's offer had been accepted, twenty-five more Venetian patricians had offered to become galley commanders,[113] with sharp competition among those chosen for priority in manning their ships (10:43, 126, 154) and at least one party of celebration given on board by a successful candidate that was attended by a number of distinguished guests (June 3, 1510; 10:500).[114] Moreover, a week and a half after Emo's proposal, another patrician, Tadio Contarini, made an offer involving a higher loan but with no commitment to man and command a galley:

---

112. Further details on Emo's terms—to be applied to the ten other patricians as well—are supplied in ASV, CX, Miste, filza 25, fol. 1, 6 March 1510, and ASV, CX, Miste, reg. 33, fol. 68 *n.m.,* 6 March 1510: that is, upon Emo's return from his sea duty, his salary as commander would be added to his share on the Monte Novissimo together with that remaining part of his 500 ducats that had not been applied to his taxes. This measure was passed with twenty-five supporting votes and only one dissenting vote.

113. For the twenty-five candidates, see ASV, CX, Miste, filza 25, fols. 18 (13 March, 1510), which lists twelve names; 29 (18 March 1510), which lists two names; 51 (10 April 1510), which lists ten names; and 70 (16 April 1510), which lists one name.

114. Cf. Gilbert 1983, 8–10.

March 17, 1510 (10:44)   And in this Council of Ten a bill was passed allowing [new privileges for financial support]. Up to ten patricians who are thirty years of age and older will nominate themselves. When they have actually loaned our Signoria 2,000 ducats, of which 1,000 will be credited to them in the Monte Novissimo and 1,000 [will be used] to pay future taxes, these candidates will be eligible to be voted on by the Council of Ten with the zonta. Those obtaining the support of more than half of the members will be permitted to come to the Senate for one year, though without the vote, and will have the title senator. Today the vote was taken on Tadio Contarini; he passed and was elected.[115]

There was also the interesting case of Vicenzo Priuli, one of the young men who followed Leonardo Emo's example and stepped forward with a loan that would make him a commander in the fleet and at the same time secure him a place in the Senate for one year. His offer was initially accepted but later refused because he would be too young to enter the Senate when his ship service ended. After further discussion, it was decided that he could man his galley but that he could not enter the Senate until he was thirty.[116]

However, there were further problems. On February 15, 1511 (11:819), in a list of fifteen "sopracomiti dil Consejo di X," as these appointees by the Council of Ten were called, the word *non* appears next to seven names, including Vicenzo Priuli's, indicating that they had not yet kept their promise to loan these funds and prepare their ships. Such behavior was not to be tolerated: Vicenzo and another young man were called in before the Council of Ten the next day and told that were they to default, they would never thereafter be allowed to enter the Senate. The young men loaned the funds *promptissime,* and the ships were outfitted within the next few weeks.[117]

Meanwhile, Vicenzo Priuli became betrothed to the daughter of Alvise Pisani "dal Banco," one of the wealthiest and most powerful patricians in Venice. Sa-

---

115. Cf. ASV, CX, Miste, filza 25, fol. 26 (17 March 1510); and ASV, CX, Miste, reg. 33, fol. 7 (17 March 1510). For the wealth and extensive trading interests of Taddeo Contarini and for his patronage, together with his brother-in-law Gabriele Vendramin, of Giorgione (1477–1511), whose canvases hung in their homes, see Settis 1990, 15, 39, 152–55. Cf. Kaplan 1986, linking Giorgione's painting *The Tempest* to the defense of Padua in 1509.

116. On Vicenzo Prioli's offer of a loan and subsequent negotiations for a ship to command and the privilege of entering the Senate, see diaries, 13 March 1510 (10:31). Cf. ASV, CX, Miste, filza 25, fol. 18, 13 March 1510. See also diaries, 16 March 1510 (10:43) and 4 April 1510 (10:94).

117. See the Council of Ten's statement of 15 February 1511, about Vicenzo Prioli and Magdaleno Contarini (ASV, CX, Miste, filza 26, fol. 216, and ASV, CX, Miste, reg. 33, fol. 119). Sanudo's report on that day does not mention Contarini's negligence, but it does include, besides Prioli's, the names of six other unwilling *(renitenti)* patricians. Contarini's name appears in the diaries as both *Madalin* and *Natalin.*

nudo described the betrothal party as one of two events that cheered the city up in a dark season of military danger:

March 3, 1511 (12: 16)   I note that this evening two small festivities were held in connection with betrothals. One took place in the home of ser Zorzi Corner, the knight and procurator, for the marriage of his daughter to ser Zuan Antonio Malipiero. The other was held at the home of ser Alvise Pixani dal Banco for the marriage of his daughter to ser Vicenzo di Prioli. There were many women at both festivities, and many maskers. Although the city is financially pressed and in mourning [for its military losses], three very lovely momarie were held today. First were the Compagni Eterni, all of whom wore ducal sleeves of silk, stoles of silk and gold, and silken caps. The lord of their festivities was ser Daniel Barbarigo. Each one was preceded by a squire carrying a torch of ten libre, and there were ceremonial trumpets. They went to Ca' Pixani and took part in the festivities, dancing in the square with the women and staying on to supper there.

Item: there was another momaria, of peasant men and women all in good order, that made its way through the city, and then [a third] by other performers. Thus they have cheered the city considerably.

Immediately below this entry, Sanudo adds this information:

March 3, 1511 (12:16)   To be noted: Yesterday morning ser Madalin Contarini and ser Vicenzo Prioli enlisted the crew for Contarini's intermediate-sized galley and Prioli's light galley just as the law stipulated.

It appears that Vicenzo Priuli's marital plans and financial commitment to the city's needs went forward simultaneously. But it turned out that they were not entirely compatible. For Vicenzo Priuli to go to sea on his ship for six months now would be tantamount to forsaking this important marriage. It would be, he claimed, "the complete ruin of my affairs."[118] Moreover, he had the example of Tadio Contarini to follow. He now committed himself to pay the entire sum of fifteen hundred ducats right away, in exchange for which he would enter the Senate as others had, but he would not go to sea:

March 6, 1511 (12:23–24)   After dinner the Council of Ten met with the zonta. A bill was passed concerning Vicenzo Prioli, who had manned a galley in order to serve as a galley commander and is betrothed to the daughter of Alvise Pixani dal Bancho. He has offered to loan the Signoria 1,500 ducats immedi-

---

118. "Cum gran ruina de le cosse mie." ASV, CX, Miste, filza 27, fol. 9, 6 March 1511.

ately, with the following provisions: five hundred will apply to his taxes and those of other [members of his family], and he will be credited with 1,000 [in the Monte Novissimo]; then, just as the others [who have paid for the privilege] have entered the Senate, he will enter it and no longer have to serve as galley commander. The bill passed, and there was a great deal of grumbling about it in the city, and it was an unjust thing. Nonetheless, [the Ten] have done it to be able to use the money, which is in very short supply.

That Vicenzo's offer was accepted was owing not only to the money he could make immediately available but also to his powerful connections. His father, Lorenzo Priuli, was the influential controller of finances *(provveditore sopra i danari)*, whose warnings about the lack of funds in state coffers had prompted the government's extraordinary measures (September 25, 1510; II:416). And his prospective father-in-law, Alvise Pixani, commanded respect. In due course, the wedding was held, with parties most likely attended by many of the powerbrokers in Venice:

May 6, 1511 (12:178)   A sumptuous meal was given at Ca' Lippomano today by Lorenzo Prioli. It celebrates the wedding of his son Vicenzo to the daughter of Alvise Pixani dal Bancho, which took place yesterday. We were 362 guests at table, including the women.

"Everything is for sale"

During the succeeding years there were permutations of these arrangements whereby entry to office was achieved by loans. This had become so common that in early August 1515 a "general loan to deal with the great need" was declared. Neither patriotic actions nor native ability seemed to sway the subsequent elections, which went to the high bidders (August 3–5, 1515; 20:447–51).[119] Sanudo regretted that previous service counted for so little.

August 16, 1515 (20:520–21)   All those who made loans were elected to the Senate, as will be seen from the list below, [except for] Lorenzo Falier, who had also made a loan [but] failed to acquire [the requisite number of votes]. Many senior patricians who are entitled to serve were nominated but received few votes because the Great Council wants money. They are concerned with nothing else except getting those who loan money elected; neither age nor great service matters. . . .

---

119. Not necessarily, however, to the highest bidders. For a round of competitive bidding, see diaries, 16 September 1515 (21:85–86). Cf. Gilbert 1983, 16.

The others who loaned money stood around to see about entering the Senate because by order of the Signoria they were informed that they would do so. Therefore they were coming to the Signoria to offer their loans, which was both a fine and a ridiculous sight. In this way 4,600 ducats were found. Worthless [to the electors] were the important services of Bernardin da ca' Taiapiera: he was a member of the zonta, he lost all of his worldly belongings at the battle of Caravazo [Caravaggio], and he spent fifty-two months as a prisoner in France. He nominated himself and came last in the voting. So it is clear that at the present time these credentials are useless, as is service at the siege and defense of Padua. The only ones deemed qualified are those who loan money; the others are not. In fact, Sebastian Foscarini, university laureate, who is a lecturer in philosophy, was nominated to the Senate today, and the Great Council had a good laugh over it as if to say "we need money, not philosophy!"[120]

At the same time that these entries to the Senate were being purchased by loans, certain offices were "for sale" (20:150). Sanudo himself uses that term to describe a ten-year lease for the huge sum of five thousand ducats involving purchasable privileges in the viscountcy of Cyprus and goes on to say: "They [the Council of Ten] do everything to find money, and they would sell anything if they could find a buyer for it." And this same Council of Ten on the same day "sold" the lifetime occupancy of the chancellery in Candia (Crete) for five hundred ducats, "so that everything is for sale" (April 28, 1515; 20:150). The posts of commissioner for health (*provveditore di sanità*) and commissioner for the commune (*provveditore di comun*), the consulship in Alexandria, the highest administrative position (*capitanio e podestà*) in Sacile, a town in western Friuli important in the defense against imperial attacks, and the post of *provveditore* in the Salt Office—all these were awarded in exchange for loans (see August 16 and August 24, 1515; 20:520 and 553–55). So effective in raising funds was this system that soon new positions were being created for this very purpose.[121]

---

120. For Sebastian Foscarini, see chapter 8 under "Public Education in Venice." Sanudo may have grumbled that service to the city-state mattered less than money in obtaining office, but he recognized the financial exigency and listed in thirteen columns the names of all the lenders and nonlenders in the elections of that August (diaries, 20:456–68). Of two bankers who only gave 50 ducats each, he wrote that "being bankers, this is shameful thing" (5 August 1515; 20:451). He himself in August 1516 gave 500 ducats to enter the Senate, and a year he later pointed out that from 1515 to 1517, 474,870 ducats were raised by this system of loans (29:529).

121. Strictly speaking, only lower offices were really sold, and these purchases were usually for life. See the diary entry for 8 March 1510 (10:27), where a number of *officij di populani* are listed as for lifetime sale after their current incumbents had died. Higher offices were "bought" for loans, and as service to the state became a commercial object, the impression grew that positions of power were now "for sale." Cf. Finlay 1980b, 173–81. The phrase "sale of offices" appears in the Florentine observer Donato Giannotti's *Libro della Republica de' Vinitiani*, Giannotti 1974,

The opportunity to do so presented itself when the procurator Luca Zeno died on April 26, 1516 (22:166). The procuratorship was the highest office next to that of the doge, and there were only nine of them. Sums ranging from five thousand to ten thousand ducats were offered by contestants for the vacant position. Zacharia Gabriel was the winner. While he had offered only seven thousand ducats, he waived interest on his loan and promised to supply the money forthwith (April 28, 1516; 22:169–72). And he had set a precedent soon to be followed.

The Fortunes of Alvise Pisani

Appetites—both the government's fiscal appetite and the patricians' appetite for power—were now whetted. By June 1516, eighty thousand to one hundred thousand ducats would be needed. The Collegio, where opinion was divided, was reluctant to act. So the doge, "in high dudgeon," called on the Senate to approve a bill proposed by the controller of finances. The bill proposed that three more procurators, one for each branch of the magistracy, be elected from those offering loans at the next Great Council. This, it was thought, would bring in at least 45,000 ducats (May 15, 1516; 22:214–15). Those who had offered the higher sums the previous month renewed their offers, and Alvise Pisani, who had offered ten thousand ducats, was chosen. It was for him, as Sanudo wrote, a "supreme" achievement:

May 18, 1516 (22:223)   So today Alvise Pisani dal Bancho was elected procurator. He is forty-eight years old, and yesterday he celebrated the betrothal of one of his daughters to ser Zuan Corner, son of ser Zorzi Corner, knight and procurator. The dowry was 10,000 ducats, that is, 6,000 in cash, 2,000 to be paid in four years, 1,500 in Monte Novissimo shares, and 500 in material goods. He had the greatest joy at the betrothal; today, he achieved another supreme happiness, helped greatly by his new family bond [with Zorzi Corner]. And today he came to the council with these proposed terms: that if, on the second ballot, anyone else made an offer, he, Pisani, would increase his offer by 4,000 ducats. No one came forward [with a competing offer], and he saved himself those ducats. . . . And he brought and lent his 10,000 ducats, some of

---

1:138–42, written in 1525–26, only to have the Venetian spokesman M. Trifone Gabriello indicate that it is an inaccurate term for the loans: "Cominciò questa usanza (che molti falsamente chiamano—vendere i magistrati)." Gabriello then explains that in addition to offering money, one has to win the election, and he concludes: "I do not think that this is as great a corruption as many think and say." Sanudo's similar use of the verb *vendere* ten years earlier indicates that it was already a common usage. In any case, the practice referred to accomplished its purpose. It is estimated that between August 1515 and January 1517, the government collected enough to maintain the army for about ten months. See Cozzi 1973, 315; and Pezzolo 1996, 736.

which were sent right away to the military camp for its current needs, so that it was timely and in gold.[122]

Alvise's career up to this pinnacle is an example of what a wealthy Venetian patrician could aspire to. In 1499 his bank was the only large one to survive the general panic.[123] In 1500 it was liquidated, paying in full (March 23, 1500; 3:158), and it was refounded in 1504 (March 4, 1504; 5:942). Through his bank Pisani invested in the western voyages to England and Flanders, trading in wool and cloth (September 18, 1518, February 25, 1519; 26:48, 495). He participated in the spice trade with Alexandria and the voyages of merchant galleys to Barbary.[124]

So rich a man was bound to make his mark. Sanudo has much to say about him, but one incident reminds us that for all his wealth, Pisani could behave with the same cupidity as his colleagues. In 1515 the sultan sent a collection of presents to the Venetian government, and the patricians fell upon them in a paroxysm of greed:

March 6, 1515 (20:41)   This morning the chest sent from Cyprus with the gifts from the sultan was brought from the customs into the Collegio. It was opened and rapidly looted by those in the Collegio. One took one thing, another took another, with so much frenzy that it was shameful to witness such activity. The doge took for himself the cap [*corno*] of civet and —— ; in a fury others seized turban cloths and ornamented daggers[125] and porcelains, and the remainder was plundered. Ser Antonio Trun, the procurator, did not want things done in this way, but thought the gift should be sent away and given to the office of the Raxon Vecchie and sold for the benefit of San Marco. Nothing availed him, and he left with the intention of bringing the matter up before the next meeting of the Senate. Ser Alvise Pisani, the councillor, took the golden robe lined with ermine; ser Francesco Foscari, councillor,

122. Within the next year, the War of the League of Cambrai ended with a treaty signed on 7 January 1517 with Emperor Maximilian. On 16 January 1517 in the Senate (Finlay 1980b, 195) and on 25 January in the Great Council, the system of loans for offices was ended by the Venetian patricians, who viewed it as a necessary measure but "contrary to our ancient practices" (contra l'antiquo instituto nostro). ASV, MC, Deliberazioni, reg. 25 (1503-21), fol. 151 *n.m.* This measure passed with 1,416 votes for, 132 against, and 5 abstaining. But a few years later, in the early 1520s, the practice was revived, in spite of Sanudo's vigorous opposition. See vols. 32, 33, and 34 of the diaries as cited in Finlay 1980b, 195-96.

123. Lane 1987a, 7. See the diary entry of 17 May 1499 (2:726-27), above.

124. Lane 1966a, 41-42; 1966c, 77; 1973b, 350, for the transport of African gold to Venice.

125. The Fulin edition has *fese et iscari*, but based on the manuscript, the present editors read *sesse*, meaning a long cotton cloth to be wound as a turban; the editors take *iscari* to be the same as the Turkish *ışkı*, meaning an ornamented dagger or knife, similar to the Greek word *sicarios*. Diana Wright kindly supplied this explanation and related vocabulary for *iscari*.

took quite a few daggers and turban cloths; ser Zuan Francesco Bragadin, a head of the Quarantia, took the saddle. In this way all of those present got something. The savi ai ordeni got nothing, nor did ser Zuan Barozi, another head of the Quarantia. It used to be the custom, when I was savio ai ordeni, that these presents were shared: five members of the Collegio, one for each committee, were sent to the Procuratia to divide [the gifts] there, but the almond-oil camphor and the cloths to make chasubles stayed in the Basilica of San Marco, as did the aloe. In this way everyone had his share, and it would not be snatched away [*andava a la zaffa*], as happened on this occasion. The city was full of this news and this deed.

At the same time that he was trading and acquiring, Pisani used his wealth to perform extraordinary service for the state. He offered many loans to assist in paying war expenses, so that by the end of the war he had loaned the government 150,000 ducats.[126] In September, 1516, his bank guaranteed repayment of loans made by others to the state.[127] It is no wonder that the Council of Ten declared on one occasion that "it is quite superfluous to describe the good-will and patriotism with which our highly beloved Alvise Pisani has served this state during the war years. He has placed at the disposal of the state a gigantic sum of money when it was most needed and with the promptness and eagerness which can be expected from a Venetian noble."[128]

Part of Pisani's program was to increase his family's network through patrician alliances. In November 1520 his son Zuan married the granddaughter of Andrea Gritti, who became doge in 1523, an election Alvise Pisani helped to bring about.[129] His other four daughters married into the prominent Corner, Grimani, Priuli, and Capello families, as Sanudo reported in 1524:

---

126. For example, on 8 February 1512 he loaned 400 ducats, anticipating an appointment three days later to the zonta of the Council of Ten (diaries, 13:452, 461). On 5 August 1514 he sent 1,000 ducats to help defray expenses in Padua (18:417). On 22 October 1514 he gave 200 ducats to the state, matching Zorzi Corner's contribution and tying with him for the third largest loan on that day (19:153). On 20 April 1515 he loaned 1,000 ducats to the Signoria (20:129). On 3 August 1515 he loaned 300 ducats to the Signoria (20:448, 456), again the third largest loan after the doge's offer of 500 ducats and Zorzi Corner's offer of 400 ducats. For the totals, see Tucci 1996, 801 (up to 1519); and ASV, CX, Miste, filza 36, 18 January 1516, as cited in Gilbert 1983, 25.

127. To cover that guarantee, Pisani received the income from the Polesine (the fertile area at the mouth of the Po River), reckoned at 30,000 ducats, as well as the salt tax from Padua (2,950 ducats) and the customs duties of Treviso (3,500 ducats) and Udine (3,000 ducats). See diaries, 1 September 1516 (22:507–9); cf. Lane 1966c, 82.

128. Gilbert 1983, 25 (ASV, CX, Miste, filza 36, 18 January 1516).

129. Alvise Pisani was a member of the Forty-one, the final group in the complex voting process that elected the doge. See Finlay 1980b, 158–59, for this election and Pisani's role in it. For a possible pictorial reference to this relationship, see the description of Titian's lost painting of Andrea Gritti in chapter 8 under "Venetian Artists and Artworks," excerpt of 6 October 1531.

June 18, 1524 (36:410)   Today in the home of Alvise Pisani dal Bancho, the procurator, the families met for the betrothal of his fifth and youngest daughter to Zuan Capello. Her dowry is 8,000 ducats.

It should be noted that he has married five daughters: the eldest to Vicenzo Prioli; [the next three] to Zuan Corner, son of Zorzi Corner the knight and procurator, Antonio Prioli dal Bancho, and [Antonio][130] Grimani, the grandson of the doge; and this last one to Zuan Capello. Thus in daughters' dowries and wedding costs he has spent more than 40,000 ducats. In addition, he had his son made a cardinal, which also cost him a great deal.[131]

As early as 1514, when Alvixe Pisani, at "the young age of forty-six," became a head of the Council of Ten (April 28; 18:170) and a ducal councillor (June 11; 18:263), Sanudo commented that "he has enormous power in this city" (June 6; 18:250). His statement was borne out in the years that followed. Pisani also had strong enemies; because of his close relationship with Gritti, he was called in one graffito "a big traitor" who would try to "sell the Ducal Palace."[132] But he served his city well to the very end, meeting an untimely death from disease in 1528 while he was acting as proveditor with the Venetian-French army outside of Naples. Shortly thereafter his bank was closed, with full restitution made to all its depositors. Marin Sanudo witnessed that ceremony and described it as the honorable civic event it was:

November 3, 1528 (49:124–25)   This morning Zuan Pisani dal Banco, the son of the late Alvise, procurator, having decided to liquidate his bank, [sponsored a ceremony to this effect]. The bank was founded on March 1, 1504, in the name of Alvise alone, having previously been chartered in the names of Francesco and Zuan Pisani [his uncle and father]. Zuan invited many patricians to come today to the High Mass in the church of San Zuane di Rialto wearing colors; among these I, Marin Sanudo, was invited by him. He also went to the

---

130. The name was erroneously given by Sanudo as Jacomo, but see diaries, 33:614.

131. Alvise Pisani had funded Francesco Pisani's acquisition of the cardinalate in 1517, just as he had his daughters' dowries. See diary entries of 4 July 1517 for news of the appointment arriving in Venice (24:447) and for celebrations and the following comment from Sanudo: "It cost 20,000 ducats and a ruby" (24:450). The news was brought by Francesco's brother-in-law, Zuan Corner, whose own brother Marco Corner was already a cardinal (since 1500) and, along with Domenico Grimani, a cardinal since 1493, represented Venice among the cardinalate. See Cardinal Francesco Pisani's accumulation of rich benefices (Padua, Vicenza, Treviso) and his request, one year after the above ceremony, of the bishopric of Treviso (15 October 1529; 52:79–80, 82–83) and the speech of Alvise Mocenigo in opposition. This "trade" in benefices was another kind of patrician commercial activity. Lane (1987b, 324) writes that Francesco Pisani in 1535 derived 5,000 ducats per year from just the bishopric of Padua. See also Carroll 2000a, 965–66.

132. "Alvixe Pixani rebellazo, sotto sto Doxe tu venderà il palazo." Diaries, 29 October 1523 (35:148).

Collegio to invite the Collegio. Thus today he [went to Mass], dressed in plain black cloth with ducal sleeves in observance of the death of his father and accompanied by Lorenzo Loredan, Hironimo Justinian, Lorenzo Pasqualigo, and other procurators, knights, and patricians dressed in color and in silk. The Collegio came next, led by Nicolò Trivixan, the councillor. After the mass, they left the church. Then Antonio da Mula with Domenego Trivixan, the knight and procurator who is savio di Consiglio, Francesco Donado the knight and Hironimo Barbarigo, both councillors, with other procurators, Piero Arimondo and Aurelio Michiel, who are heads of the Quarantia, then other patricians and savi di Collegio all came to the bank. There were sacks of ducats and crowns, and plenty of coins [on the table]; however, it was draped with black cloth.[133]

Afterward, this announcement was called out by Nicolò the herald, who was dressed in scarlet: "In the name of God and of the Virgin Mary and of St. Mark, the patrician Zuan Pisani, son of the late Alvise Pisani the procurator, makes known to all that he wishes to liquidate the bank. Let all those who are creditors come to take their money, which will be given to them fully and willingly. Long live St. Mark."

It should be noted that a wind ensemble played; the guests left the church to its accompaniment. This intention to liquidate the bank redounds greatly to the honor of the city and to that of Zuan Pisani.[134]

Alvise Pisani was a true example of the interwoven economic, social, and political networks of Renaissance Venice, a living embodiment of the 1526 placard reading, "Whoever has wealth may sail with fair wind and govern fortune as he wills." But it was his political as well as his financial service to the city that made him remarkable. Even after his death, his reputation and that of his family were honored by the successful liquidation of his bank. So was the reputation of the city: "Eviva messier San Marco!"[135]

---

133. The symbolic role of fabric and color is well illustrated here: Zuan Pisani and the bank bench itself are appropriately draped in plain black cloth as signs of mourning for Alvise Pisani, dead just over four months. Diaries, 30 June 1528 (48:237). But Zuan Pisani also made sure that his guests wore "color and silk" to indicate the celebratory occasion of the bank's fully meeting its financial obligations to its investors.

134. Sanudo's praise here contrasts with his condemnation of the banker Girolamo Prioli, his fellow diarist, in 1513, when the Prioli bank failed and "the banker did not wish to reimburse [his creditors], behaving in a bestial manner" (18 November 1513; 17:328).

135. Economic historians have concurred with Sanudo's note of resilience here. See Hocquet 1982, 2:702: "Enfin si un siècle nous semble réaliser un heureux équilibre pour la cité de Venise, grâce à la diversification des activités e des revenus, c'est bien plutôt le XVIème siècle, que ceux qui l'ont précédé, depuis le XIIIème siècle." At the same time, Hocquet wrote: "L'histoire de Venise ne fut jamais facile, elle est un combat permanent, une constante adaptation à des situations nouvelles." Cf. Pezzolo 1996, 744; and Lane 1966a, 54–55, on the opportunism and flexibility of Venetian family partnerships.

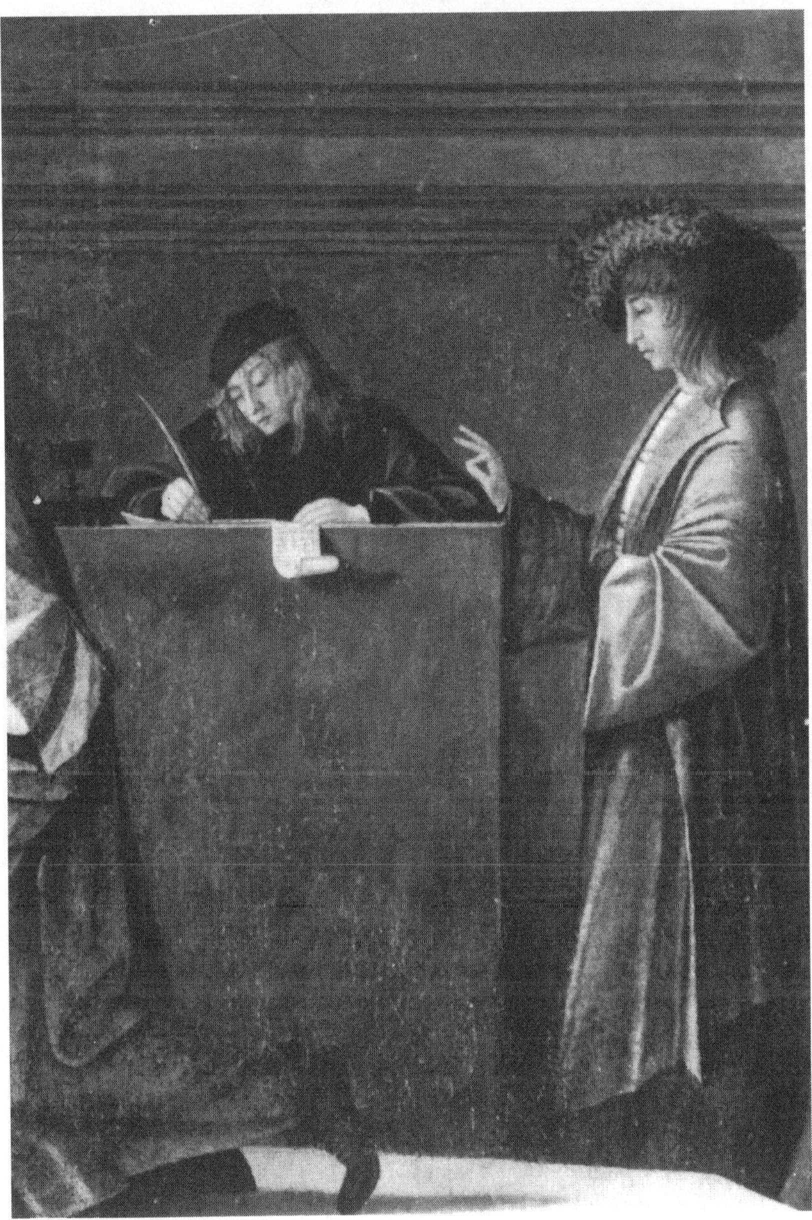

Venetian scribe, detail from Vittore Carpaccio, *Departure of the Ambassadors*, c. 1500.
Accademia, Venice. Photo by Osvaldo Bohm, 2064.

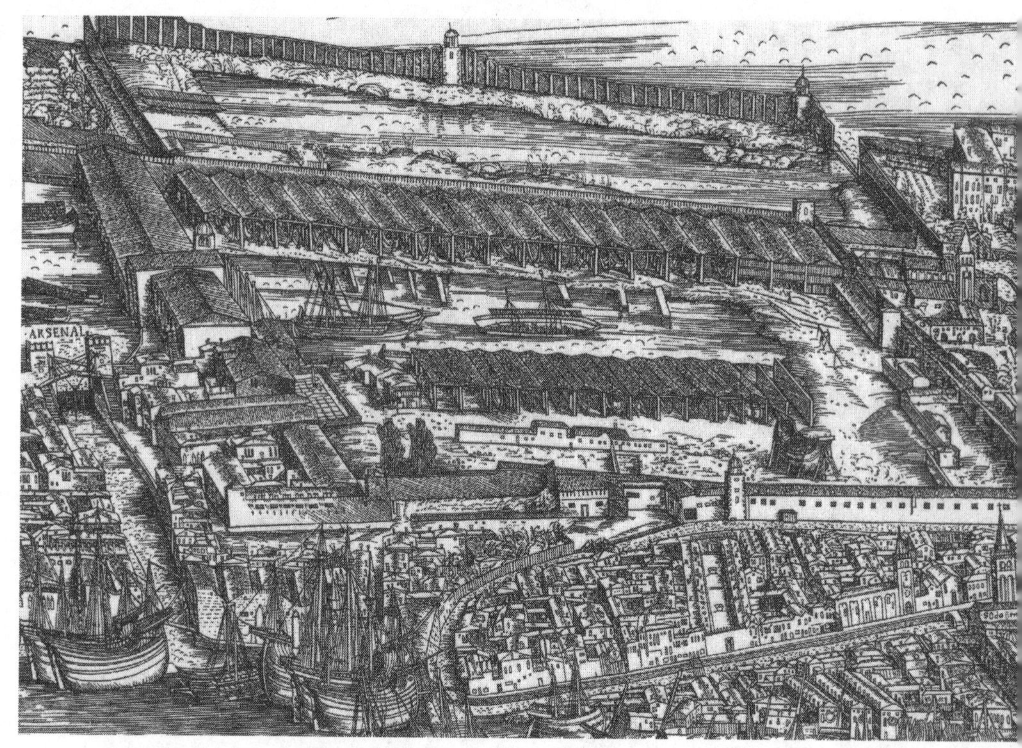

The Arsenal, Venice, detail from Jacopo de' Barbari, *View of Venice,* woodcut, 1500. Photo by Osvaldo Bohm.

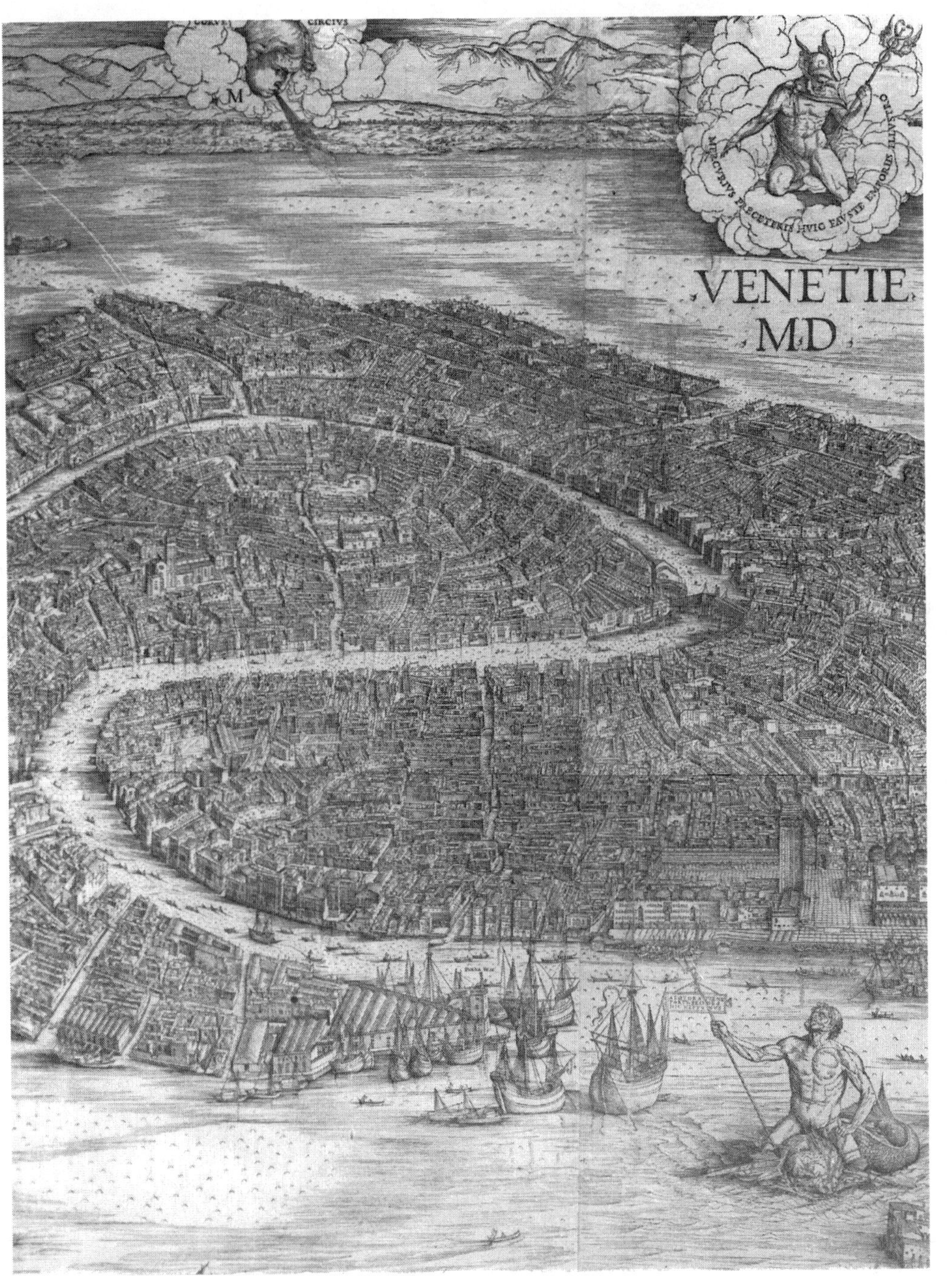

Detail from Jacopo de' Barbari, *View of Venice*, woodcut, 1500. Photo by Osvaldo Bohm.

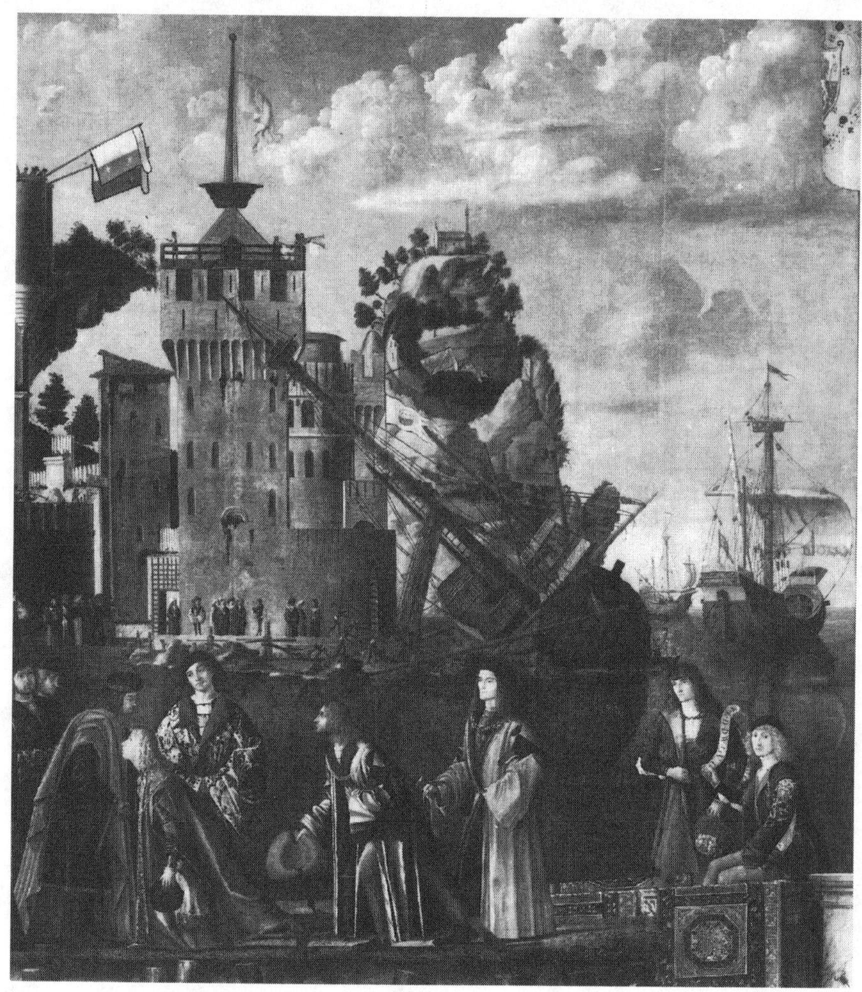

Shipwreck, detail from Carpaccio, *Leavetaking of the Betrothed Pair,* from the St. Ursula cycle, 1495. Accademia, Venice. Photo by Osvaldo Bohm, 2064.

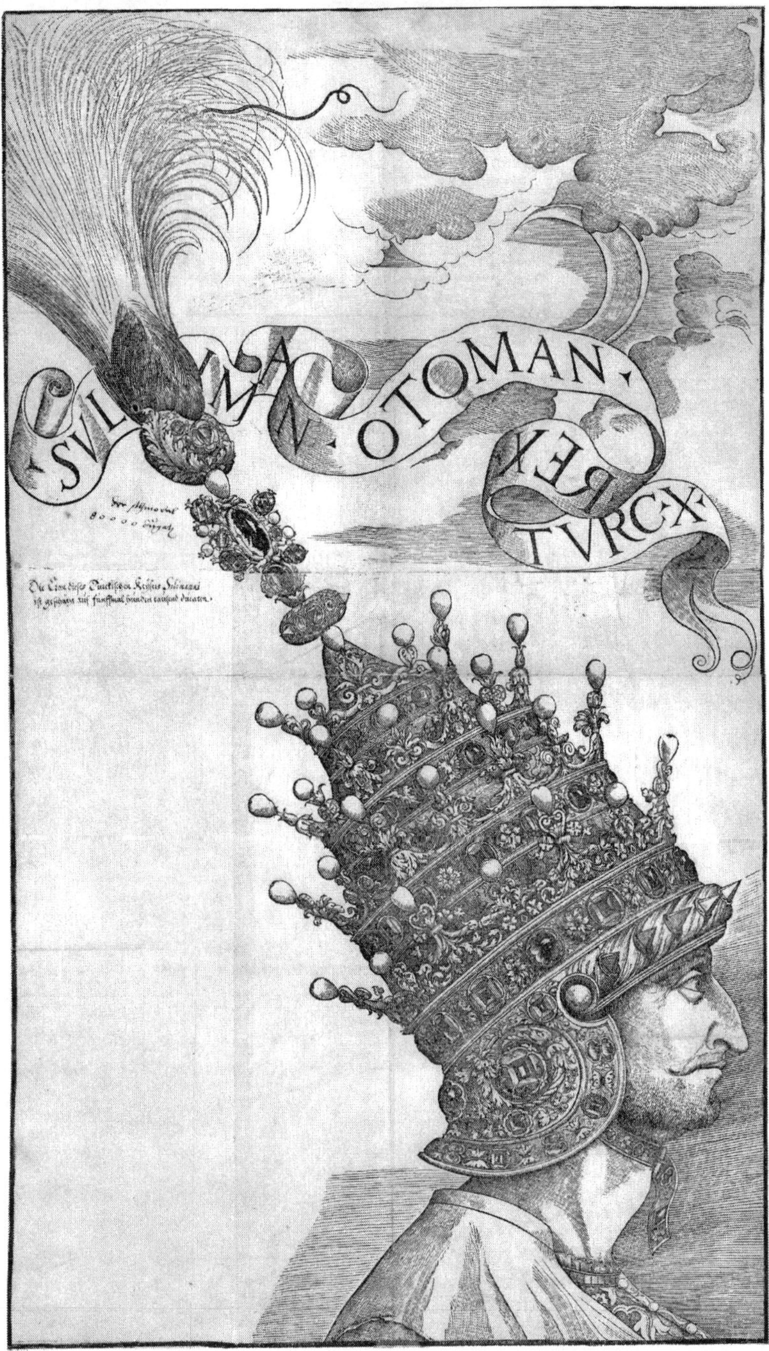

Anonymous, portrait of Sultan Suleiman wearing the gold helmet made in Venice in 1532, Venetian woodcut in two blocks, c. 1535. The Metropolitan Museum of Art, Harris Brisbane Dick Fund, 1942 (42.41.1). Image © The Metropolitan Museum of Art.

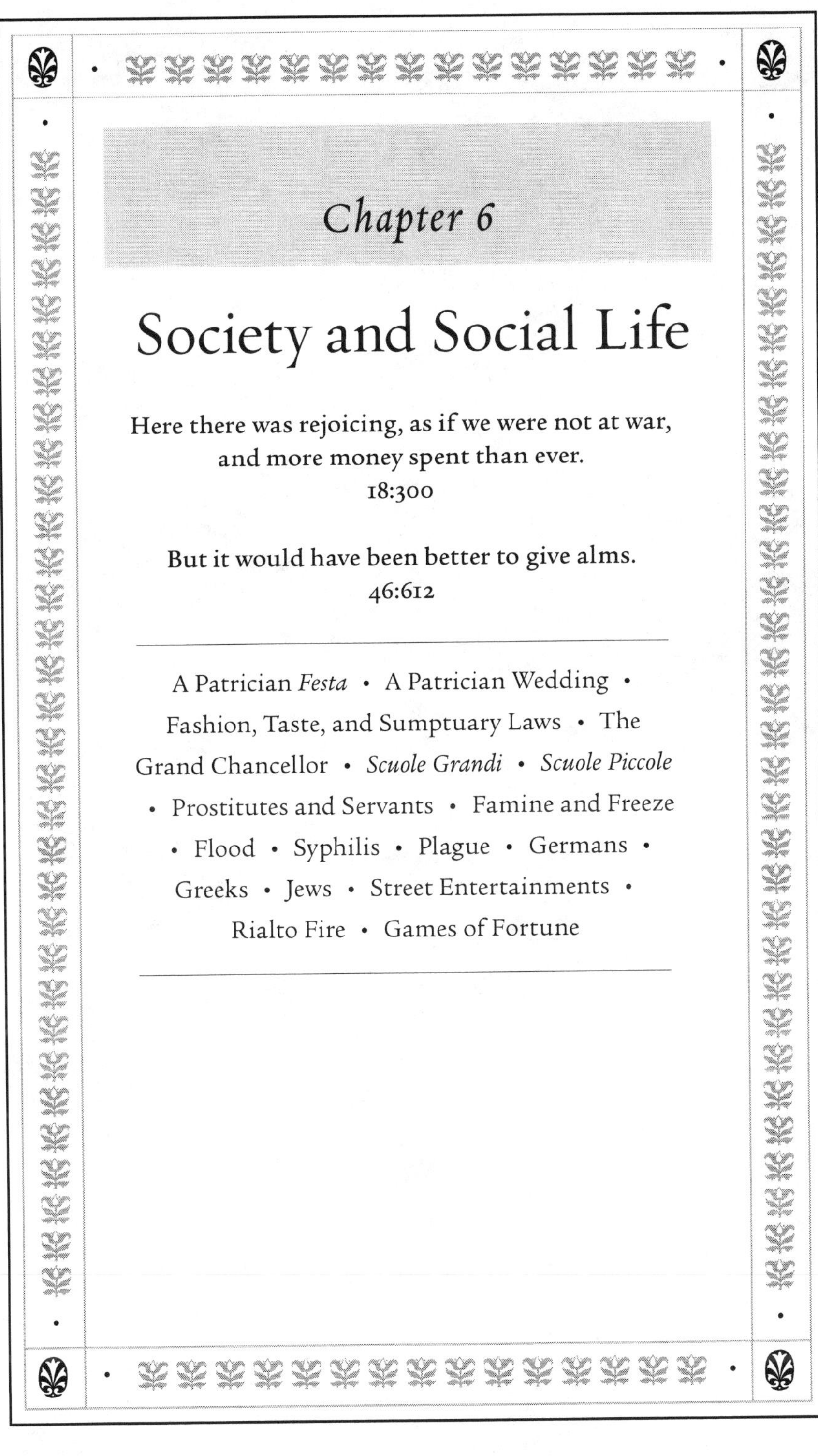

Chapter 6

Society and Social Life

Here there was rejoicing, as if we were not at war,
and more money spent than ever.
18:300

But it would have been better to give alms.
46:612

A Patrician *Festa* · A Patrician Wedding ·
Fashion, Taste, and Sumptuary Laws · The
Grand Chancellor · *Scuole Grandi* · *Scuole Piccole*
· Prostitutes and Servants · Famine and Freeze
· Flood · Syphilis · Plague · Germans ·
Greeks · Jews · Street Entertainments ·
Rialto Fire · Games of Fortune

"There are three types of inhabitants: the patricians, who govern the city and the Republic . . . , citizens, and artisans, or the lower class."[1] So Sanudo described the society of Venice in his *De origine,* and these estates were legally defined, each with its own privileges, duties, designated activities, and entertainments. Within each group there were further distinctions, but Sanudo's focus was on his own patrician class, which made up about 5 percent of Venice's population at the time. It was a highly self-aware class, protecting its prerogatives and guarding its bloodlines. It is not accidental that in more than one place Sanudo lists the patrician houses and comments on those that had become extinct by his time, a source of some concern to a society so dominated by its nobility.[2]

Of modest wealth himself, Sanudo was keenly aware of the range of both economic and political power enjoyed by the Venetian patriciate.[3] While he himself had failed to achieve the higher ranks of governmental offices, his patrician status permitted him to attend governmental discussions and observe the full range of patrician activities. Sanudo seems to have taken particular interest and pride in the social life of those able to afford the more extravagant pleasures of communal celebration and private revelry.

A Patrician *Festa*

At the center of Venetian patrician social life was the *festa*. The festa, which was more than the banquet itself, was most often organized for a particular occasion: to honor visiting dignitaries, to celebrate a wedding, to observe a religious holiday. But a festa could also take place, especially in Carnival season, simply because a *compagnia della calza* organized it.

---

1. Sanudo 1980, 22. The Venetian population at this time has been estimated at about 115,000 (or excluding clergy and religious orders, about 102,000). See Chambers and Pullan 1992, 6; J. C. Davis 1962, 55; and Beloch 1902, 40, where Beloch estimates, on the basis of extant partial documentation of the 1509 census, which Sanudo used, a population of 110,000. Cf. Beltrami 1954, 59. Romano 1987, 31, 36, prefers to distinguish between *popolo grande* (nobles and well-to-do commoners) and *popolo minuto* (workers), with clergy and slaves as additional groups. We have retained Sanudo's tripartite distinction, imprecise as it is.

2. See diaries, 6:117–18, 45:569–72. Sanudo was keenly aware, as were his contemporaries, of the *casade morte,* the "dead houses" of certain patrician families. See also Sanudo 1980, 68–70, 178–79, 206; and diaries, 6:117–18. The *Libro d'oro,* which contained the names of the current patricians old enough to take their place in the Great Council and occupy governmental positions, had come into existence in August 1506, after a century of gradually increasing awareness of those families that were extant and those that had become extinct. See Chojnacki 1996.

3. On the range between rich and poor nobility, see Pullan 1971, 267–78.

These compagnie della calza were an important feature of Venetian social life. Societies of young patricians who were identified by their colorful stockings, they were frequently commissioned by the government to add brilliance and festivity to diplomatic and ceremonial occasions. But they also participated in private gatherings, where they themselves funded the entertainment. Membership in these societies was often sought by young foreign nobility as well as Venetian nobles, and elections to them were honorary events. Sanudo lists thirty-four such compagnie (58:184–85). They were ephemeral organizations, lasting usually for a year or two and then replaced by others.[4]

In 1507 Sanudo described the founding of a new compagnia, its officers, and its obligations to the festa:

October 24, 1507 (7:169)   This morning a compagnia of youths was formed. They are about eighteen years old, very wealthy, calling themselves the Immortali (Immortals) and numbering thirteen, including one who is absent [from the city]. They have chosen a prior for one year, and they must [each] now give a festa, first the prior, then all the others, with a penalty [for not doing so], etc. And they can accept no one else until all these parties have been given. They come dressed in purple velvet trimmed with vair. Their sleeves are gathered, with one red stocking and the other half-purple and half-grey. The lord of the compagnia wears a garment of crimson two-pile fabric with open sleeves lined with ermine; on his head is a cap of black velvet in the French fashion, with a jewel attached. The compagnia attended Mass at the Madonna di Miracoli and then came to San Marco.

There follows a list of the members of the new compagnia, comprising three Contarinis from two different branches and one each from the Diedo, the Vendramin, the Dandolo, the Malipiero, the da Lezze, the Grimani, the Moro, the Foscari, and the di Priuli, plus one unidentified patrician.

And it should be noted that they call themselves the Immortali. There are three compagnie with similar names, using other terms, that is, the Sempreviva [Everliving], the Perpetui [Perpetuals], the Eterni [Eternals], and now these Immortali. Other compagnie in my time are these: the Puavoli [Dolls], the Felici [Joyful], the Principali [Chiefs], the Sempreviva [Everliving], the Liberali [Generous], the Sbragazai [Baggy Pants], the Fraterni [Fraternals], the Potenti [Powerful].

---

4. Historians have identified at least forty-three over the period of their existence (1441?–1564). See M. T. Muraro 1981, 321.

A typical evening's entertainment took place on a February evening, and therefore in the midst of Carnival, in a patrician house on Murano, where many of the wealthier patricians had their "country" homes. This festivity included theatrical entertainments as well as dinner and dancing, all typical components of a Venetian festa.[5]

February 16, 1512 (13:483)   This evening, at the Lippomano house on the island of Murano, a *comedia* and entertainments involving characters dressed as peasants were staged by a compagnia of noblemen called the Zardineri [Gardeners], numbering about twenty-five in all. The members of the compagnia themselves performed the comedia and did it well. Quite a few people attended the presentation and the festa that they gave. [The compagnia members] invited twelve of the city's demimondaines.[6] However, they were all[7] respectably dressed in silk and seated on the platform. The lord of the festivities was Gasparo Contarini,[8] who is one of the signori di notte. The compagnia members all wear white stockings to these festivities. Next they held a sumptuous feast, followed by a dessert of marzipan fruitcake and then a momaria of buffoons. They danced with those women all night, so that when the party was over it was daylight. I spent[9] the night there without sleeping, a most unusual thing, but in fact it was quite a sight.

Such extravagant and protracted parties were not unusual, especially if high-ranking guests were involved:

January 9, 1521 (29:536–37)   After dinner, there was a festa at Ca' Pesaro, at San Benedeto, given by the compagnia of the Ortolani [Farmers] and paid for by Count Antonio da Martinengo, a nobleman who is our condottiere and who has been accepted into that compagnia.[10] There were about sixty women, the most prominent and beautiful in the city, and everyone supped on sweets, partridges, oysters, etc. After supper a beautiful new comedia was put on by

---

5. For a fuller discussion of theatrical entertainments, see chapter 9.

6. Sanudo's term is *scosagne*, which Battaglia 1961–2000 cites, relating it to *nascondiglio*, "hiding place," and deriving it from *scoso*, the participle of *scondere*, "to hide."

7. The manuscript has *tutte*; the Fulin edition omits it.

8. This is not the famous religious reformer whose father's name was Alvise. This Gasparo Contarini's father was Francesco Alvise. Gasparo had participated in a tournament the year before (diaries, 12:277) and in March 1522 hosted a performance of another peasant comedy *a la vilanescha*, in the country style (see below, n. 27), also with the Zardineri (33:9).

9. The manuscript has *trovai*; the Fulin edition has *tornai*.

10. The Martinengo were an important Brescian family whose members were often employed by Venice as military leaders.

Ruzante and Menato, the Paduans,[11] attended by a large number of people. Then at three hours after sunset some of the members of the compagnia and Count Antonio went to invite the Prince [of Bisignano, Pietro Antonio di Sanseverino] and some of his friends to the festa and to supper, and four of our patrician university laureates went to accompany him. He came with about ten of his principal advisers. After arriving, he wished to dance dressed just as he was, in cloth of gold, with the wife of ser Zuan Cosaza, who is his cousin, as well as with the wife of ser Andrea Diedo, who is a Prioli and a very beautiful woman. He danced with no one else. Afterwards, a supper was prepared on the upper floor; tables were arranged around the hall, with one in the middle, at which the prince and his retinue and the laureates and the abovementioned ser Zuan ate from a silver service, and it was very sumptuous for him.[12] This too was paid for by Count Antonio. Next, the comedia was put on, and it ended at eleven hours after sunset.

A week later the same compagnia celebrated the acceptance of the prince himself as a member. Sanudo took evident satisfaction in describing the luxurious details of this party at his nephew's house:

January 16, 1521 (29:546–47)   This evening, at San Anzolo, on the Grand Canal, at Ca' Lando, the home of ser Marco Antonio Venier, lord of Sanguanè [Sanguinetto], my nephew, a very rich party and supper were given by the Ortolani at their expense for the Prince of Bisignano, who has been accepted into their compagnia.[13] First the hall and rooms of the house were beautifully decorated with tapestries and paintings, and there was a large credenza of silver dishes worth 5,000 ducats, and a cloth of gold had been spread out where the prince and the lord of the festivities were to sit. Forty or more of the most beautiful women of the city had been invited; they were dressed in trimmed and quartered cloth of gold and in silk.

First a ball was held, and the lord [of the festivities] danced a great deal, being young, handsome, and vigorous and ready to fall in love. Next came the buffoons in various costumes according to the act. Then came all the virtuosi of music and song that anyone could wish: a wind ensemble, bagpipes, cornets, and flutes were played. Next came the supper for the prince and twelve

---

11. See chapter 9 for these actors.

12. The manuscript has *a lui;* the Fulin edition omits it.

13. Sanguinetto was a castle that belonged to the Venier family, of which Sanudo's mother was a member. The Prince of Bisignano had wanted to join this compagnia because, as Sanudo says earlier, "he loves to dance and is a youth of 18 years and a half" (diaries, 29:543). On the Prince of Bisignano, see Carroll 2000b, 39–42.

of his retinue, ser Zuan Cosaza,[14] Julio Manfron, Ferier Beltrame [the knight of Rhodes], and about the same number of women. They dined in the side rooms and had twenty-two courses: peacocks, pheasants, partridges, wood grouse, etc., dressed, with gilded bread, gilded oysters—even the wax candles were gilded.[15] Two wax torch [i.e., torchbearers] preceded[16] the dishes, and the compagnia members served. Outside, in the area of the portico, the other women and their husbands had supper. . . . After that they danced the hat dance, which went on a long time.[17]

The party lasted until thirteen[18] hours after sunset, when the prince was accompanied to his home by the members of the compagnia. No one was allowed to enter except his retinue and about forty patricians; none of the silver was lost except a cup. . . . There were —— members of the compagnia, and they made a tree with the coats of arms of the compagnia members and of the prince and the following inscription: "Pietro Antonio of Sanseverino, Prince of Bisignano,[19] Duke of San Marco, Count of Tricari, Claremont, Coriolano, Mileto, of the Kingdom of Naples and elected member of the Ortolani."

Parties could also be quite unruly, as was the case with one party organized some days later by the same compagnia:

January 23, 1521 (29:567)   I note that yesterday evening at Ca' Corner, at San Benedeto, on the Grand Canal, a party or supper was held by the compagnia [of the Ortolani] for the betrothal of ser Agustin Contarini, who is marrying the daughter of ser Alvise Corner. Attending was the Prince of Bisignano, a member of the Ortolani, who supped with them. Antonio, the Count of Martinengo, who is also a member of the compagnia, came armed to the house after supper because of certain insulting words that had been said to him by

---

14. Count Giovanni di Cosazza, a close relative of the prince's.

15. On gilded foods, see below, n. 56.

16. The manuscript has *avanti;* the Fulin edition omits it.

17. The *ballo del cappello,* or "dance of the hat," was popular at this time. Molmenti 1973 describes this as a "contraddanza," which ordinarily concludes a feast (2:379). Molmenti also quotes Simeon Zuccolo, who in his *La pazzia del ballo* (Padua, 1549), 28, said that the *ballo del cappello* was also called the *ballo dell'adulterio* and proceeded in this fashion: the lover was invited with a sweet smile and loving glance by his beautiful lady, and he placed his hat, which he had courteously kissed, on her blond tresses. The two found themselves happy, joyous, and full of contentment, especially the giddy and bold woman, for it seemed to her that in this dance she was superior to the man, having his cap on her head in this delightful hour and being able to trick and lead this foolish and hatless man wherever she pleased through the large rooms.

18. The manuscript has *hore 13;* the Fulin edition has *hore 14.*

19. The name Bisignano is in the manuscript but omitted in the Fulin edition. The Prince of Bisignano belonged to a noble house of Naples and Lombardy, as indicated below.

the other compagnia members. And when these members of the compagnia saw him arriving at the festivity with arms, they too [pulled out] their swords; thus the prince drew his, as did ser Zuan Cosaza. More than twenty swords were drawn in the room and were being brandished about, and no one knew against whom. Antonio da Martinengo did not draw his sword, but his people did. The women were terrified, and once the noise died down, the party was called off, at nine hours after sunset.

For all that excitement, the Prince of Bisignano left the next day highly pleased with his visit. He had, after all, been royally entertained:

January 23, 1521 (29:567)   [The Prince of Bisignano] left highly satisfied with this city of ours, saying that all other cities are but villages, but this one seems to him a most excellent city.

Visiting dignitaries considered worthy of entertainment were of all sorts. Even the wife of a captain general received a reception in 1514 (18:238). In the following excerpt a visiting cardinal, that is, a prince of the church, was entertained by two Venetian cardinals, one not yet confirmed.

September 23, 1518 (26:53-54)   There were neither letters nor news of any importance in the Collegio. Cardinal Cibo paid visits to the Bell Tower of San Marco and to view the jewels [of San Marco] and to see the rooms of the Council of Ten, which are in the Ducal Palace.[20] He went to dinner where he wished; it is believed that he went with his own people to the tavern. This evening at Ca' Corner, where he is staying, festivities were held with a wind ensemble; — women guests attended, and maskers wearing mid-calf robes of silk danced.[21] There were three cardinals seated next to each other: Cibo, Pisani, and Corner, who, because he is in his own house, took the inferior position.[22] I also saw the following bishops: [Cristoforo] Marzello of Corfù,

---

20. Innocentius Cibo, a nephew of Pope Leo X (1513-21), had received his cardinal's hat in 1513. As noted earlier, these three sites were part of the typical "tourist itinerary" of the period included these three sites, along with the Arsenal, Rialto, the glass factories of Murano, and several others.

21. In another passage Sanudo cites a 1513 letter from London describing male dress there (15:575) and defines these robes *(roboni)* as "garments pleated at the shoulders . . . , reaching to the mid-leg, lined with every kind of beautiful fur" (veste increspade su le spale . . . , longi a meza gamba, fodrade di più sorte pelle belletissime). Newton 1988, 78–80, writes that *roboni* and *saioni* indicated very elegant garments that did not reach to the ground but, on the other hand, did not conform to the current French fashion of reaching only to the knee.

22. Marco Corner had been a cardinal since 1500; Francesco Pisani was confirmed as cardinal in 1517. Both the Corner and the Pisani were among the most powerful families of the Venetian patriciate.

[Giovanni] Lando of Candia, [Giacomo] Pesaro of Pafo, and the bishop of Famagosta; also in the room was ser Andrea Corner, the cardinal's brother, who is archbishop of Spalato. The guests danced for a long time. Then the women and their husbands had supper and danced the hat dance; they brought all of the cardinals onto the dance floor.

On another occasion the guests of honor were fugitives from Florence, from which the Medici were already fleeing, prior to the reestablishment of the Republic a few months later (May 17, 1527):

January 8, 1527 (43:616)   This evening ser Marco Foscari, the father of don Hironimo, the bishop of Torcello and former ambassador to Rome, held a lovely banquet in the courtly style with silver settings. It was given in honor of a son of the late Lord Zanin de' Medici, who is — [eight] years of age and whose name is — [Cosimo], and a son of Lord Jacomo Salviati, who was the brother-in-law of Pope Leo. . . , and several other Florentines.[23] They left Florence a number of days ago for reasons of personal safety and have come to live in this city. Also attending were women guests, the procurator ser Marco da Molin, and other patricians. There were comedie and instrumental and vocal music; in short, it was a lovely supper.

It should be noted that it has been said that the Salviati boy is to marry the only daughter of ser Marco Grimani, the procurator, and that the pope will name ser Marco's brother Marin, the patriarch of Aquileia, to a cardinalate and that ser Marco will give the pope money, they say about 25,000 ducats.[24]

Sanudo always noted the presence of women: their number, elegance, and sometimes their behavior. Women were considered an enhancing presence, with their display of jewelry and costly attire, a reminder of the power of the city and, in this case, a sign of its liveliness:

February 16, 1533 (57:525–26)   I wish to note that this evening a very lovely party was held at Ca' Corner, at San Polo, for the betrothal of the daughter of ser Zuan Corner, whose dowry amounts to 10,000 ducats, that is, 9,000 in

---

23. Zanin de' Medici was Giovanni dalle Bande Nere, the famous condottiere, who died in 1526. His son, Cosimo, born in 1519, became Cosimo I, Grand Duke of Florence from 1537 to 1574. Leo X (1513–21) and the current pope, Clement VII (1523–34), also belonged the Medici family. At the end of 1526, imperial troops were sent into Italy with orders to march against the Papal States and Pope Clement VII, threatening as well the Medici power in Florence. Giovanni Salviati was the nephew, through his mother, of Leo X and, through his sister, the uncle of Cosimo I, as well as his cousin.

24. In fact, negotiations for the Grimani daughter to marry a relative of the pope's continued until 1534, when Clement died, and then were terminated.

cash and 1,000 in goods and money. She is marrying ser Piero Morexini, of the San Cassan [branch of the family], who is very rich. Many women were invited, and they danced all day. So that the tables on the first platform might be prepared at four and a half hours after sunset, the members of the compagnia ... went with fifty women to Campo San Polo and as far as Rialto, and they surrounded the bridge,[25] dancing the *chiaranzana* with the women, who fell on the ground.[26] Some of them lost their caps and were bareheaded, some lost gold medallions that they kept in their caps, some suffered one damage, some another. Then they returned home accompanied by a wind ensemble and went to supper. Cardinals Grimani and Ridolfi were there incognito, and they had supper in an upper room.

On one occasion a compagnia invited women without their husbands, which led to a fracas:

January 22, 1516 (21:471)   This evening, at Ca' Donado, near the church of the Servites, some members of the compagnia called the — held a supper and party. Women were invited, but their husbands were not allowed to attend, and the doors were locked. Many young men wanted to enter the house and broke the windowpanes with stones, making a great disturbance. The lord of this festivity was ser Nicolò Donado.

There might be an element of disorder at even the most elegant dinners. In 1526 a politically awkward situation developed when a plucked and mutilated rooster was used as a metaphor for the condition of the French king, causing discontent and open reproach from the diarist for what he considered an inappropriate display:

February 7, 1526 (40:789–90)   This evening, on the island of the Giudecca, at Ca' Trivixan, a beautiful banquet was held, and three comedie were recited: one by Cherea, one by Ruzante and Menato in the country style, and one in the buffoon style by Cimador and the son of Zuan Polo.[27] This party thrown by the patriarch of Aquileia [Marino Grimani]. Attending were sixteen women, among the most beautiful in the city, and the following ambassadors: the papal legate [Tommaso Campeggi], two from the emperor [Charles V], two

---

25. The manuscript has *e torniorono Rialto;* the Fulin edition omits it.

26. A popular dance, the *chiaranzana* was danced in a circle. The name derives from *Carinthia,* where it supposedly originated. See Battaglia 1961–2000.

27. Plays in the country style often had to do with peasant wedding; the buffoon style tended toward courtly entertainment, with jugglers and acts of physical virtuosity.

from France [whose king was Francis I], one from the English king [Henry VIII], two from [Ferdinand] the Archduke of Austria. Absent were [the ambassadors from] Milan, Ferrara, and Mantua. Present also were the primicerio of San Marco, the bishop of Baffo, [Giacomo] Pesaro, the bishop of Concordia [Giovanni Argentino], the knight [of Jerusalem, Zaccaria] Garzoni, and a few others. It was a lovely dinner, with all the various dishes one could want, and served on silver, but there was a lot of confusion because the hall was filled with foreigners, especially the servants of the ambassadors, who created a lot of commotion. Because of this, the supper did not proceed in a very orderly way. And then a certain impudence was committed by a Spaniard, who threw a wine jug at ser Agustin Nani and cut him a little on the forehead. This party lasted until twelve hours after sunset.

It should be noted that at the meal there were many dishes, including some pastries. From one dish, crabs were spilling; from another, little rabbits,[28] and out of another, birds. And out of another came a rooster that had been plucked and whose comb had been cut, [which] ran around the table knocking over glasses and wine jugs.[29] Since the French ambassadors were there, this was not a wise thing to do, and there was a lot of grumbling about it around the city.[30] Four young procurators were present: ser Marco da Molin, ser Francesco di Prioli, ser Marco Grimani, and ser Vetor Grimani. One noteworthy episode occurred when ser Marco Grimani the procurator, dressed in black velvet, climbed onto the table [to persuade those present] to make some room: the hall was full of young people who didn't want to leave because the comedia was put on after supper.

A Patrician Wedding

The principal occasion for a patrician festa was a wedding, the bonding—economically and politically, as well as socially—of two prominent families. Sanudo describes a number of these occasions, carefully recording the dowries, which, in spite of legislation to control them, grew to significant sizes; the number of guests; the elegant costumes of the bride, the groom, and the attendants; the

---

28. The manuscript has *conieti;* the Fulin edition has *confeti.*

29. See Padoan Urban 1993, 169, where it is pointed out that these live creatures were produced not to be eaten but for effect.

30. The plucked and mutilated rooster represented the French king, Francis I, who had been taken captive by Emperor Charles V at the battle of Pavia on 24 February 1525 and had not been released until the Treaty of Madrid on 14 January 1526, only a few weeks prior to this party. See Lovarini 1965, 94–96, 100–103, which connects this episode with the proimperial and anti-Venetian sentiment evident in Ruzante's circle and notes that thereafter he is not mentioned in Sanudo's diaries. For Ruzante, see chapter 9.

courses served at dinner; and the wedding entertainments. All these were set forth as a statement of the city's wealth and power.[31]

So important were weddings as a barometer of the public mood that in 1511, two years into the War of the League of Cambrai and two years after Venice's disastrous defeat at Agnadello at the hands of a French army, Sanudo reported on two weddings with "many women and maskers at both, so that although the city has expenses and is in mourning, three very beautiful momarie were put on today and . . . they have cheered the city considerably" (March 3, 1511; 12:16). And three years later he reported on the affirmative political significance of an elaborate series of nuptial activities:

June 26, 1514 (18:299–300)   Today the entire city is celebrating because after this morning's wedding of ser Beneto Grimani to the daughter of ser Vetor Pixani, the members of his compagnia decided, after many difficulties, that they would obtain from ser Vetor the party that they had planned for today on the Grand Canal. They prepared a bucintoro[32] by adorning a wine barge with tapestries and covering tables[33] with galley awnings and pennants. It was a very attractive sight, and they made places to seat the women; and they procured everything necessary to hold a supper on it. So that today after dinner most of the young women who had dined at Ca' Pisani, at San Patrinian, boarded the bucintoro along with the members of the compagnia, who were dressed in short fitted jackets and mid-calf robes and carried batons and musical instruments.[34] They chose a lord [of the festivities] from among them, . . . and allowed only members of the compagnia and their servants on board. The barge was towed by six boats from San Nicolò with —— oars apiece. They left from San Benedetto and followed the Grand Canal to the columns of San Marco, dancing all the while and stopping in many places. Then they turned around and came back along the Grand Canal as far as Santa Croce. Many boats[35] followed them in order to watch, and women and others came to the balconies of their houses to see the spectacle.

Another compagnia of young men about the same age, called the Immortali, decided to compete by making their own bucintoro. Three of them went to the Collegio and asked for a light galley for today, offering to loan the Signoria 200 ducats for a year. A few members of the Collegio, including ser

---

31. For a more extensive discussion of patrician weddings in Sanudo's diaries, see Labalme and White 1999.

32. This was obviously an unofficial, probably informal copy of the official state ceremonial galley. See appendix B under "Boats, Ships, and Nautical Terms."

33. The manuscript has *e fato il coverto;* the Fulin edition has *e fato il convito.*

34. See Newton 1988, 11, 80.

35. The manuscript has *assaissime;* the Fulin edition has *moltissime.*

Christofal Moro, savio di Collegio, and ser Gasparo Malipiero, savio a Terraferma, opposed the request. After the young men had left the Collegio, they prepared another big barge like the first one, with boat covers and the ducal pennant of Doge Foscari [1423–57] and other pennants, so that it was quite a fine sight. Then the Collegio voted to give them the barge, but they no longer wanted it. This second bucintoro was put together at Ca' Corner di la Piscopia, with ser Fantin Corner in charge. The compagnia members had invited some very beautiful women, whom they brought there, and when the other bucintoro departed, so did this one from its berth. There were six boats from San Nicolò pulling it, and it was preceded by two fishing boats with trombones and canvas galley pennants. With the women dancing on its deck too, it sailed down the Grand Canal; when it caught up with the other one at San Marco, it went on to the Zuecha [Giudecca], while the other barge, which belonged to the Fortunati, returned down the Grand Canal. The barge of the Immortali came along later, with the women dancing on board and boats following it. The French ambassador, the bishop of Asti, and the Ferrarese ambassador boarded it[36] to look it over and stayed a while; then they left.

In the evening the boats were equipped with wax torches, and in this manner they floated along the Grand Canal, with the barge of the Fortunati going first. It stayed out until five hours after sunset, and the other one [stayed] until nine hours after sunset, that is, until full daylight, so that day and night there was celebrating on the Grand Canal. The women guests and the Fortunati had supper on the barge, but the women invited by the Immortali had supper at ser Fantin Corner's house. The expense was borne by the compagnia. The number of ducats spent on both boats together was ——.

I will not hesitate to write that today's publicly held[37] festivity led many to say that it would have been better to spend the money on the war; nevertheless, it honored our [mainland] state, given that the enemy was camped thirty miles away, and yet no one paid any heed, and here there was rejoicing, as if we were not at war, and more money spent than ever.

A particularly important wedding was that of the granddaughter of Doge Andrea Gritti in 1525. The War of the League of Cambrai was well past, and Gritti was a doge committed to the pomp and glory of his city. The festivities lasted more than ten days, beginning with the ritual presentation of the bride-to-be to the extended families. Sanudo's account is almost pictorial in its depiction of Venetian high society.

---

36. The manuscript has *vi montò;* the Fulin edition has *et montò.*
37. The manuscript has *fata;* the Fulin edition omits it.

January 16, 1525 (37:445)   After dinner the betrothal of the granddaughter of the Most Serene Prince with ser Polo Contarini took place. His Serenity was seated in the new Audience Chamber of the Ducal Palace with the Signoria around him and ser Francesco Contarini, brother of the groom, dressed in purple with ducal sleeves, standing; the prince was dressed in bluish crimson velvet. The groom was at the door of the palace dressed in black, and his [other] brothers were also in black.[38] Many patricians attended, and all took the doge's hand, so that he became very weary. And the bride was led around by the dancing master who is instructing her, but she did not dance. Nothing more was done today.

The next day, affairs of state were suspended because of these festivities:

January 17, 1525 (37:447)   No meetings were held after dinner because the Ducal Palace was the site of a party for the betrothal celebrations. Women were being received in the upper room where the Senate meets, and people were dancing. A very large number of women attended; in the evening the supper tables were prepared and the dividing partition was removed to create more space. . . . It was a most elegant dinner, with pine-nut cakes, partridges, pheasants, baby pigeons, and other dishes. And although more guests appeared than were expected, each one had enough to eat. The compagnia responsible was the Ortolani; ser Dolfin Dolfin was lord of the feast, nor was there any activity beside the dancing. The party concluded at eight hours past sunset, and not without a rain that ended days and months of drought, a good sign that this ceremony is taking place in a time of abundance.

Eight days later, after a procession through the Piazza San Marco to the music of trumpets and the sound of bells, the actual wedding ceremony took place in the Basilica, an unusual venue and one only for a distinguished bride.

January 25, 1525 (37:470–71, 473–75)   Today was the feast of St. Paul, when the stars take on a special aspect.[39] This day has been designated for the wedding

---

38. The purple *(paonazo)*, crimson *(cremexin)*, and violet *(violato)* colors of Venetian garments were all varieties of the aristocratic *porpora*, worn by particular magistrates on special occasions, and their mention here is an acknowledgment of the importance of the occasion and the status of the participants. *Paonazo* could also be a color of half-mourning (see Newton 1988, 18–21), and since the groom and his other brothers were wearing black, they may have been in mourning for their kinsman Antonio Contarini, patriarch of Venice, who had died several months earlier (see diaries, 37:38). The ducal sleeves of the bridegroom's brother were wide and open, and his wearing them indicated social privilege.

39. The day is described as *ponto di stella*, that is, one having a special astrological formation. See Coltro 1980, 65.

of the doge's granddaughter. About one hundred women guests arrived at the Ducal Palace; some were relatives of the bride and groom, and some were [guests of the] members of the Ortolani. They followed the bride into church, all well dressed except for one, the wife of the late ser Vincenzo Gritti. All told, I counted ninety-five women. In advance of the bridal procession came the captains and officials, clearing a way as they passed through the Piazza, with four large wax torches and the long trumpets and wind ensemble of the doge.[40] Next came the bride wearing the latest fashion, a rose-colored velvet dress; following her was her [future] sister-in-law, the new bride of ser Filipo Contarini and daughter of ser Antonio Pesaro; then came the other women, all of whom were wearing heavy gold chains and lots of pearls. And the wife of ser Fantin Corner wore a collar with splendid, rich, large jewels that had belonged to the king of Cyprus.[41] The last woman in the procession was the wife of ser Domenego Zorzi; she is a Tiepolo. The next to enter the church were the six ducal councillors and all the procurators; they numbered seventeen, but five were missing. . . . They entered [the church for] Mass together with ser Francesco Contarini, the brother of the groom, and ser Michiel Malipiero, [representing] the doge on the bride's side. They sat in the choir. A High Mass was celebrated with vocal and instrumental accompaniment. The church was full of people, as was the Piazza. When Mass was over and the councillors and procurators, etc., had exited the church followed by the women, the bells rang none. The bride was married in church;[42] the sponsor [*compare*] was ser Bernardo Capello. Both the compagnia members and the groom wore black, which in my opinion was not the thing to do. On a day like today they should have worn [red] silk, or at least scarlet cloth. The lord of today's festivities, chosen from among the Ortolani members, was ser Antonio Zane. . . .

Before Mass was over, [the men who were dinner guests] left the church and went to the Ducal Palace. The doge was there, dressed in gold brocade with a ducal cap of the same material. The tables had been set up in the Audience Room; when everyone had been seated in a courtly fashion, they enjoyed an excellent meal of duck, pheasant, partridge, and many other dishes. For dessert there were a whipped-cream confection [*cai di late*],[43] marzipan, and sweetmeats [*confeti*],[44] followed by performances by the buffoon Zuan Polo and other virtuosi.

---

40. See appendix B under "Musical Instruments."

41. Fantin Corner belonged to the Piscopia branch of the family, which had extensive business dealings in Cyprus and to which the last king of Cyprus had been heavily indebted. See Campolieti 1987, 47.

42. Sanudo emphasizes the location because church weddings were not usual at the time.

43. The standard Italian term would be *capi di latte*.

44. The sweetmeats were all sorts of preserved foods to complete digestion and sweeten the

After Mass, the women followed the newly wed bride out of the church. One by one they processed across the Piazza. . . . I note that among them were six women of the people [*popular*], whom the doge specially invited, and one foreigner [*forestier*].[45] And there were many people in the Piazza. These women walking by were a fine sight.

They were accompanied by the members of the Ortolani, who were dressed first in black robes with full sleeves, as were the groom and his brothers. Then they stripped down to short, plain tunics that were also black, except for the lord of the feast, ser Antonio Zane, who wore a —— of crimson velvet. When the women and the Ortolani had been seated, they were served the usual nice luncheon including partridges and two servings of roast meats. After the meal, the doge came out of his room, as did the others seated around the hall of the Ducal Palace and the women. A single dance was danced, and since by then it was only twenty-two and a half hours after sunset, they decided to board the Bucintoro.

Thereupon the bride, whose name is Viena, threw herself at the feet of His Serenity. Weeping, she took her leave; the doge too got a lump in his throat and began to weep. Accompanied by the Ortolani, they processed to the Bucintoro and boarded it. The only other guests allowed aboard were the women guests of the Ortolani, who numbered 113, the majority of whom, as I mentioned, were dressed in black velvet and adorned with pearls, heavy chains, and very long chain belts [*colari in sbara*].[46] Many others were not wearing necklaces, but all were formally dressed. Once everyone was on board, the Bucintoro, carrying the standard and emblem of the doge, was loosed from its moorings. As usual, it was accompanied by the boats from the parish of San Nicolò.[47] The entire expense was borne by the doge himself.

The Bucintoro floated down the Grand Canal as the members of the Ortolani danced with their women guests to the sound of a wind ensemble. When they drew even with the groom's house, they were greeted by the booming of artillery as blank shells were fired from the house across the canal, which

---

breath, including spices to nibble such as anise seeds, cardamon, candied ginger, and thin slices of fennel moistened with the juice of bitter oranges. This explanation was kindly supplied by Phyllis Pray Bober.

45. Probably a pilgrim en route to or from the Holy Land, for which Venice was the major port, invited, as the six *popular* guests probably were, to represent the larger community of Venice in the festa.

46. Described in Bistort 1969, 186n1; and Vitali 1992, *colari in sbara* were ornate chains draped diagonally from the waistline and reaching nearly to the floor.

47. The parish of San Nicolò dei Mendicoli had a special relationship with the doge. Populated by fishermen, the parish annually elected a doge of the Nicolotti, who was honored by the patrician doge in a formal ceremony, and members of the parish occasionally escorted the doge in their boats. See Lane 1973b, 108.

used to belong to the Duke of Milan, in celebration of the marriage. Thus the Bucintoro was brought as far as Ca' Foscari, at the bend in the canal, where it turned around and stopped in front of the groom's home, the dancing continuing all the while. Once the sun had set, thirty wax torches of — pounds were brought; fifteen were placed on one side of the boat, and fifteen on the other. Paper lanterns in great numbers adorned the top of the house, the balconies, the window sills, and the roof tiles. When lit, they cast a brilliance over the festivities.

A chill wind blew up, which the women felt even though the Bucintoro was covered, as is customary. At four hours after sunset all the women came indoors; the house and courtyard were decorated with tapestries from top to bottom, a lovely sight. Tables had been set up in the hall and the rooms all around it, and everyone sat down to dinner with the members of the compagnia. It was the usual wedding feast, but in addition there was potted pheasant and baby pigeon. . . . Many of the women and compagnia members were young and married, so that there were many people at the wedding. Once it [the feast] was over, there was a little dancing, then everyone went home. . . . The bride and groom went to give themselves pleasure; not only had they not yet slept together but the doge had not even allowed them to be [together] without a chaperone. This is contrary to what is customarily done in marriages, that the couple give their hands to each other in the morning and sleep together that night, which is not proper. Early the next morning the Bucintoro was returned to the Arsenal.

Not all weddings were as well supplied or went as smoothly, and Sanudo reported on several that went awry:

January 26, 1508 (7:256)   After dinner there was a meeting of the savi di Collegio. It happened that a compagnia of young men named the Eterni were [to be given] a dinner at the house of ser Lunardo Grimani for the wedding of his daughter to ser Alvise Morexini, one of the members of the compagnia. But [Grimani] was reluctant to give the compagnia members their dinner. They reported him to the consuls, and today they had it.[48] It is said that they were ill treated; that is why all the members of the compagnia came to Rialto in their ceremonial garb at twenty-three hours.[49] After they had done

---

48. Each compagnia had its own statutes and fines for their infringement, imposed by its own officials. Some of the rules concerned the obligation to entertain in style.

49. The Eterni are described as wearing *vesta da contor.* This term does not appear in any of the Venetian lexicons, but uses of it cited in Bistort 1969, 355, and Molmenti 1973, 2:478–79, suggest a ceremonial gown.

great damage to the Grimani house, they took two silver basins, which Father Stefano and [the buffoon] Domenego Taiacalze carried at the head of the procession. . . . The buffoons proclaimed at the Rialto that since the company members had been ill used today and no women [had been invited to the supper], they had therefore taken the basins to have a fitting supper at Grimani's expense. And they pawned them, one for wax torches and one at the tavern of the Campana,[50] where they had a nice supper at his expense.

In another case, the problem posed was not inadequate hospitality but the groom's quixotic behavior:

March 8, 1519 (27:30–31)   Since today is Mardi Gras, no meetings were held after dinner. There is one noteworthy item, however: ser Andrea Mozenigo, university laureate, former senator, and grandson of the doge,[51] got married during this past Carnival to the daughter of ser Zuan Alvise Duodo, from Sant'Anzolo. The contractual betrothal ceremony was celebrated together with the family presentations; it was impressive. The woman was not pretty, but he took her, and having taken her, he went through with the betrothal, etc. However, some days later, even though he had given his hand, he said that he no longer wanted her as his wife and he would no longer go to her. The bride's father and brother, who were amazed at this, did everything they could to keep the learned man, who had the reputation of being wise, from inflicting such an insult on them. The dowry was reasonable, the woman was not deformed, and such things are just not done. Her family is very large, and they all consider themselves insulted. But he was adamant in stating that he did not want her, and neither father nor brothers[52] could persuade him to accept her. Announcing that he wished to enter a religious order, he stopped coming to public places. The whole city was talking about this, and he continued with his caprice of not accepting her all through Lent. However, after Easter he was so goaded that he took her in marriage and brought her to his home.[53]

Sanudo's entry of April 25, the day after Easter, recapitulates the story and adds that at least twice the putative bridegroom gave his hand and then refused to

---

50. An inn in which Sanudo held shares and from which he derived a tidy income. See below under "Rialto Fire," excerpt dated 10 January 1514 (17:458–62).

51. Doge Giovanni Mocenigo (1478–85).

52. The manuscript has *fradelli*; the Fulin edition has *fradelo*.

53. Since Easter was not until 24 April that year, this last sentence must have been added later.

see the girl. After he finally returned to her, he could resume his place in the society and political deliberations of his peers:

April 25, 1519 (27:209)   And so today he was at the house of this bride, and he will wed her at the agreed-upon time. But the city will not forget what he has done, and that he was ill advised to do this, and that just as [during this rejection] he was not seen around town, today he came to San Marco, and the next day to the meeting of the Great Council.

Fashion, Taste, and Sumptuary Laws

Legislation concerning proper procedure in patrician marriages included limiting patrician expenditures, whether it for excessive dowries or lavish parties or luxurious gifts. Dowry limits were so important that they were legislated separately, while wedding feasts and gifts fell under more comprehensive sumptuary laws. These laws, which date back to the fourteenth century and attempted to control this consumer extravagance, provide details of the material life of the patricians, as illustrated by restrictions on nuptial expenses in a law of 1526:

January 31, 1526 (40:751–52)   The ring sponsors may not send the bride or anyone else associated with the wedding a present of anything other than six forks and six spoons, whose value may not exceed one ducat each. Conversely, the bride may not give to the sponsor pine-nut cakes exceeding a total of ten ducats [in value]. The penalty for such transgressions will be forfeiture of the items with which they have broken the law, plus sixty ducats. The silversmiths who made the forks or spoons will incur a fine of ten ducats. . . .

It is stipulated that between the time that the nuptial contract is concluded and the [time that the] wedding ceremony takes place, the ring sponsors may not give the groom more than six small suppers, of no more than twenty guests apiece, and two large meals, one of which may not exceed fifty[54] guests, and the other eighty, including men and women and close relatives, with the exception of dinners given by the *compagnie*. The groom may give two meals, one with fifty guests and one with eighty, including men and women and close relatives. At these meals it is prohibited to serve partridge, pheasant, peacock, francolins,[55] baby doves, and no more than three nongilded dishes

---

54. The manuscript has *cinquanta;* the Fulin edition has *cinquecento.*

55. Mountain birds similar to partridges. In Venice (Comune), Consiglio comunale 1847, 2:215, they are described as "galo salvadego rarissimo. . . . Sono uccelli riservati per le tavole signorili."

may be served.[56] The food may only be served by the steward of the sideboard [*credenziere*],[57] and carpets may not be placed on the tables.[58]

Also prohibited are confections of large pine-nut cakes, pistachios, round filled pastries, sweetmeats, confections, and sweet gums, formless confections, marzipan fruitcakes, sugared fruit, and every other type of large confection that one may make or imagine.[59] The penalty for the lawbreakers will be fifty ducats, and for the pastry cook it will be twenty-five ducats. . . . The stewards and cooks who serve such meals are obligated under penalty of a ten-ducat fine per person and a prison term of four months to come to our office and record when and to whom and where such meals will be held so that employees of this office may be sent to determine whether the law has been broken. And the stewards are obligated to take them through the rooms so that they may do their job, and if they are impeded by members of the household or others and not allowed to do their job, the stewards are obligated to leave and no longer serve their employers, who must nonetheless give [them their] wages. Similarly, if more than the allowed number of guests attends a dinner or prohibited dishes are served, the servants must come to our office after the dinner is served to report what has taken place, on pain of the above penalties. And truly, those who would act so dishonestly as to throw bread or oranges at our employees or push them or kick them out will fall subject to a penalty of fifty ducats.

---

56. Gilded foods, that is, foods actually decorated with gold, were not uncommon at very important feasts. Molmenti 1973 reports that they were considered not only ornamental but beneficial to the heart (2:390). See also Bistort 1969, 209. The term *dorade* might also be applied to those foods (usually fowl, as above) with a "golden" battered crust, made from a mixture of egg yolk, flour, and fat or liquid such as wine.

57. These stewards served cold courses from imposing credenzas that might display the household's rich tableware of the household, alternating them with hot (and perhaps "gilded") courses, served from the kitchen.

58. The use of luxurious Turkish rugs as table coverings is documented in contemporary paintings, such as Lorenzo Lotto's *Family Group* and *The Protonotary Apostolic Giovanni Giulino,* both in the National Gallery in London, as well as in somewhat later canvases, such as Veronese's *Wedding at Cana,* at the Louvre in Paris, and the *Last Supper,* now called *Feast in the House of Levi,* at the Accademia in Venice. We are grateful to Patricia Fortini Brown and David Rosand for these references.

59. "Grosse pignocade, pistachi, calisoni, fongi de Savonia, trazie, oldani et confecti senza corpo, spongade figure, fructe de zucaro, et ogni altra sorte confection grossa che far et imaginar si possa." *Pignocade* were a popular preprandial snack made of sugar and egg whites beaten together with a small amount of flour, a generous portion of pine nuts, and sometimes chopped lemon or orange flowers, then dropped by spoonfuls onto a baking sheet and baked in an oven at medium heat. *Calisoni* were filled pastries either fried or baked; the filling was usually marzipan, and the dough included sugar and rose water. *Confecti senza corpo* were soft or jellied sweetmeats. These definitions were kindly supplied by Phyllis Pray Bober. *Fongi di Savonia* were sweetmeats made of sugar, starch, and rose water, and *spongade* were marzipan fruitcakes molded into various shapes, such as castles, ships, nymphs, animals, and coats of arms. See Ambrosini 1996, 496.

Wedding feasts were only one of the targets of the sumptuary laws. Luxurious fabrics and jewelry had been subject to governmental regulation for more than two centuries by Sanudo's time, in an effort to keep wealth from being taken out of circulation through such expenditures. In 1507 an anonymous letter accused three patrician women of "ruining the city" through their extravagant expenditures (7:158). A new law in 1511, fifteen years earlier than the one cited in the excerpt above, repeated many provisions drafted decades earlier and would itself be reiterated in the decades to come. But neither the repetition of prohibitions nor the magistrates appointed to uphold them appear to have been very effective.

February 5, 1511 (11:796–99)   It is announced to all that the most excellent Senate has elected the honorable patricians ser Nicolò Michiel, university laureate and knight, and ser Thomà Mocenigo, both procurators of San Marco, with supreme authority, power, and freedom to correct, modify, and take steps against the unusually high expenditures that have been made, and that are being made, in this city and in its territory by men and women of all kinds and stations, as appears in the laws passed concerning these matters. So that these laws may be put into effect and no one may claim ignorance as an excuse, these honorable gentlemen have decided that notice [will] be given to all, of whatever social station, both men and women, boys and girls, that they must obey to the letter the laws that have been passed in the most excellent Senate. If they do not obey, the honorable proveditors will punish those who transgress against the mandate in such a way that they will serve as an example to others.

First: Concerning ornaments to the head, it is permissible to wear gold or silver work, both spun continuously and pieced, as long as its value does not exceed fifteen ducats. No pearls or jewels of any kind or type may be worn on the head or on the neck or on any other part of the body, except one strand of pearls at the neckline, which may be worth no more than fifty ducats. Nor may the neckline be ornamented in any other way.[60]

The sleeves of dresses may be made of cloth of gold or of silver and measure two *braccia*[61] per pair of sleeves. Sleeves made of silk cloth, woven, plain,[62] of one cloth and of one color, may measure four and one-half *braccia* per pair of sleeves, using a silk *braccio* of the usual width. These sleeves may not be slashed or open at any point, nor ornamented in any other way, but plain. These sleeves also may not be baggy at the elbows and closed at the wrist,[63]

---

60. See Giovanni Bellini's *Sacra Conversazione* in the Accademia.

61. On the *braccio,* about two feet in length, see appendix B under "Fabrics and Garments."

62. That is, not having the lined slashes that were popular at the time; see below.

63. Such sleeves were known as *a comedo* or *a comeo.* See Newton 1988, 11.

nor may they follow the bodice in the back down to the waistband, nor may they be in the new fashion. Sleeves made of wool cloth, or of any other sort of cloth, cannot be of more than two *braccia,* using the measure of the silk *braccio,* and must all be banded at the wrist.

Item: all fringes, large or small, of any kind are prohibited, whether they be placed at the waistline of dresses or at the hem or in the middle of dresses. Similarly, it is not permitted to put large or small fringes on robes.

Dresses must be of a cloth of a single color, plain and simple, of no more than eighteen *braccia* of silk cloth, including the border at the hem, woven of silk being of no greater value than two ducats per *braccio,* measured in silk *braccia* and of no greater width than a quarter of a [*braccio*] of silk cloth. No ropes or cording or fringes or any other kind of fancywork may be placed at the hem, but everything must be completely simple.

Pelisses [overgowns] may not be lined with lynx, sable, marten, ermine, or squirrel-back, nor may they have a covering of iridescent silk or silk, nor bodices of gold or silver, nor any other type of work. No waistbands, mantles, kerchiefs, or aprons may have any work in gold or silver or silk or linen. They must be plain and without any decoration at all.

Robes truly must be plain and simple and of one same color and cloth, with no ornamentation at the neckline nor a border at the hem. No ornament can be worn over robes, except for a jeweled collar, which may not be worth more than 500 ducats, on those robes that do not have a veil. They may be made with thirty-two *braccia* of silk cloth, whether they have open sleeves or ducal sleeves. Those that have open sleeves may have a train as long as one pleases, provided it does not exceed the total of thirty-two *braccia,* not including the lining. Those with ducal sleeves may not have more than a quarter of a train; the same holds for those of woolen cloth, which may be made of twenty-eight *braccia* of cloth and no more, of the width of serge. Totally prohibited are chains in place of belts, hoop-belts, sashes, both decorated and plain pockets, and ribbons or cords of gold or silver net and heavy cords. The only thing[s] that may be worn are woven belts with their silver fittings, the total value of which may not exceed fifteen ducats. The total value of all rings for the fingers may not exceed 400 ducats. Be it also declared that all the new fashions are banned, which is to say that from now on, no one may wear any new fashion that may be described or imagined. All such ornaments are forbidden to the women of this city or who are residing in this city, both inside the home and outside the home, both in this city and in all cities and locales governed by our Signoria.

With regard to household decor, all silk and wool hangings, whether of open cutwork or appliqué, are prohibited. The same holds for rugs under settings at meals, as well as horsehair comb cleaners, brushes, mirrors, and combs of gold and silver, bejeweled, or ornamented in any way. Also forbidden are chests and small chests, gilded grates, and andirons of gold or silver or inlaid with gold and silver filaments. Similarly, one may not put on beds or use sheets embroidered with gold, silver, or silk, nor pillowslips, nor pillows, nor blankets, nor bedspreads, nor any other type of bedclothes adorned with gold, silver, jewels, nor may they be made of velvet, satin, or heavy silk. What are permitted are blankets, bedspreads, curtains, and bed drapes [*tornoleto*][64] of sendal, taffeta, velveteen, *catasamito*,[65] and ormuzine;[66] and these bedclothes must be plain, without gold, without border, and without any other type of work except gold [leaf] applied by painters.

But passing the law and administering it were two different matters, and the difficulty for the responsible officials, the *executori sopra le pompe,* may be surmised from the penalties the law proposed:

February 5, 1511 (11:799)   In order that these laws be duly applied, it was decided in the excellent Senate, on the fourth day of the present month, that the most honorable proveditors and executori sopra le pompe may not pardon any of those found guilty, who are to be immediately treated as lawbreakers. [Those administrators granting illegal pardons] will be required to pay a penalty from their own property. The notary assigned to this task is obligated to take a list of those who will be declared guilty each month to the Collegio and to the doge so that His Serenity, seeing that the law was flouted, may have these honorable proveditors and administrators who did not uphold the law inscribed as debtors to the state. These administrators are also required to conduct diligent investigations of lawbreakers, making use of the ample freedom granted their office to inquire, undertake legal action, examine, decide penalties, and obligate each one as they see fit. Moreover, the administrators may not be petitioned about anything pertaining to their office, on pain of all of those strictures and penalties contained in the law. It is declared that those women who will have been found to have broken the law in any way, or who have worn the forbidden items, even some of them, will be stripped of the garments and will forfeit them. In addition, they will be condemned without possibility of pardon, according to the terms of the law, without any lightening of the sentence. *Item:* if the person who accuses someone of wear-

---

64. This might mean *attorno al letto,* which could be the kind of curtain that was used around the bed, mentioned by Boccaccio in the *Decameron, 4.1;* or the kind of decorative border seen in Carpaccio's *Dream of St. Ursula.*

65. Battaglia 1961–2000 defines *catasamito* as a heavy silk cloth shot with silver or gold thread and commonly used for bedspreads and cloaks.

66. A light silk cloth.

ing the forbidden items be a slave, male or female, he or she will be freed; and
if it be a manservant or maidservant, whether indentured or salaried, his or
her time of service will be considered completed and he or she will receive the
entire salary, as well as a portion of the fine.

But in spite of all these strictures, women continued to circumvent the laws:

May 8, 1529 (50:305)   Many laws have been enacted at many times by this
council concerning the clothing styles of the men and women and boys and
girls of this city, as may be seen by the contents of those laws. The wearing
of chains and pearls having been forbidden as a way of avoiding excessive expense, it appears that the women of this city with new ingenuity have devised
a substitute for chains of gold and pearls. They wear chains, belts, and necklaces and such like decorated with alabaster, crystal, lapis lazuli, carnelian,
green quartz, mother-of-pearl, quartz, jasper, agates, porcelain, rock crystal,
and every other kind of pastiche and, similarly, embroidery and filigree. People pay thirty, forty, fifty, and one hundred ducats for such things, and yet
their resale value is barely four to six ducats or even less, which causes terrible
damage and loss to this glorious city and is completely contrary to the holy
intentions of this most illustrious Senate. Therefore:

There will be a new law that all of the additional aforementioned wom-
en's ornaments will be completely prohibited, and they may neither be made
nor worn. But because it is fitting that women wear something around their
necks, which will be of little expense and harm, the recent proclamation of
this body notwithstanding, they are permitted to wear around the neck and
on no other part of the body one gold chain or small gold chain worth forty
ducats or less, including the expense for manufacturing it, which cannot exceed five ducats. No other ornament may be worn but the chain or small
chain of the value described above. These chains or small chains may not
be worn until they have been stamped by our sumptuary office; by law this
stamp will be given without any emolument whatsoever; transgressors will
be condemned to whatever penalty the sumptuary office will decide upon.
Additionally, no woman may use as a belt any object ornamented with more
than handwork made with woven silk.

For all its determinations, this was not to be the last sumptuary law. Luxurious
dress and objects continued to circulate and be esteemed by those who could
afford them, a group not limited to the patrician class. *Pagar le pompe,* "paying the sumptuary fines," became so proverbial an expression that it has been
suggested that such laws and fines were intended as a form of supplementary

taxation on wealth, with those able to afford the tax entitled to display their luxurious possessions.[67]

The Grand Chancellor

The *cittadini,* or citizens, were the second group named by Sanudo in his tripartite division of Venetian society. As a general category, they formed, as did the patricians, about 5 percent of the population, and they were likewise divided into several groups, though more legally than economically distinct. The highest group was represented by the *originari,* or "original" citizens, and those who were naturalized. Among these original citizens, those at the top level were close to the nobility, participating with them in the economic, social, and religious life of the city and, through the civil service, sharing in many of the government's activities. The naturalized citizens were again divided into two groups: those who could practice internal and external trade *(de intus et de extra)* and those whose trade was restricted within the city *(de intus).*

It was from the higher levels of cittadini that the grand chancellor and the secretaries to the various organs of the Venetian government were elected and appointed. The grand chancellor was the most important citizen in Venice.[68] His position, achieved after a competitive election by the patriciate, was held for life. In processions, he walked just in front of the doge, and in importance he ranked directly below the procurators of San Marco and the savi and above the members of the Senate. In 1517 an election roster for the grand chancellorship—the incumbent had died a week earlier—provided a summation of the kind of service such men at the pinnacle of their careers had provided and an indication that the higher civil-services offices tended to be monopolized by a few families:

January 25, 1517 (23:529–30)   Nominees put forward by the Most Serene Prince and councillors [for the position of] chancellor of Venice, to replace the most worthy don Francesco Fazuol, may God forgive him:

Gasparo di la Vedoa, secretary, who has already for forty-six years served the most illustrious Signoria in all important matters within this city as in Italy and beyond; he has served with *provveditori generali* in the army and with *capitani generali* in the navy, and for twenty-four years as secretary to the illustrious Council of Ten;

Nicolò Aurelio, secretary to the illustrious Council of Ten, son of the late Marco, secretary to the same council, who has in addition this further quali-

---

67. Bridgeman 2000, 220.
68. Sanudo 1980, 277.

fication: that he has served in fourteen legations with diverse distinguished ambassadors and has for thirty-eight years served this illustrious state with integrity and loyalty;

Zuan Piero Stella, secretary, the son of the late Domenego, who was secretary to the illustrious Council of Ten, who has in addition this further qualification: that he has served in twelve legations with ambassadors and served alone in nine, most recently [in a legation to] the Swiss, where he was imprisoned for thirty months at peril to his life and with the ruin of his health;

Alexandro Capella, secretary, son of the late messer Phebus, chancellor of Venice;

Alberto Tealdini, secretary of the most illustrious Council of Ten, who was the son of the late Chimento, secretary of the most illustrious Council of Ten,[69] [who was himself] son of Davit, secretary to this most excellent Republic;

Zuan Battista di Adriani, secretary of the most illustrious Council of Ten, son of the late Alvise, who has in addition this qualification: that he has already served twenty-one years with that diligence and loyalty apparent to all and for that reason has suffered the greatest infirmities.[70]

The names were balloted, and of the six contestants, Zuan Piero Stella was the clear winner, with 1,303 votes. Gasparo della Vedoa was the runner-up, with 965 votes. All had lobbied among the patricians (23:523), as the runner-up would continue to do with an eye to a future election:

February 21, 1517 (23:599)   This evening there was a festa at the house of Gasparo di la Vedoa, the secretary of the Council of Ten, at which eclogues and comedie were staged. It began at twenty-one hours and [continued] until[71] — hours after sunset. Then he gave a supper for all the guests, who included all of the current members of the Council of Ten except ser Francesco Contarini, the head, and ser Priamo da Leze, all of the members of last year's Council of Ten, and a number of other patricians. The supper was excellent, with partridges, pheasants, fried oysters, marzipan, sweetmeats, little doves, and other things, with all the music and arts this city offers. He did this because he wants[72] to be the grand chancellor in place of the man who was recently elected.[73]

---

69. The Fulin edition does not include *fo fiol di Chimento, secretario dil conseio illustrissimo di X.*

70. See Chambers 1998a, 12, on Sanudo's familiarity with these candidates, who were important sources of information for him. Neff 1985, 348–599, supplies background information on nearly all of these candidates.

71. The manuscript has *fino hore;* the Fulin edition has *finì hore.*

72. The manuscript has *desidera;* the Fulin edition has *desiderava.*

73. His entertainments did not secure him the position. Six years later, Gianpietro Stella died

Scuole Grandi

The most visible organs of citizen life were the scuole. In origin the Venetian scuole, or confraternities, were religious and devotional societies, inspired by the penitential flagellant groups of the thirteenth century. From the start they were essentially citizen and lay organizations, with their own rules and rituals, and as active entities, they soon came under the careful supervision of the Council of Ten. Their concerns were pious, moral, and charitable: the support of impoverished members, dowry provision for orphans and needy virgins, funeral obsequies, prayers for the dead, and the administration of charitable endowments.

As religious organizations, their account might just as properly be found under the rubric of religion (see chapter 7). By Sanudo's time, however, they had evolved into more broadly conceived associations that, while retaining their religious and charitable responsibilities, were also valued for their display of pomp and splendor on ceremonial occasions and their financial support of the state. It was for the *scuole grandi,* with their sense of magnificence, that some of the greatest art of Venice was produced, including Gentile Bellini's famous *Procession in San Marco* (1496), which depicts long lines of scuole winding about the Piazza to the sound of instruments and for the edification of the populace. It is because of their function as part of the social fabric of the city that they are included here.

By the early sixteenth century there were five scuole grandi: Santa Maria della Carità, San Giovanni Evangelista, Santa Maria della Misericordia, San Marco, and San Rocco. The following description of a solemn procession in 1515 illustrates well their mix of religious and political functions, along with demonstrations of wealth by each of the five scuole grandi. The procession celebrated a decree regarding the French king's return to Italy (which Venice then favored) and was held on the feast day of the Birth of the Virgin Mary.[74]

September 8, 1515 (21:45–47)   [This is] the feast of the Birth of the Virgin, the date designated by the recent law for a solemn procession acknowledging the French king's arrival on this side of the Alps. . . .[75] Around the Piazza, awnings of white cloth were set up on poles, and on the beams were clusters of gold torches belonging to the *scuole piccole* [smaller confraternities]. It was a lovely day, and the entire Piazza was full. Our[76] Most Serene Doge, dressed in dam-

---

(see below for his funeral) and Nicolò Aurelio was selected as his successor. See diaries, 23 August 1523 (34:376–77).

74. Francis I, the new French king, who had acceded to the throne in 1515, had reactivated the terms of the Treaty of Blois (23 March 1513) and thereby secured the support of Venice against the emperor with his new invasion of northern Italy.

75. For the embassy of welcome sent to greet Francis I in August 1515, with four ambassadors, each with thirty horses, see chapter 4 under "Francis I."

76. The manuscript has *nostro;* the Fulin edition omits it.

ask of white gold, wearing a robe and mantle decorated with ermine, that is, at the collar, and a cap of the same white gold on his head, was carried down on a chair from the Ducal Palace. With him were the ambassador, the bishop of Asti,[77] and the ambassador from Ferrara,[78] don Bernardin di Prosperi; next came many bishops, as I will recount later. They entered the Basilica of San Marco and heard Mass, said by the most reverend don Antonio Contarini, our patriarch. [The doge] returned [through] the Piazza, which was full of people, and there was good news, and letters had arrived from the battlefield dated [September] 6 at — o'clock, which I will summarize below. The procession began at fifteen hours, and it was splendid. . . .

First came the scuole, at the head of which was the Scuola di San Marco, which won the toss of the dice held by the heads of the Council of Ten. They had forty-four double candles on gold poles, followed by the scuola's banner, then forty small boys dressed as angels carrying silver objects, then three insignias—of the king of France, of St. Mark, and the coat of arms belonging to our doge Loredan, and no others. Next came three umbrellas, under which were relics housed in tabernacles and carried on small platforms, among which was the finger of St. Mark. Before them went the flagellants[79] carrying large white wax torches to honor the relics; following them were thirty flagellants with large silver goblets and basins. It was quite something to see thirty of the objects, of such great worth, as well as the flagellants. Next came the Carità with a similar number of gilded wax torches, and forty large hand-held candles, and forty little boys carrying silver objects. Last came a four-year-old boy[80] in the garb of a Swiss [soldier]: he was all in black with a pike in his hand, which was quite a sight, and bearing the scroll [reading,] "Duke of Geler the Captain," which made everyone laugh.[81] Next came the three insignias as above and two umbrellas, under one of which was the icon belonging to Cardinal Bessarion and under the other an icon made—so it is said—by the hand of St. Luke.[82] After that came the Scuola di San Zuanne, with forty-four gold double candles, and little boys with twenty-six silver pieces, and two umbrellas preceded by hand-held wax torches. Under one of the umbrellas was St. Martin's leg encased in silver, along with other relics belonging to the

77. Antonio Trivulzio, ambassador from France.

78. The manuscript has *France;* the Fulin editors have corrected this to *Ferrara,* which was clearly intended, given the context.

79. The flagellants, so called because the original religious discipline of these lay groups was self-flagellation, were members of the scuole.

80. The manuscript has *putin,* "little boy"; the Fulin edition has *patron.*

81. The Duke of Gueldres was a general in the French army.

82. The Hodegetria and the Nicopeia, two famous icons in Venice. The first depicts the Virgin "who guides." She supports the Christ child in her left arm and points to him with her right fin-

scuola, and under the other was the piece of the Holy Cross, also belonging to the scuola, and then one hundred[83] flagellants carrying silver objects, lovely basins and sweetmeat dishes. First among these objects was a silver damascene chair once belonging to the Duke of Milan and now owned by ser Zuan Antonio Dandolo. Next came the Misericordia with golden double candles, forty children carrying forty silver objects, two umbrellas held above some icons, and twenty-eight large, hand-carried wax torches. The flagellants had no silver objects, and this scuola, whose head is Michiel da Ponte, was in disarray. Then came San Rocho with forty-four gilded double candles, as above, and forty little boys with silver objects, and then four large platforms. On one was a large San Rocho dressed in gold, made out of wood, accompanied by a small child dressed as an angel to whom [San Rocho] showed the plague sores. On the next was San Zacaria, the prophet, bearing a particular scroll that read ——. Another bore the twelve tribes [of Israel] and the rod of Aron and Moises; worshippers knelt in front of them wafting incense from a censer. The fourth depicted Christ's arrival in limbo to free the souls of the holy fathers, and it showed limbo with the devils, etc.[84] Next were two umbrellas, under one of which was a tabernacle containing a relic of San Niceto, and under the other another tabernacle on small golden platforms containing the finger of San Rocho. Before them went a goodly number of flagellants carrying silver objects and also forty large wax torches. Thus this scuola did itself great honor, and its guardian, ser Zuan Calbo, who is a silk draper, deserves praise.

Some descriptions dwell particularly on the demonstration of wealth belonging to the various scuole (and by extension to the city), as does the following description of a later celebration of another political league, with an entirely different cast:

January 1, 1530 (52:435–36)   This day has been chosen for the publication of the peace and the league. Although there was mud and fog and bad weather, the Basilica of San Marco was beautifully adorned with tapestries and cloth of gold. On the high altar were great lamps remaining from the eve and day of Christmas. However, the exterior of the church was not decorated, and there was no hanging of the customary array of tapestries and standards of doges and captains general; they say that the reason was the bad weather. The

---

ger. The second shows the Virgin "who gives victory." She presents the Christ child, who holds forth his arms to the viewer.

    83. The manuscript has *n° 100*; the Fulin edition has *numero 108*.

    84. A scene familiar to the period as the Harrowing of Hell.

ambassador of the signor Turco was given lodgings above the tavern, at the house of Piero de Lodovici, the procurators' administrator, together with don Thodaro Paleologo, the interpreter. They are comfortable and are enjoying seeing everything. They then dined there, and a most worthy banquet was given for them. . . .

Mass was said in the Basilica of San Marco by our patriarch; then the procession began. The customary cloths stretched on frameworks were not put around the square since there were no clean ones available; in addition, it is winter and the sun is not a problem. The scuole that processed were San Zuanne, the Carità, the Misericordia, San Rocho, and San Marco, all in good order and well furnished with silver objects. First came the gilded double candles, with three large cups attached to each. Then came a great number of silver pieces, some on platforms, some in large wicker baskets, some in conical baskets ——, others under umbrellas on platforms; a large quantity. *Item:* all of the scuole had many flagellants carrying silver objects that were lovely and of great value. The Scuola di San Rocho did itself honor both with silver objects and with platforms and the rest. The Scuola di San Marco had [a platform with] a statue of Justice seated and one of San Marco standing. There was also one with the five members of the league seated together on it, that is, the pope, the emperor, King Ferdinand, the doge, and the Duke of Milan. It was something to behold. The silver objects carried by the scuole were judged to be of great worth; this was done by order of the Signoria so that people would see that although a war has been fought in our territory, there are still many silver objects in the city. . . . The San Marco group did not go all the way around the square; rather, once they had reached the Piera del Bando,[85] given the lateness of the hour, they broke away from the route and went around the church with the patriarch, who wore vestments and his miter on his head. When the Most Serene Doge arrived at the Piera del Bando, the peace pact and league were publicly announced by Nicolò, the government herald, who was dressed in a light crimson damask with a slashed crimson mantle [*scarlato a fanestrele*].[86] The text will be written below. The procession and the celebration were completed to the sound of trumpets and pipes and a great ringing of bells. It was twenty-two hours after sunset, so everyone went to dinner. There was a great crowd in the Piazza, but it was a bad idea for the doge not to make the circuit of the Piazza as is customary but rather to cut the procession short because of the lateness of the hour.[87]

---

85. The *pietra del bando,* or *piera del bando,* was the stone from which the city herald made announcements.

86. Having a longitudinal cut of the sleeve characteristic of Renaissance costume.

87. Sanudo often deplored deviations from ceremonial custom.

For all its secular aspects, the religious mission of the scuole remained paramount. This included sharing in the religious feasts of the year, such as that which took place on Holy Thursday, accompanied by a significant number of flagellants:[88]

April 14, 1530 (53:144)   This evening the scuole came in good order to San Marco to see the blood of Christ. Among them were the Scuola di San Rocho with ninety flagellants beating themselves, many lamps, and many patricians stripped [of their usual finery] with each scuola. Then they went to Santo Antonio to obtain the indulgence.

As the excerpt above indicates, patricians often sought to join these scuole because of the power of their prayers for the dead, as well as the numbers they could muster as funeral mourners. Admission might be quite costly, it might have to wait until the applicant was *in extremis,* and even then it could take place only by permission of the Council of Ten and only shortly before the applicant died:

April 22, 1505 (6:154)   At about twenty-three hours after sunset don Marco Sanudo, my in-law and first cousin, who had been elected a savio di Collegio, died of the illness from which he had been suffering for less than two months. At the time of his death he enjoyed a fine reputation as a savio and one of the most outstanding patricians who had ever lived in this city or who will live in it for years to come. He was —— years old. I must say that everyone mourned his death. It was noted that he apparently was accepted into the Scuola di San Zuanne at the moment of his death. After he died he was clothed in their robes. The guardian of the scuola went to the heads of the Ten to say that there is a law that all acceptances into the scuola must take place at the altar; it is also necessary that before the new member dies, the acceptance be approved by all seventeen members of the Ten. Thus it was decided that on the following day, Wednesday, even though there was to be a meeting of the Great Council, the Council of Ten would be convoked to grant this permission. The meeting took place, but they were unable to do anything because he was already dead. Thus the body had to be stripped of the flagellant's robes and dressed in a velvet robe.[89]

---

88. A separate occasion, on the vigil of the Sensa, had been established for women to visit the relic of the blood of Christ in order to prevent disturbances. See diaries, 23 May 1498 (1:966). On 5 April 1531 (54:369) it was mandated, conversely, that women not be allowed to visit this relic on Holy Thursday, which would henceforth be reserved for men.

89. This did not prevent a large ceremonial funeral complete with a learned epitaph. See diaries, 6:154–55.

On the two occasions described below, a more timely procedure was observed, and the dying patrician was admitted into the scuola.

September 7, 1514 (19:25)   It was decided [by the Council of Ten] that ser Lorenzo Zustinian, who is very ill, may be accepted into the scuola of the flagellants and wear their habit. He had the Passion read to him and is indeed very ill. He was a ducal councillor but then was made governor of Cyprus, and there has never been a better one. He is seventy-six years of age.

   March 14, 1532 (55:629)   After the zonta was dismissed, the simple Council of Ten remained in session and decided that the guardian of the Scuola della Misericordia may accept into the scuola ser Francesco Contarini, of the Crosechieri branch, who is dying.

The accession of nobles (for a price) and the gifts of rich cittadini made possible the great wealth of the scuole grandi, a resource of which the state did not hesitate to avail itself, especially in times of need such as that imposed by the War of the League of Cambrai in 1509, as can be seen in this preamble to a new tax decree:

October 11, 1509 (9:247)   It is clear to everyone that there is currently a pressing demand for money to meet the extremely urgent needs of our state. Since, up until now, the means for obtaining funds has been restricted to levying taxes and tithes on the few, the resulting funds have been meager and consequently have not been sufficient to satisfy our great need. It is thus necessary to find a general tax that will be tolerable and still yield a good sum to our Signoria so that everyone will pay it the more willingly.

After mentioning a series of types of boats that would be subject to the new tax, the law continued with taxes to be paid by the scuole according to their size and wealth:

The five scuole grandi are obligated to pay a one-time sum, per the above, according to the following plan: the four most important ones, 200 ducats apiece, and the Scuola di San Rocho, one hundred, because it is poor. The scuole piccole will pay from one to twenty-five ducats according to their means. This will be judged for the most part by our proveditori del Sal, to whom the enforcement of this law and the handling of the money are entrusted. All of the aforementioned scuole are obligated to go and register with the proveditori within the next eight days, on penalty of paying double. Within the eight days following, they must pay what they owe.

A similar measure in the form of a forced loan was taken in 1527, when Venice was threatened by imperial troops:

May 11, 1527 (45:77–78)   This morning the entire city was filled with the news from Rome.[90] Some believed it and some did not, especially as no announcement came until none, which amazed everyone. Discussions were held in the Collegio about finding money, at least 100,000 ducats, to make military provisions. Since the members of the Scuola della Misericordia have six thousand ducats that was left to them by Grifalconi, who died recently, to be used for ——, the guardian and the members were summoned before the Collegio. The heads of the Ten were present, and the guardian . . . was persuaded to loan this money to the Signoria to be sent into the field because of the great need that we have. He was promised that the scuola would be given a credit at the Monte for the additional subsidy at a rate of seventy-five ducats per hundred for the aforementioned sum. And so they are willing to give the money and brought it to the state treasurer today.

Scuole Piccole

In addition to the five scuole grandi, there were more than one hundred scuole piccole, which unlike the scuole grandi were organized by parishes. Often attached to a church or convent, they included members from various social levels and occasionally non-Venetians as well. Certain of these scuole piccole had particular missions within their charitable functions, as did the Scuola di San Fantin, whose traditional ministry was to comfort prisoners and console the condemned. In this work the presence of women participants was notable:

November 24, 1525 (40:349)   Today at vespers, by a decision of the Council of Ten, one Cristoforo da Crema was hanged between the two columns [of the Piazzetta]. . . . As he was going to the gallows, I observed that there were three elderly women dressed in veils and robes accompanying the Scuola di San Fantin out of devotion because they are affiliated with the scuola. After the hanging was over, the body remained there until the evening and then was buried at San Zaccaria.

In the following excerpt, Sanudo describes a visit to Santa Agnese (St. Agnes), which devoted much of its care to orphan girls born legitimately to members.

---

90. For the sack of Rome, see chapter 4.

January 21, 1526 (40:696–97)   Sunday, the feast of Santa Agnese. Today I went to her church to see something new. On a small platform were six girls between eight and nine years of age, daughters of the scuola's members, half of whom were dressed in red and half in white, with their hair loose on their shoulders and a wreath of greenery on their heads. They are staying in a house in the San Barnaba neighborhood set aside for this purpose with a governess who is paid forty ducats a year. These girls are supported and are taught to read and to work [embroidery] until they are at the right age for marriage or something else. Their dowry is paid with monies of the scuola from a bequest that the procurators used to draw upon. But as the result of a bill that passed [in] the Senate this year, the management has been given to the members of the scuola. They have —— ducats per year for this from the Office of Loans of the Monte Vecchio and from other sources. They are supposed to keep twelve girls, but at the present time they have six, who are chosen by the members of the scuola according to a particular and attractive procedure.[91]

The Scuola della Pietà cared for foundling girls, whom it raised. In 1525, recognizing its good works, the government intervened to rescue it from financial ruin:

August 11, 1525 (39:300)   A bill concerning the Pietà was posted by the entire Collegio as before. The Pietà is in a state of direst poverty: the number of infants has grown such that some wet nurses have to feed four children apiece and the institution is 3,000 ducats in debt to pay for their services. Thus it is proposed that as soon as vacancies open up at the ferry stations, the procurators of the hospice may place a boat at each one. These boats will belong to the Pietà and may be rented or sold, not increasing the number, however, and the money they make with this must be used to pay only the illumination fee.[92] *Item:* if almsgiving has dropped off, they may send their banner around the city to raise more; it may be accompanied by musicians, and no one else may go with them. *Item:* a letter should be sent to Rome to obtain an indulgence from the pontiff for those who will give them alms. *Item:* be it resolved that the fines that will be levied in future by our councils and all offices be increased by two soldi per lira. The two soldi will go to the Pietà, and the procurators of the Pietà will keep the accounts. The bill passed 185 [for], 5 [against], 4 [abstaining].

Perhaps most noticeable to contemporaries were the funeral corteges provided by the scuole grandi and the scuole piccole. One hundred nineteen members

---

91. See Pullan 1971, 260.
92. That is, the cost of illuminating the altars of the church, a considerable expense.

of the scuole piccole joined the funeral procession for Doge Leonardo Loredan in 1521, along with clergy, seamen pallbearers, and accompanying patricians, a reminder that in great public events like these, all the elements of Venetian society participated. Sanudo's account of the funeral includes the following description:

June 25, 1521 (30:399–400)   Next came 119 banners of the scuole piccole, each one preceded by two gilded candleholders topped with wax torches, and some even had four torches. Then came the four flagellant scuole grandi; and the fifth, which is the Misericordia, to which His Serenity belonged, came last to carry the body.[93] These scuole carried twenty-four gold candleholders apiece. Next came all of the mendicant and Conventual friars of Venice and Murano and the regular canons and all the black and white [Dominican] monks. First among them were the Jesuati, and last were the canons regular of San Zorzi in Alega (Alga) and Santa Maria di l'Orto.[94] Then came the new congregations of priests, then the chapter[95] of Castello, and lastly the chapter of San Marco and one hundred priests, each carrying a four-pound double candle.[96] They received ten soldi apiece, a donation made in accordance with the wish of the [sponsor] paying these expenses. Next came the Scuola di la Misericordia with one hundred wax torches on gilded candleholders, paid for by His Serenity's sons, and one hundred of the doge's [candles] on black candleholders, and the cross of the scuola with four long, fat gilded candles on gilded candleholders. Next came the commanders, dressed in light blue, the shield-bearers and household of the doge, with black cloaks, followed by the prison scribes and the captains and the stewards of the doge. It should be noted that the ducal secretaries are not attending because the Signoria is not attending.[97] At length came fifty seamen, one by one, carrying double candles weighing ten pounds apiece, which the doge had paid for. Next, brought by order of the members of the scuola, came the doge's escutcheon, borne on poles and reversed, also carried by the sailors. It later was taken to the church of San Marco and affixed there to bear eternal witness. Next came the ballot boy of the doge, wearing a long mantle. The coffin was picked up by the sea-

---

93. The doge was an honorary member of this scuola grande. It was usual for a doge to be an honorary member of one of the major confraternities. See Muir 1981, 276n75.

94. This was the order founded by Beato Lorenzo Giustiniani in the first part of the fifteenth century.

95. The manuscript has *il capitolo;* the Fulin edition has *li capitoli.*

96. The pound weight referred to here, *libbra sottile,* was equivalent to 301.23 grams (or .66 English pounds). We thank Reinhold Mueller for this information.

97. Muir 1981, 274–75: "The Signoria remained aloof from the vigil and funeral procession to signify . . . that, although the Doge was dead, his authority, now vested in the Signoria, lived on." See also below.

men and carried under the scuola's canopy, which has silver rods and was carried by the flagellants. Ahead and behind them came the twenty-eight gentlemen dressed in scarlet with scarlet hoods, signifying that the doge is dead but that the Signoria is not.[98]

Zuan Piero Stella, the grand chancellor whose election Sanudo had carefully followed earlier, died two years after Doge Loredan:

August 8, 1523 (34:355)   This morning at sixteen hours after sunset, don Zuan Piero Stella, our grand chancellor, died. May God grant him peace. He was extremely fat. It was ordered that the funeral be held Monday; as is customary, the body will be taken to San Zuminian [San Gemignano], and the funeral will be held in the church of San Zacharia. The doge will accompany him as usual, and a funeral oration will be delivered. He named the doge his executor.

In 1522, when Zuan Piero Stella wrote his will, Andrea Gritti, whom he named as executor and whom he had earlier served as secretary, was not yet doge. But now he was, and the death of Gritti's granddaughter the day after Stella's death postponed the latter's funeral a few days. It was attended by many patrician dignitaries and included *popolani,* just as had the earlier funeral of the doge. But there were fewer mourners, as Sanudo noted:

Friday, August 14, 1523 (34:362-63)   This morning the funeral of don Zuan Piero Stella, the grand chancellor, was held. The coffin was covered first with the cloth of the scuola and then with cloth of gold and the doge's gold cushion, and spurs and a sword, since he was knighted by the emperor. The coffin was displayed in the baptismal chapel of San Marco. Present were the nine congregations,[99] his Scuola di San Marco with a number of sailors carrying torches, and twelve Jesuati with torches. Next came the secretaries, but in a departure from custom they were not wearing capes. They were followed by the doge, dressed in a scarlet robe and cap, the same that he wore in the council on Sunday because of the death of ser Agustin Foscari's daughter, his granddaughter and the wife of ser Nicolò Venier. The papal legate and the two imperial ambassadors accompanied the doge. When he is in mourning,

---

98. Ibid., 74: "During the three days that the body of Doge Loredan lay in state in the Senate Hall, each member of an elected contingent of twenty-eight nobles spent several hours a day in an official vigil over the body," a further sign of the continuity of the Venetian government. Cf. diaries, 3:390–92.

99. On this ecclesiastical body peculiar to Venice, see Betto 1984.

there is usually a mourner near the doge, but this time the mourners followed him and were with the ambassadors and the councillors, that is, the ambassadors from Milan, Ferrara, and Mantua. . . . The only procurator was ser Antonio Trun, in a black robe. Then came the heads of the Forty, dressed in purple, and other patricians who have been assigned to accompany the doge this month, dressed in black. There were only eight mourners in the church of San Zacharia. The coffin was carried to the large baldacchino that had been prepared for it. The oration was given by don Marin Bezichemi, the professor of humanities in Padua, because the chancellor had arranged for him to do so. The body was buried in San Zuminian, where the tomb will be built.[100]

Prostitutes and Servants

The third *generatione,* in Sanudo's language, after the patricians and the citizens were the artisans or lesser folk, that is, the rest of the Venetian populace: scribes, notaries, public accountants, guildsmen, shopkeepers, Arsenal workers, seamen, and the poor. Here too there was a wide economic and social range. These groups did not often attract Sanudo's attention unless they shared in some unusual event, such as a lavish wedding of commoners (May 5, 1533; 58:133), or as mourners in the funeral of a doge or grand chancellor, or as victims of a catastrophic famine or freeze. But Sanudo occasionally commented upon prostitutes and courtesans because of their reputations and also because of their occasional intrusions into the patrician world.

Prostitution was generally recognized by the government as an unavoidable activity. Prostitutes were even allotted a particular district near the Rialto and protected from the competition of male homosexuals.[101] But their presence elsewhere was considered inconvenient. For example, one month after the defeat of Agnadello, prompted by the pressure of war and a concern for military discipline in the camp near Mestre, only a few kilometers distant from the invading impe-

---

100. Marino Becichemi was a lecturer in the School of San Marco during the years of the War of the League of Cambrai and was also a professor at the University of Padua. See chapter 8. In his will, Stella had designated as his burial place the church of San Gemignano, which lay directly across the Piazza San Marco from the Basilica, so that he might be close to that patron saint who had so honored him that had he not sufficiently served him (and his city) in his lifetime, he might do so now in his death. See Gilbert 1976, 508, 512.

101. Labalme 1984, 247–48. On the numbers of prostitutes in Venice during the early months of the War of the League of Cambrai, scholars have tended to cite Sanudo's diary entry of 15 June 1509 (8:414). But the term Sanudo uses for his figure of 11,654 is *femene da partido,* which can also mean "girls of a marriageable age," that is, those who are neither adult females (*femene*) nor children (*puti*) in the language of Sanudo's passage. This possibility was pointed out by Grandi 1997, 81. The editors are indebted to Reinhold Mueller for this reference and have concluded that it is better not to rely on this passage for the number of prostitutes in Venice in June 1509.

rial troops, an attempt was made to remedy an undesirable condition in that camp:

June 18, 1509 (8:414)   I note that today in the military encampment it was proclaimed that all prostitutes and their pimps must clear out within two hours, on penalty of being whipped. So immediately, despite the outcry of the soldiers, about 1,000 got up and left, although a few remained in disguise or in hiding. I don't know what the cause of the proclamation was, but it was a good idea.

Among the prostitutes, as among members of the other classes, there were differences of style and wealth. Those styled *sontuose,* implying both sumptuous costume and a sumptuous way of life, were the courtesans, noted for their elegance, their frequenting of professional and patrician circles, and occasionally their artistic or intellectual talents:

October 16, 1514 (19:138)   This morning Lucia Trivixan, who was an excellent singer, was buried at Santa Catarina. She was the consummate courtesan of her day and was held in much esteem by musicians; all of the virtuosi met at her house. She died last night, and eight days from today, at Santa Catarina, the musicians will have a solemn funeral mass and other offices said for her soul.

January 27, 1524 (35:375)   This evening on Murano, at the house of ser Lunardo Justinian, some of our patricians held a little party with about fifteen sumptuous prostitutes, who danced and supped with the virtuosi there with great pleasure. . . . Three procurators, ser Marco da Molin, ser Francesco di Prioli, and ser Marco Grimani, came in costume to dance and did so in a room with some of the prostitutes, etc. The party lasted until ten hours and later.[102]

Sanudo reports some occasions when prostitutes were involved in disorders of a serious nature:

July 28, 1513 (16:555)   On this day, ser Andrea Loredan was wounded by ser Orsato di Prioli in the courtyard of the house of Alvise da Molin at San Zulian. The cause of it was a certain whore, and they say that Loredan will die.

May 9, 1522 (33:233)   At today's meeting of the Council of Ten, in the first

---

102. The costumes did not disguise the identity of their wearers. The procurators involved were all young men who had achieved this prestigious position *cum oblatione,* with large monetary loans and gifts. Chambers 1997, 38–43.

part of the meeting, when it met without its zonta, it was decided that a reward will be given to anyone providing evidence against those who, on a recent night, went armed and in disguise to the house of Julia Lombardo, a sumptuous prostitute, and rebuked her at length, intending to knock down the door. For this purpose it was decided to give 1,500 lire to anyone providing evidence, so that through this evidence the truth may be discovered. This money will come from the guilty parties, if they have any; if not, it will come from our Signoria, as the proclamation states. Nonetheless, nothing further was heard.

But the most serious disorder, in Sanudo's view, was the corruption of the patrician stock by a prostitute's marriage to a patrician, as the two examples below indicate.

April 11, 1526 (41:166)   Today one heard publicly about the wedding between ser Andrea Michiel da San Canzian, a widower, and a certain Cornelia Grifo, a most beautiful and sumptuous widowed prostitute. She has been publicly kept by ser Ziprian Malipiero and then belonged to ser Piero da Molin dal Banco and to others. She is rich, and she has brought him a dowry of — thousand ducats. The wedding was held at the monastery of San Zuan on Torcello and has cast great shame on the Venetian patriciate.[103]

Even more distressing to the patrician government was a misalliance compounded with bigamy:

April 24, 1532 (56:95–96)   Today after dinner the Quarantia Criminal met. It is an unusual thing to have any council meet when the doge is away from the Ducal Palace. Ser Filippo Trun, the state attorney, introduced the case of ser Paulo da Canal, who took two wives. First he married a prostitute named —. Then he married a sister of ser Bertuzi Valier — months ago; he had received about 400 ducats of the dowry. The said [ser Paulo] was subpoenaed in Castello by his first wife, who obtained a judgment against [him] that she was the true one. Therefore the state attorney recommended, and it was unanimously decided, that he be detained. Ser Paulo absented himself.[104]

---

103. San Zuan on Torcello was a special monastery for the *convertite,* that is, those women who had turned away from a life of prostitution. As such, it appears an appropriate place for this wedding. The "shame" cast on the patriciate to which Sanudo refers may have led to the debates and legislation, within the following fortnight, concerning the preservation of the nobility's "purity and status" through marital registration with the state attorneys. Diaries, 41:201, 203. See also Chojnacki 1998b, 142.

104. There is no further mention of this case in Sanudo's diaries, but the state attorneys'

If courtesans and their less sumptuous colleagues kept to their own functions, which included the entertainment of visiting dignitaries, no prejudice was expressed by Sanudo in their description:

October 20, 1532 (57:111–12)   When the Great Council descended the stairs, Cardinal [Ippolito] Medici was present in disguise with Monsignor [Antonio] Valier and two others, who watched them descend. In the evening the cardinal went to spend the night at the house of a courtesan called La Zaffetta.

So much a part of Venetian society were prostitutes and courtesans that on at least one occasion they proved economically useful to the government:

October 25, 1514 (19:165–66)   I note that in the last few days, that is, on Sunday the 22nd, it was proposed by ser Hironimo Contarini, the proveditor of the Arsenal, that since the Arsenal is being fortified and since it is necessary to excavate [for its reconstruction], for which there is no money, all the prostitutes of the city should be taxed and that this will produce[105] enough money to complete the project. The proposal was praised by the doge and the Collegio, and they commissioned Contarini, together with ser Andrea Barbarigo, lord of the Arsenal, and ser Andrea Loredan, one of the savi ai ordeni, to undertake this project.[106] Thus the order was given by the captains, the head watchmen of the signori di notte, and the heads of the sestieri.[107] And all the prostitutes [were required] under oath to bring a written statement to the arms depository, and these were brought, and the prostitutes are being taxed. So they are serious about imposing this tax. It is a new thing, and they say that it will bring in a great deal of the money we need.

What is clear from the diaries is that in this hierarchical society prostitutes were expected to observe certain societal boundaries. Such standards also applied to household servants, whose mimicry of aristocratic practices on one occasion aroused Sanudo's disapproval:

---

records show that one month later, on 28 May 1532, for a deed declared to be of such "corrupt audacity and iniquity," a sentence of perpetual banishment was pronounced by the Quarantia against Paolo da Canal, allowing him to pursue his life only on the island of Cyprus or in service on Venetian merchant or armed ships. This record also reveals that both wives were named Cecilia, the prostitute also bearing the sobriquet "Balla le oche" (Geese Dance). See ASV, Avogadori di Comun, Raspe, reg. 3667, fol. 20v *n.a.*, 28 May 1532. Cf. Labalme and White 1999, 65.

105. The manuscript has *trazerà*; the Fulin edition has *trazeva*.

106. The proveditor of the Arsenal was the patrician administrator of this vast shipyard where military and commercial ships were built and weapons stored. The lord of the Arsenal was a patrician supervisor. See chapter 5 under "The Arsenal."

107. For the signori di notte, see appendix B under "Governmental Terms." The sestieri were the six divisions of the city.

February 14, 1525 (37:578)   This evening at Santa Maria Formosa, in the house overlooking the bridge to the Morexini house, a party with dancing was put on by a compagnia of gentlemen's servants. Every man contributed a ducat, and they chose a lord of the festivities. Each came with his harlot, and they danced all night, and they had supper there, and they did not admit anyone else. Thus the servants are competing with the nobles to hold parties. It was a bad thing to do, and the heads of the Ten should have done something about it.

Famine and Freeze

Beyond the courtesan group, Sanudo did not record much about the *popolo* unless they were affected by tragedies such as famine, a great freeze, a flood, or disease. In 1527 there were two natural disasters: a famine in the spring and a freeze in November. Of the first, Sanudo left a vivid account wherein he describes the populace giving unusual expression to their need:

May 19, 1527 (45:141)   Sunday His Serenity the doge had sent messengers to invite all the members of the Senate to come in the morning to accompany him on barges to the church of Saints Job and Bernardino. This because it was on the eve of that feast four years ago that he was elected doge, and he must keep his vow to go hear Mass in that church, tomorrow being the feast of St. Bernardino. The Signoria gathered, but not many patricians were present; there were no ambassadors, only two procurators, ser Alvise Pasqualigo and ser Marco da Molin, and not one head of the Council of Ten. The doge was dressed in crimson velvet; after he heard Mass, as he was boarding the barges, children, women, and the crowd began to cry, "Abundance, abundance!"[108] They followed him along the length of the canal. This was quite a sight and has never occurred with any other doge. Flour is expensive; it was going for twelve lire and more, although it has dropped to nine lire. There is no meat in the butcher shops, etc. The craftsmen have ceased working, the fair is not being held, and there is a war on.[109]

Word has come that ser Alvise Dolfin's ship that was coming from Cyprus with 4,000 bushels of wheat and 2,000 of barley and 180 sacks of cotton encountered a great storm above Cerigo[110] on Easter night. It seems that it was swamped, and it is believed to have broken up. People saw barrels and sacks of cotton in the water.

108. "Abundantia, abundantia!" It is as if the people were charging the doge with having plenty, when they had nothing.

109. The imperial troops were marauding the Italian peninsula and had sacked Rome on 6 May 1527.

110. An island in the Greek archipelago.

In addition to the stress of the famine, which continued all through the summer, a killing freeze occurred in the late fall:

November 26, 1527 (46:326)   It was very cold in the morning and began to snow rather heavily, but then the snow stopped and the wind died down. . . . *Item:* the extreme cold of the last few days caused the deaths of several tramps and galleymen staying under the porticoes in Piazza San Marco and at Rialto, who were also starving.

By December of that same year the condition of the populace both within the city and on the Terraferma was even more pitiable:

December 16, 1527 (46:380)   I note that . . . wheat, barley, etc., have been brought by these ships coming from Cyprus and other ships in the past few days. Nonetheless, the cost of wheat is rising . . . so that it is an extremely severe famine. And [the cost] not only of grains but of wine. . . . Thus everything is expensive, and every evening in Piazza San Marco and in the streets and in Rialto there are children crying, "I want bread—I am dying of hunger and of cold," and it rends your heart. And in the morning bodies are found under the portico of the Ducal Palace. Yet no steps are being taken.

And I do not wish to omit that in Padua, because of the great famine, ser Mafio Michiel, the civil governor, and ser Santo Contarini, the military governor, seeing entire crowds dying of hunger, have made a ruling together with those appointed by the city that all the civic, professional, and religious groups [must] give so many loaves a day according to the limit set. So that bread has been distributed. . . .

As part of their charitable function, the scuole in Venice too participated in the famine relief effort:

December 28, 1527 (46:413)   *Item:* given the great shortage of coarse grain and other foodstuffs that exists in this city, and the large number of poor men and women, be it legislated that 1,000 ducats be taken from the Procuratia and 300 ducats apiece from the five large flagellant scuole and put with the twenty soldi added to the fixed price of the flour of St. Mark at the [city's] warehouses and that this money, which will amount to about 6,000 ducats, be used to make bread out of coarse grain and that this bread be distributed in the parishes every week by the parish priest, a nobleman, and a non-noble. They will be elected by our Collegio together with the heads of this council [the Ten] and will be sworn to distribute the number of loaves entrusted to them to the destitute throughout that parish. The bill passed. Some wanted money to be given, but this bill passed.

The famine was not much relieved two months later, but the city and those who could still enjoy Carnival in Venice went about their pleasures:

February 20, 1528 (46:612)   Not to omit something important, which I wish to live on forever in human memory, I must write of the terrible famine now in this city. Besides this city's poor, who are crying out in the streets, the poor are also coming from Burano by sea, the majority of them with their outer skirts over their heads and their children in their arms, begging for alms. Moreover, large numbers of peasant men and women have come here, and they stand on the Rialto bridge with their children in their arms, begging for alms. And so many have come from the countryside around Vicenza and Brescia that it is stupefying. You cannot go to hear Mass without ten poor people coming up and asking for alms; you cannot open your purse to buy anything without poor people asking for a coin, and until late in the evening people go about beating on doors and crying out in the street, "I am dying of hunger." Still the government has made absolutely no provision to deal with this.

Again this evening, in the Procuratia residence of Procurator [Marco] Grimani, a beautiful banquet was held. Present were the cardinal of Trani, Cardinal [Marino] Grimani, the English ambassador, the Milanese ambassador, Archbishop Corner of Spalato, Archbishop Podacataro of Nicosia, Bishop Pesaro of Paphos, Bishop Grimani of Ceneda, the primicerio of San Marco, and several others, who ate a magnificent meal in chambers. Then — very beautiful women arrived and some eighty other young men and husbands. There was a splendid banquet . . . , and there was dancing; indeed people did nothing else until eleven hours after sunset.

Let it be noted: every evening in that procuratia since Grimani was named cardinal, there has been dancing, and whoever wants to go can go. But it would have been better to give alms.[111]

---

111. On the elevation of Marino Grimani, patriarch of Aquileia, to the cardinalate, see Chambers 1997, 72; and diaries, 46:580, 582–83. A few weeks later, on 14 March 1528 (47:83–84), the government debated what measures to take and eventually voted to register the beggars and refugees, put up emergency shelters for the sick and weak, and give a quarter-ducat to those who were healthy and send them on their way.

Flood

More frequent than severe famine such as that of 1527–28 were the occasional inundations of Venice, which were not so different then than they are now, and like all urban blights, they were harder on the poor than on anyone else. Sanudo described such an *acqua alta* in 1517:

November 16, 1517 (25:84)   Monday morning, the 16th. Because it rained heavily during the night and in the morning, and there was a high sirocco in the morning, about tierce the water rose very high in the city, the highest it has been in many years. The Piazza San Marco on the Grand Canal side and Rialto and all the walks were full of water. It was almost impossible to move about on land and even more so by boat because of the bridges, except that by boat one could travel over some flooded *fondamente*.[112] It was terrible to see the water continually rising, which it did until the twentieth hour. If the wind had not been blowing against the tide, no doubt it would have been much higher. In the memory of living man it has never been so high. The high water ruined many wells, with damage, it was said, of ten thousand ducats. It destroyed much merchandise in warehouses, especially ashes[113] and other goods. In many houses of poor people, everything on the ground floor was flooded, inflicting great damage. It is likely that this flood will give rise to many diseases in the city, which God forbid. In my courtyard, although it is elevated, there was more than a foot and a half of water. By the twenty-second hour the water had returned to normal, and one could walk everywhere in Venice. I wanted this to be noted and remembered.

Syphilis

Always subject to the severities of weather and to fluctuations in the availability and price of grain, the city was also exposed to epidemics and most regularly the plague. But in the late fifteenth century a new disease appeared, brought into Italy by the invading armies:

July 1496 (1:233–34)   It should be noted that as a result of heavenly influences, in the past two years, that is, since the arrival of the French in Italy, a new infirmity has been discovered in human bodies. It is called the French disease and has spread throughout Italy, Greece, Spain, and nearly the entire world. By its nature, it weakens the limbs with gout, especially the hands and

---

112. Dry passageways along the banks of waterways.
113. Ashes were used in the manufacture of soap.

feet, and gives rise to pustules and swollen, liquid-filled blisters all over the body and on the face, accompanied by fever and pain in the joints. All of the skin is covered with pimples, including the face up to the eyes, as happens with smallpox, and women's thighs to the vagina. It is such a tormenting disease that the patients cry out for death. This illness originates from the private parts and is spread by intercourse and no other means. It is said that even children have it. It takes a long time for people to recover, and all told, it is a filthy disease, yet few die from it. Many say that it was brought by the French, yet they have also had it for the past two years and call it the Italian disease.[114]

In the following decades, as syphilis became a more familiar disease, syphilitics attracted the charity of some patrician men and women:

March 24, 1524 (36:102-3)   Today after dinner in the hospital [of the Incurabili], the washing of the feet took place with great devotion. The patrician [hospital] guardians and others, twelve altogether, with great humility washed the feet of the impoverished and ill syphilitic men, and the gentlewomen washed the feet of the women, that is, the females sick with this disease. There was quite a crowd watching, and many were moved to piety seeing this pious work performed by the prominent people of the city. . . .

This hospital is a wonder, having grown so greatly in two years. It was in Lent of 1522 that it was founded by two women, one named Maria Malipiera Malipiero . . . and one [other] lady, Marina Grimana, who undertook to cure three poor women from San Rocho who were afflicted with the French sickness. They brought them to a house near Santo Spirito, where the hospital now stands. With the help of don Caietan —— the apostolic protonotary from Vicenza,[115] a learned and good servant of God, it grew to such a size that now it feeds eighty mouths . . . including a doctor and apothecaries and others—men and women—who serve, and all this is done with alms, which are very abundant.[116]

---

114. Syphilis first appeared in the Venetian territories in 1495. Some historians have suggested that the disease came from South America or originated in Haiti; others, that it was already known in antiquity. In the seventeenth century, Africa was added as a candidate for its origins. What was certain was that it struck western Europe as an epidemic, although the novelty of the disease at this date prevented Sanudo from realizing its potential mortality. See Eamon 1999.

115. Gaetano da Thiene.

116. For additional background on the Incurabili and Sanudo's references to them, see Aikema and Meijers 1989, 131ff.; and Cicogna 1824-53, 5:299-405.

Plague

The plague recurred at various times during the fifteenth century, and by the end of that era a contagion theory had developed and methods of dealing with the disease had been devised. Houses in which the plague had appeared were immediately quarantined for fifteen to forty days and/or their inhabitants sent to the Lazzaretti.[117] The Lazzaretto Vecchio was founded in 1423 on the island of Santa Maria di Nazareth, near the Lido, as one of the earliest permanent hospitals for the cure of plague victims. The Lazzaretto Nuovo was decreed by the Senate in 1468 on the island of Sant'Erasmo for the isolation of those suspected of having the disease. In addition, a magistracy, the Magistrato alla Sanità, was established in 1486 to enforce the rules and to take further measures to prevent the spread of the disease,[118] which recurred at intervals of five to six years during this period.

June 5, 1497 (1:645)   In recent days many cities in Italy have been in grave danger from the plague. The disease had already taken hold in some places, facilitated by the wars and the food shortages.[119] For that reason, our Signoria took every due precaution to prevent our city from becoming infected, may God spare us. Three *proveditori sora la sanità* were designated to handle these matters, and in the past few days two were elected to fill vacancies.[120] They are: Lunardo Marzelo, Jacomo Venier from San Samuel, and Hironimo Bon. They have announced publicly that no one arriving from the affected cities may enter our city until forty days have passed, at the risk of incurring very severe penalties. . . . These are the cities and localities in which this year there has been and [now] is the disturbance of plague: Cesena, Rimini, Ancona, Recanati, Loreto, Ortona da Mar, Lanzano, Rome, Naples, Florence, Pisa, the Abruzzi, Trieste, Muggia, Castelnuovo de Istria, San Lorenzo [da Pamadego, in Istria], San Vincenzo, Segna, Durazzo, Albania, Valona, Salonicca [in Macedonia], and Cologna.[121]

---

117. Institutions to cure those with the plague, to isolate those exposed to the plague, and to quarantine those arriving from places afflicted with plague. Named for the biblical Lazarus, who was saved from death.

118. Pullan 1990, 275.

119. While a theory of contagion existed by this time, it was also thought that the plague could be spontaneously generated by the putrefaction of corpses or spoiled food and that famine contributed to its spread. See Camporesi 1998.

120. See Sanudo 1980, 118, 250, on savi sora la sanità or provveditori sora la sanità.

121. Ambassadors and merchants abroad—and the towns and areas mentioned were all part of Venice's economic network—were required to report to the Signoria on the presence of the plague.

Spring often signaled the beginning of a new epidemic:

June 26, 1514 (18:299)   I do not wish to omit the fact that in the past few days the city has begun to show signs of infection. Four to five people are falling ill or dying every day; they are sent to the Lazzaretto. Today seven went there, and from various places. God help us, especially because it is June. I will record what happens.

The following year, Sanudo reported the commencement of the plague in March: "May God protect us, lest great harm be done to our affairs!" (March 20, 1515; 20:66). While the records Sanudo kept tended to focus on the patricians, disease was no respecter of rank, and as in so much of the social life of the city, servants and masters, doctors and patients, high and low were all caught up in the webs of life and death.

April 5, 1515 (20:97)   Today in the Querini house, in which three have already died, two more died. They were a girl who was the daughter of ser Alvixe Zorzi and the daughter of some woman. Both bodies were sent to the Lazzaretto. There are many people in the house, and they wanted the proveditori sora la sanità to let them go. Doctors, barbers, and others already move about freely and are mixing with everyone.[122]

Germans

In addition to Venetian patricians, citizens, and *popolo,* groups of foreign nationals constituted a significant proportion of the population in this most cosmopolitan of cities. They were such a recognized element that in a speech Sanudo made toward the end of the War of the League of Cambrai, in December 1516, he referred to the need to raise funds from "citizens and artisans and foreigners" who had paid no taxes for two years: "They should support this city, which they enjoy as do we" (23:341). Among the most important foreign groups were the Germans, Greeks, and Jews, but there were also Flemings, French, Slavs, Albanians, Armenians, mainland Italians (Tuscans and Milanese had their own altars at the Frari, the church of the Friars Minor), as well as pilgrims en route to the

---

122. See Venice (Commune), Assessorato alla cultura e belle arti 1979, 113; and Titian's *St. Mark Enthroned,* now in the Salute, originally in Santo Spirito in Isola, with four saints of healing: Cosmos, Damian, Rocco, Sebastiano. It is possible that this painting refers to the plague of 1509-14, which was particularly severe because it occurred during time of war. Plague attacked a society without immunity. See diaries, 6 May 1528 (47:370): "In these days, quite a number of people in the city, including many patricians, are dying of plague" (In questi zorni, in la terra muor assaissime persone da petechie, tra li qual molti zentilhomeni).

Holy Land. All these were in addition to a large diplomatic community, including the Turks, who in this period came only on specific diplomatic missions. Philippe de Commynes, the French ambassador to Venice in the late fifteenth century, commented that "most of the people are foreigners."[123]

Some of these groups, such as the Germans and later the Turks, who came to do business in the city, were transient and fluctuating communities but over time formed their own commercial establishments.[124] Because in Sanudo's time the Turks' visits were transient and essentially diplomatic, they are discussed in chapter 4. The Greeks were more of a stable and cultural presence, with domestic quarters in the city and eventually the privilege of practicing their own religion within that defined area. The experience of the Jews was even more unusual.

The foreigners who were most important to the economic life of the city were the Germans, or *tedeschi,* as they were called. In the thirteenth century they were allowed a large area in the commercial heart of the city on which they built a residential warehouse, the Fondaco dei Tedeschi. So vital was this group to the economic well-being of the city that when the *fondaco* burned down in 1505, the government voted to contribute one-half of the cost of raising a new one, whose facade would be frescoed by Giorgione and the young Titian a few years later.

January 27, 1505 (6:126)   This past night, between the twenty-seventh and the twenty-eighth, the German Warehouse at Rialto caught fire. There was little damage to the things kept there since they were intent on getting their stuff out even before the doors were thrown open. Now the building is all burned, including the gold storerooms, etc. The Germans have found lodgings here and there. The entire following day it burned. Some who went to help were killed by a wall that collapsed. And together with the news from Coloqut [Colocut], it is an ill omen that the warehouse burned.[125]

February 6, 1505 (6:131)   After dinner there was a meeting of the Signoria to deal with the question of the German Warehouse. They want to rebuild it immediately and make it very beautiful, and they listened to Zorzi Spavento, the [building] foreman of the Basilica of San Marco.[126] It was then decided to get started and to put the project in the care of ser Francesco di Garzoni, provedador al Sal. So that the Germans may find lodgings, two things

---

123. Commynes 1970, 2:591.

124. The Germans occupied the district that became the Fondaco dei Tedeschi, or German Warehouse, from the thirteenth century; the Fondaco dei Turchi, or Turkish Warehouse, dates from the late sixteenth century.

125. See the introduction under "Venice and the Battle of Agnadello" for the chronological connection between this misfortune in 1505 and the new Portuguese trade route to the East.

126. This office of the *proto,* which still exists today, had charge over all repairs and improvements to the Basilica.

were decreed: one is that whatever house they choose, the Signoria will pay one-half [of the rent] until the warehouse is completed; the other is that the bales of goods will be tied up under the loggia at Rialto and the area closed off with planking [for protection]. And so began the demolition of the warehouse in preparation for rebuilding. The Germans wanted the Foscari house . . . , [whose owners] are asking a very high rent, and the Signoria was not of a mind to rent it. They have now settled on the Lippomano house, which they have rented for two years at 500 ducats per year.

The Germans were valued and protected as participants in Venice's economy. For their part, the Germans shared in the city's entertainments (23:583; 28:252), as well as in its charitable efforts in times of famine.

March 6, 1528 (47:42)   It should be noted that so great is the scarcity of food that about 200 peasant women, with their children, stand in a row on the Rialto bridge, and alms are given them, and out of pity the Germans from the warehouse have had large cauldrons of vegetable soup prepared, . . . and they have sent it to be distributed to each of them. And it is heartrending to see the numbers of the destitute and above all, the poor women from Burano, who go seeking alms with their outer skirts over their heads, as is their custom, and many who have taken the feathers from their beds and large numbers of them stand with sacks of feathers on this side of the Rialto bridge, and they sell their feathers to survive, which invokes the deepest compassion.

Greeks

The Greek community was an even more integral part of the city than the German merchants. Not only a mercantile but often a highly cultured presence, the Greeks began to permeate Venice after the Venetian conquest of Constantinople in 1204. During the fifteenth century, as Turkish pressure upon the Eastern Roman Empire led to an influx of fugitives from Greek lands, the Greek presence in Venice accelerated, especially after the fall of Constantinople in 1453.

Cardinal Bessarion, bishop of Nicaea, churchman, diplomat, and bibliophile, who was himself part of that influx, had left his remarkable collection of Greek books and manuscripts to the city of Venice. Marco Musuro, a scholar from Crete, was hired to teach Greek at the University of Padua. Greeks were employed as editors and printers at presses such as that of Aldo Manuzio, whose gatherings of learned men formed an Aldine Academy, in which the mandated language of communication was Greek.

There were copyists and dealers in Greek manuscripts and teachers of the Greek language, not to mention artists and the artistic influence of Greek icons and mosaics. And on a less elevated level, there were galleymen and *stradioti*. It was in the name of the *stradioti* that the Greek community began to press for their own church, leading to the long-drawn-out negotiations in which Sanudo took an intense interest.

From the early fifteenth century on, the Greeks had sought papal approval for the freedom to celebrate, with their own priests, their religious rites *alla gre-cha,* according to the orthodox Greek ritual. Permits had been granted by the papacy and by the Venetian authorities to use particular churches for such rites when these churches were not preempted for Roman Catholic practices. Such freedom was often resisted by the Venetian patriarch, who considered it an infringement upon his control of the Venetian church and an unwarranted permission for heretical practice.[127]

January 26, 1504 (5:766)   In the Collegio. The patriarch came [to speak] about certain Greeks who are holding ceremonies at San Biagio, which is against the decisions of the Council held in Florence, etc. The doge answered him and reminded him of other things, etc.

Because of such difficulties, the Greeks pressed to have their own church, and in a brief of June 3, 1514, Pope Leo X granted the Greeks in Venice the right to construct a church with jurisdictional immunity from the Venetian authorities, confirming this in a bull of May 18, 1521. The patriarch continued to object:

July 11, 1526 (42:101)   It was decided to allow the Greeks, i.e., don Thodaro Paleologo and the others who petitioned, to build a Greek church on a piece of property they bought for 3,000 ducats from ser Piero Contarini. . . . The Greeks have briefs from Pope Leo, and this Pope [Clement VII] has confirmed that they may hold services in the Greek manner in that church.[128] Therefore, they ask that by giving 500 ducats to our Signoria they might be allowed, etc. The bill was proposed and approved. Nevertheless, they have their church at San Biagio, where they practice the Greek rite,[129] but it is a parish.

---

127. Technically, since the Council of Ferrara-Florence in 1438–39, the Roman and Greek Catholic churches had been in communion, recognizing a common set of principles. But many Greeks rejected this "union," and many Roman Catholics distrusted it.

128. On 5 September 1526 Clement VII strengthened Leo's permission by appointing three prominent ecclesiastics as supporters of that exemption. Both of these Medici popes were concerned above all to retain Venetian support for their efforts against the Turks but also, as humanists, to permit the Greek community its live according to its own culture and practices.

129. The manuscript reads *dove officiano a la Ghrecha;* the Fulin edition has *dove officiano a la chiesa.*

More than a year later the problem of the Greek church was still unresolved, owing especially to the intransigence of the patriarch, who since 1524 had been a conservative Dominican (46:356). So heated did the controversy become that the patriarch, considering these Greek practices heretical, excommunicated their fledgling church:

December 18, 1527 (46:381–82)   Many Greeks, including don Theodoro Paleologo, addressed the Collegio complaining that the patriarch had excommunicated their new church three days ago and does not want them to say the offices, something that was permitted by the pope and the Council of Ten with the zonta. In addition, the patriarch detained one of their "popes," that is, one of their priests, who had come from Corfù and was going to Ancona. Thereupon the Collegio expressed its regret for these things. But the patriarch is obstinate and wants them to have Catholic priests. The Collegio concluded that they would summon the patriarch to speak after dinner with the doge, who would persuade him to release the priest from prison.

But the mandates of the Signoria had no effect, and once more the pope tried to intervene by appointing an ecclesiastical panel:

December 28, 1527 (46:410–11)   Don Borgasio, the bishop of Limisso, came [before the Collegio] saying that before the recent holidays, in obedience to the mandates of the Signoria, he had gone to the patriarch to speak with him about opening the church of the Greeks at Santo Antonin for the holidays. The patriarch refused to speak with him, telling him that if he came after the holidays, he would speak with him then. In other words, he absolutely refuses. Thus, an order was posted that because the pope has chosen three judges—the papal legate, this Borgasio, bishop of Limisso, and the abbot of San Zorzi Mazor [San Giorgio Maggiore]—to consider the concession made to the Greeks at the Florentine Council, etc., on Monday morning all these three [would meet], and the patriarch would come to hear them on this matter.

December 30, 1527 (46:416)   This morning our most reverend patriarch and Bishop Borgasio came before the Collegio in the matter of the Greek church. The patriarch spoke in lofty tones, saying that in no way would he tolerate the Greeks' having a public church. Borgasio opposed him, saying that the church has promised[130] them to do so.

It took nearly a year for the dispute to be resolved:

---

130. The manuscript has *promesso;* the Fulin edition has *permesso.*

October 25, 1528 (49:93)   This morning an agreement was struck between the two sides by the bishop of Chieti, who is living at the Scuola di San Nicuola da Tolentino. He is the commissioner delegated by the pope to settle the dispute between our patriarch and the Greeks over the new church [to be] built in the parish of — with the name of San Zorzi. The Greeks had been excommunicated because they were not Catholics; the matter was suspended by the papal legate, and the case referred to the bishop of Chieti. He heard both sides and brought them together; that is, they are to be good Catholics under the patriarch, and therefore this appointed bishop absolved them and consecrated their cemetery. The Greek Mass of Santo Zuan Crisostomo was celebrated there in a most solemn way. I was among those who attended, and I saw the consecration of wheat bread, which, by the way, they gave to everyone. And then this bishop went to celebrate a Low Mass at the church of the Pietà.[131]

Jews

Sanudo's diaries contain numerous references to the "Ebrei" or the "Zudei," as he variously calls the Jews, commenting on their activities in the Venetian dominion and occasionally elsewhere. For example, in his first volume, under the date June 5, 1497, he summarizes an ambassadorial report from Spain about the marriage of Ferdinand and Isabella's daughter to the Portuguese ruler and includes this information: "This king and queen of Spain would never have given or promised their daughter as a wife to this king of Portugal had he not first effectively expelled the Jews from his entire kingdom. And so it was done, so that the Jews experienced another persecution in these times in being expelled from Spain. And so they had to leave and go elsewhere." Then Sanudo adds this interesting comment: "I wish to write something about these Jews below, about their persecution and their opinion that the coming of the Messiah is near" (1:646).

Sanudo never fulfilled that wish, but its formulation best expressed his curiosity and intention, here as elsewhere, to provide historical explanation as well as contemporary accounts. Two weeks later, however, he reported a more local story concerning a poor peasant from Piove di Sacco (near Padua) who, having no grain to sow, was given some by Jews. The crop produced in the peasant's "Christian" fields gave forth an unusual grain that was large but blighted and seen "as God's miracle against the Jews" (June 20, 1497; 1:653).

It is somewhere between these two modes—that of a curious and sympathetic reporter and that of the mirror of bouts of contemporary prejudice—that Sanudo must be placed in the following accounts of the Jews in Venice. For the

---

131. The bishop of Chieti was Gian Pietro Carafa, who would play a less conciliatory role in the Reformation controversies between Roman Catholics and Lutheran Protestants.

story that these excerpts tell is different from Sanudo's reports about Germans or Greeks, because the Jews of Venice occupied a place that was both figuratively and literally quite different from that of the Germans and the Greeks.[132] Although no Jews lived permanently in Venice before the fourteenth century, they had been a commercial presence since the Middle Ages. And since Jews could have no legal residence in the city (except for the brief period 1382–97), they made their homes in Mestre, a town at the edge of the lagoons nearest to Venice.[133] But by the sixteenth century, Jewish activities had been reduced to banking and trade in secondhand goods. Jewish communities elsewhere in the Veneto had suffered from bouts of prejudice aroused by Lenten preachers and stories of Jewish ritual murder of children, the most famous of which concerned the child Simon of Trent in 1475.[134] But the enormous economic usefulness of Jews as purveyors of loans, especially to the urban poor, and as objects for high taxation and forced loans to the government also led to their protection and a long series of negotiated contracts between this foreign community and their rulers.[135] However, their economic usefulness did not mitigate, and often contributed to, the resentment felt by their debtors.[136]

The defeat of the Venetians at the battle of Agnadello in 1509 and the subsequent occupation of the Venetian Terraferma by imperial and French troops, including the conquest of Padua and the burning of Mestre, enormously increased the refugee Jewish population of Venice itself. By 1515 Sanudo reports an increasing distress at their visible presence and free circulation, although Sanudo himself is viewed as generally "level-headed and no fanatic."[137]

April 6, 1515 (20:98)   [Good Friday.] I do not wish to ignore a depraved custom that has developed from the continuous commerce that people have with these Jews, who inhabit this city in great numbers at San Cassan, Santo Agustin, San Polo, Santa Maria Mater Domini. It used to be that from before Palm Sunday to after Easter they were not to be seen. This year they were out and about until yesterday [Holy Thursday], and this is a very bad thing. No one says anything to them because, with these wars, they need them; thus they do

---

132. Pullan 1971, pt. 3, esp. 431–509 for this period, provides a thorough introduction to the experience of the Jews in Venice and includes many passages from Sanudo.

133. Ravid 1997, 112–13.

134. Simon's body was discovered on Eastertide 1475. The local bishop immediately accused local Jews of ritual murder; several were eventually executed. The boy's body became a cult center attracting pilgrims from both Italian- and German-speaking regions.

135. Benjamin Ravid has pointed out that these contracts or charters were issued continuously from the first granted to the Jews of Venice in 1513 down to the end of the Venetian Republic in 1797. Only in 1571 was a charter not renewed, but no expulsion followed. Ravid 2003.

136. Sanudo 1980, 136, 195.

137. Pullan 1971, 486.

what they want. The preacher at the Frari, Fra Giovan Maria di Arezzo, thunders against them and against Jewish doctors, especially Master Lazaro.[138] He has made Christian women become dissolute and has frequented Christian women, and no measures have been taken. The preacher concludes that it is all right to take everything [Jews] have and put it toward the defense of the state, since they are our servants.

On April 23, 1515, it was suggested in the Senate that all Jews be removed to the Giudecca, where it was believed the original Jewish merchants from the Levant had first established themselves (20:138). Jewish leaders were able to forestall this decree, but during the following year the military situation so worsened and the mood of the city became so dark that a similar proposal in the spring of 1516 went forward in a renewed effort to placate a deity viewed as angry with the city's sinful ways (including its toleration of a Jewish presence). A new location was proposed: the Ghetto Nuovo, named for an iron foundry that had once stood on the site.[139] In the context of the previous proposal, this one could be viewed as a compromise: the Ghetto Nuovo was certainly less remote from the city centers than was the Giudecca, accessible by foot as well as by canals. Sanudo questioned neither the rationale of the decision nor the location proposed; it was the specific details that interested him:

March 26, 1516 (22:72–73)   News of the morning: ser Zacaria Dolfin, the savio di Consiglio, proposed in the Collegio in recent days that it is bad to have the Jews in this city, given that preachers are preaching that the afflictions of our state derive from this and from their having synagogues, which is not in conformity with the laws. He is thus of the opinion that they should all be sent to live in the Ghetto Nuovo, which is like a castle, and [that it be closed] off with a wall and drawbridges.[140] They are to have only one gate, which is to be closed so that they remain within; and two of the boats of the Council of Ten are to go there and stay there all night. [The boatmen] are to be paid for by the Jews since they will benefit from the added security measure. As a result,

---

138. See chapter 7 for this overzealous friar. Master Lazaro was a particularly famous Jewish doctor with a patrician clientele and special privileges of visitation, which led to the friar's charges that Lazaro had taken sexual advantage of his female Christian patients.

139. Ravid 1999b: The Venetian Ghetto was built on the site of the municipal foundry, where iron was poured and cast into artillery.

140. Zaccaria Dolfin had previously served as *provveditore all'Arsenale* (in 1504 and 1513–14) and may have conceived of this area to be walled off as a similarly discrete urban space. Or the idea may have reflected the development of the Lazzaretto Nuovo as a well-furnished castle. See Concina 1991, 30–32. Dennis Romano suggests that removing the Jews to the Ghetto should be seen in the context of increasing patrician control over the cityscape in this same period, which marginalized the poor, the sick, and women (1989, 348).

the doge and some councillors, warming to the idea, sent for the owners of the houses of the Ghetto. Those who don't live there were happy; some who do live there told the Collegio that they had bought those houses and put a good deal of work into them and spent a lot of money and that it would be hard to leave them.

Then Anselmo the Jew and two other Jewish leaders were summoned, and the doge told them that [the government] wanted them to go live in the Ghetto Nuovo and that their keeping a synagogue here was against the law.[141] Anselmo replied that this was an injustice for several reasons. First, he said that since they will not be surrounded by gentlemen and other Christians, their houses will be sacked, something that has already begun to happen even though they live near the guards at Rialto, [and it would be worse if they were] much farther away. Also, they had been promised by the Council of Ten with the zonta that no new measures would be undertaken concerning them, and this would be breaking that promise, particularly since the secondhand dealers spent a great deal of money to have shops on the Rialto and now they will be ruined. In addition, he said that the poor Jews will not want to go live there and will leave the city and that he, Anselmo, has promised to pay for everyone but will not be able to pay since he will have no one to tax.[142] He beseeched [the Collegio] not to make this change but instead, when the Venetian territory had been reclaimed [from the enemy], . . . to allow the Jews to go out and live[143] in the mainland towns where they used to live, although they would not be able to live in Mestre since there are no longer any houses there. He then left, and Dolfin, more impassioned than ever, wanted the bill to go before the Senate. I will record what becomes of it.

It was to no avail that the Jews demurred through their leaders. The bill was passed a few days later,[144] and its introduction indicates the unusually intense atmosphere of prejudice in which it was conceived.

March 29, 1516 (22:85–88)   According to the provisions[145] of various laws of the Senate and our council, Jews are not permitted to live in this our[146] city

---

141. Anselmo dal Banco (Asher Meshullam of Mestre), a banker and head of the Jewish community in Venice during this period, had great power: "Anselmo dal banco à gran poder," Sanudo wrote in his diary (20:71). See also Pullan 1971, 479.

142. Anselmo "guaranteed" the taxes by paying them and then collecting from individual Jews what they owed.

143. The manuscript has *habitar;* the Fulin edition omits it.

144. The actual bill was dated 20 March 1516.

145. The manuscript has *provisto;* the Fulin edition has *previsto.*

146. The manuscript has *nostra;* the Fulin edition omits it.

beyond a total of fifteen days over the course of a year. . . . However, given the [financial] necessities and the extremely urgent conditions of the times, Jews were allowed to come and live in Venice. This happened principally so that the possessions of Christians, which were in the hands of the Jews, would be preserved. However, it cannot have been the wish of any citizen of our state who wants to live in the fear of God that, once the Jews had arrived here, they would disperse themselves throughout the entire city, sharing houses with Christians and going about day and night wherever they wish. . . . Therefore, it is entirely necessary that appropriate and valid measures be taken.

To avoid such disorderly and unsuitable situations, it is proposed that the following provisions and decisions be made: that all Jews who currently live in the various parishes of this city of ours and those that will come here from now until further provisions are taken . . . are obligated and must go immediately to live together in the group of houses that are in the Ghetto, near San Hironimo, a very spacious locale for them to inhabit . . . two high walls are to be built to close off the other two sides that look onto the canals; all of the banks along which the houses run are also to be walled. Moreover, the guardians are to live in this place day and night alone, without family, in order to guard it well, and they will observe whatever other regulations are established by this Collegio. In addition, the Collegio will assign them two boats, with which they will patrol this place day and night and which will be paid for out of the money of the Jews. All of these regulations are to be voted on in the Collegio by ballots and ballot box, and those that will obtain a majority will become the law just as if they had passed [in] this council. . . .[147]

Plans went forward for ensuring the separation of the Jews through the appointment of guards and boat patrols, with special treatment provided for Jewish physicians, a number of whom were famous and had prominent connections.

July 29, 1516 (22:392)   Many Jewish doctors are living in the Ghetto who are likely to be called during the night to treat the sick living outside the Ghetto and who sometimes will stay out very late for some consultation. In order that they not run afoul of the law for this reason, let it be law that each time these doctors go out at night to tend to the sick or remain out late for a consultation, they must inform our guards in writing of the details of where they have been, who the sick persons are, and what consultation they attended.

---

147. Pullan summarizes the function of the Ghetto as follows: "This was 'like a fortress,' with a single entrance that could be guarded at night by boats belonging to the police force controlled by the Council of Ten. It could therefore perform the double function of protecting the Jews from violence and plunder, and of enabling an effective curfew to be imposed upon them." 1971, 487.

The guards are obligated to present the written information the following day to our Cataveri, on pain of losing their job and spending six months in prison and paying fifty lire de pizoli to our Cataveri.[148] The officials must immediately make diligent inquiries concerning whether the said doctors were in the stated places; if they find that it is not true, they must punish the doctors according to the provisions of the law passed by this council on March 29 of the present year.[149]

These legislative measures were of particular interest to Sanudo, who considered himself in this instance, as on many other occasions, the depository of the law. The Ghetto itself, unusual in its time, later became a destination for visitors; its name was to have an enduring history.

Also of interest to Sanudo, as major religious and social events, were a number of conversions, especially if the convert came from a prominent Jewish family such as the dal Bancos, whose leader, Anselmo, had negotiated with the government in 1516:

January 19, 1528 (46:501–2)   This morning, in the church of the Friars Minor, which had been beautifully decorated with tapestries and other adornments and [where] above the choir the figures of the children and apostles [were] clothed with albs and copes, on a large platform built near the pulpit . . . a seventeen-year-old Jew named Vivian was solemnly baptized. He is the son of Jacob, the son of Anselmo dal Banco, who, being worth 100,000 ducats, is the richest Jew in the city. The young man was a student and wanted to marry a cousin of his who had a large dowry, but persuaded by several friars, especially Master Bortolomio of Venice, he decided to become a Christian. His father and mother came to persuade him to stay in his faith, but he remained firm in his desire to become a Christian. Thus the baptism is to take place today. The church was so packed that there was not an empty space from the choir to the main door; the crowd was estimated at more than 10,000.[150]

The Jew came very well dressed in black: a jacket of black satin, a tunic

---

148. The magistracy of the Cattavere had been designated executors of the Ghetto arrangement and assigned one-third of the fines. See appendix B under "Governmental Terms"; and Ravid 1999a, 238–39.

149. Such exemptions from curfew restrictions, as well as the requirement to wear an identifying yellow badge or red hat or the privilege of wearing the patrician's black hat *(bareta negra),* might as easily be revoked (see diaries, 24:50–51, 59) or allowed to lapse (50:67) and then restored (50:474, 51:32, 53:177).

150. As noted earlier, Sanudo tended to exaggerate numbers. Three of Vivian's siblings also were baptized Christians, as was his father, Jacob, in 1533. See Roth 1930, 480; and diaries, 5 July 1533 (58:563–69). Jacob was Asher Meshullam's son, renamed "Marco Paradiso, cavalier of St. Mark." See Pullan 1971, 480, 507, and 1987, 674. For another conversion, see diaries, 31:291.

of black cloth, and a black cap on his head. He took his seat in front of the pulpit that had been adorned for his baptism. First a sermon was preached by Master Fra Bortolomio, who is a learned man. Present were the bishop of Baius [Bayeux],[151] who is the ambassador of the king of France, and the ambassador of the Marquis of Mantua. Then he was solemnly baptized by a bishop wearing his vestments and a miter on his head; his name is —— [Antonio di Beccaria], and he is the bishop of Scutari and the suffragan bishop of Verona. The godfathers were the two ambassadors and several others. But first a collection was taken up, and everyone gave something. Indeed, collection boxes where people could toss in money for him were placed at the doors as if it were a jubilee. In all, the alms today added up to twenty ducats and no more. Once it was over, the Monsignor of Bayeux raised him up to the accompaniment of a wind ensemble for having converted to the faith of Christ. He then took him to dine at his house, where they say he will live. To give him an income, they want to start a subscription list for a sum of 300 ducats and use it to purchase an annuity for him. What will come of it, God only knows. ... They say that his father told him that he will not want for anything. Thus the morning was occupied with this ceremony.

Sanudo reports little about Jewish culture. He does state that he acquired "a beautiful Hebrew bible" (8:525), but he makes no mention of the important printing in November 1516, only a few months after the Jewish Ghetto was founded, of the Pentateuch in Hebrew by Daniel Bomberg of Antwerp, to be followed by Rabbinic bibles and Talmudic works. But Sanudo did report on one form of Jewish culture that particularly interested him, the theater, and that only on one occasion. However, he states neither how he heard about the performance nor whether, in spite of the prohibitions, he attended, although the fact that he praised the event and knew when it ended suggests that he did attend.

March 4, 1531 (54:326)   This evening, in the Ghetto, the Jews put on a very nice comedy for themselves; the heads of the Ten had forbidden Christians to attend. It was concluded at eight hours after sunset.[152]

Street Entertainments

Hierarchically divided as Venetian society was, much of the social life of the city was shared by its populace—patriciate, citizens, artisans and all, including foreign elements, whether transient or fixed. In addition to the religious festi-

---

151. Ludovico Canossa.

152. The date of the performance suggests that it may have been connected to the Jewish feast of Purim, which falls in the month of Adar, in midspring.

vals, the solemn funerals, and the patrician parties that spilled out from the palaces into the campi and onto the banks of canals, Sanudo also described the daily happenings in the streets and waterways, sometimes with a few lines, sometimes in a long entry for one or two days, sometimes over several months. The small and the large events of his city's society all formed part of his record, whether the subject was a strolling minstrel; a boat race between men or women (36:459); a bridge battle that drew its audience from the entire population; a communal disaster such as the great Rialto fire of 1514; or a communal excitement such as the lottery craze of 1522.

As an example of a passing street entertainment, Sanudo includes this brief description of a young minstrel whose performance he found pleasing.

June 13, 1500 (3:392)   This month a well-favored young man arrived in town. Dressed in a short jacket, he strolled around town singing the following song while beating time with a cane that he held in his hand:

> Take her now, country boy,
> The girl in the jumper,
> You will make her work hard
> With a hoe and rake.

It continued in the same vein and was lovely to listen to.[153]

Bridge battles *(battaiole)* were a peculiarly Venetian entertainment. Prints of a later period show the crowds who both participated and attended, with patricians taking space on the adjacent rooftops to enjoy a show that was often a hazardous free-for-all. Sanudo reports the government's desire, in the early years of the War of the League of Cambrai, to control these events:

November 1, 1510 (11:571–72)   This morning a law passed yesterday by the Council of Ten was proclaimed from the Pietra del Bando in San Marco. It deals with the [bridge] battles that have been going on in the city, with some fatalities, . . . and whose contestants have refused to obey the captains, etc. It states that such battles may no longer be held anywhere in the city, under these penalties: for those above the age of ——, three yanks of the rope and exile from Venice for —— years, and for those below, a fine of forty lire each. And the same for those who prevent the captains and officials from performing their duties.[154]

---

153. This topos (farm tools as a metaphor for male genitalia and the earth as a metaphor for female genitalia), popular in medieval and Renaissance literature, may be found in Ruzante's short monologue *Lettera giocosa* and sporadically in other works.

154. These popular "bridge battles" continued for several more centuries. See R. C. Davis 1994.

Rialto Fire

Among the major events that affected the whole city in Sanudo's lifetime was the great fire of 1514, which destroyed much of the Rialto. Sanudo's description, made vivid by the details that he himself had witnessed, conveys his shock: "the most dreadful and horrifying thing that was ever seen in Venice or anywhere else."

January 10, 1514 (17:458–62)   Today was the feast of St. Paul the first hermit.[155] Tuesday . . . a fire broke out in the monastery of the Crociferi and spread from the head doctor's room.[156] Because a strong wind was blowing, it took only a short time, less than three hours, for the entire monastery and several houses behind it to burn. Nevertheless, the church, which houses the body of St. Barbara, was not damaged. As this fire was blazing and the tocsin was being rung at Rialto, according to custom, another fire was discovered in a dry-goods shop, the one that uses the diamond as its insignia. It happened because they keep a fire in a brazier to heat the store. A spark fell from it and set the cloth on fire, and the Rialto guards did not arrive soon enough to prevent the fire from consuming this and other shops. It was two hours after sunset, and one shop after another caught fire, both dry-goods shops and ropemakers' shops, producing an enormous blaze. A very strong wind was blowing from the north-northeast, and the cold was unbearable. The tocsin was rung at Rialto, and everyone came running, those who have vaults and warehouses full of merchandise as well as the shopkeepers and others who have business establishments at Rialto, including myself, Marin Sanudo. I too ran since I own part of the tavern of the Campana, from which I draw my livelihood; it pays 205 ducats in rental income, in addition to the income from the shops below it.

The fire was burning, and no one was doing much about it because they were all busy emptying out everything they could from the shops, vaults, warehouses, and offices. A number of foreigners rushed there, as did others who showed up to loot once they heard that there was a fire at Rialto, which is the most important and richest spot in Venice. Soon the place was so jammed that one could no longer reach it. People were removing the merchandise and things from their shops, some of which got stolen; others were renting small boats and boats used on the Padua line and laden wine barges, onto which

---

155. St. Paul of Thebes, distinct from St. Paul of Antioch, "Apostle of the Gentiles."

156. The monastery had owned and run a hospital nearby, with a capacity of forty to fifty persons, up to the early fifteenth century (1414). It had then become a hospice for indigent women. See Lunardon 1985.

they intended to load the merchandise that was in danger of burning. No one was trying to put out the fire, [which was] already making great gain by going along the street toward the Agustini and especially the Pixani banks, which were open. The books and the cash that were there were removed, as happened also at other banks, that is, the Vendramin bank, which is still standing, and the books of the others who have banks, that is the Agustini, Prioli, and Lippomani. Meanwhile, the fire continued to blaze at Rialto, whipped up by the strong wind, and no one was taking measures against it. Ser Hironimo Tiepolo and ser Stefano Contarini, heads of the Ten, and the signori di notte were actually there, but they could do nothing because no one would obey them, everyone being occupied with saving their own goods and not Rialto. Those who were not just stood around watching.

Many well-regarded patricians were there, busying themselves with emptying the offices and saving the books, especially salvaging the money that was in the office of the governors of the fisc.[157] The parish priests of the churches at Rialto—San Jacomo, San Zuane Evanzelista, and San Matio—carried the body of Christ around Rialto [to try to stop the fire], but to no avail. The fire continued to spread, and in a short time[158] all of Rialto had burned; along the Grand Canal the vaults and offices were destroyed as far down as the public treasurers' offices, and on this side to where the stairs begin to ascend the bridge.

The tocsin was rung at San Zuane di Rialto and in the nearby parishes, and many people responded. But no one helped, and they seemed more interested in stealing what they could; even women came to steal the goods that were out in the streets, especially things from the inns and from some shops above the Pescaria [Fish Market] that were hard to reach. By chance there were piles of stones at the Pescaria because it was going to be repaved by the proveditori del comun on the orders of the Signoria.[159] Some of these stones were used to seal the windows of the inns because of the fire that was burning all over Rialto.

I must report that in less than six hours all of Rialto burned, including the dry-goods shops and the vaults above them. On this side the fire entered the Monkey Inn, which belongs to the nuns of San Lorenzo and was new. On the other side, on Jewellers' Alley, the fire progressed as far as the vaults of the friars of San Zorzi; on the other side all of old and new Rialto and the Riva dil Ferro burned, and the flames spread from house to house. On this side,

---

157. In listing the damaged buildings, Sanudo crisscrosses the bridge, reflecting the confusion of the moment.

158. The manuscript has *e in poco;* the Fulin edition has *e in poche ore.*

159. The provveditori di comun were in charge of streets, canals, bridges, and public wells.

the church of San Zuane di Rialto, which had a piece of wood from the True Cross, was consumed by the flames, which spread to the top of the Campanile, where two figures of men rang out the hours. The top of the Campanile burned along with the figures of men that were on it and the entire roof. The fire burned all night because of the strong wind, and people stood watching, and in the streets people were running as if they were going to get indulgences. . . .

The fire burned all night and all day on the eleventh, as I said.[160] It was still burning at sunset, when I left. All of Rialto burned, and all of the Flour Warehouse, but the blaze did not spread beyond the canal bank. . . . Only the church of San Giacomo di Rialto, with its leaden roof, remained standing, even though it was in the middle of the fire; so it was God's wish that it be spared. For this was the first church built in Venice, begun on March 25, 421,[161] as may be read in our chronicles, and God did not wish a ruin so great as to destroy with fire the first church [of Venice]. . . .

Today the head of St. Barbara, which is kept in the church of San ——, was carried in procession around the burning areas because it is believed to have great preventive powers in such matters, yet the fire continued to burn. Today the Collegio did not meet, nor were there any meetings after dinner. Only the Collegio and the heads of the Ten gathered in the doge's chambers in the morning and after dinner to decide what measures to take, which I will describe below. These measures will be taken during the night out of concern for safeguarding this city, given that it is engaged in a war and that the enemy is at Este—not far distant—and Maran, and there are so many rebels and foreigners here.[162] Moreover, at this critical moment the *populo* were much quicker to busy themselves with robbing than to protect Rialto, which shows their ill will. Those who could find nothing better stole boards and firewood and then left. But the Arsenal craftsmen did their duty in making sure that the fire did not go beyond San Silvestro and Santo Aponal. They deserve much praise also because they were in great danger; it is believed that some of them were killed by walls that collapsed. The ladders and the buckets that the Council of Ten had ordered placed in the various neighborhoods were nowhere to be found. All the same, people brought water by whatever

---

160. The entry is all under the date of 10 January indicating that Sanudo's entries were occasionally written after the date cited and backdated to the day when the event began.

161. This traditional date—the day of the Annunciation—for the building of the first church formed part of Venetians' claim to the special sanctity of their city. See Labalme 1969, 267.

162. Este is about thirty kilometers southwest of Padua; Marano and the Gulf of Marano are at the northern end of the Adriatic, slightly west of Aquileia and to the east of Venice. See above, chapter 3 for these "rebels," who were mainlanders sequestered in Venice after siding with league forces against Venice at the beginning of the War of the League of Cambrai.

means they could. Finally, at about twenty-three hours the fire began to abate somewhat and to lose its former intensity, and the wind died down. . . .

Today, with the terrible cold and the high wind, fires broke out in a number of chimneys, but they were extinguished. Indeed, it seems as though these fires have been preordained: God has brought them upon us as punishment for our sins and the injustices committed. This past night the *populo* were saying, "Oh, what a sentence! Oh, what revenge!" And more than one was saying, "Even the half-rents were injustices." The fruit and cheese stalls were all spared, and the wine barges were all unmoored [and spread out] along the Grand Canal. The people standing on the Rialto bridge had to leave because of the intense heat from the great fire. You could not see anything but boats full of goods and barges and other vessels, whose owners and porters earned good money carrying things here and there. The whole scene looked like the fall of Troy and the sack of Padua, which I myself witnessed. . . . I thought it was the most dreadful and horrifying thing that was ever seen in Venice or anywhere else.

Games of Fortune

It was not only disasters like the fire of 1514 that generated general excitement. In February 1522 the lottery appeared in Venice, and Venetians plunged into this new form of gambling as brokers set up lotteries not only in Rialto but also in San Marco and the refectory of the Franciscan monastery.

February 18, 1522 (32:467–68)   A newsworthy event has taken place in the last few days: a new way of making money by betting a small amount of capital has appeared at Rialto. It began with small amounts and originated with Hironimo Bambarara, the secondhand-cloth dealer, but then it moved to larger sums. First, each person who wanted to play gave twenty pence, then it went up to three lire, then to a ducat, and the prizes were rugs, cushions, and other things.[163] Now silver items worth about 200 ducats have been added, and others have put up a piece of gold brocade, which you can take a chance on for one ducat per person. This is the way it is done: whoever wants to play writes his name down on a piece of paper and gives the specified amount in cash. There are those who play their entire capital and considerably more. All of those who have placed a bet gather in certain designated shops, where there are two bags. In one are the slips of paper deposited by the bettors. In the other are an equal number of slips, some with a particular prize written on

---

163. A ducat was a month's wages for a working-class occupation such as that of foot soldier. See "A Comparative Scale of Annual Wages and Salaries" in appendix A.

them and some with only "Patience" written on them. Once they are all gathered around, they call a child and thoroughly mix up the slips in these bags. Then he pulls out a name from the first bag and goes to the second. If a prize comes up, it belongs to the person whose name is on the slip, but if he pulls out a slip with "Patience" on it, that person wins nothing, and it is his bad luck. Every day now such things happen at Rialto. It seems that Lodovico da la Faità wants to set up a pot of 4,000 ducats, and all those who want a ticket can buy as many as they want for ten ducats apiece, and once the amount for the pot has been reached, they will hold a drawing. The first prize will be 1,000 ducats, and so on in like manner, and this will be an excellent and honorable undertaking. The lottery announcement has been drawn up and is circulating. I will record what comes of it.

February 27, 1522 (32:500–502)   I have written earlier of how no one in this city cares about anything except betting money on lotteries at Rialto. Prizes are decided upon, as is a ticket price, whether it be ten soldi or twenty soldi, thirty-one soldi, three lire, one ducat, two ducats, until the amount has been reached. The value of the prizes goes up to about 1,500 ducats, some more and some less. Prizes in these lotteries include silk and wool cloth, paintings, lining materials of different kinds, a large number of silver items, and beautiful objects, including large pearls and fine jewels of all kinds, large amber-bead necklaces, and even a live large simian and caparisoned white horses, Neapolitan steeds, and other [kinds of horses].[164] Everything is put up for the lottery—many tapestries, silk robes, dresses of silk or gold brocade, and other items—so that both sides of Goldsmiths' Street and Jewellers' Alley all up and down are devoted to this, and it is impossible to pass through these places. There are so many people that it seems like the feast of the Ascension. . . .

So that no fraud will occur, the heads of the Council of Ten commissioned the proveditori di comun . . . [to ensure that] no lottery can be set up without their knowledge, items must be valued at a fair price, and a scribe will be sent to watch the drawing of the tickets. These are drawn in the following way: All of the tickets that have been purchased for the prize in the lottery are placed in a little cabinet. A little boy pulls one out and then pulls out another from a second cabinet, in which the other tickets, which are equal in number to the tickets purchased, have been placed. Part of them are blank, and part of them are marked "Prize" with the number of the prize on them. . . . If it is blank, someone who is there calls out, "Patience." If it is for a prize, they say what

---

164. The amber beads were known as *pater nostri*. See Molmenti 1973, 1:379. The simian was called *uno gato mamon vivo*, a kind of monster monkey, and the steeds were referred to as *chinee*, the sort offered each year by kings of Naples to the pope as a feudal gift.

prize it is, and it is written down on a slip, which is taken to the office of the proveditori di comun, and the winner goes and picks up his prize.

Many women have bet money on the lottery; everyone is running off to put up a small amount of money in order to win a large amount because they see that someone who bet one ducat won one hundred gold ducats, and someone else won pearls worth 180 ducats, and the like. And there were some who bought a large number of tickets, and yet each one turned out to have "Patience" on it. There are some who buy tickets under various names and some who say bizarre things and get the slip with the prize on it. Among the other things that happened, I was there this morning with a very dear friend of mine who is a wealthy patrician, who put in several tickets for silver pieces bearing the following phrase: "Felix concordia" (Blessed be peace), but he has not yet won anything. Drawings remain to be made in the other lotteries, not just here at Rialto but also in Piazza San Marco. I, Marin Sanudo, have not yet risked any money in these lotteries, because they seem to me to be illicit and perhaps even fraudulent. The signori di notte or the proveditori di comun arrested someone who put more tickets than he should have in the lottery; he was made a public laughingstock, etc.

Today a lottery was opened; Zuan Manenti, the broker, is in charge and will earn 3 percent.[165] The pot will be 4,000 ducats, with tickets at ten ducats apiece. And the most important people in the city are putting their money down so they can win the first prize of 1,000 ducats, the second of 500 ducats, the third of 300[166] ducats, and so on. There are one hundred prizes and 400 tickets. This lottery is now closed, and today after dinner, in the new refectory of the Friars Minor, the drawing of the approved tickets was held; they were drawn by a child of the Balbi family. It lasted until three hours after sunset.

. . .

There followed a list of one hundred prizewinners in this lottery. Some disguised their names with initials such as "Z.F." or "M.V and friends." Some chose hopeful pseudonyms such as "God send me good luck" or "I recommend myself to the Madonna" or "Father, Son, and Holy Spirit—if not the first at least the second."[167] The first prize, one thousand ducats, went to one Marco Aurelio, an illegitimate son of ser Nicolò; the second, of five hundred ducats, went to ser Piero Gradenigo; and the third, of three hundred ducats, went to madonna Cecilia Ba-

---

165. See Carroll 1990, 24–25, for information on Zuan Manenti, who was also an *autor*. For this term, see appendix B under "Vocabulary Used in the Original."

166. The manuscript has 300; the Fulin edition has 100.

167. "Pare, fio e Spirito Santo, se non el primo el segondo al mancho."

doer, wife of ser Jacomo. The compagnia of the Triumphanti had three winning tickets, one for one hundred ducats and the others for forty and twenty. There were a few others for fifty and thirty ducats, and all the rest were for twenty or twelve ducats. As early as the following day another lottery was in progress, and disapproval of the activity, including Sanudo's, began to be expressed.

February 28, 1522 (32:504)   Nothing important happened in the morning, and no letters arrived. The only thing of note is that people are waiting for the closing of another lottery with a pot of 6,000 ducats, which was also organized by the broker Zuan Manenti. The tickets cost ten ducats apiece, and his fee is 3 percent. The first prizes are 500 ducats each, and there are — of them, and this lottery closed quickly. [Additional lotteries are being planned], one with a pot of 5,000 ducats and two with pots of 4,000 ducats apiece. And Sunday, after dinner, the drawing will be held in the monastery of San Zane Polo [Santi Giovanni e Paolo]. . . .

I note that today the preacher at San Zane Polo, a most worthy man . . . , spoke at length against these lotteries, saying that they are illicit and that steps should be taken to stop them.[168] And I, Marin Sanudo, have declared publicly to everyone that if I were in the position to do so, I would put a stop to these lotteries. I even sent this message to the Most Serene Doge.

Later that same day a measure was passed by the Council of Ten that those lotteries in process should be speedily wound up, and further lotteries forbidden under pain of two years' imprisonment and a stiff fine of five hundred ducats. The craze continued for a few more days before the prohibition took effect:

March 5, 1522 (33:14)   *Item:* many patricians and others appeared before the heads of the Ten requesting permission to draw the lotteries that have already closed. In light of the law that has been passed, the heads decided to do nothing. Indeed, since people were saying that they were going to go to Mestre to draw them, the heads of the Ten wrote to the civil and military governors of Mestre telling them not to let anyone draw a lottery. The money will be returned to the ticket holders.

But it was not long before gambling returned to Venice. Playing with fortune became a growing passion during the succeeding centuries, and it has been sug-

---

168. He was undoubtedly a visiting preacher who spoke out against the practice in his host church.

gested that the risk of these games replaced the older, mercantile risk of Venetian commerce.[169] Certainly, the games of Fortuna became a permanent part of the Venetian social scene, providing one of its tourist attractions, as well as, according to the eighteenth-century playwright Carlo Goldoni, one of its ills.[170]

169. Crouzet-Pavan 1992, 2:858.
170. See Goldoni's *La bottega del Caffè* and *Le avventure della Villeggiatura*.

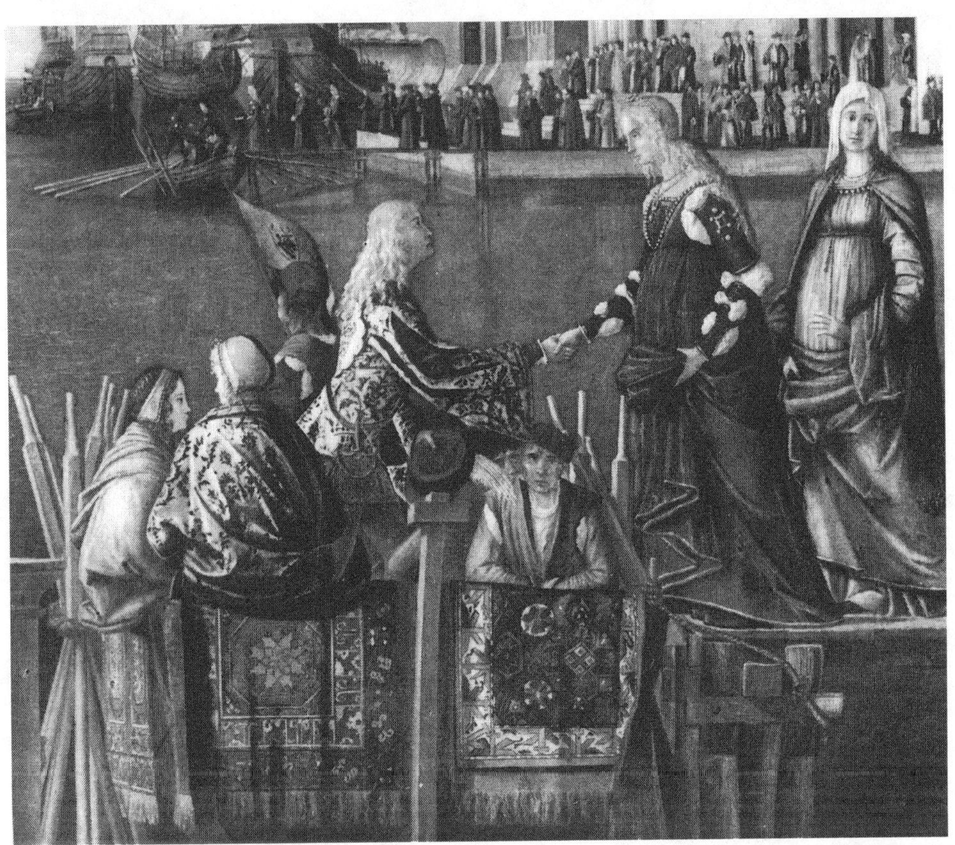

Carpaccio, *Leavetaking of the Betrothed Pair,* from the St. Ursula Cycle, 1495. Accademia, Venice. Ursula's fashionable outfit features the slashed sleeves prohibited in sumptuary legislation. Photo by Osvaldo Bohm, 542N.

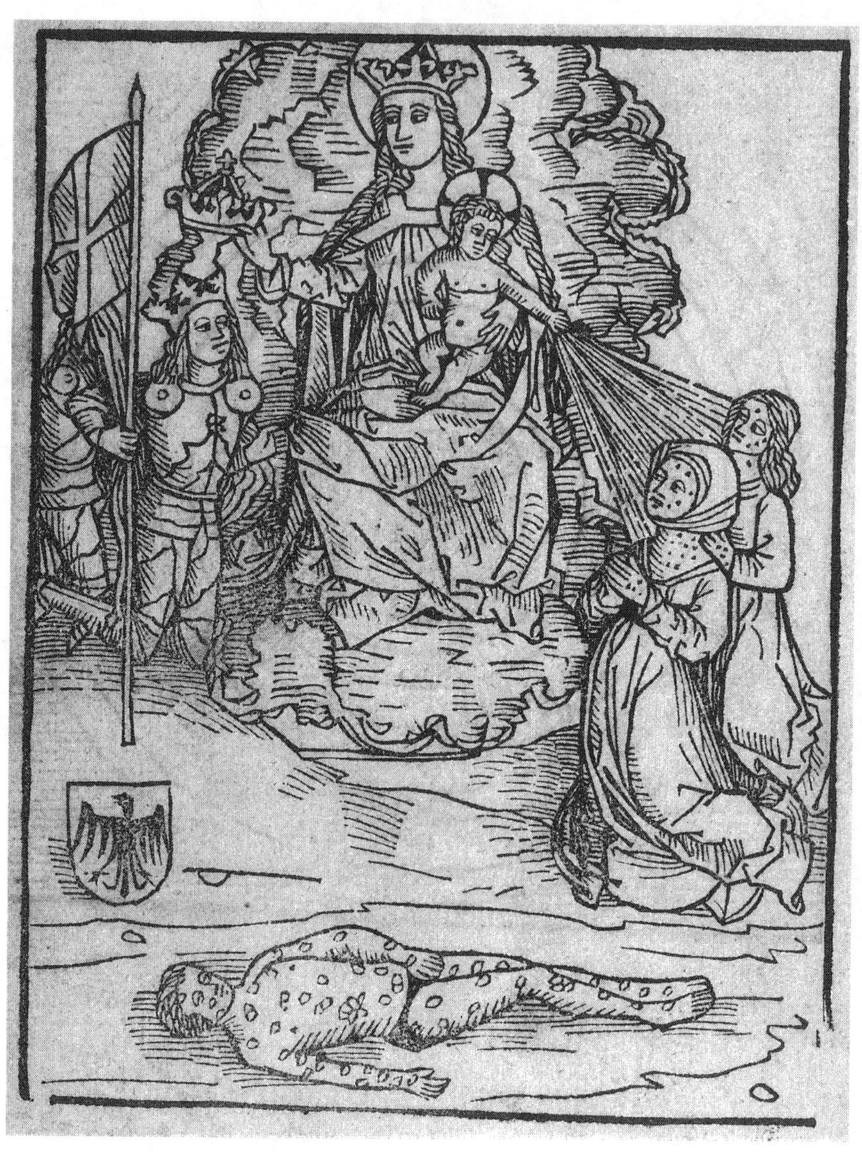

Madonna and Child with syphilis sufferers of both sexes, from Joseph Grunpeck, *Tractatus de pestilentiali scorra sive male de Franzos* (Magdeburg, Germany, 1498). © British Library Board. All rights reserved. IA.6830.

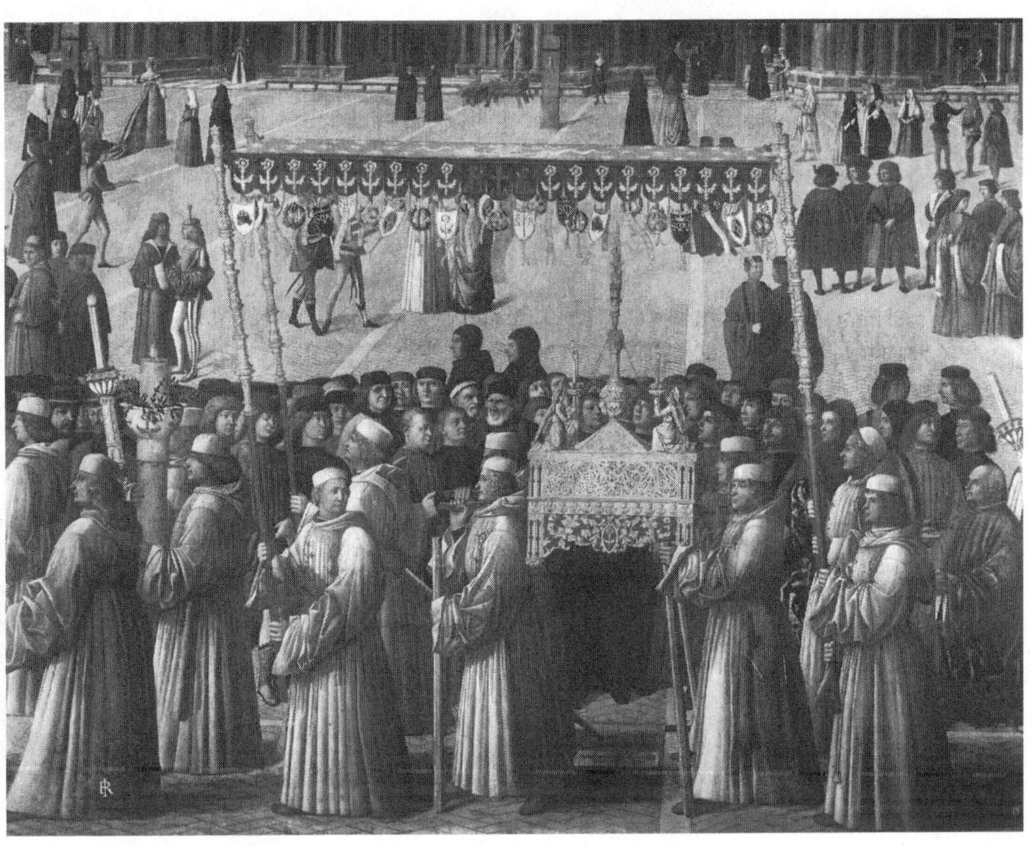

Detail from Gentile Bellini, *Procession in Piazza San Marco,* 1496. Accademia, Venice. The Scuola Grande di San Giovanni Evangelista proudly carries its relic of the True Cross in the annual procession on the feast day of St. Mark. Hanging from the baldachin are the coats of arms of all the scuole grandi. Visible in the background are Venetian men and women, German merchants, Greek priests, beggars, and young members of the compagnia della calza. Photo by Anderson, 11681.

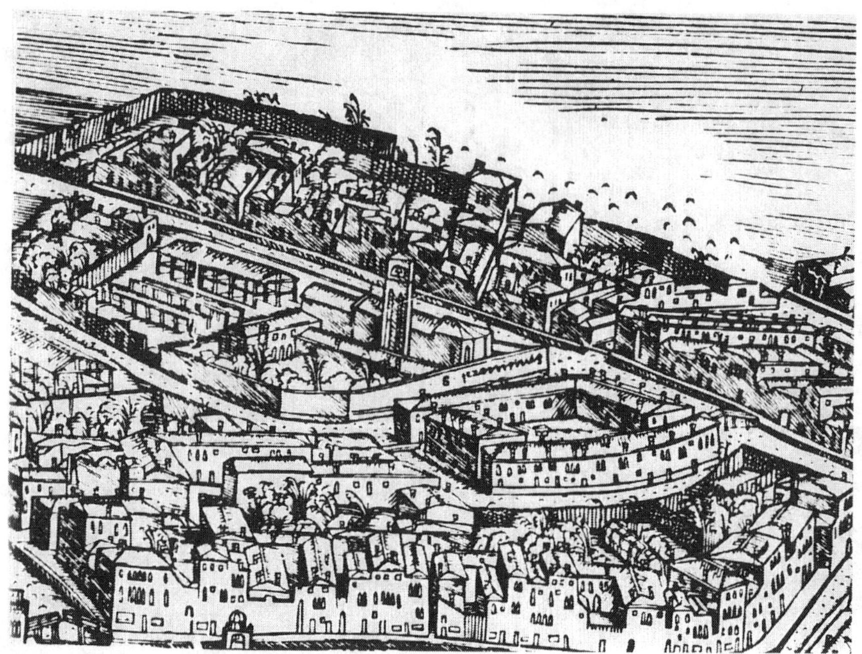

Ghetto Nuovo, detail from Jacopo de' Barbari, *View of Venice*, woodcut, 1500. Photo by Osvaldo Bohm, 916A.

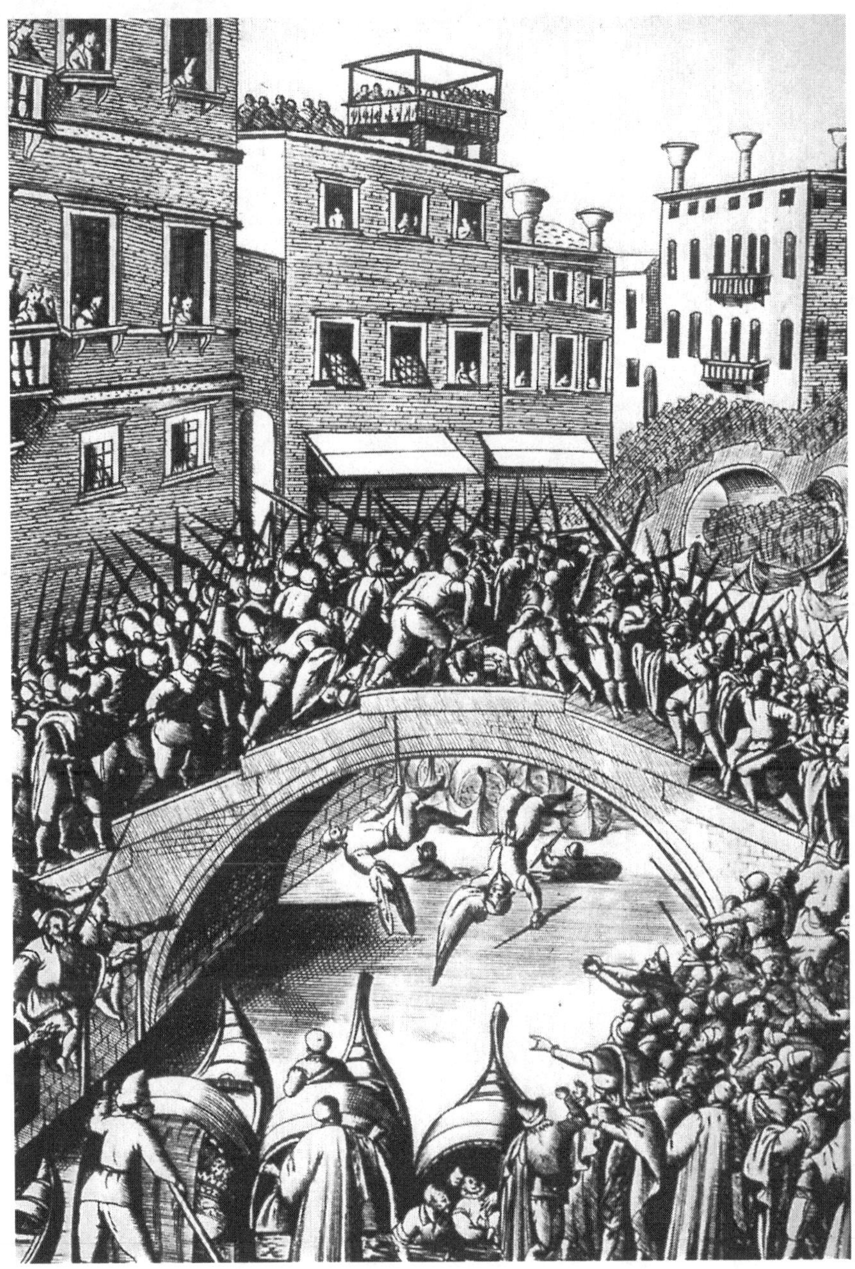

Giacomo Franco, *Fistfight at the Ponte dei Pugni,* from his *Habiti d'huomeni et donne venetiane. . .* (Venice, 1610).

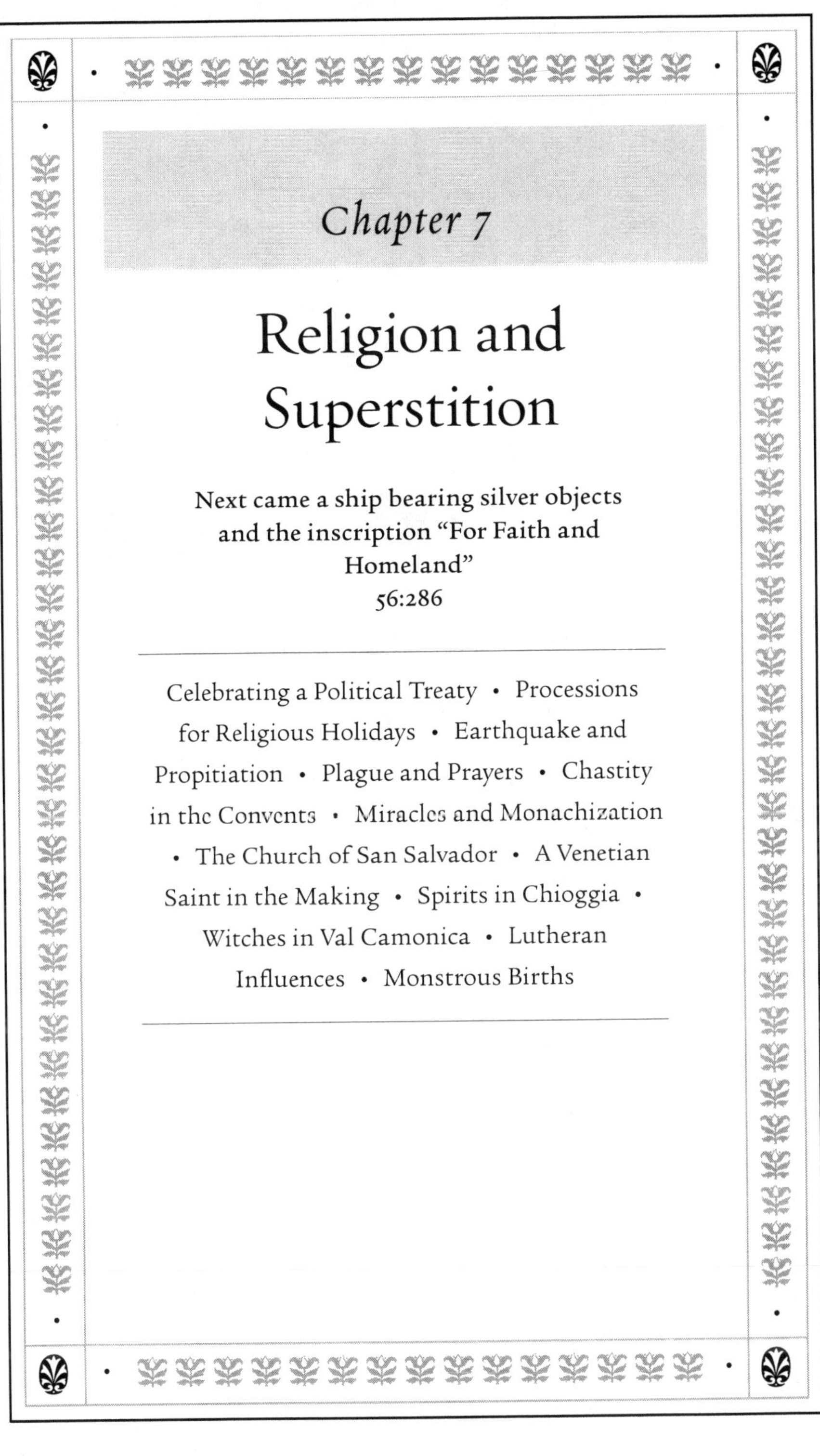

Chapter 7

Religion and Superstition

Next came a ship bearing silver objects
and the inscription "For Faith and
Homeland"
56:286

Celebrating a Political Treaty · Processions
for Religious Holidays · Earthquake and
Propitiation · Plague and Prayers · Chastity
in the Convents · Miracles and Monachization
· The Church of San Salvador · A Venetian
Saint in the Making · Spirits in Chioggia ·
Witches in Val Camonica · Lutheran
Influences · Monstrous Births

According to some early historians and mythmakers of the city, Venice was founded on March 25 in the year AD 421, the day of the Annunciation. Divine providence, so the story went, had led a group of Paduans who were fleeing from foreign invasions to the safety of the lagoons, where, again by divine guidance, a great city slowly arose. Such a miraculous creation built upon the sea would be preserved only so long as it in turn preserved its Christian devotion and morals. Even later Venetian historians, while adducing other accounts of the city's origins, endorsed its religious and moral obligations as its best defense and protection.[1]

Religion, therefore, with its spiritual commitments, its charitable offices, and its rituals, was at the heart of the Venetian Republic. In addition to the prescribed church holidays, some form of religious ceremony was part of every political, social, and civic celebration. The churches in Venice were many and splendid, the religious orders were active and powerful, and the scuole, those religious-social guilds for the citizenry, played important roles in the ceremonial life of the city.[2]

Moreover, through this major international metropolis and gateway to the East there was an incessant flow of prelates, preachers, and pilgrims. These itinerants, like the letters from ambassadors, merchants, and travelers, brought news and rumors from mainland Italy: reports of monstrous births and prophecies. All these are described by Sanudo, as are the great catastrophes within the city—the earthquake of 1511 and the plague—seen by many as divine retribution for the sins of the age. Other kinds of tremors, such as those caused by the Lutheran revolt in Germany, were felt more slowly. But occasionally Venice itself was visited by fiery preachers, at least one of whom was considered tainted by the northern heresy.

Sanudo's own interest in these phenomena was great: he reports everything, not without discrimination, praising ceremonies and sermons that promoted the spiritual pride of Venetians and the cohesiveness of their civic life and rejecting those that were disruptive. Certain prophecies and signs he relates without comment; on others, he expresses his doubts. He was moved by ceremony, both political and spiritual, and appears to have been pious. Like most of his Venetian

---

1. The holiness of this day is affirmed by Sanudo on 25 March 1530 (53:72), when he conflates the foundation of the city at Rialto not only with the Annunciation but also with the formation of the world, the Crucifixion, and the reedification of the church of San Salvador in 1507.

2. On the scuole, see chapter 6.

contemporaries, he took for granted the Christian framework and foundations of his daily life, just as he automatically identified each diary entry with whichever saint might be associated with that day. But because his attention was attracted by the exceptional, his diaries convey less of the normal and steady cycle of religious observance, the ordinary sacramental life of the parish, the daily devotions, or the deep piety that observed the boundaries of decorum and went unnoticed because it was so basic to the life of the Venetians. It is against this background that the extravagant ceremonies, the unusual preachers, and the unorthodox behavior, beliefs, and phenomena must be set.

Celebrating a Political Treaty

In 1511, two years after the grievous military losses caused by the War of the League of Cambrai and the diplomatic isolation that defeat betokened, Venice had begun to recover its mainland territories and cobbled together an alliance with some of its former foes: the papacy and the kings of Spain and England. The elaborate celebration and procession that surrounded the proclamation of this league involved the entire population of the city and many of its subject territories. Although the procession was prompted by a political triumph, it was a triumph sanctioned by spiritual affirmation and serves here to introduce the role of religion in Venice, intimately interwoven as it was with the political and social fabric of the city.

All the themes of this chapter are here set forth: the city's special relationship to Christ through St. Mark, whose powerful protection was continually invoked, visually and ceremonially; the city's consequent sense of its own sanctity as a holy city, *civitas sancta,* and its claim to have served, from its very foundation, as sanctuary from the ultramontane "barbarian" invaders; the procession itself, in which patricians and populace celebrated their relationship to God, whose intercession would secure their victory over hostile forces, whether spiritual or political, and certify their purity, power, and endurance against whatever was unorthodox, deformed, or destructive of the Venetian glory.

October 20, 1511 (13:130)   This morning, Monday, October 20,[3] was the day chosen for the procession in Piazza San Marco and the proclamation of the league, because twice before, last Wednesday and yesterday, which was Sunday, the order to perform the ceremonies had been posted, but because of rain they were put off until today. And so they took place, as will be noted below. First, all the shops in town were closed and remained so all day today.[4]

---

3. The Fulin edition has *October 10,* which is incorrect.

4. Sanudo always specifies those holidays and festivals when the shops were closed, a sign of the importance attributed to the occasion.

Before daybreak the bells in San Marco and in all the parishes began to ring in celebration. At an early hour the streets were teeming with people headed for Piazza San Marco, which quickly filled up. So did the balconies of the houses around that Piazza, where the procession was to pass and where viewing stands were constructed. There was an enormous throng of people; in addition to the usual inhabitants of this city, there were many outsiders, both men and women. The most numerous were those from Vicenza and other places who had fled here to escape the barbaric persecutions [of the war], as if [Venice] were their safest haven. Indeed, Vicenza is almost empty. Also present were inhabitants of Padua and Treviso, many of whom are staying in Venice.

There follows a passage describing first the decoration of the Campanile and facades of the Basilica of San Marco and the Ducal Palace with the banners of Venetian military and political leaders and then the cloths and treasures on display within the church, where religious ceremonies were held and the great procession began. Throughout the text a kind of guidebook didacticism is evident, a reminder that the diarist was explaining Venetian rituals to the Venetians themselves and to others requiring instruction in Venetian history.

October 20, 1511 (13:131–32)[5]   The interior of the Basilica of San Marco was splendidly decorated. First, the [statues of] all the Apostles above the choir were dressed in silk chasubles.[6] A length of gold brocade served as a wall hanging. The pulpits were adorned with crimson velvet embroidered in gold, as is the custom; the cloth was taken from the tent that was made for His Serenity, Doge Cristoforo Moro, when he departed aboard a galley for the crusade.[7] The choir around the high altar was decorated with the gold cloths that are presented by the doges to the church, while the Pala d'Oro,[8] studded with jewels of enormous value, stood open upon the high altar. The two roses that Pope Sixtus IV and Pope Alexander VI sent to our Signoria were affixed above the wrought-iron gate to this chapel.[9] And above the altar of St.

---

5. The following excerpts in this section are sequential, and like the preceding excerpt, all are dated 20 October 1511.

6. The manuscript has *pianee;* the Fulin edition has *pianede.*

7. Cristoforo Moro, doge from 1462 to 1471, undertook to participate personally in a crusade along with Pope Pius II, but the death of the latter upon his arrival in Ancona in 1464 dissolved the enterprise.

8. The famous gold and jewel-encrusted screen still visible in the Basilica of San Marco today.

9. These golden roses were ceremonial symbols of papal favor, distributed on special occasions with much fanfare. Pope Sixtus IV had sent one to Doge Andrea Vendramin in 1476, and Pope Alexander VI had sent one to Doge Agostino Barbarigo in 1495. It was appropriate that they should be prominently displayed in a ceremony celebrating a renewed entente between Venice and the papacy.

Mark, which is made of silver, were silver crosses and candleholders embedded with beautiful jewels and the crown[10] that has recently been found in the Procuratia.[11] Not displayed today were the other jewels of St. Mark that are usually exhibited on the feast of the Ascension, that is, the pectorals, crowns, carbuncles, and unicorn horns, etc.[12] Such items usually are not displayed on a day like this because once they have been put out, the procurators of the church are obliged to sit next to them to guard them, but today they are going to accompany the Signoria in the procession. The chair upon which the doge was to sit was decorated with cloth of gold, as was the spot where he kneels in front of the altar of San Climente, the usual place that doges and ambassadors occupy during such processions. Women and others filled the pews of the church. Once the patricians had gathered at the Ducal Palace, His Serenity the doge proceeded into the church with a distinguished retinue that I will describe below. No sooner had he arrived than the most reverend Antonio Contarini, our patriarch of Venice, began to celebrate a Solemn Mass in a grand ceremony accompanied by vocal and instrumental music.[13] When it was over, the procession was allowed to enter the church. As is customary, it was led into the church by the first scuola to arrive in the Piazza, which entered the choir and passed in front of the doge. Upon leaving the church, the procession wound around Piazza San Marco, starting at the door to the Ducal Palace. The procession did honor to the city and is worthy of being recorded, and it took place with the great pleasure and jubilation of the city. Therefore I will explain here exactly how it was organized.

Each of the five scuole grandi, with its attendants, reliquaries, and relics, is described in turn. Two of the five descriptions are given below. Included in the descriptions are the religious apparel and objects that emphasize the demonstrable spiritual and material wealth of the city's religious organizations and therefore of the city itself:

---

10. The manuscript has a word after *corona,* possibly *conzilij* (*con gigli,* "with lilies"), which is omitted in the Fulin edition.

11. See below for the discovery of this crown and jewels at the time of the earthquake a few months earlier, in the spring of 1511.

12. At this time the treasury of San Marco contained three highly prized "unicorn horns," the most recent of which had been acquired a year earlier. See Gallo 1967, 267–69. These horns, in actuality tusks of a male narwhale, were symbols of purity and religion, for common belief held that only a virgin could approach and capture a unicorn. (The identification of Venice with the "inviolate Virgin" is suggested here.) The dust of these horns was considered an antidote for every sort of poison. The carbuncles were red precious stones.

13. Only by invitation and on special occasions did the patriarch, whose episcopal church, San Pietro di Castello, was located in the eastern corner of the city, come to the doge's chapel, the Basilica of San Marco, to celebrate Mass.

October 20, 1520 (13:132–33, 134–35) First of all came the Scuola di la Misericordia bearing gilded double candleholders with —— wax torches in them and the standard of the scuola, then twenty-seven little boys dressed like angels, all carrying silver objects in their hands, while others bore the arms of the league, that is, of the pope, the king of Spain, the king of England, and St. Mark, who represents our government. Next came fifty-eight flagellants [*batudi*] arranged in pairs carrying in their hands various silver objects, such as pastry trays, vessels, and basins [*confetiere, ramini et bazili*].[14] These were followed by an icon carried on a little platform, sheltered by an umbrella. This icon had belonged to Cardinal Nicenus, who gave it to that scuola when he was a papal legate here.[15] Next came the hand of Saint Theodosia encased in silver, followed by the thorn from the crown of Christ, housed in a tabernacle and also carried on a small platform and sheltered by an umbrella whose ribs were made of silver. Following that came more flagellants carrying beautiful silver objects, among which I spied an elaborately worked hand-held cross and a silver ship decorated with everything that a ship requires and weighing —— marks. Last came a large number of flagellants with their green candles in their hands.

Among the five scuole described, the Scuola di San Rocho was notable for its elaborate tableaux, carried on platforms upon which religious, symbolic, and contemporary figures were represented, displaying pertinent legends. Several of these represented Venice in different roles and guises—as blessed by the Holy Spirit, as supplicant of St. Mark, as attended by Peace and Mercy, as Justice:

October 20, 1511 (13:134) They were followed by the Scuola di San Rocho, carrying their gilded candleholders and crucifix. Since the scuola does not have a standard, they next carried an umbrella that sheltered a small platform bearing a tabernacle with the finger of San Rocho. That scuola has his body, which they put on public display. There were also four Greek icons of silver and mosaic. . . . Next came the flagellants, carrying a large basket lined in crimson satin piled high with silver objects of great weight, that is, pastry trays, vessels, basins, and such silver pieces. These were followed by a silver tray surmounted by a horse and rider,[16] also in silver, with an inscription that read "Zuan Paulo Baion."[17] Next came two other baskets full of silver items, and finally twenty-eight little [children dressed as] angels, walking

---

14. The objects carried by the flagellants turn up frequently in this and other religious processions, here as silver vessels demonstrating the wealth of the scuola.

15. On Cardinal Bessarion (Nicenus), see chapter 8.

16. The manuscript has *uno homo a cavallo;* the Fulin edition has *uno homo e cavallo.*

17. Recently made governor general of the Venetian army.

two by two and carrying silver objects. They were followed by two beautiful, elaborately decorated Parisian-style silver coffers, which were quite large,
then two large silver goblets,[18] containing two crocodiles [*do cocodrili dentro*].[19]
Following them on foot came a figure dressed to resemble Justice and carrying a sword and silver scales. Next appeared a life-size wooden statue of San
Rocho dressed in a gold mantle and preceded by [a young boy dressed as] an
angel. Then came flagellants carrying six large basins; they were followed by
trumpets and a platform upon which was seated a figure of St. Mark dressed
as an apostle, in front of which stood a clothed woman representing Venice.
[Above her was] a little dove[20] representing the Holy Spirit; it carried a scroll
in its beak that read, in Latin, "I have seen your tears."[21] The figure of Venice carried another scroll that read, "I give thanks to you because you have
shown me everything." St. Mark carried another scroll, whose comforting inscription was directed toward [the figure of] Venice: "Do not fear to confront
them for I am with you." The float also bore two young handmaidens. One
was Peace, who carried this scroll: "God has restored peace to us." The other
was Mercy, whose scroll read: "The city is full of the mercy of God." Preceding the platform was a gold banner with an image of St. Mark to show that it
symbolized Venice.[22] Then came a platform carrying the king of England on
horseback, a remarkable sight, with a scroll reading, "Fear not: I will multiply
your seed and your city." Next came another[23] platform bearing a ship, and
its legend read: "Fear not, for the wind has ceased." Then came the king of
Spain on horseback; he too had a scroll, which read, "I have never found so
much faith as was and abides in you." Next came the fourth platform, with
the pope, who was seated, and two cardinals, one standing on each side of
his chair. The king of France stood before him enveloped in gilded flames; his
scroll read: "Help me, O Lord, for I am being tortured in this flame."[24] The
pope responded by saying, "Why has your faith grown cold?" One cardinal's
scroll read, "It would have been good,"[25] while the other's read, "Had he not
been born." The pope wore a miter and a cope of gold brocade. Borne along
on one of these platforms was the world in the form of a globe and a woman

---

18. The manuscript has *do cope grande;* the Fulin edition has *do cape grande.*

19. The coffers were decorated *a la Paresina,* "in the Parisian style," a term of refinement that
connoted exaggerated elegance.

20. The manuscript has *pareva che una colombina;* the Fulin edition has *pareva con una
colombina.*

21. From 2 Kings 20:5: "Thus saith the Lord, . . . I have heard thy prayer, I have seen thy tears.
Behold, I will heal thee." All of the scrolls were in Latin.

22. In all likelihood, this image was of the lion of St. Mark.

23. The manuscript has *altro;* the Fulin edition omits it.

24. The king of France was still Venice's enemy.

25. The manuscript has *bonus;* the Fulin edition has *bonum.*

dressed as Justice, a magnificent sight. The platforms were decorated around the edges with various silver items of great value; they were followed by the flagellants carrying ash-colored torches rather than candles in their hands.

After the scuole came the monastic communities, such as those described here, displaying their wealth, both material, such as objects of silver, and spiritual, such as holy relics:

October 20, 1511 (13:137)   Next came the Servite friars and the friars of San Jacomo on the Giudecca, one by one, numbering fifty. Thirty-four of them were dressed in copes and [vestments] to celebrate Mass. They carried many of their silver items and relics, crowns of Our Lady, and tabernacles. Indeed, they have very beautiful things, including a large silver bust of St. John the pope and martyr[26] and another bust of about the same size, which is of St. Mary Cleophe[27] and which was carried in a large chalice. All in all, these friars were well appointed with various kinds of relics.

Some of the monastic communities displayed, in addition to their silver and relics, the special relationship Venice claimed to the Savior, with whom it traditionally shared the same day of conception, March 25.

October 20, 1511 (13:137)   The friars of San Stephano and San Cristoforo di la Pace came next in single file, numbering sixty. First came the young friars, twenty-eight in number; they were dressed in surplices and carried various silver objects, that is, basins, pastry trays, and goblets . . . , and clothed statues of saints decked with jewels, among which I noted a small St. Hironimo dressed as a cardinal with a cardinal's hat on his head. Next came the friars wearing vestments, thirty in number, who carried chalices, tabernacles, and other relics. Among these [relics] I spied two heads in chalices, which were said to belong to two of the 12,000 virgins [who accompanied Saint Ursula]. Borne on a small platform came a beautiful cross . . . with other crosses, silver items, and chalices upon it. And then came six friars wearing Mass vestments; their chasubles were all embroidered with pearls of great value, and they carried silver objects in their hands. A platform bearing the seated pope appeared next, with the two kings of the league flanking[28] him. A small manger scene was also included, and pastry trays were placed along the edges.

---

26. Pope John I (AD 523–26).

27. Mary, wife of Cleophas, who stood, according to John 19:25, at the foot of the Cross with the mother of Jesus and Mary Magdalen.

28. The manuscript reads *per lai,* for *per lati,* meaning "at the sides"; the Fulin edition has *per cai.*

Finally, there came twenty elderly friars who are masters in theology; they carried candles in their hands and were dressed in their usual black habits; they are called elsewhere Heremitani.

Included in addition were 110 Dominican preachers, followed by those having theological degrees; numerous reliquaries, including two arms, one of St. Luke the Evangelist and one of St. Matthew the Evangelist, both "with pens in their hands" (13:139); various groups of canons, the nine congregations of the clergy (13:140), the chapter of San Marco, followed by the doge and other dignitaries. The procession made its way to the Pietra del Bando, where the league was publicly proclaimed to the cries of the crowd, the blaring of brass instruments, and an artillery salute.

October 20, 1511 (13:141–42)   At this point the doge exited the church, and the bells of San Marco began their usual peal. The procession made its way to the Pietra dil Bando, where such accords are normally made public. Many trumpets and battle trumpets having sounded and then fallen silent, the league was proclaimed by Baptista, the steward of the Zudegà di Proprio, as [the document] had been consigned to him by Gasparo di la Vedoa, the doge's secretary.[29] A copy of it will be included below. The announcement concluded to great cheers of "Long live St. Mark" [*Viva missier San Marco*], the playing of a wind band, and the booming of artillery from the ships that were in port. While music continued to play in the Piazza San Marco, following the procession as it made its way around the square were. . . .[30]

The entire celebration was both an affirmation and an assertion of Venetian glory to hearten the Venetians themselves and to send a message of strength to those who lived in the Venetian dominion, so recently challenged and now being recovered.

October 20, 1511 (13:144)   The procession that began at sixteen hours ended at twenty-one hours to the great jubilation and happiness of the entire city and the confounding of the rebels.[31] It is worth noting that the Vicentines re-

29. On the Giudici del Proprio, see appendix B under "Governmental Terms." For Gaspare dalla Vedova, later grand chancellor, see chapter 6.

30. Here Sanudo lists the participants in the procession: government officials, young women, musicians, men carrying relics, prelates, and scores of patricians. The list occupies seven columns.

31. These rebels were the inhabitants of the cities of the mainland domain who had rebelled against Venice after its loss to the French army at Agnadello in May 1509, and had allied themselves with Emperor-elect Maximilian.

joiced greatly, being true partisans of Venice.[32] Indeed, the Vicentine knights who are here wished to participate in the procession dressed in gold, to honor this day and to express their great joy; but the Signoria let them know that they were not to come because of the danger that the enemy would rise up and burn Vicenza, and so they did not come. After the procession, the Piazza was so full of people and the streets were so tightly packed that those who wished to leave and go home found it impossible to move. So people had to wait until the crowd thinned out.[33]

Processions for Religious Holidays

More regular than the celebrations of exceptional political events such as the proclamation of the league of 1511 were the feast days of the Venetian year. Among these was the feast of Corpus Christi, celebrated in the late spring; even in this ceremony honoring the sacrificial body of Christ the secular presence was visible and strong.[34] Indeed, the intimate connection between religion and a defeated and vulnerable state was demonstrated in the measures taken to protect the city during this feast day in the grim month after the rout at Agnadello and in the absence of splendid objects, costumes, or a rejoicing audience:

June 7, 1509 (8:372–73)   It was the feast of Corpus Christi, on which there is a solemn procession in San Marco, and so it was done. But first the heads of the Ten ordered that there should be no ladies on the balconies of the Piazza, nor should any children or women be allowed inside the Piazza. Instead, there were about one thousand men armed with swords and shields and breast-plates under their cloaks, and twenty of these, under the [command of the] six deputies and the captains, were posted at the corners of the Piazza, where the entrances are, to watch those entering the Piazza. And this was started at an early hour. The scuole processed, and the friars, but not those of San Zorzi Mazor [San Giorgio Maggiore], who had all left the city; then the priests and canons without silver objects, but well vested, although not sumptuously; then came the body of Christ under its canopy and the patriarch wearing

---

32. Sanudo calls these loyal Vicentines *marcheschi*, i.e., followers of St. Mark.

33. This long description—it took up nineteen columns in Sanudo's diaries—concluded with an individualized listing of the 130 patricians who participated in these celebrations, telling which of them wore *scarlato* and which of them wore *seta*, clues to the differentiating role of costume upon which Sanudo often commented. See appendix B under "Fabrics and Garments"; and Newton 1988, 18.

34. See Vicentini 1990, esp. 385, on the institution of the feast of Sacro Santo Corpore di Christo in the thirteenth century and its celebration in the sixteenth century. See also Sanso-vino 1968, 511.

vestments. This is the first time he has said Mass in San Marco.[35] Then the doge, dressed in crimson velvet, followed him, trembling, between ser Bortolo Minio and ser Nicolò Pixani, councillors. The area encircling the Signoria was full of these armed men, for fear of disturbances, which gave the city much to talk about. Nevertheless, it was said that there would be an uprising, and many avoided going to the Piazza. There were few patricians with the Signoria, nearly all of them dressed in purple,[36] with about eight in scarlet and others wearing black. There were no pilgrims, as there usually are on this occasion.

Even two years later, on June 19, 1511 (12:243), only a few months before the league was proclaimed, the Corpus Christi procession was a sorry sight, "without angels, or platforms, and very few pieces of silver [displayed], because they had been melted down and used in the mint." All this was to change by the following October, when the new league of 1511 was celebrated.

Over the succeeding years, Sanudo reported on a number of Corpus Christi and other processions, commenting on the doge's presence, his costume and bearing, the important attendees and their dress, the participating scuole and the platforms and candles they carried, the size of the crowd, and the presence of pilgrims. On June 23, 1519 (27:404), he notes that apart from the patriarch, there were no other bishops with white miters, "as there used to be," and that of the seventy-two patricians attending, only eighteen wore scarlet cloth. "All the rest wore [black] silk, which provided a meager spectacle. There were many pilgrims, so that every patrician was preceded by one and followed by several more, even though some had already left" for the Holy Land.[37]

Later, the more sumptuous festivities returned, and toward the end of the diaries Sanudo notes about a Corpus Christi procession that Christ himself was represented, along with the Venetian ship of state and its blazon, "For faith and homeland," which might appropriately epitomize the Venetian relationship with God:

May 30, 1532 (56:285–86)   May 30, Thursday, was the feast of Corpus Christi. His Serenity the doge, dressed in gold brocade and wearing a corno of beauti-

---

35. Antonio Contarini, elected patriarch by the Senate on 17 November 1508, had been consecrated as patriarch on 4 February 1509. See above, n. 13, on his celebrating Mass in the Basilica of San Marco.

36. A color worn on solemn occasions.

37. So proud were Venetians of the solemnity and the beauty of their Corpus Christi processions that only a few weeks later the Venetian ambassador in Rome (who had not witnessed this last "meager spectacle") commented that the papal procession, "if one took away the majesty of pope and cardinals, is, in my opinion, less solemn and less beautiful than our beautiful [processions] that are held in Venice." Diaries, 13 July 1519 (27:469).

ful iridescent gold cloth, received the ambassadors and others but then did not wish to attend the church services, so as not to tire himself. Ser Polo Donado, the councillor, dressed in crimson velvet, served as the vice-doge,[38] accompanied by the ambassadors from the Empire, France, England, and Milan, the one from Ferrara being absent from the city, the bishop of Baffo, the bishop of Chisamo, Veia, and Puola,[39] and ser Gasparo Malipiero, councillor, dressed in plain black cloth,[40] in all ——. Absent were ——.

A very stately mass was celebrated by the bishop of Traù, whose family name is Scardona. Only forty-one pilgrims attended, and the Scuola di San Rocho put on a fine procession. First came twenty-four gilded candleholders, each with two large wax torches, for a total of forty-eight candles, then a platform bearing silver objects, then three platforms with [scenes from] the Old Testament, the twelve patriarchs, then a wheel with six putti on it that turned around, which was quite a sight. There were also thirty-three pairs of flagellants carrying silver objects. The other scuole had nothing but angels. Also there were the friars of San Zane Polo [Santi Giovanni e Paolo] with platforms, upon one of which were Adam and Eve, represented as naked children; upon the other was Christ with the four religious orders beneath him: the Franciscans, the Dominicans, the Carmelites, and the Augustinians. And Christ recited a few verses. Next came a ship bearing silver objects and the inscription "For faith and homeland" [*Pro fide et patria*]. It was followed by representatives of the scuole, sixteen each, in gowns with full, gathered sleeves. There were eighty of them in single file, carrying wax torches each weighing eighteen libre. Then came the rest of the procession, which was over at sixteen hours. The weather was good, and it was not too hot.

But the civic element remained equally powerful, for these processions were never merely commemorative but served as barometers of the current mood and portents of things to come. In the procession described in the following excerpt, the very splendor of the accoutrements served to impress the diplomatic corps and even evoked some criticism from the Turkish ambassador, who may have resented the insistent self-advertisement of the procession even as he sported his own finery for the occasion.

June 15, 1525 (39:77–78)   Today was the feast of Corpus Christi. . . . His Serenity the doge, dressed in cloth of gold with a mantle of crimson satin and a crimson corno, entered the Basilica of San Marco with the ambassadors

---

38. That is, he was the senior councillor.

39. Pafo, Veglia, and Pola.

40. The manuscript has *zambeloto, nº,* for *zambeloto negro;* the Fulin edition has *zambeloto, numero.*

of the papacy, England, Austria, Milan, Ferrara, and Mantua. The imperial ambassador was absent because he was ill. Following them came the ducal councillors together with the nephew of the king of England [Reginald Pole], who is studying in Padua, and ser Jacomo da Pexaro, the bishop of Baffo. Accompanying the councillors were some pilgrims, of whom the two important people were ——. Four procurators attended: ser Alvise Pasqualigo, ser Andrea Gusoni, ser Marco da Molin, and ser Francesco di Prioli.[41] Then there were many other patricians dressed in silk, each one accompanied by a pilgrim, as is the custom.[42] Our patriarch, who usually dresses in the habit of his order, celebrated the mass and wore pontifical vestments.[43] Although the procession took place on a workday, the Scuola di San Rocho had quite a few platforms, etc. And the Turkish ambassador went up to the top of the Basilica with ser Todaro Paleologo to observe the procession, which went on until quite late.

It is worth mentioning that many believed that the Turkish ambassador's presence atop the Basilica was a bad omen, and especially because only two of the usual three standards could be flown today, one of them being broken. . . . The ambassador said to Paleologo, who served as his interpreter, that while he liked to watch people, he did not like this procession, and he particularly disliked the parading about of all those objects. He was told that these objects related to the laws of the Old Testament, and he replied, "Are they not written down? So why carry them around?" Then he said that he would have liked to watch a joust in the Piazza. He was told that horses are not used in this city but that in earlier times jousts had been held and that many noblemen had come from all over Italy to participate and to watch. Then he went on to other topics. All [his business] had been expedited on Saturday, and he was wearing the clothes that were given to him [as ceremonial gifts]. He will appear before the Collegio to take his leave; it is believed that he will depart after Monday, the 19th of this month.[44]

---

41. There were as many as twenty-two procurators in 1525 (see diaries, 37:471), although traditionally there had been only nine. The office had been made available for loans to the government during the War of the League of Cambrai. See Finlay 1980b, 180–81; and, for loans and elections in May 1516, diaries, 22:214–15, 219–21, 223, 227–28.

42. Pilgrims in Venice of pilgrims en route to Jerusalem were made part of this religio-civic celebration. Those who were *signori* walked behind the ambassadors, and the others went one by one as ranked by the state attorneys. Diaries, 11 June 1517 (24:347–48). On Corpus Christi processions, see Vicentini 1990, 385–86.

43. Girolamo Querini, patriarch of Venice from 1524 to 1554, was a Dominican and generally insisted on wearing his plain monk's robe, of which Sanudo disapproved. Diaries, 2 August 1525 (34:271).

44. This Turkish ambassador has been identified as "Chaius Heinechen," elsewhere described by Sanudo as having a dark complexion (diaries, 39:23). His may have been in ill humor on this occasion precisely because such displays served to assert Venetian power and because of their

Religious processions were organized not only on feast days and to celebrate political events but also in conjunction with natural disasters, frightful visions, or events seen as divine punishment for the sins of humanity. In such cases, the procession was a form of penance, together with fasting, prayer, and preaching to placate the divine wrath. Sanudo's narrative of the earthquake of 1511 interweaves, into a description of physical devastation, the moralizing attitudes of those who experienced this catastrophe even as he disassociated himself from identifying a "phenomenon of nature" with supernatural forces.

Earthquake and Propitiation

March 26, 1511 (12:79–80)   Today, March 26, Wednesday, at twenty hours and three quarters, the weather being somewhat unsettled, an earthquake suddenly hit this city of Venice. It was so powerful that it felt like the houses were collapsing. The chimneys were swaying, the walls bursting open, the bell towers tottering, things on high were tumbling down, and the water in the canals—even the Grand Canal—was boiling as if it had a fire under it. Indeed, even though it was high tide, people said that some canals ran dry when the earthquake struck, as if there were a great drought. This earthquake lasted as long as a *miserere*,[45] so that it was felt by all and was terrifying, considering how greatly endangered were the inhabitants of this city, unused to such earthquakes, which have not been experienced for many years. The bells in the bell towers, because of the movement of these towers, rang in many places and especially in Piazza San Marco, which was very fearsome. By chance the Senate happened to be in session, deliberating the affairs of this Republic. They had barely entered the chamber and begun to read the first dispatch when they heard the noise and felt the shaking of the room. Everyone rose; the doors were opened; each man headed down the wooden staircase as best he could, with such haste and in such a crush that many, carried along by the crowd,[46] reached the bottom without their feet ever having touched a step of the stair.

For all his fear and astonishment, Sanudo went right to work interpreting the meaning of the event:

---

special claim to divine support. The interpreter, Todaro Paleologo, had been a local magistrate in the service of the Turkish government before his service to the Venetian government.

45. Psalm 50 in the Vulgate, asking for God's mercy. Comparing the length of this event to that of a prayer captures the religious import of the event.

46. The manuscript appears to have the following punctuation: *tanto era la calcha. Dove seguite cosse . . . ;* the Fulin edition has the period after *seguite.*

In the midst of all this, some events occurred that are worthy of being record-ed: first of all, four marble statues of kings[47] standing upright fell from their place atop the facade of the Basilica of San Marco. Other than this there was little damage to the church, except to a few of the small columns. However, on the side facing the church of San Basso[48] a marble statue of a woman was toppled. This was Prudence, who had stood erect among the other virtues. At the Ducal Palace, the top part of the decorations over the large balcony of the hall of the Great Council fell down. It had been quite tall and included a statue of Justice. But the marble statue of St. Mark stood firm and did not fall. I do not wish to omit the fact that half of the battlement above the hall of the Great Council fell into the middle of the courtyard of the Ducal Pal-ace—the half that is of marble and bears carvings of lilies. The force of the fall drove it into a piece of hard stone at the base of the stone staircase,[49] with the head of the lily pointed down. Many took it as a good omen indicating that the lily, which is the emblem of France, will fall and be ruined. May God so will it for the good of Italy, scourged by these barbarians! Some also took the fall of Prudence to be an omen, and if augurs existed today, they would say, "Take care, take care, Venice; mind you be prudent[50] in these times, for these are evil days. Take no false step as you did two years ago, for if you will not govern yourself wisely, this Republic could suffer great damage. Behold the statue of St. Mark, which has remained intact atop the Ducal Palace; it signifies that this city will remain faithful to Jesus Christ. It will remain the preserver of the Catholic faith, the defender of the church, one who used to love justice. If Justice has fallen, let it now be restored!" Many say that there was no Justice atop the balcony, but I believe there was.[51]

Particularly strange to the city was the silence imposed on the Bell Tower of San Marco, whose bells normally gave rhythm to the Venetian day, while in the other center of the city, Rialto, the cross from San Giacomo di Rialto, knocked over by the tremors, fell onto the portico in an upright position:

---

47. See below, where Sanudo explains that these "kings" were really saints.

48. Now the location of the Piazzetta dei Leoncini. See Lorenzetti 1926, 142.

49. The "hard stone" here referred to is called *pietra viva* or *piera viva* in the text, sometimes identified as a stone quarried on the Dalmatian coast or the Istrian peninsula and used ex-tensively for statues and facades in Venice. See Sanudo 1980, 24, 33; and Sansovino 1968, 383. Generically it indicates a type of stone known for its hardness and worked only with special tools.

50. In the manuscript there is a raised period after *prudente;* it is not present in the Fulin edition.

51. It is typical of Sanudo to engage in wordplay to link the effects of the earthquake to the political-moral situation of the day.

The upper part of the Campanile of San Marco suffered a great deal from the movement; it was so cracked that the next day it was impossible to ring tierce, half-tierce, none, vespers,[52] or any other bell. It has never before happened in this city that a day has passed without the canonical hours being rung. The stones that fell from the top of the Bell Tower smashed the leaden roof of the *loggetta* below, where patricians used to foregather. Moreover, in the Basilica of San Marco a part of the upper mosaic fell, although not much damage was done. At Rialto, an iron cross upon a pedestal of hard stone was knocked down. It had stood atop the church of San Jacomo, and it landed on the leaden roof of the portico, still standing upright. That church was the first in Venice, and its founding on March 25, 421, the anniversary of which was yesterday, initiated the building of the city, then called Rivoalto. So this is a sign that this city will be the savior of Italy and of the Christian faith and will chase the barbarians[53] out of Italy, provided that it is supported in true faith by Italians.

After listing all the other bell towers and chimneys damaged by the earthquake, Sanudo continues:

March 26, 1511 (12:81–82)   In conclusion, the entire city was terrified, but the earthquake was a short one; had it lasted longer, without doubt there would have been great damage and destruction of buildings in this most excellent city, which God founded and has preserved to this day for the enhancement of the Christian faith. The church of the Carità lost the marble statue of Christ, which fell from the front facade. There was damage in other parts of the city, which we will learn about over the course of the day. Everyone was stunned by this frightful event. Some ran out into the public squares, some into the streets, some began to pray, and some did not know what to do. I was at home, and I ran out into the street, which was a bad idea in the midst of such a dangerous thing as this earthquake. Many women were taken ill, and some of them died; fear caused pregnant women to give birth prematurely and without labor pains, among them the wife of ser Thomà Tiepolo, the galley commander—she is the daughter of ser Pancrati Justinian. One noteworthy item is that today Francesco Fasuol, university laureate, who has been elected grand chancellor, made his entrance into the Senate. The four marble "kings" that fell from the Basilica of San Marco are four saints: San Constan-

---

52. See "About the Translation" under "Canonical Hours."
53. The "barbarians" were the French, German, and Spanish troops whose presence in Italy since the invasion of 1494 had been alternately invoked and condemned by the different Italian powers.

tin, San Dimitri, San Zorzi, and San Thodaro, who are all Greek saints and look like kings. Later, in the evening, the parish priests led processions in the parishes, followed by a multitude carrying double and single candles in their hands and singing litanies; it was something very fearful to see. Everyone felt endangered because these earthquakes usually last several days. Last night a number of groups stayed outdoors to sleep, either in boats or in gardens or in the public squares, fearing that the earthquake would return and destroy their homes.

The following day, the patriarch declared the earthquake a sign of God and exhorted the authorities to address the sins of sodomy, incest, and irreligion, as well as the need for more preaching (which had been curtailed to avoid contagion from the plague):

March 27, 1511 (12:84–85)   This morning the entire city was frightened because tremors were again felt twice during the night, that is, yesterday evening at one and a half hours of the night and then at about the eleventh hour, but they were not very strong. Therefore no one talked about anything else, and everyone had something to say. Since the top of the Bell Tower of San Marco suffered a fair amount of damage, including a crack, no bells were rung, neither the Marangona[54] nor half-tierce nor tierce, which has never happened in this city, this silence of the bells, except on Good Friday. . . . Then our patriarch, don Antonio Contarini, appeared [before the Collegio], saying that the earthquake is a sign from God: it is because of our sins that misfortunes afflict us [*Signa Dei, et propter peccata veniunt adversa*]. He said that this city is full of sin, especially sodomy, which is everywhere recklessly committed. The prostitutes have sent him word that they cannot make a living; no one comes to them, so rampant is sodomy. Even old men get themselves worked over [*e fino vechij si fanno lavorar*]. Also, the patriarch has heard from confessors that fathers meddle with their daughters, and brothers with sisters, and so forth. Moreover, the city has become irreligious; the preachers told him that it was wrong to suspend the preaching of the divine word this Lent because the city has recovered from the plague, and it was a bad idea to eliminate sermons. He also said that in other years, by now, halfway through Lent, confessors ordinarily would have heard the confessions of half the city. This year they have heard only the confessions of the female tertiaries,[55] and very few oth-

---

54. See "About the Translation" under "Bells."

55. Female tertiaries—the *pizochere*—were lay women attached to religious orders, sometimes referred to as third-order nuns, who took only simple vows and were not formally bound to a monastic order. See Sperling 1999, 281n54.

ers. Then he said that he wants to order a three-day procession in Piazza San Marco that will pass through the parishes in the evening. He also wants three days of fasting on bread and water to placate God's wrath, and he said some other things. The doge and members of the Collegio praised him and said that measures would be taken to deal with the problem of blasphemy and of bringing people to justice, etc. Today the Council of Ten will make provisions concerning sodomy.

Thus it was ordered that all preachers assigned to churches should preach, beginning tomorrow morning. The patriarch ordered a three-day fast of bread and water and processions singing litanies around the campi in the evening and in Piazza San Marco in the morning. I applaud these measures as far as good habits and religion go, but as far as preventing earthquakes, they accomplish nothing, for these are a phenomenon of nature.[56]

For several days the aftershocks continued, as did the processions and the preaching:

March 28, 1511 (12:87)   I wish to record that this morning at nineteen hours an aftershock was felt, but it did not last long. I was at Santa Lena [Sant'Elena], where I had gone to dine with several patricians. While we were at table we felt the quake, and all of us went into the garden. The quake completed the job of toppling several stones from the decoration over the large balcony of the hall of the Great Council, but there was no other damage.

A meeting of the collegio of the savi had been scheduled for the afternoon, but fear of the earthquake kept all but a few from attending. Everyone was very frightened. Some took to their boats, some to the campi, and some made other provisions, such as sleeping in boats. Today, Friday, is the first day of fasting; thus some had only bread and water and will continue tomorrow and Monday.[57] The processions that were held in the evening in the parishes included both priests and friars, and many people followed them carrying large candles. It should be noted that the churches were full of women and others going to confession. Tierce was rung in the Basilica of San Marco.

Meanwhile, the preachers, invited back to the pulpits and campi, took up their task of reminding their audience of the consequences of their sins, which for some preachers included toleration of the Jews, whose numbers were swelled by Jewish refugees from the Terraferma.

---

56. On the earthquake of 1511, see Chambers and Pullan 1992, 188–89. The translations presented here are based in part on the translations there.

57. The church did not allow fasting on Sundays since by definition Sunday was a feast day.

April 2, 1511 (12:98–99)   During these days, notice was taken of what the friar Rufin Lovato, preaching in the campo of San Polo, said against the Jews: that it would be good to take away everything they had and sack [their houses], because the city is full of Jews who have fled here. Yesterday he preached a lot, and this morning the Jewish bankers Anselm and Vivian, fearing an uprising against them, went to the heads of the Ten to complain about this. The heads went to the Signoria, who decided to admonish this preacher and likewise the ones at the Frari and at San Cascian, who were preaching such things, so that there would be no disturbance against the Jews.

Meanwhile, there was some cause for celebration: the earthquake's damages seem to have led to the discovery of some relics and what had been thought to be lost treasures.

April 5, 1511 (12:104)   After dinner no meetings were held, neither the Great Council nor anything else. This was for fear of the earthquake that people said was supposed to occur.

A solemn procession was held at Castello; participating were the scuole, the clergy, the patriarch, and a very large throng of people. This was because some relics had been found there. A [reliquary in the shape of a] cross that had been made for them was carried in the procession. On top it held a wooden fragment of the True Cross, and underneath, some hairs from the beard of Jesus; on the right arm of the Cross was a stone of the chalice; on the left, one of Christ's nails [from the Crucifixion]; and other relics.

April 6, 1511 (12:106)   I note that in the last few days a strongbox was found in the procuratia of the Basilica of San Marco. This is the procuratia of ser Andrea Venier, ser Antonio Grimani, and ser Andrea Gritti, who is absent. The strongbox is ninety-seven years old and was unopened, and [no one] knows whose it is. Inside were 3,000 ducats of the Foscari era[58] and a jeweled gold crown and other jewels embedded in bands of gold. The total value is about 10,000 ducats, which will be used to rebuild the top of the Bell Tower of San Marco.[59]

Plague and Prayers

More frequent than earthquakes were the periodic visitations of the plague.[60] In their effort to control the spread of the disease, the city's officials had to bal-

---

58. Doge Francesco Foscari (1423–57).

59. Gallo 1967, 42n3, suggests that the contents were saved from the fall of Constantinople (1453) and belonged to private persons who died in that siege. By February 1512 this windfall had been used to gild the Campanile. Gallo cites Priuli, who wrote that one of the procurators of San Marco, Antonio Grimani, had anticipated such a find, "looking everywhere for it."

60. For other excerpts on the plague, see chapter 6.

ance the attraction of propitiatory preaching against the threat of contagion in overcrowded churches. In the excerpt below, churches were ordered closed for a few days before Christmas. On that holiday a Franciscan Observant preacher invited by the doge to preach in San Marco excoriated his Venetian audience—which included the doge, leading officials, and the ambassadors from Spain, Naples, Milan, Monferrato, Rimini, and Pisa, among others—for the sins of the city and the corruption of its institutions, which he said had brought God's retribution upon its inhabitants. Then, to moderate the severity of his sermon, the preacher ended with a light remark:

December 16, 1497 (1:836–37)   In this month and in this city, at San Domenego in Castello, several people died of the plague. The *proveditori sora la sanità*, who are Lunardo Marzelo, Anzolo Trivixan, and Hironimo Bon, took many precautions to make sure that the plague would not spread to the rest of the city; [that it did not] is a miracle, since almost all of Italy has suffered from it, most recently Ravenna, Padua, Treviso, Istria, and the Friuli. Those who are infected but still alive are quarantined in the Lazzaretto, and their things are burned. Now Christmas is approaching, the season in which the city celebrates the papal pardon and holds festivals at the churches of the Madonna di Miracoli and San Zuan Crisostimo. Therefore, on the twenty-second of this month, members of the Senate proposed a bill that [the Venetian government] write to the pope and ask him to grant this pardon at another time of the year and to close churches that draw crowds during the holidays, that is, Madonna di Miracoli, San Zuan Crisostomo, San Fantin, and Santa Maria dil Ponte di la Fava. They did this so that people would not gather, because a woman who died in the Lazzaretto in the last few days confessed that on the feast day of Santa Lucia she had gone, infected with the plague, to the church of Santa Lucia and said that two women from [the nearby parish of] San Marcuola had caught it from her there. The Senate also decided that there would be no preaching for now in any of the churches of this city. They sent word to all of the parish priests that they were not to hear confessions of any sick person without the Senate being informed of it and that the barber-surgeons were not to bleed people.

But on Christmas Day[61] the doge wanted a sermon to be delivered in the Basilica of San Marco, as is the custom. This was done by a certain Fra Thimoteo, from Lucca, of the Observant Franciscans, who had been preaching at San Francesco a la Vigna. He gave a fine sermon. Among other things, he said: "My lords, in keeping the churches closed for fear of the plague, you are acting prudently. But if God wishes [the plague to strike this city], closing the

---

61. Sanudo does not indicate in the text that he is writing this entry after Christmas Day.

churches will be of no avail. You must remedy the causes of the plague, which are the horrendous sins committed in this city: the blasphemy against God and His saints, the sodomitical associations, the infinite number of usurious contracts made at Rialto, and everywhere the selling of justice with decisions in favor of the rich and against the poor.[62] And what is worse, when some nobleman comes to town, you show him the convents, which are not convents but bordellos and public whorehouses. Your Serenity, I know that you are not ignorant and that you are even more aware of these things than I am. Take care! Take care, and you will take care of the plague." Then at the end he asked for forgiveness, saying, "I know, Your Serenity, that you know how to make some excellent stiff caps,[63] so I will come to get one!" And he said it in so pleasant a way that everyone laughed. When he came down from the pulpit, the doge greeted him with good humor.

Chastity in the Convents

The spiritual health of the city was attested to not only by its extravagant processions, its religious festivals, and its support of the Christian teachings of itinerant friars but also by its resident clergy, its multiple parishes, and its many monastic establishments. Among these monastic establishments, certain aristocratic women's convents played a special role. For the nuns in these convents were closely related to the governing class and could serve the state through their piety, purity, and prayer. Conversely, they could create difficulties for the state through a derogation of their religious duties, which their contemporaries equated with sacrilege, a lese majesty against God.

At their best, female convents represented the religious dedication of Venetian society. Such a relationship found expression in ceremonies such as the "wedding" of the doge to every newly appointed abbess of Santa Maria delle Vergini (Virgins), a convent founded and endowed by Doge Pietro Ziani in 1219 and remaining within the doge's right of patronage.[64]

June 14, 1506 (6:353)   Sunday. The doge went with ceremonial galleys to wed the abbess of the Verzene [Vergini]. She is of the Badoer family, and the doge [always] comes to marry the abbess in the year of her installation since the church is under his patronage. He was accompanied by the Signoria and pa-

---

62. These were the standard "sins" preachers cited as responsible for God's disfavor.

63. The manuscript has *sa far;* the Fulin edition has *fa far.* The preacher used the words *belli capelli et bruschi,* probably a reference to the distinctive ducal cap, which doges had made in sumptuous fabrics.

64. This right was known as *ius patronatus* and included the right to appoint its clergy, procurators, and employees.

tricians. They heard Low Mass. Then the patriarch celebrated a High Mass, for which the doge did not stay. And the church was beautifully decorated, more so than any church in the city was ever decorated, at a cost of sixty ducats. And one could go inside as far as the refectory, where more than 500 women and a few men were fed. And [the display on] the credenza was magnificent.[65]

But at their worst, and there were some shocking incidents, the aristocratic female convents might justify Girolamo Priuli's labeling of them as "bordellos and whorehouses" and charging them with the ruin of Venice.[66] This was because these convents for patrician women often housed daughters whose families were unable to provide them with a dowry for an appropriately aristocratic marriage and for whom convent life had to be made agreeable in order to attract them. Among their privileges were the freer reception and entertainment of visitors than a strict enclosure would permit. Such liberties occasionally led to scandalous abuses, and then, as now, the scandal made the news.

February 12, 1506 (6:294)   It should be made known that in the last few days it was learned that the abbess of Ogni Santi, who is no longer abbess, was made pregnant, along with other nuns, by one Father Francesco Persegin, who has been arrested.[67] Thereupon the patriarch, in a great uproar, went to the convent with the state attorneys, who are ser Francesco Orio, ser Hironimo Querini, and ser Antonio Zustignan, a university laureate. They surrounded it with boats full of officials. They intended to seek out the truth. The abbess was arrested, and I will report what comes of it.[68]

---

65. See chapter 6 for other credenza displays. The "wealth" displayed in this symbolic wedding paralleled that of other patrician weddings. For the background to this occasion, see Sansovino 1968, 19–20. Originally called Santa Maria Nuova in Jerusalem, the convent was founded with the mandate that it remain within the patronage of the founding doge's successors; "therefore the Doge ceremonially in person weds the new abbess in recognition of his ancient authority." To confirm the abbess's position, the doge gave her two rings, one with St. Mark's lion on it, the other, a precious sapphire to represent her pastoral office. Ibid., 22; Pedani Fabris 1995, 113–14. The convent of the Vergini was attached to the regular canons of San Marco di Mantova, which may explain why the symbol of St. Mark on one of the rings. See Fabris 1988, 75, 90, 92.

66. For "publici bordelli et publici lupanari," see Priuli 1912–41, 4:34. Shortly thereafter Priuli blamed errant nuns for recent disasters: "Per il peccato gravissimo di queste monache meretrici se indichava fusse proceduto in grande parte la ruina del Statto Veneto" (4:115). Both quotes date from June 1509, shortly after Agnadello.

67. Fois 1989, 168, identifies Francesco Perseghin as the vicar-general of Cardinal Marco Corner. This would have made him a privileged figure in Venice.

68. See Chojnacki 1998a, 72, describing the talismanic role of holy women in Venice, where they were seen as "providing protection and moral validation for the regimes that harbored them."

In combating even the possibility of such scandals, the government sought also to control young male patricians who were accustomed to visiting these convents and who, because of their illicit relationships with nuns, were known as *muneghini,* or frequenters of nuns.

May 25, 1509 (8:307–8)   This morning the cases of several young patricians were brought before the Quarantia Criminal at the request of the state attorneys ser Bernardo Bembo, university laureate and knight, ser Marin Zustignan, and ser Daniel Renier, with Marin Zustignan speaking for the group. The Quarantia decided to arrest them. In the past few months, at the time when the newly elected abbess held her ceremonial meal in the convent of the Celestia, these remained locked in the convent [when the other guests departed] and, to a wind band, danced all night with the nuns. This is against the law for the nuns and for the *muneghini* as well. Thus it was decided that they should be arrested. There are sixteen of them....[69] I will write down later what becomes of them, but in my opinion this was not the time to stir up these things. It should be noted that nothing came of it.

Sanudo's closing comment that the time was not propitious for this investigation refers to the fact that only eleven days earlier Venice had suffered the crushing defeat at the battle of Agnadello. That is why he adds, in what appears to be a later note, "0 fu poi" (zero happened later). But in the Senate a month later, severe measures were proposed. The details of these measures reveal how difficult it was to implement these strictures against aristocratic resistance:

June 29, 1509 (8:454–56)   Preserving all our laws[70] and ordinances in this matter that deal with the wicked and sacrilegious transgressors against the convents of consecrated nuns dedicated to divine service and worship, and especially that of May 30, 1486, it is proposed that [a new law] be added that all those who have traffic with nuns, within the convent or outside it, and likewise those who take nuns away from the convents, even if they claim they have not had commerce with them, shall, in addition to the penalties of imprisonment and fines that the preceding laws imposed, be perpetually banished from Venice and its environs and be prohibited from holding office or enjoying any benefit or emolument of our government in any of our territories. And if they shall be found within our boundaries and captured, they will be confined to our Strong Prison for two years and then returned to exile, and

---

69. Here Sanudo lists the names of all those arrested. It is no wonder that some patricians may have resented his scrupulous recording.

70. The manuscript has *ordeni nostri;* the Fulin edition omits *nostri.*

this as many times as they violate their exile. And those who apprehend and present to our authorities any of these sacrilegious men will receive 500 gold ducats, at 124 soldi to the ducat, of the criminal's goods, which will forever remain obligated to this reward. . . . Truly, nuns who leave their convents for any reason shall be immediately detained and consigned to the most reverend patriarch, whom the Signoria prays and entreats to punish them so as to make them a most significant example to others. Indeed, those who dare to accept any of these nuns into their homes or arrange for others to accept them, whoever they may be, shall be banished for five years from Venice and its environs. . . . In truth, the servants, boatmen, and others who, in whatever fashion, transport these nuns away from the convents either through this city or elsewhere must be imprisoned for six months and shall be whipped from San Marco to Rialto. And the same penalty will be applied to those who row anyone around the convents. And because in these convents of Conventual nuns are employed female servants in secular dress, who come and go out of the convent as they please, causing much trouble with their go-between activities, it is decreed that these servants must depart from the convents within fifteen days. . . . But if the aforesaid nuns wish to have persons in their service, they must be servant nuns, according to the constitution of their rule, who will wear religious habits outside the convent. . . . And no pardon, favor, revision, or compensation may in any way be made of these penalties or of the above statute . . . on pain of a penalty of 2,000 gold ducats, at 124 soldi per ducat, imposed on anyone who proposes or consents to the contrary. . . . Moreover, no reduction of sentence will be considered valid unless it is posted and passed by the six councillors, the three Heads of the Ten, forty of the Quarantia, and five-sixths of the Great Council.

Such severe measures elicited at least one skeptical response, that of Sanudo's fellow diarist Girolamo Priuli, who remarked that "for about one month this law will be observed, but then everything will be as before, because 'a Venetian law lasts but a week' [*parte veneziana dura una septimana*]."[71] Over the next decade and a half the old Venetian proverb proved both right and wrong. For there was now in Venice a patriarch determined to pursue the *reformatio* of the Venetian church. On November 17, 1508, the Senate had elected Antonio Contarini, prior of the regular canons of San Salvador, to serve as patriarch of Venice.[72] Among

---

71. Priuli 1912–41, 4:115.

72. Antonio Contarini had been prior at San Salvador from 1503 to 1508. It should be noted that like all patriarchs and other senior ecclesiastics in the Venetian dominion, Contarini was elected by the Senate, then his election was approved by the pope. In a parallel example of independence from Rome, parish priests in Venice were chosen by their property-owning parishioners. The relationship between the Venetian church and Rome is discussed in chapter 4.

the many ecclesiastical concerns he inherited from his predecessors, all of whom had belonged to monastic orders and several of whom had already begun to impose higher standards, none was more urgent than the reform of the patrician convents. This reform was put off for a few years were while the Venetian government and the church dealt with the problems caused by the War of the League of Cambrai, from Julius II's excommunication in 1509 to the military dangers posed by hostile armies on the Terraferma. By the spring of 1513, however, a Lateran Council in Rome was proposing its own general reforms. And in the next year the Council of Ten in Venice addressed the problem of the *muneghini* with new strictures, which met with spirited resistance on the part of the nuns.

July 1, 1514 (18:323)   Today a noteworthy event occurred by order of the heads of the Ten, who have again taken up a bill against the *muneghini* proposed by the former heads of the Ten that also brings this matter under the council's jurisdiction, as they had earlier done with blasphemy.[73] Now, wishing to close the parlor of [the Convent of] San Zacaria in the interests of chastity, the vicar of the patriarch, don Zuan Anzolo di Santo Severino, of Vicenza, university laureate, went there for this purpose, accompanied by some captains and officials. Seeing this, the nuns drew together [and defended themselves] with stones and forced the officials and the vicar to leave against their will. So they have decided that on Monday the patriarch himself will go to take care of this matter. Moreover, the Council of Ten ordered that grilles be installed.[74]

It was not a simple matter. The patrician families of the nuns actively defended the privileges of their daughters and sisters to come and go, to put aside their veils, keep servants, and in general lead lives in keeping with their social status. But the patriarch continued to remind the government of his concern "over the vices of the city, especially those of the nuns" (January 14, 1516; 21:452). And gradually, even in the face of patrician opposition from the families of the nuns, the patriarch, when he had the support of the secular arm, had his way. Or so he described it with regard to a skirmish with the nuns of Santa Catarina, who refused to consecrate an oblate whom they declared had married and whose husband was still alive. The patriarch visited the convent, interviewed the can-

---

73. In 1513 the Council of Ten had assumed jurisdiction over cases of sacrilege committed in the monasteries; in April 1514 it extended its jurisdiction to cases of blasphemy. Eventually, this led to the creation of new permanent committees. The Magistrato sopra i monasteri, originally established in 1521 as a temporary magistracy, later became permanent; and the Esecutori contra la bestemmia (Executors against Blasphemy) was established in 1537.

74. The privilege withdrawn here was a more open *parlatorio* (conversation room) where, instead of there being a grille to separate the nuns from their visitors, a more salonlike arrangement prevailed.

didate for an hour, and "was certain that the marriage had not been consummated" (25:9, 11).

October 10, 1517 (25:25–26)   There was a great fuss in the Collegio made by many patricians who are relatives of the nuns of Santa Catarina. This was because the vicar of the patriarch had wanted to enter the convent to make sure that the consecration of a woman from the Michiel family took place, acting on a brief from the pope. . . . But the nuns did not wish her to be consecrated, claiming that her husband is alive. Now, the patriarch intends to be obeyed, and he secured the support of the secular arm of captains [of the guard], and this past night he had the gates of the convent forced open, and he went inside. The nuns locked themselves in the Bell Tower and rang the tocsin; therefore, there was great turmoil in the parish. And this morning these relatives came to the Collegio to complain. The patriarch was sent for and told to appear in the Collegio tomorrow. The patriarch is determined that the abbess and the others whom he has excommunicated ask his pardon, and then he will decide whatever he deems appropriate.

In 1519 the patriarch began a series of reforms in the convent of Santa Maria delle Vergini, scene of the symbolic wedding of the doge to the abbess in 1506.[75] Similar reforms would be pursued in other convents, such as San Zaccaria, Santa Anna, and Santa Maria la Celestia. The method was relatively simple: to introduce Observant nuns, that is, nuns following a stricter rule, alongside the Conventuals. The execution of the plan, however, did not go unchallenged.

May 21, 1519 (27: 317)   Yesterday morning the patriarch, with ser Benedeto Zorzi, state attorney, and his vicar and other notaries, went to the convent of the Verzene, and he summoned the abbess and nuns to the chapter and said that the Signoria wished to cloister them and make them Observants, and he asked for their opinions. And first the abbess and then the others answered that they in no way wished to become Observants; they were Conventuals, and the ones who were misbehaving should be punished, etc. These convents are under the *jus patronatus* of the doge; they take no vows, nor is any prelate their superior, according to bulls that they have from the pope. And the doge sent Lorenzo Rocha, the secretary of the patriarch, to record and in his name give necessary authority [to the patriarch] to reform these monasteries through closure, etc.

---

75. On the reforms of 1519, see Sperling 1999, 143–45, 208–12.

Three days later, the patrician relatives of the nuns took up the battle on behalf of their daughters and sisters, but without success:

May 24, 1519 (27:321)   Some relatives of the nuns of the Verzene went to the Collegio to complain that these nuns did not wish that other nuns be placed [in their convent]. They preferred that they be cloistered and become Observants. And the doge sent them away, saying that he did not wish to hear them speak and that they should all obey the laws passed by the most excellent Council of Ten.

A month later, a dividing wall went up in the convent:

June 21, 1519 (27:402)   This morning the state attorneys went with captains and officials and masons to the convent of the Verzene, which is the second to be closed. They were following orders given by the Collegio together with the Council of Ten, who themselves were following the wishes of the patriarch because the doge has ceded to him all the authority he had over the convent of the Verzene in order to have it reformed. They entered the convent by force, having broken down the doors, and partitioned part of this convent, that is, the new section toward the patriarchate, closing up doorways, etc. . . . [This section] they wish to turn over to Observant nuns of Santa Justina, who will enter there. The nuns of the Verzene cried out that they were being coerced and impeded from using their usual paths, etc.; nevertheless, they had patience. And the task of closing and partitioning this convent, where they wish to place the Observant nuns, was given by the doge and Signoria to ser Alvise Barbaro, knight, procurator, and *provedador al Sal.*

Meanwhile, the patriarch had taken the precaution of obtaining papal support, and his vicar came to the Collegio with a papal brief fully authorizing the reforms (June 24, 1519; 27:405). But while the secular and ecclesiastical officials were pursuing these measures, the nuns of the Vergini were taking matters into their own hands. The next day, June 25, which was the feast day of the Apparition of San Marco, the news of their actions reached the Signoria:

June 25, 1519 (27:407)   This morning, after the procession, the doge and the Signoria having heard that yesterday the nuns of the Verzene had torn down the wall put up to separate them from the nuns of Santa Justina, intended for that section [of the convent], [the doge] sent the Signoria with the heads of the Ten and the three state attorneys, who were dressed in silk, to this convent. When they saw what [the nuns] had done, they strongly berated them and sent for the patriarch. . . . He arrived and entered the chapter room with the state attorneys; they called the nuns, saying that what they had done would harm them. And the nuns asked pardon, saying that it was very difficult to be expelled from their home, and this patriarch, although he threatened to punish them, in the end is not their superior, and so they left without doing anything more. Nevertheless, the masons are working to divide the convent.[76]

Three days later it became apparent that the nuns and their families had also had recourse to Rome to protect their rights. The patriarch was temporarily outmaneuvered by another brief from the pope.

June 28, 1519 (27:409)   In the morning our patriarch came to the Collegio, where he had an audience with the heads of the Ten and the state attorneys after the others were sent out of the room. And he complained that[77] the nuns of the Verzene yesterday and all night long had rung their bells to signal their joy because they had received a brief sent from the pope to his legate [saying that the pope] wishes the nuns to be reformed but not that other nuns be placed in their convent, etc. There was considerable discussion about what to do about this matter. Because they had a previous brief from the pope authorizing the patriarch to reform these Conventual convents and turn them into Observants, taking whatever measures he thought necessary, the doge, the patriarch, and the whole Collegio with the heads of the Ten were of the opinion that they need not obey this second brief, and they summoned to the Collegio don Panfilo Rasmin, the Veronese auditor of the legate, and told him that they wished their decision to be implemented and that he should report this to the monsignor legate. . . .

Barely a week later five Observant nuns and two servant nuns had been introduced into that part of the convent of the Vergini prepared for them. Meanwhile, the families of nuns in San Zaccaria had managed to have the patriarch cited in the Papal Rota, a papal court in Rome, for his interference in the government of that convent. The patriarch complained to the Signoria, which committed to the state attorneys the execution of the decision to introduce Observant nuns there (July 5, 1519; 27:450). And the Venetian ambassador in Rome, having been enjoined to have the second of the pope's briefs (the one suspending the reform of the Vergini) revoked, counseled patience lest "all that money spent on briefs and citations be thrown into the water." He would try to introduce some order and prevent similar reversals in the future. He did not enjoy such a task, but he would obey his orders (July 13, 1519; 27:473).

76. Pedani Fabris 1995, 118, suggests that the nuns tore down the wall to retrieve their possessions, from which they had been separated by the new construction.

77. The manuscript has *dolse che le monache;* the Fulin edition has *dolse de le monache.*

By late August, a bull from the pope (in response to requests from the doge and the patriarch) indicated that the ambassador had done his job: the patriarch's reformation of the convents was approved, and he had every authority to complete the reforms even though several of the convents were under the jurisdiction of outside orders. "And the Conventual nuns could no longer lead private lives; they were to eat together and sleep together. . . . For which reason all the Conventual nuns are in flight, sending their things away from the convents to their relatives" (August 26, 1519; 27:593). A few months later two papal briefs, one for the patriarch and one for the doge, confirmed these measures:

November 3, 1519 (28:50)   Our most reverend patriarch came to the Collegio and showed to the full Collegio [*ploeno Colegio*] a brief written him by the pope, approving everything he had done in reforming the convents of the nuns in Venice and its environs and giving him full authority to complete the reforms for the remaining convents even if they are under someone else's authority. . . . He wishes that the patriarch himself reform them with strong authority and forbids all from intervening except the pope himself. . . . The patriarch presented a brief for the doge in which the pope asked and ordered him to give every support to the patriarch toward this end. At this, the doge greatly rejoiced, and he and the patriarch warmly entertained each other for some time, thanking God that their good intentions will be realized. . . .

At Celestia, Santa Chiara, and Santa Anna the dividing walls continued to go up, the Observants were introduced, and the reforms went forward. The patriarchal vicar, who arranged for these changes, became so hated in Venice that he had to leave town:

December 29, 1519 (28:142)   The heads of the Ten proposed to write a letter to the Venetian ambassador in Rome [instructing him] to press the pope to give the first vacant benefice in our dominion yielding 200 ducats of income to don Ottavian — da Pexaro, vicar of our patriarch, because of the great effort he has made in the reformation of the convents and the enormous hostility he has aroused. And ser Francesco Foscari, councillor, was very much opposed to the proposal. Luca Trun, head of the Ten, spoke in its favor, and so did the doge, who wished to take part in the proposal; nevertheless, it did not pass. There were 10 for it and 20 against.[78]

---

78. A contemporary chronicler, probably a Conventual nun in the Vergini, labels the vicar "a treacherous dog . . . descended from the seed of Judas. . . . a diabolical schemer." See Pedani Fabris 1995, 117–18.

In order to maintain the reforming momentum, a new law was passed in February 1520 reaffirming the strictures against visits from those not closely related to the nuns; even those relatives could only speak through the grille, and then only during specified hours. Furthermore, boatmen who brought nonrelatives to the nuns would be whipped, branded, fined, and exiled (February 11, 1520; 28:257–58).

At the same time, unrest and resistance continued, partly for economic reasons and partly because on June 22, 1521, the old doge, Leonardo Loredan, died. The new doge, Antonio Grimani (1521–23), was more responsive to the plight of the Conventual nuns, especially as his son, Cardinal Domenico Grimani, was the official protector of the Conventual convent of Santa Chiara:

August 2, 1521 (31:162)   The Abbess of Santa Chiara di Venezia, Sister Anzola Boldù, who is 106 years old, appeared before the Collegio with six other patrician women, Conventual nuns of this convent, together with maestro Zerman of the Friars Minor [Franciscans] and other relatives of theirs, and with the permission of her protector, the most reverend Cardinal Grimani. When the doge entered the Collegio, she lamented that because of the Observant nuns, they were not given their subsistence and they were starving to death, which could not be tolerated. The doge and his councillors were very sympathetic. Present was the patriarch's vicar, who had come especially [for the hearing of her petition]. Then the doge, acting according to the will of the councillors, committed the matter to his son, Cardinal Grimani, and to our patriarch; they are to hear [the parties] and make the determination that seems[79] best to them.[80]

The time seemed ripe for protest. A few weeks later the four Conventual patrician abbesses of the Vergini, San Zaccaria, the Celestia, and Santa Marta, accompanied by many relatives, went to the Collegio, where the patriarch had also been told to appear:

August 21, 1521 (31:276–77)   These women threw themselves on their knees before the doge, and the abbess [Chiara Donà] of the Verzene spoke in Latin, almost giving an oration. Then they were seated next to the savi ai ordeni; ser Nicolò Michiel, who has sisters and daughters at San Zacaria, spoke, and

---

79. The manuscript has *pareva;* the Fulin edition has *aparerà.*

80. Cardinal Grimani's special interest in this convent may also have derived from the fact that its sister convent, Santa Chiara di Murano, was a depository for parts of his artistic and literary collections. See Paschini 1943, 102, 149. On Marino and Marco Grimani, see Chambers and Pullan 1992, 221n21.

spoke well, of the cruelty used against the nobility, how our gentlewomen will go wandering homeless and dispersed, all because of a vicar of the patriarch, from Romagna, banned from Rome and crowned [*incoronato*],[81] who has brought enormous difficulties upon these nuns in order to rob or lust with whomever he chose. He [Nicolò Michiel] cited San Zaccaria, where everyone used to be noble and where nuns of other orders, other rules and habits, bastard Greeks, and women of the popular class are now being placed. For 760 years [the convent] has been the same; they spent 46,000 ducats on the church and the convent and the beautiful refectory, and all this has now been taken away from them . . . , and the entire Collegio was moved. . . . Then all the relatives blamed the vicar of the patriarch, don Octaviano di Pesaro, who was present there, saying very harsh things to him, etc.

In response the patriarch said that if his vicar had erred in his methods, he would be punished; that he had acted in order not to offend the Divine Majesty and with the sanction of the now deceased doge, according to the law of May 4, 1519;[82] and that he had done nothing without the permission of the Council of Ten and the Collegio. And the patriarch complained that the nuns, who could not leave their convents under pain of excommunication, had appeared here in the Collegio. He criticized in turn each of the convents for their resistance, their laxity, their using their connections to thwart reform. Sanudo continues with the savi's intervention:

And here the savi spoke out strongly against this patriarch, speaking harshly of his vicar. And then ser Michiel Trevixan, who had been a state attorney, spoke, saying that his sister was the abbess of San Zacaria, and he spoke vigorously against the vicar, etc., and begging that the bulls be made public so that all could see what they really are and whether that papal bull has been executed. Then ser Piero Trun, head of the Ten, got up, saying that he saw that there was agreement, because the Conventuals wish to be reformed and the most reverend cardinal has worked toward that end, but it remains to be seen how to achieve it. In the meantime, the bulls and the briefs will be taken and reviewed one day by the Council of Ten with the zonta, who will attend to this matter because it was initiated by them. And everyone praised this solution. But when the aforesaid vicar wished to speak, he was thoroughly rebuffed by the senior patricians of the Collegio.[83]

---

81. The term carries a derisive implication. The vicar, according to his accuser, had been *incoronato*, metaphorically speaking: miscreants were often forced to wear a mock crown and be subjected to ridicule. Sanudo's sense is that the vicar was widely despised and derided.

82. The manuscript has *Mazo;* the Fulin edition has *Marzo.*

83. See Pedani Fabris 1995, 121–22, which adds that the eloquent abbess, to the loss of her cause,

The patriarch persisted. In September 1521 he issued an excommunication against those who favored or aided the Conventual nuns. No sooner was the excommunication posted on the Basilica of San Marco and elsewhere than it was torn down (September 10–11, 1521; 31:384–86). The reforms and the resistance to them now elicited a more formal mechanism to cope with the economic burden of supporting two parallel monastic rules within each reformed convent.

September 17, 1521 (31:424)   The Council of Ten again raised the matter of the Conventual and Observant nuns, and there was a great deal of discussion.... It was decided to elect by *scrutinio* in this council with the zonta three honorable patricians from among our most prominent who, together with the most reverend patriarch, would oversee the provision of a living to both the Conventual and Observant nuns, with authority to suspend and annul any mortgaging and leasing of the goods and properties of the aforesaid convents, as seems to them best, as in the bill.[84]

Three patricians, "all three friends of the Observants," were chosen (31:425), and in this way was founded the commission that eventually evolved into the Magistrato sopra i monasteri. But the situation remained troubled, and there were occasional incidents of conflict, such as the following, involving Patriarch Antonio Contarini's successor, Hironimo Querini (1524–54), a very strict Dominican who brooked no interference with his prerogatives and zeal.

August 25, 1525 (39:345)   Again this morning our patriarch, together with ser Piero Contarini, the state attorney . . . , the heads of the Ten, and other officials, went to the Celestia because those Conventual nuns are very unchaste, wearing their hair long, etc. They arrived so early in the day that the nuns were not yet dressed. When they came before the patriarch, and they all saw a daughter of —— Taiapiera with her hair in braids, the patriarch grabbed her and with his own hand cut her hair. He wanted to put two nuns in prison outside the monastery, but all the others began to scream and to gather around the door and would not allow him to do it. Wherefore he could only admonish them, and nothing else happened.

---

died a few months later. As for the maligned vicar, he continued to attract the ire of these patricians. On 29 August 1521 (diaries, 31:311) ser Nicolò Michiel wanted him disciplined by some prelate for his misdeeds; on 1 September 1521 (31:340) he was charged with having appointed a chaplain to the Celestia in return for fifty ducats; and the vicar was cited again on 17 September (31:423).

84. Cf. Chambers and Pullan 1992, 203–4.

It would be wrong to take these accounts of what were exceptional events as evidence of widespread moral corruption, notwithstanding an occasional preacher's alarm. Aristocratic nuns led what for them was a normal aristocratic life, cared for by personal servants, who catered to their comforts and tastes to the extent possible. Many were learned and accomplished women; their talents were among those "notable things" offered to visiting dignitaries.[85] Patrician brides-to-be honored their cloistered relatives with a visit, as did other family members who might use the nuns as intermediaries in their pursuit of political deals. The nuns' political power was subtle, but recognized, as was the economic independence of those who had brought considerable funds with them. If the convent itself was wealthy, its abbess enjoyed considerable economic power.

It was the loss of this economic power, as well as the imposition of a stricter rule, that the nuns described above were protesting. Sanudo's evident interest in the power struggles between the various political and ecclesiastical authorities involved with the fate of the aristocratic convents suggests how integrated these convents were in the larger aristocratic society of the city. The occasional scandals should not obscure the contemporary concern for their psychological and economic plight, which was real, or for their independence, which, in spite of their protests, would shrink in the following decades.[86]

Miracles and Monachization

Even before the reform within the convents of Venice there were many devout nuns and religiously observant communities. Occasionally the deep piety of a convent might give rise to a belief that certain holy women were capable of miraculous deeds and perceptions, as in the case of a Franciscan abbess described by Sanudo in the following entry:

March 31, 1507 (7:40)   *Item:* it seems that many miracles are being performed by the abbess of a monastery of cloistered religious women of the Hordine di Santa Chiara [Poor Clares], recently founded in the hospital formerly belonging to the Vioni family, near the sepulcher. The abbess is named Sister Chiara di Bugni, and she is thirty-five years old. It is said that she goes forty days without eating, that on Fridays she goes into spiritual transports, and finally that she performs great miracles. It is said that on Good Friday everything

---

85. Sanudo includes in his list of notable sights shown to important visitors "the singing of the nuns at the Vergini or San Zaccaria," and he underlines this item three times in red. Sanudo 1980, 62. For a balanced assessment of the patrician nuns' culture and living conditions, see Pedani Fabris 1995, 122–25. On education and literacy in the convents, see King 1991, 171–72, 175.

86. On the government's attempts to control convent expenses, see Sperling 1999, 176–78.

will be known, that she will certainly die, etc. Fra Francesco Zorzi, the father superior [*guardian*] at [San Francesco di] la Vigna, who is her executor [*comissario*], has been inside but does not wish to speak about it. But he does say that these are great matters: "You will know hereafter." I note that Cardinal Grimani, who, on the pope's orders, went inside to see, said when he came out, "It is a wondrous thing."[87]

The ceremony of induction for such nuns continued to be an important event in the lives of patrician families. Sanudo comments appreciatively on a ceremony he attended:

May 17, 1529 (50:336)   I went to Mazorbo[88] with ser Pandolfo Morexini, the councillor, and some other relatives of ours to see three young daughters of ser Ferigo Morexini, who is his brother and my cousin, take the veil in the convent of Santa Catarina. Their names are Lodovica, Catarina, and Vitoria. Six other girls also took the veil: two from the Badoer family, a Quirini, a Zorzi, a Barozzi, and a Michiel. It was very lovely to see the ceremonies in which they were given their habits; I saw all of it, something I had never seen before.

The Church of San Salvador

The role of Patriarch Antonio Contarini in the religious life of Venice was marked not only by the reform of the convents but also by the reconstruction of the church of which he had been prior before his elevation to patriarch. As Sanudo wrote at the time of Contarini's death, this reconstruction was among his most cherished projects:

October 7, 1524 (37:17-18)   The canons of [San Pietro di] Castello came to notify the Serenissimo of the death of the most reverend patriarch, domino Antonio Contarini.... This patriarch was appointed in 1508, on November 17, by the Senate and confirmed by the pope. He was the prior of San Salvador ..., a good and devout person. ... He exerted himself greatly in reforming the convents of nuns. He wore his habit [as a canon regular of San Salvador] of white with a black mantle. He did not live ostentatiously, but rather in a simple manner. With his own means he had a chapel built in San Salvador,

87. On Chiara Bugni, Fra Francesco Giorgio, and the spiritual ambience of San Francesco della Vigna, see Kuntz 1999, 8:121–22. Cardinal Domenico Grimani was a Venetian cardinal from 1493 until his death in 1523 and the cardinal protector of the Franciscan order, of which the Poor Clares were a part.

88. An island in the Venetian lagoon.

arranging for mosaics in the upper part, and it was he who had the church pulled down in order to rebuild it, as is happening now.

San Salvador was the church of the Savior, a church of immense importance for its foundation and location. According to Sanudo's *De origine,* San Salvador was founded in the seventh century by San Magno, bishop of Oderzo. Christ had appeared to San Magno, ordering him to establish a church in the middle of the city, that is, within the boundaries of what would come to be the city, and the church would be called San Salvador.[89] It was at this holy center of the city, halfway between the oldest church, the church of San Giacomo di Rialto, and what later, in the ninth century, came to be the Basilica of San Marco, that San Salvador was established and endowed with precious relics. To this church were brought, in the thirteenth century, the remains of Theodore, an important patron saint of Venice.[90] And it was the intention of its prior, Antonio Contarini, to make San Salvador not only a fitting receptacle for Theodore's relics but also worthy of its titular namesake. Therefore, the day on which its rebuilding began was chosen with this in mind, as Sanudo recalled many years later:

March 25, 1530 (53:72)   Today was Friday, the 25th, the day of the Annunciation to the Virgin, on which day in 421 the city of Rialto was founded with the laying of the first stone; it is the same day on which the world was formed and, according to Saint Augustine, the day on which Our Lord Jesus Christ was crucified. On this same day in 1507, the rebuilding of the church of San Salvador in this city was begun with the placing of the first stone. Thus it is a very illustrious day.

The reconstruction of the church, which took more than two decades, was a project dear not only to the patriarch but to the government as well, and funds were drawn from both governmental and ecclesiastical sources.[91] Sanudo records both the pope's and the doge's letters of support at one point when the work had stalled, with Doge Leonardo Loredan insisting on the importance of completing this work for the embellishment of the city, "in whose navel the church sits" (in cujus umbilico situm est) (April 30, 1515; 20:156–57, 159). A few years later the government intervened again to force the canons regular of San Salvador to fulfill their financial commitment:

---

89. Sanudo 1980, 15–16.

90. Theodore's remains were brought to the church in 1267. On the importance of Venice's patron saints and the evolution of Theodore's position among them, see Labalme 1995, esp. 236n9. For the confusion and blending of the two holy Theodores, see Muir 1981, 92–95.

91. In 1517, for example, the pope granted income from Lenten ceremonies for the reconstruction of San Salvador, "as it has had other times." Diaries, 11 March 1517 (24:50).

February 2, 1519 (26:445)   It should be noted concerning the church of San Salvador, which was torn down some years ago and whose reconstruction was begun and has now ceased, that the friars of San Salvador made a commitment to the Signoria to give 500 ducats of their income each year for it. Nevertheless, for —— years they have given nothing, and the building is unfinished. Therefore, ser Marco Trun, who is in charge of this construction and is a formidable man, with the backing of the patriarch . . . will have these friars excommunicated if they do not give the money they owe within fifteen days so that the construction can continue.

Not only was the building to be reconstructed but Saint Theodore, who gave the church its most important relic, was to be restored to his rightful role as copatron of Venice. For many years the feast day of Saint Theodore had gone unobserved. The government again intervened:

November 8, 1519 (28:57)   Noting that for several years the feast day of Saint Theodore, who was the first protector of this city and whose body is in San Salvador, has not been observed, with shops staying open, the Signoria has on this day made a public proclamation that according to the law passed on another occasion, and with the penalties therein described, the day [of November 9] shall be a holiday, and the shops may not be opened, under penalty of twenty-five lire and other penalties, including excommunication, as our most reverend patriarch has ordered.

This first attempt to restore Theodore's feast day seems not to have been effective, since the order had to be given again the next year, when Sanudo added a reference to the relevant "law of September 21, 1457 in book 2 of the Senate's Terra records, on folio 151," which he intended to copy into his diaries but did not include (November 8, 1520; 29:380).

Meanwhile, the rebuilding of the church itself had been sufficiently completed for Mass to have been celebrated a few months earlier, on August 6, the feast day of the Savior, in the large chapel of San Salvador, "which is a very beautiful church" (August 6, 1520; 29:97). By 1530 the church had been completed and could assume its role as emblem of the sanctified city, the *civitas sancta,* and the city of regal display. During the ceremonial visit of the Duke of Milan it would serve as a venue for the compagnia della calza of the Reali [Royals, or Kingsmen] to entertain that dignitary, and so the church entered fully into the renewal of the city, its religion, and its politics.

October 16, 1530 (54:54–55)   This morning, in the church of San Salvador, which had been prepared with tapestries, flags, etc., and where an enclosure[92] had been built in which the Duke of Milan would attend Mass along with the Duke of Ferrara and High Mass would be sung with all the virtuosi of the city. And the lord of the compagnia of the Reali, ser Zacaria Gabriel, was dressed in cloth of gold with vair and a mantle of two-pile velvet over it, with a large gold chain at his neck and a cap of crimson velvet . . . and all the others in crimson velvet with gathered sleeves and many in stoles of double-height black velvet, their stockings embroidered, with a single message above their emblem, adorned with pearls, which read, "May his name soar straight to heaven." And their jackets were of cloth of gold, and there was a wind band. They came to hear a Solemn High Mass, as I have said, in San Salvador.[93]

A Venetian Saint in the Making

One other project was dear to Patriarch Antonio Contarini, one in which his reforming concerns and his dedication to the sanctity of the city were combined: the canonization of Lorenzo Giustiniani, the first patriarch of Venice. Lorenzo Justinian (1381–1456) had come from a family as distinguished as Contarini's. His life as a canon of San Giorgio in Alga, as a prior, and as a reforming bishop had been exemplary.[94] His able administration and strict personal observance of the religious life had led to his appointment as patriarch of Venice in 1451, when the patriarchate of Grado and the bishopric of Venice were combined. He died in 1456 and was soon associated with a number of miracles, all recounted by his nephew in a *vita* prepared for the canonization process launched in 1474.

That first effort came to nothing, but Sanudo's awareness and interest in it provides us with what information we have about it. In 1518 Sanudo recorded renewed efforts by the family, the patriarch, and the government, beginning with the appearance in the Collegio of Leonardo Giustiniani, a great-great-nephew of the holy patriarch.[95]

---

92. A similar enclosure—*seraia* or *serraglio*—was built for the Duke of Milan later that same day in front of the Ducal Palace as a viewing stand for the naval battle. See chapter 2.

93. On the importance of the reconstruction of San Salvador as part of the spiritual *reformatio* and material *renovatio* of Venice, see Concina 1988; and Tafuri 1983. Tafuri suggests that the reconstruction of this Venetian church, with its enormous interior space, may have been a response to Julius II's grandiose plans for St. Peter's in Rome, whose reconstruction began on 18 April 1506. Cf. McAndrew 1980, 455.

94. Lorenzo Giustiniani reformed the convent of the Celestia in 1442. See Fois 1989, 159.

95. For the story of this attempt to canonize Lorenzo Giustiniani and Sanudo's many references to the negotiations, see Labalme 1993. Giustiniani did not become a saint until 1690, and then under a Venetian pope.

December 9, 1518 (26:248)   In the morning ser Lunardo Justinian came to the Collegio. He is the son of the late ser Lorenzo who was the son of ser Bernardo, procurator, a close relative of the blessed Lorenzo Justinian . . . who was most holy. . . . In life and in death he performed many miracles. He was a friar of the order of the canons of Santa Maria di l'Orto. . . . This ser Lunardo explained that he was seeking the canonization of this blessed Lorenzo, and he offered to contribute to the expense. Moreover, our most reverend patriarch will contribute, for he has a great desire to see Lorenzo canonized, and the friars of his order and even the government will also be willing to contribute. Lunardo requested that letters about this matter be written to the Venetian ambassador at the papal court and to the pope as well. And so the whole Collegio, especially the doge, praised this request and ordered Bartolomeo Comin, the secretary, to write in appropriate form.[96]

Numerous and complex negotiations followed. But by the spring, a new *processo,* or trial, was to be held concerning Lorenzo Giustiniani's canonization. The patriarch ordered the city to celebrate:

May 10, 1519 (27:264)   This morning, Tuesday, was the feast day of Saint Job, and following the decree issued by the most reverend patriarch, the government bodies were not in session, except for the Quarantie, and all the city shops were closed for two hours after tierce, upon pain of excommunication. Whoever obeyed will have an indulgence, and this was because today was the start of the canonization of the blessed Lorenzo Giustiniani, the first patriarch of Venice. That is, the [sanctification] process will be initiated as prescribed in the commission that the pope and cardinals gave to the reverend legate, bishop of Pola, don Altobello de Averoldis of Brescia, and the reverend don Hieronimo [Trevisan], bishop of Cremona and abbot of St. Tomà di Borgognoni. The legate is not in town but in Paluelo, in the home of Filamati, where he broke his leg, but he is better. Therefore, the abbot and the legate's substitute — started the process.

Solemn High Masses were sung in the churches, and there was a procession, and in Castello, where the body of this blessed Lorenzo lies, there was a solemn procession of the scuole, etc., which I will fully describe below. This morning, therefore, the offices in Rialto were closed, but they were open after

---

96. There were only two previous Venetian-born saints to look to, according to Sanudo (diaries, 40:622): the seventh-century Pietro Orseolo (Piero Ursiol), who had been doge, then a monk and was buried in Aquitania (southern France), and while unofficially venerated, not formally canonized until 1731; and the eleventh-century San Gerardo Sagredo, martyred in Hungary and canonized in 1083, who was buried in Murano.

dinner, and there was a great crowd in the church of St. Job in support of this cause.

But the celebration was premature. Diplomatic efforts to secure a canonization over the next six years were thwarted by changes in papal incumbents, political factors, and the many other preoccupations of the Venetian government. It was only possible, in 1524, to secure an *indultum,* a papal order establishing Lorenzo Giustiniani as a holy confessor, a Beatus, whose first official veneration Sanudo witnessed and described:

January 8, 1526 (40:620–21)   Today was the feast of the blessed Lorenzo Giustiniani, first patriarch of Venice, who died in 1453[97] on the 8th of January. According to a papal brief issued by the current pope, we may venerate him on this day and say an office and celebrate a mass [in his name] as if he were a saint. And so at San Pietro di Castello, at vespers, in the presence of the friars of Santa Maria di l'Orto and of San Zorzi Mazor, the marble tomb wherein his body lies was opened. . . . His body had decayed, except for his head, which still had its beard and tonsured fringe. Placed over the bones was a panel of cloth of gold with a wooden grating above that, and his remains were shown to everyone with great devotion yesterday and all day today. And so this morning a High Mass was sung in this chapel, attended by ser Jacomo Soranzo, the procurator, ser Marco Dandolo, university laureate and knight, ser Antonio Sanudo and myself, Marin Sanudo, and many other gentlemen, and a large crowd from the Castello district. And after the mass was finished, I saw the aforesaid blessed Lorenzo, and the church was draped with cloths embroidered [with the arms] of the Justinian family. . . . Then our patriarch, in pontifical vestments because it was his anniversary, celebrated a High Mass at the high altar, and in the afternoon there was a sermon and vespers with a great crowd in attendance. . . . And because I, Marin Sanudo, had recommended it to the doge, the shops of the city were ordered closed; the government offices and banks were not open for business, except for the Quarantie and the *savi sopra li extimi.*[98] But it would have been better if the doge had gone to Castello with the Signoria and others to honor one of its own most holy gentlemen, who was the first patriarch,[99] a most learned theologian and true servant of God, who wrote eighteen works in Latin, on behalf of whose canonization the Senate has written so many letters to Pope Leo in Rome.

97. Sanudo incorrectly gives the year of Lorenzo's death as 1453; he actually died in 1456.

98. Supervisors for the accounts. They had jurisdiction over property taxes levied on individuals.

99. Lorenzo Giustiniani was the last patriarch of Grado, whose ecclesiastical authority included the city of Venice. His title was changed in 1451 to patriarch of Venice.

Sanudo's disapproval of the government's absence on this occasion was echoed a year later, on the first anniversary, when instead of holding a proper civic celebration of this Venetian holy man, the city went indifferently about its business. The authorities may have felt that Venetian sanctity lay more in the integral city than in any single human representative. For whatever reasons, the government did not appear interested in institutionalizing an annual observance for a member of its patriciate.

January 8, 1527 (43:599)   It was the feast day of blessed Lorenzo Justinian, but it was not observed as it was last year, and the governmental offices and banks were open, and shops were open throughout the city. And it was not well done.

Spirits in Chioggia

This was an era when society was prepared to accept the miraculous, the divine intervention in human affairs, signs, portents, prophecies, and ritual wonders. For witness there are the contemporary paintings of Carpaccio, none more imbued with Venetian urban reality than *The Miracle of the Cross* (1494), in which an obsessed man is cured with a miraculous relic in the hands of a fourteenth-century holy man, the patriarch Francesco Querini. Or there is the reported observance of a cross on the moon (April 1, 1507; 7:41) or of saints with lit candles in the skies (March 27, 1517; 24:25), or visions of battles in the heavens (March 18, 1510; 10:48–49). Comets were seen as "merciful God sharing his divine grace with us," which contemporaries of Sanudo published "so that everyone will pray to God for universal peace among Christians" (February 29, 1520; 28:295–96). It was also a society in which religion and superstition, credence and skepticism, respect for the clergy and anticlericalism coexisted, as the following tale about "spirits" in Chioggia illustrates.

May 12, 1519 (27:267–68)   Thursday. In the morning, the reverend don Bernardin Venier da Pyran, bishop of Chioza [Chioggia], came to the Collegio.[100] Seated next to the doge, he talked about a certain spirit who had appeared there in Chioza. For several days the news of this has already been bruited about in the city. But I did not want to record it until I better understood the matter. And it became known after Hironimo Barbarigo went there to assume the *podestaria* because those who accompanied him there heard about it.

---

100. Chioggia was the site of the southernmost mouth between the lagoon and the Adriatic, an important strategic city of the Veneto. Pirano is a small town on the coast of Istria south of Trieste.

Now this bishop, who is a learned man, said: "Most serene prince, it seemed to me that I should come to tell you what has happened in our city of Chioza. This past Lent, an Observant Franciscan friar, a Savorgnan from Friuli, preached at — and strongly warned people in Chioza to amend their sinful lives." There is, in the bishop's residence, a room in which several of his priests sleep. On Easter Monday they heard a lot of knocking under the bed, and they did not know what it was. This continued for several nights, and thinking that these might be spirits, they began to pray, and one of them began to exorcize the spirits. But the spirit did not answer while it was knocking. Seeing that the spirit did not wish to answer, they asked it if it had come with good news. The spirit did not knock. [They asked if it had come] with bad news. The spirit knocked. And so they learned that it wished to answer by knocking. They asked, "Bad news for Venice?" It did not knock. "For other cities?" It did not knock. "For Chioza?" It knocked, as if to say, "Yes." A certain priest named Father — asked it if there would be plague, or war, or famine: it did not knock. Then he asked about high water [*acqua granda*], and it knocked. Submersion of the city? It did not knock. Flood? It knocked. It was asked whether this would be at Venice or elsewhere. It did not knock. At Chioza? "Yes." And when? This April? "No." This May?[101] It knocked. And when? The fifteenth day. It knocked. That is, Sunday. The time? It knocked eight times, that is, the eighth hour. Asked if there would be signs first, it knocked, namely that on the preceding Monday there would be a big storm, and that happened; but by knocking it said that the water would rise considerably.

This story was heard by many persons—the chancellor of the city government, the doctor, and others. But the bishop himself did not wish to go. But the priests asked the spirit whether they should tell the bishop. It knocked. And so they told him, and they asked the spirit to make a sign to the bishop so he would believe them. The spirit responded with its knocking that it would do so, and so one night the bishop felt his nose squeezed, which gave him great fright and convinced him of the spirits.

Then they did what they could to see whether this was a trick. They took the bed apart, and still the spirit knocked during the night. And so all of Chioza was in a panic. And it seems that Our Lord God is doing this because of four sins: blasphemy, incest, sacrilege, and sodomy.

Twice each morning, the bishop has led processions intoning the litanies. Many women in Chioza have miscarried from fright. Prayers and fasts have been ordered. The bishop has asked the nuns of San Francesco di la Croxe, here in Venice, to pray. In this convent the bishop has a sister, who has let him know that God revealed to her that this event will take place, and she asked

---

101. The manuscript has *Mazo;* the Fulin edition has *Marzo.*

him to leave Chioza. Therefore, it seemed best to him to come to relate such an important matter to the Signoria in the full Collegio.

The doge told him to go to report this to the patriarch, and he left to do so. This bishop is in a great fright. Nevertheless, there are no letters from the podestà to the Signoria about this affair, but there are some to his brothers.

Many Chiozoti [Chioggians] are in fear; others say it is a trick devised by these priests, because the spirit never knocks unless priests are in the bed. I will relate what follows.

What followed over the next week and a half was the unraveling of the story. The podestà Hironimo Barbarigo wrote to his brothers that he would go with others to test the spirit and that they "will make every possible effort to hear these things, but doubtless will hear nothing." He was concerned, however, that the panic that had gripped the city could empty it of enough people to create a problem (May 12, 1519; 27:271–72). He wanted to get to the bottom of it all. Meanwhile, he urged his colleagues in the Council of Ten to get the distraught bishop, now lodged with his sister in San Francesco della Croce in Venice, back to Chioggia, but the fearful bishop refused to return to dispel the fears of his flock.

May 13, 1519 (27:278–79)   The heads of the Ten sent Lorenzo Quarto, the notary of the Chancellery, to San Francesco di la Croxe, where the bishop was lodged, to order him to return to Chioza. He is terrified,[102] and he came right away to the heads of the Ten, and in audience he told the whole story and brought with him one priest, Bernardino da Pyran, his relative,[103] dressed as a pilgrim, recently come from Rome, who had been in the room where the spirit knocked, and he affirmed these great events. And I, Marin Sanudo, talked to him there, where the Council of Ten gathers, while many listened. He recounted to me the questions he had put to the said spirit, who was able to tell him the truth: namely, whence he had come, where he had said Mass at the Madonna of Loreto and at which altar, who was with him on this pilgrimage. So that he was certain this was a spirit sent by God to announce this. . . . He concluded that on Sunday the 15th, at the eighth hour, just as the spirit had said, the city of Chioza will be submerged under twenty-four feet of water for its sins, and yet only ten people had gone to confession. . . . He concluded that it is very frightening to be there in Chioza.

The heads of the Ten, having heard this bishop, persuaded him to return to Chioza: they said that the city was in a great panic and that nothing would happen. The bishop, in terror and humility, began to say, "Signori, put me in

---

102. The manuscript has *grandissima paura;* the Fulin edition has *gran paura.*
103. Wrongly identified earlier by Sanudo as the bishop himself. See diaries, 27:267.

prison; do[104] what you like. I shall never return [to Chioggia] until Sunday has passed, because I have heard many things with my own ears." And so he was dismissed by the heads and returned to San Francesco di la Croxe.

Meanwhile, this bishop went to the patriarch, who ordered processions, fasting, and indulgences to placate God's wrath against the city of Chioza.

The next day, May 14, a letter from the podestà of Chioggia reported the unraveling of the hoax: a priest, under threat of torture, had confessed. The confession was sent to the heads of the Ten. The news had reassured the city, and everyone was happy. The bishop himself was not unhappy to hear that it had been a trick and said that that had been his own thought. However, he lingered on in Venice, "afraid of the people." "A very ridiculous affair . . . ," concluded Sanudo, "and one hears nothing more about that thing which was so much discussed" (May 14, 23, 1519; 27:298–99, 320).

Witches in Val Camonica

At the opposite end of the spectrum of credulity were those who, through what were considered diabolical manipulations, believed themselves to have been led, or were believed by others to have been led, into necromancy. As such, they were declared enemies of the Christian faith. But was it so? Already in the early sixteenth century, when the presence of witchcraft in the countryside around Brescia—the Bresciano—was under discussion, the reports of envoys were *in contraditorio*, under appeal (March 10, 1517; 24:50), and controversy continued to surround the charges of witchcraft and whether those declared to be involved in its practice were truly a threat to Christian society.

In the summer and fall of 1518 Sanudo was particularly attentive to the letters and reports about witchcraft in the Bresciano.[105] Included in his diaries are a number of documents and reports concerning the witches of Val Camonica, a valley north of Brescia, two of which are given below. The first, although it appears a few weeks later in the diaries than the second, provides some background for these episodes. It is a letter to a Venetian patrician from someone who signs himself "Joseph da i Urzi nuovi" and "Joseph Servitor." It appears somewhat learned and literary, but it is also based more on prejudice and hearsay than on experience. The writer begins with an apology for not writing more frequently and then announces that he has something novel to relate, something the like of which has not been heard since the time of the sorceress Medea and

---

104. The manuscript has *fe'*, "do"; the Fulin edition has *se*, "if."

105. For example, in late August he includes a full record of a trial that took place from 19 to 29 June 1518 (27 August 1518; 25:632–50). R. Martin 1989, 15, comments on this 1518 outbreak of witchcraft.

involving such a crowd of people that it is hardly to be believed. He tells the story dramatically, beginning with the scene itself:

August 20, 1518 (25:602–3)   There is a valley located in the northern part of Brescian territory whose official name is Val Camonica. It is near the border with the Germans, where our butchers go every year to provision our city with lamb. This place, however, is more mountain than valley, more sterile than fertile, and its inhabitants for the most part are more ignorant than anything else, people afflicted with goiter, almost all of them with the grossest deformations and completely lacking in the forms of civilization.[106] Their customs are most frequently rustic and wild; rare are those who are familiar with, let alone observe, the commandments of the Lord. One can say that in a sense there is as much difference between these valley folk and the other inhabitants of the Brescian territory as there is between the Portuguese and the people of Colocut. As rumor has it, for a number of years warlocks and witches have [practiced] there, such as used to exist in the time of Medea in Thessaly, of whom the ancients write.

It seems that in the intervening centuries the art of witchcraft was transmitted from Albania to the Val Camonica. This accursed activity has multiplied to such an extent there over the years that if the proper measures were not to be taken against it immediately, the sickness of this plague would spread so far and so fast that the inhabitants of the entire valley on the heights and on the plains, those poor priests and lay people, would lose their faith in God's divine majesty. More of them would be unbaptized than baptized, and therefore they would turn to the devil's works and learn the techniques for casting spells on men and bewitching little children. Wherefore, whether by the actions of some good Christian and public official of the valley who saw that it was rapidly moving toward perdition if someone did not root out such enormities and ward off such a curse or even by divine providence, the inquisitor of San Domenico finally went there several days ago with priests representing our bishop to look into this matter. In making their inquiries throughout the valley and its regions in order to cure it, they learned that there are an incredible number of warlocks and more followers of the devil than Christians. This is so because certain priests, whose duty should be the care of souls, were not truly baptizing infants at the baptismal font but only pretending to, with the result, it is said, that more than two thousand may be found there in this condition. Some, who were also priests of that valley, celebrated Mass either in the godly manner or in that of his [God's] adversary but

---

106. Goiter, resulting from a lack of iodine, which is found principally in seafood, was a common problem among mountain people.

were not consecrating the Host; and they have lived this way for some time. These priests were themselves the chief warlocks, [feeding upon the people] as wolves do on sheep, secretly serving the devil and not the true God. They committed all manner of evil, having, as the poet says, "a thousand harmful arts from Satan."[107]

The letter continues with a description of how the devil's followers are won over:

August 20, 1518 (25:603–4)   There is great talk about how these kinds of people become rebels against their living and true God and how they become, body and soul, possessions of the devil, and about how they have proliferated faster than weeds. Some, as I said above, because they were not truly baptized by their priest; some, being poor, were promised great riches so that they could triumph without having to work hard for their livelihood; some lascivious old men were promised pleasure, which they could not get in any other way; some women with the goiter, whom no one but the devil would want, [went along] to get themselves well and truly laid, and [in a way] contrary to the way men should be with women.[108] Several of the most important warlocks, telling their friends about the pleasures of feeding the fleshly appetites with such delicate treats, caused those of similar inclinations themselves to go along with them. Once they had entered this "academy" [*ginnasio*], one thing led to another, especially for those who are desirous of the things I have mentioned. The most common and popular explanation is that some, especially the head warlocks, having been promised by their king, the devil, that they would rise in his hierarchy in proportion to the evil they committed and the souls they acquired, upon seeing a person in despair would seemingly console him with sweet and artful words, pretending to be a friend or to have been moved to compassion. They would promise the desperate person that they could obtain for him the greatest good and the paradise of delights and happiness if he would do whatever they told him, for his own good. Undoubtedly those in despair, seeing that they were promised good things, wealth and lots of pleasures, agreed to do everything.

Thus each senior or master warlock, having converted the ignorant or desperate person to evil, took him into the forest to some remote spot or secret dwelling to undertake the actions that initiate one into the warlocks' guild.

---

107. Virgil *Aeneid* 7.338 ("mille nocendi artes"). Virgil's reference is to Alecto, one of the Furies.
108. "Alcune femene gozute, che altri che il demonio non le lavoraria, per farsi ben ficar, et è contra masculi *cum* femine" (25:603). The use of *contra* here might imply that it was intercourse *contra naturam,* or sodomy.

Like a good teacher, [the warlock], having drawn a circle with a cross inside and having obtained a promise of secrecy, began to instruct the new disciple. First he has him stomp on the cross to show contempt for such mystery; then he must disavow his baptism and all of the church's sacraments, which enhance the life of the soul, promising to give his body and soul entirely to his lord, that is, the devil. These rituals having been completed, in order to turn the promises into effective reality, the initiate is made to have sexual relations, a male initiate with a woman and a female initiate with a man, of a beauty greater than Paris or Helen, at once represented to them as their lover. Apelles, the greatest painter of antiquity, could not have painted[109] more beautiful figures than those presented to the initiates at this moment.

The description of the satanic kingdom, its delights and its deceptions, continues for several more columns, flavored with classical references and Latin phrases, contributing to the standard contemporary literature on the subject (25:604–8).

The following account is from an unnamed and unidentifiable eyewitness anguished by what he perceived as travesties in the procedures against some of these unfortunates and by the cruelty of their punishment. Part of the account is in Italian, part in Latin, which made the more explicit passages less available to uneducated readers and, in a way, less realistic. It is possible that this description of satanic activity, as well as the one above, was influenced by the ideas and questions of the inquisitors, which predetermined to some extent the answers provided by the accused.[110]

August 12, 1518 (25:586–88)   Section of a letter concerning the witches of Val Camonica composed in Brescia. . . .

Since Your Magnificence has asked me to write to you about these witches, I will tell you that it is true that this evil heresy and repudiation of the Lord God and the saints exists in the Val Camonica and here in Brescia as well and has spread throughout the world. In four places in the Val Camonica, approximately sixty-four people, both men and women, were burned;[111] the same number and more have been sent to prison and — there are about 5,000 of them, which is hard to verify. Since I wrote that I was at Pisogne[112]

---

109. The manuscript has *non liniaria più belle figure;* the Fulin edition has *non li haria più belle figure.*

110. For similar cases from a later period, see Ginzburg 1983, 147–71.

111. Cf. the diary entry for 25 September 1518 (26:58), which reads, "In Val Camonica, a total of sixty-six people were burned alive for witchcraft, that is, ten men and fifty-six women."

112. A town on the eastern shore of Lake Iseo.

to watch eight of these witches be burned, the honorable podestà made me write a record of what I had seen and heard. To tell the truth, I wish I had never gone there, because my account was sent to the heads of the exalted Council of Ten, and they have required me to write a deposition in my own hand; I am sending a copy of it to your magnificent lordship. As soon as the most honorable podestà returns from the Val Camonica, this coming Saturday, I will write something to your magnificent lordship, if there is anything noteworthy to write.

It is quite true that in the Val Camonica there are many witches and warlocks, as I wrote in my report, but it seems to me that in the legal proceedings some inappropriate means are being used. I have been there, and I am sending you what I heard and saw.

This, then, is my account, which I myself have written.[113] Requested by the magnificent and most learned university laureate and knight ser Zuan Badoer, the most worthy podestà of Brescia, to say what I saw and heard in the town of Pisogne on July 17, 1518, concerning the burning of eight women that don Bernardino de Grossi, the vicar of the Inquisition, had declared to be definitely unrepentant and heretical witches, I say the following. It is true that on the day before the burning of these women I and a number of other people asked Father Bernardino to be allowed to see the witches. He replied, "I do not wish you to bother them, because they have made their confessions, and I would not want them to be disturbed."

I say further that at the time that their sentences were read I saw that these women, in my opinion, were truly repentant, because they were saying many prayers and commending themselves to God and the Blessed Virgin, crying out continuously, "Oh, God, have mercy." And among other things, one of them in my presence said to Father Bernardino, the vicar, "Do you not know that you are doing me a great wrong, because I did not want to speak as you wanted me to? You called me a 'filthy cow' and other insults; and you even promised to let me go if I spoke as you wished. You hold my soul up as one does a piece of cloth, and you are worse than I am. God knows this, and He is up in heaven." And almost all of them were told by him that he promised to release them if they would confess. . . .

And I say that the sight I saw seemed to me of great cruelty. As the fire spread among the women to be burned alive, I shrank in horror: three or four of them were dead and almost completely consumed before the flames had reached the others. And I heard it said publicly that these witches were being given excessive torture and that among other things, fire of such intensity

---

113. Beginning with this sentence, the language shifts to Latin, except for the direct quotations.

was being used to make them[114] confess that it caused their feet to break off. I believe that this caused them to confess many lies. And I say that these trials must be conducted by men who are experts, theologians and canon lawyers who are God-fearing men of good conscience, since it is a question of life and death.[115]

On the other hand, I wish to inform your magnificence that some of these women are truly witches and that the first thing that they confess is their repudiation of their baptism and Jesus Christ and his mother. They say that they have sexual relations with the devil on a cross and that in order to increase the pleasure he gives them, he forms a bifurcated penis for himself and that in that moment they truly[116] have a double enjoyment. They say that every time they want it, they ask for it, and he is always equipped to serve them. However, they confess that they have greater pleasure with men but say that the devil serves them in his way in quality and quantity. But they say that what they feel is something frigid. Similarly, the men say that they have a woman lover whom they consort with but whom they really know to be the devil. They see him in the clothing of a refined man, transformed into a handsome young man or a beautiful young woman, but retaining some vestiges of the devil, for instance the feet of a —— or another animal, and horns ——. . . .[117]

I realize that these are grave matters to relate, and I am amazed and beside myself. I believe them, but yet I do not believe them. May God, who sees and knows all things, uproot this evil seed from the land of the living I have given a written account of these things to your magnificence, and if I have included anything that might be offensive to your ears, please forgive me, because I wrote my report in obedience to your wishes and I phrased things in as veiled a way and with terms as veiled as I could while yet communicating the information to your lordship.

By September the subject was prominent in the diaries. There are several entries dated September 11, 1518, including a contemporary priest's graphic confession; an exemplum of a 1485 senatorial decree issued to the authorities mandating the extirpation of "demonic deceptions" in order to prove the Christian devotion

---

114. The manuscript has *quidem mulieri;* the Fulin edition has *damcui mulieri.*

115. Archival records demonstrate the struggle that sometimes took place between the local clergy and their inquisitors, on the one hand, and the Venetian officials, on the other. See ASV, CX, Miste, reg. 42, fols. 36v, 72v–73r *n.a.* (8 May, 31 July 1518); and ASV, Sant'Ufficio, busta 160, for a similar situation in 1534.

116. The manuscript has *et vere eodem tempore duplici luxuria;* the Fulin edition has *et utere eodem tempore duplici luxuria.*

117. In the following paragraph Sanudo returns to Italian only.

of the Venetians; an exemplum from 1499 of a letter directed to the doge from the inquisitor's vicar complaining about papal interference in his judicial procedures; a summary of the heresies of three priests condemned to death by the inquisitor of Brescia; and two more priestly confessions (26:29–37).

Much of the literature describing the witches' activities, whether in Sanudo's reports or in contemporary accounts, is repetitive, mentioning the desecration of the Cross and the Host; the transportation to the devil's mountain (Mount Tonal); a demon lover; delightful feasts; the commitment to harm humans, animals, and crops by means of demonic unguents and powders; corporal punishment for disobedience; and sometimes cannibalism (26:325, 413–14). It was not unusual for these descriptions to include the questions asked by the interrogator, so that the Inquisition's concern for motive and for the accused's awareness of his deed is evident. For it was the Inquisition's purpose to get the accused to make a full confession and fully repent his deeds.[118] At the same time, the repetition of elements and allusions seen in the other descriptions suggests that a narrative pattern may sometimes have been imposed on a description since it verified that witchcraft was indeed being practiced.

September 11, 1518 (26:29–32)   These are some of the answers given by a certain priest, [who has been] detained and confined by the authority of our monsignor, to some interrogatories and articles put to him. And first, as to how he became a warlock and who was the cause, he answered that for ten years he has been enamored of a woman and he felt himself dying for her. Unable to satisfy his longing and do his will, he pined away in continuous sighing, so that he could neither eat nor drink nor sleep. His mother, herself a witch and very expert in that art (although the aforesaid priest, her son, did not know this), taking pity on his misery, boldly undertook to reveal this thing to the priest to liberate him, and she did it in this way, using such words: "My dear son, if you wish to do things in my way and do what I will order you to do, I offer to bring about the fulfillment of your wish and satisfy your great and burning desire."

The priest eagerly answered that one hour seemed to him a thousand years. Thereupon, they planned to leave the house together the evening of that same day on which this conversation took place, at about two hours after sunset. When the time arrived, and they had gone out, the mother turned to her son, the priest, and said to him: "My dear son, if you want to achieve your longed-for wish, it is necessary that you do everything that you will see done by me, your mother, in your presence; it is only for your benefit and to assuage

---

118. R. Martin 1989, 84.

your turbulent soul." And the priest, curious about what would happen, said, "Mother, hasten your speech and all this talk."

So she began to explain: "My son, it is necessary that you renounce faith in Christ, baptism, and everything else believed by the Christian church." And he did it forthwith. Then this mother took a cross from her bosom and, trampling it beneath her feet, said: "My son, do you likewise." When the priest had done so, the aforesaid mother took from her bosom a little vessel in which there was a certain unguent, and taking two sticks, she anointed them, and immediately [the sticks] were transformed into two goats, which lifted them [the priest and his mother] into the air and swiftly carried them to a very high mountain, at the summit of which was heard a wonderful harmony of music and singing.

They presented themselves before someone who sat upon a somewhat elevated tribunal. He had a red beard and was dressed in a long gown of black velvet that hung to the ground, with a hat also of velvet, such as is now the fashion, and next to him were seated many of his barons. This signor asked him what he wanted, and this priest responded: "My lord, I wish to belong to you, body and soul." And as witness and confirmation of this, the lord made him perform all the abovementioned ceremonies that his mother had made him perform earlier. And after he had taken the lord's hand and those of his attendants, the lord gave him an ointment to anoint his rod [*il suo bastone*] in the future, and then he gave him a certain powder, which he would sprinkle on that woman whom he loved and on whom, three times sprinkled, he would be able to work his will.

And then he gave him as his lover a young woman with a most attractive figure and of outstanding beauty, who was a demon. In two ways this priest knew her to be demonic: first, she had a web between her toes as do geese, and then, on her head, two little horns. And one day, the priest asked his love casually why such great beauty had such a deformity imposed upon it among both the [demon] men and the [demon] women. She answered: so that those who had renounced Christianity could never, ever excuse themselves claiming, "We did not know we were demons."[119]

Furthermore, this priest was asked whether there was a great multitude on the aforesaid Mount Tonal, and he answered that sometimes there were 4,000 persons. Asked whether they talked one with another, he answered, No, because the demons did not wish them to do so. But dancing, they recognized

---

119. The With the change from direct to indirect discourse beginning in the following paragraph and the use of the Latin term *item* in the next paragraph, there appears to be a shifted from what had become a narrative back to the more formal citing of the actual trial records.

one another, for each wore his own clothes, such as they wore every day in their towns and homes.

When he was asked how long this dance, which they call a *rigoletto*,[120] lasted, he answered: Until six hours after sunset. *Item:* [he was asked] what they do next. He answered that they all have intercourse and take carnal pleasure according to their tastes. Then they go to where tables have been prepared with every sort of food you could desire, and everyone eats and drinks. And then they present themselves before their lord to take leave. With great threats, he orders every one of them to perform every day, in his honor, some evil deed or to kill men, or women, or children of whatever sort, or animals, or to cripple them, or to desiccate trees, or make storms, or cast other spells, and to everyone he gives powders and ointments designed for such evil deeds. And when they return, which is every Thursday and at the beginning of the month, they have to render an account. And if by chance they have done no ill, they are thoroughly beaten.

Because the priest was an educated man, he was asked whether he could discern whether people actually go there in the flesh, and he answered that since it was now ten years since he had last consecrated a Host in his masses, he was pricked in his conscience on Pentecost in May when he was about to consecrate, so he determined to do so and did. When he next went to the mentioned dance, several demons came and began to beat him so severely that if his lover had not asked mercy for him, they would have killed him. And he returned home with eight or ten wounds, so that his blood poured from his head and he had to stay home for about twenty days. This priest said that had he not gone [to Mount Tonal], and had he not gone there physically, he would not have had to stay in bed so long.

Furthermore, this priest said that for a time he had wondered whether this was an illusion, aware that when he happened to go to that feast without dinner, no matter how much he dined there on the mountain, he was starving because that food did not nourish him, so that he needed to eat again. Nevertheless, he could certify [his being physically there] with those beatings that had forced him to stay in bed.

Asked whether the flesh of his lover that he touched felt like real flesh, he answered that one could not imagine any flesh more delicate, to the point that if [that of] the Greek Helen [of Troy] were compared with it, she would lose, and that it was such that he would never return to his first love. . . .

Item: asked how he was caught, he answered that he was suddenly surrounded by guardsmen and that in taking him they dealt him two head wounds and took from him 200 ducats and put him in prison, and [while he

---

120. An old group dance performed in the round.

was] in prison, his [demon] lover once appeared to him to persuade him to be faithful. [But] the priest rebuffed her in such a way that she did not appear again. He is so unhappy that he himself confesses that he deserves death, and he says that he asks only one favor in the world, that he be allowed to speak to the heads of the Ten, whom he would make understand, among other things, that unless they take timely measures against this [witchcraft], the greatest mishaps will very soon occur. And when asked why he remained in such error, when he knew that these were demons, he answered that many times he would have departed, but he was afraid the demons would kill him, because they often threatened to do so.

And much else might be written, which would make a long tale.

In Brescia, September 1, 1518.

The debate over how to curb deviant beliefs and these reputed practices continued over the next four years, with ecclesiastics claiming that diabolical instigation was at work, while a prominent patrician, Luca Tron, a friend and patron of Sanudo's, vehemently urged the government not to act, "because it is all craziness, and people do not go to Mount Tonal!"[121]

The government found itself dealing sometimes with competing lay and spiritual jurisdictions, for witchcraft was considered a *crimen mixti fori,* that is, a crime that could be judged by either secular or ecclesiastical authorities. Sometimes the government encountered the same overzealous patriarchal vicar who had so aroused the patriciate in his imposition of reforms in the convents and who was now accused of using the charge of witchcraft for purposes of extortion. Then there was the papal inquisitor who apparently behaved incorrectly: "he had not conducted himself properly" (October 3, 1518; 26:95). An active role was played by the papal legate, who tried to balance the conflicting pressures and appoint appropriate inquisitors, while ecclesiastics such as a Brescian bishop appointed to make judgment were convinced that witches were at work.[122]

For all the efforts of the Collegio and the Council of Ten to control the procedures, especially the execution of sentences, sometimes it must have seemed as if only the machinery itself was in charge of the events.[123] Sanudo's own sympa-

---

121. For "diabolical instigation," see diaries, 3 January 1521 (29:506–7), 3 September, 1521 (31:353); for Luca Tron, 1 February 1519 (26:411), 28 September 1520 (29:211), 12 December 1520 (29:465), 3 January 1521 (29:506–7), 8 March 1521 (30:13).

122. For competing lay and spiritual jurisdictions, see R. Martin 1989, 2. For the overzealous vicar, see diaries, 1 February 1519 (26:411–12), 5 February 1519 (26:436); for the unsatisfactory papal inquisitor, 3 October 1518 (26:95); for the papal legate, 11 September 1518 (26:23), 30 December 1519 (28:144), 24–25 February 1520 (28:273, 287), 3 January 1521 (29:506–7), 21 March 1521 (30:44), 3 April 1521 (30:103).

123. For the government's concern about controlling the procedures against the witches, see diaries, 1 February 1519 (26:412), 25 July 1520 (29:65), 28 September 1520 (29:211), 12 December 1520

thies seem to have lain with the views of his friend Luca Tron, for he cited the Venetian ambassador's response to the pope when asked what sort of people these witches were: "they are foolish and ignorant people [*siochi et ignoranti*]" (26:95). And he described two witches identified by the patriarch as practicing witchcraft in Venice as follows: "they are women who do this to earn a living" (tamen sono femene che fanno questo per vadagnar) (26:396). In a report in March 1521 on a contentious debate he concluded with this statement: "These poor folk died as martyrs, and there is nothing on Mount Tonal" (March 8, 1521; 30:13).

Lutheran Influences

During the period when Sanudo wrote the reports above concerning witchcraft in the Bresciano and in Venice itself, a far more profound challenge to the established church appeared in the form of the Lutheran movement in Germany. It is first mentioned in the diaries in an ambassadorial report from Rome:

September 7, 1518 (26:18)   The pope has decided to send the Duke of Saxony the rose that was blessed this Lent as usual on Laetare Sunday.[124] He is hoping through his intervention to root out a sect that has arisen there from the sermons of a friar of the Order of Preachers [Dominicans]. This friar condemns life as it is practiced at this time and refuses to accord any value to indulgences as they are currently given. In Rome this matter is viewed as a great heresy.[125]

A year and a half later, in another report from Rome, Luther is named, and it is clear that the dimensions of his movement are better understood:

February 13, 1520 (28:256–57)   Copy of a section of a letter sent on February 4, 1519 [*m.v.*], from ser Marco Minio, our ambassador to the papal court.

A convocation of all of the fathers general of the mendicant orders was held the other day. Those who were not present were represented by the procurators of their orders. The assembly was headed by the most reverend cardinals Ancona and Caietano.[126] It was called to condemn some of the propositions of Brother Martin Luther, who for a long time has been preaching in Ger-

---

(29:465), 3 January 1521 (29:506–7), 14 January 1521 (29:544), 8 March 1521 (30:13), 11 March 1521 (30:15), 21 March 1521 (30:44), 3 April 1521 (30:103).

124. The fourth Sunday of Lent, regarded as a day of rejoicing because it marks the midpoint in this period of sacrifice.

125. Sanudo was misinformed: Luther was an Augustinian friar whose challenge to the papal practice of indulgences had begun almost a year earlier, on 31 October 1517. The pope's attempt to persuade Duke Frederick of Saxony to abandon Luther was unsuccessful.

126. Pietro Accolti was the cardinal of Ancona, and Tommaso de Vio Cajetan was the cardinal of San Sisto.

many against the authority and the powers of the pope. He has a very large following and is much favored by the Duke of Saxony. By this means, the convocation intends to eliminate the favor and the following he enjoys and is preparing a bull [against him]. But the convocation was not conducted very well, because unexpectedly the friar's propositions were read, and when the vote was called, it was evident that this Brother Martin demonstrates that he takes his foundations principally from the Gospels and from those doctors of the church who [hold views that] are like [those of] St. Augustine, but not from other church doctors. He derides St. Thomas Aquinas, Duns Scotus, and others like them. It is quite scandalous.

By May 1520 Sanudo was referring to this "scandalous" more often, but it was not until August that he mentioned its effect in Venice: Lutheran books had begun to circulate in the city, and a preacher was echoing Lutheran beliefs from a Venetian pulpit. The authorities took immediate action against the spread of heretical doctrine:

August 25, 1520 (29:135)   August 25, Sunday. Domino Octavian Britonio, the vicar of the most reverend patriarch, appeared before the Collegio today and presented a printed brief from the pope that had come from Rome. It condemns the writings and works of the German brother Martin Luther, of the Augustine Friars; no one, under pain of excommunication, is to read or to keep any of the aforementioned books in his home. The vicar obtained permission to send the police captains to the home of the German bookseller Zordan,[127] who lives at San Mauritio, to confiscate these aforesaid works, which were printed in Germany and sent to this city to be sold. Thus the Collegio sent Thomà di Freschi, secretary of the Council of Ten, with the vicar to take care of this, and they seized the works that he had. Nevertheless, I have had, and still have, one of these in my study.

Lutheran books might be confiscated, but Lutheran teachings were less easily silenced:

December 25, 1520 (29:492)   Today was Christmas Day. The Signoria was in church with the ambassadors of the papacy, France, Ferrara, and Mantua; also present were two Frenchmen of status who had been on a pilgrimage to Jerusalem, as well as other guests who had been invited to dine tomorrow with the doge.

---

127. Grendler 1977, 73, suggests that this may have been Giordano de Dislach, a longtime assistant to Aldo Manuzio.

After dinner the preacher of the church of the Carità . . . gave a homily at San Marco. Another sermon was preached in Campo San Stefano by Master Andrea of Ferrara, who draws a large crowd. The campo was full, and he stood on the balcony of the home of Pontremolo, scribe[128] to the Ten Offices,[129] and spoke ill of the pope and the Roman court. He follows the teaching of Brother Martin Luther, who lives in Germany and is a very learned man, a follower of St. Paul. Luther is much opposed to the pope and has been excommunicated by him.

The next two excerpts from reports of the Venetian ambassador in Rome indicate the pope's concern and the Venetian government's ready response:

January 18, 1521 (29:552)   The Venetian ambassador writes that yesterday he was at the papal palace; when the pope saw him, he called him over and said, "Write to the Signoria that a certain Brother Andrea of Ferrara, a great scoundrel, has been preaching in Venice. He talks too much and [in an] offhand [way] and walks in the footsteps of that Brother Martin, and he has written a book. Tell them not to let him print it." He also called don Pietro Bembo over, telling him to write a brief to the Signoria on this matter. Then Bembo told our ambassador that it would be a good idea for the Signoria to have Andrea of Ferrara arrested.

Another letter from the Venetian ambassador a month later shows his efforts to reassure the pope of Venice's orthodoxy:

February 9, 1521 (29:615)   As soon as the pope arrived in Rome on Thursday, and despite a heavy rain, our ambassador went to the papal palace. Upon entering the pope's chamber, he expressed his delight at the pope's return and kissed his feet. The pope embraced him and kissed him on both cheeks, offering affectionate words of thanks to the Signoria. Then the ambassador related to the pope that Brother Andrea was no longer in Venice and that neither his conclusions nor anything else against the pope had been or would be printed. The pope thanked the Signoria, saying, "This crazy man wants to follow the path of Martin Luther, who is favored by many." The ambassador responded, "These people end badly." The pope said, "That is the truth."

But for all the professed cooperation of the Venetian authorities, it was not until 1524 that Venice took an official stand against Luther. And even after that,

---

128. The manuscript has *scriva,* for *scrivano;* the Fulin edition has *serviva a.*
129. Not the Council of Ten but a tax magistracy.

Lutheran beliefs and practices continued to penetrate the city and its religious communities.

April 14, 1525 (38:185)   After dinner His Serenity attended the sermon in San Marco with the ambassadors.[130] was preached by a member of the Order of Observant Dominicans — who is a Venetian and the son of Matio di la Torre, the broker, and who normally preaches at San Lorenzo. He has a good voice and gave a good sermon. Among other things, he said that many in this city have been eating meat this Lent and that as a result the butchers' tax during Lent this year has brought in a higher revenue than in other years because of the large number of Lutherans.

It should be noted that the majority of the Germans at their *fondaco* ate meat. The preacher at the church of San Zane Polo said from the pulpit that this year the friars of his monastery heard half as many confessions as in previous years because many hold Lutheran views.[131]

Monstrous Births

Strangest among the deviant phenomena reported by Sanudo were monstrous births. Whether these occurred in Florence, Bologna, the Paduan territory, or Venice itself, they were generally viewed as portentous and attracted the vigilance of governmental and ecclesiastical authorities and the curiosity of Sanudo, who even reproduced a drawing in one case and included a lengthy political interpretation in another.[132]

August 9, 1506 (6:390)   Word reached us today from ser Alvise Contarini, podestà and capitanio of Rimini, who apparently wrote a letter specifically about this to his son Zacaria, that in Florence a lower-class woman recently gave birth to a monster. It is a horrible creature, as in the image drawn below. He also sent a picture of it, which was shown yesterday to the Council of Ten:

130. It was Good Friday.

131. Lutheran followers refused to observe the laws of fasting and abstinence and rejected five of the seven sacraments, including confession. It would have been hard to keep Lutheran ideas from circulating in such a cosmopolitan city as Venice, especially given the German population. But Luther's ideas never constituted any real threat to the Roman Catholic establishment in Venice, and the reasons for the decline in the number of confessions may well have included factors such as indifference alongside Lutheran influence. For a comprehensive collection of excerpts dealing with the Lutheran reformation, taken from the unedited diaries, see Sanudo 1883b.

132. Monstrous births belonged to the category of prodigies capable of interpretation. For a review of the phenomenon and explanations of monstrous births in a European context, see Daston and Park 1997, 173-90.

ser Zorzi Emo, head of the Ten and brother-in-law of the abovementioned podestà of Rimano [Rimini], brought it to show to the doge and others.[133] He [Contarini] says that it lived —— days and then, at the command of the [Florentine] Signoria, food was withheld and it died. The mother took the dead monster to have it embalmed so that she could show it to the world, and she went to Rome.

November 27, 1513 (17:347)   In the last few days a monstrous baby boy was taken to the foundling home, the Pietà. It had no nose, its two arms were attached ——, it had all its teeth, and its tongue was attached to its gums. It had six fingers on the right hand and six toes on the right foot and a hairy tail like that of an animal. The monster lived three days. The patriarch sent people to question all of the midwives to learn who the mother was, but her identity was not discovered. The child was allowed to die.

Elaborate interpretations might be offered for such "monstrous births." The following diary entry shows how contemporary politics, and especially difficulties imposed on Venice by the War of the League of Cambrai, might color the meaning attributed to these misshapen creatures.

January 31, 1514 (17:515–16)   Copy of a letter from Rome, sent on January 25, 1514, and received by the papal ambassador to Venice, Pietro Dovizi of Bibbiena.[134]

You will by now have seen the drawing of the monster of Bologna, which has two faces, three eyes, and on top of its head the open vulva of a woman.[135] An astonishing and profound interpretation could be given to such a portent after the fire that there has been in Venice.[136] I will omit two parts of it, since not all things should be committed to writing. [The first part] is the one about the little church that stood unharmed amidst the roaring flames, as is consistent with its ancient founding and primitive condition.[137] I will also remain silent about the second part, but I believe that a suitable meaning can

---

133. See the photo gallery following p. 421.

134. This unsigned letter is discussed in Bowd 1999, which proposes Pietro Bembo as the author of the anonymous letter. Bembo was papal secretary to Leo X at this time.

135. See Bowd 1999, 42n7, for a medical description of this condition: "The infant was probably afflicted by craniofacial duplication (diprosopus). In such cases the infants have a single trunk and normal limbs, but varying degrees of facial duplication. They may have four eyes, or a fusion of medial eyes. Two, three, or four ears may be present, while some have only partial or complete doubling of the nose. The 'vulva' may in fact have been a vestigial ear."

136. The great fire of three weeks earlier, on 10 January 1514. See the entry for that date in chapter 6. The fire is viewed here as sharing in the portent.

137. The reference is to the preservation from the fire's destruction of San Giacomo di Rialto, held to be the first church built in Venice, on 25 March (the day of the Annunciation) 421.

be found for that double forehead with three eyes, because two of them are completely closed and even though the third one, which is in the middle, is open, it is impossible to tell what and how much it sees.

I turn to the third figure, of the vulva, with tears in my eyes, for Italy has become this monster with closed eyes and two faces looking in two different directions because of its division—one part looking west to follow its inclinations and its own convenience, the other looking north according to its passions—and thus divided and blinded, O miserable wretch! it has become a monster.[138] The open vulva on its head is that homeland and province that has so long preserved and defended the beauty, the virginity, and the modesty of calamity-stricken Italy. Since she has been so prostrated, and with her vulva open, many outsiders, as we have seen with our own eyes, come to indulge their lust and debauch [her].[139] Even in this hour she continues to invite more outsiders. And note well that this two-faced monster born in the Bolognese [countryside] takes by its two mouths—as the governor of that city writes—milk and nourishment, which descend through a single channel to the stomach, because the two faces are connected to one neck, and the rest of the body is that of a female, like poor Italy, which every man uses as he wishes, as [is the case] with a female and a prostitute. With all my heart I pray to almighty God, and I invite all religious persons and true Christians in Italy to pray that he turn his merciful eyes upon us, "He who alone has the spirit and the ministers and the burning fire; He truly is the Lord of hosts, who alone performs great feats; and He regards not our sins but our faith and the mystery of His Church." I am certain that these modern "sages" who advise princes with their tricks and their subterfuges, and "do not fear God but trust in their own cunning," would laugh at my words.[140] And I laugh at theirs, knowing that I communicate and write to a man who is Catholic and well-mannered, serious, experienced, old, and prudent, and removed from all passion and avarice, as I find myself to be, by divine grace.[141]

The sense that such monstrous births were connected with the political and moral state of Italy and the world reaches an apogee with a 1526 broadsheet on "the monster of Castelbaldo," an anonymous and untitled text without publisher or place of publication, attached by Sanudo to his diaries. Here the inter-

---

138. In this passage, France represents the west, and the Holy Roman Empire the north.

139. The Venetian Terraferma is "that homeland and province" that has defended Italy, now prey to foreign troops.

140. The quoted passages are in Latin and are pieced together from Psalms 103:4; 76:14, 102:10 (Vulg.). See Bowd 1999, 42n8.

141. The translation of the paragraph above is largely based on Cochrane's translation in Niccoli, who documents the actual existence of this deformed child. Niccoli 1990, 52–56.

pretation alludes to the sins of vainglory, lasciviousness, and sodomy and finds these degeneracies due to the deceptions of a pseudoprophet (Luther) and his books:

January 12, 1526 (40:652–53)   The lack of faith that today reigns in this world, my most illustrious lords, is the reason why many times God the Father sends us monsters so that we may see the evils we failed to believe. Although they arise from natural matter that is ill-formed and badly organized or stained, or from a superfluity of sperm, nevertheless God, who is in charge of nature, lets things happen that he could prevent, because of our enormous sins. His purpose is the one that I mentioned in my other treatise on the German monster: by seeing that we were born unblemished, we have cause to praise our eternal God the Father and to fear him, considering that he could have made us equally monstrous as or more monstrous than the deformed and monstrous child born recently near Castelbaldo at Maxi [Masi] in 1525, on the 28th day of December.[142] It has three legs; the third leg, between the two [normal ones], is turned upward. Between the right leg and the middle one it has the genitals of a woman, and around back it has a male member. In the stomach it has something like a round ball or a head, and around back, a defective arm. Such phenomena give much cause for thought about their meaning, and with my small and low intelligence I will try to explain it as God composes it in my head. Thus I beg you, my very dear readers, to excuse my ignorance if the explanation is not to your taste. If, on the other hand, you wish to praise it, your praise should be directed to the Prime Mover, to whom all praise belongs and who deserves to be praised for all centuries to come [*per infinita saecula saeculorum*].

The monster was born with three legs, the third of which is located between the other two, descending from the lower part of the body. Above this is a sort of round ball, while around back is a male member, and between the right leg and the middle one are the genitals of a woman. I say, first of all, that the round ball, which is in the stomach, signifies that the entire world is full of wind, that is, pomp and vainglory. Or perhaps it signifies the princes who are full of, that is, pregnant with, thoughts that they do not dare bring forth because they do not trust one another; they therefore are reluctant to give birth to their thoughts for fear of being deceived. And the leg that sticks out of the stomach and points upward signifies a leader or a prophet who will preach falsehoods. Just as a foot cannot walk if it is unnaturally twisted, so this one will not be able to walk; that is, it will not be long before [the false prophet] is annihilated. The defective arm signifies the imperfect works with

---

142. Masi is in the province of Padua.

which he will make a show of observing the holy faith of Jesus Christ [but which instead] will damage it. And just as his back side goes against nature, so will he go against the holy faith. And from the female genitalia it may be understood that he will promise that lust is not at all a sin. The male member, which is on his back, signifies that enormous and reeking sin against nature that today rules the world, for which God will promise through this false prophet that he will come to flagellate Christianity.[143] And attesting that this is true, at the present time people use books to teach the diabolical art of sodomy in as many ways and means as the damned devil is able to come up with. I believe that certainly some diabolical spirit has brought the cursed book up from the center [of hell] to poison and pollute the entire world. Oh God, Oh God, Oh Christ Jesus, Oh Jesus Christ, Oh Redeemer, Oh Savior, Oh Lover of true Christians, I pray that by the infinite love that moved you to descend from heaven to earth to take on human flesh in the virginal womb of Mary, your mother, I pray you, and again I pray you, by the passion that caused you to carry the beam of the holy Cross, we beseech you, for the sake of us miserable and ungrateful sinners, extinguish that burning flame, that putrid sin that without your help will continue to spread. Oh God, Oh Lord God, do not repay us according to our sins, but according to your holy mercy. Amen.[144] Praise be to God. . . .

With this penitential prayer the writer of the letter brought together the deviant and the devout. Having preserved this document without attribution or commentary, in his next diary entry Sanudo simply states that on January 13, in the morning, nothing of moment happened (40:653).

143. To Sanudo and his contemporaries, the "reeking sin against nature that today rules the world" was sodomy. Luther is here alluded to as the false prophet whose teachings were reputed to allow for sexual license. See, e.g., Gasparo Contarini's report on Luther from the Diet of Worms in 1521: "Dicat a quolibet laico confici posse sacramentum Eucharistiae, matrimoniumque dissolvi posse, fornicationem semplicem peccatum non esse, ac innuit mulierum illam comunitatem de qua Plato in sua Republica." Diaries, 30:212. For his part, Luther also interpreted the birth of a deformed child, called the "monk-calf" because of a cowl-like protrusion on his neck, as proving divine displeasure with the state of contemporary monasticism. See Soergel 1998.

144. Portions of this translation are based on Cochrane's translation in Niccoli 1990, 129–30. The broadsheet with this illustration was pasted into the original manuscript of Sanudo's diaries, BNM, Ital. Cl. VII, 268 (9255), fol. 435r. The creature was brought to Venice where Sanudo saw it (diaries, 40:650).

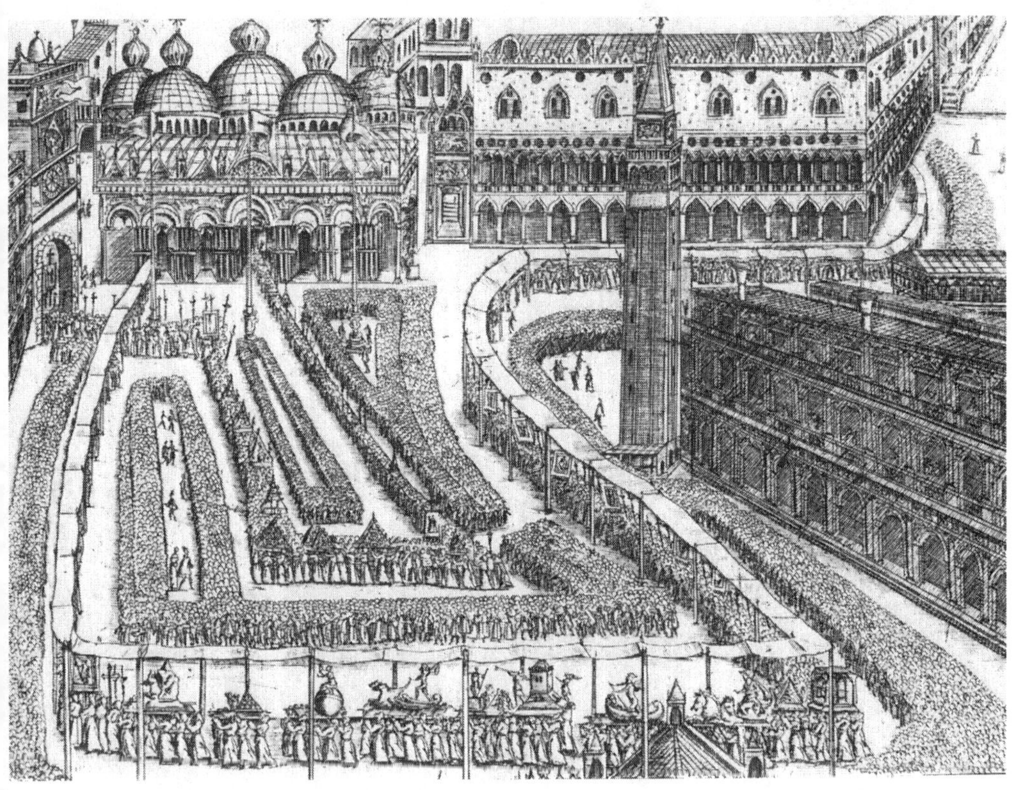

Cesare Vecellio, *Corpus Christi Procession,* late 16th century. Sanudo would have seen a similar display in the 1520s and 1530s. Museo Correr, Venice.

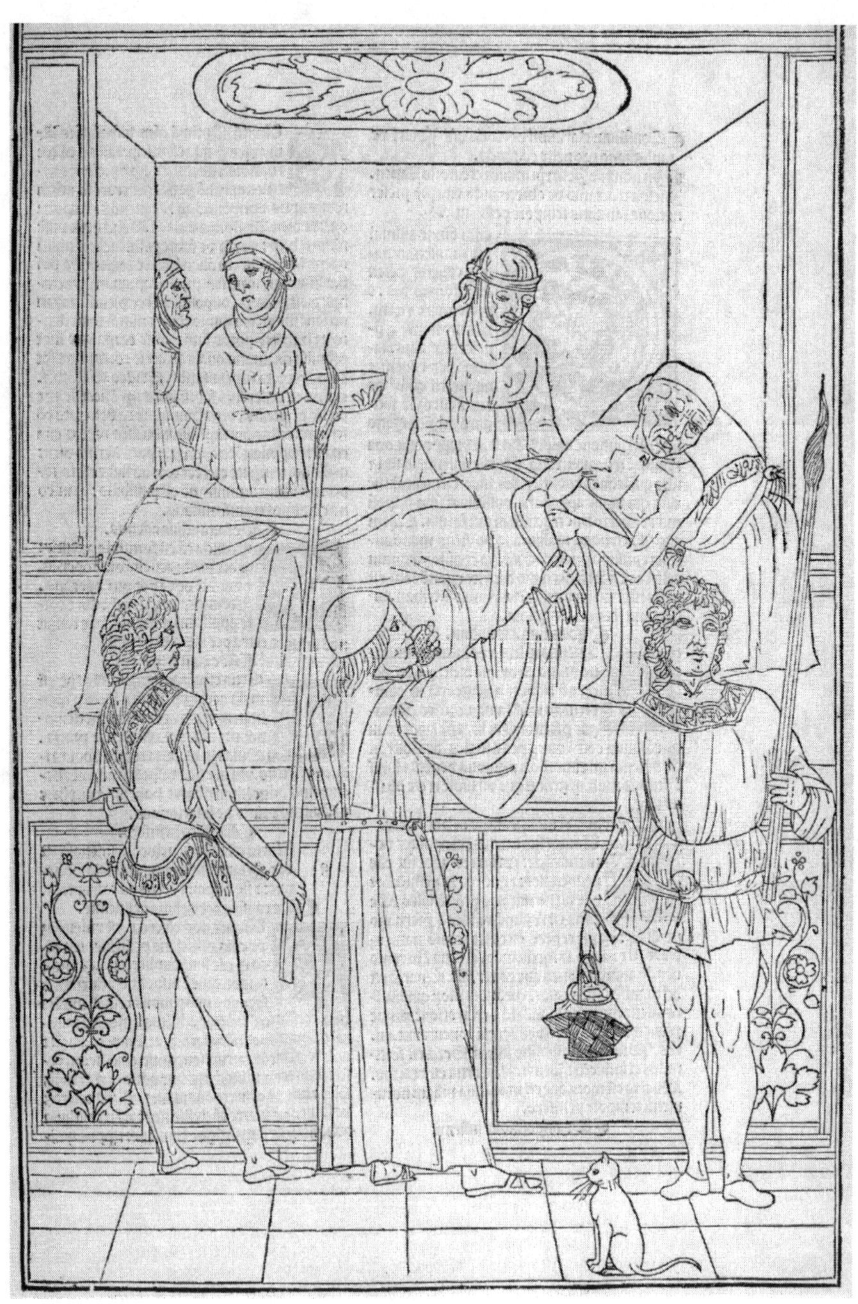

Johannes Ketham, *Fasciculus medicinae* (Venice: Giovanni & Gregorio de' Gregori, 1493/94).
© British Library Board. All rights reserved. IB.21101.

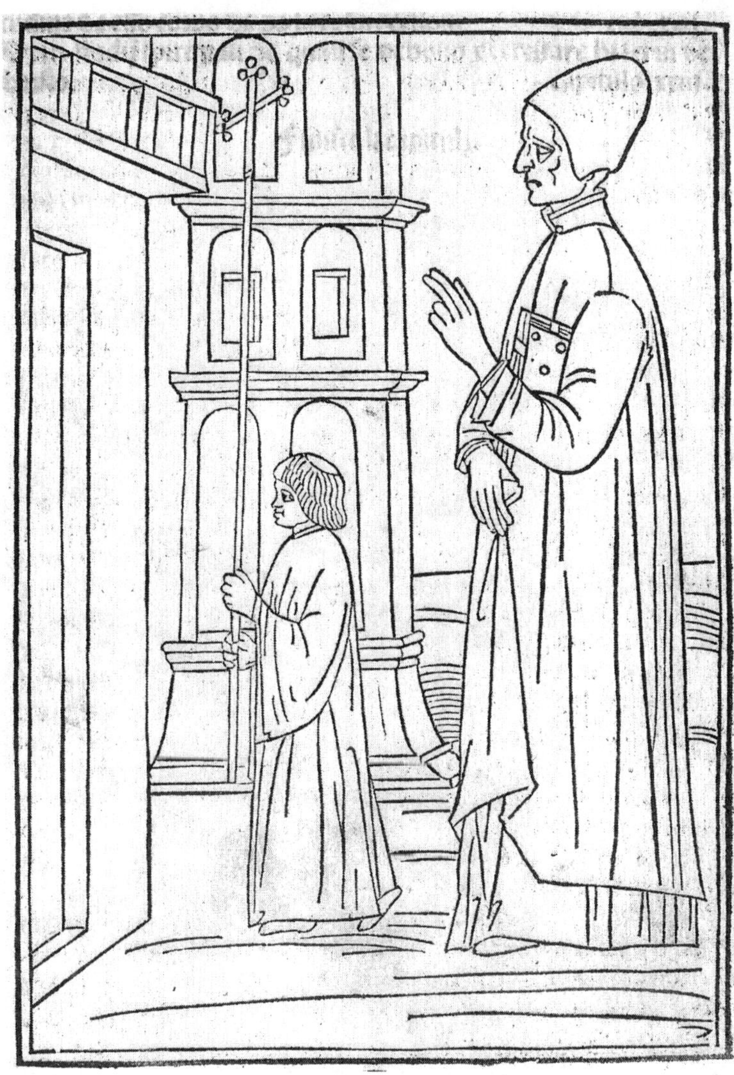

Lorenzo Giustinian, from *Dottrina della vita monastica* (Venice: Bernardino Benali, 1494). Biblioteca Nazionale Marciana, Venice.

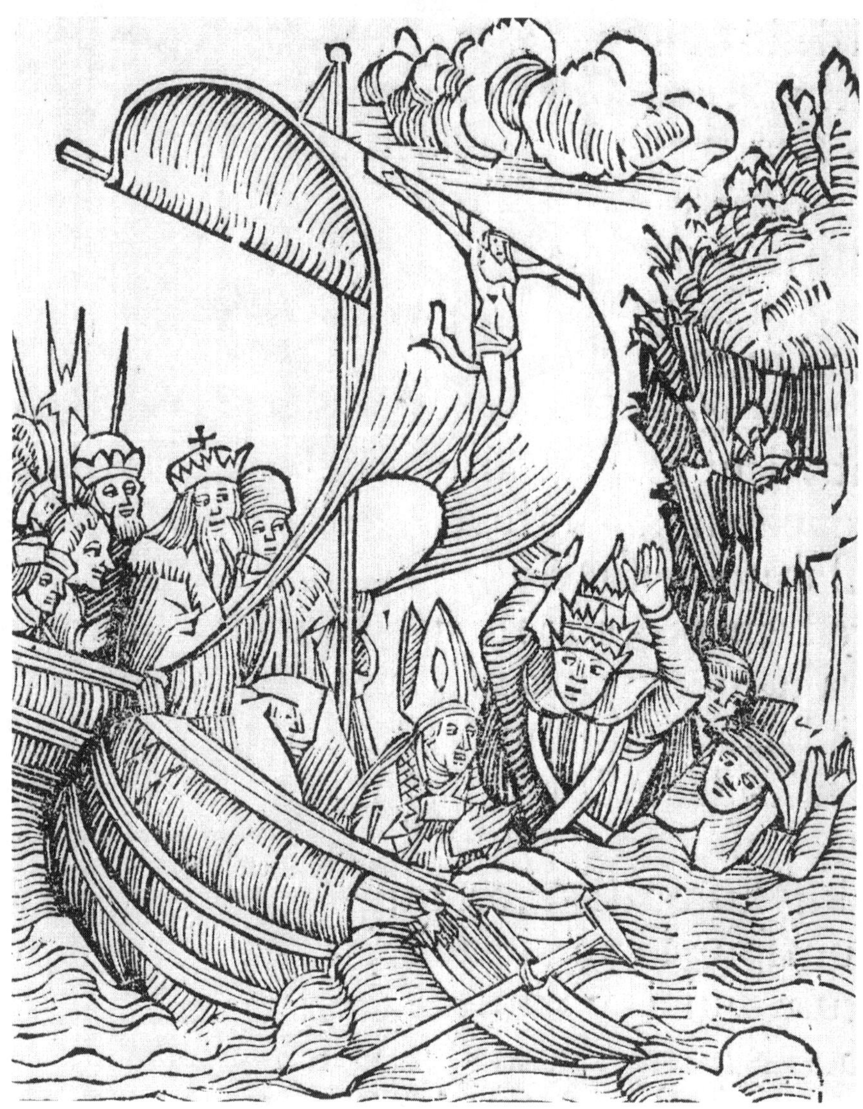

Hans Suss von Kulmbach, *The Sinking Ship of the Catholic Church,* woodcut from Joseph Gruenbeck, *Speculum naturalis coelestis & propheticae visionis* (Nürnberg, 1508). © British Library Board. All rights reserved. c.70.g.5.

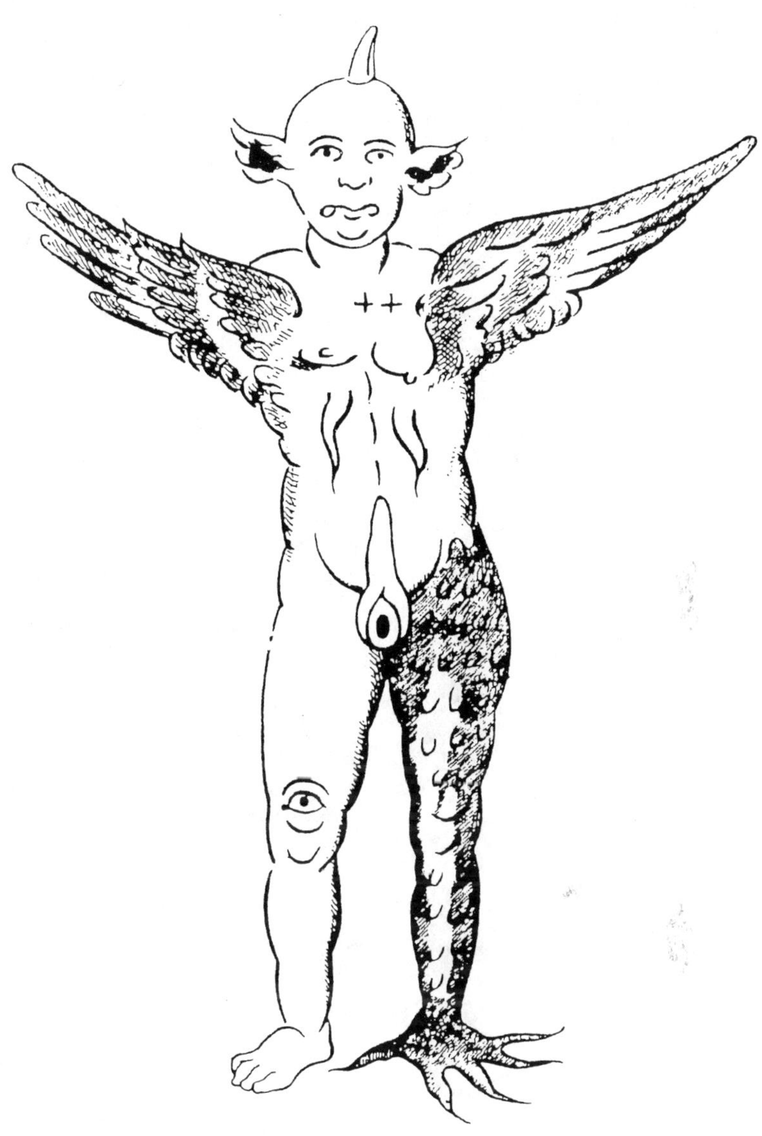

Marin Sanudo, drawing of a monster born in Florence in 1506, from Sanudo, *I diarii*, vol. 6.

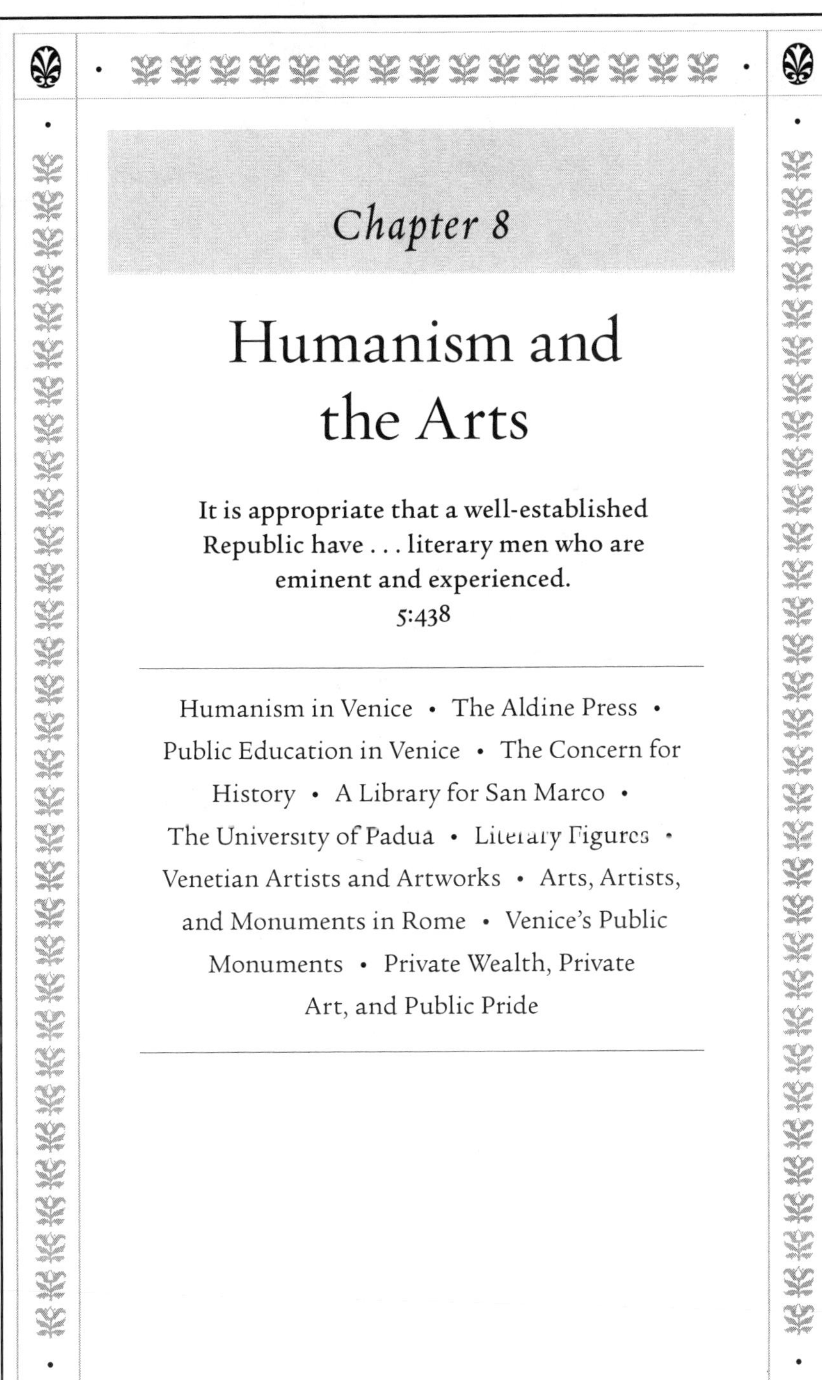

Chapter 8

Humanism and the Arts

It is appropriate that a well-established
Republic have . . . literary men who are
eminent and experienced.
5:438

Humanism in Venice · The Aldine Press ·
Public Education in Venice · The Concern for
History · A Library for San Marco ·
The University of Padua · Literary Figures ·
Venetian Artists and Artworks · Arts, Artists,
and Monuments in Rome · Venice's Public
Monuments · Private Wealth, Private
Art, and Public Pride

To what extent did Sanudo represent the culture of Venice and Italy in a period so rich in literature and art, so much of it retrieved from and reflective of the glories of antiquity, that it later was labeled the Renaissance, the Revival of Arts and Letters? Sanudo's own classical schooling in Venice—for he never studied at the university in Padua—enabled him to read and translate Latin, produce Latin verse and prose, and acquire a reputation for erudition. For witness, there was Sanudo's association with the group around Aldo Manuzio and the Aldine press, at least in an earlier phase of its existence (1498–1503), and there was the admiring literary circle in Verona within which, during his sixteen months there as *camerlengo,* or treasurer (1501–2), he played a significant role.[1]

But it was not a role he duplicated in Venice, where he never achieved a position comparable in importance to being treasurer in Verona, a position he could combine with his cultural activities. He would have liked to do this in Venice because his sense of *humanitas*—the contemporary term closest to our notion of culture—was truly Venetian, defined by civic and political activity, by learning exercised, not apart from, but in the interest of the state.[2] His hope had been to lead that life of cultural-cum-political endeavor; instead, he was increasingly forced to settle for a description of it. But in spite of his personal disappointments, his own view of *humanità,* to use his word, remained clear, and where he perceived it, as in the figure of Bernardo Bembo, he praised it for what it was.

Humanism in Venice

Bernardo Bembo was born in 1433. He studied in Padua with the faculties of arts and jurisprudence, acquiring the doctoral degree in both areas. This was followed by a long life of service as a politician and incumbent of many important

1. On Sanudo's schooling in Venice and his abilities in Latin, see Cozzi 1970b, 335–36. Sanudo himself describes the kind of exercises schoolboys in Venice demonstrated for their admiring families, in which expositions of classical texts were made and oral impromptu translations from the vernacular into Latin were performed "to the great praise" of the audience. Diaries, 8 April 1524 (36:181). For his reputation and "rather ostentatious social and literary life" in Verona, see Chambers 1977; and Murari 1898, 1899, 1900 for extensive explorations of Sanudo's literary activities during this period. See also Sanudo's own anthology of material, mostly eulogies of himself, in BNM, Ital. Cl. IX, 364 (7167), fols. 104v-187r. Although he was no Ciceronian, it is worth noting that Sanudo copied into his notebook Juan Luis Vives's letter of 18 September 1528 to Calcerano Cepello in Venice, in which Vives proposes the imitation of Cicero *per ben vivere,* there being no better model to follow for doctrine, style, or a well-lived life. See BNM, Lat. Cl. XII, 211 (4179), fols. 276r-278v; and Kristeller 1967, 261–62.

2. There is an extensive literature and bibliography on Venetian humanism. See esp. Branca 1973, 1981, 1998; Caracciolo Aricò 1980; and King 1986.

[429]

government positions, including service as a diplomat and orator on behalf of the Venetian government.[3] His service as podestà in Verona, which began on April 10, 1502, when he was nearly sixty-nine, overlapped for five months with Sanudo's tenure as camerlengo there and contributed to a relationship that lasted until Bembo's death in the spring of 1519. Sanudo reports Bembo's death in such a way as to define an ideal Venetian humanist: a man whose considerable learning was expended in the service of the state; who even in his declining years served his society with elegant and erudite communications; who could still be remembered, eighteen years after the fact, as one of the forty-one electors of the current doge, Leonardo Loredan (1501–21):

May 28, 1519 (27:324–25)   Today at the hour of vespers don Bernardo Bembo, a most worthy senator, university laureate, and knight, died. He was the father of the most reverend Pietro Bembo, who is on his way from Rome to this city. He was eighty-seven years old and had been sick for nine days. He was an excellent and most learned patrician and senator, especially in the humanities. He served in many ambassadorial missions and governorships. For several years now he had withdrawn from the Republic's affairs, nor would he let himself be nominated for the zonta or anything else. He dedicated himself to his life, continually writing, until the final hour of his illness, fine and well-composed letters filled with every sort of erudition. And he was the thirty-fifth elector to die of the forty-one who elected the doge. In addition to His Serenity, only five other electors are still alive. He was buried with worthy ceremony on the thirtieth in San Salvador, in a vault containing the family tombs.[4]

Bernardo Bembo's son Pietro Bembo would go on to achieve a literary prominence far greater than his father's, but not as a servant of the Venetian government.[5] Even the history he wrote for the Venetian government, and for which he

3. While a student in Padua, Bernardo Bembo copied Leonardo Bruni's translation of the *Phaedo of Plato,* commenting on it with marginal references to Petrarch, Cicero, Lucretius, and Aristotle. During his stay in Ravenna as podestà and capitanio, Bembo restored Dante's tomb (1483). His philosophical and literary interests continued all of his life and found particular resonance during his embassies to Florence, when he formed close ties with members of the Medici family and with humanists such as Marsilio Ficino, who dedicated several small works to him. On Bernardo Bembo, see Frati 1904; Ventura 1968; Branca 1981; and Giannetto 1985. Bembo served as ambassador to Castile, Burgundy, Florence, Ferrara, and Rome. See King 1986, 335–39. While Sanudo comments throughout his diaries on Bembo's career, he fails to comment on his literary interests.

4. This is a good example of how Sanudo includes a later event in an entry.

5. Pietro Bembo failed to be elected to any of the Venetian governmental posts for which he was nominated and leaned increasingly toward an ecclesiastical career within the Roman hierarchy. When Giovanni de' Medici became Pope Leo X (1513–21), Pietro Bembo was appointed

was given access to Sanudo's diaries, was less useful than the government had hoped and lay unpublished until 1551, several years after the younger Bembo's death in 1547. About Bembo's appointment in 1530 as official historian of the Republic, the position Sanudo himself had so coveted, Sanudo comments respectfully, but with circumspection: "What this monsignor will do," he wrote, "I do not know" (December 21, 1530; 54:186).

That Sanudo has so little to say about this major literary figure is a commentary not just on Sanudo's personal view but on the general Venetian attitude toward patricians who opted for a career outside the political and diplomatic framework of the Venetian government or the ecclesiastical hierarchy of the Venetian church. In that respect Sanudo was more truly representative of the Venetian attitude toward *humanitas* than either Pietro Bembo or his earlier compatriot Ermolao Barbaro, a great scholar who also lived outside the Venetian political system and earned Sanudo's respect but not his praise.[6]

The Aldine Press

Sanudo was far closer to Aldo Manuzio, the famous printer who took up residence in Venice about 1490 and from whose press a series of carefully edited Latin, Greek, and Tuscan classics was to issue forth.[7] Aldo's esteem for Sanudo

---

to the papal curia as a secretary *(segretario ai brevi)*. His father, now too closely related through his son to papal politics, withdrew from his own political activities, as Sanudo relates. After his father's death, Pietro Bembo dedicated himself to literary studies in Padua, was nominated a cardinal by Paul III in 1539, and died in Rome in 1547. As a poet, essayist, and theorist, he wrote enormously authoritative and diverse literary works such as *The Asolani* (1505), a fictional dialogue on Platonic love that takes place in Caterina Cornaro's villa in Asolo, where this queen of Cyprus had retired after abdicating her throne and transferring it to the Venetian Republic. Pietro Bembo's *Prose della volgar lingua* (1525) established the canon, for the Renaissance era and several centuries to come, of the literary language of Italy. For a summary of Pietro Bembo's career and works, see Dionisotti-Casalone 1966. On Bembo's history of Venice and the government's reaction to it, see Cozzi 1963-64, esp. 234-35. Berchet 1903, 100n1, states that Bembo "sacked Sanudo to compose his twelve books on the history of Venice 1472-1513." Gilbert 1965, 226, calls Bembo's Venetian history a "lifeless, rhetorical exercise." For a more balanced evaluation, see Cozzi 1963-64, 231-34.

6. Sanudo was fully aware of Barbaro's achievements and refers to him in the prefatory dedication of his *Commentari della guerra di Ferrara* (1484) to Ermolao's father, Zaccaria Barbaro, as a "giureconsulto, peritissimo nel greco e nel latino" (jurisconsult, most expert in Greek and Latin). Quoted in Cozzi 1970b, 337. Sanudo copied into one of his notebooks in 1492 Ermolao Barbaro's verses on Ludovico Sforza. BNM, Lat. Cl. XII, 211 (4179), fol. 256. On why both Ermolao Barbaro and Pietro Bembo had to live outside the Venetian system, Gilbert remarks: "The 'vita contemplativa,' an existence devoted to scholarship and literature, remained Ermolao's ideal.... It was no accident that he had to live in exile from Venice in the last years of his life. Pietro Bembo's genius also led beyond the political and intellectual limits of Venice into a world which had rules and values quite outside the control of a particular social body" (1979, 23). On this other world, which some have called the Republic of Letters, see Branca 1998, 129ff.

7. For a survey of Aldo's contribution to Venetian culture, see M. Zorzi 1996, 896-910.

is already evident in the dedication to Sanudo of Aldo's edition of the works of Poliziano in 1498, where he praises Sanudo for his "sharp intelligence and singular learning" and speaks of having recently visited Sanudo's library, "crammed with every sort of book." Of Sanudo's character and work, Aldo said: "Deeply modest and devoted to public affairs, he never stops writing and compiling whatever is worthy to be read."[8]

Aldo went on to dedicate publications of other classics to Sanudo: Horace in 1501 and Catullus, Tibullus, and Propertius, as well as three works by Ovid in 1502–3. During the time when Sanudo was in Verona he corresponded with Aldo and other friends about the publication of a corrected edition of Pliny's *Natural History*. In a letter to Matteo Rufo, a learned priest in Verona and a member of Sanudo's literary circle there, Aldo wrote that Marin Sanudo was the "delight" of the Venetian nobility, a man filled with *humanitas* and courtesy, a man of great character and unusual judgment.[9]

Sanudo, for his part, was instrumental in securing for Aldo his patent for italic type, devised as a means of converting cursive script into print, a way of making Aldine books fully competitive with the most beautiful Greek and Latin manuscripts and permitting the development of the octavo book form: small, portable, and capable of being mass-produced. Piracy of texts, typefaces, and book forms was rampant at this time; by 1500 there were two hundred competing printing presses in Venice. Shortly after returning from Verona, Sanudo mentioned his role in sponsoring Aldo's exclusive license for his innovations and indicated how supportive the government was of Aldo's contribution to Venice primacy in this new industry:

October 17, 1502 (4:369)   At my instigation [*me fauctore*] the council proposed a bill to grant the request of m[agistr]o[10] Aldo the Roman, who prints books,

---

8. Berchet 1903, 41–42. In 1498 Sanudo's library contained five hundred volumes, some undoubtedly inherited from his father, Leonardo, who had commissioned the transcription of humanistic texts. See M. Zorzi 1996, 821, 855–58. Sanudo's library, which would grow to number more than sixty-five hundred volumes, would enjoy a reputation sufficient to attract distinguished visitors such as the Prince of Salerno (see chapter 1). For contemporary praise of Sanudo's library, see BNM, Lat. Cl. XII, 211 (4179), fols. 1r–6v, 9r–10v. For a letter from the Chancellery secretary Lorenzo Rocca in praise of Sanudo's "suntuosissima Libreria," see BNM, Lat. Cl. XIV, 246. And for other significant contemporary Venetian libraries, see Lowry 1974; and King 1986, 5–10.

9. See Murari 1899, esp. 279n3. Aldo indicates that Sanudo's humanism included both erudition [*paideia*] and love of mankind [*philanthropia*], considered the two critical aspects of Renaissance humanism in this period. However, Aldo's multiple dedications to and praise for Sanudo must be considered in the light of this printer's active self-promotion through flattery. See Lowry 1979, 1991.

10. The manuscript has *M°,* for *magistro;* the Fulin edition has *Marco.*

works, and new letters and things that no one else may print for the next ten years, etc. The vote for it was unanimous.[11]

Sanudo's relationship with Aldo Manuzio is not mentioned further in the diaries, perhaps because Sanudo's subsequent career did not put him in a position to be of further use to the printer. But Sanudo notes his death and public funeral with a full and appreciative description of Aldo's contribution to the cultural reputation of Venice:

February 8, 1515 (19:425)   Two days ago don Aldus Manutius the Roman died here in Venice; he was an excellent humanist and Greek scholar and was the son-in-law of the printer Andrea [Torresani] of Asolo. He produced very accurate editions of many Latin and Greek works with prefatory letters addressed to many, dedicating a number of little works to me, Marin Sanudo. He also wrote an excellent grammar. But now, after lying ill for many days, he is dead. Since he was tutor to the lords of Carpi and was made part of the Pio household, he ordered that his body be taken to Carpi for burial and that his wife and children go to live there, where those lords gave him some property. This morning, the body having been placed in the church of San Patrinian with books surrounding it, the funeral rites were held. An oration praising him was recited by Raphael Regio, public lecturer in *humanità* in this city. The body was then placed in storage until it can be taken away.

Public Education in Venice

The participation of Raphael Regio, a publicly employed humanist, in Aldo's funeral ceremonies indicates the degree to which the government fostered academic and humanistic studies. Since the mid-fifteenth century, when the Venetian authorities first subsidized public lectures in logic, philosophy, and theology, a number of publicly funded academic chairs had been established. By the early sixteenth century, these also included chairs for grammar, rhetoric, poetry, and history, that is, those subjects called the *studia liberalia* or *studia humanitatis*, "because it is appropriate that a well-established Republic have, especially in this type of lectureship, literary men who are eminent and experienced" (5:438). Of particular importance to the government was the training of young clerks for the Chancellery, where classical Latin was needed to prepare letters, proposals,

---

11. The government's decree may be found in the Senate's records under the date 11 October 1502: ASV, Senato, Terra, reg. 14, fol. 112. For a review of early printing in Venice, see M. Zorzi 1996, 872–92.

and decrees.[12] But attending the lectures were many people who were there less to be trained than to be edified. Even during the most difficult years of the War of the League of Cambrai (1509-17), so active was the intellectual life of the city that Aldo Manuzio could refer to Venice as "another Athens."[13]

Sanudo was intensely interested in the public lectures of the city, the humanists' provenance, talents, salaries, and their keen competition for vacant chairs. His references document how closely involved the Venetian government was in promoting and controlling the teaching of the humanities.

January 23, 1500 (3:90-91)   Yesterday don Zorzi [Giorgio] Valla, who was born in Pavia, died in this city. A man who was equally learned in Greek and in Latin, he wrote many works and was a public lecturer in the Ospedaletto at San Marco, receiving 150 ducats per year from our Signoria. He was a lecturer here for — years; he took the place of Zorzi Merula of Alexandria.[14] Now, in the space of two days, he has died at the age of — years. He was buried at the church of the Carità. And it should be noted that many learned men are maneuvering to obtain his job, including Scyta [Giambattista Scita] and Raphael Regio, while some would like Demetrius or even Lascharis [Lascaris] the Greek, who used to be a lecturer in Sicily, etc.[15]

Sanudo attended many of the public lectures and commented especially on debates, which formed some of the learned entertainment in the city, a reminder that in an oral culture such as Venice enjoyed at this time debate, whether in the governmental bodies or in the makeshift venues for humanistic lectures, was considered a cultural event worth attending.[16]

December 8, 1500 (3:1146)   Nothing happened after dinner. At the church of San Zane Polo an oration was delivered by don Gregorio Amaseo of Udine praising especially the humanistic arts and rhetoric. There were a lot of people

---

12. On public education in Venice, see Labalme 1969, 91-106.

13. On Venice as the new or another Athens, see Marcus Musurus's preface to the Aldine Aristophanes, or Aldo Manuzio's preface to his 1514 edition of Pindar et al.: "We return to Venice, which we can now call another Athens." These are cited in Murphy 1998, 484-85 and nn. 23, 25.

14. Cozzi 1970b, 335, states that Sanudo had studied with Giorgio Merula.

15. Of these various scholars, Scita had the worst reputation. On 22 April 1500 (3:249) Sanudo reported that he was "non ben grato a li scolari" (not well viewed by the students). Scita died in November 1500. For Greek scholars in Venice such as Demetrius Chalcondyles and Constantine Lascaris, see Geanakoplos 1962.

16. The contemporary appreciation of rhetorical skill and improvisation is illustrated by Sanudo's account of a visiting Florentine poet called Cristoforo Fiorentino *lo Altissimo*, who so skillfully improvised verse to music as to arouse Sanudo's suspicion: "In my judgment, it was a written work that he had composed in Florence, because he delivered it so well." Diaries, 10 May 1518 (25:391).

present, including many learned men. Now, Amaseo had posted many theses outside [the church], especially against Raphael Regio. Believing that Regio wished to engage in a debate, Amaseo left the pulpit once he had finished his speech. Raphael Regio climbed up and said a few words extemporaneously and included his theses concerning the points he wished to debate and what he thought of the art of rhetoric, etc. Amaseo and his brother Hironimo argued against him, and then the debate was postponed until later.[17]

In 1503 a new lecturer arrived in the city and caused quite a stir. He had already taught in Rome and Perugia and had evidently done some services for the Venetian government while attending the apostolic legate in Hungary (December 22, 1503; 5:592):

October 29, 1503 (5:228)   This morning I went to hear a new reader who has come to lecture in the Ospedal of San Marco. He is called Calbero da Forlì,[18] and he is lecturing on Pliny. He shows great scientific knowledge, is fluent in his delivery, and is very erudite. A large crowd was there. He hopes to have a public chair. And the Amaseo brothers lecture there.

This challenge to the Amaseo brothers was evidently orchestrated by a group of young patricians led by Gabriel Moro:

November 17, 1503 (5:333)   In the Collegio. . . . Many young patrician scholars and others who are interested in learning arrived, and ser Gabriel Moro made a speech in the vernacular on behalf of the group. He exhorted the Signoria to hire as lecturer don Hironimo [Girolamo] Maserio da Forlì, who has come from Hungary and is very learned and for twenty-four days has being trying out as a lecturer. When Moro was asked what he wanted, he replied that Hironimo should be hired and implied that Hironimo would replace don Gregorio Amaseo, who is lecturing in the place of Valla. The Collegio

---

17. In April 1500 Girolamo Amaseo had been recommended to the Signoria by the French ambassador, Accursio Mainier, to whom Amaseo had dedicated a pro-French *Vaticinium* (Prophecy), published by the Aldine press in 1499. Diaries, 22 April 1500 (3:249). Girolamo Amaseo was an established man of letters who taught in Rome and Perugia and served as secretary to the papal legate in Hungary. See Tognetti 1960; and Gilbert 1971, 292n52. In June the savi proposed giving the lectureship to Gregorio Amaseo, but the Collegio demurred and opined that there should be a competition for the chair. Diaries, 29 June 1500 (3:429). Sanudo appeared particularly interested in Raphael Regio, whose death he noted twenty years later in his diaries and whose epitaphs of praise he copied into his notebook. See BNM, Lat. Cl. XII, 211 (4179), fols. 288ff.

18. While he is clearly identified as Calbero in this passage, elsewhere Sanudo refers to him as Hironimo Maserio or, more frequently, Hironimo da Forlì.

responded that the lectureship [previously held by] magistro Beneto Brognoli was vacant, and they would see. And so the group was dismissed.

Shortly thereafter the Senate yielded to pressure from Girolamo da Forlì's backers and announced a competition to be held on November 22, 1503. Sanudo recorded the Latin text of the proposal for the competition and its results. The winner was, predictably, Girolamo da Forlì:

November 30, 1503 (5:438)   After the death some years ago of the most learned don Giorgio Valla, expert in both [classical] languages, who was publicly employed to teach humanities here, this Senate determined that in his place [Gregorio][19] Amaseo be appointed. But because this decision was taken contrary to the custom of our city, which is that before this kind of lectureship is conferred, a contest of many competitors is held and followed by a vote in the Senate so that the most erudite is chosen, the proposal was quashed by ser Francesco Foscari, at that time state attorney in our government. And because it is appropriate that a well-established Republic have, especially in this type of lectureship, literary men who are eminent and experienced, it is proposed that by the authority of this body the lectureship bestowed upon the abovementioned Amaseo be suspended, and whoever is interested in this lectureship should have himself registered in our Chancellery within ten days.[20] This having been done, all those registered should be voted upon in the Senate, and whoever shall obtain the most votes above the majority of the Senate will be appointed, with the same salary, terms, and conditions that pertained to the late don Giorgio Valla but at no loss of income to the aforesaid Amaseo, who ought to have what he has earned up to that day, as is just. . . .

Chosen: Don Hironimo da Forlì, university laureate.

A month later, Girolamo thanked the Signoria for his appointment:

December 24, 1503 (5:599)   Don Hironimo Maserio da Forlì, who has been hired to teach the humanities in place of Giorgio Valla, as voted in the last meeting of the Senate, came to the Collegio. He was accompanied by many patricians and students, and he gave an extemporaneous speech thanking the Signoria for hiring him. He promised that he would work hard to satisfy

---

19. Sanudo erroneously calls him Giorgio.

20. The manuscript has *in termino dierum decem;* the Fulin edition has *in termine — decembri.*

his audience's expectations.[21] The doge answered him graciously, praising him warmly and encouraging him in his work.

So promising a start had an unfortunate finale six years later. At the outset of the War of the League of Cambrai, Girolamo da Forlì, who in addition to teaching practiced astrology, made an unfortunate astrological prediction that Venice would enjoy an early victory. After Venice's disaster at the battle of Agnadello on May 14, 1509, he found it prudent to decamp:

June 8, 1509 (8:384)   *Item:* Hironimo da Forlì used to be a lecturer in this city at San Marco in the Terra Nova.[22] His many predictions as an astrologer had included one that we would have a complete victory, and many people believed it. Now, seeing that things have gone quite the opposite way, he recently left Venice and went to Forlì. He was drawing a salary of 200 ducats per year for lecturing to the members at the Chancellery.

Scholars came and went and continued to compete, with the government assigning different lecture times to different scholars and arranging for open competitions to avoid the promotion of favorites.

July 20, 1511 (12:296)   *Item* to be noted: a new lecturer must be named by the grand chancellor to teach humanities to the members of the Chancellery, taking the place of don Hironimo da Forlì, who left. Thus, in the last few days, by order of the heads of the Ten and the Signoria, two men have been chosen who want the post; they will teach on alternate days in the Terra Nova in the storage rooms of the Council of Ten. The two are don Hironimo Calvo, from Vicenza, and don Marin[o] Becichemi, from Scutari;[23] they will lecture to the members of the Chancellery on Pliny, on the orations of Cicero, and on Virgil. There will be two lectures in the morning and one in the afternoon; in the evening they will debate each other, which will be a fine spectacle.

With Girolamo da Forlì's disappearance, Gregorio Amaseo pressed his followers to help him get reappointed:

---

21. The manuscript has *sarà satisfatione;* the Fulin edition has *farà satisfatione.*

22. The Terra Nova was an area near where the Giardinetti Reali (Royal Gardens) are now. It had been cleared of boatyards in the fourteenth century to house the magistracies for health (Magistrato alla Sanità) and wood supplies (Magistrato delle Legne) and the Flour Warehouse (Fondaco della Farina). Certain prisons were also located there in the late fourteenth century. See Tassini 1970, 426.

23. On Becichemi, see Clough 1965. Scutari is a town near the Dalmatian coast.

January 23, 1512 (13:406–7)   A bill was proposed by several savi di Collegio to give the lectureship in humanities at San Marco in this city to don Gregorio Amaseo, university laureate, who has served as a lecturer in the past in this city. They are cognizant of his loyalty demonstrated in Friuli, as he was completely faithful to don Hironimo Savorgnan, et cetera,[24] and lost all he had.[25] In opposition to this, the councillors proposed a bill that within fifteen days all who wish this lectureship must have themselves registered in the books of the Chancellery so that balloting may then take place, as has been the customary way of handling this matter in the past. Ser Mafio Lion, savio ai ordeni, went to the podium and spoke in favor of Amaseo, who is learned, etc. The response was given by ser Alvise Bembo, savio ai ordeni, who had never spoken before, [speaking] on behalf of the councillors. Seeing that this was the will of the council, the savi concurred. Without a bill being proposed, it was decided to vote on each of those seeking to be registered. They are: Raphael Regio, Marin Becichemi, Hironimo Calvo, and any others who shall come forward.

A few weeks later, Sanudo reported on the results of the competition, putting a cross next to the name of each winner, as was done in Venetian government documents unless the winner was the only candidate. In this case, Gregorio Amaseo was not among the winners; Regio and Musuro were.

February 17, 1512 (13:486)
　　Lecturer in humanities:
　+ Don Raphael Regio 139
　　Don Hironimo Calvo 57
　　Don Gregorio Amaxeo, university laureate 65
　　Don Marin Becichemi of Scutari 100 or 127
　　Lecturer in Greek:
　+ Don Marco Musuro 167

Sometimes, however, a competition required the direct intervention of the heads of the Council of Ten, who in 1513, for example, had to settle a quarrel between two distinguished humanists, Raphael Regio, who a year earlier had won the humanities chair, and Marino Becichemi, who had found a private position subsidized by his supporters:

---

24. The manuscript has *et cetera;* the Fulin edition omits it.
25. On the troubles in Friuli in 1511 and the Savorgnan clan, see chapter 2.

January 26, 1513 (15:517)   This morning the heads of the Council of Ten had a hearing about the dispute between two excellent humanists who are public lecturers. One, don Raphael Regio, lectures in the Terra Nova as a public employee; the other, don Marin Becichemi, from Scutari, lectures publicly in San Provolo to a group of students who pay him, and anyone who wants to hear him may attend. It turns out that this Marin Becichemi has drawn many students away from the aforesaid Raphael Regio, who complained to the heads of the Ten. It was finally determined that both could lecture, that the city is free, that one could not keep Becichemi from lecturing.

Such rivalries were endemic to the humanists' profession. When Raphael Regio died, two of his students vied for the honor of pronouncing his funeral oration, and once again, the government had to step in:

July 16, 1520 (29:52–53)   Don Raphael Regio died yesterday, after none. He had lectured publicly in the Terra Nova to the Chancellery. His salary was —— ducats per year. He was an old man, learned in Greek and in Latin, and above all a fine orator. He left his books to the friars of San Zorzi Mazor [San Giorgio Maggiore] and by spoken request asked to be buried in Santo Anzolo, near where he lived. He made no will. He has a nephew and was from Bergamo. Now, on the seventeenth, the feast of Santa Marina, his funeral was held before none in the church of Santo Anzolo. It was attended by ser Sebastian Foscarini, university laureate, who lectures in philosophy, and some others, including myself, Marin Sanudo. There was an argument about who should give the oration. One of his Venetian students, called Albertazo, wanted to do it, and a Paduan named Terentio —— also wanted to do it. They appealed to the Signoria, who decided that the Venetian should do it, but that decision was revoked, and first the Paduan gave one in the morning and then the other [gave his] after dinner.[26]

A particularly interesting scholar was Marco Musuro, a Cretan Greek, whose abilities and reputation were such that his appointment to the chair of Greek in 1512 was apparently uncontested. Musuro edited most of Aldo Manuzio's Greek editions, he taught Greek literature to numerous scholars at the University of Padua, and for several decades he lectured in Venice on Greek texts, a reminder that this city, more than any other in Italy, was steeped in Greek and Byzantine culture. A scholar fluent in the currently spoken Greek as well as in its classical

---

26. The manuscript has one comma after *padoan* and one after *disnar;* the Fulin edition omits them.

form could provide useful service to the government. Sanudo had little to say about Musuro, probably because he knew too little Greek, if indeed he knew any, to attend Musuro's lectures. But in 1512 he did report that Musuro was employed, only a few months after his election to the chair in Greek, to translate a letter in Greek from the Turkish sultan:

June 23, 1512 (14:414–15)   A copy of the letter of June 1512 from the Turkish sultan written to our Signoria, brought by his ambassador Ruis and translated from Greek into Latin by Marco Musuro from Crete, public lecturer in Greek in this city.

Sultan Selim by the grace of God most high king and emperor of both continents of Asia and Europe, etc., offers a dignified and suitable greeting to the most illustrious and esteemed and in all things honorable doge of the most illustrious dominion of the Venetians, Lord Leonardo Loredan; sent with appropriate affection to your most illustrious lordship.

Be you informed that, by the grace of God, my lord father of his own will and inclination sent for us[27] and has conferred upon us and assigned us his seat and his empire, both in the West and in the East. Thus our majesty, in consideration of the fact that you are our friend and have been the friend of our ancestors for many years, sends you our slave Zanne Sius, who will bear witness to our affection toward your lordships. We have done this to reassure and cheer your lordships and so that we may be informed that you are well.

Written in the room of our sultan, ruler of Constantinople, on the fourth day of May in the year of the Prophet Mohammed 918, and of the true descent of Christ[28] 1512.

While the lecturers in the humanities were all non-Venetians, the chair of logic and philosophy eventually was monopolized by Venetian patricians such as ser Sebastian Foscarini, upon whose retirement three patricians lobbied for the job, while a fourth announced a philosophical challenge to be held in the church of San Zane Polo (July 15, 1521; 31:60). Such debates and lectures often attracted a number of patricians and government dignitaries:

February 2, 1526 (40:763)   After dinner in the church of San Zane Polo, Alexandro Corner, the illegitimate son of ser Fabricio Corner, held a public disputation in philosophy and theology. He performed very well. Among our people who debated were ser Sebastian Foscarini, university laureate and lecturer, and ser Hironimo Taiapiera, university laureate, and some others,

---

27. The manuscript has *ne ha mandato;* the Fulin edition has *me ha mandato.*
28. The manuscript has *Christi vero cô desensione;* the Fulin edition has *Christi vero descensione.*

friars and physicians. Present were four savi di Consiglio, that is ser Daniel Renier, ser Francesco Bragadin, ser Marin Zorzi, university laureate, and ser Francesco Donado, knight. Also present were four savi di Terraferma, ser Antonio Surian, university laureate and knight, ser Marco Antonio Venier, university laureate, ser Jacomo Corner, and ser Gasparo Contarini; two state attorneys, ser Piero Contarini and ser Federigo di Renier; and other patricians, [including] ser Alvise Mocenigo, knight, ser Marin Corner, ser Jacomo Michiel, ser Polo Trivixan, as was I, Marin Sanudo. Also present was the papal legate.[29] When the members of the Collegio had been there a while, they got up and went to the Collegio to consult about what should be done tomorrow in the Senate.

On many occasions, whether for a philosophical debate or an oration for the opening of the academic season, Sanudo provides a long list of the distinguished officials present, among which company he often proudly cites himself. Their presence illustrates the link between politics and *humanità* in Venice. The case of Sebastian Foscarini serves as an example. Foscarini was a prestigious teacher at the School of Rialto, but since he was often called on to perform politically important tasks, he had to have a cadre of colleagues and substitutes to take over his academic responsibilities. Such an occasion is noted on August 10, 1521, when Foscarini had to go to Cyprus as a councillor and a new reader in philosophy had to be appointed. Foscarini's place was taken by ser Nicolò da Ponte, a former senator, "who often debated in logic, philosophy, and theology" (31:205–6).[30]

The Concern for History

The government's close surveillance of public lectures, patricians' partisanship for competing humanists, and the high attendance of patricians at certain lectures indicate Venetian rulers' concern for the quality and content of whatever humanistic culture was being publicly displayed. This concern was particularly evident in the Republic's search for a historian who could set forth with eloquence and panache the recent history of the city. Since the mid-fifteenth century, prominent humanists had been courted or had volunteered for this undertaking, and Marco Antonio Sabellico, a humanist who taught at Udine, had produced an encomiastic (and well-received) history of Venice up to 1487.

But by the second decade of the sixteenth century, great events had occurred that deserved their own narrative: the French invasion of 1494; the participation

29. For other lectures well attended by the patriciate, see diaries, 7 November 1525 (40:213–14) and 8 November 1527 (46:283); and Nardi 1963, 116–17, 120–22, 133.

30. See also diaries, 28:237, 37:150–51, 46:533, 53:140. For Foscarini's career, see Nardi 1963, 116ff.

of other foreign and Italian states in the subsequent struggles; the defeat of Venice at Agnadello in 1509 by a combination of powers that then fell apart, so that by 1516 Venice had regained nearly its entire dominion and much of its old confidence. The Venetian government, more than ever sensitive to the importance of how its recent history should be presented, determined that it was time to commission a Venetian epic worthy of these events. Many of the resident or transitory humanists in Venice had vied for such a commission, but the choice, when it was made, was clearly arranged behind the scenes by prominent patricians and skirted proper procedure, as Sanudo bitterly comments. Moreover, the appointment included other responsibilities of importance, and its language reveals an effort to keep a valuable humanist employed in Venice rather than have him seek his fortune elsewhere.[31]

January 30, 1516 (21:484–85)   After dinner the Council of Ten met with the zonta. But before that the Council of Ten without the zonta considered a very long proposal with a big introduction recorded by the grand chancellor, [namely,] that ser Andrea Navajer [Navagero], proficient in Greek and Latin, be hired because otherwise he intends to leave us, and he will have the responsibility for the library of Cardinal Nicenus[32] and will have to write the history of Venice from where Marco Antonio Sabellico left off to the present. In addition, no one will be able to publish in the humanities without Navagero's first seeing and correcting the publication. And he will have 200 ducats a year . . . , and this until he has arrived at 600 ducats, as was decided in the Senate. This proposal received 4 negative votes and 12 positive votes, and it was proposed by the heads of the Ten, ser Zulian Gradenigo, ser Alvise Barbaro, and ser Piero da chà da Pesaro. The author and promoter of this proposal was ser Alvise Mozenigo, knight, who is a member of the Council of Ten. And so it was decided; nevertheless, they were not empowered to do this, since it is not a matter pertaining to the Council of Ten.[33]

Furthermore, the Council of Ten may not vote to dispense funds without the zonta, and they did wrong to pass over ser Andrea Mozenigo, university laureate, who has been writing in Latin the history of the League of Cambrai up to this day and is nearly finished.

---

31. For the interest in such a commission, see Tognetti 1960, 654, for the Amaseo brothers; Foffano 1892, 473, for Gregorio Amaseo; Clough 1965, 514, for Marino Becichemi, who said he could write the history of Venice if he could consult the secret documents of the Chancellery (diaries, 4 February 1526; 40:778). On Venice's concern for the crafting and presentation of its history, see the seminal articles Cozzi 1963–64 and Gilbert 1971.

32. Cardinal Bessarion, of Nicaea.

33. The manuscript has *Et cussì fo presa, tamen non si potea far per non esser materia dil Consejo di X;* the Fulin edition omits the sentence.

It had nothing to do with me, because my writings are in the maternal tongue, but they will be read more willingly by everyone than any other, for I have written fully and truthfully from the arrival in Italy of Charles, king of France, up to this day. I swear to God that if I were given 500 ducats a year as a salary, I could not sustain the burden. Nevertheless, I did it and I do it for my pleasure, and I pray God that I may complete it when we have regained our dominion, and then I shall make an end, for now nearly fifty years weigh me down, and I can no longer bear the fatigue.

The story behind this cry of grief from Sanudo is not hard to trace. Andrea Navagero, a clever and well-known humanist, had already made his mark as a learned man and orator. A collaborator in many of the learned editions of the Aldine press, he had also delivered, in 1510, the funeral oration for Caterina Cornaro, the famous former queen of Cyprus. As the widow of James II of Lusignan, she had ruled that island from 1474 to 1489, when she resigned her throne in favor of the Venetian Republic (July 12, 1510; 10:764). Most significantly, Navagero was an employed protégé of Bartolomio d'Alviano, the captain general of the Venetian army, who, although temporarily disgraced by his loss of the battle of Agnadello, had been brought back into favor when a treaty was signed with the French in 1513. Two years later, on September 13–14, 1515, d'Alviano had led the Venetian-hired troops to a stunning victory against the imperial Swiss troops at Marignano. Within weeks of this "beautiful and most glorious victory," in which the whole city rejoiced (September 18, 1515; 21:114), d'Alviano died, on October 7. The government decreed that he would be ceremonially buried as a military hero and that his follower Andrea Navagero, "who received a retainer of —— a year from the aforesaid captain," would deliver his funeral oration (Nov. 8, 1515; 21:273).

So it took place. Navagero paid his friend due honors and referred to his patron's affection: "He loved me especially" [*Qui me unice amabat*].[34] Sanudo reported extensively on the ceremony and tersely on the oration, which "lasted —— hours and was much praised. I was not present" (November 10, 1515; 21:275–76). Sanudo's description concludes with his own muted assessment of d'Alviano, Navagero's patron and Venice's great hero: "He was a man of considerable wealth, very loyal to the Signoria, and conscientious, but a little boastful" (21:276).[35]

---

34. See Libby 1973, 9, for a discussion of Navagero's funeral oration for d'Alviano; and Libby 1971. For the relationship between d'Alviano and Navagero, see also Perocco 1992. D'Alviano was a man of culture who gathered about him "a veritable academy" in Pordenone. On 5 May 1515 he spoke in the Collegio about the need to "free the books of Cardinal Nicenus from their long imprisonment and build a library," a matter he had raised on other occasions. See diaries, 20:176–77; M. Zorzi 1987, 98; and Pieri 1960, 591.

35. "È stato homo d'assai, et fedelissimo a la Signoria et solicito, ma un poco sbarajoso."

D'Alviano's patronage, it has been suggested, was decisive in the choice of Navagero as the custodian of Bessarion's library and the official historian of Venice. But Navagero was also a strong candidate. The decree of his appointment speaks of the Council of Ten's concern to preserve the memory of the recent events, which were "as worth remembering as those of the foundation of the city" and whose proper presentation "can often accomplish more with [foreign] powers than force." It cites Navagero as a patrician "wonderfully endowed especially with Greek and Latin learning and style of expression." At the same time, here was a noble in need of immediate succor lest he seek his fortune elsewhere and give to the enemies of Venice the opportunity to "deprive this famous city of such a great ornament." As to his supervision of the humanistic products of the Venetian press, the council averred that "everywhere in the world, in all the celebrated cities of Italy and the barbarian provinces, public honor does not permit that humanistic works be published that have not been reviewed by the most learned persons possible." And they went on to state that incorrect and faulty publications served to dishonor the city and that henceforth nothing should be printed without citing Navagero's permission, at the risk of being "lost and burned."[36]

Of all the responsibilities this degree gave to Navagero by this decree, only the one concerning Bessarion's books was fulfilled.[37] Navagero's account of recent Venetian history appears never to have been written, and the supervision of Venetian printing presses was never enforced. On October 10, 1523, Navagero was elected ambassador to the emperor in Spain. He left for that post the following July and died abroad, in France, in 1529. Sanudo records the news of his death:

May 25, 1529 (50:372)   After dinner the Council of Ten met with the zonta, and letters from France were read. They stayed very late to deliberate; no action was taken. And among other matters, I heard that letters from the ambassador to France brought news of the death there of ser Andrea Navagero, ambassador.[38] His body was placed in a lead coffin and on the tenth was sent

36. ASV, CX, Miste, reg. 39 (1515–16), fol. 39. On Navagero's humanistic accomplishments, see Cicogna 1824–53, 6:169–346.

37. See Perocco 1992, 330n10, which cites an inventory Navagero made and his efforts to reclaim volumes that had been lent out from this library. See also M. Zorzi 1987, 102–4; and Cicogna 1824–53, 6:309–10. The care of Bessarion's book collection had already been associated with the appointment of the previous historian of Venice, as the decree of the Council of Ten makes clear: "He [Navagero] will also have, as was imposed upon the aforementioned Sabellico, the responsibility for the Nicene Library, when it will have been built according to the deliberation of our Senate" (Habia insuper, come al prenominato Sabellico fo imposto, el cargo de la Biblioteca Nicena, quando la sarà erecta juxta la deliberation del Senato nostro). See Perocco 1992, 330.

38. Cermenati 1912, 204, records that at the time of his death Navagero was on a mission to Francis I.

to Italy, accompanied by his brother. [Navagero] had ordered his brother to burn his writings concerning Venetian history—for which he had received 200 ducats annually—because he had not revised and corrected them.[39] I maintain that it was because he had written nothing, nothing good.

Discouraged as Sanudo may have been by Navagero's appointment in 1516, he continued to believe in his own work and in 1519 asserted that what he was producing (or would someday produce) was "an important text and a record for eternity of things that have occurred, very good for instructing those patricians, senators, and others who take pleasure in history and who aspire wholeheartedly to the governance of the state" (March 1, 1519; 27:5–6).[40]

That may be why, one month later, he chose to record in his diaries a summary of letters from Marcantonio Michiel, a Venetian patrician who at the time was attached as secretary to the household of Cardinal Francesco Pisani in Rome. This summary lists many humanistic personalities and shows the circulation of literary manuscripts, the role of patronage, the collection of historical texts, and the connections between political service, rhetoric, and historical literature. This was clearly the company and the subject matter for which Sanudo had a personal affinity:

April 30, 1519 (27:223–24)   Summary of letters from ser Marco Antonio Michiel[41] in Rome to don Nicolò Tiepolo, university laureate, dated 17 April 1519.

According to what ser Piero Sumontio [Pietro Summonte] has told me, when he has completed having the works of Pontano copied in fine and elegant form on good paper, he would like to come to Venice to present them to our most illustrious Signoria.[42] This matter was planned by Pontano while he was still alive. And although this ser Piero could send someone in his stead

---

39. Navagero's request that his works be burned is recorded in the opening lines of Pietro Bembo's *Historiae Venetae libri XII*. See Bembo 1551.

40. "Opera di gran scriptura et eternità di le cosse passate, optima a instruire li patricii, senatori, et altri che hanno piacer de historia et si danno a voler ascendere al governo dil Stado." David Chambers, who has analyzed Sanudo's introductory statements to his volumes, suggests that this statement was made in a rare and passing moment of elation (1998a, 29). But it should not be forgotten that Sanudo's commitment to his diaries and to the idea of creating a historical account based on them was an enduring and deeply felt civic commitment, part and parcel of his abiding love for his homeland, which guided both his political and his literary endeavors. See diaries, 1 March 1523 (34:5–7).

41. For Marcantonio Michiel (c. 1484–1552), see the section "Arts, Artists, and Monuments in Rome," below.

42. Giovanni Pontano (1429–1503), born in Spoleto, had joined the service of King Alfonso of Aragon at eighteen, and from that time on his name as politician, writer, and poet was linked to the Aragonese court in Naples. Pontano's *Opera* had already been published by Aldo Manuzio in 1505 and by Manuzio and Torresani in 1513. Summonte was Pontano's agent.

rather than taking the trouble himself . . . ;[43] he fervently wishes to see this city and Republic of ours, as do nearly all the other scholars; he is not well,[44] and for this reason he wishes to have this worthy event take place before any accident prevents it. Therefore, he would like ser Andrea Navagero, as director of the library, to see to it that he receives a greater remuneration than many of those illiterates who are governing the Republic would like to give him.

I wish to find out via Egnatio[45] if all the orations and histories of Bernardo Justinian[46] are available; I particularly wish to know which orations and in which shop [they may be found], as well as the price and number of the orations, so that I may arrange to have them bought and sent to ser Jacomo Sannazaro.[47] He is more desirous of them than he is of the missing eleven decades of Livy, his eagerness having been aroused by the great and admirable reports made to him by His Serenity Federico and other nobles of earlier times about ser Bernardo's thoughts when he was ambassador to the old king Ferdinand of happy memory.

But for all his interest and sense of affinity, Sanudo was not in that company. His work was known, even appreciated, but it was as yet unorganized and it was in the vernacular, whose use he defended in his *Spedizione di Carlo VIII*, stating that only this form would allow "learned and unlearned" alike to profit from his writings.[48] A vernacular history was not yet equivalent to a Latin history in the eyes of contemporaries, and Sanudo later acknowledged that his lexicon was "coarse, unadorned, and low" (July 1, 1521; 31:7). And in 1531, when he had to share his diaries with Pietro Bembo, Navagero's successor, to provide substance for Bembo's officially commissioned work, he could at least comfort himself with what he was contributing to the historical culture of the city: "Without a diary, one can hardly write anything that is true and good."[49]

---

43. The manuscript has two unclear words at this point; they are omitted by the Fulin edition.

44. The manuscript has *non ben sano;* the Fulin edition has *desiderano.*

45. Giovanni Battista Egnazio (1473-1553) was a Venetian citizen and professional humanist.

46. Bernardo Giustiniani (1408–89) was an eminent Venetian statesmen and humanist whose *Orationes* and *De origine urbis Venetiarum* had been published in Venice in 1493 and whose ambassadorial mission to Ferdinand of Naples occurred in 1458–59.

47. Jacopo Sannazaro (1457–1530) was a Neapolitan pastoral poet.

48. Chambers 1998a, 8n34. See Sanudo 1873, 17: "Acciò tutti, dotti et indotti, la possino legere et intendere, perchè molto meglio è faticarsi per l'università che per rari e pochi." Cf. Berchet 1903, 95–97, letter to the Council of Ten. On Sanudo's interest in history and his justification for his use of the vernacular to record it, see the introduction; Cozzi 1970b, 336–38, 340–47; and Lepschy 1993. Also to be noted is the government's increasing use of the vernacular over the period of Sanudo's diaries, as the language of the majority of laws shifted from Latin to the vernacular. See Frassón 1980. See also "About the Translation."

49. "Senza una diaria malissimo si pol scriver cosa che bona e vera sia." BNM, Ital. Cl. VII, 375 (8954), Sanudo to heads of the Council of Ten, September 1531, newly edited in Caracciolo

A Library for San Marco

All of Venice's officially appointed historians—Marco Antonio Sabellico, Andrea Navagero, and Pietro Bembo—had as a principal duty, along with producing an elegant and flattering account of Venice's recent history, the supervision of Cardinal Bessarion's library. Cardinal Bessarion, also called Nicenus, was the learned fifteenth-century bishop of Nicaea and patriarch of Constantinople who had first come to Venice in 1438 as part of the entourage of Emperor John VIII en route to the Council of Ferrara-Florence. He had been given a cardinal's hat in 1439, and later, after becoming a refugee from the Turkish conquest of Constantinople in 1453, he had come to Venice as papal legate. Impressed by the stable organization of the Venetian government (he had been made an honorary member of the Great Council in 1461) and by Venice's potential capacity to help in a crusade against the Turks, in 1468 Bessarion bequeathed his great collection of manuscripts to the city of Venice, to be placed in a library bearing the name of Venice's patron saint, located near the Basilica of San Marco and accessible to the public. It was a tribute to this city that Bessarion's library, the result of his effort to save as much as he could of the Greek heritage after the fall of Constantinople to the Turks, was deeded to Venice, which he called "almost another Byzantium." It was a tribute and a trust that the Venetians recognized and wished to honor so as to enhance their cultural reputation.[50]

During the decade following Bessarion's gift the 752 manuscripts, 482 of which were in Greek, arrived from Rome, but there was no building to place them in, and the fifty-seven crates in which they were packed were stacked in government offices. Over time, some manuscripts were borrowed, some lost, some deteriorated. Mostly the collection went unused and uncared for. In 1515 the government was still debating where the library should be built, and with what funds. Clearly this was a matter of governmental concern, but not yet a priority, given that the War of the League of Cambrai was still going on.

February 7, 1515 (19:424)   The Council of Ten talked about making a library where lectures are currently held in the warehouses facing the Flour Warehouse in the Terra Nova, where they would deposit the books of the late Cardinal Nicenus. It would be paid for out of the money obtained from the rebels[51] up to —— ducats. The head of the Ten ser Marin Zorzi, university

Aricò 1980, xv–xvi, from the Marciana manuscript, partially correcting Berchet's transcription in Berchet 1903, 97.

50. On Bessarion's library, see Labowsky 1979, 148; and M. Zorzi 1996, 862–72. On Bessarion and other Byzantine scholars in Italy, see Monfasani 1995.

51. Inhabitants of the mainland cities who had rebelled against Venice in the War of the League of Cambrai and whose goods had been confiscated and sold.

laureate, promoted this, and ser Zorzi Emo agreed and spoke in favor. On the other side were ser Francesco Bragadin, savio di Consiglio and ser Luca Trun, who is on the Council of Ten; they maintained that it should not be put there because that is the most dismal spot in the city,[52] and the books will be completely eaten by insects [*tarmar*], etc. No decision was made.

But a few months later a decision was made, and the language of the decree reflects the importance the government now attributed to this precious collection of books, whose proper shrine would certify the intellectual preeminence of Venice, approximating it to the two greatest cities of antiquity and supporting its claim to have inherited their cultural superiority:[53]

May 5, 1515 (20:178)   The savi dil Consejo and the savi a Terraferma proposed making a library on Piazza San Marco in one of the new buildings that are being built for the Procuratia, the one in the middle, where the procurators have agreed to give [the space]. The 800 volumes left by the very reverend Cardinal Nicenus, which are in the hands of the procurators, will be put[54] there as is stated in the bill. There were 17 votes against, 149 votes in favor, and it passed. I shall write a copy of the bill here below.

May 15, 1515 (20:181–82)[55]   Libraries are often used to celebrate and add special luster to well-founded cities. Such was the custom in Rome, Athens, and other ancient wealthy cities. For, beyond providing an ornament, [libraries] also encourage minds toward learning and erudition, whence good morals and other virtues are wont to arise. Therefore, since the late most reverend Cardinal Nicenus, who was so gracious to our Republic, gave to our government, now some time ago, the gift of about 800 Greek and Latin books of great beauty and value, thinking that nowhere else than in this city of ours could this donation shine more brightly, it is fitting at last to erect a most precious repository [for the treasure] that the vicissitudes of time held nearly hidden, especially since the procurators of our church of San Marco have willingly donated a place in the Piazza itself, in the area of new building. There could be no lovelier location in this city, nor one more convenient to the learned, in addition to the fact that once the library has been finished, it will present a perpetual monument to our heirs and a mirror and light to all Italy. It is therefore decreed:

That in the aforesaid location in the Piazza San Marco be built a library,

---

52. The dungeon for prisoners of war was also located nearby. See above, n. 22.
53. See above, n. 13.
54. The manuscript has *posti;* the Fulin edition has *posati.*
55. The senatorial decree is in Latin.

in that manner deemed most appropriate by the procurators themselves, in which the aforesaid books are placed as decorously as possible. . . . In addition, let a caretaker or governor be responsible for the care of the books themselves, to be appointed at a salary that shall seem [proper], and let there be enacted whatever other provisions and ordinances shall seem useful for their preservation.[56]

Eight months later Andrea Navagero was appointed curator of the collection. Even if he failed as the historian of Venice, he did help protect this intellectual legacy, as did his successor Pietro Bembo, until the Biblioteca San Marco could assume that responsibility.

The University of Padua

The major center of Venetian academic learning was not located in the several academic chairs or incipient public library of Venice, however, but in the Studio, the University of Padua, some thirty miles away on the mainland. After Padua's conquest by Venice in the early fifteenth century, its university became the privileged *studio* of the Venetian state, run by local authorities and later by specially chosen Venetian *riformatori*, elected in Venice's Great Council. From 1407 on, the Senate forbade subjects of the Venetian state from studying or matriculating at any other Italian university. Sanudo never fails to attach the title *dotor*, "university laureate," to those patricians who earned it, and he occasionally mentions the honor and celebrations that accompanied a newly awarded degree.[57]

The largest faculty at the University of Padua was that of law. It attracted many Venetian nobles, who used it to prepare themselves for government service, and its professors were the most highly paid. But the arts faculty (which comprised theology, philosophy, rhetoric, and medicine) was also important, and its prominent teachers had their defendants, as the following letter from the Venetian bishop of Padua shows:

February 23, 1504 (5:884–85)   Copy of a letter of don Pietro Barozi [Barozzi], bishop of Padua, written to our Signoria.

---

56. In spite of this positive statement, the discussion about location and payments was to go on for seventeen more years. Cf. diaries, 22 April 1532 (56:94). A contract was not awarded to the architect, Jacopo Sansovino, until 1537, and it not until three decades after that that Bessarion's collection was finally moved into the new Biblioteca San Marco (to which was later added the building formerly housing the Mint), where it remains to this day.

57. See diaries, 15 July 1519 (27:480) and 19 December 1520 (29:467). But he did not overvalue the prestige of the doctoral title and boasted once that he had successfully argued in the Great Council against a patrician with a university degree: "Io vadagni un dotor—I have won out over a university laureate" (5 August 1500; 3:587).

Most serene prince and excellent lord, whom I hold in the highest regard, a most humble greeting.

My offices of the chancellorship of the university and of the bishopric, which I received and hold through the grace of Your Sublimity, make me appear to be importunate in matters pertaining to the university, especially in the reading of theology according to Scotus's interpretation, which is like an antidote for the errors, swarming out of philosophers, concerning "the eternity of the world, the unity of the intellect, whether nothing may come from nothing," and other similar positions.[58] If it were not for [Scotus's philosophy], one could say that everything studied in that university could be studied in a pagan university, from canon law on out, something that is far from Your Sublimity's mind, you who try to govern your subjects in God, from whom you have your governing authority, as a most Christian governor. Your Serenity knows that I have written you several times in a very persuasive way concerning a salary increase for the reverend master Mauricio de Gelanda [Maurice O'Fihely] of the Order of Friars Minor, who has been appointed by you to lecture in theology according to Scotus's interpretation. He is an extremely learned and experienced man who, in my opinion, has no equal in Italy, except for the reverend teachers Antonio Trombeta and Gratia.[59] You also know that I made it clear to you that he should not be looking for a large increase, but only an amount that will allow him to live decently according to his rank.

Now I am letting you know that he will soon go to France to the general assembly [of his order] that will be held there. Due to his learning and other good qualities, he may be retained there or he might remain there of his own volition "because the love of the homeland is sweet" [*Quia dulcis amor patriae*]. If Your Sublimity gives him a salary increase right away, he may perhaps return. And if he does not, he will have reason to glorify to those others the liberality of this Signoria. Otherwise I respectfully advise you that he is about to remain there, and as for us, we will have to work hard to find a teacher of similar quality for twice as large a salary as would have been his once the increase had been computed.

---

58. The bishop was concerned because some unorthodox theories held by a number of theologians in Padua challenged the orthodox scholastic tradition of the great medieval scholar John Duns Scotus (1266–1308). Most of these theories were derived from the twelfth-century Spanish Mohammedan scholar Averroes, who wrote commentaries on Aristotle's philosophy and whose ideas remained influential in the sixteenth century. On Pietro Barozzi (1441–1507), see Gaeta 1964. For Scotist and Thomist theologies, see Grendler 2002, 369.

59. Trombeta was a Franciscan and Scotist scholar who held a professorship of metaphysics in Padua. He earned 150 florins in 1509–10, while the Scotist theologian Maurice O'Fihely earned 100. See Grendler 2002, 370. We have been unable to identify Gratia. The editors thank Jill Carrington for her advice.

Your Sublimity, who is very learned and very religious and knows the importance of that lectureship, should do as you think best, and I will be completely satisfied. I humbly recommend myself to your grace.

Sent from Padua, on the 23rd day of February 1504.

The servant of Your Most Excellent Sublimity,

Pietro, Bishop of Padua.

Faculty salaries were only one concern of the authorities; unruly students were another. In the following instance, the students rebelled because they had not been granted a Carnival holiday.

January 20, 1507 (6:534)   A newsworthy item: this month something very memorable happened in Padua. The students, wishing to take a vacation for Carnival, did not permit the professors to give lessons at the schools. As a result, ser Polo Pixani, knight and capitanio of Padua and at the moment also the vice-podestà because ser Andrea Gritti was here [in Venice], issued an edict that the students must let the professors teach or face a penalty of yanks with the rope.[60] Angered by this, the students smashed all the benches in the school and the chairs of the professors, so that they could not lecture. And when certain professors wanted to lecture at the Carmine,[61] the students opposed it. Now, seeing this, the capitanio ordered the professors to take a vacation; the students, when they heard this, grabbed the professors and forced them to lecture. All of this was done because the students did not want to be subject to our rectors in this matter.

The role of the university and its students both in serving the cultural reputation of Venice and in securing support for the Paduan economy was significant. Disrupted by the War of the League of Cambrai, the temporary occupation of Padua by imperial forces, the adherence of prominent university professors to the imperial cause, and the revenge exercised upon them when Venetian troops retook the city (8:523), the university's normal operations were restricted. But in January 1517, as the war begin to wind toward its close, a group of Paduan citizens requested that the university be reopened.[62] The following September, three patrician *dottori,* probably laureates of this university, were deputed to reopen the University of Padua. In the ensuing debate in the Senate, the political and commercial significance of the university to the Venetian state was emphasized:

---

60. *Scassi di corda,* a standard form of punishment as well as torture in which the arms are tied behind the back and a rope suspended from a pulley is tied to the wrists, then yanked upward.

61. The monastery or church of the Carmelites.

62. See diaries, 25 January 1517 (23:527); and Dupuigrenet Desroussilles 1981, 626–29.

September 15, 1517 (24:670–71)   A bill was posted by ser Zorzi Pixani, university laureate and knight, ser Marin Zorzi, university laureate, and ser Antonio Justinian, university laureate, who have been charged with the reconvening of the University of Padua, to appoint some professors to lecture in Padua, that is, to the second-position chairs in law,[63] because they do not have first-rank professors. They have good professors in the arts and in rhetoric, including the following three: don Bernardin Spiron [Speroni], the physician, who is in this city [i.e., Venice]; for medicine, don Antonio de Fantis, of Treviso; in philosophy, don Marin Becichemi, of Scutari. In rhetoric there are other professors whom I do not know. Altogether, these professors draw a salary of about[64] 2,000 ducats.

Ser Lunardo Emo, the councillor, went to the podium taking the opposite position: that now is not the time to rebuild the University in Padua, [that it should not be rebuilt] until we know how things will stand with the emperor. He said that the foreign[65] students could give away Padua [to the imperial forces] that and the possession of Padua is the key to this city. He said a few more words and proposed postponement for the moment, a delay of two days until Corner and Gritti are here; they left Verona today and will be able to give information about the fortification of Padua, etc. Ser Francesco Bragadin, savio dil Consejo, responded, saying that a decision had already been made to reconvene the university in February, that everything had been written and agreed upon with the professors, and therefore it should be done. This countermotion not to do so would cause great harm because we should not distrust the students, in the first place because [many of them] will be our own patricians, of whom there were twenty-four at the beginning of the war, and because [other students] will be our subjects, from the Romagna and such. Then he said that when Marsilio di Carrara came to retake Padua [in 1435], the patrician students defended Padua, and that thus [the city] will be more secure if the university is open. He also said that the university budget was 7,000 ducats, including the payment and the tariff on the carts, and that for this reason the revenue produced by the tariffs is considerable, as is the money that the students will leave in Padua and the money they will spend living there; he said a few other things. Ser Lunardo Emo returned to the podium to respond to him. Next ser Zorzi Pixani, mentioned above, went to respond to him, praising the reopening of the university as a means of securing the city. Then the savi proposed to affirm the earlier decision [to proceed with the opening of the university]. The ballots were cast: one negative vote,

---

63. The manuscript reads *videlicet in leze al secundo locho;* the Fulin edition omits *in leze.*
64. The manuscript has *di zercha;* the Fulin edition omits it.
65. The manuscript has *forestieri;* the Fulin edition has *fo restreti.*

zero abstentions, 40 positive votes for the councillor's proposal [not to re-open the university], 121 [positive votes] for the proposal of the savi; the latter passed.[66]

A report from the returning podestà of Padua a few years later indicates that the university was once again thriving and attracting wealthy students, whose large retinues helped to strengthen the economies of both Padua and Venice:

November 13, 1521 (32:132)   In the morning there were no letters of any importance, nor any noteworthy events. Ser Marin Zorzi, university laureate, appeared before the Collegio dressed in black velvet to make his report. He has just returned from being podestà of Padua, having been replaced Sunday by ser Piero Marzello. First [he spoke] about justice and the procedures of that palace,[67] complaining that the [state] attorneys[68] prevented justice from being done by suspending sentences.[69] He recalled certain measures that had been praised by the savi, who wanted to propose them in the Senate. He spoke of the university and the quality of the professors, describing it as a flourishing and excellent university, more so than it has been for many years, with a good number of students, among whom are twenty noblemen who maintain retinues of twenty, thirty, and forty persons apiece. He spoke a little about the fortifications and the city. Then he wanted the heads of the Ten to be called and related some things [to them]. He was praised according to custom by the doge in the usual way.

Literary Figures

The competition for public appointments in the humanities, the search for an official historian, the establishing of a library, and the reestablishment of the University in Padua—Sanudo seems to have been more interested in the activities and processes than in the individuals involved, though dedicated as he was to particulars, he did name names. Not only did he scant the *literati* of Venice but he had little to report on the great literary figures of Italy's past or present. For example, Baldassare Castiglione, author of the enormously popular work *Il libro*

---

66. There follows a list of the faculty to be appointed, along with their teaching duties and salaries. See Grendler 2002, 32.

67. The Palazzo della Ragione, the seat of the Venetian government in Padua, where judicial procedures were administered by a variety of local and Venetian bodies.

68. The manuscript has *dolendosi li Avogadori;* the Fulin edition has *dolendosi di Avogadori.*

69. These suspensions of justice, in the form of *gratia,* were a problem throughout the various judicial bodies in Venice. In this case, sentences determined in Padua were reversed by the *gratia,* or exonerations, obtained in Venice (see chapter 2).

del cortegiano (The Book of the Courtier), is mentioned only once, upon his death, and then more for his position as papal envoy to Spain, with particular emphasis on his ecclesiastical income, his perquisites, and his possible successors:

March 15, 1529 (50:62)   From the Venetian ambassador in Rome.

He writes that Baldissera da Castion [Baldassare Castiglione], the papal nuncio, has died in Spain. A man of letters, Castion had obtained the bishopric of Avila, which gave him an income of twelve thousand ducats. Just eight days after the emperor agreed to give it to him, he suffered an attack of spleen and died. He writes that the reverend bishop of Verona, who was at one time the datary,[70] wanted to return to his bishopric but that the pope refused to grant him leave; however, he writes, the pope's confessor has been working to arrange for the leave. But since the news of Castion's death has arrived, people are saying that the pope wants to send one of the following three in Castion's place to the emperor's court in Spain: this former datary or the archbishop of Capua or the bishop from Vicenza, who is the pope's chief of staff.[71]

Two iconic literary figures of the past—Dante and Boccaccio—are not mentioned in the diaries. However, he does mention Petrarch, the third member of the great triumvirate. Petrarch had spent much of his later years (1362–74) in Venice and the Padovano and extolled its freedom, justice, and peace, naming it "a port to which men can repair . . . who seek the good life."[72] Sanudo had written a *notarella,* a little commentary, on Petrarch in his younger years and had visited his tomb and final home in Arquà, near Padua.[73] It is not surprising that the last volume of the diaries contains a letter from the Venetian envoy to France describing Avignon, where Petrarch had long lived and loved his Laura, and nearby Nîmes, with its great Roman aqueduct:

September 4, 1533 (58:741–42)   A letter from Avignon, from ser Marin Justinian, the Venetian ambassador, written to ser Tomà Lippomano, his brother-in-law.

Having left Montpelier, we proceeded to Nîmes and then here to Avignon. . . . At Nîmes I saw an arena, or theater, that is smaller than the one in Verona; the exterior is better preserved and more beautiful, but the interior is smaller

---

70. The bishop of Verona was Giovanni Matteo Giberti; the datary was the office in the Vatican that vetted candidates for benefices and, together with the pope, dispensed them.

71. The pope's chief of staff was Girolamo de Bencucci da Schio. Sanudo was as interested in the income from Castiglione's benefice as he was in who would succeed him as papal envoy to Spain. Such ecclesiastical benefices provided a form of patronage for men of letters.

72. See Petrarca 1966, 234.

73. See Sanudo 1857; and P. F. Brown 1996, 157.

and less beautiful. I also saw an extremely old church [originally] dedicated to the ancient gods; it was small but exquisite. It belongs to the Benedictine nuns and the good women associated with them. In addition, I saw an ancient building, possibly the treasury, which had multicolored columns and, in front, a peristyle. On our way to Avignon, a little way off of the road, we came upon an aqueduct that consists of three arched structures, one on top of the other. It is an enormous structure, very beautifully built, beneath which flows the Gard River. The first bridge has six arches; the second, which is built atop the first, has eleven arches; the third has thirty-five, somewhat smaller. It is among the most beautiful things I have seen in France, perhaps the most beautiful.

Here, in Avignon, the tomb of Petrarch's madonna Laura was recently discovered in the church of St. Francis of the Friars Minor; the sepulture is in the floor, surmounted by a large stone. Found beneath the stone was a small leaden vase on which was sculpted the figure of a woman, and inside it was a sheet of parchment upon which the following lines were written, allowing us to identify this without question as the tomb of madonna Laura:

> Here chaste and blessed the bones abide
> Of one unique in life, a courteous soul.
> Cruel obdurate stone, you now keep beneath you
> Her fame, true worth and lost beauty.[74]

Venetian Artists and Artwork

It may come as a surprise that such an assiduous observer as Marin Sanudo devoted so little attention to Venetian art and artists in a period that has come to be seen as the golden age of Venetian painting. Sanudo's interest in artists, like his interest in the few literary figures he mentioned, tended to be more historical and practical rather than aesthetic or analytical. He recorded the names of artists he thought important, the works they produced, how they were paid, when they died, and where they were buried, thus providing precious clues about the lives of some of Italy's greatest painters, among them the Bellini brothers, Carpaccio, and Titian.

---

74. "Qui riposan quei casti et felici ossa / di quella alma gentile et sola in terra. / Aspro e dur sasso hor ben techo hai sotera / il vero honor la fama e beltà scossa." While Sanudo reproduces the entire sonnet, we give only the first quatrain here. However, this is not by Petrarch, nor is the tomb Laura's. Moreover, this error was already known to men of literature such as Pietro Bembo. The editors are grateful to Sarah Sturm-Maddox for this information. See Giudici 1980, 12, which says that most likely the poem was not Petrarch's and the tomb was not Laura's and that Bembo held this opinion in 1533.

February 23, 1507 (6:552)   I note that today Zentil Belin [Gentile Bellini] was buried in the church of San Zane Polo. An excellent painter, he was sent several times to the father of the present Turkish lord, from whom he gained a knighthood.[75] Since he is so famous, I wished to mention him here. He was —— old. He is survived by his brother Zuan Belim [Giovanni Bellini], who is the best painter in Italy. Also in recent months Andrea Mantegna died in Mantua.

November 29, 1516 (23:256)   It has become known that Giovanni Bellini died this morning. He was an outstanding painter; he was —— years old and famous throughout the world. And old as he was, he still painted with great skill.[76] He was buried in San Zane Polo in the tomb where his brother Gentile, also an excellent painter, is buried.

Like the Bellini brothers, Titian was known by reputation. Of particular interest are the remarks regarding the remuneration for the civic projects undertaken by these artists:

May 31, 1513 (16:316)   Today, the Council of Ten, meeting without the zonta, voted that Titian the painter should work in the hall of the Great Council, as the other painters do. However, he will not earn a salary, but will have the usual expectation[77] of those who have painted. Among them were Gentile and Giovanni Bellini and Vetor Scarpaza [Vittore Carpaccio], and now it is the turn of this Titian.

That several governmental bodies might be delegated to supervise the financing of artistic projects bears witness to the integration of politics and the visual culture of the city:

December 30, 1515 (21:425–26)   A bill was posted by the savi today with the following content. With the money being spent on painters for the hall of the Great Council, ser Francesco Valier, the *provedador al Sal,* was charged with looking for—and indeed he has found—among the paintings commissioned

---

75. Mehmed II gave Gentile a heavy gold necklace and the title "Eques Auratus" (Golden Knight). See P. F. Brown 1988, 55.

76. Giovanni Bellini was born c. 1434 and was about eighty-two when he died.

77. An *expectativa* (also *spettativa*) was the promise of a *sansaria* (also *sanseria*), which was a sinecure awarded to an individual for certain services rendered to the state. A *sansaria* normally became available upon the death of a person holding one. At this time there were thirty, of which only a few were given to artists. The one Titian eventually received gave him a lifetime income from a brokerage at the Fondaco dei Tedeschi.

two whose painters have not yet begun the drawings. These two cost about 700 ducats, and he said he could contract the job[78] for 250 ducats. Therefore, it was proposed that these painters be removed and better, more experienced ones be selected, that the new painters be approved by a vote in the Collegio, and that the review of these accounts be delegated to the three savi over the Kingdom of Cyprus. Against: 6; in favor: 150. I note that this was a pointless decree since the painters clarified everything with the Signoria, the terms were approved by the Collegio, and a new agreement along these lines had been made with the painter Titian himself.

In addition to governmental commissions, the artists were also at work in the scuole and churches of Venice. Two commissions of Titian's are described below, the first being his great *Assumption of the Virgin* in the church of the Frari:

May 20, 1518 (25:418)   Today was the feast of St. Bernardino, which, according to a bill passed in the Senate, was observed: government offices were closed. And yesterday the large altarpiece painted by Titian was installed on the altar of Santa Maria di Frati Menori (dei Frari). Earlier, a great work in marble had been constructed around the altar at the expense of Maistro Zerman, who is the guardian now.[79]

The second was a painting, now lost, portraying Doge Andrea Gritti and, in what must have been a familiar detail, Gritti's "little amber-colored dog behind him":

December 6, 1523 (35:254–55)   Today, Sunday, was the feast of St. Nicholas. The doge, together with the Signoria, the savi, the state attorneys, and the heads of the Ten, went to Mass in the new church of San Nicolò. The doge was dressed in a crimson damask robe with modified ducal sleeves and lined with fox fur; over it was a squirrel-lined mantle of crimson satin with the sleeves showing. He also wore a crimson velvet corno. The doge is responsible for the work, almost completed, at San Nicolò, and there is a very fine portrait of him there painted by Titian that even includes his little amber-colored dog behind him. Also figured in the painting are St. Nicholas and the four Evangelists writing the Gospels.[80] Now that the gilding of the altar has been completed,

---

78. The manuscript has *si faria;* the Fulin edition has *li faria.*

79. Germano da Casale, guardian of the Frari and its high altar, had commissioned Titian's *Assunta* in 1516, probably using bequests to the Frari to pay for it. Goffen 1986, 73, 84.

80. Although part of the fresco that included St. Nicholas, the four Evangelists, and Doge Andrea Gritti has been lost, a fragment survives: *Madonna and Child with Angels,* now in the Sala della Quarantia Criminal in the Ducal Palace. See Wethey 1967–75, 1:100.

religious offices were said there yesterday and today. So the old church of San Nicolò will be demolished; it is very beautiful, decorated with paintings, frescoes, and mosaics. At the door there is a marble plaque inscribed with the text of a papal bull issued when ser Lorenzo Celsi was doge [1361–65]. . . . When Mass was over, everyone went home.

In another entry, Sanudo reports more on the political gossip about a painting of Doge Andrea Gritti than on the painting itself, relaying a "clever commentary" the diarist wished to preserve for posterity:

October 6, 1531 (55:19)   I saw, newly installed in the Collegio, the full-length painting of the doge. He is pictured kneeling before Our Lady, who is holding the Christ child, and he is presented to her by San Marco; behind her are San Bernardin, Santo Alvise, and Santa Marina. It has been suggested that these three saints are quarreling over which of them made him doge. San Bernardin is saying, "He was elected on my feast day." Santa Marina is saying, "He was elected because he retook Padua on my feast day, July 17." Santo Alvise is saying, "I am the namesake of ser Alvise Pisani, the procurator, who is his supporter, who was a member of the Forty-one and was responsible for his being elected doge." Thus, given this dispute among the three saints, it appears that St. Mark is presenting him to Our Lady and her son so that they may decide which of the saints determined the election of His Serenity to the dogeship. It is a beautiful painting made by Titian the painter and an amusing commentary, which I wanted to preserve for posterity.[81]

Patronage of the arts in Venice was also exercised by wealthy Venetians such as the Corner family (see above) and the Grimani. Cardinal Domenico Grimani was well known not only for his library[82] but also for his collection of furnishings and art, parts of which are described here two and a half years after the cardinal's death in 1523:

February 1, 1526 (40:758)   As is the custom [for Candlemas], the doge, eleven ambassadors, most of the Signoria, and sixty nobles went to vespers at Santa Maria Formosa; the new parish priest —— had the church beautifully decorated. Among the other items were two embroidered golden brocade hangings

---

81. Doge Andrea Gritti (1523–38) was closely related to Alvise Pisani by marriage. The Committee of Forty-one was the final group in a series of nine to elect the doge. See chapter 2. Since Titian's votive painting of Gritti was destroyed in the fire of 1574, this entry is one more example of the value of Sanudo's diaries as a unique record. The painting was replaced by one on the same subject by Tintoretto c. 1581–84 that is still there today. Cf. Finlay 1980b, 158.

82. See chapter 4 for a 1505 ambassadorial visit to Grimani's library in Rome.

decorating the doors of the church.[83] They belonged to Cardinal Grimani, as did others made of silk cloth of gold.[84] On view in addition were some paintings made in Rome by Michiel Angelo [Michelangelo]; they are very beautiful and also belonged to the late cardinal. I saw two portrait busts in bronze that looked very real; they were of the late Doge Antonio Grimani and his son Cardinal Grimani.[85] Indeed, the church was well furnished with tapestries. The ceremonies concluded with the parish priest's invitation to the doge and all present to take refreshments, which he repeated twice. Then they went to the bridge for the annual ceremony, and the doge gave the priest the coins called "bianchi," which are small copper coins about the size of *bagatini*[86] but having no value, and the parish priest in turn gave the doge two paper hats decorated with his own arms and those of the doge and the patriarch.[87]

Art, Artists, and Monuments in Rome

Sanudo's most informative passages on art came to him secondhand, occasionally from ambassadorial reports and *relazioni* but also, and primarily, from the letters of the Venetian Marcantonio Michiel, writing from Rome. A patrician, connoisseur of antiquities and painting, and art patron, Michiel was also well known in the literary circles of Venice, which Sanudo frequented. Michiel spent two years in Rome in the entourage of Cardinal Francesco Pisani, and his letters to friends in Venice during this period (1518–20) testify not only to Michiel's discerning eye but also to Sanudo's interest in antiquities and in the famous artists of the day who worked outside Venice.[88]

The following excerpt is from the end of a long letter Michiel's wrote on May 4 to Antonio Marsilio, a successful lawyer in Venice for the government and for private clients, who later (1523) had himself painted, together with his wife, in a marriage portrait by Lorenzo Lotto that now hangs in the Prado Museum in Madrid. The letter evidently reached Sanudo on May 12, for he copied it into the

---

83. "Do antiporte d'oro a ago . . . soprarizo." See Newton 1988, 16.

84. See Molà 2000, 114.

85. Antonio Grimani was doge from 1521 to 7 May 1523; his son, Cardinal Domenico Grimani, whose palazzo is described in chapter 4, died unexpectedly on 27 August 1523. See T. E. Martin 1998 for a discussion of these busts.

86. *Bagattini* were small Venetian copper coins of little value; twelve were equal to one soldo.

87. The annual ceremony referred to celebrated the rescue of Venetian women from marauding Slavs by members of the Scuola of the Casselleri (the makers of furniture, including marriage chests). As a reward, they asked for the doge to make an annual visit. "What shall I do if it rains?" he is supposed to have said. "We shall give you a hat," they replied. See chapter 7, entry of 16 December 1497 and n. 63, where these symbolic hats are mentioned. See also Sanudo 1980, 59, 181, 183, 233.

88. For more on Marcantonio Michiel, see Fletcher 1981.

May 12 entries to his diaries. The recipient's interests, as well as Michiel's own, may explain the content of this particular letter, which describes religious, social, and literary events in Rome and concludes with this reference to Michelangelo's work in Florence and a survey of several major artists at work in Rome:

May 12, 1519 (27:274)   I have yet to make good on the debt I incurred when I promised to write you about the paintings and the painters of Rome. If you had been more courteous in writing me about what is happening where you are, I would have already satisfied your curiosity. However, putting aside your negligence, I will undertake to satisfy your curiosity soon. For the moment I will tell you only that Michelangelo is in Florence to work on the facade of the church of San Lorenzo. At the Vatican, Raphael of Urbino has painted four of the pope's rooms and a very long loggia and has set about painting two other loggias, which will be truly beautiful. In addition, he is in charge of the building of St. Peter's Basilica, which is progressing slowly for lack of money. Sebastiano [del Piombo] has completed his altarpiece, which will be shipped to France, so I must go round and see it tomorrow.[89] I am in the process of making friends with another Sienese painter, named Master Baldassare [Peruzzi], who is a clever inventor and an accomplished[90] master of his craft. When I have more time, I will write you in greater detail in further letters. I am sending you some inscriptions and epitaphs that I obtained from the chapel where Pontano is buried in Naples. Please show them to my lord ser Nicolò Tiepolo and my other friends.[91]

---

89. Sebastiano's altarpiece, *The Raising of Lazarus,* painted for the cathedral of Narbonne, is presently in the National Gallery, London. Two months later after this letter, a letter from the Venetian ambassador to Rome reports "a great feast for discerning eyes was present in a canvas by the hand of our painter Sebastiano, placed on an altar in front of the house of the most reverend Corner. Its subject is the visitation of the Virgin Mary and St. Elizabeth. It is a gift destined for the most Christian queen of France, and it will always stay in her room" (diaries, 13 July 1519; 27:469). [Fu gran pasto agli occhi giudiciosi quel zorno uno quadro di mano del nostro Sebastiano pittore, posto sopra uno altare avanti la casa del reverendissimo Cornaro, el cui argomento è la visitatione di Santa Maria et Santa Elisabetta, dono destinato a la Cristianissima regina di Franza, et che averà a stare sempre ne la sua camera.] This painting, *The Visitation,* now in the Louvre, may have been a Venetian state commission intended for the queen of France. See Fletcher 1981, 456n44.

90. The manuscript appears to have *pronto;* the Fulin edition has *proto.*

91. Marcantonio Michiel kept a diary from January 1511 to February 1520; it is an important supplement to the information provided by Sanudo for this period. According to Fletcher 1981, 459, it was Antonio da Marsilio who passed on to Sanudo the letters of 4 May 1519 and 11 April 1520 (diaries, 27:272–74, 28:424–26). We know that Marsilio was familiar enough with Sanudo to have visited his library and, together with Giovanni Battista Egnazio, estimated the value of his books. See Caracciolo Aricò 1980, xii n10; Berchet 1903, 104; and Conto 1994, which refers to R. L. Brown 1837–38, 3:221.

Raphael was particularly concerned about the remains of antiquity in Rome, whose despoiling also alarmed others. In the excerpt below, a summary of a letter from the Venetian ambassador in Rome written on July 9, 1519, the clerical authorities are blamed for allowing such destruction.

July 13, 1519 (27:470–71)   For many years priests and Romans have been despoiling the tomb of Caesar Augustus, which is located between the Tiber[92] and the Via Flaminia. The greed and worthlessness of our times have inflicted a similar fate upon the rest of the venerable antiquities. But in the last few days the leader [of these thieves], who is the brother of Cardinal Ursino [Franciotto Orsini], has arranged to put the finishing touch on things, once the marbles have been stripped, by having some [accomplices] demolish it.[93] When the accumulated earth was removed,[94] they discovered the foundations and, nearby, an enormous obelisk that had fallen to the ground, broken in the middle, and eventually been covered by earth. And it seems to me that I have read that there were two of them; perhaps if they look on the other side, they will find [the second one],[95] if it has not already been broken or removed. The one that was found was rather badly burned by a lime kiln that used to be nearby. Raphael of Urbino, that refined and inventive painter and architect, has offered to transport it to St. Peter's Square for 30,000 ducats,[96] but I do not know if this will take place. If my memory serves me, both Suetonius and Strabo wrote extensively about this tomb, which has finally been located. It breaks my heart to see such a beautiful thing destroyed

Less than a year later Raphael was dead. Sanudo summarizes a letter from Marcantonio Michiel written on April 11 and addressed to Antonio da Marsilio in Venice describing Raphael's activities in the last phase of his life. Michiel praises the artist's love for antiquity and his volume of drawings in which he reconstructed the sites, architecture, and ornamentation of ancient Rome. He grieves for the interruption of this fair project and describes, in an elegiac tone, the sorrow of pontiff and people, the impressive funeral procession, and the burial in the Pantheon. The entry ends with news of Michelangelo's illness and an expression of concern for the health of the Venetian artist Vincenzo Catena:

92. The manuscript has *Tevere;* the Fulin edition has *teatro.*

93. The manuscript has . . . *marmi, cum alcuni c' hanno pigliato;* the Fulin edition omits *cum alcuni c' hanno.*

94. The manuscript has *scoperta;* the Fulin edition has *soto.*

95. The manuscript has . . . *coperto. Et già parmi avere leto che ne erano dui; forse se cercheranno da l'altra, parte lo troveranno;* the Fulin edition has . . . *coperto. Erano do forse; se cercherano da l'altra parte troveranno.*

96. The Fulin edition has *ducati 90 milia;* the manuscript has *ducati 30 milia.*

April 15, 1520 (28:424–25)   On the night between Good Friday and Holy Saturday, at three hours after sunset, Raphael of Urbino, that most refined and superior painter, died. He is mourned by everyone, and especially by the learned more than others, although most of all by painters and architects. Just as Ptolemy mapped the universe, so Raphael was compiling in one volume drawings of the ancient buildings of Rome, showing their proportions, forms, and ornamentation so clearly that one who had looked at the book could claim to have seen ancient Rome.[97] He had already completed the first section. Nor was he limiting himself to showing the floor plans and sites of the buildings, information that with great effort and industry may be gathered from the ruins. In addition, he was producing eloquent drawings of the facades and their ornamentation. Those that could no longer be found among the ruins he painstakingly reconstructed by consulting Vitruvius, the architectural plans,[98] and ancient histories. Now death, filled with envy of him, has robbed[99] us of this young master too early, at the age of thirty-four on the very day of his birth, interrupting his important and praiseworthy endeavor.[100] Even the pontiff is beside himself with grief; in the fifteen days of Raphael's illness His Holiness sent messengers to visit and comfort him six times. Think what others must have done.

Because the papal palace in these days is threatening to collapse, the pope has gone to stay in the apartments of Monsignor de Cibo. There are those who say that the [weakening of the papal palace] was not caused by the weight of the superimposed arcades but that it was an omen that its adorner would soon pass away. And truly one has been lost whose excellence was equal to the task, whose absence should be mourned and lamented by every sensitive spirit not only in simple and fleeting voices but in well-executed and lasting works, which, if I am not mistaken, are already being undertaken by myriad authors.

They say that Raphael left 16,000 ducats, of which 5,000 are in cash, to be distributed chiefly among his friends and servants. His house, which used to belong to Bramante and which he bought for 3,000 ducats, was left to the cardinal of Santa Maria in Portico [Bernardo Bibbiena]. A stately funeral

97. The notebook referred to here is no longer extant. That Raphael was deeply concerned about the antiquities of the city is attested to by a report he made to Pope Leo X in 1516–17, about one or two years after the pope had, in 1515, appointed him "maestro della fabrica" of St. Peter's and ordered him to oversee the preservation of ancient inscribed marbles. Cf. Jacks 1993, 184–86, 190, 192.

98. The manuscript has *ragione della architectura;* the Fulin edition has *regione della architectura*.

99. The manuscript has *expresissimamente;* the Fulin edition omits it.

100. Raphael, who was born on 6 April 1483, was exactly thirty-seven when he died on 6 April 1520.

procession brought him to the Rotunda [the Pantheon], where he was buried. His soul has certainly gone to contemplate those celestial halls that suffer no deterioration, but his memory and his name will long remain here on earth in the thoughts and minds of good and noble men. . . .

Michelangelo has fallen ill in Florence, they say. Please tell our Catena[101] to take care of himself because this seems to be the fate of great painters. God be with you.

The following excerpts, dating from a few years later, are from an account written by four special envoys sent to offer obeisance to the Flemish Hadrian VI on his ascent to the papal throne in 1523. The excerpts below, all from the much longer description (34:204–25), provide a guide to the civilization of Rome as it appeared to cultivated Venetian patricians in the early sixteenth century. The report was entitled "Summary of the journey of our ambassadors who went to Rome on an embassy of obeisance to Pope Hadrian VI."

May 25, 1523 (34:217–18)   [While the ambassadors were in a secret audience with the pope] the other gentlemen set out to see Rome, going to the seven churches,[102] which is a wonderful devotional[103] practice. They began at San Paulo [fuori le Mura], which is a good distance from Rome. It is an old church, but large and very beautiful, and supported by a number of handsome and very large columns. It belongs to the Benedictine friars. From there they proceeded to San Sebastiano, a lovely church that has steps that take you quite far underground.[104] Indeed, [the authorities] have almost forbidden people to go down there since so many have vanished because they insisted on going in too far, and either their light went out or they lost their way and did not know how to return. Next was San Lorenzo fuori le Mura, because it is another of the Roman [devotional churches], and it is a beautiful church. Then to Santo Jani (San Giovanni) in Laterano, outside Rome, where there is an infinity of wonderful relics. And outside [that] church, in another church with its own round shape, is the baptistery of the emperor Constantine; the roof of that church is supported by twelve columns of high-quality porphyry only slightly smaller than the columns of the Basilica of San Marco [in Venice]. They are a marvel to behold. The church is adorned all around from top to bottom with mosaics that look like intarsia and are made from porphyry, serpentine, and

---

101. Vincenzo Catena (c. 1480–1531), a successful Venetian painter.

102. This itinerary, known as the Via delle Sette Chiese, was and remains a popular route for pious visitors to Rome.

103. The manuscript has *ch' è devotioni bellissime;* the Fulin edition has *de devotioni bellissime.*

104. There are catacombs on four levels at this site.

alabaster. Their beauty is impossible to describe. Every inch of the church, no matter how old, is covered with them, and there are great quantities of porphyry, serpentine, alabaster, and other stones that appear to be jewels.

Next, [the gentlemen went] to Santa Croce in Jerusalem, the titular church of the most reverend cardinal of Santa Croce. It is a new building, commissioned by His Reverence, and still under construction. At the time, they were working on the cornices and arches of some doors in a stone that had been taken from the ruins. It is of such extreme beauty that certainly a small piece of it would be worth setting in gold and wearing as a precious ring.

From there one goes to Santa Maria Maggiore, which is inside the city: a church most beautiful in its grandeur and full of lovely columns and precious stones that have been composed into mosaics. It is a most cheerful church. It is here that they celebrate the feast of Our Lady of the Snows, [whose origin is as follows:] A Roman gentleman who was very rich and noble, not being able to have children with his wife, made a vow to the glorious Virgin Mary that if a son were born to him he would build a church in her name. His prayer was answered, so he asked God to reveal to him where to build the promised church. The following day, August 6, he found an enormous snowfall covering a piece of ground exactly the size of the plot upon which this lovely and spacious church is built. The result is that it is the most beautiful of the seven churches, and it cost a lot of money. The next church on the itinerary is St. Peter's, so that one begins at St. Paul's and ends at St. Peter's.

On St. Mark's feast day, the [Venetian] ambassadors were at his church to participate in a procession with the most reverend Cardinal Grimani because he holds the title to it. They then joined him there for the repast that he gives every St. Mark's Day for all Venetians in Rome. Then on to Sant'Agnete [Agnese] fuori le Mura; among its many other treasures is the tomb of Bacchus, which is like a large square chest of splendid porphyry. The sides and the top are decorated with figures sculpted in almost full relief, joined with a long and very intricate vine whose leaves and grape clusters wind around the head and other limbs of those little figures with great comeliness. On the way back, one sees the baths of Diocletian, most of which are still standing, as grandiose as they once were. It is breathtaking to imagine how immense they must have been. It is one of the most beautiful things to see in Rome, although there are others, like the baths of Antoninus, and so on, but none of them has such a large portion still standing.[105]

---

105. These baths, which once covered thirty-two acres, were more visible and monumental in the sixteenth century than today, since now they are but one part of the Piazza della Repubblica.

The next section of this long excerpt describes a feast in Cardinal Grimani's palazzo (still extant in Rome as Palazzo Venezia), a sample of the princely life led by a Venetian cardinal in Renaissance Rome. This bears comparison with the feast described eighteen years earlier in another Grimani palace (see chapter 4). Once again, the decor, the cuisine, and the entertainment are carefully reviewed, for the visiting dignitaries would have found these as culturally important and worth reporting on as the architectural and sculptural wonders they saw. The table set in a courtly manner, the elegant room overlooking a pleasant Mediterranean garden (a *locus amoenus*), and the illustrious guests convey all the elements of the grand dinner in which certain details stand out: the abundance of fish because it was Saturday, the gigantic, expensive sturgeon, the flowing wine, the contrast between the ability and the physiognomy of the woman lute player. Finally, there is the shrewd and revealing cultural judgment of the wise and gracious Cardinal Campeggio, whose function as master of ceremonies in the uncouth Flemish papal court proved so essential.

May 25, 1523 (34:218–19)   The Venetian ambassadors and gentlemen went to dinner at the palazzo of Cardinal Grimani, the second largest in Rome after the palazzo of San Zorzi. It is enormous in size and in number of rooms and is most handsome. The tables had been set up on one side of an open corridor, with a roof to block the sun, like a monastery cloister; it overlooked a garden of lovely fresh grass, in the middle of which was a beautiful fountain surrounded by the most beautiful orange trees, laurel, and cypresses, which were a wonder to behold. There were four tables lined up one after another, with spaces between them so that diners could pass through to seat themselves on the inside, where everyone was placed. At the head of the first table was the most reverend cardinal, then the ambassadors, and on the outside, nearby, his lordship the illustrious Duke of Urbino, who was staying in the palace in the rooms below.[106] These were the people seated at that table. At the other were the patriarch of Aquileia[107] and many Venetian bishops and archbishops. Next came the table of gentlemen and others. . . . Both sides of the table were full; there were about forty people. Since it was Saturday, fish was served; there was a great quantity of it prepared in various ways, and people remained at table for just under six hours. Being the bishop of Porto,[108] the cardinal has access to large amounts of fresh-caught fish, yet eighteen gold ducats were spent on a single fish, a sturgeon whose head was bigger than that of a large

---

106. Cardinal Grimani was also bishop of Urbino, where Francesco della Rovere was duke.

107. Marino Grimani, nephew of the cardinal.

108. Rome's seaport.

steer. There was an infinite quantity of wine. After dinner some musicians were brought in, including an extremely ugly woman who sang and played the lute admirably. Once the envoys had risen from the table and taken their leave of His Reverence, they went to the pope's palace with the ambassadors, both of whom, being knights, were dressed in gold brocade with ducal sleeves lined in crimson. They spent a short time there, visiting the most reverend [Cardinal] Campegio, who has his apartments in that place. He is the most wise, refined, and humane cardinal at the court; he is about thirty-six years old, handsome, and very gracious. He must initiate all of the court functions, since those Flemish friends of the pope are ill-versed in such customs and slow to learn them. Then the ambassadors returned home.

Sanudo's summary of the description then returns without a break to the buildings and public places of the city. Two, the Colosseum and the Pantheon, because of their size evoke comparison with Venetian spaces familiar to those to whom the envoys would be addressing their report:

May 25, 1523 (34:219–21)   Many vestiges of beautiful ancient buildings may be seen in Rome today, among them, near Monte Cavallo [Horse Mountain], part of the palazzo of that father of literary men, the good Maecenas. But it is impossible to fathom the shape and quality of that building. It is called Monte Cavallo because at the brow of the densely populated hill there is an imposing piece of very thick wall; on top of one corner there is a horse made of what seems to be Istrian stone, very old and corroded by time. On top of the other corner of the wall there is another horse. Both are only half-figures, that is, with only the head, neck, hooves, shoulders, and half of the back. Next to them are two enormous naked giants, twice life size, who hold the horses with one arm. These figures are very well proportioned and made of the same stone as the horses; each is as beautiful as the other. Under one there is an inscription in lovely antique capital letters that reads "Opus Fidiae" [Work of Phidias], and under the other, "Opus Praxitelis" [Work of Praxiteles]. They are beautiful figures, and the workmanship is exquisite. The word *Fidiae* is written without aspiration; it should be spelled *Phidiae*.

There are also many beautiful arches [in Rome] still standing intact. And then there is the Colosseum, which surpasses all other works of art; it was truly said, "Every achievement cedes to Caesar's."[109] From the part that remains standing, which is quite large, one realizes what an imposing and wondrous structure it was. Outside, the form is round, with a very large cir-

---

109. "Omnis Caesareo cedat labor amphiteatro." Martial *De spectaculis* 1.7; the original has *cedit*.

cumference; inside it has the shape of an egg, half as large as the Piazza San Marco [in Venice], measuring from where the columns are. And there are still many vestiges of the Capitoline Hill, where [civic] discussions continue to be held. In the splendid palazzo where the Roman senator lives there are an infinite number of admirable marble and bronze figures, the most beautiful and famous in the world. There is a bronze statue of a peasant pulling a thorn from his foot; it is made in such a natural, rustic way that to the admiring onlooker the peasant seems to be trying to speak, lamenting the pain of this thorn—an amazing sculpture! There is also a bronze she-wolf suckling two little boys, that is, Romulus and Remus, which is very well done. And there are other things, etc.

Then there is Santa Maria Rotunda, the most beautiful church in the world; it used to be the Pantheon, or the temple of all the gods, but these days the feast of All Saints is held there. One used to ascend ten or twelve steps upon entering; now, with the passing of time, the [surrounding] earth has risen so much that one descends more than eight steps. In the vestibule of this church there are fourteen columns, which are certainly larger than ours at San Marco. They are arranged in front of the door in groups of three and support a canopy made of metal beams. The door is as large and ancient as the rest of the church; it too is made of metal and contains so much gold that many say that it is of the quality of raynes,[110] but that cannot be true, because Pope Leo would not have let it stand if it were.[111] It is undeniable, though, that it is of a very yellow color that looks like gold, and it has sustained many dagger blows made by those who wish to see if the blade resists[112] inside as it does outside.[113] . . . The church is as round as if it had been made with a compass; inside it is full of altars. At the foot of one of them, which is magnificently decorated with serpentine, porphyry, and marble, lies the tomb of ser Raphael of Urbino. The roof is all round and concave like a vault and cut out of living rock. Nor does any light enter into the church except through the door and a great hole in the middle of the roof about the size of a wellhead, which makes the interior very luminous. The church is so tall that it is visible a good distance from Rome.

The final excerpt from the report describes three of the most famous ancient sculptures in Rome, the statues of Apollo, Laocoön, and Venus, with an appreciation confirming the fascination that the art and architecture of antiquity

---

110. Gold coins minted in Cologne, of exceptional purity. German coinage would have been well known in Venice.

111. The avarice of Pope Leo X (1513–21) was proverbial.

112. The manuscript may have *resiste;* the Fulin edition has *reense* ("penetrates"?).

113. This would test whether it was high-grade gold, which is very soft.

held for Sanudo's contemporaries and the reverence with which these were discussed. The following excerpt describes the famous Belvedere sculpture court built by Bramante for Julius II:

May 25, 1523 (34:224–25)   Facing each other in the middle of the pope's garden are two enormous male figures in marble, twice life size, reclining on the ground as if they were sleeping. One is the Tiber, and the other the Nile; both are very ancient figures. Two beautiful fountains spring from them. At the first entrance to the garden, on the lefthand side, is a little chapel embedded in the wall, where, on a marble base, stands the statue of Apollo that is famous all over the world. A life-size figure made of very fine marble, it is extraordinarily beautiful and praiseworthy. Somewhat farther along the same wall that leads to the arch, in a similar niche and even on a similar base about the size and height of an altar, and in the middle of a perfect basin, one sees the most famous [*famosissimo*] statue of Laocoön. It is a figure of superb quality, very lifelike, about the size of a normal man, with a flowing beard. The figure is entirely naked, so that you could not see the joints, veins, or even the nerves better in a living person: the only thing that is missing is the breath of life. He is seated with his two little boys, one on each side, and both encircled—as is he—by serpents exactly as Virgil describes. The statue so beautifully displays the creator's skill that it could not be improved: you can clearly see [the figures] weaken and die. The serpent has wound itself twice around the waist of the child on the right, gripping him tightly; one of the coils crosses the boy's little chest, squeezing so hard that his heart stops. The other boy, on the left, gripped by a second serpent, tries with his little arm to free one leg from the rabid beast. His every effort failing, he turns to his father with tears [coursing down] his face, crying out to him and grasping his father's left arm with his other hand. But seeing his poor father's travail to be much greater than his own, the child expresses two sorrows: the first for his own death, which he knows to be close at hand, and the second because his father cannot help him. Indeed, he is dying and soon to give up the spirit. It is impossible for human skill to create such a work of art so closely resembling real life. The entire statue is intact except that Laocoön's right arm is missing. He appears to be about forty years old and resembles ser Hieronimo Marzelo from San Thomado; the boys look about eight or nine years of age. When the king of France was in Bologna, he asked Pope Leo to give him the statue as a gift. The pope promised that he would, but so as not to deprive the Belvedere of it, he would have a copy made to give to the king. The figures of the two boys have already been made and are stored there in a room, but if the sculptor had lived to be 500 years old and had made a hundred copies, they would not look like the original.

Not very far from here is a beautiful Venus displayed in a similar fashion. She is life-size and naked, with a bit of drapery over her shoulder that covers some of her private parts. It is as lovely a figure as you can imagine, but the excellence of the Laocoön makes everyone forget both her and the Apollo, which before had been so famous.[114]

Venice's Public Monuments

The Venetians' fascination with Rome, with the standards of art and material luxuries set by the cardinals in what was called *Urbs*, "the City," in no way diminished Venetians' appreciation for their own monuments, public statuary, and styles of luxury. From his first volume to his last, Sanudo comments on the various works of his own city, such as the Colleoni monument near San Zanipolo, which was unveiled shortly after the diaries began:

March 30, 1496 (1:96–97)   I note that in Venice on Monday, March 21, the bronze equestrian statue of Bortholamio Coglion (Bartolomeo Colleoni) of Bergamo, the former captain general of our army, was unveiled in the campo of San Zane Polo. Until now, the statue, which is a very handsome work, had been in the hands of master craftsmen, who were gilding it. Everyone went to see it, and I must note, too, that the master who made it, whose name is Alexandro de Leopardis and who is from the Veneto, has been given a lifetime pension of one hundred ducats a year, above and beyond the considerable sum that the Council of Ten paid him when he completed it. And written on the base of this equestrian statue is this inscription: "Bartolomeo Colleoni of Bergamo, in honor of his fine military deeds on behalf of our empire." And on the other side is written "Under the supervision of Johanni Mauro and Marino Venier, 1495." And under the belly of the horse: "Alexander Leopardus F[ecit]."[115]

About the same time that the Colleoni monument was completed, work began on the Torre dell'Orologio, or Clock Tower. There had been a clock at the north

---

114. This sculpture of Laocoön, which made an enormous impression on contemporaries, had been found on 14 January 1506 on the Esquiline Hill and placed in the Belvedere court by Julius II. Sanudo copied into one of his notebooks a letter commenting on this statue. See BNM, Lat. Cl. XII, 211 (4179), fols. 200–226.

115. The statue had been commissioned by Colleoni himself, who also supplied the funds. Colleoni had commanded the Terraferma Venetian armies from 1454 to 1475, the year of his death. The model was created by the Florentine Andrea Verrocchio (d. 1488), and the statue was finished and fused by the Venetian Alessandro Leopardi, who also designed the pedestal. In Sanudo's manuscript there are two rubrics next to this item: "Statua equestri Bartol. Coleoni Bergomensi" and "Nota eiusdem statue littere."

end of the Piazza San Marco for a century, but it had become decrepit, and in 1493 a new one was ordered. In due course it was decided to house it in a tower of its own.[116] On June 10, 1496 (1:205–6), the work of demolishing existing structures where the retail street of the Merceria entered the Piazza had begun, to make space for a monument that Sanudo declared would be "the most beautiful in all of Italy." By December 1498 the great bronze giants had been put in place, and six weeks later the clock itself was unveiled:

December 15, 1498 (1:833)   On the 11th day [of December] the bronze giants were placed above the clock tower that was recently built in Piazza San Marco, where they will ring the hours. This I have recorded so that it will be remembered for all time.

February 1, 1499 (2:396)   Today, February 1, as the doge was crossing the Piazza to go hear vespers at Santa Maria Formosa, the clock was uncovered and seen for the first time. It is located on the Piazza, above the street that leads to the Merceria. It was made with great ingenuity and is most beautiful.

The Ducal Palace, the central governmental building of the city, was often under reconstruction. It was appropriate, Sanudo wrote in his *De origine*, that this should be "a most beautiful and worthy work" (33), one comparable to the excellent public buildings of Rome (34). Sanudo remarks in the excerpt below on the obligation of the Venetian nobility to maintain their public buildings.

March 10, 1497 (1:552)   Recently, the hall of the Great Council in Venice was restored, that is, along the edges where they had rotted, and the entire hall was shored up. It was solid work and cost 500 ducats. The pieces of the edges that had rotted were put on display so that everyone could see them. Had this not been attended to, there would have been a great outcry against the nobility.[117]

Such repairs were ongoing, and given the large sums of money spent on these public works, it is not surprising that there were occasional cases of fraud:

April 5, 1498 (1:927–28)   In the past few days, it was discovered that master Antonio Rizo, the stonemason who is in charge of the rebuilding of the Ducal Palace, and who has received a salary of 200 ducats per year for thirteen years already, had embezzled more than 10,000 ducats by adding expenses to

---

116. See McAndrew 1980, 382.
117. That is, for allowing such an important civic monument to fall into a ruinous state.

the bills for the Ducal Palace. Francesco Foscari and Hironimo Capelo, who were charged with reviewing the accounts of the Signoria, found that up to this point 97,000 ducats had been spent. This is an incredible sum, but a large part of this money has been stolen, not spent. Now this Antonio, seeing that even the shirt on his back was about to be requisitioned, sold everything he had, including a piece of property, and fled toward Ancona or Foligno. He was called to appear on the 10th of this month, and maistro Simon Faxan the stonemason and others who worked with him were arrested because they stole large amounts.[118]

Another important edifice that required fairly frequent attention was the bridge at Rialto, the commercial center of the city and the only place where the two sides of the Grand Canal were connected. The earliest structure may have been a bridge of boats that connected the parishes of San Giovanni de Rialto and San Bartolomeo.[119] By the mid-thirteenth century a wooden bridge had been raised on posts, and successive wooden bridges continued to be built on that spot thereafter. In January 1514 the existing bridge and much of the surrounding area were destroyed by fire (see chapter 6). In the months that followed, a variety of artists, humanists, and politically powerful spokesmen made themselves heard,[120] an indication that Rialto had, for Venetians, an importance equivalent to Piazza San Marco, matching the governmental heart of the city with its economic vitality, "of all the world the richest part," as Sanudo put it.

The range of models proposed during that summer is an indication of the cultural forces circulating at that time. Fra Giocondo, a well-known architect, proposed a geometric reconstruction, one of rigid hierarchies, which Sanudo dismissed because "he does not understand the location" (July 28, 1514; 18:401). On the same morning, Alexandro de Leopardis, the sculptor, presented his model to a committee predesignated to consider models for Rialto.[121] Indeed, every August morning "the committee for rebuilding the Rialto meets and deliberates on how the models should be" (August 30, 1514; 18:483).

By September, it seemed that a decision should be made, and the Senate turned to discussing its financing:

---

118. On Antonio Rizzo, *proto* of the Ducal Palace, see Sanudo 1989–2001, 1:226; 2:397–98, 494, 497.

119. Bisà and Masobello 1991, 7; Romano 1987, 17.

120. Sanudo 1980, 27. See Calabi and Morachiello 1987, 294–97, for some of the important participants in the debate.

121. "In questa matina, il Collegio deputado sopra i modelli de Rialto *etiam* si redusseno come eri, e alditeno Alexandro de Leopardis per il suo modello." Diaries, 28 July 1514 (18:401); cf. 9 August 1514 (18:401).

September 28, 1514 (19:94–95) Now that the collegio of the [seven][122] savi has chosen the model for the bridge at Rialto, the construction must begin without further delay.[123] The bridge will serve both as an ornament for this city and as a profitable convenience for our merchants. To provide for such work, a bill for the election by this council of three savi by ballot is proposed. The savi, together with the purser of the Salt Office, who is assigned to construction projects, must be present at Rialto to give orders and supervise the construction.[124] No one may refuse the office, under pain of a fine of 500 ducats, to be collected by the state attorneys.[125] And because it is necessary that those who have shops and storerooms contribute the money to pay now for the walks along the canal and later for the other matters necessary to the construction, the aforesaid savi are charged with inspecting for the Salt Office the storerooms that have been built above the shops, vaults, and stands of the Rialto. . . . The entire construction of Rialto must be supervised by the foreman [appointed by] the savi so that it will all be under the authority of one person, as is proper. The monies designated to be disbursed for this construction must be kept in a truly separate and specific account, credited to those who made the payments. Their money will be repaid. . . .

With regard to the allocation of shops and vaults, each merchant should be allotted an amount in proportion to his storerooms, and the remaining space should be given to the Signoria. . . .

Because there are many disagreements about the reconstruction of the buildings in the areas of the Rialto island that burned, these savi are also appointed as judges. Appeals concerning their decisions will be made to the twenty *savi sopra le vendede,* with all of the procedures and conditions made by the seven savi, their predecessors.[126] These savi are also free to provide whatever reward they deem fit to the notary, who has labored this entire past year without recompense. Thus he will have good reason to continue to do his job. For: 148; against: 15; abstaining: 2.

As it turned out, the rebuilding of the bridge was no simple matter, largely because it served, as stated above, as both an ornament for the city and a conve-

---

122. Sanudo erroneously wrote "forty-seven."

123. By July 1514 ten models had been proposed. The one mentioned here was not the one finally used. See Calabi and Morachiello 1987, 297. For a survey of sixteenth-century discussion of different models, see Calabi and Morachiello 1987; and the review of this work, Lieberman 1991.

124. The Salt Office, which was responsible for much of the government's revenue, dispensed a large part of the money appropriated by the Senate for construction. See Lane 1973b, 58, 447.

125. The problem of Venetian patricians refusing to accept certain offices to which they were elected was a serious and continuing one. See Queller 1969, 1986.

126. Sanudo defines these groups elsewhere as bodies of senators who sat on alternate days as

nience for its merchants. Over the next two decades, models came and went, and the debates continued, such as the one below, which shows how expediency (which served the merchants) clashed with and even obscured the search for a fine design that would redound to the city's reputation. Sanudo's summary of a discussion in 1526 conveys the conflicts and his own unwillingness to be involved in what he declared to be a discussion of an inferior subject, *cosse basse:*

February 22, 1526 (40:855) The savi dil Consejo and the savi a Terraferma, except for ser Jacomo Corner, who was absent, posted a bill to grant the request of those who had owned shops on the Rialto before it collapsed to be allowed to rebuild the shops at their own expense on the sides of the current bridge, atop pilings. The Salt Office being satisfied through its examination of the directors of the works that they would not damage the bridge or cause a risk of collapse, and indeed that they will strengthen it, let it therefore be law that those shop owners may rebuild [their shops] on pilings along the bridge as they were before, having the quality and the dimensions that are [registered] in the Salt Office, on the condition that when a desire arises to rebuild the bridge, they may not petition our Signoria for any [reimbursement] for the construction and demolition of the shops. So that the bridge may be open on both sides, let it also be law that all of the stands and whatever else on the stanchions has been rented by the Salt Office be taken down. And those who have paid will be reimbursed. . . . It passed, having 128 [yes votes], 53 [no votes], 11 abstentions.

And I opposed this bill for four reasons. The first is that it shames our city, because there will be no more talk of completing the bridge; the second is that it will cause damage by impeding the flow of the waters in the Grand Canal; the third is that the bridge will not be safe because it will be loaded down with sacks and other things; the fourth is that they have shops near the bridge on which they pay rent. But I did not wish to speak because this is an undignified subject, and those who are new to the Senate might say that Marin speaks of undignified things.

The difficulty in resolving the Rialto bridge design was also compounded by the relative antiquity of the structure, which gave it a mystique and status that was quasi-sacred.[127] The Venetians could not compete with the Romans in the area

courts of appeal for cases concerning debts to the state and the wine tax. See Sanudo 1980, 251, 310.

127. Calabi and Morachiello 1987, 294, cites a reference to a statement by the Council of Ten that the Rialto should be considered *un sacrario* (a shrine or sanctuary) of the city and comments that a *sacrario* is difficult to transform.

of ancient ruins and remains. They collected, purchased, and abducted what portable pieces of antiquity they could. What they had might be fragmentary, but it was valued. During all the construction and reconstruction of Renaissance Venice an effort was made not to destroy or even move older artifacts to make way for new monuments.[128]

Private Wealth, Private Art, and Public Pride

Apart from the main civic buildings of the city, much of the wealth and artistic patrimony of Venice lay in its private buildings. These palatial homes were called *case* or *ca'* in Venice, for only the doge's abode was allowed to bear the regal title *palazzo.* In 1532 one of the most remarkable of these *case* burned down, to Sanudo's horror, taking with it an emblem of the city's material stature and pride:

August 16, 1532 (56:751–54)   During the night, at the fifth hour after sunset, a terrible fire took place in this city. It was an awful and lamentable event for the public sector as well as for the private[129] that the palace, which is the home of the children of the late and illustrious knight and procurator ser Zorzi Corner, [burned down]. Located on the Grand Canal at San Maurizio and formerly called Ca' Malumbra, it was purchased in — by ser Zorzi for 20,000 ducats. He spent an additional 10,000 ducats, making it a very beautiful house, indeed the most beautiful house in Venice and, one could even say, in all Italy: aristocratic, magnificent, and spacious. Yet it burned to the ground in — hours; one could say it was like the fire of Troy, but worse, since there was nothing left standing except for some columns on the canal side. All the rest is burnt and in ruins. In a few places the shells of the walls are still standing, but it is frightening to look at them.

The incident occurred in the following way. Ser Zuan Corner's son,[130] who has the benefice of Cyprus, which brings him thousands of ducats per year in income, had sent his father sugarloaves and bales of cotton. The sugarloaves had gotten wet in the crates, and to help them harden, they were put

---

128. See Sanudo's successful protest two years earlier against moving two stone lions from the baptistery to the "columns of Acre" because "it is a very shameful thing to move those ancient pieces." See chapter 1, diary entry of 9 September 1530 (53:541). His respect for antiquities was combined with a sense of Venice as a perfect product of its own civilization, the display of whose treasures should not be lightly altered. Such an attitude of respect for original locations did not apply, however, to Sanudo as a collector; we learn from Federico da Porto's poem praising Sanudo's library, copied by Sanudo into his notebook, that during his military service in Padua Sanudo acquired two ancient vases for his library. See BNM, Lat. Cl. XII, 211 (4179), fol. IV. For a comprehensive discussion of Venice's relationship to antiquity, see P. F. Brown 1996.

129. The manuscript has *privato, che il;* the Fulin edition omits it.

130. Alvise di Giovanni, cardinal comendator of Cyprus. See Howard 1975, 134 and fig. xvi, 135.

on an upper floor in a room above the courtyard. During the day the sun beat down on them, and at night braziers filled with burning coals were brought to heat and dry them. And whether by the will of God or of the devil, ser Zuan was treating his gout with Indian wood, having been told that he would be cured of it if he did but that he must also keep warm. This is the particular disease of the family, and he has the inflamed kind. And so he was taking it according to the prescribed regimen. So that evening many of the braziers in his room were taken upstairs. A great heat, which had perhaps already built up before then, got under the beams, which caught fire. In a flash the roof and the crates of sugar were ablaze. There was no one in this sugar [storage] room.[131]

In the Corner house they dined late, so everyone was asleep. Someone saw the fire and pounded on the door, but either the family did not hear it or, as rumor has it, they did not want to open up. Thus the shout went up along the Grand Canal, "Fire in the Corner house!" At about the fifth hour the family members got up; all of them were dazed and half-dead. Some of their friends and relatives having arrived, they decided that the lesser evil would be to lock the doors and salvage as much as possible of their great wealth. They carried out their plan, not letting anyone enter until the best had been carried away. A great number of baskets of mixed silver pieces were taken to the house of ser Zuan Antonio Malipiero, their brother-in-law, who lives nearby in Ca' Zorzi, as well as three strongboxes full of money, almost all the furniture that was on the first floor and the mezzanines, the family papers, and other things. When the barges[132] arrived, they were loaded down with the sugarloaves and cotton that had been in the warehouse. The large items were thrown into the courtyard and later taken away.

The Corner were all in a daze, but the upper part of the house continued to burn. No one would put them [all] up, [so] the women[133] and the children and mother and wife of ser Jacomo Corner went to Ca' Malipiero[, while the] wife and children of ser Zuan Corner went to stay with her brother ser Zuan Pisani, the procurator. Immediately ser Nicolò Venier, the former councillor, and his sons came, as well as ser Antonio da Mula, the councillor, and ser Agustin,

---

131. Cf. ibid., 134: "Zuan . . . had retired to bed with some heated Indian wood to relieve the pain. The process of preparing the remedy had led to such overheating in the attic above this room that during the night the roof beams began to smoulder." See also Calabi 1991, 790. On the "cure" using this Indian wood (also known as *guaiacum* or *guaiaco*), a treatment that may have been for syphilis rather than for gout, see Arrizabalaga, Henderson, and French 1997, 100-102. On the wealth of the Corner and their development of sugar plantations in southern Cyprus (Piscopia property), see Lane 1987b, essay 2, 72ff.

132. The manuscript has *piate*; the Fulin edition has *pute.*

133. The manuscript has *le done*; the Fulin edition has *la dove.*

his brother, ser Antonio Dandolo, ser Francesco Barbaro, [and] ser Domenego Mozenigo, who was particularly helpful. They kept watch at the doors so that nothing would be stolen. When it was God's will, the doors were opened and people went upstairs, some to put out the fire[134] and some to steal.

The description of the fire continues, mixing what amounts to an inventory of the wealthy family's possessions with a record of human losses involved:

The fire, however, continued to burn because the first floor did not have a tile covering. All of a sudden the beams caught fire, and the flames spread below. Many of the possessions of the queen of Cyprus, their aunt, were up there.[135] Some of them were recovered by several brave men who threw the items out of the window. These men had been promised a quarter of what they saved, though later they were simply given one hundred ducats, which they accepted. [Among the goods stored up] there were about seventy beds, the sugar, all burned, 400 bushels [*stara*] of wheat, all the crates, and the paintings that had been in the grand salon [*portego*], including the *Supper at Emmaus*, a beautiful painting by Vianello. The chapel burned, and the Roman marble bust of — that was worth a king's ransom broke into pieces and was destroyed in the fire. The hot flames continued burning their way through the house; someone who was on the upper floor and wanted to come down could not because the staircase had burned. There were no more stairs; there were no water buckets. A rope was thrown up to him, and he came down. The fire continued until tierce, at which time the facade collapsed and those beautiful marble columns of the balcony[136] fell all at once into the Grand Canal, never to be recovered. As it happened, four people were under the *portego;* three of them, to save themselves, jumped into the water. The stones fell on them, and they were seen no more. One who was closer to the bank escaped, though he was half-dead. If they had all stayed under the *portego,* they would have been saved.

The fire continued to burn the entire house and mezzanine rooms, including the very beautiful gold one that was built by the cardinal,[137] who is now the bishop of Brescia, as well as the one on this side, used first by the most illustrious ser Zorzi Corner and now by Jacomo, his son. Beneath it, the Corner kept their silver and their strongboxes in a very secret and secure place, which allowed them to be saved though many other things were stolen.

134. The manuscript has *studar;* the Fulin edition has *stridar.*
135. This was Caterina Cornaro (*Cornaro* was the alternate spelling of *Corner).*
136. The manuscript has *di la balconadi;* the Fulin edition omits it.
137. Francesco Corner.

Indeed, many things were destroyed by the fire, though in general they were not of great value. The fire also penetrated the wood storage area, which contained 600 cartloads of wood, the casks of the wine cellar, and the other storage rooms: everything burned. The bank along the canal was full of people, but no one helped. The Grand Canal was full of boats, and the people [in them] were watching the fire. At first the sparks even fell on the far side of the canal. It was a huge conflagration. Much later the tocsin was rung at the churches of San Maurizio, Santa Maria Zobenigo, and San Vidal. It was a terrible thing that in such a short time, that is in — hours, a house that was so beautiful and magnificent and so large both in length and width of facade should be completely burned, nor did any part of it remain standing, except the shells of a few walls on the Ca' Duodo side, which really ought to be knocked down, although that will not be easy to do.

Sanudo concludes his account with his personal reaction to what he judged to be a great civic tragedy, as well as a summation of the Corner wealth and of the loss imposed on the family by this conflagration:

I was so full of sorrow that I cannot give expression to it, both for the private reason that this house of Corner are very dear friends of mine and for the public reason that it is the most beautiful house in Venice and that [the house] at the head of the Grand Canal should burn. Thus, toward none I went by boat along the Grand Canal with ser Gasparo Contarini, the councillor, to see the fire, which was so great and had such high flames that I took fright and was unwell the rest of the day. And because there was a council meeting today, afterwards I went to Ca' Malipiero to see ser Jacomo Corner and comfort him, saying, "The Lord giveth and the Lord taketh away."[138] Ser Zorzi Corner, knight and procurator, recently deceased, had entailed [*conditionò*] the house to his sons and male heirs. If all of them are dead, it will pass to the males of Ca' Corner, nor can it be divided or broken up, as stated in the will. And it was written also that if ever the house should come to ruin or burn or anything else, it should be rebuilt by his executors.[139]

These Corner are extremely rich. They have an income of about 10,000 ducats, in addition to 10,000 ducats from three abbeys, including Carara San Zen on Cyprus. Then, Cardinal Francesco, who was a knight and procurator and is bishop of Brescia, has an income from this and other benefices of 3,000 ducats. In addition, they have a great quantity of cash, jewels, silver, etc. It is

---

138. "Deus dedit, Deus abstulit." Sanudo here misquotes Job 1:21, which reads "Dominus dedit, Dominus abstulit."

139. On the entailing of property in Venice, see J. C. Davis 1975, 74–83.

believed that they will rebuild the house and perhaps make it more beautiful than ever, but it will take a long time to assemble all the wood and the hard stone. Then again, they will not be able to find the columns from the facade, although the columns facing the side canal remain. They also have a house in San Polo that belonged to Gatamelata,[140] where they lived before they bought this one, and a house in San Cassan, on the Grand Canal, where the queen of Cyprus lived. Ser Jacomo Corner is going to stay in the latter home for the time being; ser Zuan, his brother, will also go there at first, but then they will move to his house in San Polo.

To conclude, the members of the Corner family suffered a loss of — thousands of ducats and more in this fire, losing the value of the house and the improvements that were made after they bought it, the goods that burned, the merchandise and what was stolen.

But it was the loss to the grandeur of the city that most affected Sanudo, grieving privately for a house he loved and publicly that "the most beautiful house in Venice and [one] at the head of the Grand Canal should burn." The diminishment of that grandeur was a personal and civic tragedy. For Sanudo, as for his patrician contemporaries, the city itself was the central material artifact, the physical realization of their culture.

That was true not only for the Venetians: the great de' Barbari map of the city, completed in 1500, on which the urban fabric of the city is recorded in amazing detail, was a paid for by a German merchant, Antonio Kolb:

November 30, 1500 (3:1006)   To be noted: On the thirtieth of this month a decision was made by the Signoria that since the German merchant Antonio Kolb had incurred great expense in printing [a map of] Venice, which is being sold for three ducats [per copy], he may transport it from the city and carry it away without paying duty.

The government's grant for a four-year copyright and free export license for the print exists in the archives along with Kolb's statement that he was issuing this view "principally for the glory of this illustrious city of Venice."[141] The city's geography was indeed its fame, its glory, and its culture. It was also its stage, within and upon which its daily dramas took place, as well as its own formal and informal entertainments, to which we turn in the concluding chapter of this volume.

---

140. Gattamelata (Honey Cat) was the nickname for Erasmo da Narni (d. 1443), a famed mercenary captain who had commanded Venetian forces.
141. Schulz 1978, 473.

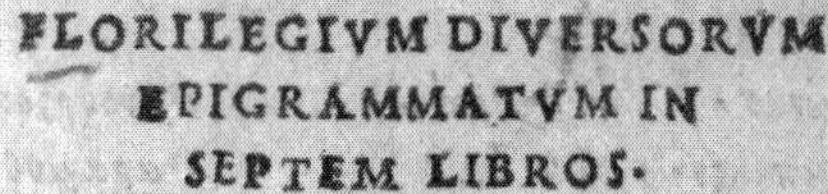

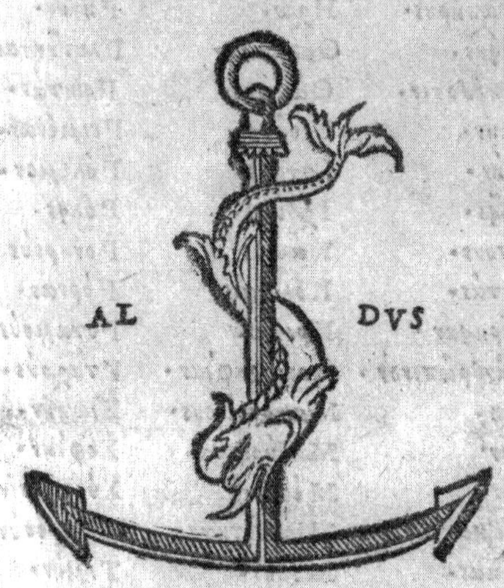

Title page from *Florilegium diversorum epigrammatum in septem libros* (Venice: Aldine Press, 1525). Rare Books Division, The New York Public Library, Astor, Lenox and Tilden Foundations.

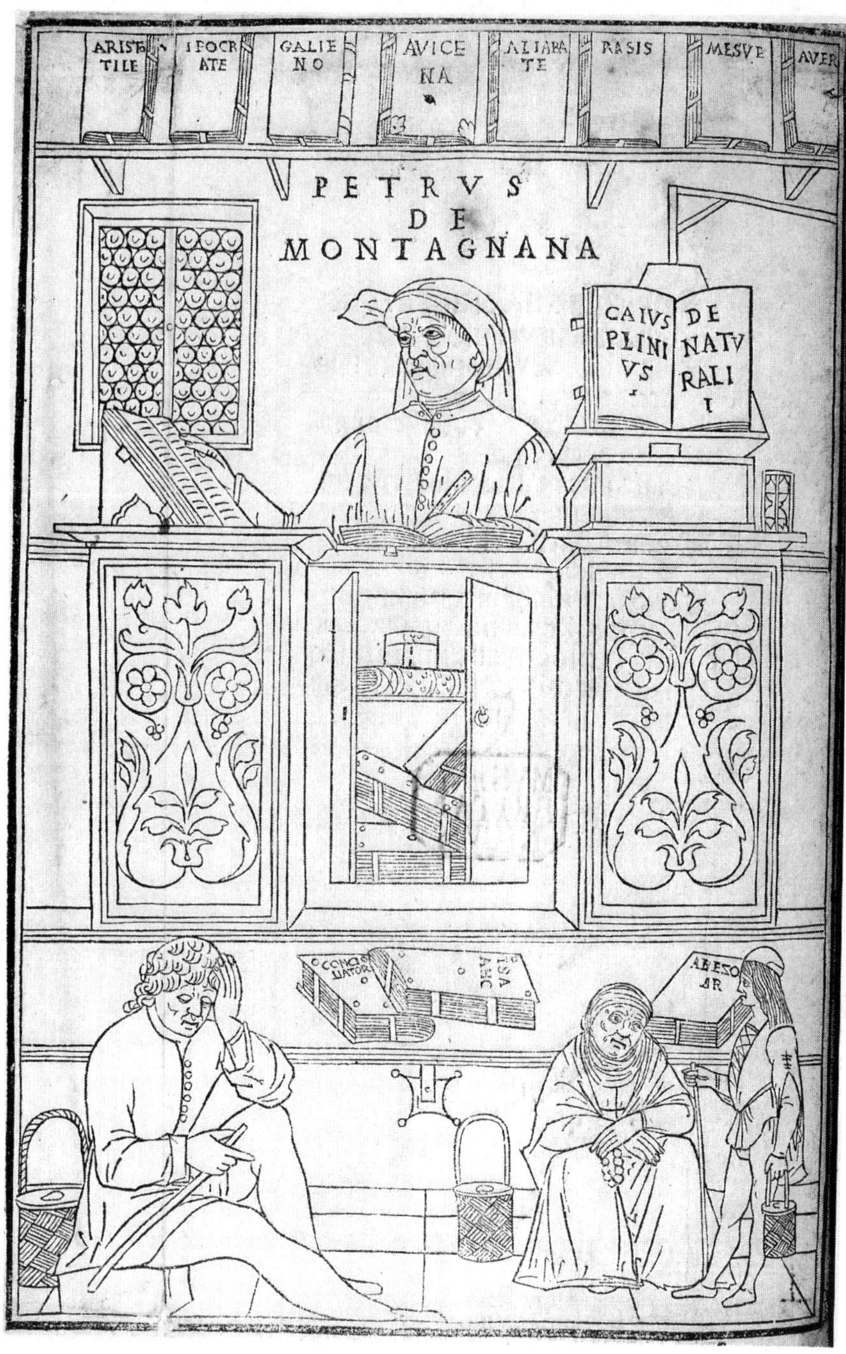

Pietro da Montagnana lecturing, from Johannes Ketham, *Fasciculus medicinae* (Venice: Giovanni & Gregorio de' Gregori, 1493/94). © British Library Board. All rights reserved. IB.21101.

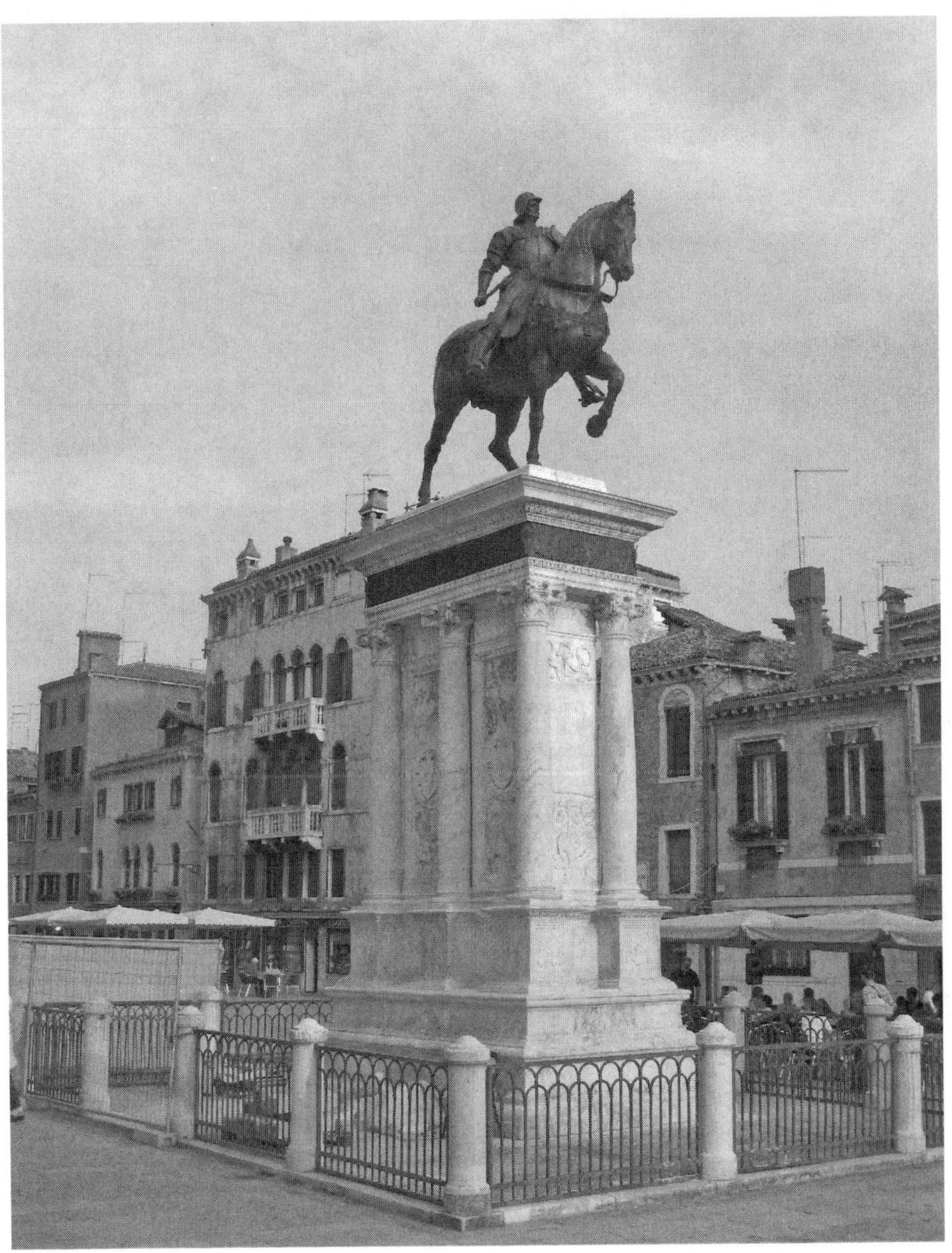

Andrea del Verrochio and Alessandro Leopardi, Monument of Bartolomeo Colleoni, Campo Santi Giovanni e Paolo, Venice. Photo courtesy of P. F. Brown.

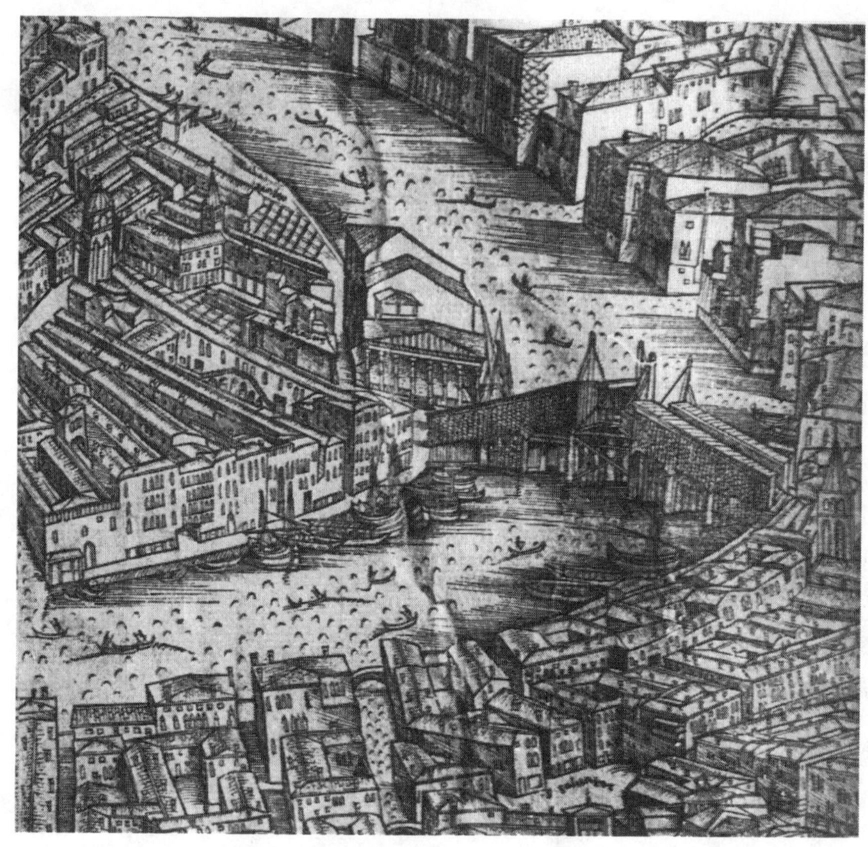

Rialto area, detail from Jacopo de' Barbari, *View of Venice,* woodcut, 1500. Photo by Osvaldo Bohm, 550.

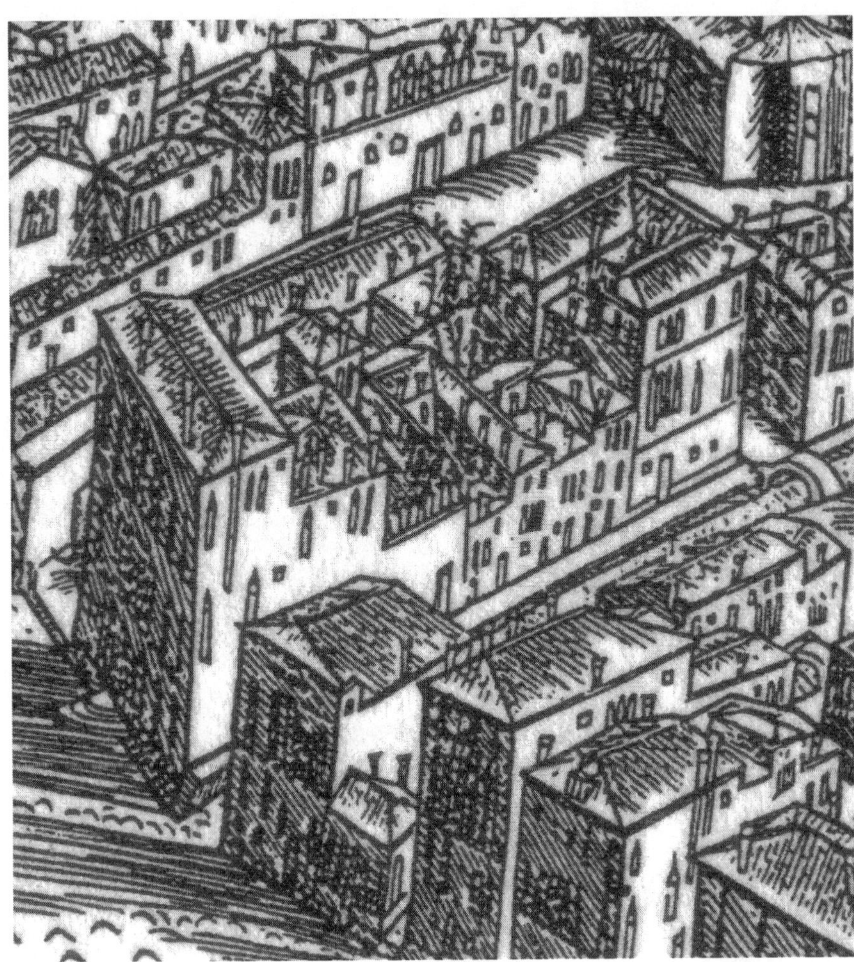

Ca' Corner della Ca' Grande before the fire of 1532, detail from Jacopo de' Barbari, *View of Venice*, woodcut, 1500.

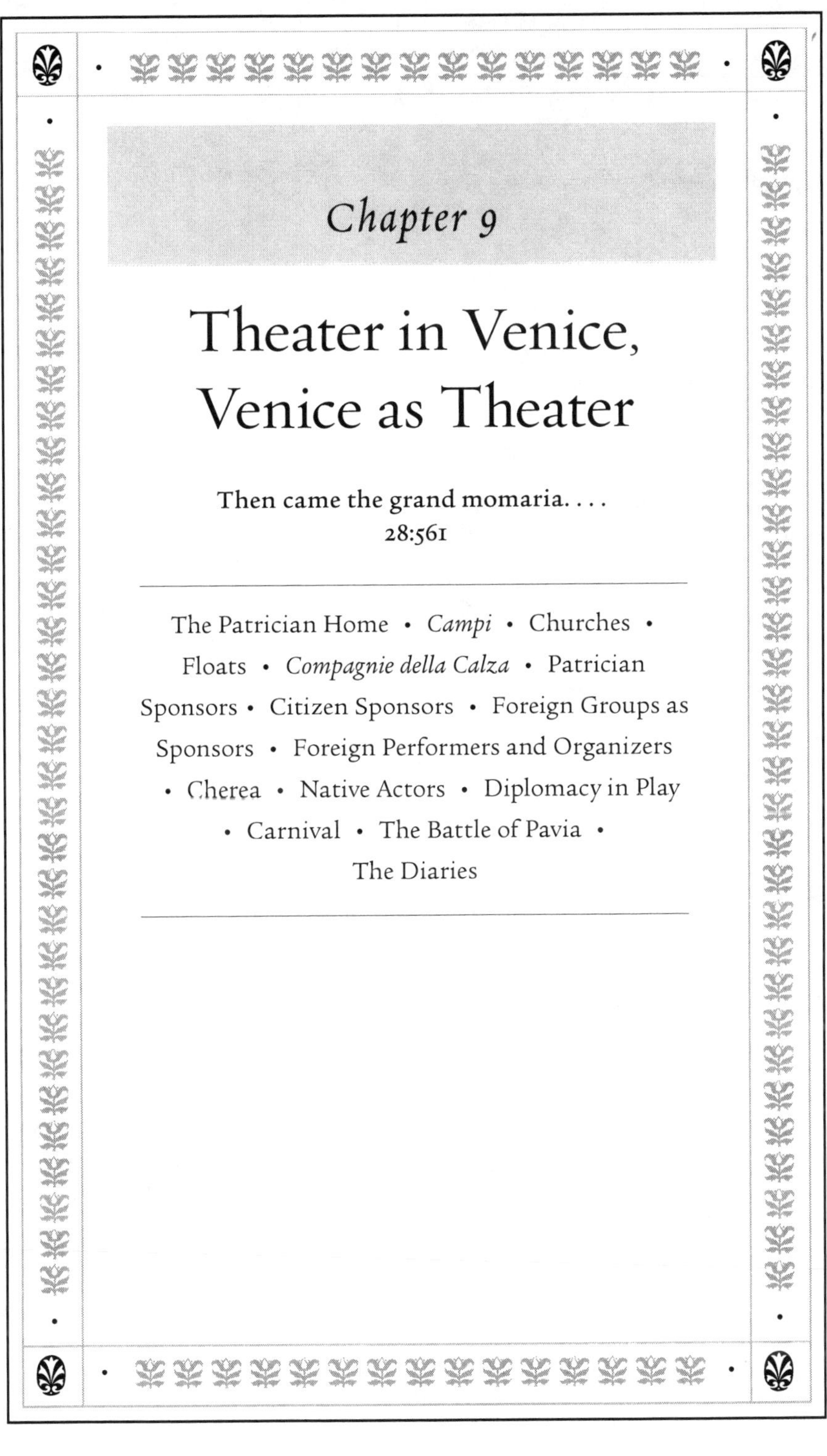

Chapter 9

Theater in Venice, Venice as Theater

Then came the grand momaria. . . .
28:561

The Patrician Home • *Campi* • Churches •
Floats • *Compagnie della Calza* • Patrician
Sponsors • Citizen Sponsors • Foreign Groups as
Sponsors • Foreign Performers and Organizers
• Cherea • Native Actors • Diplomacy in Play
• Carnival • The Battle of Pavia •
The Diaries

Corpore suscepto gaudent modulamine recto;
Et Ducis, et Cleri, populi processio meri.
Ad Theatrum cantuque plausuque ferunt sibi sanctum
Currentes latum venerantur honore locatum.

[Having received the body, they rejoice with fitting melody,
The pure-hearted doge, clergy, and people in procession.
They themselves carry the saint with song and cheers to the theater,
Hastening to venerate him whom they brought and installed with honor.]

The earliest and perhaps the greatest "theater" in Venice was the Basilica of San Marco, where the above inscription was placed in the late thirteenth century.[1] According to the accepted story, it was in this gathering place—and the word *theatrum* originally meant just that—that the Venetians placed the body of their patron saint, a theater built to accommodate this precious relic after its daring theft from Alexandria in the ninth century. And it was in the great forecourt of this Basilica, the Piazza San Marco, that much of the dramatic celebration of Venetian polity, heritage, and wide dominion, believed to have been achieved through the saint's sanction, took place.

But theater in Venice went beyond religio-civic commemoration. Theater was an essential and vital part of Venetian life. The features of the city itself—the glittering reflections of lights, the land intermingled with water that mirrors and doubles reality, the configuration of its unique urban spaces, and the expansive vistas offered by the surrounding lagoons—can be seen as dramatic elements that gave Venice its special theatrical quality. It was in this natural stage setting that the Venetians entertained themselves and their guests with theatrical performances of one sort or another.

The varieties of Venetian theater can be traced throughout Sanudo's diaries: from the classical tradition of Plautus and Terentius to the urban comedy of Machiavelli's *Mandragola,* from the *comedia a la vilanescha* (rustic peasant comedies) of Ruzante to *intermezzi* (short interval entertainments of music, dance, and buffoonery), from *momarie* and elaborate tableaux to folk dances, bullfighting in the streets, and mock naval battles. All of these were faithfully recorded by Sanudo. Himself a collector of plays, he had in his own library texts of comedies by Plautus and other Latin playwrights, which he had translated for performance

---

1. Demus 1984, 2:201. The inscription is located above the fourth doorway to the left of the central porch, where the transportation of St. Mark's body to the Basilica is depicted.

by Venetian nobles.[2] But he also liked the rustic comedies. Whatever he could see, he did see and judge: "well done" (7:311), "very lovely" (14:325, 37:671), "most beautiful" (37:653), or "very ugly" (44:171–72). In his accounts, sketchy as some of them are, lies the theatrical lexicon and topography of Renaissance Venice.[3]

It was a variegated topography, for its physical settings reflected the nature of the city itself, an ensemble of theatrical indoor and outdoor stages, according to the season and the nature of the event. There were enclosed private spaces such as palace loggias and courtyards; there were borrowed or rented convent refectories; there were the more public campi, the Piazza San Marco, the loggia of the Rialto, the canal embankments, the Grand and Giudecca canals, the lagoons themselves. These more open spaces offered a natural venue for a popular audience whose presence, whether on the embankments or in boats, may have trespassed the thin divide between *mondo* and *teatro,* between world and stage. The theater space itself expanded onto the water as large floating stages glided through the canals, lit with torches and animated with music, dance, and pantomime.

The Patrician Home

Of all these stage settings, the patrician home was the most frequently mentioned in the diaries, where the audience might be restricted but might include a large number of patricians and distinguished visitors. Typical of his accounts of theatrical performances was that of the entertainment provided at Ca' Pesaro, at San Beneto, on February 3, 1515. Sanudo indicates the care taken in the preparation of the set, the costumes, and the props (including animals or men dressed as animals), in addition to the juxtaposition of a classical comedy, a comic intermezzo with dances, songs, and percussion instruments, and a tableau based on a classical myth. The substance of the performances is only cursorily described, while the quality of different aspects of the evening is emphasized. Indeed, the entire event presented such successful entertainment that it competed with the business of government:

February 19, 1515 (19:443)   This evening, in the Pexaro home at San Beneto, in the courtyard, the compagnia of the Immortali sponsored a comedia[4] that

---

2. See Uberti 1985, 16–19, for discussion of a number of Sanudo's manuscripts, including BNM, Ital. Cl. IX, 368 (7170); and Caracciolo Aricò 1980, xii n15.

3. Much of the commentary in this chapter is based on Giorgio Padoan's many writings on the Venetian theater, in particular Padoan 1978a, 1981a, 1981b. Also important was M. T. Muraro 1981. For an informative survey of theatrical texts, as well as the locations of performances, see Mancini, Muraro, and Povoledo 1985–2002, vol. 1. See also the several works by Linda L. Carroll listed in the bibliography.

4. It should be noted that *comedia* was used in a general rather than a specific sense. Padoan

they put on themselves, Plautus's *Miles gloriosus*. A beautiful stage set had been constructed, especially a sky over the courtyard,[5] and the players were beautifully dressed. Between the acts, Zuan Polo put on another new comedia, pretending to be a wizard who had been to hell, and he made a hell with fire and devils appear. Then he pretended to be Cupid, and he was taken to hell, where he found Domenego [Domenico] Taiacalze chasing wethers [*castroni*].[6] Taiacalze came out with the wethers, who danced together. Next came a chorus of nymphs on a triumphal chariot, who were singing a song, each one beating a hammer in time on an anvil, pretending they were beating a heart. And when the principal comedia was over, they also gave the *dimostration*[7] of Paris and those goddesses [who competed over] which of them he would give the apple, [and he gave it] to Venus.[8] It was a beautiful thing, and many important people were there, including the French ambassador and the captain of the infantry, many senior patricians and the doge's sons. Many women were present, showing off their rich clothing. Among them I saw the wife of ser Zuan Emo dressed in cloth of gold and over it a lightweight black silk, as a sign of mourning, but cut so that the gold was visible. And there were other women wearing other fashions.[9] The entertainment wound up at seven hours after sunset; then there was the supper for the women and their husbands, and a ball. It lasted almost until daybreak, and there was almost no one in

---

1978a, 34–35. Apparently, the one element that various types of comedie had in common was dialogue. Other terms used by Sanudo, such as *momaria, fabula* (fable), *demonstratione,* or *rapresentation,* tended more to mime or speech in the form of a monologue than to the dialogues of comedie. In some cases the presentations were more pageantry and tableaux than drama. For a discussion of the meanings and possible derivation of *momaria,* see M. T. Muraro 1981, 328–31; Tichy 1997, 12–23; and Molmenti 1973, 2:391–401.

5. These makeshift stages were typical of such productions. They could easily be set up and later dismantled to make room for the dancing. As for the scenery, Sanudo does not provide much description. What the text suggests here is some kind of covering over the courtyard, which, given the season, would have been useful.

6. Zuan Polo Liompardi was a well-known actor-producer who appears in many of the performances of this period. See Ambrosini 1996, 494. His occasional partner, Domenico Taiacalze, whom Sanudo considered an *optimo bufon* (excellent buffoon), had died a few years earlier (diaries, 14 February 1513; 15:543), so this was an actor impersonating the buffoon who was found in hell, cavorting with men dressed as wethers, or castrated rams.

7. A secondary comedia. Sanudo uses several spellings: *demostration(e), demonstration, dimonstration,* and *dimostration.*

8. This series of entertainments—a *comedia principale,* an intermission of buffoonery, and then a *demostration*—was not unusual.

9. The government had expressed concern about the wearing of lavish dress the week before, after women who were dressed *molto pompose,* "very extravagantly," attended a performance by the Zardinieri (Gardeners) in Murano. "And for this reason a law was proposed in the Collegio regulating sumptuary matters." Diaries, 7 February 1515 (19:424). For Sanudo's disapproval of such extravagance, see 19:418; and chapter 6 under "Fashion, Taste, and Sumptuary Laws."

the Senate today because everyone wanted to get there in time and get a good seat.[10]

In the excerpt above, the line between a private venue and a public celebration might appear thin, given the large and elegant audience including governmental and diplomatic officials. In the following excerpt the same ambiguity pertains, for the entertainment is referred to as a "public festa" that took place in either in the courtyard of a home or a semiprivate area attached to the local church, and by its very nature as a "grand momaria" it was expansive:

March 6, 1508 (7:342)   Today there was a public festa in the Ca' Moro, near San Zuan Digolado, in the courtyard. It lasted all night, and the grand momaria cost a great deal. And a certain comedia was performed.[11] This was for the engagement of ser Domenego Bragadin to the daughter of the late ser Vido Morexini.[12]

Campi

Far more exposed to the general public were the performances in the *campi*,[13] those open spaces of varying dimensions that were found throughout the city. Such an occasion was a momaria performed as part of a betrothal celebration held in the Campo San Polo. A venue of this kind might have been chosen by a family whose home lacked the proper space for a theatrical presentation, for example, a courtyard, garden, or embankment. Or it may have been an intentional demonstration of the family's wealth, for the momaria concerned Jason's quest for the golden fleece and it was followed by a dinner at which part of the bride's dowry was actually presented in bullion and coins:

October 14, 1507 (7:161)   On this day a party was given by the compagnia of the Eterni on raised platforms in Campo San Polo to celebrate the betrothal of ser Luca da Leze to the daughter of the late ser Zuan Batista Foscarini. It lasted until four hours after sunset. There was a splendid momaria about Jason's quest for the golden fleece. It should be noted that at the dinner hour,

---

10. This translation follows Mancini, Muraro, and Povoledo 1985–2002, 1:14.

11. Sanudo occasionally uses *certa*, "certain," to describe a comedia whose moral or political subject matter he found distasteful.

12. Sanudo uses three spellings: *Morexini, Moresini,* and *Morosini.* Because this was an engagement party, the audience, like most audiences in patrician homes, was very likely composed exclusively of aristocrats or people in direct contact with the ruling class. See Padoan 1978a, 36.

13. In Venice, the only public square that could be termed a *piazza* was Piazza San Marco; all other squares were termed *campi*. In the early sixteenth century they might be paved over with brick but perhaps not yet stone. The editors thank Dennis Romano for this suggestion.

when I was present, about 4,000 ducats was brought in in six basins. The first one contained gold, the rest coins, all part of the bride's dowry. Well done, for those who can afford it!

The campo in the excerpt above served for a betrothal celebration. The campo in the excerpt below was used to entertain the public at large with what appears to have been a traveling show.

February 19, 1506 (6:297)   A castle was constructed in Piazza San Marco, the same one that had been in Campo San Stefano, along with quite a few viewing stands. There was a huge crowd, and it was a beautiful festa, with a momaria of twelve floats that moved around the Piazza. And they performed a splendid fable; and then there were fireworks that traveled down a rope from the Campanile to the Clock Tower and from the Clock Tower to the castle, in the shape of a serpent, and the fireworks consumed the castle, but without damage. The doge was there with the French ambassador and the two Moldavian ambassadors and the cousin of the Marquis of Mantua.

Churches

Besides campi, spaces that were more clearly public included some churches and monasteries, such as the monastery of San Stefano where Plautus's *Asinaria* was presented by a group that included nonpatricians:

February 16, 1515 (19:439)   Today, in the refectory of the monastery of San Stefano, a comedia, *Asinaria,* was excellently recited in vernacular verse by several learned men and young men who were not patricians. . . . So many people attended that they filled the room, which was all decorated with tapestries. Present were Lorenzo Loredan, son of the doge, and many other prominent men. The play began at the twenty-second hour and ended at the fourth hour.

Among other public ecclesiastical locations, the convent of the Croceferi on the Fondamente Nove was well known for its performances, including those of a secular nature, which might seem inappropriate for a monastery. Even after the building burned down in 1514, its neighborhood continued to serve as a venue for performances. In 1522 the participation of well-known actors attracted a large, heterogeneous crowd who were willing to pay for the entertainment:

February 9, 1522 (32:445–46)   This evening, at the Crosechieri, with permission of the Council of Ten, although the Council of Ten [itself] passed a law against giving permission,[14] a comedia—that is, a tale of love—was put on by Cherea, from Lucca,[15] recently arrived from Rome. It tells of Philarete, who loves Charitea and is counseled by one Caliandro. By means of a blind man, Philarete is helped and obtains his beloved. And Zuan Polo and his son did the intermezzi; they were rather good. The granddaughters of the doge, who are staying in the Ducal Palace, were there, and other ladies, and a considerable crowd who paid one marcello each.[16] And I was among them.

Two weeks later another play was performed in the same neighborhood, and the proceeds were appreciable:

February 23, 1522 (32:487)   This evening, at the Crosechieri, a prose comedia, the story of Calandro,[17] was performed, which, however, has already been staged on other occasions in this city. There were many people, so that the profits were good,[18] but there were no intermezzi.

Meanwhile, between these two performances, Machiavelli's *Mandragola*[19] was staged at the Crociferi. The crowd was so large that the actors did not have sufficient room to complete the last act:

February 13, 1522 (32:458)   This evening at the Crosechieri another prose comedia was put on by Cherea, from Lucca, and his troupe. Its subject was a certain elderly Florentine doctor who had a wife but could not have children, etc. There were many people there, and the intermezzi were performed by Zuan Polo and other buffoons. The stage was so full of people that the fifth act was not performed; it was impossible to do so with so many people.

This comedia was repeated successfully, and in its entirety, three days later, but Sanudo did not attend that performance:

---

14. See below for a discussion of restrictions on theatrical performances.

15. For background on Cherea, see Padoan 1978a, 39ff.; Bregoli-Russo 1995; and Tichy 1997, s.v. "Nobili, Francesco de'."

16. Sanudo, who was always interested in the economics of theatrical productions and every type of festa, notes the charges for this performance and many others. See diaries, 10 January 1508 (7:243), 21 February 1517 (23:598), 29 May 1520 (28:561), 23 February 1522 (32:487), 5 February 1526 (40:785), 28 February 1527 (44:171–72), 3 February 1530 (52:553), 16 February 1531 (54:297), 24 January 1533 (57:459). See also Padoan 1978a, 35, 38.

17. It seems clear that this was Cardinal Bibbiena's play the *Calandria*. For the staging of the *Calandria* in Venice, repeated on 3 February 1523 (diaries, 33:607), see Padoan 1978a, 42ff., esp. 42n25.

18. The manuscript has *vadagnono*; the Fulin edition has *vadagnano*.

19. While the play is not named, it can be identified from Sanudo's summary of the plot.

February 16, 1522 (32:466)   At the Crosechieri, the comedia about the Florentine left incomplete the other day was recited again. I did not attend, having attended already.[20]

An additional public space was a room or loggia of San Canciano in Biri,[21] mentioned in 1508 as the setting for performances of a comedy and a play by Plautus:

February 26, 1508 (7:311)   A country comedia was put on this evening at San Cancian in Biri; that is, it was performed, and it was good. And last night there was the *Truculento* of Plautus. It was well attended and well played.[22]

Among the locations that were used as both private and public spaces was the Ducal Palace. In 1523 a grandson of Doge Antonio Grimani treated his wedding guests to an "indecorous" comedia by Ruzante. Sanudo, who never commented on the apparent anomaly of an ecclesiastical setting such as San Stefano or the Croceferi for some of the more controversial comedie, remarks on the inappropriateness of such a performance in the doge's palace because of the presence of the Signoria, an indication that the governmental presence created a more morally sensitive ambience than did a religiously consecrated location:

20. These performances of Machiavelli's *Mandragola* have led to an interesting commentary by Padoan (1978a, 37–51), who points out that the popularity of the first performance was due to the reputation, not of the playwright, who was unknown in Venice at the time, but of the actors, Cherea and Zuan Polo. Padoan suggests that Sanudo did not attend the second performance (whereas in other instances he saw performances both in rehearsal and at their opening) and asserted his indifference in so dismissive a tone because he resented Machiavelli's jibes at the French in this play (e.g., in act 2, scene 6, and act 4, scene 8). Such remarks discomfited Sanudo, who always adhered to the governmental posture, at this time favorable toward the French. Moreover, Sanudo was not inclined to praise the Florentines, with whose state Venice was often at odds. Two later performances of the *Mandragola* in 1526, after its author had become better known in Venice and its success had been acknowledged, were not even mentioned by Sanudo, although his personal library contained two copies of the play. See Padoan 1978a, 37–51.

21. For other mentions of San Canciano in Biri in the diaries, see entries dated 10 January 1508 (7:243), 21 February 1517 (23:598), 31 January 1521 (29:593), and 14 March 1528 (47:84), where it is cited as a location "dove si recitava le comedie." Padoan concludes that it was no longer being used as a theater by 1528 (1978a, 36).

22. While San Stefano, the Crociferi, and San Canciano in Biri were used for secular drama, some churches and convents were the settings for religious theater, whose audiences tended to be limited. See Padoan 1978a, 37–38. The topics were usually episodes of saints' lives. See references in diaries, 15 February 1515 (19:434), to "Santo Alexio" at San Salvador; and 28 May 1515 (20:234), to "Santo Ylarione convertito da Santo Antonio" at San Donato on Murano. But on Sunday, 17 May 1523, at San Trovaso, we find Cherea as the impresario of "certa istoria in modo de comedia" (34:148); and on 18 February 1533 at San Zanipolo "tra loro frati una comedia" was performed.

May 5, 1523 (34:124)   After dinner the collegio of the savi met, and a lovely banquet was held for patricians and invited ladies in the dining room of the Ducal Palace to honor the wedding of ser Antonio Grimani, son of ser Vicenzo, son of the doge. The councillors, heads of the Quarantia, state attorneys, and heads of the Ten and some procurators of San Marco who had been invited dined on the lower floor. They then came upstairs, and there, in the hall, a comedia of Ruzante's was put on, the one that was staged this winter at the Crosechieri.[23] It was a very indecorous thing to do in front of the Signoria. When it was over, a dance was held. The compagnia was the Ortolani [Farmers]. . . . Some of the women stayed for the supper and danced until five hours after sunset, then everyone went home. Meanwhile, the doge is ill.[24]

A gathering such as the one above, even when attended by government officials, retained something of a private nature, for the Ducal Palace was also the house of a family. However, the courtyard of the palace was a fully public space, as is evident in these descriptions of two "beautiful momarie" performed there on February 5 and 7, 1526. Later, the second one went out "through the whole city."[25]

February 5, 1526 (40:785)   After the Council of Ten came down [from the upper floor of the Ducal Palace] after the second hour of the night, a beautiful momaria arrived in the ducal courtyard. Six principals, exquisitely dressed, danced with twelve persons who were dressed as Saracens and carried torches in their hands, and they performed several new dances that greatly pleased those who saw them, and there were many people in the courtyard and the doge on the balcony of his palace.

February 7, 1526 (40:789)   This evening, at the third hour of the night, a beautiful momaria came into the courtyard of the Ducal Palace, all performed by young gentlemen, in number ——, dressed as Moors and in good order carrying twenty-four torches each weighing —— pounds, with trumpets, shawms, cornets, and singers, and with Zuan Polo dressed as a doctor in scarlet cloth. There were five principals, or mimers, who danced, dressed in the ancient style with golden garments and their heads covered.[26] The first was Neptune with a sign whose letters spelled "Neptune." Then came Spring with

---

23. See Padoan 1978a, 113, identifying this comedia as Ruzante's *Betia,* a play with explicitly vulgar language. On Ruzante, see Lovarini 1965; Carroll 1990, 2000a; and below.

24. Doge Antonio Grimani died two days later, on 7 May.

25. This second momaria was performed only a few days after the sumptuary law of 31 January 1526 forbade all such entertainments. See diaries, 40:749–54. See below for the first of such prohibitions in 1508, which was ignored after an interim of three years.

26. The manuscript has *velli;* the Fulin edition has *veli.*

flowers crowning a cornucopia. Then there was Summer with ears of wheat, and then Autumn with bunches of grapes, then Winter with dry firewood. There were two women for Spring and Summer and two men for Autumn and Winter. First Neptune danced alone, then Spring joined him, then all the others, so that finally all five danced, and it was lovely to see. There were 3,000 people in the palace courtyard. That is how it happened, and the momaria will go out tonight through the whole city. . . . The *autor*[27] of the *momaria* and the dances was maestro Pellegrin.[28] And it is in competition with the one that will be produced tomorrow in the Piazza San Marco, where the platform has been constructed.[29]

Floats

Just as the momaria of Neptune above was first performed in the Ducal Palace courtyard and then moved out into the city, *per tutta la terra*, so many of the theatrical productions sought out an even wider audience by circulating along the Giudecca and Grand canals. Some of these used mobile, open stages to create imaginative and daring structures. By means of platforms and bridges made of boats, they converted palace, embankment, and canal into a continuum between land and water, an extraordinary terrestrial-aquatic stage.

May 29, 1520 (28:561)   Today, soon after dinner, the festa of the compagnia of the Immortali in honor of the Marquis of Mantua was begun. First, a large platform was prepared on the quay at Ca' Corner de la Piscopia, upon which fifty invited ladies were seated, and the compagnia members went to fetch the marquis at the house of his ambassador at Santa Sofia. He was brought, with those other gentlemen [accompanying him], to the platform, and while the ladies and the members of the compagnia began to dance, two large fishing boats were prepared, one bearing the Contarini coat of arms, while some maskers performed certain dance steps; it was lovely to watch. And there was another, smaller fishing boat bearing the Molin coat of arms, and a joust began with six boats, and two men were thrown into the water. . . . Then, as

---

27. In Venice at the time the term *autor* usually referred to the organizer of an event, who might also contribute his artistic talent to its creation; it could also refer to the sponsor. See Padoan 1978a, 116n77; and Carroll 2000a, 967n11.

28. Pellegrin del Doge, whose name appears a number of times in the diaries: 24 January 1513 (15:511), 20 February 1528 (46:611), 17 July 1530 (53:355), 20 February 1533 (57:530-32). This last reference explains his name: he had been a squire to Doge Agostino Barbarigo (1486-1501). Another dancing teacher was maestro Marco Tonin. See 13 February 1520 (28:253-54), 3 July 1524 (36:457-58), 28 February 1527 (44:172).

29. No other such theatrical competitions are mentioned by Sanudo, so this must have been of an informal nature. Sanudo's reference here to a crowd of 3,000 is most likely an example of his often exaggerated numbers.

people waited for the women's and men's races, there was a downpour. A fine collation was offered; it was carried on rafts down the Grand Canal by many [servants], and the compagnia came with it. Then everyone, the lord of the festivities and the ladies, boarded two barges that were tied together and well decorated with tapestries and the coats of arms of the marquis and compagnia members. There were two seats, one for the marquis and the other for ser Andrea Dandolo, the lieutenant of this festa. Also present were the brother of the Marquis of Saluzzo who is a student at Padua, Count Mercurio, and other Mantuans and foreigners in abundance. Our governor[30] was invited but did not attend. And so, while the women were dancing, the marquis danced with my niece, who is the wife of ser Marco Antonio Venier and the daughter of the late Marco Zorzi.

The regatta passed them as they proceeded to the Zuecha [Giudecca]. . . . There they all disembarked at Ca' Dandolo, near San Zuane di la Zuecha, where they dined in the garden in a courtly fashion, using silver.[31] It was twenty-two hours after sunset. Then they mounted the platform raised in front of the house, and another for dancing, on which a lot of dancing took place. There were 200 lit wax torches of ten libre each. They went for the herald, and it was a fine sight to watch him approach along the embankment. . . . The canal was full of boats. I was there, and it was impossible to move with so many notable men and women in their boats. Many rockets and artillery salvos were fired. Then came the grand momaria on a number of floats, and they performed the fable of Hercules, who goes to carry Persephone off from Hades, which took a while. This was a momaria put on by Pelegrin dil Doxe [Pellegrin del Doge], and it cost seventy-five ducats.

In 1530, on the day celebrating the recovery of Padua in the early months of the League of the War of Cambrai (July 17, 1509), after a procession to Santa Marina (whose feast day this was) and another mass in San Marco, the secular festivities began. A "large and commodious theater"—and this was one of the few times Sanudo used the term *theater*[32]—was built on two barges. This was an open, circular structure large enough to accommodate a momaria, dancing guests, and balladeers.[33] It proceeded by water to the Rialto and then returned to San Marco:

---

30. The manuscript has an abbreviation that we have interpreted as *governador;* the Fulin edition has *governo.*

31. Because of the sumptuary laws, special permission was required for the use of silver.

32. See diaries, 8 and 21 June 1533 (58:263–64, 350).

33. Schulz 1961, 500n4, 506n23. Such structures may have been influenced by the humanistic concept of ancient theaters. See Padoan Urban 1966, 140, 143, and fig. 164, a 1497 woodcut illustrating a "Coliseus sive theatrum."

July 17, 1530 (53:355–56) Today was the day designated for the festa of the compagnia of the Floridi [Flourishing] on the Grand Canal; the lord of the festivities was ser Francesco Diedo. . . . The party was held after dinner, so there was no meeting of the council. A large and commodious theater with a beautifully constructed sky was set up on two barges; one could board it, and it was decorated with tapestries and with two marine monsters, an old man and a woman, the front half at the stern and the back part, with fishtails, on the prow. The theater, where the eighty-seven women were seated, was towed by many boats; all of the women disembarked at the house of the lord of the festivities at San Polo, that is, the ferry at San Beneto. Then they got [back] on, and they danced. In the aft part a certain momaria was staged by maistro Pelegrin, a fable, with a few well-dressed principals, by ——. Wandering among the dancers were some singers, who sang a song about the tale. Thus the theater moved toward the Rialto bridge and then returned to San Marco. In the meantime, wind and rain blew up, to the point that the plan was changed, and although they were supposed to have supper on the temporary bridge of boats that crosses over to the Zuecha, they went to eat at the home of the lord and stayed until six hours after sunset.

These barges were decorated by ser Zuan Vituri with tapestries and banners, including a beautiful one that belonged to the Marquis of Guasto [Vasto, Alfonso d'Avalos] . . . , and the tapestries and banners were thoroughly soaked.

Five fishing boats had been well prepared by the members of the compagnia; upon one of [them] some people were dancing very nicely. The whole city was full of festivities today, when the rain did not interfere. And at twenty-three and a half hours after sunset there was a boat regatta, the prizes having been donated by the compagnia. Tuesday, God willing, the real festivities will be held, namely, on the bridge, with a supper . . . that will be served entirely on silver. Then in the evening the momaria will pass along the Zuecha quay, and there will be dancing on the bridge, and it will be a lovely sight to behold. The money for all of these expenditures comes[34] from the compagnia.

And it should be noted that there were four inscriptions on the boat-theater, in white on a red background, which said: "The ship of the Argosy was less rich than am I"; "More powerful is virtue than the murmur of the crowd"; "If I am lacking in skill, I will never lack in good will"; "You were brought among the favored people"; "The fragrance of our flowers has such distinction that it will bring glory and fame to our country."[35]

---

34. The manuscript has *si fa;* the Fulin edition has *si farà.*

35. Although Sanudo says there were four verses, the editors of the Fulin edition listed five; since Sanudo does not punctuate, the second and third verse might well belong together, as

Two days later the festa was still in progress. The ladies once again boarded the barges, which had been made into a theater, and danced as they were towed to the Rialto bridge, where races were held. Then this structure was brought to where another had been built on five galleys and two barges, forming a bridge to the Giudecca. The ladies disembarked. A collation was served, but it was a disorderly and inadequate affair, "a shameful collation." Finally came the momaria, about which Sanudo had less to say than he did about the poorly presented repast:

July 19, 1530 (53:361–62)   Later, at twenty-three hours, the meal was brought in. It had been prepared at Ca' Marzello on the Zuecha, and there were only 225 presents, which was very shameful. First there were only [figures of the lion of] St. Mark made of sugar and certain poorly made figures, no marzipan cakes in the shape of castles, ships, galleys, the Bucintoro, etc., as used to be done, nor were[36] there basins and candy dishes, with round pastries and pine-nut cakes, but [merely] cups with the abovementioned things inside. It was therefore a shameful collation. And then there were neither doughnuts nor cookies,[37] but it was all confections, pine-seed cakes, round pastries, mushroom-shaped pastries, confections, scallop-shaped pastries, sweets, sugared fruits, etc. This meal was carried along the Zuecha by inept waiters and in disarray as far as the boat bridge at the house. . . .

And so the herald came and finally the momaria with . . . wax torches along the Zuecha quay, and there were platforms in the shape of animals carried by porters. There was a world in the form of a sphere, a city with the shape of Venice, and an Inferno.

In another water-borne event three years later the constructed theater was not the setting for a performance but part of what Sanudo called a "triumph on the Grand Canal." The compagnia of the Cortesi [Polite] organized the event to welcome a new member, Francesco d'Este, son of the Duke of Ferrara, and the physical theater not only contained the audience but also became a prop in the pageant, in which the whole city celebrated the event along its main thoroughfare:

they are in the manuscript. It is interesting to note that in preparation for this event the sponsoring compagnia paid a ceremonial visit to the Great Council the week before; however, the reason for the visit, which probably involved obtaining some permission, is not specified. See diaries, 10 July 1530 (3:338–39).

36. The manuscript has *mal fate, niuna sponga . . . nì bazili;* the Fulin edition has *mal fate in una sponga . . . fu bazili.*

37. Perhaps Sanudo complained about the omission of *storti* and *bozoladi* because he felt that without these traditional local festivity foods, it was not a proper festa.

June 8, 1533 (58:263–64)   In the past few days a most beautiful round wooden structure was built upon two large barges. It was covered and festooned all around with a light blue sailcloth held by golden cords, and it had a square shape with benches in the middle forming a theater. The lord of the festivities and the son of the Duke of Ferrara together with the councillors sat on the top tier; below them on the benches that went around were 115 women; above—out of sight—was the wind band, and above all were the standard of Doge Vendramin [1476–78] and three tall gold banners; below, just above the level of the water, [the structure] was encircled by a painted cloth, and no other boat could approach it. The compagnia members danced with the women, and some of their servants were present, and everyone could watch. This took place on the Zuecha on the quay at Ca' Vendramin because one of those Vendramin belongs to the compagnia. This structure was designed and built by a maistro Domenico ——. It cost in all 500 ducats, a beautiful sight to behold. It was towed along and in the morning was brought to San Polo, to the ferry crossing on the quay where ser Fantin Diedo, a member of the compagnia, lives. All the women embarked, and then the theater was towed toward the Rialto bridge, with the compagnia members dancing on the lower level[38] with the women and a Frenchwoman who danced in slippers ——. And there was instrumental and vocal music. . . .

The canal was full of boats, which was a fine sight, and certain larger fishing boats or brigantines, well supplied with banners of gold and coats of arms, and instrumentalists went along the canal. The Duke of Ferrara viewed the festa from Ca' Foscari, and all the houses were full of ladies and gentlemen. This structure was towed along the Grand Canal to the Ponta de la Doana.
. . .

The structure, surrounded by lit wax torches held by servants of members of the compagnia, came with its dancers as far as the San Polo canal to the lower level of Ca' Loredan.[39] Ser Vicenzo Grimani, procurator, lent them the house, which had been well decorated for their dinner and the conclusion of the festa. And he himself also gave a dinner at his own expense for his friends, with more than one hundred at table. When the compagnia with the theater arrived at the quay at the third hour of the night, all the 107 ladies disembarked. Fifteen went home; the rest stayed for supper and danced the night through until it was nearly daylight.[40]

---

38. The manuscript appears to have *sotto;* the Fulin edition has *tutti.*

39. "A chà Loredan nel soler da basso," possibly the *androne,* or water entrance.

40. For another festa that extended from the land to the water, see the final excerpt in this chapter.

Compagnie della Calza

The sponsors most frequently mentioned in Sanudo's diaries—as in the excerpt above—were the various compagnie della calza.[41] In February 1515, for example, the city was so full of festivities that three comedie were put on by three compagnie: in Murano at Ca' Capello, by the Zardinieri; on the Zuecha at Ca' Trevisan, by the Ortolani; and at San Beneto at Ca' Pesaro, by the Immortali (February 3, 1515; 19:418). Sanudo never fails to mention which compagnie were involved, and his interest in these groups is evidenced by his summation, toward the end of his diaries, of their names and numbers (May 18, 1533; 58:184–85). The words he chooses—"visto et conossuti li compagni" (I have seen [the companies] and known the Companions)—convey his sense of historic witness to a phenomenon he knew to be ephemeral, and at a time when his own powers were failing. Each of these societies existed for only a brief period, but during that time their role was critical in the artistic and celebratory life of the city.

In the fall of 1530 the Duke of Milan made a state visit to Venice. For his entertainment, 500 ducats and the use of the Bucintoro were given to the compagnia of the Reali [the Royals, or Kingsmen]. The justification for this support of a great variety of events, including two momarie, was the diplomatic usefulness of such compagnie to the Venetian state, which was in this case a cosponsor.[42]

October 13, 1530 (54:46–47)   In the Senate. . . . The compagnia of the Reali greatly desiring, no less for their own than for the public reputation, to pay honor to the most illustrious Duke of Milan and his entourage in every way possible, they have for many days now begun to prepare those things that are necessary. Because in so doing they have not stinted on expenditures, which have up to now amounted to a large sum, it is appropriate and worthy of the gratitude and munificence of this state that it should partially aid this compagnia of the Reali, as our Signoria is accustomed to doing in similar cases when it has been opportune to hold public feste in the Ducal Palace to honor an important person, for this also redounds to the honor of our own state.

It is therefore proposed that by the authority of this council, a gift of 500 ducats at six lire and four soldi per ducat be made to the compagnia of the Reali for their present needs so that they can increase their funding and fulfill their aforementioned desire.

And similarly, it is proposed that the compagnia be granted use of the Bucintoro for the one day on which they wish to use it.

In favor, 164; opposed, 36; abstaining, 3.

---

41. See chapter 6.
42. For a fuller description of the duke's entertainment, see chapter 2.

Patrician Sponsors

In addition to the government and the *compagnie della calza*, there were many other types of patrician sponsors. Occasionally an individual is named, such as the lawyer ser Luca Donado, who put on a theatrical mock battle in the Campo Santa Maria Formosa in February 1515:

February 18, 1515 (19:441)   Today, in the campo of Santa Maria Formosa, there was a beautiful festa with a bull chase, and a wooden castle was constructed in the middle of the campo that was attacked by a detachment of infantry in block formation led by signor Zuan Cosaza on horseback, who was armed but wearing a [Carnival] mask. At the end, the castle was taken and a kind of container was burned—a fine sight! The campo was full of people . . . with quite a few maskers and platforms around the campo. The sponsor of this festa was ser Luca Donado, the attorney.

Two days later another individual patrician put on a Latin comedy featuring his sons as actors:

February 20, 1515 (19:444)   After dinner the collegio of the savi met, and there was no new business. Many parties were held on the island of Murano, and there were many balls and masquerades throughout the city. Everyone has had a good time, and it has been a festive Carnival. And in the evening Plautus's comedia was put on . . . by the sons of ser Lazaro Mocenigo at his house near the church of the Carità.[43] They recited it in Latin, and it was lovely to see and hear those young people, and a number of patricians were there.

Yet one other individual theatrical patron was Marco Grimani, another grandson of Doge Antonio Grimani, who sponsored a theatrical performance in the Ducal Palace:

February 2, 1522 (32:439)   And in the evening there was a small festa in the Ducal Palace put on by Marco Grimani, his grandson. Invited to dinner was the bishop of Ivrea ——. He is young and is studying in Padua, and twelve of the most beautiful women of the city were invited. There was dancing in the Golden Room upstairs, and instrumental and vocal music, and a tragedy was recited by Cherea, and then there was a supper in the room where the Collegio meets.

43. Santa Maria della Carità, now the Accademia.

In other instances the sponsors might be a single patrician family or several patrician families who were related, as in 1512 and 1513, or a group of patrician families who had combined to support the dramatic efforts of their sons, such as happened in 1532:

August 31, 1512 (14:641)   Yesterday evening, in Ca' Moroxini at San Zuan Lateran, a comedia by Plautus, namely, the *Miles gloriosus,* was performed by four of our gentlemen, that is, ser Lunardo Contarini, ser Stefano Tiepolo, ser Marco Antonio Memo, ser Fantin Corner, and five others who were commoners. It was excellent and lasted until the third hour of the night. There were about 200 men invited, a set number for each [performer], and some women who are relatives.

February 8, 1513 (15:535)   This evening, in Ca' Moroxini at San Zuan Lateran, a comedia by Plautus was staged. It was called the *Pseudolo* and had been translated into vernacular verse, and the *demostratione*[44] was performed by our patricians, ser Stefano Tiepolo, savio ai ordeni, ser Lunardo Contarini, ser Marco Antonio Memo, ser Francesco Zen, ser Fantin Corner and his brother Gabriel, ser Jacomo Duodo, all of them virtually first cousins, and several who are commoners. The set was excellently decorated, and their garments were of gold, silver, and silk. And then there was a *demostration* concerning certain problems,[45] which was delightful. The actors invited several guests each and only ten women, so that in all there were not even 300 of us,[46] nor was anyone admitted but those who had been invited. There were instrumental ensembles of every sort and songs. It ended at the fourth hour of the night, and because it was a beautiful production I wished to mention it here.

June 15, 1532 (56:405–6)   Today at twenty hours a very fine Latin comedia was performed in the home of ser Marco Morexini, university laureate, and his brothers, at San Marzilian. It was given under a loggia overlooking[47] the garden by some young students who are the sons of ser Jacomo Gradenigo, ser Filippo Donato, ser Thomà Michiel, ser Francesco Lippomano, and ser Bartolomeo Morexini; they were all excellent.[48] First came Temerity, then Momus, then Virtue, who lamented, then Fortune, then Mercury, and finally Jove, who got everyone to make peace. Then came the three Fates, Cleto, Antropos, and Lachesis, spinning the thread of life, accompanied by

---

44. See above, n. 7.

45. "Fu fato certa demostration di problemi." In the manuscript the word *problemi* is not clear.

46. The manuscript has *sichè in tutto non fossemo 300;* the Fulin edition omits *non.*

47. The manuscript has *soto;* the Fulin edition has *fato.*

48. Although the play, of uncertain provenance and authorship, was held in the Moresini home, it is likely that the other fathers mentioned would also have contributed to the production.

instrumental and vocal intermezzi. And when it was over, a fine collation was brought in. . . . Attending were Monsignor Garzoni, knights, university laureates, ser Antonio Mozenigo the procurator, all three state attorneys, many senators, among whom [was] I, Marin Sanudo, and quite a few other learned and talented people.

Citizen Sponsors

More rare than patrician sponsors were citizen sponsors. Occasionally a wealthy, important, and cultured citizen such as Gasparo dalla Vedova, secretary to the Council of Ten, might offer to a patrician audience in his own home eclogues and comedie (February 22, 1517; 23:599) as a way to cultivate political favor.[49] In similar fashion, a citizen group might be the sponsor, as in the case of a customs official and his associates who put on Plautus's *Menaechmi* in a patrician setting, although they had to sell tickets to cover the costs, and even then the production failed to meet Sanudo's critical standards.[50]

February 5, 1526 (40:785)   A comedia was put on at Sant'Aponal in Ca' Morexini by Zuan Francesco Beneti, a customs official, and some of his colleagues, for which one had to have tickets to be admitted. The place was small, and Cherea acted, and it was a play by Plautus about two brothers, not very well done; it ended at the fourth hour of the night.[51]

In one instance Sanudo writes of "a few rich commoners" who, in 1517, put on "a most beautiful momaria" with golden garments and instrumental music in the Ducal Palace courtyard (January 6, 1517; 23:425), but that was probably exceptional.

Foreign Groups as Sponsors

More usual, probably because the funding was more available, were the performances put on by foreign groups: the Florentines, the Germans, and the Jews. In 1498 the Florentines sponsored and acted in a momaria that appears to have

---

49. Gaspare dalla Vedova had a special interest in theatrical texts. An important manuscript containing many of Ruzante's works was assembled in the first three or four decades of the sixteenth century by copyists under his supervision. See Padoan 1978a, 105; see also diaries, 10 May 1518 (25:391), describing him and Sanudo together attending the *declamazioni* (declamations) of Cristoforo Fiorentino, "detto l'Altissimo."

50. Padoan 1978a, 35, suggests that initiatives such as these were an attempt by nonpatricians to imitate the parties given in a more systematic and sumptuous manner by the compagnie della calza, which did not charge admission.

51. This may have been the *cosa morta* described by a friend of Machiavelli's in a letter to him, contrasting it to the success his *Mandragola* achieved that same night in a performance about which Sanudo says nothing. See Padoan 1978a, 46.

been quite elaborate. Sanudo tended to be ill-disposed to the city of Florence, especially since Venice at that time was actively supporting the revolt of Pisa against Florence:

February 14, 1498 (1:873–74)   On the evening of the 14th some Florentine merchants who were in the city, under the leadership of Bortolo di Nerli, son-in-law of the late Zuan Freschobaldi, put on a momaria either to celebrate the treaty between France and Spain or because their ambassador in Rome had been honorably received and they have high hopes of retaking the city of Pisa, which our Signoria has defended and guarded and promised to maintain in its liberty, or to make people talk about them and say that the Florentines do such things.

And so, at the first hour of the night, they emerged from Nerli's house. They were nearly all Florentines, and they performed in this way. Eight men riding hobbyhorses, armed and armored for the joust, were surrounded by other young men dressed identically with silvered masks, who carried torches and lances and helmets for them, and there were many little bells. . . . Then there were many others dressed as Moors, in tunics and blackface, and one king or lord surrounded by some foot soldiers. There were many torches, and they spent some money on it. But it did not succeed as they expected—I might say it was a Florentine frivolity.

Nevertheless, they went to the courtyard of the Ducal Palace, and there they jousted. The doge was on the balcony, and the courtyard was filled with people. But they soon tired of watching this fable.

More approved of by Sanudo were the German momarie of 1517 and 1520 in the Fondaco dei Tedeschi:

February 12, 1517 (23:583)   Today, at the German Warehouse, the German merchants put on a lovely party to celebrate the pact or truce that has been reached with His Imperial Majesty [Maximilian I].[52] They set up viewing stands, and the party began in the morning and lasted until three hours after sunset. There were jousts and bull chases and bearbaiting with dogs. Zuan Polo, the buffoon, came and wanted to join the joust, but he fell off his horse and hurt his leg, so he was not able to perform any of his buffoonery. Then eight players excellently costumed came in and danced upon a platform that had been erected in the middle of the courtyard. Finally, when hobbyhorses and triumphal chariots had appeared on the platform, the players, dancing, enacted the *dimonstration* of a fable ——. It involved the god of love, nymphs,

---

52. This was the truce that ended the War of the League of Cambrai. See Carroll 2000b, 17.

lovers, sacrifices, births, and burials, interpreted in the dance. It was a very decorous and expensive performance. There were lots of people, women, maskers, and others, and the Germans spared no expense from their coffers to provide dinner, etc.[53]

February 12, 1520 (28:252) This evening a lovely momaria was put on by several German merchants and others elegantly dressed. Six of them danced, and there was excellent instrumental and vocal music. They held a ball in the Warehouse, which a number of patricians came to see. They went on with ceremonial trumpets and wax torches until nine hours after sunset.[54]

Foreign Performers and Organizers

Many non-Venetians served a variety of functions in Venetian festivities, for which most were probably paid. Well-known buffoons included Zuan Polo (who was a mime, acrobat, and actor) and his son; Zuan Cimador; and Domenico Taiacalze, who appeared in private and public feste and whom Sanudo almost invariably praised.[55] Their intermezzi were often more appreciated than the principal entertainments they accompanied. Some festivities were organized by foreigners, such as Zuan Manenti and Cherea; Cherea also acted in them. Upper-class actors formed a special group; the most famous were the Paduans Angelo Beolco (Ruzante) and Marc'Aurelio Alvarotto (Menato), the core of a troupe that approached semiprofessional status.

Certain dancing masters also became well known in Venice, as did Maestro Pellegrin del Doge, who was first mentioned in 1513:

January 24, 1513 (15:511)   This evening a beautiful momaria of twelve players came forth, that is, six dressed as women and six men, splendidly costumed in gold brocade and decked with jewels, and two dressed as Saracens led the twelve, holding large torches. They were foreign commoners, and their director was Maestro Pellegrin, who conducts a dancing school. They performed a number of new dances and had a great crowd following them.

---

53. Here, as elsewhere, Sanudo is less concerned with the meaning of the production than with its preparation, duration, audience, and general effect.

54. Sanudo also mentions a *bellissima comedia* performed by Jews in the Ghetto. See above, chapter 6.

55. Sanudo remarked at the time of Taiacalze's death that "è homo in queste cosse fazete di primi di la città nostra" (diaries, 14 February 1513; 15:543) [in these humorous matters he is one of the top men in our city]. Zuan (or Giovanni) Manenti and the Paduan Menato (Marc'Aurelio Alvarotto), Ruzante's stage companion, were also well-known theatrical figures in this period, as was Tizzone Gaetano da Toti *napoletano*. See Carroll 1990, chap. 3; and diaries, 25 February 1525 (37:653).

Cherea

Of all the foreigners in performances, there was one, known as Cherea, whose intermittent career in Venice spanned much of the period of the diaries and whose earlier appearances in Venice were connected by Sanudo with the first Venetian legislation against theatrical events.

Cherea was an actor from Lucca, and therefore Tuscan, whose proper name was Francesco de' Nobili but who was best known by the name adopted from a character he had played in Terence's *Eunuch*. More than an actor, he was an autor and entrepreneur who had collected theatrical scripts, translating a number from Latin and Greek into Italian. Cherea may even have been responsible for introducing into Venice his translations of Plautus in 1507–8.[56] We know that in January 1508 he put on (and probably acted in) the *Maenechmi* of Plautus, as well as an *Asinaria* and a pastoral eclogue in the public space of San Canciano in Biri (7:243). These were undoubtedly among the collected texts and translations for whose protection he sought a copyright from the Venetian government on September 10, 1508. During the same period he attempted to secure the loggia at the Rialto for a production.[57] This was a highly public venue, and Cherea was a foreigner. His actions may have sufficiently alarmed the Venetian authorities about the spread of lascivious and raucous stage comedies to provoke the prohibition of all performances on December 29, 1508. Or so Sanudo suggests:

December 31, 1508 (7:701)   After dinner there was a meeting of the Great Council. And a law was announced that had been passed by the Council of Ten on the 29th of this month that, among other things, stipulated that there be no more recitation of comedie, tragedies, and eclogues in this city, neither at weddings nor in any place, with a penalty for the householder hosts of one hundred ducats and the exclusion for two years from offices and councils, and for the performers as is stated in the bill, etc. And it should be noted that the cause [*l'autor*] of this law was one Cherea from Lucca, who was intriguing to have from the provedadori dil Sal and the heads of the Ten the use of the loggia at Rialto for the recitation of these comedies; whereupon this law was passed by the Council of Ten upon the recommendation of the doge and the councillors.[58]

This prohibition was issued in the uneasy days after the forming of the League of Cambrai against Venice (December 10, 1508), when all such entertainments in the

---

56. Padoan 1981b, 397.

57. For a view of the Rialto loggia, no longer extant, see Carpaccio's *Miracle of the Relic of the Holy Cross* in the Accademia.

58. The prohibition may be found in ASV, CX, Miste, reg. 32, fol. 55v, 29 December 1508.

approaching Carnival season might have appeared frivolous and possibly subversive. Cherea's foreign background, his connections with hostile powers such as Mantua and Ferrara, may also have aroused the government's distrust.[59]

But the prohibition, like sumptuary laws, which also addressed Carnival activities, was soon ignored. Theater was too exuberant an expression of confidence to be long suppressed.[60] By 1512 Cherea was back in Venice performing at weddings and carnival festivities:

June 14, 1512 (14:325)   This morning at Santo Alvise a daughter of ser Marco Antonio Contarini was married to Count Collalto. The wedding took place in the home of these counts . . . and there was a splendid dinner. . . . It was served on silver, there was dancing, and women with masks, etc., because they had permission to wear them, and a pine-nut cake was served at the table. Moreover, in the evening after the dancing, there was a recitation by Cherea and the *demostration* of a tragedy and a pastoral eclogue that was quite lovely.

The next year finds Cherea performing a pastoral comedy at a home on the Giudecca (February 6, 1513; 15:531).[61] Shortly after that he moved to the papal court of Leo X (1513–21), not returning to Venice until the busy theatrical seasons of 1521–22 and 1522–23. He was hired by Marco Grimani to perform a tragedy in the Ducal Palace (February 2, 1522; 32:439), the first time the chambers of the Ducal Palace were so used.[62] On February 13, 1522 (32:458), he acted in Machiavelli's *Mandragola* at the Crociferi. In 1523 he appeared in "a true tale presented as a comedia" in the church of San Trovaso (May 17, 1523; 34:148). He also appeared in performances in 1525 (January 2; 37:396) and 1526 (40:789; 41:215–19). In April of that year he participated in the festivities for the feast of St. Mark, one of the

59. Sanudo mentions Cherea later, in 1510, as a courier between the Marquis of Mantua, a prisoner of the Venetians, and his wife, Isabella d'Este Gonzaga (30 April; 10:223).

60. It is interesting that the 1508 prohibition of comedie was republished on 1 February 1521 (diaries, 29:606) and on 16 February 1530 (52:583) was referred to as still valid—"se dia publicar ogni anno"—to explain why a new prohibition was not passed. But the law went unobserved—see the entry of 26 February 1530, below, for the subsequent performance by the Reali. Cf. the sumptuary law of 25 January 1526 (40:749–54), whose stricture against momarie (40:752) was ignored in the following weeks: on 5 February 1526 (40:785) "una bellissima mumaria" was performed in the Ducal Palace courtyard; on 7 February 1526 (40:789–90) a number of comedie were performed; on 8 February 1526 (40:791) a momaria was performed with Maestro Tonin. On 28 July 1533 new restrictions were imposed after the performance of a comedia that Sanudo described as "very dirty and shameful" (22 July 1533; 58:465). See also Bistort 1969, 225–31; and Padoan 1981b, 396, 422n.

61. An important patron during this period was Gaspare di Sanseverino detto Fracasso. See Padoan 1981b, 415. He was present at a number of Cherea's recitals in 1512 (diaries, 14 June; 14:324) and 1513 (6 February; 15:531).

62. Padoan 1981b, 409.

most important celebrations of the Venetian state. In this case his performance simply completed a day of theatrical religiosity and civic representation:

April 25, 1526 (41:218–19)   Today, the 25th, was the feast day of St. Mark. The doge [Andrea Gritti] was dressed in gold brocade under a mantle of crimson silk with an ermine collar and a cap of crimson silk. . . . Alvise Minio, departing [to serve as] civil and military governor of Caodistria [Capo d'Istria], carried the ceremonial sword and was dressed in crimson damask, and his companion was ser Domenego Capello, wearing crimson velvet. Neither the primicerio nor the bishop of Baffo was present, but there were two Englishmen with their ambassador, who were also invited to the meal; the remainder of the delegates and the Signoria, numbering fifty-two, were also among the dinner guests, most wearing silk. They went to the church of San Marco to hear Mass, and the doge was met by the canons carrying double candles and a cross,[63] as was customary, and the vicar, who was to celebrate Mass, in his vestments, together with the deacon and subdeacon. According to the ducal ceremony, [the ducal party] entered the church through the door near the canonry and, encircling it, passed through the ambulatory and entered the church [proper] through the main portal. After the ritual solemn confession had been completed at the altar, with the doge responding, the doge and ambassadors went up into the reserved area [*pergolo*], as is customary, along with the sword-bearer and his companion. The others stayed below. After the Solemn Mass had been celebrated, the five scuole passed by. The guardian [of each scuola] first gave to the doge a large candle and to each of the ambassadors and others a thinner candle. And each scuola carried under a baldachin crosses or icons and relics, and the Scuola di San Marco carried the ring of St. Mark. Then two of the artisan guilds passed in review, the Tuscan [luxury-fabric makers] and the tailors [*toscani et sartori*], each with an offering. And when it was completed, everyone went to the palace to dine. . . .

It was a most beautiful meal, as is usual with this doge. There were eighty-two of us dining at the table, and there was a variety of dishes, but neither whipped-cream sweets nor cookies.[64] There were the usual sweets, and everyone had his own. There were many songs during the meal,[65] and then there was a short comedia performed by Cherea, who pretended to be taken prisoner by some pirates, together with some little boys and girls, and then they were freed. Then the party began with dancing, and they danced the *lodesana*,

---

63. In the manuscript, *croce*, "cross," is always indicated by the symbol †.

64. The manuscript had *torti*; the Fulin edition has *torte*.

65. The manuscript has *canti assai fo manzando, e poi*; the Fulin edition has *canti assai. Fu manzado, e poi*.

which was very energizing. A make-believe horse was brought in, [complete] with hide, that appeared to be alive; Cherea mounted it, and together they jumped in a wonderful way, and then another performed marvelous and daring jumps, and it was a great success. Finally, the women danced, and one named Perina took the doge's hand, and the ambassadors' and everyone's, and there was great laughter—she was a pretty young thing. And when it was over, the doge stood at the door of his palace with the Signoria and bade goodnight to everyone who had dined there, thanking them.

This may have been the high point of Cherea's Venetian career. The next year, he devised an elaborate pantomime that failed to please.[66]

February 28, 1527 (44:171-72)   After dinner on the day assigned for the chase in Piazza San Marco, because it had been decided that the Council of Ten would give fifty ducats every year for the festa, Cherea took on this task. He had a large platform built in the middle of the Piazza, where the doge and the ambassadors will sit, and he had long canvases hung around it, so that the rumor spread that he would do something splendid. Many viewing stands were built around the Piazza, more than usual, and a reserved area on which a place was secured by a payment of three to four ducats in advance, and it also cost plenty to be in the stands, where there were many maskers, women and others. There was a substantial crowd in the Piazza, where there were not many maskers and only a few horses. But there were two little carts carrying women in costume that were drawn by horses about the Piazza. . . .

Now, the doge arrived with the ambassadors of the pope, France, England, Milan, Florence, Ferrara, and Mantua and many patricians who accompanied the doge to see the festa, as well as many senators who had paid to be elected and others who are not in the Senate this year. . . . Then the bulls ran in the Piazza, and the heads of five pigs were cut off by the doge's squires, and the bull's head by a butcher. It began to drizzle a little, so the canvases were let down over the platform, in the middle of which appeared a large old world and a little world on one side with four giants, one at each corner of the platform. Then there emerged out of a grotto four poorly costumed players, two women and two men dressed as ——, and [they] did a kind of dance. Then others came . . . and sang about the world they wished to renew. Then came twelve armed men, who one by one and one after the other danced, as it were a morris dance [*moresca*], and each had a halberd in his hand. These men made certain thrusts, then tossed away the halberds, and each drew his sword from

---

66. See Padoan 1981b, 415; Tafuri 1984, 9; and Muir 1984b, 66. Muir gives this momaria the title *Trionfo del Giovane sul Vecchio*.

his side, dancing all the while and beating time, and then they went into the grotto.

Finally, out came two dancers who performed very well with jumps, each with four [others] dressed as nymphs, but not in good order, and they danced certain dances. But then a serpent-shaped firework emerged, and it went around the platform with fire in its mouth. There was someone who sang and a child dressed as an angel who recited some verses about the old world, and the big old world was set on fire and it burned. And this fire was the intermezzo. And with this the festa ended, and the new world remained on high. Thus it was a very poor festa, and Cherea was reproached by everybody. The one that maistro Tonin produced last year with floats, etc., was much better; I conclude that this was a very bad showing.

The doge thereupon retired to the Ducal Palace, where there was dancing, music, and a feast. And then in the palace courtyard the entertainments continued:

And about two hours after sunset a most beautiful momaria came into the courtyard of the palace made up of well-costumed young gentlemen with eighty torches and hobbyhorses, serpents, and other things numbering — carried by porters. After these came the Compagni, beautifully dressed in the Greek fashion, and they performed the fable of Perseus and Andromache[67] with dances and marvelous music, so that this was as praised by all as the performance today by Cherea was criticized. This was produced by Tonin.

After this fiasco, Cherea left Venice to take employment with the Count of Caiazzo, as his chancellor.[68]

Native Actors

Theater in Venice may have been too decentralized and spontaneous to support a professional like Cherea, who, unlike Zuan Polo and Ruzante, had no native connections to the city or its dominion. Venetian theater was essentially amateur-driven. It was the Venetians themselves who acted in most of the productions, for example, in the family productions mentioned above or those put on by the young patrician members of compagnie, as in the following excerpt.

---

67. This should be *Andromeda,* but both the manuscript and the Fulin edition have *Andromaca.*

68. Sanudo mentions Cherea's later activities as a liaison with the Hungarians in 1531 (15 January; 55:338) and 1532 (21 April; 56:77).

June 12, 1514 (18:265)   Today, on Murano, in Ca' di Prioli, a certain party was held and a comedia performed by the Compagni Zardinieri, and some prostitutes were there, and the group did not want anyone else to attend.

February 13, 1515 (19:433)   This evening, at San Thomado, in the house of ser Leonardo di Prioli, a new comedia about some shepherds was performed by certain compagnia members called Virtuosi and women, and there were no others. And I went this morning to see the rehearsal—it was very good.[69]

February 13, 1520 (28:256)   Today there was also a rehearsal for a comedia at the Loredan house in San Marcuola, which the compagnia of the Triumphanti will stage tomorrow. The comedia is Terence's *Adelphoe,* and the members of the compagnia will recite it themselves. The set was constructed in the courtyard. There were many important senior patricians and women and others, so the courtyard was full. The rehearsal lasted until three hours after sunset. Tomorrow they are going to do the actual performance,[70] and the women and their husbands will all stay to supper. Thus it was staged the following day and lasted until eleven hours.

February 26, 1530 (52:601)   This evening, at Ca' Loredan, on the Grand Canal, there was a rehearsal for a comedia to be performed by the compagnia of the Reali on the last day of this month, which will be Monday. They invited many senators, and I also attended. It lasted until five hours after sunset. There was the ambassador from Milan . . . and procurators, the state attorneys, the heads of the Ten, old ser Michiel da Leze, and many senators. The comedy was very good and well performed. The scenery presented the Temple of Mars, which was closed to become the Temple of Peace. The autor of this comedia was Zuan Ortica. The members of the compagnia who performed were the following: ser Francesco Justinian, ser Domenego di Prioli, ser Piero Loredan, ser Tomà Mozenigo, ser Zuan Donado, ser Marco Justinian, ser Piero Morexini.[71]

Diplomacy in Play

The line dividing theater in Venice and Venice as itself an actor upon its own stage was often invisible. In May 1513, in the midst of the War of the League of Cambrai, a compagnia della calza staged an elaborate re-creation of Venetian diplomatic

---

69. Rehearsals were themselves sought-out occasions, well attended and widely discussed. See below, excerpts dated 13 February 1520 and 11 and 25 February 1525.

70. The manuscript has *l'ordinaria;* the Fulin edition has *Aulularia,* followed by a question mark.

71. Other occasions when native actors performed are described in the entries for 16 February 1512 (13:483), 8 February 1513 (15:535), and 3, 7, 16, and 20 February 1515 (19:418, 424, 439, 444).

receptions in which members of the compagnia danced, acted, and recited a series of complex scenes full of historical references and symbolic gestures. Among the audience were three real ambassadors, to whom were presented theatrical imitations of diplomatic ceremonies at a time when it was important to show Venice's political position in a favorable light. The occasion was a wedding feast involving the granddaughter of the doge and 420 guests, who were seated for "a fine meal."[72] This was followed by the elaborate entertainment:

May 2, 1513 (16:206–7)   Then preparations were made for presenting a comedia, that is, certain representations. A platform was set up for the women to sit on; another one was constructed in the middle of the room for the recitation. The three ambassadors and other high-ranking men were seated there, although the Spanish ambassador left early to write, he said, to the viceroy.[73] One of the kings of the compagnia of the Eterni, ser Francesco Zen, came onto the platform dressed in a silver robe with a gold, Greek-style tunic [*caxacha*][74] over it and a hat on his head, with his councillors, ser Francesco Barbaro and ser Luca da Leze, and his interpreter, or chancellor, ser Stefano Tiepolo, all of whom were well costumed.[75] After these members of the compagnia had danced for a while on the platform with the women, the first *demostration* was put on by ser Marco Antonio Memo, dressed in old-rose-colored vestments as a bishop and legate of Pope Calixtus.[76] He presented the king [of the Eterni] with a brief from the pope declaring that he had sent this bishop *de nulla tenentis* [i.e., without a see] to congratulate him. He also presented him with a letter of [diplomatic] credentials and, after delivering his oration, gave him a kingly crown, placing it on his head and blessing him. The king

---

72. See chapter 4 under "Foreign Diplomats in Venice."

73. The Spanish ambassador may have been displeased with the Venetian government for diverting France from forming an alliance with Spain and the empire by making its own treaty with France at Blois on 23 March, less than six weeks earlier. Thirteen days later this same Spanish ambassador would excuse himself from the ceremonial investiture of Venice's captain general, Bartolomeo d'Alviano, although he had previously—as on the earlier occasion—accepted the invitation to attend. Diaries, 15 May 1513 (16:251); see also Romanin 1853-61, 5:282-83.

74. A long garment that, unlike the Venetian official robe, was open in front. See Newton 1988, 30; and Vitali 1992.

75. Honorific titles and offices such as that of king, councillor, interpreter, or chancellor may have been bestowed by the compagnia upon their members for this specific occasion.

76. The color of the vestments was described as *ruosa secha,* a newly fashionable old-rose color. A decade later Andrea Gritti would adopt the color for some of his ducal vestments. See Newton 1988, 30. In 1122 Pope Calixtus II had given the Venetian a papal banner bearing the words "Vexillum beati Petri" (Banner of St. Peter) to carry in a crusade, and this became part of their standard regalia. It was a well-chosen reference to convey Venice's desire for an optimal relationship with the new pope, Leo X, who only two months earlier, on 19 March, had ascended to the papal throne.

thanked him and invited him to watch a dance, which was performed there[77] on the platform by two women and two members of the compagnia. When it was finished, the legate invited the king to listen to a member of his retinue, Galeazzo da Valle, from Vicenza, who improvised a song, accompanying himself on the lyre, and left. [Next] to arrive was ser[78] Zuan di Cavali, dressed in the German manner, as the ambassador of the emperor. He carried a letter of credentials from the emperor Otto.[79] He delivered his oration in German and presented a scepter to this King Pancratio of the compagnia of the Eterni.[80] Then the women performed a dance, and the ambassador asked his musicians to play a piece on flute and bagpipe.

After he had left, ser Santo Contarini came on stage dressed as a Mamluk.[81] Taking the role of the soldan's ambassador, he presented a letter and a lynx.[82] After the women had danced, the ambassador had his retinue perform a morris dance. Next to arrive was the French ambassador, ser Zuan Contarini, very nicely dressed in the French style. He brought a letter from King Louis; having read it in French, he presented the king with a dog.[83] Once

---

77. The manuscript has *li;* the Fulin edition omits it.

78. The manuscript has *sier;* the Fulin edition omits it.

79. Otto was the son of Emperor Frederick Barbarossa. According to the Venetian legend, Otto had persuaded his father to accept the doge's offer to make his peace with Pope Alexander III, a Venetian ally, in 1177. This was the famous Pax Veneta, and the reference to Otto here would remind the Venetian audience of that most glorious occasion and the acquisition, from a grateful pope, of their most prized regalia: an umbrella to be carried over the doge as a sign of regal authority; a lit candle to carry in processions as a sign of devotion and nobility; a lead seal bearing images of St. Mark and the doge (as the papal seal carries the image of St. Peter); a sword as a sign of the doge's faithful defense of the church against the emperor; and most important for the ritual life of the city, the privilege of wedding the Adriatic Sea in the annual ceremony of the Sensa, the *sposalizio del mare.* See Padoan Urban 1968.

80. The presentation of a scepter (which implies *imperium*) to the Venetian "king" by the German "ambassador" must have been understood by the audience as guaranteeing Venetian jurisdiction over the imperial lands, which included imperial territories in northern Italy conquered by Venice in the fifteenth century, then lost in the earlier years of the War of the League of Cambrai, and in 1513 being regained. Venice had recently been negotiating with Maximilian for the investiture of these lands. See Romanin 1853–61, 5:280.

81. *Mamluk* here refers to a member of a politically powerful military class in Egypt.

82. This was a lynx (*lovo cervier*) fur piece, much prized as an accessory. See Bistort 1969, 386; Boerio 1856; and Newton 1988, 167, which describes similar sable fur pieces with jeweled collars that could be hung from the waist and were like toys. The lynx was traditionally considered a sharp-sighted animal, far-seeing and percipient, an apt metaphor for Venetians' diplomatic acumen in dealing with their Egyptian trading partners, sometimes as enemy and sometimes as ally.

83. The dog was a symbol of fidelity, a reference to the renewed alliance between Venice and France represented by the Treaty of Blois, signed on 23 March 1513. Allegiance to France was dominant in much of Venetian diplomacy during this period, as were French modes of fashion.

the women had performed their dance, he had cornets and trumpets play. The Spanish ambassador then appeared, played by Zuan Falier, who spoke in Spanish. He presented the letter of credentials written in Spanish, made a gift of two men from Africa [*do di Ginea*],[84] who engaged in swordplay, after which the women performed their dance. Lastly, the bridegroom, ser Ferigo Foscari, came as the Hungarian ambassador with a letter from King Ladislaus. He presented the king with a lidded gold cup, and after the dance, he had some of his Hungarian retinue play the *violeta* and other instruments.[85]

It should be noted also that the interpreter, ser Stefano Tiepolo, cleverly translated into our tongue the speeches of the ambassadors and the replies of the king. A little hobbyhorse ridden by a pygmy [*pygmeo*] courier came on next, along with the ambassador of the pygmies, ser Jacomo Dandolo. . . .[86] Once he had read and presented the letter from his king, he gave our king a crane.[87] When the women's dance was over, he instructed his four pygmies to perform their own dance, which they did well, waving hatchets and dancing to a four-meter beat [*a tempo in 4*].[88] Then came three Venetian ambassadors: ser Beneto Zorzi, dressed in gold brocade, and ser Daniel Barbarigo and ser Baptista Contarini, wearing silk mantles. The letter of credentials from Doge Michiel Sten was presented, and the ambassadors were introduced: the first as a member of the Storlado family, a university laureate and knight; the second as a Participazo; and the third as a Bonzi, all families that are now extinct.[89] Then Zorzi delivered the oration, made a gift of a silver ship,[90] and

---

84. In an entry of 14 August in this same year (16:622) Sanudo records a letter from Pope Leo X to Manual of Portugal addressing him as "rex Portugalliae et Algarbiorum citra et ultraque mare in Africa, dominus Guineae et conquistae navigationis ac commertii Ethiopiae, Arabiae, Persiae atque Indiae." The vocabulary of these exotic lands was well known to the Venetians.

85. The Spanish ambassador had left early, but the papal envoy and the Hungarian ambassador were still there to witness their counterparts enacting these ceremonial courtesies to a Venetian "king" for the evening. Venice's alliance with Hungary was a key element of its defensive policy toward the Turks.

86. The pygmy courier rode "uno cavalo marian picolo," which was a prop horse probably made of wood and moved by the actor. See M. T. Muraro 1981, 331n64. The father of the pygmy ambassador was "ser Alvise gobo," a hunchback.

87. The crane could have symbolized the vigilance and loyalty of the Venetians. See Ferguson 1961, s.v. "crane."

88. The editors thank Ellen Rosand for her suggested translation of this phrase.

89. On Sanudo's awareness of the *casade morte*, the "dead houses" of certain patrician families, see chapter 6, n. 2. The "reincarnation" of three extinct families here from a century earlier is suggestive of this sense of loss, as is the fact that these "ambassadors" came from Doge Michele Steno, who ruled from 1400 to 1413.

90. Perhaps a little silver model, such as the sixteenth-century thurible of hammered and engraved silver, partially gilded, in the treasury of the Basilica of St. Anthony in Padua. Pendent earrings in the form of a ship were also popular in fifteenth-century Venice. See Pazzi 1995, 104. We owe both these references to Doretta Davanzo Poli. Phyllis Pray Bober has suggested that

presented a buffoon, Zuan Polo. After the women's dance was over, two servants cut capers, and four peasants from the countryside sang songs. After Zuan Polo told a few jokes and performed sleights of hand on top of a stool, the festivities ended. It was three hours after sunset and very warm because of the crush of the crowd.[91]

Carnival

That the chief participants in the theatrical productions of Venice were the Venetians themselves is perhaps best exemplified in the activities of Carnival, that most theatrical period of the city's year. Carnival was the annual event that turned all of Venice into a theater and Venetians into actors of freely chosen identities, the period when the entire population of Venice took to its streets and canals, often extravagantly costumed and masked, to the sound of instruments, songs, and the shouts of crowds at play. It was the period in which daring behavior, extraordinary forms of entertainment, and identity reversals might be risked, as the governors intermingled with the governed in celebration of their city, its history, and its continuity.[92]

Carnival in Venice ran from St. Stephen's Day (December 26) until the beginning of Lent, the moveable date of Fat Tuesday, which varied from February 3 to March 9. Festivities during this long season took various forms: patrician parties and weddings; momarie and comedie; races, or regattas, as these water races were called; and fireworks. The following account of the various participants in the revelries suggests the explosion of energy and the multiple activities of a fine Carnival season:

February 4, 1524 (35:392–93)   The weather was good today, and after dinner the bull chases were held as usual in Piazza San Marco. And there was something extra: there were fireworks on ropes from the Campanile to the church that all exploded at once. The doge was there, with the ambassadors and those assigned to accompany him; there were numerous maskers.

Among others were twenty-two members of the compagnia of the Ortolani, whose lord was ser Domenego Zorzi; also present was ser Marco Grimani, the procurator. Everyone was dressed in robes of crimson velvet with ducal

---

the silver ship might be a nef, a silver or gold container for salt or spices in the form of a ship. See, e.g., the January miniature in the *Très riches heures* of the duc de Berry.

91. Povoledo 1995, 628, entitles this comedia the *Demonstration del Re Pancrazio* and describes it as a long, fragmentary, itinerant action during which the earthly powers send gifts, through their ambassadors, not to the young marrying couple but to the Eterni, with every gift corresponding to a symbolic act concerning the *vestizione*, or accouterments, of the "king."

92. See Muir 1981, 156–81; and Carroll 1985.

sleeves or in other colored silks; they wore stoles and caps on their heads, some of satin, some of velvet. [They wore] masks with noses, and each one was preceded by two servants, dressed as peasants, with a wax torch in hand. . . . One of them was wearing cloth of gold, and there were many virtuoso performers. First came the buffoons, Zuan Polo and others, next Ruzante the Paduan, others dressed as peasants who danced and performed acrobatics beautifully, and six dressed as peasant youths who sang *villote*.[93] They carried various rustic implements, such as hoes, shovels, spades, rakes, etc. They also had wind instruments, bagpipes, and ceremonial trumpets. They took a turn around the Piazza; then in the evening, with the torches lit, they went around the town. At one hour after sunset they arrived in the courtyard of the Ducal Palace to demonstrate their virtuosity. Next they went to the procuratia of ser Marco da Molin, the procurator, who was hosting a small party, then to various other places. They ended up at the Tavern of the Monkey, where they had supper. . . .

Sometimes, however, as part of the performances and merriment, costume inversions involved a mock assumption of religiosity or authority, and these earned Sanudo's disapproval, as he states at the end of a long and detailed description of an elaborate Carnival festivity marred by rain and a diplomatic squabble:

February 4, 1529 (49:421–22)   After dinner, even though it was raining and there were few people in the Piazza, the usual festivities were held. There were very few masks and horses, and the platforms were empty. The doge attended, dressed in crimson velvet, over which he wore a mantle of slashed crimson satin lined with squirrel; with him were the ambassadors from the pope, France, England, Hungary, Milan, Florence, Saint Pol, Ferrara, and Urbino. The ambassador from Mantua did not come because of a concern for precedence. He does not wish to follow the ambassador from the Duke of Urbino in the procession, and he is wrong. The other ambassadors and the doge told him he was wrong. He has written to Mantua, and it is believed he awaits their response. . . .

After the heads of six pigs had been cut off, some by the butchers and some by the doge's pages, and the bull's head had been cut off—there were about twelve bulls in the Piazza—a platform was erected in the middle of the Piazza.[94] A momaria was performed on it by four young men and four

---

93. Popular and traditional country songs from Friuli.

94. See below for an explanation of the traditional bull chase, the famous *caza (caccia)* of Carnival Thursday.

women, four real women [*vere done*],[95] who danced. Then up climbed four wild men with their women; the wild men fought with the dancers and took their women away. Then the young men came out again alone and fought with the wild men and were captured. Again the young men came out with halberds, and again they were defeated; finally they emerged with firearms and defeated the wild men. Next an anvil was brought out, inside of which were a little boy and a little girl. Four young men, dancing in time, beat on the anvil with hammers, and out came the two children, who danced most excellently. Then came the wild women, who, after they had danced with the other women, fought[96] them and were defeated by their firearms. And lastly, all the wild men came out; they had been tied up by the women, who held arrows in their hands; dancing, the women stuck them with the arrows. They all were wearing bells on their feet. Finally, the young men appeared with the wild women, who were tied up, and all sixteen of them danced the *tarintera* [tarantella]. When the entertainment was over, they all left the platform, and there were no other platform performances.

There was a firework display with lots of fire and rockets burning, but nothing else was done, and it rained all day, so it was a very meager festival. Indeed, because of the death of the doge's daughter-in-law, there was no feasting at all in the Ducal Palace.

Today in the Piazza one merrymaker took as his costume the veil of a flagellant;[97] this is really insufferable.

Some years later a similar inversion of costume, this time mimicking official dress, drew similar criticism from the diarist:

February 25, 1533 (57:548)   After dinner the savi did not meet, and there were many maskers around the city. Some people wore scarlet robes with ducal sleeves, and silks, and velvet stoles, and one had a gold chain and was preceded by a grand chancellor. Others were dressed like heralds and like the keeper of the archives, while still others had wind bands precede them as if they were announcing the Signoria.[98] In my opinion this was not a proper thing to do.

---

95. That is, women rather than boys dressed as women, evidence that women occasionally performed in Venetian theatrical productions in this period.

96. The manuscript has *combatuto*; the Fulin edition has *combatute*.

97. The term used was *batudo*, meaning a member of a penitential community.

98. The manuscript has *coladena d'oro con il canzelier grando davanti e altri secretado et vestiti da comandadori . . . in segno che era la Signoria*; the Fulin edition has *coladena d'oro come il canzelier grando davanti e altri da comandadori . . . in segno che va la Signoria*.

The *zuoba di la caza,* the Thursday of the chase, was a central event in Venetian Carnival celebrations. This was a ritual reenactment of a historical event that brought together all the strata of Venetian society, from its highest leaders to its poorest onlookers. It referred to a twelfth-century rebellion led by the patriarch of Aquileia against the patriarch of Grado, a Venetian ecclesiastical puppet, in which it was said that twelve castellans of Friuli participated. According to the story, the miscreants were captured and condemned to death, but the pious intervention of the pope commuted their sentence to a perpetual annual tribute of three hundred loaves of bread plus twelve pigs and one bull. Therefore, the reenactment concerned the ritual public slaughter of the pigs and the bull (representing the castellans and the patriarch of Aquileia) after the bull had been chased through the streets.[99]

The entire city witnessed these events—the doge, the Signoria, and guests from the balcony of the Ducal Palace and the populace from the Piazza.[100] The doge further participated through a "formal" condemnation of the animals to such capital punishment, and councillors armed with sticks enacted a symbolic destruction of toy castles especially built for this purpose. But sometimes, as in the early years of the War of the League of Cambrai, Friulan pigs were not to be had, or had to be purchased. In the excerpts below, Sanudo regrets the wartime curtailment of the city's traditional revelries:

February 7, 1510 (9:516)   Today was February 7, the Thursday of the chase. I note that this year was unusual in that no pork treats[101] were given to the patricians. This was because the pigs, which the castellans are obliged to donate, are not to be found in the Patria of Friuli. This is because of the wars that have taken place. Therefore, this good custom will be suspended.

February 23, 1514 (17:574)   After dinner the chase was held in the Piazza San Marco, but it was very bad. There were few masks, and the city seemed depressed, which is just what it is. And it should be noted that this spectacle is put on by the Patria of Friuli, and the castellans were obliged to send the pigs. But now Friuli is lost, and the pigs had to be purchased, and so they were, and the festa took place.

With the end of the War of the League of Cambrai, pigs once again became plentiful, and this "good custom" was resumed. But a few years later it was again suspended to avoid diplomatic ridicule:

---

99. Muir 1981, 160–61.

100. Sanudo 1980, 58.

101. Sanudo uses the word *zozolo,* a cognate of the Friulan *zozzul,* meaning "little pieces of pork." These were distributed to senators after the annual pig chase in the Piazzetta. The editors are grateful to Edward Muir for this definition. Cf. diaries, 27:12 and 28:31, for additional uses of the term.

March 7, 1520 (28:330–31)   It was decided that two councillors will no longer be appointed to go as judges to the Court of the Proprio to deliver the sentence on behalf of the doge to the pigs that their heads are to be chopped off after dinner on the Thursday of the chase. This signifies [the punishment of] the castellans of Friuli, according to the ancient custom. In addition, neither the doge nor the Signoria will any longer go to smash the wooden models on this day in the meeting room of the signori di notte or the [Sala di] Piovego, as is customary—and signifies the destruction of the Friulan castles. But they will hold a chase on the designated Thursday, and the pigs' heads will be cut off by the doge's squires and given to the prisoners as usual. The rest will be discontinued. And the reason for this decision was that this past Thursday of the chase the papal legate, the bishop of Pola, was in the Collegio when two councillors rose to go to the Court of the Proprio to give the sentence to the pigs, and the legate asked where they were going. The doge told him, and the legate had a hearty laugh. Then the Collegio decided to sponsor a bill to end this custom and did so.[102]

Additional serious problems occasionally resulted from the behavior of maskers or from accidents caused by the excitement of the crowd:

January 24, 1518 (25:215–16)   In the morning, nothing of importance took place in the Collegio. In Campo San Polo many viewing stands had been set up, given the plans for holding a festivity and a chase of four bulls, and a tightrope walker, and other things. For this reason and because everyone was speaking about this festivity, organized by Albaneseto, the public executioner, and some of his colleagues, it seemed best to the councillors . . . not to convene the Great Council today and to all attend the festivities. . . .[103] And everything was crowded, the women at the windows and numbers of people on the platforms, infinite maskers, and a huge crowd in this square. Temporary viewing stands had been commissioned by the organizers[104] themselves. Those who wanted to view the festivities from them paid from four to ten soldi. Once they were filled, the bulls were released into the campo, where they were chased by dogs. This continued until the twenty-third hour, [when] an announcement was made that nothing else would be done today, so they dismantled the tightrope . . . and everyone went home. And the crowd was disgruntled: they had spent their money to go on the stands and had not seen anything, not even the beheading of the bulls. Some were cleverly dressed as

---

102. The suspension was only temporary.

103. The day was Sunday, when the Great Council usually met.

104. The manuscript has *soleri fati far per loro auctori di tal cosa;* the Fulin edition has *soleri fati per loro per veder tal cosa.*

old men. It happened that one petty trader masked as an old man had a cage with a Priapus inside: it was quite a sight, and he was going around showing it off to the women. Now, it seems that at Santa Maria Zubenigo, while he was showing it to a young woman on a certain balcony, a man who had some connection with her came out and stabbed him with a spindle, and the masker died. He was sixteen years old. So the next morning, it was announced at San Polo that by order of the most illustrious Signoria, the stands should be taken down, and nothing more was to be done.

In spite of all the precautions taken, the government could not anticipate every eventuality, since the crowds and beasts were uncontrolled and shoddy construction methods were occasionally employed:

February 6, 1520 (28:239)   A noteworthy event occurred yesterday in the campo of Santa Maria Formosa, where preparations had been made for a festivity, a chase, and other [entertainments] as usual. A number of people had gathered to see the festa, and viewing stands had been set up. By chance a large stand placed off to one side collapsed. Many people were underneath it: seven were killed outright. Others were on it, and some were twisted, some were injured, and it was a horrible experience to see brains dashed out on the ground, heads without bodies, crushed heads,[105] and pieces of bodies awful to behold. Several who were on the platform were injured, and so the festa ended. The stand was built on barrels without boards being affixed to the top.

A few years later, fireworks went astray, striking a priest in the eye and burning the garments of several onlookers, including a patrician woman's dress of crimson velvet (February 8, 1526; 40:791). But one accident in 1530 elicited particular sympathy from Sanudo:

February 16, 1530 (54:296–97)   Today there occurred a most unhappy event. Antonio Beneto, seventy-two years old, a notary of the *sopragastaldi* since 1485, a wise man of great discretion and experienced in governmental matters, was in the Piazza, where there were thirteen bulls. In trying to escape one who was being chased, he hit the back of his head on the ground, and after two hours he died. May God have mercy on his soul.

Restrictions of masks and/or costumes and rules prohibiting the carrying of arms were occasionally imposed by the Council of Ten to prevent disorder. For

---

105. The manuscript could read *teste frachade;* the Fulin edition has *teste stachade.*

example, in 1518 the council required those who wished to disguise themselves to get permission to do so, prohibited maskers and soldiers from carrying arms, and forbade all visits to convents (February 11, 1518; 25:248). The next year, maskers could not participate in the bull chase, "which seemed very strange, and it had never been done" (March 3, 1519; 27:12). The following year, this restriction was modified:

February 16, 1520 (28:264)   After dinner the chase took place in Piazza San Marco as usual. Attending were the Signoria and the vice-doge, ser Francesco Foscari, with the ambassadors. It was over quickly. There were quite a few maskers since for the present the Council of Ten has given permission for disguises, but they required the maskers to go in groups of four and no less and to have received permission.

The term Sanudo used for costume disguises was *stravestir,* which generally meant disguising one's identity and sometimes one's class by adopting patrician or religious garb. Yet some forms of disguise might be permitted in spite of a prohibition, for whatever its accidents and extravagances, Carnival fulfilled a great need. It was an assertion by the entire Venetian society of the happiness, the *felicità,* of the Republic:

February 13, 1526 (40:810–11)   By order of the heads of the Council of Ten it was publicly proclaimed that this Lent no one may any longer dress in costume under penalty, etc., and thus no one did. And this evening brought the conclusion of Carnival, a Carnival that has been the most festive in many a year. First an enormous number of people wore masks of many styles, but a majority of those were old peasant fools,[106] with a lot of women dressed in their usual clothes with just a mask on their face, draped with pearls and gold chains. Others wore a gown and veil and had servants who held up their trains behind them and old women following. Furthermore, some men were dressed like senators in scarlet and silk, and some had ducal sleeves.[107]

In addition, at night there were many splendid momarie with wind bands, ceremonial trumpets, and wax torches. Every evening that they went out, the revelers came to the courtyard of the Ducal Palace to hold a dance. Sunday evening, yesterday evening, and this evening at an hour and a half after sun-

---

106. Sanudo's phrase is *barbachieppi vilani,* roughly "wild bearded peasants." Boerio offers as a synonym for *chiepo* the word *rapa,* which figuratively can denote thickheadedness. *Barbachieppi* was such a peculiar term that Fulin put a question mark next to it.

107. See above for other costume inversions (1529 and 1533); and see Carpaccio's St. Ursula cycle, at the Accademia, for a monkey dressed in senatorial robes.

set there was a momaria of eighteen people wearing leaves of light blue paper, so that they looked like men from ancient times. Each one carried a slender stick in his hand, and they danced complicated variations of the *chiaranzana*,[108] keeping time with the sticks. They all showed great alacrity in waving them to the beat, and the dance lasted a long time. Then they had two little boys play a rousing fencing game, which was fun to watch, but they had only six torches. They were Germans merchants from the Warehouse.

Beyond that, many expensive banquets were held, including three sumptuous ones given by ser Fantin Corner da la Piscopia, by the patriarch of Aquileia, [Marino] Grimani, and by the knight Garzoni,[109] which I have already described. And not only these but others in private homes among friends, companions, and relatives, to the point that pheasants these days are selling for thirteen lire a pair, and partridges for —— lire a pair, and capons and chickens in great quantity.

In conclusion, it has been years since we have seen a Carnival as festive as this one, and there was no disorder caused by maskers because people were carrying neither arms nor clubs. May God grant that these festivities add to the happiness of our Republic.[110]

The festivities and felicity associated with Carnival in Venice could also be found throughout the Terraferma. Over the many Carnivals Sanudo described during the thirty-seven years of his diaries, he referred often to celebrations throughout the Venetian dominion:

February 16, 1518 (25:253)   It should be noted that at Treviso, on Carnival Sunday . . . there was a festa in the palace [of the civic and military governor] . . . and that evening Plautus's comedia the *Amphytrion* was performed. It was well done, and many of our young patricians went to see it, in spite of the great muds caused by the rains. But most went by boat.

February 17, 1533 (57:528)   It should be noted that in Treviso a beautiful comedia and feste took place; in Padua, another excellent comedia was performed by Ruzante in Ca' Corner, near the Santo;[111] in Verona, there were comedie and jousts, so that our cities are rejoicing, for we are at peace, and the Thursday bull chase in the Piazza will be a fine occasion, [even though]

---

108. A vivacious folk dance.

109. Zaccaria Garzoni, Knight of Jerusalem.

110. This passage continues with Sanudo's fear that this happiness might not continue. The sultan's army was marching against Hungary, and his navy was being prepared for war, "which news has stunned many, and it happened on the last day of Carnival."

111. On 25 February another "bellissima comedia nova" was performed in the same Ca' Corner. Diaries, 25 February 1533 (57:549).

the doge did not wish viewing stands to be placed around the Piazza as is usually done.[112]

The Battle of Pavia

To separate the theater and Carnival texts and performances from the narrative of Sanudo's diaries is to deprive them of their context within the quotidian events of Venetian life and to mute their relationship to the specific moment in the life of the city when they occurred. Theater and Carnival were simply particular aspects of the daily drama that was life, especially Sanudo's life, in Renaissance Venice. For this was a city that, with its settings and scenery but most of all its intense political life, provided a sense of personal and civic drama just as powerful as that enacted upon its improvised stages.

Venice as theater is nowhere better illustrated than in the interweaving of a major military event with the Carnival life of the city in 1525. The event was the battle of Pavia, on February 24, when the Carnival season was well under way. The first two excerpts below illustrate the normal Carnival events, with performances commanding the attention of government councils, which chose entertainment over their political business.

February 9, 1525 (37:559–60)   After dinner few members of the Collegio convened, because some of the savi di Consiglio, including ser Lorenzo Loredan, procurator, ser Hironimo Justinian, procurator, ser Luca Trun, and ser Nicolò Bernardo, went to see the rehearsal of a comedy at Ca' Arian, at San Raphael. It will be staged on Monday the 13th of this month for the festa that the compagnia of the Triomphanti is sponsoring; the autor is Zuan Manenti. Ser Marin Capello is lord of the festivities. . . .

Other procurators came . . . and two heads of the Ten . . . [and numerous state officials] and more than forty senators were there, people of quite different ages and conditions, including myself, Marin Sanudo. It rained while we were going over there, and soon the hall was full. For that reason, neither the Senate nor the Council of Ten met. Two brothers of the doge, ser Michiel and ser Polo Malipiero, attended.

The performance began at sunset and lasted six hours. There were nine intermezzi and three comedie in prose [presented] as one,[113] by Zuan Manenti, called *Philargio et Trebia et Fidel*. Then the Paduans Ruzante and Menato, dressed as peasants, put on a rustic-style comedia that was very lascivious

---

112. This was the last Carnival about which Sanudo wrote. His diaries end with the entry of 30 September 1533.

113. The manuscript as emended by Padoan 1978a, 115n74, has *per una, fata;* the Fulin edition has *per una fiata.*

with very dirty words, to the point that it was condemned by all and they were yelled at. There were almost sixty women on the stands wearing veils, and the young ones with their hair in coifs, and they shuddered at what was said in their name. The whole ending was about messing around and cuckolding their husbands.

But Zuan Polo did a good job, and the intermezzi were very nice, with all the virtuoso instrumentalists and singers that it is possible to have. They were dressed in various costumes, some as Moors, some as Germans, some as Greeks, some as Hungarians, some as pilgrims, and in many other kinds of costumes, but they did not wear masks. Zuan Polo came first in his costume and called himself Nicoleto Cantinella. And the last to come were eight dressed as crazy women with distaffs, and they performed a nice dance to a bagpipe. The rehearsal of the aforementioned comedia was completed to universal condemnation, not of the members of the compagnia, who spent [a large sum of] ducats, but of the autor, and this was out of money[114] they won a year ago in the lottery.[115]

February 13, 1525 (37:572)   Today, although the weather was bad, the comedia of the Triumphanti was put on at Ca' Arian, at San Raphael, and it was very lovely and chaste. About one hundred women attended, and the comedia that the Triumphanti had [the players] recite was not the dirty one . . . but instead the one by Ruzante in the rustic style. And Zuan Polo did a good job; there were a number of lovely intermezzi. It concluded at seven hours after sunset. It was followed by a supper for a large number of people . . . that went on until ten hours after sunset.

Into this festive season of Carnival an international political event of high importance intruded. Two weeks after the "lovely and chaste" comedia and dinner party at Ca' Arian, disturbing news arrived from Brescia (37:648). The French army under their king, Francis I, and the Spanish-imperial army had met the day before outside the city of Pavia. The French had been defeated, their king wounded and possibly slain, their leaders killed or taken captive.

The Venetians, although originally allied with the victors, had made a secret treaty with the king of France on December 12, 1524. The pope, Clement VII, was also a party to this secret treaty, which assured the Venetians that their traumatic defeat in 1509 at the hands of a Franco-papal enemy would not be repeated. But the Venetians had miscalculated the strength of the French king, which they tended to overestimate, and now, alarmed to see Emperor Charles V able to as-

---

114. The manuscript has *fo di denari;* the Fulin edition has *fo denari.*

115. For excerpts on the lottery, see chapter 6, where Zuan Manenti's role as lottery organizer is described.

sert his power in Italy, they considered the French defeat very bad news.[116] The doge hastily assembled the Council of Ten and the Collegio and sent a courier posthaste to Rome with the disturbing news, which reached Sanudo as he left his home to attend a rehearsal at Ca' Dandolo:

February 25, 1525 (37:648–49)   This morning, Saturday, after the Collegio had come down from its meeting and the doge had come for dinner, a messenger arrived with letters from ser Piero da ca' da Pexaro, procurator and proveditor general, written in Brescia yesterday at the —— hour. The doge read them: they brought the news that the armies clashed yesterday, the 24th, St. Matthew the Apostle's Day, and that the army of the Most Christian King[117] had been defeated, and that nonetheless the fighting continued the whole day. [Pexaro] had had this news in a letter from Paulo da Bologna in the imperial camp, written on the 24th, at the —— hour. And a little later came another letter from the proveditor general written at the 24th hour, describing how this Paulo da Bologna, having left the [imperial] camp this morning, had arrived in Brescia and reported that the French army had been defeated, the King wounded and captured—some say he is dead—and Monsignor the admiral[118] killed. . . .

When the doge heard this, the heads of the Ten, ser Paolo Donado, ser Pandolfo Morosini, and ser Hironimo Barbarigo, were called into his chambers. They were still in the palace, since a meeting of the Council of Ten with its zonta had been scheduled for this day. Only two secretaries were in the palace, Zuan Jacomo Caroldo and Lorenzo Roca. Then the doge immediately summoned the Collegio; ser Domenico Trevisan and ser Hironimo Justinian, procurators and savi di Collegio, who live in the Piazza, came right away.[119] Then the others arrived, but they were the first, and so the letters were read, to the great sorrow of everyone. And in the last letter to arrive, it appeared that twenty of the French troops had not been killed and that the king was not captured,[120] and the Swiss and the men-at-arms in block formation were heading in the direction of Milan. And the letter told how the Spaniards . . . had assailed this camp, breaching its stockades, and how the rest of the troops had fled across the Ticino with the Spaniards in pursuit.

And it was agreed that this was very bad news for this state. Letters with copies of these reports were dispatched to Rome posthaste to ensure that the

---

116. See Gilbert 1977, 309.

117. The French king is always referred to in the diaries as *re Christianissimo.*

118. Guillaume Gouffier, seigneur di Bonnivet.

119. The procurators had lodgings in the Procuratie, surrounding the Piazza San Marco.

120. Actually the French losses, both killed and wounded, numbered about eight thousand men, according to Dupuy and Dupuy 1993, 475, and the king was indeed captured.

pope was informed. The courier was ordered to take no other letters; he was to make a swift journey, and he was promised twenty-two ducats if he arrived Monday morning, the 27th. These provisions having been made, the doge and the others went to have their dinner. . . .

The news spread through the city. And I, Marin Sanudo, by chance was about to[121] go out after the noon bell to see the rehearsal of a comedia at the Ca' Dandolo by the compagnia of the Valorosi [the Valiant]. All the senior patricians were going there because [it was said] to be very good. When I arrived in the Mercerie near San Bartolomeo, ser Leonardo Contarini, who was coming from the barber, told me the news, and when I arrived at San Marco I heard that it was true.

And today there was an engagement party at San Lunardo for the daughter of ser Lunardo Emo and ser Justinian Contarini. And when this terrible news became known, they all were struck as if dead. The doge immediately sent word of the news and the letters to be read to the imperial, English, and Milanese ambassadors, who rejoiced and gratefully thanked the doge. At the same time, word was sent to the papal legate, and condolences to the French ambassador, informing him of all the news that had come in.

February 25, 1525 (37:650)   To be noted: all five ambassadors[122] gathered together with great jubilation and joy with a large group of their people and the exiles from Milan. They went to the Madonna di Miracoli to hear a solemn Te Deum with voices and instruments and a solemn vespers that they had arranged.

The next several pages of the diaries summarize the letters that continued to arrive with news of the French king (he was alive, but wounded and a prisoner). His admiral (Bonnivet) and several other of the French leaders had been slain or taken prisoner. But before this one day was out, Sanudo had gone on his way to the rehearsal, which was much to his liking:

February 25, 1525 (37:653)   This evening, in Ca' Dandolo, in the street of the Rasse,[123] which is the house of the Paduans, upstairs there was a *demonstration* and a rehearsal of a comedia whose autor was Tizone the Neapolitan, who is staying at Santa Marina. It was put on by the Valorosi. . . . The lord of the festa is ser Agustin Foscari. The play will be presented on Carnival Monday, February 27, along with a supper and festa. Many important senior patricians were invited. The papal legate was there in mask, as was the ambassador of

121. The manuscript has *hessendo per;* the Fulin edition has *escito per.*
122. That is, two imperial, two Milanese, and one English. See below, n. 126.
123. *Rassa* was the heavy cloth used to make gondola covers. Tassini 1970, 538.

Mantua, a cousin of the king of England who is studying in Padua,[124] and a number of mature gentlemen—though not so many—including myself, Marin Sanudo.

The comedia was most beautiful, with intermezzi of poetry and instrumental music. Everyone praised it. It ended at the seventh hour of the night, and among other things, those who performed were very well costumed in gold brocade and silk, and the stage was marvelously decorated, as was the room, and in place of decorative roses there were basins and large cups of silver, forty-two in all.

That day's entries concluded with further summaries and more letters from Bergamo, Crema, and Cremona describing the ongoing military skirmishes of the various troops involved and such matters as the lack of nails for shoeing the horses. The next day's entries began with the speeches made in the Collegio by the imperial ambassadors and the doge. When one of the former chided the Venetians for their military timidity (and perhaps their muted expressions of joy), the doge defended the Venetian position of military reserve and protested (duplicitously but, it appears, effectively) how much the city shared the victor's exultations. It was, in its own way, a stellar "theatrical" performance, and one fully praised by the doge's colleagues:

February 26, 1525 (37:656–57)   February 26, Carnival Sunday. After the Collegio had convened . . . the ambassador of Ferrara arrived full of ill humor, saying that the news that had arrived was of great importance, and he [had come] to hear something about it, and he had had no word from his lord.

Then the five ambassadors entered, namely Carazolo [Caracciolo], protonotary, and Sanzes [Sanchez], wearing a tunic of cloth of gold and a chain around his neck, who are the imperial ambassadors; Pazeo [Pace], the English ambassador; the two ambassadors of the Duke of Milan, Taberna [Taverna] and the knight Bilia [Billia],[125] full of happiness and good humor, with a huge escort of Milanese who are in this city, Genoese belonging to Adorno's faction, and Spaniards. There were about one hundred of them. After they had entered the Collegio, Sanzes said: "You are timid; in spite of this, we won." Once they had sat down, Carazolo spoke in a wise and conciliating manner, saying that he rejoiced in the victory achieved and in the capture of the Most Christian King, which will bring peace and quiet to Italy. Just as the impe-

---

124. This was Reginald Pole, actually a nephew of Henry VIII.

125. Marino Caracciolo and Alfonso Sanchez were the imperial ambassadors; Richard Pace was the English ambassador; and Francesco Taverna and Luca Billia were the Milanese ambassadors.

rial and Catholic Majesty [Charles V] was born on St. Matthew's Day, and he is twenty-four years old now,[126] and this day is much honored in Spain and his dominions, so Eternal God gave him a great victory on that day. He said that they would have so liked for the forces of this most excellent state to be united with the imperial forces. And he said other judicious things.

To these, the Serenissimo answered that as soon as he heard the news, he had sent word of it to all these ambassadors, together with whom the city rejoiced. As to our forces, there was a good reason why they had not joined their allies: since the imperial forces had moved so close to the French forces, there could easily have been some contretemps; and [if] those [imperial] forces had remained together with the Venetian forces, they could have reinforced each other in the defense of [our] conjoined territories. The other reason was for the conservation of the Venetian state, because this Signoria has only its own state, and if it had not been protected, the French might well have had some thought to attack us. But, he said, let us thank God that there was a good conclusion, which certainly will bring peace to Italy. He sent our respects to the Imperial Majesty and the most gracious king of England and the illustrious Duke of Milan. And he spoke other words that were praised by the Collegio.[127]

As proof that Venice continued to honor its alliance, the imperial and English ambassadors were granted permission to take gunpowder and pitch from the Arsenal for their victory celebrations:

As they were leaving, the ambassadors asked for some powder to set off artillery and some pitch for illumination because they wanted to hold great festivities for three evenings at the houses where they are staying, namely, the imperial ambassadors at San Severo in Ca' Zorzi, the English ambassador at San Zorzi Mazor, and the Milanese ambassadors at Santa Justina in Ca' Pasqualigo. The Collegio voted to provide them with everything they had requested from the Arsenal stores. And so this evening they celebrated with artillery, illuminations, etc.

---

126. According to Setton 1976–84, 3:229, the battle took place on Charles V's twenty-fifth birthday.

127. This masterful speech of Gritti's and its careful use of dissembling language is an example of what Felix Gilbert has called the "finesse and subtlety" of Venetian patricians, trained in the debates of the Senate. "Discussions in the Pregadi were concerned not only with broad questions about what course to take in foreign policy but also with finding the most appropriate language in the formulation of an instruction or treaty" (1977, 313).

Meanwhile, given the concern of the Venetians for their military and diplomatic situation, Carnival activities were few and subdued:

February 26, 1525 (37:660)   There has been little masking, so that it seems as if the city is mourning the capture of the Most Christian King, because in fact almost everyone laments it.

The reports continued to come in—from Bergamo, Brescia, Crema, and Cremona. There were letters from Innsbruck, Spain, Rovere di Trento, Pavia, and Buda. Sanudo records them all. At the same time, he does not fail to mention on February 27 (37:671) that the comedia at Ca' Dandolo whose rehearsal he had attended took place and that it was "bellissima," lasting until 3:00 AM, while the Senate gathered in the doge's palace to hear an eclogue "that was quite nice and humorous."

But in general the city did not rejoice. Only the imperial ambassadors and those of Milan and England made merry with feasts and music and the fireworks their Venetian hosts had made available to them:

February 27, 1525 (37:674)   After dinner on Carnival Tuesday nothing happened. There were very few maskers in the Piazza. The city is unhappy, and moreover female masking is forbidden. In the evening there was a festa, with music and fireworks, at the houses of the imperial ambassadors at San Severo and those of the Milanese and English ambassadors.

The Diaries

A thematic deconstruction of a diary such as we present in this volume can be justified, but its also distorts. For example, in order to illustrate a point the excerpts from the last three days of the theatrical and Carnival season of 1525 focus on the effects of a great military battle and on a number of theatrical performances. Yet during that same period Sanudo's diaries mention a great variety of other matters, among them a decision that the procurators of San Marco could show its treasures to a visiting delegation sent by Teodoro Trivulzi (37:648); the sale of the possessions of rebels (37:648); the prices of the Monte Nuovo and the Monte Novissimo shares (37:648); the arrival in Spain from the Indies of four caravels laden with gold and pearls and reports of others possibly carrying spices and senna (37:661); the charge of heresy levied against Martin Luther's protector, the Duke of Saxony (37:665); the need to subsidize the ship tax of Damascus, which was calamitously low (37:670); and the return of the young women's shelter of the Scuola di la Chiesia di Sant'Agnese to its own governance

(37:670–71). All of these were important enough to Sanudo to be entered into the diaries, even against the backdrop of a great battle and its effect (or lack of effect) on the Carnival activities of Venetian life.

If it was Sanudo's conviction that he must bear witness to the major events of his era—a drama in which Venice's role was central—that led him to begin this immense work, it was his eclectic curiosity and eye for detail that rendered his accounts so vivid, such as his descriptions of the arrival of the news of Agnadello at the moment when he and fellow patricians were studying the great map of Italy in the Ducal Palace; the execution of traitors in Piazza San Marco and their last words; the departure of a tearful bride from her tearful grandfather, the doge, and the rest of her natal family.

The intense activity of Venetian life, with its casts of characters, its paraphrased and quoted dialogues, its colors and costumes, kept Sanudo committed to his record for so many decades, little sustained as he was by monetary or official recognition. But he persisted, often catching, owing to his ability to recognize the essential theatricality of the moment, the significant human element, or describing, with an almost painterly skill, as if a literary Carpaccio were at work, the scenery and the costumes of some festive event.[128]

It therefore seems fitting to end this selection of his life's work with two more events from a Carnival season, two successive feste that seemed to Sanudo to epitomize the city he loved:

February 9, 1520 (28:248)   A dinner was put on this evening for the members [of the compagnia of the Ortolani] at San Polo at Ca' Capello, on the Grand Canal. It was given by ser Zuan Jacomo Bembo, who had been inducted into the compagnia of the Ortolani, and at the festa there was a kind of armed scuffle between ser Nicolò Bondimier and one of the members, ser Francesco Gritti. After dinner the members and their ladies went dancing in Campo San Polo, and the party continued until the ninth hour of the night, and until later in the house. So our city rejoices and celebrates! And Monday there will be a festa at Ca' Foscari put on by the compagnia of the Immortali, as well as a comedia. Then there will be another at Ca' Loredan, at San Marcuola, put on by the young members of the Triumphanti, with a fine comedia that will be performed in the courtyard by the members themselves. In sum, our city is triumphant. And a couple of betrothals also occurred this year. May God bless the city during this peace![129]

128. See M. Muraro 1971.
129. The manuscript has *Iddio la prosperi;* the Fulin edition has *le prosperi.*

Four days later the next festa took place, as anticipated, at Ca' Foscari. According to Sanudo, it was "the most beautiful that has been held in this city." As in many of Sanudo's descriptions of theatrical performances, the sequence of events and characters is somewhat confusing, and the probable classical allusions are opaque.[130] But the rich mixture of episodes, dancing, and fireworks convey the exuberance of a splendid Venetian festa:

February 13, 1520 (28:253–55)   Today a wonderful festa was given at Ca' Foscari at San Simion, on the Grand Canal, by the compagnia of the Immortali. . . .[131] They built a viewing stand on the quay in front of the house, partly covered and partly open, and it extended both into the house by way of the balconies and down onto a bridge laid on barges across the Grand Canal. The lord of the festivities was Francesco Sanudo, and the party was paid for by the compagnia, which is admitting three new members: first, Marquis Federigo of Mantua—they let him know they had accepted him because he wanted to join a compagnia of people his own age. The others were ser Stefano Querini and ser Ferigo di Prioli. The women were brought to the viewing stand after dinner, eighty in number and very well dressed, including some wearing dresses quartered with cloth of gold. Three bull chases were then begun on the quay. Lots of people had come to watch, and there were boats all over the place, and the Grand Canal was crowded, with people on the balconies of the houses on this and on the far side of the Grand Canal.[132] They started dancing up on the open side of the stand I mentioned, and there were even some people dancing on the barge bridge.

Then, at three hours after sunset, came the herald for the main momaria, which was organized at the church of Canaregio by Marco Tonin, the dance instructor, and cost 300 ducats. The pantomime was to come later, with a large number of torches, about forty, carried by servants and accompanied by some members of the Immortali.[133] Ser Zuane Cosaza, who belongs to the

---

130. Several of the references have to do with Troy. The story of Troy's construction, in which Apollo, Poseidon, Priam, his sister Esione, and Hercules all play a part, had special meaning for the Venetians, who claimed their descent and freedom from this ancient and famed great city and who were partial to romance poems about Troy, called "Troiani." See M. Zorzi 1996, 833–34. Sanudo's library contained one such "Troiano" among thirty-one romances he listed about 1528–29. See Harris 1993–94, I, 5, 126–27.

131. On this particular theatrical spectacle, see Mancini, Muraro, and Povoledo 1985–2002, 1:30–32, for a more elaborate interpretation of Sanudo's text. However, in several places Mancini's printed version of the text is unsupported by both the manuscript text and its printed edition. See also Tichy 1997, 94–110; and Carroll 2000b, 30–33.

132. The last clause, *poi a li balconi di le caxe, di qua et di là dil Canal Grando*, appears in the manuscript but not in the Fulin edition.

133. The manuscript has *parte l'acompagnava;* the Fulin edition has *per tre la compagnava.*

compagnia, came on horseback dressed as a military commander and made everybody make way. Then came three maskers on three hobbyhorses carried by porters; they were beautifully dressed, as used to be the custom. Among these was the herald with the letter to the lord of the festivities about when the momaria was to come. Great fireworks accompanied his ascent to the stand.

After the herald descended, people started dancing on this stand, and at the fourth hour the momaria arrived, accompanied by the torches, as I said above, and it was a beautiful sight. Beyond the stand, lit torches were continuously burning, and there were a lot of lamps around the bridge. Then came the momaria: first, on horseback, was ser Zuane, whom I mentioned; then there were two men armed for a joust on horseback, with lances in their hands to joust, but there was no time for that; then these three that had come with the herald, and another three on various animals, one on a hydra, etc. Then there was a huge giant with a snake wrapped around him like Laochonte [Laocoön], then a sow [*una troja*],[134] and last came an idol. At the end . . . there were six that were dancing and a king with his daughter in a city. There were lots of fireworks, which, when they got to the bridge and were about to climb up on it, were set off. A number of flares were thrown by some people dressed as peasants, who were also part of the momaria. As a finale they used powder to fire some mortars that were in the campo at San Symion square, a most worthy spectacle observed by a large crowd.

On the women's stand there was dancing, and there was a certain *demonstration* about the building of Troy in which a certain devil came out from under the stand with lots of fireworks, so that this momaria lasted a long time. Its route of approach [to the stand] followed the quay as far as Corpus Domini, then it doubled back to cross on the bridge I mentioned. At last, when the momaria was over, everyone went to supper, and about 350 people stayed and ate there because the house had been prepared for the presentation of another peasant comedia after supper. It was done by someone called Ruzante the Paduan, who speaks the peasant dialect extremely well.

The concluding lines of this entry may serve as a conclusion to the entire volume. Just as the diaries themselves were created to immortalize a city that Sanudo believed to be the center of all that mattered in his time, so these ephemeral revelries, put on by young men who called themselves the Immortals, celebrated a Venice that transcended the lives of those who inhabited it, lives that Sanudo

---

134. The audience would have recognized this sow as an allusion to the city of Troy, especially given the additional figure of Laocoön.

did not hesitate to criticize but whose petty failings did not mar either his heroic undertaking or diminish for him the ideal Venice he served, a Venice that was "truly excellent."

And so it was done, and with all of that the festa continued until daybreak. The members of the compagnia paid for this wonderful and generous festa; in living memory it is the most beautiful that has ever been held in this city, and let this be noted to glorify this city, which is truly excellent, although people are bad. And the name of the compagnia is the Immortali.

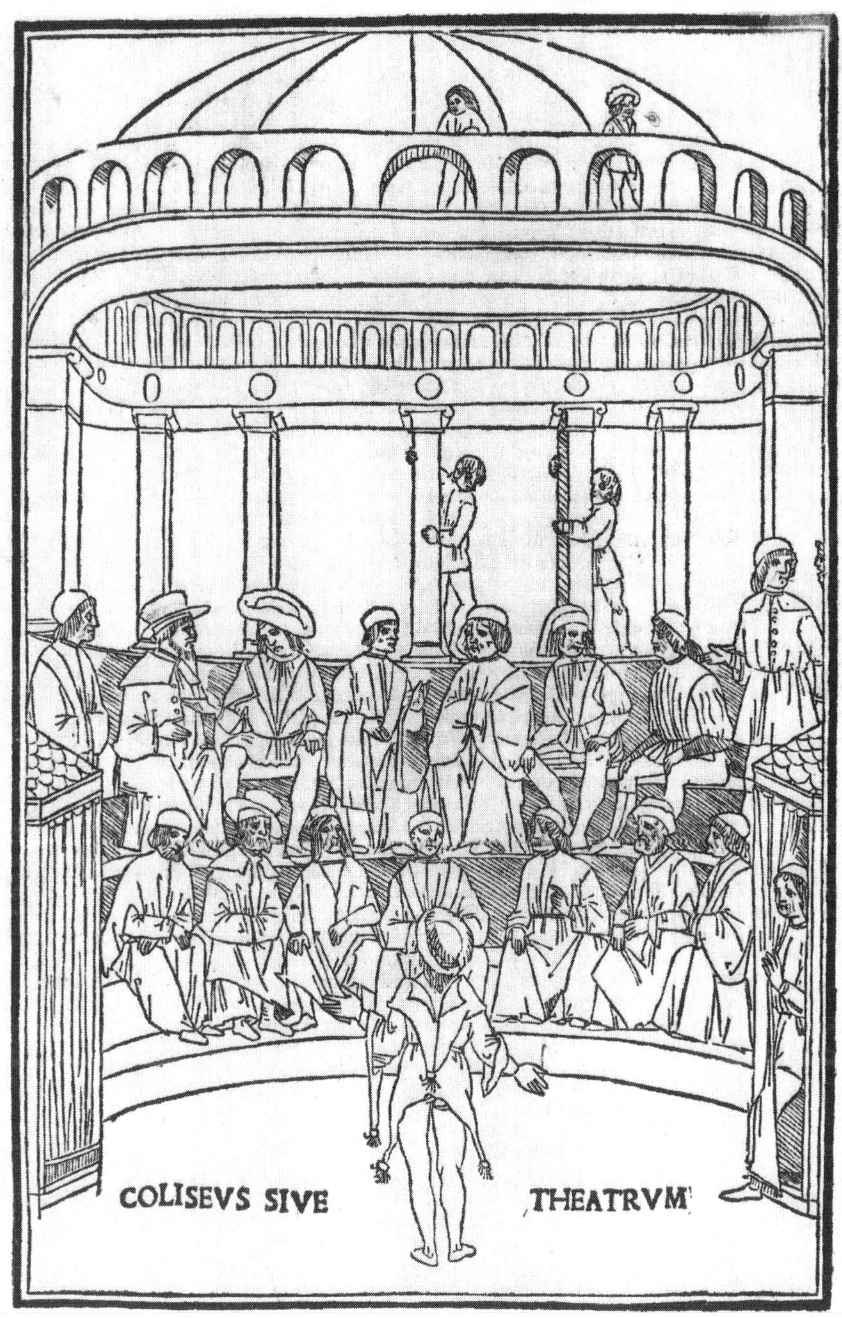

Theater of Sanudo's time, from Plautus, *Comoediae XX* (Venice: Lazarum soarsum, 1511). The British Library.

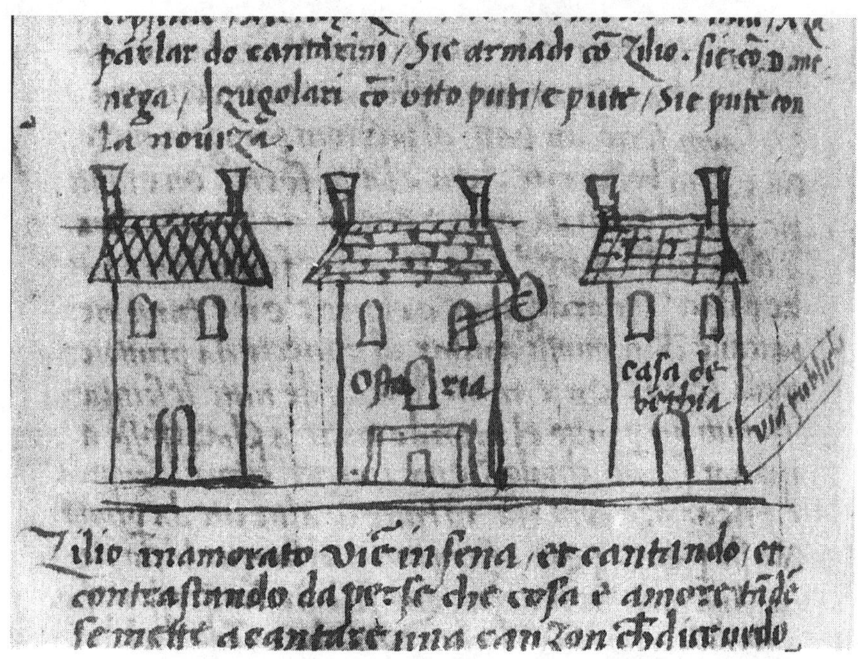

Drawing for the setting of Ruzante's *Betia,* c. 1525. Biblioteca Nazionale Marciana, Venice, Ital. Cl. XI, n. 66 (6730), fol. 173v.

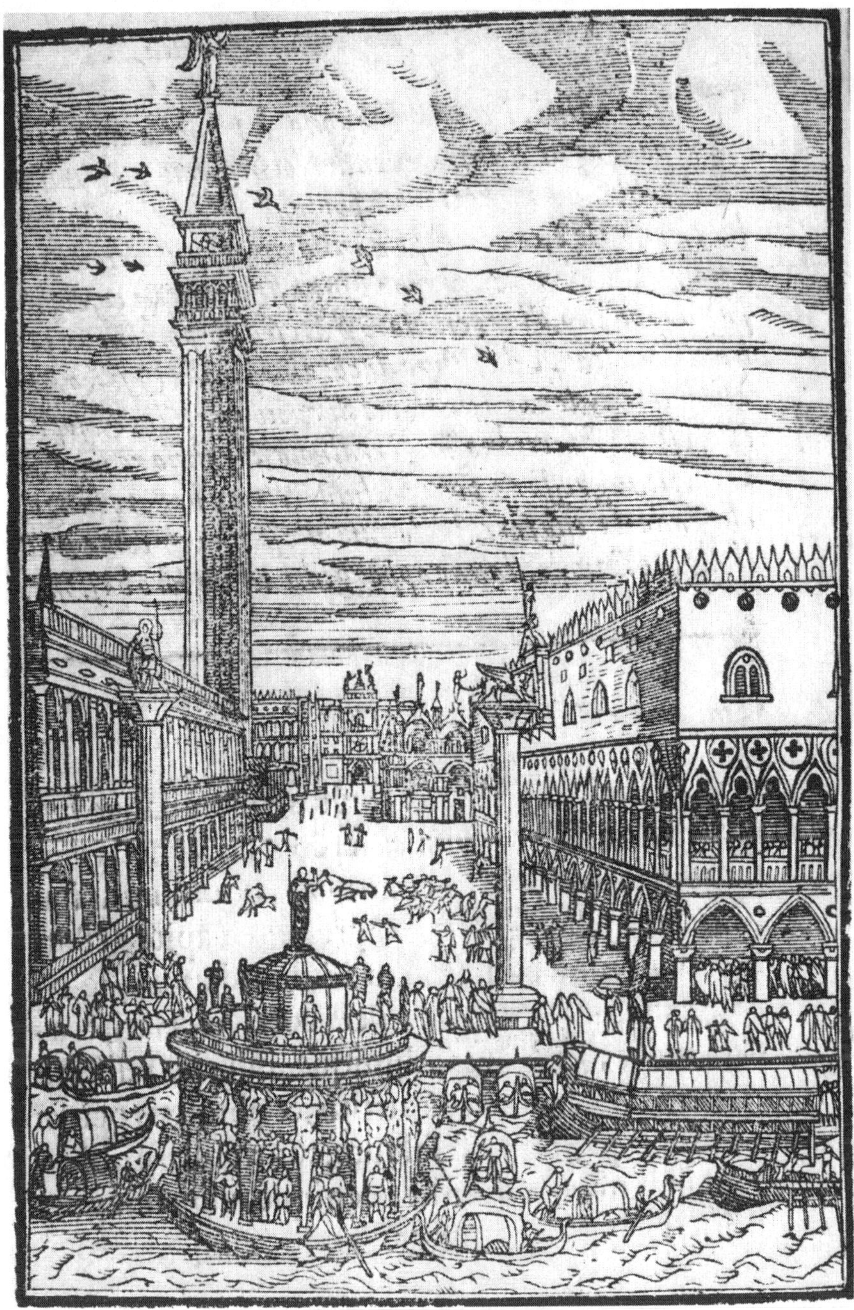

Cesare Vecellio, perspective drawing of the first Piazza San Marco, woodcut from his *Degli habiti antichi et moderni de diverse parti del mondon* (Venice, 1590). The print depicts festivities organized by the compagnia della calza in June 1564 to celebrate the visit of Francesco Maria della Rovere, Prince of Urbino. The floating "theater" is similar to such platforms described by Sanudo in the 1520s and 1530s. Museo Correr, Venice.

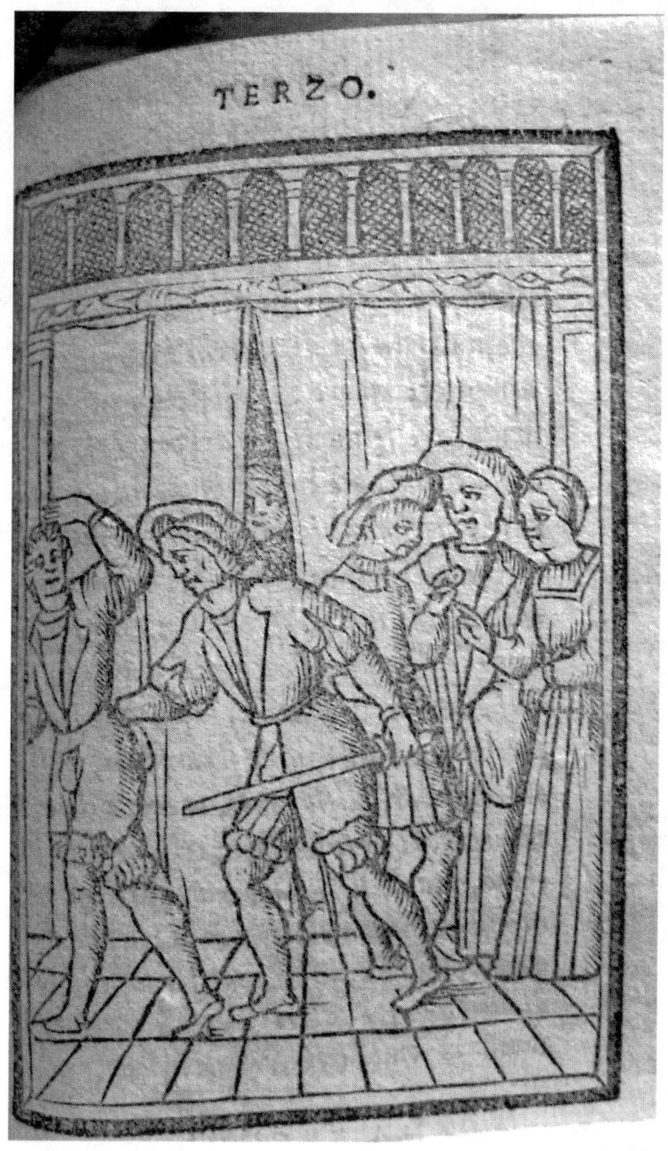

Cardinal Bernardo Dovizi da Bibbiena, *Calanddra, comedia . . . Di nuouo ricorretta e ristampata*. The British Library.

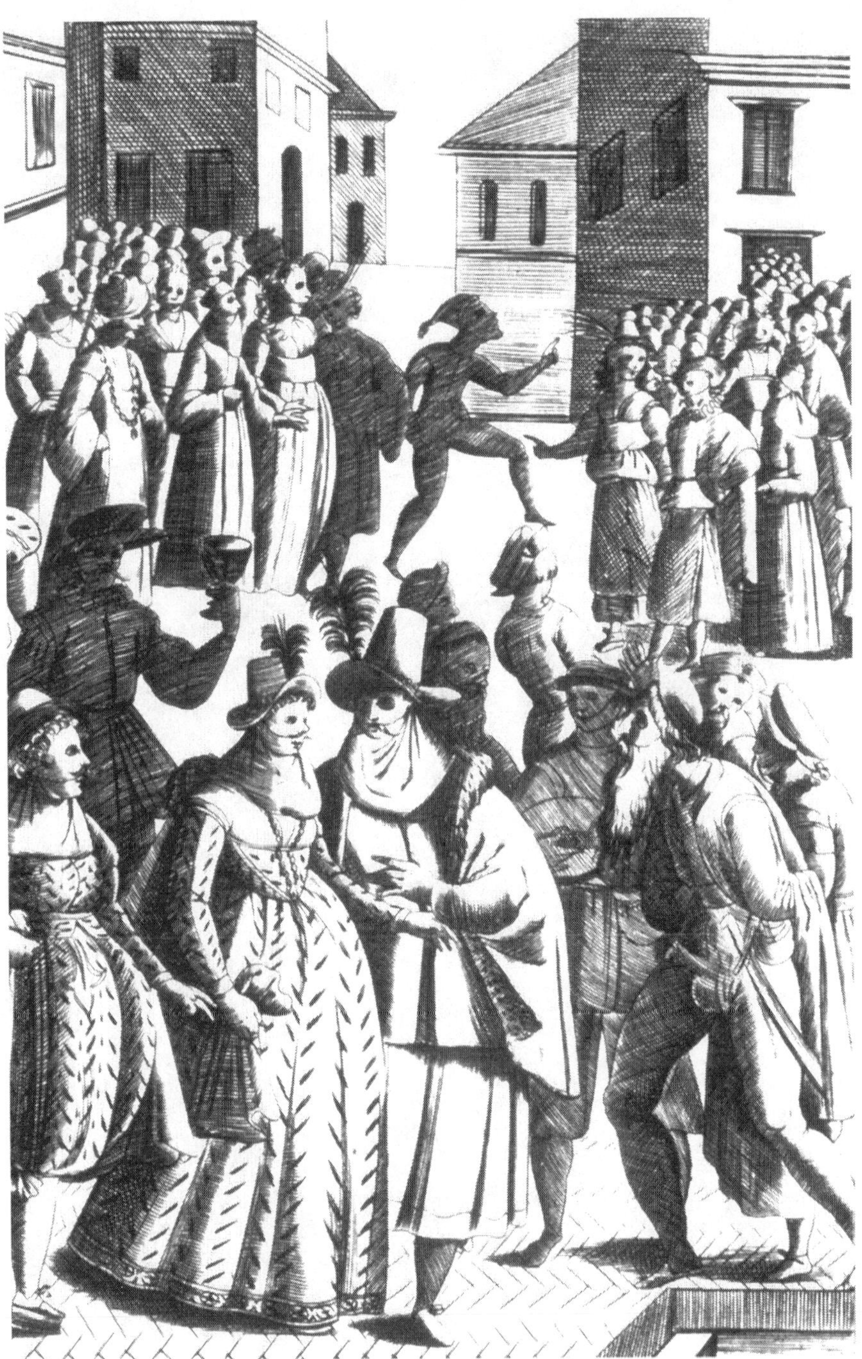

Giacomo Franco, Carnival Maskers, engraving, c. 1610. Although fashions in dress had changed by Franco's time, the print documents Carnival celebrations that would have been familiar to Sanudo.

Appendix A

Money, Wealth, and Wages

Money and Coinage

Venice had two different *lire* (pounds) in the Renaissance. The *lira di piccoli* (*pizoli* in Sanudo) was the basic money of account used in retail trade and in setting laborers' wages (Lane 1973b, 326). The *piccolo* (penny), of impure silver, was the base coin in Sanudo's period. Twelve piccoli constituted a *soldo* (shilling); twenty soldi constituted the lira di piccoli. Here, as in most texts, *lira* by itself refers to the lira di piccoli.

The *lira di grosso* was Venice's larger money of account. Like the lira di piccoli, it was divided into twenty soldi (di grosso, in this case), each of which was divided into twenty piccoli (di grosso). But the lira di grosso was worth far more than the lira di piccoli: each was valued at ten *ducats*, or sixty-two lire di piccoli.

Several silver coins were in circulation, with different weights and values. These often bore the name of the doge in whose reign they were first minted (e.g., *tron* or *marcello*).

In Sanudo's diaries, *ducat* can refer either to a money of account or to an actual coin. Either way, its value was pegged at 6 lire, 4 soldi di piccoli. After 1509 the ducat coin was kept at 3.5 grams of almost pure gold (Lane 1973b, 148).

In translating Sanudo with regard to money and wages, the guiding principle has been that of Frederic Lane: "Prices and wages have invariably been given in the text in the same moneys of account in which they were given in the sources. No attempts have been made to transform the sums into modern equivalents because there would be more delusion than meaning in such conversions. The figures are significant for comparison among themselves" (1934, 251–52).

A Comparative Scale of Annual Wages and Salaries

The following notes are offered in order to give some idea of comparative wages and salaries in Sanudo's period. In judging the relative meaning of such figures, the reader should keep in mind Gino Luzzatto's statement that "determining the purchasing power of money is, for economic historians, a little like trying to square the circle" (1954, 286).[1]

---

1. The figures in the list below have been gleaned from the diaries and from the following secondary sources: Gilbert 1976; Lane 1992, table J, s.v. "wages in the Arsenal," and 1973b, 333; Sardella 1948, 52–53; Zille 1992; G. Zorzi 1958–59.

Position	Average wage or salary (ducats)
Domestic (with board)	7 (4–10)
Agricultural laborer	13
Unskilled Arsenal laborer	16–20
Skilled Arsenal worker	20
Sailor or soldier	22
Arsenal guard	24 (2 per month)
Arsenal porter	36 (3 per month)
Chancellery notary	40 (30–50)
Government page	48 (4 per month)
Arsenal skilled craftsman	50
Supervisor of fortifications	60
Turkish-language interpreter	72
Military instructor	78 (36–120)
Production foreman, Mint	80
Arsenal foreman	82 (54–110)
Customs secretary	88
Cinque della Pace	94
Engineer	100 (80–120)
Chancellery secretary	125 (50–200)
Signore di notte	144
Podestà of a commune	190 (140–240)
Customs supervisor	200
Grand chancellor	300
Professor (renowned)	350 (100–600)
Shipmaster	720
Provincial governor	840 (280–1,400)
Consul or ambassador	1,800 (1,200–2,400)
Doge	3,000
Bishop or cardinal	10,500 (1,000–20,000)
Great merchant	11,000 (2,000–20,000)

MILITARY EXPENSES

The costs of Venice's land military forces are difficult to calculate. They varied considerably between peacetime, limited war, and the full-blown conflict of the War of the League of Cambrai; and local treasuries regularly covered military expenses, which do not show up in the Venetian record. Ester Zille (1992) estimated the peacetime pay for mercenary captains at 33,000 ducats and wartime pay (i.e., 1509–17) at 50,000 ducats, but in wartime the Republic might have several captains under contract, and it also contracted with lesser commanders.

In 1506 Bartolomeo d'Alviano was employed by Venice at 15,000 ducats per year for two years, providing cavalry as well as infantry (G. Zorzi 1958–59). In 1513, in wartime, he was given 50,000 to provide a mixed force. The military engineer Basilio dalla

Scola earned 200 ducats in 1509 (Diaries, 7:56). A Venetian proveditor general (military commissioner)—the highest military position for a Venetian patrician—received 120 ducats per month for himself and his entourage; an ordinary proveditor, who was usually a Venetian commoner, might get 120–30 ducats per year (Hale 1979, 12, 19, 21).

OTHER EXPENSES

Angela Caracciolo Aricò's edition of Sanudo's *De origine* (1980) includes the following mentions of comparable costs: Giorgio Corner bought his palazzo for 20,000 ducats, and patrician *case* on the Grand Canal could be rented for 100–120 ducats per year (21); a furnished gondola cost 20 ducats (to rent?) (22); the Fondaco dei Tedeschi was leased for 100 ducats per month. And in the diaries, Sanudo mentions that a courier was given 22 ducats to take news of the French defeat at Pavia to Rome in two days (February 25, 1525; 37:6490).

Appendix B

Glossary and Terms

Vocabulary Used in the Original

autor. Organizer and/or sponsor of an event, who might also contribute his artistic talent to its creation.

campanile. A bell tower attached to a church or convent, usually that of the Basilica of San Marco.

campo. Open space in the city of Venice. Equivalent to *piazza* in the rest of Italy, or *square,* though in Venice most were irregular.

comedia. A comedic theatrical performance.

Compagnia della calza. A ceremonial society composed mostly of young patricians, identified by their colorful stockings, present at private and diplomatic and ceremonial occasions, often sponsors of theatrical events and banquets. Their primary purpose was to entertain their members; their official purpose was the festa.

domino. Title of respect used for certain laity or ecclesiastics.

festa. Holiday; festivity.

fondaco. Warehouse, usually the Fondaco dei Tedeschi, which served as both a warehouse and living quarters for German merchants.

fontego. See **fondaco.**

intermezzo. Short entertainment between main theatrical presentations or acts of a play.

marcello. A silver coin worth ten soldi.

mocenigo. A type of silver coin weighing six grams, worth twenty soldi.

momaria. A performance, often accompanying a banquet, wedding feast, state reception, or other festa, involving music, dance, mime, and frequently acrobatics.

muneghino. A patrician man accused of illicit relations with a cloistered nun.

Piazza. The great open space in front of the Basilica of San Marco, bounded by government office buildings. It was the site of important processions and performances.

primicerio. The chief priest of the Basilica of San Marco, appointed by the doge.

staio. Dry measure equivalent to eighty-three dry liters or two to three imperial bushels.

stradioto. A light cavalryman armed with lance, scimitar, and shield. Stradioti were recruited by Venice from the Greek coasts and islands, the Dalmatian coast, and Albania.

tron. A silver coin weighing 6.6 grams.

Governmental Terms[1]

auditori nuovi. Supervisory magistrates who traveled throughout the Venetian dominion, receiving appeals and judging the sentences of Venetian governors.

auditori vecchi. Intermediaries between courts of first instance in Venice and its lagoon, on the one hand, and appellate tribunals, on the other.

avocato di presonieri. Attorney for the accused before the Quarantia Criminal.

avocati pizoli. Young patricians attached to and allowed to plead before the major tribunals.

avogadori di comun. The three state attorneys, who participated in meetings of every important magistracy, having the power to suspend deliberations if legality was in question; maintained registers of nobility and citizenship; and assigned legal cases to one of the judicial magistracies.

bailo. The permanent representative of the Venetian Republic to the sultan in Constantinople.

ballotini. Ballot-box clerks, who circulated through the Great Council with the ballot boxes into which each attending patrician placed his vote.

Camera degli Imprestidi. Office of Loans.

camerlengo. Treasurer accompanying a Venetian governor in subject lands, charged with collecting taxes and disbursing monies from the fisc.

capi. Heads of magistracies, most often referring to the Council of Ten or the Quarantia.

capitanio. Military governor of a subject city.

Cattavere. Magistracy of three officials responsible for watching over state property. They also had jurisdiction over Jews.

Cinque Savi alla Mercanzia. A body established in 1506 to remedy the decline of commerce as a result of the great geographical discoveries.

Cinque Savi alla Pace. Magistracy of five officials responsible for coordinating public safety officials.

Collegio. A committee, in Sanudo usually referring to the Pien Collegio, comprising the Signoria—the doge, the ducal councillors, and the heads of the Quarantia—plus the savi (five savi ai ordeni, five savi di Terraferma, and six savi di Consiglio). The major executive council, with consultative, deliberative, and judicial functions, it prepared business for and introduced legislation into the Senate.

Collegio alle Biave. Appellate court. Its original function was to supervise the public grain supply.

---

1. Based on Finlay 1980b; Caracciolo Arico 1980; Queller 1986; Chambers and Pullan 1992; Grendler 1990; Archivio di Stato di Venezia 1994. Other earlier sources include Contarini 1599; Giannotti 1540; Rezasco 1881; H. F. Brown 1973; Maranini 1931; da Mosto 1937-40, 1977; J. C. Davis 1962; Lane 1973b; Cozzi 1973.

consoli dei mercanti. Magistrates having administrative and judicial competence in commercial disputes, including maritime matters, insolvency, exchange rates, private banks, insurance contracts, brokerage fees, and the production of woolen goods, silk, and soap.

councillors. The six ducal councillors, forming part of the Signoria. Each one represented a different *sestiere,* or sixth, of the city.

Council of Ten. The highest government agency, made up of ten patricians plus the doge and his six councillors, so that in fact it numbered seventeen. This group met by itself *(semplice)* or with its zonta, an additional fifteen members.

decima. A direct tax inaugurated in Venice in 1463.

doge. The titular and ceremonial head of the Venetian government, also called "Serenissimo" (Most Serene) or "Principe" (Prince) in the diaries. The use of the "Serenissmo Principe" set the doge above other dukes, such as those of Milan or Ferrara.

executori. Special commissioners originally (1537) charged with the extirpation of blasphemy, later given jurisdiction over printing and non-Christians.

giudici del piovego. Judges with jurisdiction over those who usurped public streets or waterways and converted other common properties to private uses. They imposed conditions for house construction, supervised the dredging of canals, and investigated suspicious cases and usurious contracts. Their purview included changes in buildings, repair of streets, maintenance of canals, encroachment onto public lands and waters, usury.

Giudici del Proprio. One of the oldest courts in Venice, with jurisdiction over dowry restitution, intestate succession, divisions between brothers, and some property disputes.

Giudici di Petizion. Court where lawsuits concerning fifty ducats or less were judged.

governadori dell'intrade. Officials who oversaw the collection of taxes on goods, as well as the sale of assets of rebels against or debtors to the state.

Monte. One of the three funded debts of the Venetian state—Monte Vecchio, Monte Nuovo, Monte Nuovissimo—incurred through the imposition of forced loans. These loans were interest-bearing; title to them could be bought, sold, bequeathed, or otherwise transferred.

patroni. Shipmasters, usually merchants who leased galleys at public auction.

patroni al Arsenal. Lords of the Arsenal.

podestà. Civil governor.

Procuratie. The buildings surrounding Piazza San Marco where the procurators had their offices and official residences.

procurators of San Marco. Officials appointed for life who administered trusts in the several sections of the city and supervised the financial affairs of the church of San Marco, its upkeep, and its chaplains. They also administered wills and served as guardians of minors and persons of unsound mind. Normally, there were nine: three *de citra,* who administered trusts on the near side of the Grand Canal; three *de ultra,* who administered trusts on the far side of the Grand Canal; and three *de* *sopra,* in charge of the Basilica of San Marco and its treasures. Doges were nearly always chosen from the ranks of the procurators. There were as many as twenty-two procurators in 1525 (see Diaries, 37:471). The office had been made available for loans to the government during the War of the League of Cambrai.

promissione ducale. Rules regulating the authority of the ducal office, which every doge on election had to swear to respect.

proveditor. Commissioner; a patrician appointed to serve as an official in charge or superintendent for military, civil, or commercial activities.

proveditori di Sal. Officials in charge of the Salt Office, overseeing both the production and sale of salt. Their treasury was a crucial source of liquidity for the state.

proveditor sora i danari. Controller of finances.

Quarantia Civile Nuovo. Supreme appeals court for civil cases originating outside the city of Venice. After eight months on this court, its judges went on to serve on the Quarantia Civile Vecchia.

Quarantia Civile Vecchia. Supreme appeals court for civil cases originating within the city of Venice. After eight months on this court, its judges went on to serve on the Quarantia Criminal and to sit as voting members of the Senate.

Quarantia Criminal. Supreme appeals court for criminal cases that could also initiate legislation. Its judges were salaried and had previously served on the Quarantia Civile Nuova and then the Quarantia Civile Vecchia. They were included as voting members of the Senate, where they formed a block, often representing the less wealthy and important member of the patriciate. Their three heads *(capi)* formed part of the Signoria along with the doge and his six councillors.

Raxon Nuove. An office established in 1396 to take on some of the duties of the Raxon Vecchie. It supervised ambassadorial finances and the accounts of the captain general and other military and naval officials.

Raxon Vecchie. An office that supervised income from the government offices of the Terraferma, the Dogado, the *stato da Mar.* It was also in charge of expenses *pro honorandis principibus* for public feasts and ceremonies.

relazione. A long report on a Venetian envoy's embassy that included, as prescribed, his assessment of the political and economic strength of the country visited and the character of its ruler.

rito. Secret and swift judicial procedures of the Council of Ten.

Savi ai ordeni. The most junior branch in the Collegio, this body of five patricians dealt with matters pertaining to any part of the dominion that had to be reached by water; it was also in charge of naval supplies and overseas trade.

Savi da Mar. See **Savi ai ordeni.**

Savi di Consiglio. This body of six patricians was the most prestigious and powerful branch of the Collegio. It could propose virtually any type of legislation.

Savi di Terraferma. This body of five patricians dealt with affairs concerning the landed dominion.

Savi Grandi. See **Savi di Consiglio.**

scrutinio. A vote in the Senate whereby a candidate was nominated from the floor to be voted on alongside those nominated in the Great Council by a group of committees—usually four—chosen by lot. The Senate candidate had the advantage of a block of votes and support of distinguished patricians.

Serenissimo. See **doge.**

Signoria. A body made up of the doge, the six ducal councillors, and the three heads of the Quarantia Criminal. It was the supreme executive magistracy of the Venetian Republic, especially in matters of diplomacy and war. It heard, as well, extraordinary appeals and petitions.

signori di notte. Lords of the Night Watch.

sopracomito. Commander of a galley.

sopragastaldi. Officials in charge of execution of civil sentences of all Venetian magistracies. They were also in charge of overseeing the conservation of all the writings of the Chancellery.

Ufficio al Sal. Office established in 1428 to regulate the provisioning of salt.

zonta. additional body added to particular councils (e.g., the Senate and the Council of Ten).

Weight and Nomenclature for Candles

Wax candles, used in many ceremonies, were a precious commodity, and their size and weight were indications of both the wealth of those sponsoring the event and the importance of the occasion. Sanudo often gives the weight of candles in *libre*, referring to *libre sottili*. One libra sottile was equal in weight to 301.23 grams (or .66 English pounds). The editors thank Reinhold Mueller for this information.

The various types of illumination referred to by Sanudo include single candles *(candele)*; double candles *(doppiere)*, such as those visible in Gentile Bellini's *Procession;* long, fat candles *(cieri)*; short, thick candles *(candeloti)*; candles for chandeliers *(candelieri)*; and wax torches *(torzi)*.

Ceremonial Containers

The following terms appear frequently in descriptions of banquets and ceremonial processions, in which the wealth of an individual or a scuola was demonstrated through its show of precious or rare tableware or ritual objects.

bazile. Basin.

bocale. Wine jug.

confetiera. Pastry tray or candy dish.

copa. Goblet.

poto. Goblet.

ramino. Copper-plated vessel or pot.

tazone. Large cup.

vaso. Tray or vessel.

Fabrics and Garments

alto basso cremesin. Crimson two-pile velvet fabric.

becheto. Rolled hood with a liripipe.

becho. Stole.

berettino. Grey green or grey brown.

braccio. A unit of measure equivalent to 63 centimeters for silk and 68.3 centimeters for wool.

cremesino. Crimson cloth of a higher quality than scarlatto.

dossi. Squirrel backs.

listato et inquartado. Trimmed and quartered.

manege a comedo. Full sleeves, closed at wrist.

manege a comeo. See **manege a comedo.**

manege dogali. Ducal sleeves, long and open at the wrist.

raso. Satin.

raso cremizin. Crimson satin.

restagno d'oro. Patterned brocade woven entirely with a gold weft; cloth of gold; cloths of gold and silver.

riccio. See **riso.**

riso. Curl, loop. Threads, especially gold or gilded threads, were sometimes looped to catch the light.

rizo. See **riso.**

roboni. Elegant mid-calf garments.

rosa secha. Old-rose color.

saioni. See **roboni.**

scarlato. See **scarlatto.**

scarlatto. Crimson silk; woolen cloth dyed scarlet.

sendal. Light silk.

seta. A plain heavy black silk with a poplin weave.

soprarizo. Looped brocade.

tabi. Heavy silk.

vair. Squirrel fur.

Boats, Ships, and Nautical Terms[2]

barza. A round ship with a capacity of 2,000 to 2,500 botte.

barzoto. Round ship with a capacity of 800 to 1,200 botte.

botta. Butt, a measure of a ship's loading capacity; approximately .7 cubic feet of a freight ton, or about 29 English cubic feet.

brigantini. Brigantine, a simplified light galley rowed by one or two men per bench.

Bucintoro. The great state galley in which the doge rode forth on Ascension Day to bless and wed the sea. Also used by the doge to greet high-ranking dignitaries and for other ceremonies.

burchiele. Small, flat-bottomed boats.

burchio. Barge.

fusta. A long-oared ship slimmer than the normal galley, with 18-20 rowers on each side.

---

2. From Lane 1992, 53n57. Lane cites Giovanni Casoni, "Forze Militari," in Venice (Comune), Consiglio comunale 1847, 1:189–209. See also Molmenti 1973; Bertoni 1937; Manfroni 1897, 182–83; and Manfroni 1898, fasc. 12, p. 479.

galia bastarda. A galley smaller than a great merchant galley and larger than a *galia sotile.*

galia sotile. Small light galley.

ganzara. Large barge.

gripo. Small lateen-rigged ship with a single mast, rowed or sailed.

maran. Mercantile ship, smaller than the large round ships, originally used to bring firewood and building stone from Istria to Venice and then adapted for more extended voyages.

paraschelma. Large sailboat for transporting goods and people; heavy fishing boat.

paraschermo. See **paraschelma.**

peota. A mid-sized boat rowed by several oarsmen; often highly decorated for ceremonial occasions.

piato. Flatboat.

schierazo. A small Turkish loading ship with square sails.

Musical Instruments[3]

pifari. Shawms, an early double-reed, straight-bodied woodwind instruments.

trombe e pifari. Trumpets and wind band or wind ensemble (when qualified by reference to the doge); otherwise simply a wind band, possibly consisting of trombones or trumpets and shawms. When the term is qualified as *dil doxe* or *del Serenissimo,* the word *trombe* very likely referred to the six long trumpets of the doge, while the *pifari* comprised an ensemble of two trombones and three cornettos when performing indoors and two trombones and three shawms when performing outdoors in processions and other contexts. When Sanudo speaks of ensembles as *trombe e pifari* without ducal reference, he probably means a wind band of almost any size and combination of instruments, including even one or more strings, but consisting principally of trombones (the *trombe*) and shawms and/or cornettos (the *pifari*). The ambiguity arises from the application in contemporary Italian and Venetian sources of the term *trombe* to any instrument of the trumpet family, including the bass instrument, and the use of *pifari* to mean either treble wind instruments, such as shawms and cornettos, or the combination of such treble instruments with trombones. *Pifari* even extended to cover any ensemble made up mainly of winds but including a variety of other instruments as well.

trombe squarzade. A straight natural trumpet about four feet long used as both a military signaling instrument and for playing fanfares in processions and celebrations.

violeta. A stringed instrument of the viol family.

viol grande da archeto. Large viol played with a bow.

---

3. Dr. Jeffrey Kurtzman kindly provided explanations of the following terms.

Abulafia, David, ed. 1995. *The French descent into Renaissance Italy, 1494–95: antecedents and effects*. Aldershot, Hamps: Variorum.

Agostini, Giovanni degli. 1752–54. *Notizie istorico-critiche intorno: la vita, e la opera degli scrittori veniziani*. 2 vols. Venice: Simone Occhi.

Aikema, Bernard, and Culcia Meijers, eds. 1989. *Nel regno dei poveri: arte e storia dei grandi ospedali veneziani in età moderna, 1474–1797*. Venice: Arsenale.

Ambrosini, Frederica. 1996. Cerimonie, feste, lusso. In *Storia di Venezia: dalle origini alla caduta della Serenissima*, vol. 5, *Il rinascimento: società ed economia*, ed. Albert Tenenti and Ugo Tucci, 441–520. Rome: Istituto della enciclopedia italiana.

Anon. 1963. Bagarotti, Bertuccio. In *Dizionario biografico degli italiani*, 5:169–70. Rome: Istituto della enciclopedia italiana.

Appuhn, Karl. 2000. Inventing nature: forests, forestry, and state power in Renaissance Venice. *Journal of Modern History* 72:861–89.

Archivio di Stato di Venezia. 1994. L'Archivio di Stato di Venezia. In *Guida generale degli archivi di Stato italiani*, 4:857–1148. Rome: Ministero per i beni culturali e ambientali, Ufficio centrale per i beni archivistici.

Aretino, Pietro. 1960. *Lettere: il primo e secondo libro*. Ed. Francesco Flora. Milan: Mondadori.

Arnaldi, Girolamo, and Manlio Pastore Stocchi, eds. 1981. *Storia della cultura veneta*. Vol. 3, *Dal primo quattrocento al Concilio di Trento*. Vicenza: Neri Pozza.

Arrizabalaga, Jon, John Henderson, and Roger French, eds. 1977. *The great pox: The French disease in Renaissance Europe*. New Haven, CT: Yale University Press.

Ashtor, Eliahu. 1975–76. Ebrei cittadini di Venezia? *Studi Veneziani* 17–18:145–56.

Balduino, Armando, ed. 1983. *Miscellanea di studi in onore di Vittore Branca*. Biblioteca Dell' "Archivum Romanicum": Serie I, Storia, Letteratura, Paleografia, 178–82. Florence: Olschki.

Ball, James George. 1982. Poverty, charity and the Greek community. *Studi Veneziani*, n.s., 6:129–46.

———. 1985. "The Greek community in Venice, 1470–1620." PhD thesis, University of London, Warburg Institute.

Baratto, Mario. 1968. *Tre studi sul teatro*. Vicenza: Neri Pozza.

Barbarigo, Niccolò. 1792. *Andreae Gritti principis venetiarum vita*. Ed. Jacopo Morelli. Venice: Caroli Palesii.

Bibliography

Barbaro, Ermolao. 1969. *De coelibatu, De officio legati*. Ed. Vittore Branca. Nuova Collezione di Testi Umanistici Inediti o Rari, 14. Florence: Olschki.

Barblan, Guglielmo. 1979. Aspetti e figure del cinquecento musicale veneziano. In *Storia della civiltà veneziana*, ed. Vittore Branca, vol. 2, *Autunno del medioevo e rinascimento*, 247–57. Florence: Sansoni.

Battaglia, Salvatore. 1961–2000. *Grande dizionario della lingua italiana*. 21 vols. Turin: UTET.

Beloch, Julius. 1902. La populazione di Venezia nei secoli XVI e XVII. *Nuovo Archivio Veneto*, n.s., 3, no. 1:5–49.

———. 1961. *Bevölkerungsgeschichte Italiens*. Vol. 3, *Die Bevölkerung der republic Venedig, des Herzogtums Mailand, Piemonts, Genuas, Corsicas und Sardiniens. Die gesamtbevölkerung Italiens*. Berlin: Walter de Gruyter.

Beltrami, Daniele. 1954. *Storia della popolazione di Venezia dalla fine del secolo XVI alla caduta della repubblica*. Collana Ca' Foscari, Istituto Di Storia Economica, 1. Padua: CEDAM.

Bembo, Pietro. 1551. *Petri Bembi Cardinalis Historiae Venetae libri XII*. Venice: Apud Aldi Filios.

Benzoni, Gino, ed. 1992. *Studi veneti offerti a Gaetano Cozzi*. Venice: Cardo.

———. 1996. Scritti storico-politici. In *Storia di Venezia: dalle origini alla caduta della serenissima*, vol. 4, *Il rinascimento: politica e cultura*, ed. Albert Tenenti and Ugo Tucci, 757–88. Rome: Istituto della enciclopedia italiana.

Berchet, Guglielmo. 1903. Preface to *I diarii di Marino Sanuto*, ed. Rinaldo Fulin, Federico Stefani, Nicolò Barozzi, Guglielmo Berchet, and Marco Allegri, 1:7–136. Venice: Fratelli Visentini.

Berénger, Adolfo di. 1863. *Saggio storico della legislazione veneta forestale dal secolo VII al XIX*. Venice: Libreria alla Fenice, G. Ebhardt.

Bertelli, Sergio. 1968. Introduction to *Opera di Niccolò Machiavelli*, ed. Bertelli, vol. 1. Milan: Salerno.

Bertelli, Sergio, Nicolai Rubinstein, and Craig Hugh Smyth, eds. 1979–80. *Florence and Venice: comparisons and relations*. 2 vols. Florence: La Nuova Italia.

Bertoni, Giulio, ed. 1937. *Dizionario di marina, medievale e moderno*. Dizionari Di Arti e Mestieri, 1. Rome: Reale accademia d'Italia.

Besta, Enrico. 1899. *Il senato veneziano (origine, costituzione, attribuzione e riti)*. Deputazione di Storia Patria, Miscellanea di Storia Veneta, ser. 2, vol. 5. Venice: A spese della società.

Bettio, Pietro. 1828. *Intorno ai Diarii veneti scritti da Marino Sanuto il giovine in volumi LVIII: Documenti per la prima volta pubblicati*. Venice: Martinengo-Malipiero.

Betto, Bianca. 1984. *Le nove congregazioni del clero di Venezia (sec. XI–XV): ricerche storiche, matricole e documenti vari*. Miscellanea Erudita, 41. Padua: Antenore.

Biblioteca nazionale marciana. 1868–73. *Bibliotheca manuscripta ad S. Marci venetiarum digessit et commentarium addidit Joseph Valentinelli*. Venice: Ex typographica commercii.

Billanovich, Myriam. 1979. Michele Ferrarini, Aldo Manuzio, Marin Sanudo. *Italia Medioevale e Umanistica* 22:525–29.

Bisà, Marco, and Romigio Masobello. 1991. *Il ponte di Rialto: un restauro a Venezia.* Ateneo Veneto, 5. Vicenza: Neri Pozza.

Bistort, Giulio. 1916. *La repubblica di Venezia: dalle trasmigrazioni nelle lagune fino alla caduta di Costantinopoli (1453): riassunto storico.* Venice: Ateneo Veneto.

———. 1969. *Il magistrato alle pompe nella repubblica di Venezia: studio storico.* Storia Patria, Miscellanea di Storia Veneta, ser. 3, vol. 5. Bologna: Forni. (Orig. pub. 1912.)

Blackburn, Bonnie J. 1992. Music and festivities at the court of Leo X: a Venetian view. *Early Music History* 11:1–37.

Boerio, Giuseppe. 1856. *Dizionario del dialetto veneziano.* Venice: G. Cecchini. Repr., Turin: Bottega D'Erasmo, 1967.

Bohde, Daniela. 2001. Titian's three-altar project in the Venetian church of San Salvador: strategies of self-representation by members of the Scuola Grande di San Rocco. *Renaissance Studies* 15:450–72.

Bonardi, Antonio. 1902. *I padovani ribelli alla repubblica di venezia (a. 1509–1530): studio storico con appendice di documenti inediti.* Deputazione di Storia Patria, Miscellanea di Storia Veneta, ser. 2, vol. 8. Venice: A spese della società.

Bouwsma, William James. 1968. *Venice and the defense of Republican liberty: Renaissance values in the age of the Counter-Reformation.* Berkeley and Los Angeles: University of California Press.

———. 1973. Venice and the political education of Europe. In *Renaissance Venice,* ed. John Rigby Hale, 45–66. London: Faber & Faber.

Bowd, Stephen D. 1999. Pietro Bembo and the "monster" of Bologna (1514). *Renaissance Studies* 13:40–54.

Branca, Vittore. 1973. Ermolao Barbaro and late quattrocento Venetian humanism. In *Renaissance Venice,* ed. John Rigby Hale, 218–43. London: Faber & Faber.

———, ed. 1979. *Storia della civiltà veneziana.* 3 vols. Florence: Sansoni.

———. 1981. L'Umanismo veneziano alla fine del quattrocento: Ermolao Barbaro e il suo circolo. In *Storia della cultura veneta,* vol. 3, *Dal primo quattrocento al Concilio di Trento,* ed. Girolamo Arnaldi and Manlio Pastore Stocchi, 123–75. Vicenza: Neri Pozza.

———. 1996. L'Umanesimo. In *Storia di Venezia: dalle origini alla caduta della serenissima,* vol. 4, *Il rinascimento: politica e cultura,* ed. Albert Tenenti and Ugo Tucci, 723–55. Rome: Istituto della enciclopedia italiana.

———. 1998. *La sapienza civile: studi sull'umanesimo a Venezia.* Florence: Olschki.

Bregoli-Russo, Mauda. 1995. Un comico dell'arte italiana: il Cherea. In *Miscellanea di italianistica: in memoria di Mario Santoro,* ed. Michele Cataudella, 41–49. Naples: Edizioni scientifiche Italiane.

Bridgeman, Jane. 2000. "Pagar le pompe": why quattrocento sumptuary laws did not work. In *Women in Italian Renaissance culture and society,* ed. Letizia Panizza, 209–26. Oxford: Legenda, European Humanities Research Centre, University of Oxford.

Brown, Horatio Forbes. 1887. *Venetian studies.* London: Kegan Paul, Trench.

———. 1891. *The Venetian printing press: an historical study based on documents for the most part hitherto unpublished.* London: Nimmo.

———. 1973. *Studies in the history of Venice.* 2 vols. New York: Franklin. (Orig. pub. 1907.)

Brown, Patricia Fortini. 1987. Honor and necessity: the dynamics of patronage in the confraternities of Renaissance Venice. *Studi Veneziani,* n.s., 14:197–212.

———. 1988. *Venetian narrative painting in the age of Carpaccio.* New Haven, CT: Yale University Press.

———. 1990. Measured friendship, calculated pomp: the ceremonial welcomes of the Venetian republic. In *"All the world's a stage . . .": art and pageantry in the Renaissance and Baroque,* ed. Barbara Wollesen-Wisch and Susan Scott Munshower, 136–86. University Park, PA: Art Department, Penn State University.

———. 1991. Self-definition of the Venetian Republic. In *City-states in classical antiquity and medieval Italy: Athens and Rome, Florence and Venice,* ed. Anthony Molho, Kurt Rafflaub, and Julia Emlen, 511–48. Stuttgart: Franz Steiner; Ann Arbor: University of Michigan Press.

———. 1996. *Venice and antiquity: the Venetian sense of the past.* New Haven, CT: Yale University Press.

Brown, Rawdon Lubbock, ed. 1837–38. *Ragguagli sulla vita e sulle opera di Marin Sanuto detto il Juniore: veneto patrizio e cronista pregevolissimo de secoli XV, XVI: intitolati dall'amicizia di uno straniero al nobile Jacopo Vincenzo Foscarini: opera divisa in tre parti. . . .* 3 vols. Venice: Alvisopoli.

———. 1871. *Calendar of state papers and manuscripts, relating to English affairs existing in the archives and collections of Venice, and in other libraries of northern Italy.* Vol. 4. London: Longman.

Brunetti, Mario. 1923. Marin Sanudo (profilo storico). *Ateneo Veneto* 46:51–67.

———. 1950. Banche e banchieri veneziani nei "Diarii" di Marin Sanudo. In *Studi in onore di Gino Luzzatto,* 2:26–47. Milan: A. Guiffrè.

Cairns, Christopher S. 1976. *Domenico Bollani, Bishop of Brescia: devotion to church and state in the republic of Venice in the sixteenth century.* Bibliotheca Humanistica et Reformatorica, 15. Nieuwkoop, Netherlands: De Graaf.

Calabi, Donatella. 1984. Rialto, 1514–1538: gli anni della ricostruzioni. In *"Renovatio urbis": Venezia nell'etá di Andrea Gritti, 1523–1538,* ed. Manfredo Tafuri, 291–334. Rome: Officina Edizioni.

———. 1990. Venice, the ghetto and the city, 1534–1797. In *Het getto van venitië: Ponentini, Levantini and Tedeschi, 1516–1797,* ed. Julie-Marthe Cohen, 46–66. The Hague: SDU-Uitgeverij.

———. 1991. Magazzini, fondaci, dogane. In *Storia di Venezia: il mare,* ed. Albert Tenenti and Ugo Tucci, 789–817. Rome: Istituto della enciclopedia italiana.

Calabi, Donatella, and Paolo Morachiello. 1987. *Rialto: le fabbriche e il ponte, 1514–1591.* Saggi, 704. Turin: Einaudi.

Campolieti, Giuseppe. 1987. *Caterina Cornaro.* Storia e Storie. Milan: Camunia.

Camporesi, Piero. 1998. *Il pane selvaggio.* 2nd ed. Bologna: Il Mulino.

Cantù, Cesare. 1888. Diari di Marin Sanudo. *Archivio Storico Lombardo* 15:49–68.

Cappelletti, Giuseppe. 1992. *Relazione storica delle magistrature venete: opera originali del prete veneziano.* Venice: Filippi.

Caracciolo Aricò, Angela. 1979. Marin Sanudo il giovane, precursore di Francesco Sansovino. *Lettere Italiane* 31:419–37.

——. 1980. Introduction to Marin Sanudo, *De origine, situ et magistratibus urbis venetae, ovvero, la città di venetia (1493–1530)*, ed. Caracciolo Aricò, ix–xxix. Collana di Testi Inediti e Rari, 1. Milan: Cisalpino-La Goliardica.

——. 1983. "Les vite dei Dogi" di Marin Sanudo il giovane. In *Umanesimo e rinascimento a Firenze e Venezia*, ed. Vittore Branca, 567–92. Florence: Olschki.

——, ed. 1990a. *L'Impatto della scoperta dell'america nella cultura veneziana*. Rome: Bulzoni Editore.

——. 1990b. Una testimonianza di Marin Sanudo umanista: l'inedito *De antiquitatibus et epitaphis. Rivista di Archeologia*. Suppl. no. 7:32–34.

——. 1996. Il nuovo mondo nei diarii di Marin Sanudo il giovane e nelle lettere di Angelo Trevisan. In *Antonio Pigafetta e la letteratura di viaggio nel cinquecento*, ed. Adriana Chemello, 47–67. Verona: Cierre.

Carroll, Linda L. 1985. Carnival rites as vehicles of protest in Renaissance Venice. *Sixteenth Century Journal* 16:487–502.

——. 1989. Who's on top? Gender as societal power configuration in Italian Renaissance painting and drama. *Sixteenth Century Journal* 20:531–58.

——. 1990. *Angelo Beolco (Il Ruzante)*. Boston: Twayne.

——. 1992. Giorgione's Tempest: astrology is in the eyes of the beholder. In *Reconsidering the Renaissance: papers from the twenty-first annual conference*, ed. Mario Di Cesare, 125–40. Binghamton, NY: Medieval and Renaissance Texts and Studies.

——. 2000a. Dating *The Woman from Ancona*: Venice and Ruzante's theater after Cambrai. *Sixteenth Century Journal* 31:963–85.

——. 2000b. Venetian attitudes toward the young Charles: carnival, commerce, and Compagnie della Calza. In *The young Charles, 1500–1519*, ed. Alain Saint-Säens, 13–52. New Orleans, LA: University Press of the South.

Casini, Matteo. 1991. Realtà e simboli del cancellier grande veneziano in età moderna (sec. XVI–XVII). *Studi Veneziani*, n.s., 22:195–251.

——. 1992. La cittadinanza originaria a venezia tra i secoli XV e XVI: una linea interpretativa. In *Studi veneti offerti a Gaetano Cozzi*, ed. Gino Benzoni, 133–48. Venice: Cardo.

——. 1996. *I gesti del principe: la festa politica a Firenze e Venezia in età rinascimentale*. Presente Storico: Saggi Marsilio, 2. Venice: Marsilio.

Casola, Pietro. 1907. *Canon Pietro Casola's pilgrimage to Jerusalem in the year 1494*. Ed. Mary Margaret Newett. University of Manchester Publications No. 26. Historical Studies, 5. Manchester: Manchester University Press.

Castellani, Carlo. 1896. Pietro Bembo bibliotecario della libreria di S. Marco in Venezia (1530–1543). *Atti dell'Istituto Veneto di Scienze, Lettere ed Arti*, 7th ser., no. 7:862–98.

Cataudella, Michele, ed. 1995. *Miscellanea di italianistica: in memoria di Mario Santoro*. Naples: Edizione scientifiche italiane.

Cecchetti, Bartolommeo. 1886. Nomi antichi delle compane della torre di San Marco. *Archivio Veneto* 32:378–80.

Cermenati, Mario. 1912. Un diplomatico naturalista del rinascimento: Andrea Navagero. *Nuovo Archivio Veneto* 24:164–205.

Chambers, David Sanderson. 1971. *The imperial age of Venice, 1380–1580*. New York: Harcourt Brace.

———. 1977. Marin Sanudo, Camerlengo of Verona (1501–1502). *Archivio Veneto*, 5th ser., no. 109:37–66.

———. 1997. Merit and money: the procurators of St. Mark and their *commissioni*, 1443–1605. *Journal of the Warburg and Courtauld Institutes* 60:23–88.

———. 1998a. The diaries of Marin Sanudo: personal and public crises IX. In *Individuals and institutions in Renaissance Italy*, 1–33. Variorum Collected Studies Series. Aldershot, Hamps: Ashgate.

———. 1998b. *Individuals and institutions in Renaissance Italy*. Variorum Collected Studies Series. Brookfield, VT; Aldershot, Hamps: Ashgate.

Chambers, David Sanderson, Cecil H. Clough, and Michael E. Mallett, eds. 1993. *War, culture and society in Renaissance Venice: essays in honour of John Hale*. London: Hambledon.

Chambers, David Sanderson, and Brian Pullan, eds. 1992. *Venice: a documentary history, 1450–1630*. Oxford: Blackwell.

Chavasse, Ruth. 1986. The first known author's copyright, September 1486, in the context of a humanist career. *Bulletin of the John C. Rylands University Library of Manchester* 69:11–37.

Chojnacki, Stanley. 1974. Patrician women in early Renaissance Venice. *Studies in the Renaissance* 21:176–203.

———. 1980. La posizione della donna a Venezia nel cinquecento. In *Tiziano e Venezia: convegno internazionale di studi, Venezia, 1976*, 65–70. Vicenza: Neri Pozza.

———. 1990. Marriage legislation and patrician society in fifteenth-century Venice. In *Law, custom, and the social fabric in medieval Europe: essays in honor of Bryce Lyon*, ed. Bernard S. Bachrach and David Nicholas, 163–84. Kalamazoo, MI: Medieval Institute Publications.

———. 1992. Measuring adulthood: adolescence and gender in Renaissance Venice. *Journal of Family History* 17, no. 4:371–95.

———. 1994. Subaltern patriarchs: patrician bachelors in Renaissance Venice. In *Medieval masculinities: regarding men in the Middle Ages*, ed. Clare A. Lees, 73–90. Minneapolis: University of Minnesota Press.

———. 1996. Social identity in Renaissance Venice: the second *Serrata. Renaissance Studies* 8:341–58.

———. 1998a. Daughters and oligarchs: gender and the early Renaissance state. In *Gender and society in Renaissance Italy*, ed. Judith C. Brown and Robert C. Davis, 63–86. London: Longman.

———. 1998b. Nobility, women and the state: marriage regulation in Venice, 1420–1535. In *Marriage in Italy, 1300–1650*, ed. Trevor Dean and K. J. P. Lowe, 128–51. Cambridge: Cambridge University Press.

———. 2000. *Women and men in Renaissance Venice: twelve essays on patrician society*. Baltimore: Johns Hopkins University Press.

Cicogna, Emmanuele Antonio. 1824–53. *Delle inscrizioni veneziane raccolte ed illvstrate da*

Emmanvele Antonio Cicogna. 6 vols. in 7. Collana di Bibliografia e Storia Veneziana, 3. Venice: Givseppe Orlandelli.

Clough, Cecil H. 1965. Becichemo, Marino. In *Dizionario biografico degli italiani,* 7:511–15. Rome: Istituto della enciclopedia italiana.

Coffin, David Robbins. 2001. The gardens of Venice. *Source: Notes in the History of Art* 21, no. 1:4–9.

Cohen, Julie-Marthe, ed. 1990. *Het getto van venetië: Ponentini, Levantini and Tedeschi, 1516–1797.* The Hague: SDU-Uitgeverij.

Coltro, Dino. 1980. *Sapienza del tempo contadino: lunario veneto.* Quaderni di Materiali Veneti, 15. Venice: Arsenale.

Commynes, Philippe de. 1970. *Mémoires.* Ed. Joel Blanchard. 2 vols. Geneva: Droz.

Concina, Ennio. 1983. *La macchina territoriale: le progettazione della difesa nel cinquecento veneto.* Biblioteca di Cultura Moderna, 877. Rome: Laterza.

——. 1984. *L'Arsenale della repubblica di Venezia.* Milan: Electa.

——. 1988. Una fabbrica in mezzo della città: la chiesa e il convento di San Salvador. In *"Progetto S. Salvador": un restauro per l'innovazione a venezia,* ed. Caputo Fulvio, 72–153. Venice: Albrizzi.

——. 1990. The origins of the Venetian ghetto: the houses, the people, the laws, 1390–1540. In *Het getto van venitië: Ponentini, Levantini and Tedeschi, 1516–1797,* ed. Julie-Marthe Cohen, 28–45. The Hague: SDU-Uitgeverij.

——. 1991. Parva Jerusalem. In *La città degli ebrei: il ghetto di Venezia, architettura e urbanistica,* by Ennio Concina, Ugo Camerino, and Donatella Calabi, 9–155. Venice: Albrizzi.

——. 1994. *Dell'arabico: a Venezia tra rinascimento e oriente.* Polis. Saggi Marsilio. Venice: Marsilio.

Concina, Ennio, Ugo Camerino, and Donatella Calabi. 1991. *La città degli ebrei: il ghetto di Venezia, architettura e urbanistica.* Venice: Albrizzi.

Connell, Susan Mary. 1972. Books and their owners in Venice. *Journal of the Warburg and Courtauld Institutes* 3:163–86.

Contarini, Gasparo. 1543. *De magistratibus et republic venetorum, libri quinque.* Paris: Ex officina Michaelis Vascosani.

——. 1599. *The commonwealth and gouernment of Venice.* London: Iohn Windet.

——. 1630. *Della republica et magistrati di Venetia libri cinque.* Venice: Giorgio Valentino.

Conto, Agostino. 1994. Ancora sui libri di Marin Sanudo. *La Bibliofilia: Rivista di Storia del Libro e di Bibliografia* 96:195–99.

Cornaro, Flaminio. 1749a. *Ecclesiae venetae antiquis monumentis nunc etiam primum editis illustratae ac in decades distributae.* Venice: Jo: Baptistae Pasquali.

——. 1749b. *Supplementa ad ecclesias venetas et torcellanas antiquis documentis: nunc etiam primum editis illustratas.* Venice: Jo: Baptistae Pasquali.

——. 1990. *Notizie storiche delle chiese e monasteri di Venezia e di Torcello.* Intro. Ugo Stefanutti. Collana di Bibliografie e Storia Veneziana, 18. Bologna: Forni.

Coronelli, Vincenzo. 1970. *Ships and other sort of craft used by the various nations of the world—Venice 1690.* Trans. Mario M. Witt. London: Francis Edwards.

Cortelazzo, Manlio. 1970. *L'Influsso linguistico greco a Venezia*. Linguistica, 2. Bologna: Pàtron.

———. 1989. *Venezia, il Levante e il mare*. Pisa: Pacini.

Cowan, Alexander Francis. 1982. Rich and poor among the patriciate in early modern Venice. *Studi Veneziani*, n.s., 6:147–60.

Cozzi, Gaetano. 1963–64. Cultura, politica, e religione nella "pubblica storiografia" veneziana del "500." *Bollettino dell'Istituto di Storia della Società e dello Stato Veneziano* 5–6:215–94.

———. 1970a. Domenico Morosin e "il bene instituta re publica." *Studi Veneziani* 12:405–58.

———. 1970b. Marino Sanudo il giovane: dalla cronaca alla storia. In *La storiografia veneziana fino al secolo XVI: aspetti e problemi*, ed Agostino Pertusi, 333–58. Civiltà Veneziana. Saggi, 18. Florence: Olschki.

———. 1973. Authority and the law in Renaissance Venice. In *Renaissance Venice*, ed. John Rigby Hale, 293–345. London: Faber & Faber.

———. 1980. La politica del diritto nella repubblica di Venezia. In *Stato, società e giustizia nella repubblica veneta (sec. XV–XVIII)*, ed. Gaetano Cozzi, 1:15–142. Rome: Jouvence.

———, ed. 1980–85. *Stato, società e giustizia nella repubblica veneta (sec. XV–XVIII)*. 2 vols. Storia, 6, 17. Rome: Jouvence.

———. 1982. *Repubblica di Venezia e stati italiani: politica e giustizia dal secolo XVI al secolo XVIII*. Biblioteca di Cultura Storica, 146. Turin: Einaudi.

———, ed. 1987. *Gli ebrei e venezia: secoli XIV–XVIII; atti del convegno internazionale organizzato dall'Istituto di storia della società dello Stato veneziano della Fondazione Giorgio Cini*. Milan: Edizioni Comunità.

———. 1988. "Ordo est ordinem non servare": considerazioni sulla procedura penale di un detenuto dal Consiglio dei X. *Studi Storici* 29:309–20.

———. 1993. Giuspatronato del doge e prerogative del primicerio sulla cappella ducale di San Marco (sec. XVI-XVII). In *Atti: classe di scienze morali, lettere ed arti, 151, 1–69*. Venice: L'Istituto veneto di scienze morali, lettere ed arti.

———. 1997. *Ambiente veneziano, ambiente veneto: saggi su politica, società, cultura nella Repubblica di Venezia in età moderna*. Presente Storico, 5. Venice: Marsilio.

Cozzi, Gaetano, and Michael Knapton. 1986–92. *La repubblica di Venezia nell'età moderna*. Vol. 1, *Dalla guerra di Chioggia al 1517*. Vol. 2, *Dal 1517 alla fine della repubblica*. Storia D'Italia, 12. Turin: UTET.

Cross, Frank Leslie, and Elizabeth A. Livingstone, eds. 1997. *The Oxford dictionary of the Christian Church*. 3rd ed. Oxford: Oxford University Press.

Crouzet-Pavan, Elisabeth. 1981. Recherches sur la nuit vénitienne à la fin du Moyen Âge. *Journal of Medieval History* 7:339–56.

———. 1992. *"Sopra la acque salse": espaces, pouvoir et société à Venise a la fin du Moyen Âge*. 2 vols. Rome: École française de Rome.

Dahood, Roger, ed. 1998. *The future of the Middle Ages and the Renaissance*. Turnhout, Belgium: Brepols.

Da Mosto, Andrea, ed. 1937–40. *L'Archivio di stato di venezia: indice generale, storico, de-*

scrittivo ed analitico. Bibliothèque des "Annales Institutorum," 5. Rome: Biblioteca d'arte.

———. 1977. *I dogi di Venezia nella vita pubblica e privata.* Milan: A. Martello-Giunti.

Daston, Lorraine J., and Katharine Park. 1997. *Wonders and the order of nature, 1150–1750.* New York: Zone Books.

Davanzo Poli, Doretta. 1999. *Arts & crafts in Venice.* Cologne: Könemann.

Davidson, Nicholas S. 1984. The clergy of Venice in the sixteenth century. *Bulletin of the Society for Renaissance Studies* 2, no. 2:19–31.

Davis, James Cushman. 1962. *The decline of the Venetian nobility as a ruling class.* Baltimore: Johns Hopkins University Press.

———. 1974. Shipping and spying in the career of a Venetian Doge, 1496–1502. *Studi Veneziani* 16:97–108.

———. 1975. *A Venetian family and its fortune, 1500–1900.* Philadelphia: American Philosophical Society.

Davis, Robert Charles. 1991. *Shipbuilders of the Venetian arsenal: workers and workplace in the preindustrial city.* Baltimore: Johns Hopkins University Press.

———. 1994. *The war of the fists: popular culture and public violence in late Renaissance Venice.* New York: Oxford University Press.

Davis, Robert Charles, and Benjamin Ravid, eds. 2001. *The Jews of early modern Venice.* Baltimore: Johns Hopkins University Press.

Delphinus, Petrus. 1943. *Petri Delphini Annalium ventorum pars quarta. A cura di Roberto Cessi e Paolo Sambin.* Istituto Veneto di Scienze, Lettere ed Arti. Diarii Veneziani del Secolo Decimosesto, 1. Venice: C. Ferrari.

Del Torre, Guiseppe. 1986. *Venezia e la terraferma dopo la guerra di Cambrai: fiscalità e amministrazione (1515–1530).* Milan: Angeli.

Demus, Otto. 1984. *The mosaics of San Marco in Venice.* 2 vols. in 4. Chicago: University of Chicago Press.

Desimoni, Cornelio. 1893. Una carta della Terra Santa del secolo XIV nell'archivio di stato in Florence: Marino Sanuto e Pietro Visconti. *Archivio Storico Italiano,* 5th ser., 11:241–58.

Dionisotti-Casalone, Carlo. 1966. Bembo, Pietro. In *Dizionario biografico degli italiani,* 8:133–51. Rome: Istituto della enciclopedia italiana.

Dotson, John E., ed. and trans.. 1994. *Merchant culture in fourteenth century Venice: the Zibaldone da Canal.* Medieval and Renaissance Text and Studies, 98. Binghamton, NY: Medieval and Renaissance Texts and Studies.

Dupuigrenet Desroussilles, François. 1981. L'Universita di Padova dal 1405 al Concilio di Trento. In *Storia della cultura veneta,* vol. 3, *Dal primo quattrocento al Concilio di Trento,* ed. Girolamo Arnaldi and Manlio Pastore Stocchi, 607–47. Vicenza: Neri Pozza.

Dupuy, R. Ernest, and N. Trevor Dupuy, eds. 1993. *The Harper encyclopedia of military history: from 3500 BC to the present.* 4th ed. New York: HarperCollins.

Durante, Dino, and G. F. Turato, eds. 1975. *Dizionario etimologico veneto-italiano.* Padua: Erredici.

Eamon, William. 1999. Plagues, healers, and patients in early modern Europe. *Renaissance Quarterly* 52:474–86.

Erasmus, Desiderius. 1963. *Opus Epistolarum Erasmi.* Ed. P. S. Allen. 11 vols. Oxford: Clarendon. (Orig. pub. 1941.)

Erdmann, Kurt. 1966. Venezia e il tappeto orientale. In *Venezia e l'Oriente fra tardo medioevo e rinascimento [testi delle lezioni],* ed. Agostino Pertusi, 529–45. Civiltà Europea e Civiltà Veneziana, 4. Florence: Sansoni.

Este, Ercole d'. 1791–98. Sanuto (Marino juniore). *Nuovo dizionario istorico,* ed. L. M. Chaudon et al., 23:360. 28 vols. Naples: M. Morelli.

Fabris, Antonio. 1988. Esperienza di vita comunitaria: i cononici regolari. In *La chiesa di Venezia nei secoli XI–XIII,* ed. Franco Tonon, 73–108. Venice: Edizioni studium cattolico veneziano.

Faccioli, Emilio, ed. 1966. *Arte della cucina: libri di ricette, testi sopra lo scallo, il trinciante e i vini dal XIV al XIX secolo.* Milan: Il Profilo, 1966.

———. 1984. Al servizio del Sultano: Venezia, i Turchi e il mondo cruistiano. In *"Renovatio urbis": Venezia nell'età di Andrea Gritti (1523–38),* ed. Manfredo Tafuri, 78–118. Rome: Officina Edizioni.

———, ed. 1987. *Arte della cucina in Italia: libri di ricette e trattati sulla civiltà della tavola dal XIV al XIX secolo.* Turin: UTET.

Favaretto, Irene. 1990. *Arte antica e cultura antiquaria nelle collezioni venete al tempo della Serenissima.* Studia Archaeologica, 55. Rome: "L'Erma" di Bretschneider.

Favaro, Antonio. 1918. Lo studio di Padova nei Diarii di Marino Sanuto. *Nuovo Archivio Veneto,* 3rd ser., 36:65–128.

Fedi, Andrea. *I Diarii di Marin Sanudo: strategia del racconto e "scienza" della storia.* Ravenna: Longo.

Ferguson, George Wells. 1961. *Signs & symbols in Christian art.* London: Oxford University Press.

Ferraro, Joanne M. 1993. *Family and public life in Brescia, 1580–1650: the foundations of power in the Venetian state.* Cambridge: Cambridge University Press.

Ferro, Marco. 1845–47. *Dizionario del diritto comune e Veneto.* 2nd ed. 2 vols. Venice: Santini.

Finlay, Robert. 1976. Venice, the Po expedition and the end of the League of Cambrai. *Studies in Modern European History and Culture* 2:37–52.

———. 1978a. Politics and family in Renaissance Venice: the election of Doge Andrea Gritti. *Studi Veneziani,* n.s., 2:97–117.

———. 1978b. The Venetian republic as a gerontocracy: age and politics in the Renaissance. *Journal of Medieval and Renaissance Studies* 8:157–78.

———. 1980a. Politics and history in the diary of Marin Sanuto. *Renaissance Quarterly* 33:565–98.

———. 1980b. *Politics in Renaissance Venice.* New Brunswick, NJ: Rutgers University Press.

———. 1982. The foundation of the ghetto: Venice, the Jews, and the War of the League of Cambrai. *Proceedings of the American Philosophical Society* 126:140–54.

———. 1984. Al servizio del sultan: Venezia, i Turchi e il mondo cristiano, 1523–38. In

"Renovatio urbis" Venezia nell'età di Andrea Gritti, 1523–1538, ed. Manfredo Tafuri, 78-118. Rome: Officina Edizioni.

——. 1994. Crisis and crusade in the Mediterranean: Venice, Portugal, and the Cape Route to India (1498-1509). *Studi Veneziani,* n.s., 28:45-90.

——. 1999. The immortal republic: the myth of Venice during the Italian wars (1494-1530). *Sixteenth Century Journal* 30:931-44.

——. 2000. Fabius Maximus in Venice: Doge Andrea Gritti, the War of Cambrai, and the rise of Habsburg hegemony, 1509-1530. *Renaissance Quarterly* 53:988-1031.

Fletcher, Jennifer. 1981. Marcantonio Michiel: his friends and collection. *Burlington Magazine* 123: 453-67, 602-8.

Foffano, Francesco. 1892. Marco Musuro, professore di greco a Padova ed a Venezia. *Nuovo Archivio Veneto* 3:453-73.

Fois, Mario. 1989. I religiosi: decadenza e fermenti innovatori. In *La chiesa di Venezia tra medioevo et età moderna,* ed. Bianca Betto and Giovanni Vian, 147-82. Venice: Edizioni studium cattolico veneziano.

Franco, Giacomo. 1610. *Habiti d'huomeni et donne venetiane: con la processione della Serenissima; signoria et altri particolar cioè trionfi feste et cerimonie publiche della nobilissima città di Venetia.* Venice.

Franzoi, Umberto. 1966. *Le prigioni della repubblica di Venezia.* Venice: Stamperia di Venezia.

Frassón, Paolo. 1980. Tra volgare e latino: aspetti della ricerca di una propria identità da porte di magistrature e cancelleria a Venezia (secc. XV-XVI). In *Stato, società e giustizia nella repubblica veneta (sec. XV–XVIII),* ed. Gaetano Cozzi, 577-615. Rome: Jouvence.

Frati, Carlo. 1904. Un codice autografo di Bernardo Bembo. In *Raccolta di studi critici dedicata ad Alessandro d'Ancona,* 193-208. Florence: G. Barbera.

Fulin, Rinaldo. 1871. Gl'inquisitori dei dieci. *Archivio Veneto* 1:1-64, 298-310; 2:357-91.

——. 1881. *Diarii e diaristi veneziani: studii del prof. Rinaldo Fulin.* Venice: M. Visentini.

Gaeta, Franco. 1959. Averoldi, Altobello. In *Dizionario biografico degli italiani,* 13:399-400. Rome: Istututo della enciclopedia italiana.

——. 1964. Barozzi, Pietro (1441-1507). In *Dizionario biografico degli italiani,* 6:510-12. Rome: Istituto della enciclopedia italiana.

Gallo, Rodolfo. 1943. Le mappe geografiche del Palazzo Ducale di Venezia. *Archivio Veneto,* 5th ser., nos. 32-33:47-113.

——, ed. 1954. *Carte geografiche cinquecentesche a stampa della Biblioteca Marciana e della Biblioteca del Museo Correr di Venezia.* Venice: La Sede dell'Istituto Veneto.

——. 1967. *Il tesoro di S. Marco e la sua storia.* Civiltà Veneziana. Saggi, 16. Venice: Istituto per la collaborazione culturale.

Geanakoplos, Deno J. 1962. *Greek scholars in Venice: studies in the dissemination of Greek learning from Byzantium to Western Europe.* Cambridge, MA: Harvard University Press.

Gerulaitis, Leonardus Vytautas. 1976. *Printing and publishing in fifteenth-century Venice.* Chicago: American Library Association.

Giannetto, Nella. 1985. *Bernardo Bembo, umanista e politico veneziano*. Civiltà Veneziana. Saggi, 34. Florence: Olschki.

Giannotti, Donato. 1540. *Libro de la republica de Vinitiani*. Rome: Antonio Blado.

———. 1974. *Opere politiche*. Ed. Furio Diaz. 2 vols. Milan: Marzorati.

Gilbert, Felix. 1965. *Machiavelli and Guicciardini: politics and history in sixteenth-century Florence*. Princeton, NJ: Princeton University Press.

———. 1968. The Venetian constitution in Florentine political thought. In *Florentine studies: politics and society in Renaissance Florence*. ed. Nicolai Rubinstein, 463–500. London: Faber & Faber.

———. 1969. Religion and politics in the thought of Gasparo Contarini. In *Action and conviction in early modern Europe: essays in memory of E. H. Harbison*, ed. Theodore K. Rabb and Jerrold E. Siegel, 90–116. Princeton, NJ: Princeton University Press.

———. 1970. Venetian diplomacy before Pavia: from reality to myth. In *The diversity of history: essays in honour of Sir Herbert Butterfield*, ed. John Huxtable Elliott and H. G. Koenigsberger, 79–116. London: Routledge & Kegan Paul.

———. 1971. Biondo, Sabellico and the beginnings of Venetian official historiography. In *Florilegium historiale: essays presented to Wallace Ferguson*, ed. John Gordon Rowe and W. H. Stockdale, 276–93. Toronto, ON: University of Toronto Press.

———. 1973. Venice in the crisis of the League of Cambrai. In *Renaissance Venice*, ed. John Rigby Hale, 274–92. London: Faber & Faber.

———. 1976. The last will of a Venetian grand chancellor. In *Philosophy and humanism: Renaissance essays in honor of Paul Oskar Kristeller*, ed. Edward P. Mahoney, 502–17. New York: Columbia University Press.

———. 1977. *History: choice and commitment*. Cambridge, MA: Harvard University Press.

———. 1979. Humanism in Venice. In *Florence and Venice: comparisons and relations*, ed. Sergio Bertelli, Nicolai Rubinstein, and Craig Hugh Smyth, 1:13–26. Florence: La Nuova Italia.

———. 1980. *The pope, his banker, and Venice*. Cambridge, MA: Harvard University Press.

———. 1983. Venetian war finances during the war of the League of Cambrai. Paper delivered to the Davis Center Seminar at Princeton University on March 25.

———. 1990. *History: politics or culture? Reflections on Ranke and Burckhardt*. Princeton, NJ: Princeton University Press.

Gilmore, Myron Piper. 1973. Myth and reality in Venetian political theory. In *Renaissance Venice*, ed. John Rigby Hale, 431–44. London: Faber & Faber.

Ginzburg, Carlo. 1983. *The night battles: witchcraft and agrarian cults in the sixteenth and seventeenth centuries*. Baltimore: Johns Hopkins University Press.

Giudici, Enzo. 1980. Bilancio di una annosa questione: Maurice Scève e la "scoperta" della "tomba di Laura." *Quaderni di Filologia e lingue romanze* (Università di Macerata) 2:7–70.

Giuliani, Innocenzo. 1961. Genesi e primo secolo di vita del magistrato sopra monasteri (1519–1620). *Le Venezie Francescane* 28:42–68, 106–69.

Giustiniani, Bernardo. 1722. *Bernardi Justiniani De origine urbis venetiarum rebusque gestis venetis libri quindecim*. In *Thesavrvs antiqvitatvm et historiarvm Italiae*, ed. Joannes Georgius Graevius, 5, pt. 1. Leiden: Petrus vander Aa.

Giustiniani, Pietro. 1964. *Venetiarum historia vulgo Petro Iustiniano Iustiniani filio adiudicata*. Ed. Roberto Cessi and Fanny Bennato. Deputazione di Storia Patria, Monumenti Storici, n.s., 18. Venice: A spese della deputazione.

Gleason, Elisabeth G. 1993. *Gasparo Contarini: Venice, Rome, and reform*. Berkeley and Los Angeles: University of California Press.

———. 2000. Confronting new realities: Venice and the Peace of Bologna. In *Venice reconsidered: the history and civilization of an Italian city, 1297–1797*, ed. John Martin and Dennis Romano, 168-84. Baltimore: Johns Hopkins University Press.

Goffen, Rona. 1986. *Piety and patronage in Renaissance Venice: Bellini, Titian, and the Franciscans*. New Haven, CT: Yale University Press.

———. 1997. *Titian's women*. New Haven, CT: Yale University Press.

Goy, Richard John. 1989. *Venetian vernacular architecture: traditional housing in the Venetian lagoon*. Cambridge: Cambridge University Press.

Grandi, Casimira. 1997. L'Assistenza all'infanzia abbandonata a Venezia: i fantolini della pietade (1346-1548). In *Ospedali e città: Italia del centro-nord, XIII–XVI secolo*, ed. Allen J. Grieco and Lucia Sandri, 67-106. Florence: Le Lettere.

Grendler, Paul F. 1977. *The Roman inquisition and the Venetian press*. Princeton, NJ: Princeton University Press.

———. 1981a. The concept of humanist in cinquecento Italy. In *Culture and censorship in late Renaissance Italy and France*, essay 6. Collected Studies Series. London: Variorum Reprints.

———. 1981b. *Culture and censorship in late Renaissance Italy and France*. Collected Studies Series. London: Variorum Reprints.

———. 1981c. Five Italian occurrences of "Umanista," 1540-1574. In *Culture and censorship in late Renaissance Italy and France*, essay 5. Collected Studies Series. London: Variorum Reprints.

———. 1989. *Schooling in Renaissance Italy: literacy and learning, 1300–1600*. Baltimore: Johns Hopkins University Press.

———. 1990. The leaders of the Venetian state, 1540-1609: a prosopographical analysis. *Studi Veneziani*, n.s., 19:35-85.

———, ed. 1999. *Encyclopedia of the Renaissance*. New York: Scribner's.

———. 2002. *The universities of the Italian Renaissance*. Baltimore: Johns Hopkins University Press.

Grieco, Allen J., and Lucia Sandri, eds. 1997. *Ospedali e città: Italia del centro-nord, XIII–XVI secolo*. Medicina e Storia. Florence: Le Lettere.

Griffo, Giuliana Chesne Dauphinè. 1988. Cronache di moda illustri: Marin Sanudo e le vesti veneziane tra quattro e cinquecento. In *Il costume dell'età del rinascimento*, ed. Dora Liscia Bemporad, 259-72. Florence: EDIFIR.

Grubb, James S. 1983. "Venetian dominion in Vicenza, 1404-1509." PhD diss., University of Chicago.

———. 1985. A major new fondo of Veneto and Venetian documents. *Studi Veneziani*, n.s., 10:173-81.

———. 1986. When myths lose power: four decades of Venetian historiography. *Journal of Modern History* 58:43-94.

———. 1988. *Firstborn of Venice: Vicenza in the early Renaissance state.* Baltimore: Johns Hopkins University Press.

———. 1991. Diplomacy and the Italian city state. In *City-states in classical antiquity and medieval Italy: Athens and Rome, Florence and Venice,* ed. Anthony Molho, Kurt Raflaub, and Julia Emlen, 603-17. Stuttgart: Franz Steiner; Ann Arbor: University of Michigan Press.

———. 1995. Memory and identity: why Venetians didn't keep *ricordanze. Renaissance Studies* 8:375-87.

———. 1996. *Provincial families of the Renaissance: private and public life in the Veneto.* Baltimore: Johns Hopkins University Press.

Guarino, Raimondo. 1995. *Teatro e mutamenti: rinascimento e spettacolo a Venezia.* Quaderni di "Teatro e Storia." Bologna: Società editrice Il mulino.

Guazzo, Marco. 1546. *Historie di M. Marco Gvazzo di tvtti i fatti degni di memorial nel mondo svccessi dell'anno M.D. XXIIII.* Venice: Gabriel Giolito de Ferrari.

Guicciardini, Francesca. 1971. *Storia d'Italia.* Ed. Silvana Seidel Menchi. 3 vols. Turin: Einaudi.

Guicciardini, Luigi. 1993. *The sack of Rome.* Trans. James Harvey McGregor. New York: Italica.

Gullino, Giuseppe. 1996a. L'Evoluzione costituzionale. In *Storia di Venezia: dalle origini alla caduta della serenissima,* vol. 4, *Il rinascimento: politica e cultura,* ed. Albert Tenenti and Ugo Tucci, 345-78. Rome: Istituto della enciclopedia italiana.

———. 1996b. Le frontiere navali. In *Storia di Venezia: dalle origini alla caduta della serenissima,* vol. 4, *Il rinascimento: politica e cultura,* ed. Alberto Tenenti and Ugo Tucci, 13-111. Rome: Istituto della enciclopedia italiana.

Hale, John Rigby, ed. 1973. *Renaissance Venice.* London: Faber & Faber.

———. 1979. Renaissance armies and political control: the Venetian proveditorial system. *Journal of Italian History* 2:11-31.

———. 1980. Terra Ferma fortifications in the cinquecento. In *Florence and Venice: comparisons and relations,* ed. Sergio Bertelli, Nicolai Rubinstein, and Craig Hugh Smyth, 2:169-87. Florence: La Nuova Italia.

———, ed. 1981. *Concise encyclopedia of the Italian Renaissance.* London: Thames & Hudson.

Harris, Neil. 1993-94. Marin Sanudo, forerunner of Melzi. *La Bibliofilia: Rivista di Storia del Libro e di Bibliografia* 95:1-38, 101-45; 96:15-42.

Hills, Paul. 1999. *Venetian colour: marble, mosaic, painting and glass, 1250–1550.* New Haven, CT: Yale University Press.

Hocquet, Jean-Claude. 1982. *Le sel et la fortune de Venise.* 2 vols. Villeneuve-d'Ascq: Université de Lille III.

Hook, Judith. 1972. *The sack of Rome, 1527.* London: Macmillan.

———. 1973. The destruction of the new "Italia": Venice and the papacy in collision. *Italian Studies* 28:10-30.

Howard, Deborah. 1975. *Jacopo Sansovino: architecture and patronage in Renaissance Venice.* New Haven, CT: Yale University Press.

———. 1980. *The architectural history of Venice.* London: Batsford.

Jacks, Philip Joshua. 1993. *The antiquarian and the myth of antiquity.* Cambridge: Cambridge University Press.

Jacoby, David. 1987. Venice and the Venetian Jews in the eastern Mediterranean. In *Gli ebrei e venezia: secoli XIV–XVIII: atti del convegno internazionale organizzato dall'Istituto di storia della società dello Stato veneziano della Fondazione Giorgio Cini,* ed. Gaetano Cozzi, 29–58. Milan: Edizioni Comunità.

Jacoviello, Michele. 1985. La lega antifrancese del 31 marzo 1495 nelle fonte veneziani del Sanuto. *Archivio Storico Italiano* 143:39–90.

Johnson, Eugen J. 2000. Jacopo Sansovino, Giacomo Torelli, and the theatricality of the Piazzetta in Venice. *Journal of the Society of Architectural Historians* 54, no. 4:436–55.

Kaplan, Paul. 1986. The storm of war: the Paduan key to Giorgione's "Tempesta." *Art History* 9, no. 4:405–35.

Kaufmann, D. 1980. A contribution to the history of the Venetian Jews. *Jewish Quarterly Review* 2:297–310.

Kidwell, Carol. 1991. *Pontano, poet and prime minister.* London: Duckworth.

Killerby, Catherine Kovesi. 1994. Practical problems in the enforcement of Italian sumptuary law. In *Crime, society, and the law in Renaissance Italy,* ed. Trevor Dean and K. J. P. Lowe, 99–120. Cambridge: Cambridge University Press.

———. 2001. *Sumptuary law in Italy, 1200–1500.* Oxford: Oxford University Press.

King, Margaret L. 1976. Calediera and the Barbaros on marriage and the family: humanist reflections of Venetian realities. *Journal of Medieval and Renaissance Studies* 6:19–50.

———. 1986. *Venetian humanism in an age of patrician dominance.* Princeton, NJ: Princeton University Press.

———. 1991. *Women of the Renaissance.* Chicago: University of Chicago Press.

Kittell, Ellen E., and Thomas F. Madden, eds. 1999. *Medieval and Renaissance Venice: essays in honor of Donald E. Queller.* Urbana: University of Illinois Press.

Klapisch-Zuber, Christiane. 1985. *Women, family, and ritual in Renaissance Italy.* Trans. Lydia G. Cochrane. Chicago: University of Chicago Press.

Knapton, Michael. 1992. Tribunali padovani e proteste veneziane nel secondo quattrocento. In *Studi veneti offerti a Gaetano Cozzi,* ed. Gino Benzoni, 151–70. Venice: Cardo.

Kristeller, Paul Oskar. 1967. *Iter Italicum: a finding list of uncatalogued or incompletely catalogued humanistic manuscripts in Italian and other libraries.* Vol. 2. London: Warburg Institute; Leiden: Brill.

Kuntz, Marion Leathers. 1999. *Venice, myth and Utopian thought in the sixteenth century: Bodin, Postel and the virgin of Venice.* Variorum Collected Studies Series. Aldershot, Hamps: Ashgate.

Kurz, Otto. 1969. A gold helmet made in Venice for Sultan Suleyman the Magnificent. *Gazette des Beaux-Arts* 74:249–58.

Labalme, Patricia H. 1969. *Bernardo Giustiniani: a Venetian of the quattrocento.* Uomini e Dottrina, 13. Rome: Edizioni di storia e letteratura.

———. 1981. Venetian women on women: three early modern feminists. *Archivio Veneto*, 5th ser., no. 177:81–109.

———. 1984. Sodomy and Venetian justice in the Renaissance. *Legal History Review* 52:217–54.

———. 1993. No man but an angel: early efforts to canonize Lorenzo Giustiniani (1381–1456). In *Continuità e discontinuità nella storia politica, economica e religiosa: studi in onore di Aldo Stella*, 15–42. Vicenza: Neri Pozza.

———. 1995. Holy patronage, holy promotion: the cult of saints in fifteenth-century Venice. In *Saints: studies in hagiography*, ed. Sandro Sticca, 233–49. Medieval and Renaissance Texts and Studies, 141. Binghamton, NY: Medieval and Renaissance Texts and Studies.

———. 1996. Secular and sacred heroes: Ermolao Barbaro on worldly honor. In *Una famiglia veneziana nella storia: i Barbaro; atti del convegno di studi in occasione del quinto centenario della morte dell'umanista Ermolao, Venezia, 4–6 novembre 1993*, 331–44. Venice: Istituto veneto di scienzia, lettere e arti.

Labalme, Patricia H., and Laura Sanguineti White. 1999. How to (and how not to) get married in sixteenth-century Venice (selections from the diaries of Marin Sanudo). With translations by Linda L. Carroll. *Renaissance Quarterly* 52:43–72.

Labowsky, Carlotta. 1979. *Bessarion's library and the Biblioteca Marciana: six early inventories*. Sussidi Eruditi, 31. Rome: Edizioni di storia e letteratura.

Lagomaggiore, Carlo. 1907–11. L'Istoria veneziana di M. P. Bembo: saggio critico con documenti inedite. *Nuovo Archivio Veneto*, n.s. 7 (1907): 5–31, 354–71; 8 (1908): 162–80, 317–46; 11 (1911): 33–113, 308–40.

Lane, Frederic Chapin. 1944. *Andrea Barbarigo, merchant of Venice*. Baltimore: Johns Hopkins Press.

———. 1966a. Family partnerships and joint ventures. In *Venice and history: the collected papers of Frederic C. Lane*, 36–55. Baltimore, MD: Johns Hopkins Press.

———. 1966b. The rope factory and hemp trade in the fifteenth and sixteenth centuries. In *Venice and history: the collected papers of Frederic C. Lane*, 269–84. Baltimore: Johns Hopkins Press.

———. 1966c. Venetian bankers, 1496–1533. In *Venice and history: the collected papers of Frederic C. Lane*, 69–86. Baltimore: Johns Hopkins Press.

———. 1966d. *Venice and history: the collected papers of Frederic C. Lane*. Ed. a committee of colleagues and former students. Foreword by Fernand Braudel. Baltimore: Johns Hopkins Press.

———. 1968. The medieval spice trade: its revival in the sixteenth century. In *Crisis and change*, ed. Brian Pullan, 47–87. London: Methuen.

———. 1973a. Naval actions and fleet organization, 1499–1502. In *Renaissance Venice*, ed. John Rigby Hale, 146–73. London: Faber & Faber. Reprinted in *Studies in Venetian social and economic history*, ed. Benjamin G. Kohl and Reinhold C. Mueller, essay 8 (London: Variorum, 1987).

———. 1973b. *Venice: a maritime republic*. Baltimore: Johns Hopkins University Press.

———. 1983. *Le navi di venezia fra i secoli XIII e XVI*. Turin: Einaudi.

———. 1987a. News on the Rialto. In Lane, *Studies in Venetian social and economic history,* ed. Benjamin G. Kohl and Reinhold C. Mueller, 1–12. London: Variorum.

———. 1987b. *Studies in Venetian social and economic history.* Ed. Benjamin G. Kohl and Reinhold C. Mueller. London: Variorum.

———. 1992. *Venetian ships and shipbuilders in the Renaissance.* Baltimore: Johns Hopkins Press. (Orig. pub. 1934, translated into French in Paris by SEVPEN in 1965.)

Lane, Frederic Chapin, and Reinhold C. Mueller. 1985. *Money and banking in medieval and Renaissance Venice.* Vol. 1, *Coins and moneys of accounts.* Baltimore: Johns Hopkins University Press.

La Rocca, Patrizia. 1993. Né altro fu fatto che balar. In *La danza a Venezia nel rinascimento,* ed. Alessandro Pontremoli, 27–62. Vicenza: Neri Pozza.

Law, John Easton. 1979. Verona and the Venetian state in the fifteenth century. *Bulletin of the Institute of Historical Research* 52, no. 125:9–22.

———. 1988. Venice and the problem of sovereignty in the *Patria del Friuli.* In *Florence and Italy: Renaissance studies in honour of Nicolai Rubinstein,* ed. Peter Denley and Caroline Elam, 135–47. London: Westfield College.

Lepschy, Anna Laura. 1993. The language of Sanudo's Diarii. In *War, culture, and society in Renaissance Venice: essays in honour of John Hale,* ed. David Sanderson Chambers, Cecil H. Clough, and Michael E. Mallett, 199–212. London: Hambledon.

Levi-Pisetzky, Rosita. 1964–69. *Storia del costume in Italia.* 5 vols. Milan: Istituto editoriale italiano.

Libby, Lester John. 1971. "Venetian patriotic humanism in the early sixteenth century." PhD diss., Brown University.

———. 1973. Venetian history and political thought after 1509. *Studies in the Renaissance* 20:7–45.

Lieberman, Ralph. 1991. Review of *Rialto: le fabbriche e il ponte, 1514–1591,* by Donatella Calabi and Paolo Morachiello. *Journal of the Society of Architectural Historians* 50, no. 2:199–201.

Logan, Oliver. 1972. *Culture and society in Venice, 1470–1790; the Renaissance and its heritage.* London: Batsford.

———. 1978. The ideal bishop and the Venetian patriciate, c. 1230–c. 1630. *Journal of Ecclesiastical History* 29:415–50.

———. 1996. *The Venetian upper clergy in the sixteenth and early seventeenth centuries: a study in religious culture.* Lewiston, NY: Edwin Hellen.

Lorenzetti, Giulio. 1926. *Venezia e il suo estuario: guida storico-artistica.* Venice: Bestetti & Tumminelli.

Lovarini, Emilio. 1965. *Studi sul Ruzzante e la letteratura pavana.* Ed. Gianfranco Folena. Padua: Antenore.

Lowry, Martin. 1974. Two great Venetian libraries in the age of Aldus Manutius. *Bulletin of the John C. Rylands University Library of Manchester* 57:128–66.

———. 1979. *The world of Aldus Manutius: business and scholarship in Renaissance Venice.* Ithaca, NY: Cornell University Press.

———. 1991. *Nicolas Jensen and the rise of Venetian publishing in Renaissance Europe.* Oxford: Blackwell.

Lunardon, Silvia. 1985. L'Ospedale dei Crociferi. In *Hospitale Santae Mariae Cruciferorum,* ed. Lunardon. 2nd ed. Venice: IRE: Istituzioni di ricovero e di educazione.

Luzzatto, Gino. 1954. Il costo della vita a Venezia nel Trecento. In *Studi di storia economica veneziana.* Padua: CEDAM.

———. 1995. *Storia economica di venezia dall' XI al XVI secolo.* Intro. Marino Berengo. Venice: Marsilio.

Machiavelli, Niccolò. 1968–82. *Opera di Niccolò Machiavelli.* Ed. Sergio Bertelli. 11 vols. Milan: Salerno.

Mackenney, Richard. 1984. Guilds and guildsmen in sixteenth-century Venice. *Bulletin of the Society for Renaissance Studies* 2, no. 2:7–18.

———. 1986. Devotional confraternities in Renaissance Venice. *Studies in Church History* 23:85–96.

Mackenney, Richard, and Peter Humfrey. 1986. The Venetian trade guilds as patrons of art in the Renaissance. *Burlington Magazine* 128:317–30.

Mahoney, Edward P., ed. 1976. *Philosophy and humanism: Renaissance essays in honor of Paul Oskar Kristeller.* New York: Columbia University Press.

Malipiero, Domenico. 1844. Annali veneti dall'anno 1457 al 1500. *Archivio Storico Italiano* 7, no. 2:5–720.

Mallett, Michael Edward. 1969. *The Borgias: the rise and fall of a Renaissance dynasty.* London: Bodley Head.

———. 1993. Venice and the war of Ferrara, 1482–84. In *War, culture, and society in Renaissance Venice: essays in honour of John Hale,* ed. David Sanderson Chambers, Cecil H. Clough, and Michael E. Mallett, 57–72. London: Hambledon.

———. 1994. Ambassadors and their audiences in Renaissance Italy. *Renaissance Studies* 8:229–43.

———. 1995. Personalities and pressures: Italian involvement in the French invasion of 1494. In *The French descent into Renaissance Italy, 1494–95: antecedents and effects,* ed. David Abulafia, 151–63. Aldershot, Hamps: Ashgate.

Mallett, Michael Edward, and John Rigby Hale. 1984. *The military organization of a Renaissance state: Venice c. 1400 to 1617.* Cambridge: Cambridge University Press.

Mancini, Franco, Maria Teresa Muraro, and Elena Povoledo, eds. 1985–2002. *I teatri del Veneto.* 5 vols. Venice: Corbo e Fiore.

Manfroni, Camillo. 1897. *Storia della marina italiana dalla caduta di Costantinopoli alla battaglia di Lepanto.* Rome: Foranzi.

———. 1898. Cenni sugli ordinamenti delle marine italiane nel medio evo. *Rivista marittima.*

Mangini, Nicola. 1974. *I teatri di Venezia.* Milan: Mursia.

Manuzio, Aldo Pio. 1975. *Aldo Manuzio editore: dediche, prefazioni, note ai testi.* Ed. Giovanni Orlandi. Documenti sulle Arti del Libro, 11. Milan: Il Polifilo.

Maranini, Giuseppe, 1931. *La costituzione di Venezia dopo la serrata del Maggior Consiglio.* Venice: La Nuova Italia.

Martin, John. 1988. Salvation and society in sixteenth-century Venice. *Journal of Modern History* 60:205–3.

——. 1993. *Venice's hidden enemies: Italian heretics in a Renaissance city.* Berkeley and Los Angeles: University of California Press.

Martin, John, and Dennis Romano, eds. 2000. *Venice reconsidered: the history and civilization of an Italian city-state, 1297–1797.* Baltimore: Johns Hopkins University Press.

Martin, Ruth. 1989. *Witchcraft and the Inquisition in Venice, 1550–1650.* Oxford: Blackwell.

Martin, Thomas Edward. 1998. *Alessandro Vittoria and the portrait bust in Renaissance Venice: remodelling antiquity.* Oxford: Clarendon.

Martineau, Jane, and Charles Hope, eds. 1983. *The genius of Venice, 1500–1600.* London: Royal Academy of Arts in association with Weidenfeld & Nicolson. An exhibition catalog.

McAndrew, John. 1980. *Venetian architecture of the early Renaissance.* Cambridge, MA: MIT Press.

Melamed, Abraham. 1983. The myth of Venice in Italian Renaissance Jewish thought. *Italia judaica: atti del I convegno internazionale,* 401–13. Saggi, 2. Roma.

Michiel, Marcantonio. 1844. Annotazioni alla *Storia veneta* di Daniele Barbaro tolte dai diarii inediti di Marino Sanuto e da quelli di Marcantonio Michiel, per cura di Emmanuele Cigogna. *Archivio Storico Italiano* 7, no. 2:1097–112.

Mitchell, Bonner. 1979. *Italian civic pageantry in the High Renaissance: a descriptive bibliography of triumphal entries and selected other festivals for state occasions.* Biblioteca di Bibliografia Italiana, 89. Florence: Olschki.

——. 1986. *The majesty of the state: triumphal progresses of foreign sovereigns in Renaissance Italy (1494–1600).* Biblioteca Dell' "Archivum Romanicum": Serie I, Storia, Letteratura, Paleografia, 203. Florence: Olschki.

Molà, Luca. 2000. *The silk industry of Renaissance Venice.* Baltimore: Johns Hopkins University Press.

Molmenti, Pompeo Gherardo. 1906. *Venice: its individual growth from the earliest beginnings to the fall of the republic.* Trans. Horatio Forbes Brown. Chicago: McClurg.

——. 1973. *La storia di venezia nella vita privata dalle origini alla caduta della repubblica.* 7th ed. 3 vols. Trieste: LINT. (Orig. pub. 1925.)

Monfasani, John. 1995. *Byzantine scholars in Renaissance Italy: Cardinal Bessarion and other émigrés; selected essays.* Variorum Collected Studies Series. Aldershot, Hamps: Ashgate.

Montenegro, Eupremio. 1907. *I dogi e le loro monete.* Turin: Edizioni numismatiche Montenegro.

Morawski, Paolo. 1987. Notizie dalle (future) "Indie d'Europa": Polonia, Lituania e Muscovia nei *"Diarii"* di Marin Sanudo (1496–1519). *Annali della Fondazione Luigi Einaudi* 21:43-88.

Morelli, Jacopo. 1793. *Delle solennità e pompe nuziali già usate presso li veneziani.* Venice: Dalle Stampe di Antonio Zatto e figli.

Morosini, Domenico. 1969. *De bene instituta re publica.* Ed. Claudio Vita-Finzi. Collectanea Caralitana, 2. Milan: Giuffrè.

Mousnier, Roland. 1970. Le trafic des offices a Venise. In *La plume, la faucille et le mar-*

teau: institutions et société en France du Moyen Âge à la Révolution, 389-401. Paris: Presses universitaires de France.

Mueller, Reinhold C. 1971. The procurators of San Marco in the 13th and 14th centuries: a study of the office as a financial and trust institution. *Studi Veneziani* 13:105-221.

——. 1972. Charitable institutions, the Jewish community and Venetian society. *Studi Veneziani*, n.s., 14:37-82.

——. 1979. The role of bank money in Venice, 1300-1500. *Studi Veneziani*, n.s., 3:47-96.

——. 1997. *Money and banking in medieval and Renaissance Venice.* Vol. 2. *The Venetian money market: banks, panics, and the public debt 1200-1500.* Baltimore: Johns Hopkins University Press.

Muir, Edward. 1978. The doge as *primus inter pares:* interregnum rites in early sixteenth-century Venice. In *Essays presented to Myron P. Gilmore,* ed. Sergio Bertelli and Gloria Ramakus, 1:145-60. Florence: La Nuova Italia.

——. 1979. Images of power: art and pageantry in Renaissance Venice. *American Historical Review* 84, no. 1:16-52.

——. 1981. *Civic ritual in Renaissance Italy.* Princeton, NJ: Princeton University Press.

——. 1984a. The cannibals of Renaissance Italy. *Syracuse Scholar* 5, no. 2:5-14.

——. 1984b. Manifestazioni e cerimonie nella Venezia di Andrea Gritti. In *"Renovatio urbis": Venezia nell'età di Andrea Gritti, 1523-1538,* ed. Manfredo Tafuri, 59-77. Rome: Officina Edizioni.

——. 1993. *Mad blood stirring: vendetta and factions in Friuli during the Renaissance.* Baltimore: Johns Hopkins University Press.

Murari, Rocco. 1898. Marin Sanudo e Laura Benzoni-Scioppo. *Giornale Storico della Letteratura Italiana.* Suppl. no. 1:145-57.

——. 1899. Per l'epistolario di Aldo Manuzio il vecchio (quattro lettere inedite del 1502). *Ateneo Veneto* 22:273-89.

——. 1900. Due epigrammi e una lettera inedita di Giovanni Cotta a Marin Sanudo. *Ateneo Veneto* 23:148-63.

Muraro, Maria Teresa, comp. 1971. *Studi sul teatro veneto fra Rinascimento ed età barocca.* Civiltà Veneziana. Studi, 24. Florence: Olschki.

——. 1981. Le festa a venezia e le sue manifestazioni rappresentative: le Compagnie della Calza e le *Momarie.* In *Storia della cultura veneta,* vol. 3, *Dal primo quattrocento al Consilio di Trento,* ed. Girolamo Arnaldi and Manlio Pastore Stocchi, 315-41. Vicenza: Neri Pozza.

Muraro, Michelangelo. 1971. Vittore Carpaccio o il teatro in pittura. In *Studi sul teatro veneto fra Rinascimento ed età barocca,* ed. Maria Teresa Muraro, 7-19. Florence: Olschki.

Murphy, David J. 1998. Greek epigrams and manuscripts of Damiano Guidotto of Venice. *Renaissance Studies* 12:476-94.

Mutinelli, Fabio. 1851. *Lessico veneto: che contiene l'antica fraseologia volgare e forense, l'indicazione di alcune leggi e statuti.* Venice: Andreola.

Nallino, Maria. 1965. L'Egitto dall morte di Qa'it Bay all'avvento di Qansuh al-Guri

(1496-1501) nei "Diarii" di Marin Sanudo. *Atti della Accademia Nazionale dei Lincei, Rendiconti Morali*, 8th ser., 20:414-53.

Nardi, Bruno. 1963. La scuola di Rialto e l'umanesimo veneziano. In *Umanesimo europeo e umanesimo veneziano*, ed. Vittore Branca, 93-139. Florence: Sansoni.

Necipoğlu, Gülru. 1989. Süleyman the Magnificent and the representation of power in the context of Ottoman-Hapsburg-papal rivalry. *Art Bulletin* 71:401-27.

Neff, Mary Frances. 1985. "Chancellery secretaries in Venetian politics and society, 1400-1533." PhD diss., University of California at Los Angeles.

Newett, Mary Margaret. 1902. The sumptuary laws of Venice in the fourteenth and fifteenth centuries. In *Historical essays by members of the Owens College, Manchester, published in commemoration of its jubilee (1851–1901)*, ed. Thomas Frederick Tout and James Tait, 245-78. Manchester: Longmans Green.

Newton, Stella Mary. 1988. *The dress of the Venetians, 1495–1525*. Aldershot, Hamps: Scolar Press.

Niccoli, Ottavia. 1990. *Prophecy and people in Renaissance Italy*. Trans. Lydia G. Cochrane. Princeton, NJ: Princeton University Press.

Nicol, Donald MacGillivray. 1988. *Byzantium and Venice: a study in diplomatic and cultural relations*. Cambridge: Cambridge University Press.

Olivieri, Achille. 1985. Eroticism and social groups in sixteenth-century Venice: the courtesan. In *Western sexuality: practice and precept in past and present times*, ed. Philippe Ariès and André Béjin, trans. Anthony Forster, 95-102. Oxford: Blackwell.

Padoan, Giorgio. 1978a. *Momenti del rinascimento veneto*. Medioevo e Umanesimo, 31. Padua: Antenore.

———. 1978b. La raccolta di testi teatrali di Marin Sanudo. In Padoan, *Momenti del rinascimento veneto*, 68-93. Padua: Antenore. An earlier version appeared in *Italia Medioevale e Umanistica* 13 (1970): 181-203.

———. 1981a. Angelo Beolco, detto il Ruzante. In *Storia della cultura veneta*, vol. 3, *Dal primo quattrocento al Consilio di Trento*, ed. Girolamo Arnaldi and Manlio Pastore Stocchi, 343-75. Vicenza: Neri Pozza.

———. 1981b. La commedia rinascimentale a Venezia: dalla sperimentazione umanistica alla commedia "regolare." In *Storia della cultura veneta*, vol. 3, *Dal primo quattrocento al Consilio di Trento*, ed. Girolamo Arnaldi and Manlio Pastore Stocchi, 377-465. Vicenza: Neri Pozza.

Padoan Urban, Lina. 1966. Teatri e "teatri del mondo" nella venezia del cinquecento. *Arte Veneta* 22:137-46.

———. 1968. La festa della sensa nelle arti e nell'iconografia. *Studi Veneziani* 10:291-353.

———. 1969. Apparati scenografici nelle feste veneziane cinquecentesche. *Arte Veneta* 23:145-55.

———. 1993. Teatro in tavola. *Studi Veneziani*, 5th ser., 25:169-216.

Palmer, Richard. 1983. *The studio of Venice and its graduates in the sixteenth century*. Contributi alla Storia dell'Università di Padova, 12. Trieste: LINT.

Palumbo-Fossati, Carlo. 1984. L'Interno della case dell'artigiano e dell'artista nella Venezia del cinquecento. *Studi Veneziani*, n.s., 8:109-53.

Papadopoli Aldobrandini, Nicolò. 1893–1919. *Le monete di Venezia descritte ed illustrate.* 3 vols. Venice: F. Ongania.

Park, Katharine, and Lorraine J. Daston. 1981. Unnatural conceptions: the study of monsters in sixteenth- and seventeenth-century France and England. *Past and Present* 92:20–54.

Paschini, Pio. 1943. *Domenico Grimani, cardinale di S. Marco (+1523).* Storia e Letteratura, 4. Rome: Edizioni di storia e letteratura.

Pazzi, Piero. 1995. *I gioielli nella civiltà veneziana.* Treviso: Zopelli.

Pedani, Maria Pia. 1994. *In nome del gran signore: inviati Ottomani a Venezia dalla caduta di Constantinopli alla guerra di Candia.* Deputazione di Storia Patria, Miscellanea di Studi e Memorie, 30. Venice: A spese della società.

Pedani Fabris, Maria Pia. 1995. L'Osservanza imposta: i monasteri conventuali femminili a venezia nei primi anni del cinquecento. *Archivio Veneto,* 5th ser., no. 144:113–25.

Pellegrini, Giambattista. 1977. *Studi di dialettologia e filologia veneta.* Pisa: Pacini.

Pelliccia, Guerrino, and Giancarlo Rocca, eds. 1974–97. *Dizionario degli istituti di perfezione.* 10 vols. Rome: Edizioni Paoline.

Pennato, Papinio. 1872. Nuove notizie intorno ad Andrea Navagero e a Daniele Barbaro. *Archivio Veneto* 3:255–61.

Perocco, Daria. 1992. Uno storico mancato, un viaggiatore involontario: il caso di Andrea Navagero. In *Forma e parola: studi in memoria di Fredi Chiappelli,* ed. Dennis J. Dutschke, Pier Massimo Forni, Filippo Grazzini, Benjamin R. Lawton, and Laura Sanguineti White, 327–39. Rome: Bulzoni Editore.

Perocco, Guido, and Antonio Salvadori. 1977. *Civiltà di Venezia.* . Venice: Stamperia di Venezia.

Perry, Marilyn. 1977. Saint Mark's trophies: legend, superstition, and archaeology in Renaissance Venice. *Journal of the Warburg and Courtauld Institutes* 40:27–49.

———. 1978. Cardinal Domenico Grimani's legacy of ancient art to Venice. *Journal of the Warburg and Courtauld Institutes* 41:215–44.

Pertusi, Agostino, ed. 1966. *Venezia e l'Oriente fra tardo medioevo e rinascimento [testi delle lezioni].* Civiltà Europea e Civiltà Veneziana, 4. Florence: Sansoni.

———, ed. 1970. *La storiografia veneziana fino al secolo XVI: aspetti e problemi.* Civiltà Veneziana. Saggi, 18. Florence: Olschki.

Petrarca, Francesco. 1966. *Petrarch, letters.* Ed. and trans. Morris Bishop. Bloomington: Indiana University Press.

Pezzolo, Luciano. 1996. La finanza pubblica: dal prestito all'imposta. In *Storia di Venezia: dalle origini alla caduta della serenissima,* vol. 5, *Il rinascimento: società ed economia,* ed. Albert Tenenti and Ugo Tucci, 703–51. Rome: Istituto della enciclopedia italiana.

Picotti, Giovanni Battista. 1936. Sanudo, Marin, il giovane. In *Enciclopedia italiana di scienze, lettere ed arti,* 30:800–801. Rome: Istituto della enciclopedia italiana.

Pieri, Piero. 1960. Alviano, Bartolomeo d'. In *Dizionario biografico degli italiani,* 2:587–91. Rome: Istituto della enciclopedia italiana.

Piovan, Francesco. 1995. Fausto, Vittore. In *Dizionario biografico degli italiani,* 45:398–401. Rome: Istituto della enciclopedia italiana.

Polano, Sergio, ed. 1988. *L'Architettura militare veneta del cinquecento.* Milan: Electa.

Povoledo, Elena. 1995. La scenografia. In *Storia di Venezia: l'arte,* ed. Rodolfo Pallucchini, 2:623–71. Rome: Istituto della enciclopedia italiana.

Preto, Paolo. 1975. *Venezia e i turchi.* Florence: Sansoni.

Priori, Lorenzo. 1738. *Practica criminale secondo il ritto delle leggi della Serenissima republica di Venetia.* 9th impression. Venice: Girardi. (Orig. pub. 1622.)

Priuli, Girolamo. 1912–41. *I diarii di Girolamo Priuli [aa. 1494–1512].* Ed. Arturo Segre and Roberto Cessi. 3 vols. Rerum Italicarum Scriptores, Nuova ed., 24, pt. 3. Città di Castello: Lapi.

Prodi, Paolo. 1973. The structure and organization of the church in Renaissance Venice: suggestions for research. In *Renaissance Venice,* ed. John Rigby Hale, 409–30. London: Faber & Faber.

Pullan, Brian S., ed. 1968. *Crisis and change in the Venetian economy in the sixteenth and seventeenth centuries.* London: Methuen.

———. 1971. *Rich and poor in Renaissance Venice: the social institutions of a Catholic state.* Oxford: Blackwell.

———. 1973. The occupation and investments of the Venetian nobility in the middle and late sixteenth century. In *Renaissance Venice,* ed. John Rigby Hale, 379–408. London: Faber & Faber.

———. 1973–74. The significance of Venice. *Bulletin of the John C. Rylands University Library of Manchester* 56:443–62.

———. 1983. *The Jews of Europe and the Inquisition of Venice, 1550–1670.* Oxford: Blackwell.

———. 1987. Jewish moneylending in Venice: from private enterprise to public service. In *Gli ebrei e venezia: secoli XIV–XVIII: atti del convegno internazionale organizzato dall'Istituto di storia della società dello Stato veneziano della Fondazione Giorgio Cini,* ed. Gaetano Cozzi, 671–86. Milan: Edizioni Comunità.

———. 1989. La nuova filantropia nella venezia cinquecentesca. In *Nel regno dei poveri: arte e storia dei grandi ospedali veneziani in età moderna,* ed. Bernard Aikema and Culcia Meijers, 17–34. Venice: Arsenale.

———. 1990. The *Scuole Grandi* of Venice: some further thoughts. In *Christianity and the Renaissance: image and the religious imagination in the Quattrocento,* ed. Timothy Verdon and John Henderson, 272–301. Syracuse, NY: Syracuse University Press.

Queller, Donald E. 1966. *Early Venetian legislation on ambassadors.* Geneva: Droz.

———. 1967. *The office of ambassador in the middle ages.* Princeton, NJ: Princeton University Press.

———. 1969. The civic irresponsibility of the Venetian nobility. In *Economy, society, and government in medieval Italy: essays in memory of Robert L. Reynolds,* ed. David Herlihy, Robert S. Lopez, and Vsevolod Slessarev, 223–36. Kent, OH: Kent State University Press.

———. 1973. The development of ambassadorial relazioni. In *Renaissance Venice,* ed. John Rigby Hale, 174–96. London: Faber & Faber.

———. 1986. *The Venetian patriciate: reality versus myth.* Urbana: University of Illinois Press.

Queller, Donald E., and Thomas F. Madden. 1993. Father of the bride: fathers, daughters, and dowries in late medieval and early Renaissance Venice. *Renaissance Quarterly* 46:685–711.

Ravid, Benjamin. 1987. The religious, economic and social background of the establishment of the Ghetti in Venice. In *Gli ebrei e venezia: secoli XIV–XVIII; atti del convegno internazionale organizzato dall'Istituto di storia della società dello Stato veneziano della Fondazione Giorgio Cini,* ed. Gaetano Cozzi, 211–60. Milan: Edizioni Comunità.

———. 1990. Ghetti, moneylenders and merchants. In *Het getto van venitië: Ponentini, Levantini and Tedeschi, 1516–1797,* ed. Julie-Marthe Cohen, 11–27. The Hague: SDU-Uitgeverij.

———. 1992. From yellow to red: on the distinguishing head-covering of the Jews of Venice. *Jewish History* 6, nos. 1–2: 179–210.

———. 1997. Christian travellers in the ghetto of Venice: some preliminary observations. In *Between history and literature: studies in honor of Isaac Barzilay,* ed. Stanley Nash, 111–50. Tel Aviv: Hakibbutz Mameuchad.

———. 1999a. Curfew time in the Ghetto. In *Medieval and Renaissance Venice: essays in honor of Donald E. Queller,* ed. Ellen E. Kittell and Thomas F. Madden, 237–75. Urbana: University of Illinois Press.

———. 1999b. The Venetian ghetto. In *Encyclopedia of the Renaissance,* ed. Paul F. Grendler, 3:48–49. New York: Scribner's Sons.

———. 2003. On sufferance and not as of right: the status of the Jewish communities in early modern Venice. In *The lion shall roar: Leon Modena and his world,* ed. David Malkiel 17–61. Jerusalem: Magnes Press-Ben Zvi Institute.

Rezasco, Giulio. 1881. *Dizionario del linguaggio italiano storico ed amministrativo.* Florence: Le Monnier.

Rigo, Paola. 1991. Donà (Donati, Donato), Girolamo. In *Dizionario biografico degli italiani,* 40:741–53. Rome: Istituto della enciclopedia italiana.

Rinaldi, Francesca. 1993. Povertà e assistenzialismo a Venezia nel primo cinquecento: la confraternita per i poveri vergognosi. *Venezia Cinquecento* 3, no. 6:141–59.

Rizzo, Alberto. 1996. Il leone di San Marco e la Lega di Cambrai. *Ateneo Veneto,* n.s., 34:297–314.

Robey, Daniel, and John Law. 1975. The Venetian myth and the "De Republica Veneta" of Pier Paolo Vergerio. *Rinascimento,* 2nd ser., 15:3–59.

Romanello, Marina. 1992. Come seminario di Santa Vita: istituzioni femminili nel Friuli del cinque e seicento tra modelli religiosi e recupero sociale. In *Studi veneti offerti a Gaetano Cozzi,* ed. Gino Benzino, 207–20. Venice: Cardo.

Romanin, Samuele. 1853–61. *Storia documentata di venezia.* 10 vols. Venice: P. Naratovich.

Romano, Dennis. 1983. "Quod sibi fiat gratia": the adjustment of penalties and the exercise of influence in early Renaissance Venice. *Journal of Medieval and Renaissance Studies* 13:251–68.

———. 1984. Charity and community in early Renaissance Venice. *Journal of Urban History* 13:63–82.

———. 1987. *Patricians and popolani: the social foundations of the Venetian Renaissance state.* Baltimore: Johns Hopkins University Press.

———. 1989. Gender and the urban geography of Renaissance Venice. *Journal of Social History* 23, no. 2:339–53.

———. 1991. The regulation of domestic service in Renaissance Venice. *Sixteenth Century Journal* 22:661–77.

———. 1996. *Housecraft and statecraft: domestic service in Renaissance Venice, 1400–1600.* Baltimore: Johns Hopkins University Press.

Rosand, David. 1982. *Painting in cinquecento Venice: Titian, Veronese, Tintoretto.* New Haven, CT: Yale University Press.

———. 1984. Venetia figurata: the iconography of a myth. In *Interpretazioni veneziane: studi di storia dell'arte in onore di Michelangelo Muraro,* ed. David Rosand, 177–96. Venice: Arsenale.

Rosand, Ellen. 1977. Music in the myth of Venice. *Renaissance Quarterly* 30:511–37.

Ross, James Bruce. 1970. Gasparo Contarini and his friends. *Studies in the Renaissance* 17:192–232.

———. 1972. The emergence of Gasparo Contarini: a bibliographical essay. *Church History* 41:1–24.

———. 1976. Venetian schools and teachers, fourteenth to early sixteenth century: a survey and a study of Giovanni Battista Egnazio. *Renaissance Quarterly* 39:521–60.

Rossi, Franco. 1996. L'Arsenale: i quadri direttivi. In *Storia di Venezia: dalle origini alla caduta della serenissima,* vol. 5, *Il rinascimento: società ed economica,* ed. Alberto Tenenti and Ugo Tucci, 593–639. Rome: Istituto della enciclopedia italiana.

Roth, Cecil. 1930. *History of the Jews in Venice.* Philadelphia: Jewish Publication Society.

Rowe, John Gordon, and W. H. Stockdale, eds. 1971. *Florilegium historiale: essays presented to Wallace Ferguson.* Toronto, ON: University of Toronto Press.

Rubinstein, Nicolai. 1973. Italian reactions to terraferma expansion in the fifteenth century. In *Renaissance Venice,* ed. John Rigby Hale, 197–217. London: Faber & Faber.

Ruggiero, Guido. 1980. *Violence in early Renaissance Venice.* New Brunswick, NJ: Rutgers University Press.

———. 1985. *The boundaries of eros: sex, crime, and society in Renaissance Venice.* New York: Oxford University Press.

———. 1993. *Binding passions: tales of magic, marriage, and power at the end of the Renaissance.* New York: Oxford University Press.

———. 2001. The strange death of Margarita Marcellini: *male,* signs, and the everyday world of pre-modern medicine. *American Historical Review* 106, no. 4:1141–58.

Runciman, Steven. 1955. The decline of the crusading idea. In *Relazione del X congresso internazionale di scienze storiche,* 637–52. Biblioteca Storica Sansoni, n.s. 24. Florence: Sansoni.

Russell, Jeffrey Burton. 1972. *Witchcraft in the Middle Ages.* Ithaca, NY: Cornell University Press.

Sambin, Paolo. 1944–45. Di una ignorata fonte dei "Diarii" di Marin Sanudo. *Atti dell'Istituto Veneto di Scienze, Lettere ed Arti* 104, no. 2:21–53.

Sansovino, Francesco. 1968. *Venetia città nobilissima et singolare: descritta in XIIII libri.* Farnborough: Gregg; Venice: Filippi. (Orig. pub. 1663.)

Sanudo, Marin. 1773. *Le vite de' duchi di Venezia.* Rerum Italicarum Scriptores, 23. Milan: Societas Palatina. Cols. 405–1252.

———. 1829. *Commentarii della guerra di Ferrara tra li viniziani ed il Duca Ercole d'Este nell MDDDDLXXXII, di Marino Sanuto per la prima volta pubblicati.* Venice: G. Picotti.

———. 1847. *Itinerario di Marin Sanuto per la terraferma veneziana, nell'anno MCCCCLXXXIII.* Ed. Rawdon Brown. Padua: Tipografia del Seminario.

———. 1852. *Narrazione della festa solenne data in Venezia dalla Compania della Calza nel MDXX adi XIII Febraro per l'acceptazione di tre socii.* Ed. Emmanuelle Antonio Cicogna. Venice: P. Naratovich.

———. 1873. *La spedizione di Carlo VIII in Italia.* Ed. Rinaldo Fulin. Venice: M. Visentini. *Archivio Veneto.* Suppl. nos. 5–6, 9–23.

———. 1877–78. *Marino Sanuto világkrónikájának Magyarországot illeto tudósításai: a szerzo eredeti kéziratábó közli Wenzel Gusztáv. I–III. 1496–[1526].* Ed. Gusztáv Wenzel. 3 vols. Budapest: A Magyar Tud. Akadémia Könyvkiadó-Hivatala. The text, in Italian, comprises books 1–42 of Sanudo's *I diarii,* ed. from the original manuscript, then in Vienna.

———. 1879–1903. *I diarii di Marino Sanuto.* Ed. Rinaldo Fulin, Federico Stefani, Nicolò Barozzi, Guglielmo Berchet, and Marco Allegri. 58 vols. Venice: Fratelli Visentini. Repr., Bologna: Forni, 1969–70.

———. 1880. *La cronachetta di Marin Sanudo.* Ed. Rinaldo Fulin. Venice: M. Visentini.

———. 1882. *Il dogado di Pietro Mocenigo nel manuscritto autografo di Marino Sanuto.* Ed. Rinaldo Fulin. Venice: M. Visentini.

———. 1883a. *Capitoli di Sebenico conservati da Marino Sanuto (diarii, XXXIV, 66–67).* Venice: M. Visentini.

———. 1883b. *Martin Luther und die Reformationsbewegung in Deutschland vom Jahre 1520–1532 in Auszügen aus Marino Sanuto's diarien.* Ed. Georg Martin Thomas. Ansbach, Germany: Brügel.

———. 1886. *Nozze Cesare Le Coultre Luigia Fabrizi, Venezia 22 settembre 1886: descrizione di una rassegna di 12,000 Svizzeri fatta da Francesco Io re di Francia nei campi presso Attigny ai 4 d'ottobre del 1521.* Venice.

———. 1898. *Il giovedi grasso in Venezia nell'anno 1533.* Venice: Fratelli Visentini.

———. 1901. *Le vite dei dogi.* Ed. Giovanni Monticolo. Rerum Italicarum Scriptores, new ed., 22, pt. 4. Città di Castello: Lapi.

———. 1979. *Sah Isma'il I nei Diarii di Marin Sanudo.* Ed. Biancamaria Scarcia Amoretti. Studi e Materiali sulla Conoscenza dell'Oriente in Italia, 3. Rome: Istituto per l'Oriente.

———. 1980. *De origine, situ et magistratibus urbis venetae ovvero la città di Venetia (1493–1530).* Ed. Angela Caracciolo Aricò. Collana di Testi Inediti e Rari, 1. Milan: Cisalpino-La Goliardica.

———. 1989–2001. *Le vite dei dogi (1474–1494).* Ed. Angela Caracciolo Aricò. 2 vols. Biblioteca Veneta, 8. Padua: Antenore.

———. 1997. *I diarii (1496–1533): pagine scelte.* Ed. Paolo Margaroli. Vicenza: Neri Pozza.

——. n.d. *Feste fatte in Venezia per le nozze di Vienna Gritti nipote del doge Andrea con Paolo Contarini il 25 gennaio 1524. M. V.: estratto dal volume 37 dei diarii autografi di Marin Sanuto da carte 282 a 284.* Venice: Tipografia della gazzetta.

——. n.d. *Venuta e soggiorno in Venezia di Francesco Sforza Duca di Milano dall' 11 ottobre al 5 novembre 1530 e feste fatte in quella occasione: notizie estratte dai diarii mss. Marino Sanuto.* Ed. Ida Parravicino-Persia and Leo Benvenuti. N.p.: Tipografia della Società di M.S. Fra Comp. Tip.

Sardella, Pierre. 1948. *Nouvelles et spéculations à Venise au début du XVI siècle.* Cahiers des Annales, 1. Paris: Colin.

Scarabello, Giovanni. 1979. *Carceri e carcerati a venezia nell'età moderna.* Biblioteca Biografica, 21. Rome: Istituto della enciclopedia italiana.

——. 1980. Devianza sessuale ed interventi di giustizia a Venezia nella prima metà del XVI secolo. In *Tiziano e Venezia: convegno internazionale di studi, Venezia, 1976,* 75–84. Vicenza: Neri Pozza.

Scholderer, Victor. 1966. Printing in Venice to the end of 1481. In *Fifty essays in fifteenth and sixteenth-century bibliography,* ed. Dennis E. Rhodes, 74–89. Amsterdam: Herzberger.

Schulz, Juergen. 1961. Vasari at Venice. *Burlington Magazine* 103:500–11.

——. 1978. Jacobo de' Barbari's *View of Venice:* map making, city views, and moralized geography before the year 1500. *Art Bulletin* 60:425–74.

Sergio, Polano, ed.. 1988. *L'Architettura militare veneta del cinquecento.* Milan: Electa.

Settis, Salvatore. 1990. *Giorgione's Tempest: interpreting the hidden subject.* Trans. Ellen Bianchini. Chicago: University of Chicago Press.

Setton, Kenneth Meyer. 1969. Pope Leo and the Turkish peril. *Proceedings of the American Philosophical Society* 113:367–424.

——. 1974. *Europe and the Levant in the Middle Ages and the Renaissance.* London: Variorum.

——. 1976–84. *The papacy and the Levant, 1204–1571.* 4 vols. Memoirs of the American Philosophical Society, 114, 127, 161–62. Philadelphia: American Philosophical Society.

Sheard, Wendy Stedman. 1977. Sanudo's list of notable things in Venetian churches and the date of the Vendramin tomb. *Yale Italian Studies* 1, no. 3:219–68.

Soergel, Philip, M. 1998. "Portraying monstrous birth in early modern Germany." In *The future of the Middle Ages and the Renaissance,* ed. Roger Dahood, 129–50. Turnhout, Belgium: Brepols.

Sperling, Jutta Giseka. 1999. *Convents and the body politic in late Renaissance Venice.* Chicago: University of Chicago Press.

Spufford, Peter. 1986. *Handbook of medieval exchange.* London: Royal Historical Society.

Tafuri, Manfredo. 1983. Pietas repubblicana, neobizantinismo e umanesimo: Giorgio Spavento e Tullio Lombardo nella chiesa di San Salvador. *Ricerche di Storia dell'Arte* 19:5–36.

——, ed. 1984. *"Renovatio urbis": Venezia nell'età di Andrea Gritti, 1523–1538.* Rome: Officina Edizioni.

——. 1985. *Venezia e il rinascimento: religione, scienza, architettura.* Turin: Einaudi.

———. 1989. *Venice and the Renaissance.* Cambridge, MA: MIT Press.

Tagliaferri, Amelio, ed. 1981. *Atti del convegno venezia e la terraferma attraverso le relazioni dei rettori, Trieste, 23–24 ottobre 1980.* Milan: A. Giuffrè.

———, ed. 1982. *Relazioni dei rettori veneti nel Dogado: podestaria di Chioggia.* Serie Monografico Di Storia Moderna e Contemporanea, 1. Milan: A. Giuffrè.

Talbot, Michael. 1985. "Ore italiane": the reckoning of the time of day in pre-Napoleonic Italy. *Italian Studies* 40:51-62.

Tamassia, Giovanni. 1910. *La famiglia italiana nei secoli decimoquinto e decimosesto.* L'Indagine Moderna, 15. Milan: Sandron.

Tamassia Mazzarotto, Bianca. 1980. *Le feste veneziane: i giochi popolari, cerimonie religiose e di governo.* 2nd ed. Florence: Sansoni.

Tassini, Giuseppe. 1961. *Feste, spettacoli, divertimenti e piaceri degli antichi veneziani.* 2nd ed. Venice: Filippi.

———. 1970. *Curiosità veneziane, ovvero origini delle denominazioni stradali di Venezia.* Venice: Filippi. (Orig. pub. 1887.)

Tenenti, Alberto. 1960. I corsari in Mediterraneo all'inizio del cinquecento. *Rivista di Storia Italiana* 72:234-87.

———. 1973. The sense of space and time in the Venetian world of the fifteenth and sixteenth centuries. In *Renaissance Venice,* ed. John Rigby Hale, 17-46. London: Faber & Faber.

———. 1980. L'Uso scenografico degli spazi pubblici, 1490-1580. In *Tiziano e Venezia: convegno internazionale di studi, Venezia, 1976,* 21-26. Vicenza: Neri Pozza.

———. 1991. Il senso del mare. In *Storia di Venezia: il mare,* ed. Alberto Tenenti and Ugo Tucci, 7-76. Rome: Istituto della enciclopedia italiana.

Teza, Emilio. 1883. *Correzioni al'istoria viniziana di P. Bembo, proposte dal Consiglio dei Dieci nel 1545.* Pisa.

Tichy, Susanne. 1997. *Et vene la mumaria: studien zur venezianischen Festkultur der Renaissance.* Akádemos, 1. Munich: Scaneg.

Tognetti, Giampaolo. 1960. Amaseo, Girolamo. In *Dizionario biografico degli italiani,* 2:654-55. Rome: Istituto della enciclopedia italiana.

Tramontin, Silvio, A. Niero, G. Musolino, and C. Candiani. 1965. *Culto dei santi a Venezia.* Biblioteca Ágiografica Veneziana, 2. Venice: Edizioni studium cattolico veneziano.

Tucci, Ugo. 1973. The psychology of the Venetian merchant in the sixteenth century. In *Renaissance Venice,* ed. John Rigby Hale, 346-78. London: Faber & Faber.

———. 1996. Monete e banche nel secolo del ducato d'oro. In *Storia di Venezia: dalle origini alla caduta della serenissima,* vol. 5, *Il rinascimento: società ed economia,* 753-805. Rome: Istituto della enciclopedia italiana.

Turato, G. F., and Dino Durante, eds. 1993. *Vocabolario etimologico veneto-italiano.* 7th ed. Battaglia Terme [Padua]: La Galiverna.

Uberti, Maria Luisa, ed. 1985. *I Menechini di Plauto.* Testi e Studi Umanistici, 3. Ravenna: Longo.

Valeri, Diego. 1979. Caratteri e valori del teatro comico. In *Storia della civiltà veneziana,* ed. Vittore Branca, vol. 2, *autunno del medioevo e rinascimento*, 221–32. Florence: Sansoni.

Vanzan Marchini, Nelli-Elena. 1990. L'Altra faccia dell'amore ovvero i rischi dell'esercizio del piacere. In *Il gioco dell'amore: le cortigiane di Venezia dall trecento al settocento*, 47–55. Milan: Berenice.

Varanini, Gian Maria. 1980–81. Altri documenti su Marin Sanudo e Verona (1501–1502). *Studi Storici Veronesi Luigi Simeoni* 30–31:290–302.

Veneroni, Giovanni. 1729. *Dictionnaire italien et françois*. Amsterdam: Chez Jacques Desbordes.

Venice (Comune). Assessorato alla cultura e belle arti. 1979. *Venezia e la peste: 1348–1797*. Venice: Marsilio.

———. Consiglio comunale. 1847. *Venezia e le sue lagune*. Ed. Giovanni Correr. 2 vols. Venice: Antonelli.

Venice (Italy). Casinò municipale. 1990. *Il gioco dell'amore: le cortigiane di Venezia dal trecento al settecento*. Milan: Berenice.

Ventura, Angelo. 1964. *Nobiltà e popolo nella società veneta del '400 e '500*. Bari: Laterza.

———. 1968. Bernardo Bembo. In *Dizionario biografico degli italiani*, 8:103–9. Rome: Istituto della enciclopedia italiana.

Venturi, Lionelli. 1983. *Le Compagnie della Calza (sec. XV–XVI)*. Venice: Filippi. Originally published in *Nuovo Archivio Veneto* 16 (1908): 161–221 and 17 (1909): 140–233.

Vicentini, Enrico Abramo. 1990. The Venetian *soleri:* from portable platforms to tableaux vivants. In *Petrarch's triumph: allegory and spectacle*, ed. Konrad Eisenbichler and Amilcare Iannucci, 383–94. Ottawa, ON: Dovehouse.

Viggiano, Alfredo. 1994. Giustizia, disciplina e ordine pubblico. In *Storia di Venezia: dalle origini alla caduta della serenissima*, vol. 4, *Il rinascimento: politica e cultura*, ed. Alberto Tenenti and Ugo Tucci, 825–72. Rome: Istituto della enciclopedia italiana.

Vitali, Achille. 1992. *La moda a Venezia attraverso i secoli: lessico ragionato*. Venice: Filippi.

Voltolina, Pietro. 1998. *La storia di Venezia attraverso le medaglie*. 3 vols. Venice: Edizioni Voltolina.

Wagner, Klaus. 1971. Sulla sorte di alcuni codici manoscritti appartenuti a Marin Sanudo. *La Bibliofilia: Rivista di Storia del Libro e di Bibliografia* 73:247–62.

———. 1972. Altre notizie sulla sorte dei libri di Marin Sanudo. *La Bibliofilia: Rivista di Storia del Libro e di Bibliografia* 73:185–90.

———. 1981. Nuove notizie a proposito dei libri di Marin Sanudo. *La Bibliofilia: Rivista di Storia del Libro e di Bibliografia* 83:129–31.

Wansbrough, John. 1963. A Mamluk ambassador to Venice in 913/1507. *Bulletin of the School of Oriental and African Studies* (University of London) 26, no. 3:503–30.

Wethey, Harold Edwin. 1967–75. 2 vols. *The paintings of Titian*. London: Phaidon.

Wollesen-Wisch, Barbara, and Susan Scott Munshower, eds. 1990. *"All the world's a stage . . .": art and pageantry in the Renaissance and Baroque*. University Park, PA: Art Department, Pennsylvania State University.

Wurthmann, William B. 1975. "The scuole grandi and Venetian art, 1260–ca. 1500." PhD diss., University of Chicago.

Zamperetti, Sergio. 1991a. *I piccoli principi, signorie locale, feudi e comunità soggette nello sotto regionale veneto dall'espansione territoriale ai primi decenni del '600*. Studi Veneti. Venice: Il Cardo.

———. 1991b. Stato regionale e autonomie locale: signorie e feudi nel dominio veneziano di terraferma in età moderna. *Studi Veneziani*, n.s., 21:111–36.

Zannini, Andrea. 1993. *Burocrazia e burocrati a Venezia in età moderna: i cittadini originari (sec. XVI–XVIII)*. Memorie: Classe di Scienza, Lettere ed Arti, 47. Venice: Istituto veneto di scienza, lettere ed arti.

Zarri, Gabriella. 1986. Monasteri femminili e città (secoli XV–XVIII). *Storia D'Italia, Annali* 9:357–429.

Zele, Walter. 1989. Aspetti delle legazioni ottomane nei *Diarii* di Marino Sanudo. *Studi Veneziani*, n.s., 18:241–84.

Zille, Ester. 1992. Salari e stipendi a Venezia tra quattro e cinquecento. *Archivio Veneto*, 5th ser., no. 138:5–29.

Zorzanello, Pietro. 1950–79. *Catalogo dei manoscritti italiani della Biblioteca Nazionale Marziana di Venezia*. 2 vols. Inventari dei manoscritti delle biblioteche d'Italia, 77, 81. Florence: Olschki.

Zorzi, Alvise. 1990. *La vita quotidiana a Venezia nel secolo di Tiziano*. Milan: Rizzoli.

Zorzi, Giangiorgio. 1958–59. Alcune notizie di Basilio dalla Scola architetto militare vicentino e delle sue fortificazioni di Vicenza e di Verona. *Atti dell'Istituto Veneto di Scienze, Lettere ed Arti* 117, no. 2:153–77.

———. 1959–60. Preoccupazioni cinquecentesche per l'interramento di Venezia e della laguna e alcune proposte di Michele Sammicheli. *Atti dell'Istituto Veneto di Scienze, Lettere ed Arti* 118, no. 2:163–210.

Zorzi, Ludovico. 1971. Elementi per la visualizzazione della scena veneta prima del Palladio. In *Studi sul teatro veneto fra Rinascimento ed età barocca*, ed. Maria Teresa Muraro, 21–51. Florence: Olschki.

———. 1977. *Il teatro e la città, Saggi sulla scena italiana*. Saggi, 587. Turin: Einaudi.

Zorzi, Marino. 1987. *La libreria di San Marco: libri, lettori, società nella venezia dei Dogi*. Collana di Studi: Ateneo Veneto, 1. Milan: Mondadori.

———. 1990. La circolazione del libro a Venezia nel cinquecento: biblioteche private e pubbliche. *Ateneo Veneto*, n.s., 28, no. 2:117–89.

———. 1996. Dal manoscritto al libro. In *Storia di Venezia: dalle origini alla caduta della serenissima*, vol. 4, *Il rinascimento: politica e cultura*, ed. Alberto Tenenti and Ugo Tucci, 817–958. Rome: Istituto della enciclopedia italiana.

Zuccolo, Simeon. 1549. *La pazzia del ballo*. Padua: Per Giacomo Fabriano. Repr., Bologna: Forni, 1969.

Index

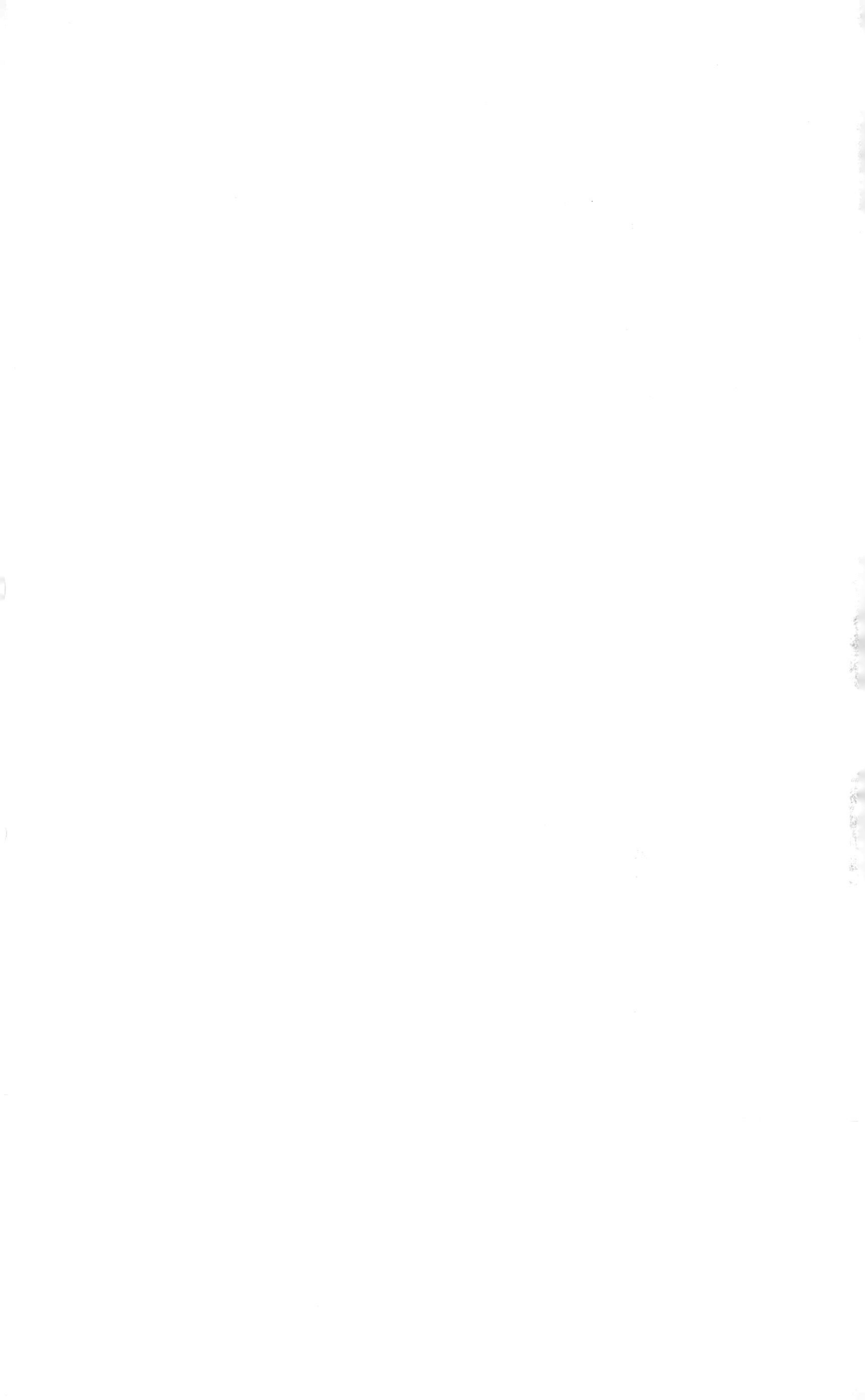